REMEMBERING THE CIVIL WAR

The Littlefield History of the Civil War Era

GARY W. GALLAGHER AND T. MICHAEL PARRISH, EDITORS

Supported by the Littlefield Fund for Southern History,
University of Texas Libraries

Remembering the CIVIL WAR

Reunion and the Limits of Reconciliation

Caroline E. Janney

The University of North Carolina Press   Chapel Hill

© 2013 The University of North Carolina Press
All rights reserved
Set in Miller by Tseng Information Systems, Inc.
Manufactured in the United States of America

Library of Congress Cataloging-in-Publication Data
Janney, Caroline E.
Remembering the Civil War : reunion and the limits of reconciliation /
Caroline E. Janney.
pages cm. — (The Littlefield history of the Civil War era)
Includes bibliographical references and index.
ISBN 978-1-4696-0706-1 (cloth : alk. paper)
ISBN 978-1-4696-2989-6 (pbk. : alk. paper)
1. United States—History—Civil War, 1861–1865—Social aspects. 2. United
States—History—Civil War, 1861–1865—Veterans. 3. United States—History—
Civil War, 1861–1865—Influence. 4. Reunions—United States—History—19th
century. 5. Reunions—United States—History—20th century. 6. Memory—
Social aspects—United States—History—19th century. 7. Memory—Social
aspects—United States—History—20th century. I. Title.
E468.9.J36 2013
973.7′1—dc23
2012046988

For Spencer

CONTENTS

ILLUSTRATIONS

ACKNOWLEDGMENTS

As most authors will concede, writing a book is far from a solitary adventure. Indeed, the debts I owe to those who have supported this project along the way are many. Seven years ago, the editors of the Littlefield Series, T. Michael Parrish and Gary W. Gallagher, offered me the opportunity to write the memory volume. Since that time, they have been unfailingly supportive. Mike has generously sent me primary sources, provided references, and given sage advice at every step along the way. Gary, too, has proved an endless source of information and wisdom. He has patiently read more chapter drafts than I am sure he can—or would like to—remember. For his faith in me as a scholar, his mentorship, and his friendship, I am infinitely grateful.

Throughout this process, it has been a pleasure to work again with the University of North Carolina Press. David Perry has been a champion of the project from its earliest stages. His support in shepherding the manuscript into existence has been much appreciated. Cait Bell-Butterfield, Ron Maner, and Eric Schramm have been immensely helpful in the fine-tuning. As a reader, Nina Silber offered excellent suggestions for the book's improvement, which I have tried to incorporate.

Much of the past seven years was spent visiting archives and Civil War battlefields throughout the country. I could not have done so without the financial assistance of several institutions. A Fletcher Jones Foundation Fellowship from the Huntington Library in San Marino, California, was pivotal to this book. Thanks to the generous support of Roy Ritchie and his staff, I was not only privileged to spend several months in one of the most beautiful spots in the United States, but I also accomplished a substantial portion of my research. The manuscript collections and rare books available at the Huntington are simply spectacular. As a Virginia Foundation for the Humanities Resident Fellow in 2010, I was fortunate to again have access to the University of Virginia's incredible archives and library. A research fellowship from the Kentucky Historical Society allowed me to spend a much-needed week in Frankfort, while the Southern Association for Women Historians' Anne Firor Scott Mid-Career Fellowship provided support for several pivotal research trips. Closer to home, start-up funds provided by my department helped me to begin my research at the Massachusetts Historical Society and Duke University. Support from a Purdue Library Scholars' grant allowed me to perform research at the National Archives on two separate occasions, while a Purdue Research Incentive grant enabled me to visit several battlefields. Finally, the College of Liberal Arts Center for Humanistic Studies fellowship provided a semester of teaching-leave to write.

At each archive and repository I visited, librarians and archivists were incredibly helpful. In particular, John Coski, at the Museum of the Confederacy, continues to be an invaluable resource. His breadth of knowledge and his generosity know no bounds. At the National Archives, Trevor Plante unearthed rich sources on veterans and pointed me in new directions. David Langbart, a friend from many summers of UVA "Civil War Camps" and an archivist at the National Archives in College Park, helped me in chasing down leads and sent me wonderfully rich references. Greg Goodell at Gettysburg National Military Park was instrumental in helping me to find images. Although I have never met her in person, Amber Paranick, a reference specialist at the Library of Congress, graciously assisted me with countless on-line searches. The interlibrary loan staff at Purdue has been instrumental in acquiring countless books and articles.

Friends and colleagues were no less generous with their time and resources. Joan Waugh has proven especially dear, inviting me to present my work at a Huntington conference, engaging in conversations about the project, and welcoming me to her home while I was in California. Steve Cushman, Pete Carmichael, Bill Blair, Matt Gallman, and Bill Freehling have all shared their wisdom. Aaron Sheehan-Dean and Barbara Gannon read numerous draft chapters, each offering deft and thoughtful commentary that pushed me to streamline my thinking. Keith Bohannon, Robert E. L. Krick, Barbara Gannon, and Keith Harris selflessly shared research materials. Commentators and fellow panelists Nina Silber, Anne Marshall, Alice Fahs, Amy Murrell Taylor, Jim Marten, Gaines Foster, Carol Reardon, Joseph Glatthaar, Elizabeth Varon, and Ed Blum provided insightful and considerate suggestions that encouraged me to make critical changes to my approach. At Purdue, Yvonne Pitts and Darren Dochuk read early versions of chapters and helped me to refine my arguments.

I owe a special debt to my students at Purdue. I have had the pleasure of teaching many wonderful students in my years here, but I have enjoyed none more than those who joined me on the spring break trips to Shiloh. Their questions and insights forced me to consider various topics from new angles, and their enthusiasm for Civil War history and memory was a sheer joy. Individual students likewise contributed to this project. Mark Johnson produced a wonderful paper on the Antietam monuments and their references to emancipation. Katie Martin, a Dean's Scholar student, spent hours teasing out the details of the Woman's Relief Corps membership. I owe a special thanks to the graduate students who participated in the Works in Progress series for their helpful suggestions about the Appomattox Peace Memorial. My appreciation for Megan Bever, a former student turned dear friend, is beyond words. She has provided access to databases, read countless drafts, and answered a million e-mail queries. I am grateful for her assistance and look forward to watching her as she embarks on the frontiers of Civil War scholarship.

Several friends and colleagues at Purdue have helped make Greater Lafayette feel like home. Doug Hurt, John Larson, Nancy Gabin, Mike Morrison, Randy Roberts, and Frank Lambert have been wonderfully supportive. Alicia Decker, Michele Buzon, Kory Cooper, Jennifer Foray, Brian Kelly, Charity Tabol, and David Atkinson have provided countless laughs and a welcome respite from work. Yvonne Pitts deserves special merit. Not only has she fearlessly helped me to take students to Shiloh, but she has also proven a constant source of humor. From our debates about southern exceptionalism to discussions about property affecting *everything*, she has kept me in stiches. Darren and Debra Dochuk have been especially treasured. As they move on to new opportunities, we will miss them fiercely.

Elsewhere, my closest friends, Pamela Adams, Julena Campbell, and Heather Gray McCoy, have encouraged me in all my endeavors and reminded me of the important things in life. "Roll On!"

It is my family, however, that has sustained me. My love for history comes in large part from my parents, Robert and Sharon Janney. But they have provided so much more than that. They have been my biggest champions and strongest supporters. My brothers, Andrew and Marc, along with my sister-in-law, Monica, have been exceptionally encouraging. Dad, Drew, and Marc have offered constructive critiques of the manuscript and sent me articles on the current state of Civil War memory. My niece and nephew, Isa and Conner, confirm what the Civil War generation understood only too well: history is as much about the future as the past. Perhaps more of a distraction than a help at times, our critters have dutifully insisted that too much time should not be spent in front of the computer. Frisbees and walks are good for the mind and body.

My deepest obligation is to my husband, Spencer Lucas. Seventeen years ago when we embarked on our first trip to Gettysburg together, neither of us could have imagined how much "the war" would become part of our lives. Nor could we have predicted the wonderful journey life had in store for us. It is Spence who keeps me grounded and reminds me that living in the present is so much more rewarding than recalling what lies in the past. It is to him that I dedicate this book.

REMEMBERING THE CIVIL WAR

To strive to forget the great war, for the sake of sentimental politics,

is to cast away our dearest experience and invite,

in some troubled future, the destruction we so hardly escaped

in the past. There can be remembrance without animosity,

but there cannot be oblivion without peril.

—Camp Fire and Battle-field, *1896*

PROLOGUE

In September 1990, Ken Burns's PBS documentary *The Civil War* captured the nation's attention, dramatically influencing American perceptions of the grueling war. For a week, millions watched as the eleven-hour series recounted the conflict from the first calls for secession to the final surrenders at Appomattox and Durham Station. Rejecting reenactors and other recreations of battles, Burns relied upon wartime photographs, newspaper accounts, paintings, lithographs, and quiet scenes at battlefield parks to tell the story of a nation divided against itself, brother against brother, countryman against countryman. But scattered throughout was footage from the early twentieth century showing the white-bearded veterans of both sides happily shaking hands, marching alongside each other, and posing for photographs.[1] No one could watch without being left with the strong impression that although the nation had erupted in civil war, its soldiers—its people—had managed to peacefully reconcile. Forgetting their past differences, they agreed that there was no North, no South, only a United States of America.

This fraternal camaraderie was never as thorough or as complete as the clips of hand-clasping former foes would have us imagine. Countless veterans did occasionally come together for Blue-Gray reunions at battlefields and in cities across the nation. But this was the exception, not the rule. "Every now and then there are reunions of Federal Blue and Confederate Gray on this or that battlefield, when the veterans of either side shake hands across the bloody chasm and conduct themselves as brethren once at variance but now happily reunited," observed a Confederate-sympathizing editorial in 1889. "But," it continued, "oftener than these occasions, may be noticed exhibitions of bitter hatred manifested by northern soldiers against those of the South." Union veterans were no less wary of the genuine sentiments expressed by former Confederates. Renewed calls for a joint reunion between the major veterans' organization of each side, the Grand Army of the Republic (GAR) and the United Confederate Veterans (UCV), aroused heated consternation in 1929. "They were wrong in 1861," declared GAR member Frank O. Cole, "and until they admit they were wrong, and not until then, will we join them." Only when they had folded up their battle flags, "the flag we fought against and carried Old Glory against to victory," and placed them in museums would the GAR truly believe that "they want reunion." Well into the twentieth century, neither side was willing to forget what it had fought to preserve, even in the name of sectional reconciliation.[2]

As early as 1865, the veterans and civilians who survived the four bloody years of war were acutely aware that people were actively shaping what should be remembered—and omitted—from the historical record. The war generation understood what historians have come to grasp only in the past few decades: that memory is not a passive act.[3] They recognized that the memorials people built, the ceremonies they made sacred, and the stories they told had immense power. They knew that shared memories held the power to unite communities over space and time, to bind people together as "Americans," "southerners," or even "veterans."[4] What individuals and communities elected to tell of the war held enormous potential for staking claims of authority and power.[5]

If most Americans agreed that they would not forget the war, the conflicts over what—and how—to remember were only beginning in 1865. Addressing a crowd at the Memorial Day services in Arlington National Cemetery in 1871, Frederick Douglass—former slave, ardent abolitionist, and the father of two U.S. veterans—identified the quandary of how a reunited nation might remember the American Civil War. "We are sometimes asked in the name of patriotism to forget the merits of this fearful struggle, and to remember with equal admiration those who struck at the nation's life, and those who struck to save it; those who fought for slavery and those who fought for liberty and justice. I am no minister of malice, I would not repel the repentant, but may my tongue cleave to the roof of my mouth if I forget the difference between the parties to that bloody conflict. I may say if this war is to be forgotten, I ask in the name of all things sacred what shall men remember?"[6] Two years later, former Confederate general Jubal A. Early offered a similar message at a meeting of his fellow officers. "If we were to attempt to erase all traces of the contest through which we have gone," he observed, "it would be a vain task." "We could not forget if we would, and I trust that there are many of us who would not forget if we could," he argued.[7] Douglass and Early understood that the postwar battles over the causes and consequences of the war carried tremendous weight. Too much was a stake for it to be otherwise.

Spanning more than seventy-five years, this book examines the deliberate efforts of the war generation, and to some extent their children, to craft and protect memories of the nation's greatest conflict and the central event in their lives. Various individuals and groups would consciously and unconsciously highlight certain aspects of the war while reshaping and neglecting others, but forgetting was what they all feared most. Despite pronouncements by some that the past needed to be forgotten in the interest of national healing, every monument, Memorial Day, Emancipation Day, soldiers' reunion, or textbook campaign was about remembering. It was the reason national cemeteries were established, the reason "Lest We Forget" adorned marble statues throughout the nation. And it is the reason bumper stickers stating "Hell no, I'm not forgettin'!" can still be found in the South. It is why the Civil War still resonates and still incites heated debate today. Remembering was—in many cases still is—paramount.[8]

Remembering was not merely a sentimental act. Indeed, it had powerful social and political connotations, not the least of which was at the very heart of the conflict: how would a nation that had been so divided that it went to war move forward as a truly *United* States of America? After Confederates laid down their guns in the spring of 1865, Unionists understood that they could not carry retribution too far if they were to truly fulfill their war goal of reuniting the nation. This is what led President Abraham Lincoln and his most important general, Ulysses S. Grant, to offer such magnanimous terms to the defeated rebels. The need to make sure that the union truly was secured tempered treatment of leading Confederates such as Gen. Robert E. Lee and even President Jefferson Davis. A lenient peace was necessary in large part because reunion *was* the Union cause. But the victorious North had vastly underestimated the tenacity of Confederate bitterness and insolence.

Even as Unionists promoted reunion, they were not necessarily calling for reconciliation. Although the words were (and are still) sometimes deployed as synonyms, subtle yet important differences existed between the two.[9] Reunion, or the political reunification of the nation, had been the chief goal of the overwhelming mass of loyal white citizens. With the rebellion suppressed, the Confederacy destroyed, the work of the founding generation preserved and made safer by the destruction of slavery, reunion was achieved in the spring of 1865 and refined during Reconstruction. Reunion occurred immediately and unequivocally after the Civil War. It was the legal reality for which Unionists had fought and died, and which former Confederates accepted—even if grudgingly.

Reconciliation was harder to define, subject to both multiple and changing interpretations. "Reconciliation," observed a columnist for the *Chicago Tribune* in 1872, "is more largely an affair of the emotions and impulses than of reason, and hence it defies calculation."[10] Even those experiencing or pushing for it often did not know precisely what it meant. It could be a sentiment, an expression of amicable harmony between Union and Confederate sympathizers.[11] For some, reconciliation implied forgiving one's enemies for their transgressions. For others, it suggested a mere silence on the issues.[12] It could serve as a mutual determination by veterans, politicians, and northern and southern boosters to gloss over past differences in order to build a prosperous political and economic future. It could be a performance, a gesture, or a ritual. Reconciliation was not necessary for reunion. But many Americans believed that only when the wounds of war had been left to the past would the United States be free to achieve its true potential greatness.

By the closing decades of the nineteenth century, reconciliation had also evolved into a memory of the war that emphasized the shared American values of valor and devotion to one's cause. Lauding the courage and sacrifice of white soldiers from both sides, a reconciliationist memory helped sell popular magazines like *The Century*; was evoked at Blue-Gray reunions; and was used to sanctify the dedications of the first national military parks. But contrary to popular notions portrayed by Burns's documentary and reinforced by much of the scholarly literature on Civil War memory, reconciliation was never the predominant memory of the war among its participants.[13] Though hand-clasping veterans served as the chief symbol of a reunited and reconciled nation, deep bitterness and a refusal to cast aside judgments about the worthiness of the two causes remained throughout the lives of the generation that had survived the war. This lingering acrimony, however, did not preclude either Unionists or former Confederates from espousing reconciliation. Indeed, both Union and Confederate veterans favored national unity—if on their own terms. Loyal citizens, including the majority of Union veterans, embraced reconciliation of a sort that left no doubt about who had been right (and by extension who had been wrong). For their part, ex-Confederates refused to concede that their cause had been unworthy. In fact, gestures of reconciliation, be they calls to return captured battle flags or appeals for a joint encampment of the GAR and UCV, often tended to reinforce sectional loyalties more than diminish them.

More resistant to reconciliation, and in many instances even to gestures toward that end, were women's organizations. Without the fraternal bonds of soldiering or political and financial incentives, members of the Ladies' Memorial Associations (LMA), United Daughters of the Confederacy (UDC), Woman's Relief Corps, and Ladies of the GAR found little reason to commiserate with their counterparts across the Mason-Dixon Line. In fact, it seemed in many instances that southern white women in particular actively sought to hinder the lovefest promoted by veterans. They could air their true feelings with little fear of the consequences. Praise for such sentiments by their respective veterans suggests that perhaps these were equally the true feelings of many men. While reunion was a legal reality, far less certain was the degree to which former Confederates and advocates of the Union had agreed to forgive and forget—to embrace true, heartfelt reconciliation.

Even when former foes came together in the name of reconciliation, most were not compelled to do so because of shared ideas about white supremacy or a tacit willingness to forget slavery on the part of Union veterans.[14] On the contrary, debates about slavery sometimes proved to be among the most powerful obstacles to reconciliation. In regimental histories, Memorial Day speeches, and even at battlefield dedications, white Union veterans recalled the centrality of the slaveholders' rebellion to the war. While some former abolitionists like Douglass believed that emancipation was being forgotten by the white North, for many white veterans the task of saving the Union could not be separated from slavery. At the eleventh reunion of the Army of the Cumberland in 1879, brevet brigadier general and U.S. congressman from New York Anson George McCook sounded a familiar and convenient moral theme when he declared that "the National authority had been reasserted over every foot of the Nation's soil, and the stain of human slavery had been washed away, and standing under the flag of the Union was a nation of freemen." Slaveholders had undermined the Union, and only slavery's demise could ensure its survival. As the years passed, white U.S. veterans not only refused to forget that slaveholders had precipitated the war, but many also increasingly highlighted their role in emancipation. The Federal armies had saved the Union, helped to abolish slavery, and now one flag would once again wave over the *United* States. Emancipation had been a crucial means and happy result of Union victory.[15]

Although race and slavery were intertwined, nineteenth-century

Americans understood that they were not one and the same. As the following chapters will show, the attitudes of white Union veterans toward slavery, African Americans, and race were exceedingly complex and varied. White veterans admitted black veterans into the posts of the GAR; in some cases white women worked alongside the wives, widows, and daughters of United States Colored Troop (USCT) veterans; and Union statues from Boston's Shaw memorial to Indianapolis's grand monument recollected the role of both African American soldiers and slaves in the conflict. White Unionists had not forgotten that African Americans—or slavery—had been part of the war. But this does not mean that most white U.S. veterans or white northerners in general sought civil and political rights for newly freed men and women. Slavery and race were not interchangeable in the minds of white Union veterans and should not be conflated by us today.

This is not to suggest that race did not shape how individuals and groups memorialized the war. For African Americans, race and slavery could not possibly be separated. Black men had fought in the U.S. armies to secure both their own freedom and the rights of citizenship. Union victory had ensured the freedom of, and promised equality for, more than 4 million men, women, and children. How could the war's memory possibly be severed from the hopes of their race and the promise of freedom? After the war, black communities staged Evacuation Day ceremonies, attended Memorial Days, celebrated Emancipation Days, and collected donations for memorials all in the name of being treated as equal citizens. African Americans waged their own battles to control the war's memory when they denounced Confederate memorials, heralded the bravery of USCT soldiers, called for a national Emancipation Day, and debated efforts to enshrine Lincoln as "the great emancipator."[16]

Both slavery and race likewise played prominent roles in the Confederate memory of the war, the Lost Cause.[17] Beginning in the war and continuing well into the twentieth century, white southerners grappled with the role of slavery in their cause. Some former Confederates, like Jubal A. Early and John S. Mosby, readily admitted that slavery had been the cornerstone of their short-lived nation. But by the 1880s and 1890s, a growing chorus of white southerners vehemently denied that their quest for independence had been anything other than a constitutional struggle to protect state rights. While Lost Cause proponents increasingly denied slavery as a cause of the war, celebrations of white supremacy escalated. Tributes to so-called faithful slaves and mammies who had "understood" their proper role in the race hierarchy became common at monument dedications and in the pages of the *Confederate Veteran* as state-sanctioned segregation and disenfranchisement became the norm in the last decades of the nineteenth century. By the twentieth century, ideas about race had gained a new-found prominence in Confederate memory. When a new generation of white southerners led by the UDC took the reins of the Lost Cause, an emphasis on Reconstruction—or more specifically the white South's triumph over it—brought with it a more emphatically white-supremacist memory of the war.

By arguing that the divisive issues of the war such as slavery and emancipation were forgotten in the name of white supremacy, both popular culture and scholars have suggested that white northerners eventually capitulated to the Confederate memory. The Lost Cause, this line of thinking goes, projected a rhetoric and imagery of battlefield bravery and valor that the North came to embrace.[18] This formulation, however, overlooks two key facts. First, Union veterans could embrace both reconciliation and emancipation. One did not preclude the other. Second, in order for reunion—the Union Cause—to triumph, the victorious North had to welcome white southerners back into the national fold. But Union veterans never forgot that they had fought against treason. Union soldiers did not "sell out" to Confederate memories. Instead, they maintained their own distinctly northern version of the Civil War in which preservation of the Union—and in many cases emancipation—remained integral to northern memories of the war well into the twentieth century.[19] Not only did Unionists fiercely celebrate what they had achieved, but they also continued to condemn the Confederate cause well into the twentieth century (just as Confederates continued to rant about barbaric and heartless Yankees). Former enemies might come together for battlefield dedications where they remained silent on the divisive issues, but beyond these occasions, Union and Confederate veterans tended to maintain that *their* cause was the virtuous one.

Like the veterans, both Union and Confederate women insisted that theirs was the righteous cause. But the women of both sides would come to play decidedly different roles in the war's commemorations. Though numerically more active than Confederate women, Union veterans largely neglected to see their women as essential to either the war or its memory. Alternatively, southern white women proved to be even more recalcitrant than their husbands and fathers in resisting the reconciliationist gush. Having in many ways initiated the Lost Cause in 1865 and 1866 through LMAs, by the turn of the century they appeared to be gaining ever more influence over the war's memory. Praised by their men for their unflagging loyalty to the Lost Cause, they remained intent on vindicating the Confederate cause and keeping its memory alive among future generations. And they succeeded marvelously. In no small part because of these women, Confederate nationalism morphed into a white, southern identity.

Although most northerners did not succumb to the Lost Cause, by the 1920s and 1930s it seemed as if the Confederate memory of the war had eclipsed that of the Union. Not only had groups like the UDC worked vigilantly to keep the Lost Cause alive, but, ironically, the very success of the Union Cause had led to its steady demise in the popular imagination. Having fought to preserve the nation, Unionists had encouraged former rebels to embrace the Stars and Stripes and identify themselves as Americans. The Union had continued to expand both in space and time. It had transformed into an American Cause, especially during the Spanish-American War and the First World War. Loyalty to the Union became enveloped in the national allegiance and patriotism of all Americans, and it was all but impossible to separate the United States of 1861–65 from the United States of the 1880s or 1920s. Even as the Union Cause became more amorphous and obscure, the Confederate Cause remained distinct. Its memory and symbols continued to stand apart, suspended in time and inseparable from the war. Increasingly, it appeared as though the Confederacy *was* the Civil War.

What follows is an examination of how a nation came to understand the Civil War between 1861 and 1939. It is not a general history of Reconstruction, the Gilded Age, or the Progressive Era. Nor is it a chronicle of every memorial organization, battlefield and monument dedication, or veteran reunion. Instead, it is a story about the contentious nature of memory, of the battles fought by men and women, white and black, Confederates and Unionists. Largely focused on the veterans who survived the war and their children, it ends in the late 1930s when most of the war generation had passed, in their parlance, to the other side of "the great divide." Their stories reveal that the categories of those who recalled a Unionist, Emancipationist, Lost Cause, or Reconciliationist memory of the war were never clear-cut, nor did they remain static.[20] Though Civil War commemorations reached a high point of visibility between the 1880s and 1910s, the understandings and interpretations of the conflict and its meaning were continually being created, negotiated, and renegotiated from the moment the first guns were fired in 1861. Perhaps most important, these stories remind us that the memory of the war had profound implications for partisan politics, government policy, citizenship, ideas about gender and race, and the future of the nation.

At the fiftieth anniversary of Gettysburg in 1913, Confederate veteran and Virginia governor William H. Mann declared, "There is no North and no South, no rebels and no Yanks." The sectional divisions of the past had been healed, he argued, so that "all is one great nation."[21] Throughout the 1890s and early 1900s others would offer the same sentiment, many employing the same words. Despite such pronouncements, sectional divisions and discord could hardly be declared vanquished. Under the mantle of Civil War memory, they had festered for too long. The notion of two separate cultures, one north and one south, had been developing well before the first shots were fired at Fort Sumter. But it was in the four bloody years of war that those ties were cemented, identities were crafted, and the memory of the war first took shape.

1

THE WAR

April 1861–March 1865

In the summer of 1863, Henry W. R. Jackson asked his fellow Confederates to consider the definition of "Yankee." In his estimation, it was a term "comprehensively expressive of all that is impure, inhuman, uncharitable, unchristian, and uncivilized (barbarian and heathen is scarcely acceptable in the case)" of these "demons of hell in the guise of men." The lone problem, he contended, was that the English language did not contain "words of sufficient force to express the baseness of the character and nature of the Yankees and the perverting influence of their self established creed, which has given birth to all the demoralizing, degrading, and hellish isms including (the last though not the least) equaltyism or negrophilism." The *Richmond Whig* offered its own definition. According to the records of a British traveler in 1791, the *Whig* said the term had derived "from a Cherokee word, *enakke*, which signifies coward and slave." Accordingly, the "epithet of Yankee was bestowed upon the inhabitants of New England by the Virginians, for not assisting them in a war with the Cherokees, and they have always been held in derision by it."[1] Regardless of its true etymology, for Confederates, "Yankee" was a foul word that came to symbolize money-grubbing, self-righteous, cold-hearted abolitionists bent on destroying all that was good and true in America. Confederate rhetoric insisted that Yankees were evil incarnate.[2]

Unionists similarly loathed their foes. In the summer of 1861, the *Illinois Daily State Journal* published a blistering account of rebel atrocities. Noting that Americans had witnessed shocking acts of barbarity by

Indians in previous wars, the paper was nevertheless shocked by the behavior of Confederates after the battle of Bull Run. "A more blood-thirsty set of pirates never took up arms in a wicked cause," observed the editorial. "When this war broke out we knew that our foes were engaged in an unholy work, and we expected some departure on their part from the established rules of war; but we did not expect to meet armies of cowardly mutilators of the dead, murderers of the wounded and slayers of women." Recounting the monstrous acts committed by the rebels, the paper declared that "a demonic spirit guides their actions." Atrocities by such savages could not be ignored. "We must retaliate," urged the paper, "by making this a war of extermination of a brood of fiends who bring such black disgrace upon their race and country." "They deserve no mercy."[3] For those who supported the Union, Confederates were not only rebels, they were also barbaric, treasonous, and decidedly un-American.[4]

For the soldiers who marched off to battle and the civilians who remained on the home front, the war was raw, it was visceral, and the stakes grew higher as the fighting continued. It was far from the romanticized accounts that would fill picture books, paintings, novels, and even television mini-series in later decades and centuries. Those who experienced the war not only recognized the brutality and devastation inflicted by the bloodletting, but they also held firm convictions about why they were willing to sacrifice so much. Confederates agreed that southern independence was the only way to ensure the survival of their slave-based social system.[5] Their desire for an independent country coupled with a deep and growing hatred for northerners fostered an intense attachment to the Confederate nation that compelled many to continue the struggle even when the odds seemed against them. Northerners were equally clear and tenacious about their war goals: they were fighting to save the Union.

As the war continued to rage for four bloody years, soldiers and civilians, white and black, men and women, Unionists and Confederates experienced and perceived the conflict in a myriad of ways. Many Unionists began to believe that only hard war would quell the rebellion, while many Confederates increasingly recognized that the stakes of their quest for independence were becoming higher with each passing day. Along the border regions, some desperately hoped only to survive the unpredictable and deadly guerrilla warfare. Many on both sides came to view their enemy as barbaric, savage, and un-American. In the postwar years, veterans would wistfully recall how enemy troops had fraternized along the lines and would contend that both rebels and Yankees were true Americans. But the voices of the war told a different story, one of bitter hatred and animosity toward the enemy that would not quickly be forgotten, shaping the memories that would follow and long complicating and limiting the process of reconciliation.

CAUSES

In the spring and early summer of 1861, young men from Minnesota to Maine bade their families goodbye and rushed to the local mustering station to enlist for their nation. Had they been asked why they clamored to take up arms they might have listed any number of reasons: for the adventure that they could not find behind the plowshare, to win the affection of their sweethearts, out of duty and obligation to the state or region from which they hailed, because of their religious convictions, to assure themselves and their communities of their courage and manhood, or simply because their brothers, cousins, and friends had enlisted. Despite this complex mixture of duty, honor, manhood, and comradeship, most would have agreed that they fought primarily for their country, for the Union.[6] As one young farmer from Michigan informed his sister, he enlisted in the summer of 1861 because "the government must be sustained." "If the union is split up the government is distroid . . . we will be a Rewind [ruined] nation," he insisted.[7]

For northern soldiers, fighting for the Union meant fighting to preserve the democratic principles established by the founding fathers that set the United States apart from other nations. Since the Constitutional Convention, Americans had recognized the fragility of the Union. Time after time, both northerners and southerners had cried disunion and threatened to destroy what their forefathers had labored so arduously to create. The crises of Missouri, Kansas-Nebraska, Dred Scott, and John Brown had all made Americans wonder if their precious democracy would survive. Moreover, the European revolutions of 1848 had reminded them that democracies were not guaranteed.[8] If northern soldiers failed they would be unworthy of the heritage bequeathed to them. "Our fathers made this country," wrote one young Ohio lawyer to his wife; "we their children are to save it."[9] The Union was their supreme motivation, allowing them to endure battlefield setbacks, the deaths of comrades, and even their own mortality. Fighting for the Union meant fighting for the principles of liberty, freedom, justice, economic opportunity, and patriotism that Americans held dear.[10] In short, it meant fighting for the country.[11]

Although abolitionists and a small but vocal minority of white northerners had been pushing for emancipation for several decades, most northerners did not initially consider attacking slavery within the South—and most white Union soldiers did not enlist in the name of emancipation.[12] Throughout the antebellum years, the great majority of northerners objected to slavery not on moral grounds but on its spread into the western territories. A loose coalition of antislavery Democrats and Republicans who believed in the "free labor" ideology maintained that the opportunity of men to achieve the status of landholder, and therefore the economic independence essential to freedom, was jeopardized by slavery. In their estimation, slavery created a world of degraded slaves, poor whites with little hope of economic betterment, and lazy aristocrats. If slavery was to spread into the West, many northerners feared their opportunities for social and economic advancement would be severely reduced. The territories should thus be reserved for free men.[13] Most white northerners had no qualms with slavery so long as it did not spread west. Even many political abolitionists directed their attacks more specifically against the slave power rather than the institution of slavery. While men like Senator (and later Governor) Salmon P. Chase of Ohio viewed slavery as morally wrong, many were most acutely concerned about what they perceived as the rising national influence of the slaveholding minority on national policies and northern rights. It was the power of the "slave oligarchy" or the "slavocracy" that they objected to the most.[14]

If they had not gone to war to free the slaves, many northerners held that freeing the great mass of white southerners from the stranglehold of the slave oligarchy was another matter. Initially, few believed the Confederacy enjoyed extensive support. Most white southerners were Unionists, or at worst involuntary rebels, they argued, deceived into secession by a handful of wealthy, slaveholding men who had for years conspired to control the federal government, nationalize slavery, and destroy democracy. "It may well be doubted whether there is, to-day, a majority of legally qualified voters of any State, except perhaps South Carolina, in favor of disunion," President Abraham Lincoln observed as late as July 1861. "There is much reason to believe," he continued, "that the Union men are the majority in many, if not in every other one, of the so-called seceded states."[15] Once freed from this slave-power conspiracy, these wayward countrymen would resume their loyalty to the Constitution.[16] This deep-seated belief in widespread Unionist sympathy not only reaffirmed the validity of the North's goal of reunion, but it also tempered any push for emancipation even among many like Lincoln who opposed slavery.[17]

When southern Unionists failed to materialize and the Union war effort faltered along the banks of the James River in the summer of 1862, however, many northern civilians and soldiers alike came to realize that not only had slaveholders precipitated the conflict, but slavery also continued to bolster the Confederate cause. The labor of 3.5 million enslaved men and women allowed the South to enlist a significant percentage of its military age white men in Confederate armies.[18] More important, slaves directly assisted the war effort when they constructed fortifications, nursed wounded soldiers, worked as pioneers, or labored in southern factories.[19] The Emancipation Proclamation of January 1863 and its provision for arming black men became a tool by which the Union might deny Confederates the use of slave labor and simultaneously place more men in the U.S. armies.[20]

As the war intensified, many white northerners increasingly acknowledged that abolition was the only means of preserving their beloved Union.[21] Col. Hugh B. Ewing no doubt spoke for many Union soldiers when he informed his wife in 1862, "If slavery is not broken, the war will last long supported & fed by it—and the loss of life on both sides will be frightful."[22] An Indiana colonel acknowledged that few of his men were abolitionists, but they desperately desired "to destroy everything that in *aught* gives the rebels strength" including slavery, "so this army will sustain the emancipation proclamation and enforce it with the bayonet."[23] Although emancipation was disdained by Peace Democrats or Copperheads (so called by their enemies for their politically poisonous, even traitorous qualities) and fueled serious antiwar opposition, by 1863 Union and emancipation had become intertwined in the northern war effort.[24] Nevertheless, for most white northerners, emancipation was not a purpose of the war so much as a necessary tool for crushing the rebellion, punishing the white South, and restoring the Union.[25]

Pro-slavery Unionists who donned the blue in border regions such as Kentucky, Maryland, Missouri, eastern Tennessee, and western North Carolina proved to be important exceptions to this pro-emancipation pattern—exceptions that would long shape the contours of Civil War memory in those regions. Kentucky, for example, had overwhelmingly voted for the Constitutional Union candidate John Bell in 1860 and sent an estimated 72,275 white volunteers to fight for the United States, many of whom believed that their interests in slavery were better protected within the Union than outside of it.[26] Throughout the war, slaveholders from the Bluegrass State steadfastly maintained their belief in the constitutionality of slavery, on several occasions turning down Lincoln's offer for compensated emancipation. Even after the Confederate surrender, many Kentuckians refused to acquiesce. As late as November 1865 the conservative-dominated legislature rejected the Thirteenth Amendment, which would abolish slavery throughout the United States. All this serves as a reminder that for vast numbers of loyal citizens in Kentucky and other border regions, Unionism never embraced emancipation.[27]

For those white Union soldiers who did believe emancipation was central to the Union war effort, it is imperative to acknowledge that they did not include nor did they demand that equal rights for African Americans must follow freedom. Instead, most white U.S. soldiers remained as racist as their southern counterparts. Fighting to end slavery did not indicate a belief in racial equality, and therefore it should come as no surprise that veterans would carry their racist convictions with them into the postwar years.[28]

The inclusion of black men within the ranks of the Union army likewise failed to change assumptions about the racial hierarchy.[29] After the battle of Olustee in February 1864, one white Union soldier commended the performance of a United States Colored Troops (USCT) regiment. "Their colonel was then shot dead from his horse, and the arms of the regiment were not loaded; but they preserved their line admirably and fought splendidly," he remarked. Four months later he praised the fearless attack of another colored division at the battle of the Crater but noted their inability to maintain themselves after the Confederate counterattack. The USCT became "panic stricken, and blindly hurl themselves back on our bayonets," he recounted, and "a wild scene of confusion ensues."[30] Perhaps Bartholomew B. S. De Forest of the 81st New York best expressed the sentiments of many white Union soldiers: "They will make good soldiers," he noted, and they should therefore be "recognized as equal with the white soldier, when they are engaged in one common cause." But, he continued, "When he lays off the blue jacket, he is a negro still, and should be treated as God designed he should be, as an inferior, with kindness and sympathy, but not as an equal, in a social point of view."[31] Loyal Americans might acknowledge African American men as first-rate soldiers who would help secure victory for the Union cause, but such praise for USCT soldiers did not indicate a postwar commitment to civil rights for USCT veterans or other freedpeople.

Confederate soldiers marched off to war in the spring and early summer of 1861 for many of the same reasons as their northern brethren. They, too, sought adventure, felt impelled to join companies along with their family and friends, and found motivation in the Scripture. Some bore arms to protect their hearth and homes from Yankee invaders, and others enlisted to protect their cherished liberty and self-determination. Like their northern neighbors, southerners believed that they were the rightful heirs of the American Revolutionary spirit. Confederates repeatedly insisted that just as their forefathers had repudiated the despotic British, southern patriots had seceded from the oppressive Yankees in order to defend their liberty. Moreover, the fact that southerners were defending their homes reminded them of their ancestors' struggles to do the same against the invading Red Coats. "If we should suffer ourselves to be subjugated by the tyrannical government of the North," wrote one Virginia soldier to his wife, "our property would all be confiscated . . . & our people reduced to the most abject bondage & utter degradation." "I think every Southern heart," he demanded, "should now respond to the language of the great Patrick Henry in the days of '76 & say give me Liberty or give me death."[32] Just like northerners, southerners conceived of themselves as the true Americans perpetuating the founding fathers' legacy.[33]

Still others recognized that the southern states had seceded to protect slavery and thus believed the war was merely an extension of that endeavor.[34] Even nonslaveholders understood that slavery provided both social and economic benefits to the white South. Foremost among the reasons for nonslaveholders to support the Confederacy were the advantages of white supremacy. The privileges of being white provided even the poorest men more respect and prestige than any free black man could ever hope to attain. And despite northern arguments of an all-powerful slave oligarchy that controlled the South, living in a slave society afforded many nonslaveholders the ability to rent slaves from their wealthier neighbors during harvest as well as access to railroads that arrived because of planters' market needs. All of that, however, appeared to be in danger with the election of Abraham Lincoln and the Republicans.[35]

Just as Union soldiers were motivated by an ardent patriotism and allegiance to their country, Confederates developed a deep and intense attachment to their new nation. During the first two years of war, a sense of national identity emerged that helped to bind soldiers and the home front to the cause of Confederate independence despite the bloodshed of the battlefield, the adversity of camp life, or even war weariness. This loyalty to an independent Confederate nation came from a variety of sources, including military service, a desire for revenge, powerful symbols such as flags, and a deep-seated belief that white southerners shared little in the way of cultural values with those from the North. By the war's midpoint, however, Robert E. Lee and his soldiers stood at the center of Confederate nationalism. From June 1862 when he took command of his newly christened Army of Northern Virginia until the end of the war, Lee and his army with their string of victories fostered solidarity among soldiers and the home front as well as confidence in the Confederate cause of independence.[36] In September 1864, Ezekiel D. Graham of the 6th Georgia reflected the attitude of many when he proclaimed "the Army of Northern Virginia alone, as the last best hope of the South." Lee's army, he believed, "will sooner or later by its own unaided power win the independence of the Confederacy."[37] Although there were white southerners who became disgruntled with the Confederacy, an unshakable belief in Lee and his army allowed Confederates from all classes and regions to believe they might secure an independent southern nation.[38]

Regardless of whether they donned the blue or the gray, Civil War soldiers understood that they were fighting to preserve their freedom and liberty as true Americans. Even as they considered their own cause righteous in the eyes of God and an extension of the Spirit of 1776, most Confederate and Union soldiers considered the other side not only the enemy but "un-American."[39]

A BARBARIC AND SAVAGE ENEMY

In 1861, Georgia planter Charles Colcock Jones Jr. declared, "In this country have arisen two races, which, although claiming a common parentage, have been so entirely separated by climate, by morals, by religion, and by estimates so totally opposite to all that constitutes honor, truth, and manliness, that they cannot longer exist under the same government."[40] Regardless of the extent to which the North and South were distinctive cultures or two separate civilizations, by the mid-nineteenth century northerners and southerners *believed* they were different and acted accordingly.[41] Even though most shared a common language, belief in the same God, history, and abiding faith in republicanism, by the 1850s Americans on either side of the line separating slavery from free labor could readily point to the differences between northerners and southerners. Increasingly, many northerners came to see the South as a barbaric, backward region where the ignorant and illiterate masses of whites were ruled by a fiery, intemperate slavocracy. White southerners like Jones looked north and envisioned a land of materialist merchants, factory workers who labored under conditions far worse than slaves, filthy immigrants, masculine women, and abolitionist fanatics conspiring to subjugate the South.[42]

Despite how one understood the enemy's motivations, fighting transformed both sides' disdain of the opposing section into a venomous hatred of the enemy and reinforced the perceived sectional differences.[43] As the war carried into a second and then third year, both sides increasingly described the other as savage and brutish. Union soldiers assigned to bury their comrades after the battle of Williamsburg were aghast to find that many "had evidently been bayoneted by the rebels, after they were shot down."[44] News that Confederates had massacred surrendering Union troops at Fort Pillow, including a significant number of USCT soldiers, outraged many Republican editors and their abolitionist allies. "Insatiate as fiends, bloodthirsty as devils incarnate, the Confederates commenced an indiscriminate butchery of whites and blacks, including those of both colors who had been previously wounded," reported the *New York Daily Tribune*. A Cleveland paper concurred, adding that the bloodletting was "without parallel in civilized warfare." Here was inexplicable evidence of the brutality fostered by a slaveholding society.[45]

Confederates were equally appalled by what they perceived as the un-Americanness of their foe. "I don't see why it should be called a *civil* war," observed one Confederate soldier; "we are not fighting our own people— but a race which is & has always been antagonistic in every particular to us—of a different country & of different pursuits."[46] Officers were not immune from such feelings of loathing. When Confederate general Richard Ewell complained to Thomas J. "Stonewall" Jackson that hogs were feasting on the remains of Union soldiers just beyond Confederate lines, Jackson chillingly retorted, "I knew a hog was not particular about what it ate but I gave them credit for having better taste than to eat a Yankee." He famously noted later that "the only objection he had to Genl Lee was that he did not hate Yankees enough."[47] Perhaps Jackson had never witnessed Lee express his own deep abhorrence of the enemy. Hearing that his beloved home Arlington had fallen into enemy hands, Lee informed his daughter that he "should have preferred it to have been wiped from the earth . . . its beautiful hill sunk, and its sacred trees buried, rather than to have been degraded by the presence of those who revel in the ill they do for their own selfish purposes."[48]

Such hatred was not reserved for the men who did the killing. Caricatures of the enemy flowed forth from pens both North and South in the form of political cartoons, songs, and poems intended to animate both fear and hatred in the popular culture. The northern press reminded its readers that the South was controlled by the slavocracy and depicted Confederate president Jefferson Davis in particular as a traitor who, at the very least, was mildly threatening. Such a South could easily be defeated. For their part, southern newspapers regularly published sketches of northerners, and Lincoln in particular, at best as incompetent and inept, at worst as handmaidens of the Devil. Confederate camp songs and poetry likewise mocked the Union war effort and bolstered southern soldiers' belief in their own invincibility. But Confederate popular culture also spread the conviction that Yankees were invading blue hordes bent on subjugating the white South and unleashing miscegenation on the region.[49] One Confederate ballad warned,

> Northern Vandals tread our soil,
> Forth they come for blood or spoil,
> To the homes we've gained with toil,
> Shouting "Slavery!"[50]

For the men of Kirk's Ferry Rangers of Louisiana who listened to this song in 1861, the meaning was clear: this was not an objection to black bondage; rather, Confederate soldiers were called to arms to prevent the savage North from enslaving the white South. Another verse, penned by Confederate prisoner of war S. Teakle Wallis and published in the *Richmond Examiner*, anticipated the race war sure to be unleashed by the savage foes:

> They are turning the slaves upon us,
> And with more than the fiend's worst art,
> Have uncovered the fire of the savage,
> That slept in his untaught heart![51]

Whether read in newspapers or sung in camp, popular images of an incompetent, brutal, inhumane, and un-American enemy pervaded both North and South.

Northerners pointed to Confederate women as particularly fiendish, especially in their adoration of ghastly war relics. Reports circulated of southern women donning rings carved from Yankee bones or exhibiting remains taken from Union soldiers as parlor ornaments. According to one account, a southern woman had requested her lover to fetch "Linken's skaalp." Mollie Sanford of Colorado was aghast after hearing of a Texas woman who demanded that her sweetheart "never return . . . without a necklace made of Yankee ears."[52] With stories such as these circulating, the following poem, which appeared in a San Francisco newspaper during the summer of 1862, no doubt held resonance with many Unionists:

> Silent the lady sat alone:
> In her ears were rings of dead men's bone;
> The brooch on her breast shone white and fine,
> 'Twas the polished joint of a Yankee spine;

And the well-carved handle of her fan
Was the finger bone of a Lincoln man,
She turned aside a flower to cull,
From a vase which was made of a human skull;
For to make her forget the loss of her slaves
Her lovers had rifled the dead men's graves.
Do you think I'm describing a witch or a ghoul?
There no such things—and I'm not a fool;
Nor did she reside in Ashantee;
No—the fair lady was an F.F.V.[53]

Some Confederate women appear to have relished their reputation for collecting such seemingly gruesome war trophies. In Savannah, one Confederate woman told Union soldiers that her prized possession was a letter from an admirer of hers sent from the battlefield of Chickamauga, reportedly written in Yankee blood. Her rebel soldier told her that he had "dipped the pen in blood as it ran from the wound that caused the yankees death." She informed the Union soldiers that she intended to keep it as "evidence of the heroism of Chivalry." Another rebel woman claimed to be the proud recipient of a Yankee jaw bone that had been transformed into a spur, while one of her acquaintances declared that she used a Yankee skull for a drinking cup.[54] Confederate nurse Phoebe Yates Pember was horrified by a conversation with several Richmond women. "One lady said she had a pile of Yankee bones lying around her pump so that the first glance on opening her eyes would rest upon them," she noted in her diary; "another begged me to get her a Yankee Skull to keep her toilette trinkets in."[55] Whether there is any truth to these tales is unknown and insignificant. What mattered was that these Confederate women clearly realized that bragging to Union soldiers of such cherished relics only served to demonstrate their deep faith in the Confederate cause and exhibit their intense hatred for their foes.

Public announcements were not the only expressions of southern white women's hatred of Yankees. Nearly every diary or collection of letters written by a Confederate woman contained some colorful phrase exuding her loathing for the "vandals in blue." Sixteen-year-old Lizzie Alsop of Fredericksburg boasted in her diary that she "never hear[s] or see[s] a Federal private or officer riding down the street that I don't wish his neck may be broken before he crosses the bridge."[56] Emma LeConte of South Carolina had hated the enemy even before she encountered them. But once they arrived at her home, she recognized that there were "no limits to the feelings of hatred" she bore for the men whose name was "a synonym for all that is mean, despicable and abhorrent."[57] Another declared she wanted no mercy for such beasts after learning that U.S. soldiers had raped a white woman in Memphis. "Shoot them, dear husband, every chance you get," she wrote in October 1863. "Hold no conference with them. They are devil furies who thirst for your blood and who will revenge themselves on your helpless wife and children. It is God's will and wish for you to destroy them. You are his instrument and it is your Christian duty. Would that I may be allowed to take up arms, I would fight them, until I died."[58]

Although the trials and stresses of war led some women to become disgruntled with the Confederacy, southern men stressed Confederate women's devotion and sacrifice to the cause in the name of national unity.[59] In an 1863 book dedicated to women's efforts, Henry W. R. Jackson had no doubt that if Confederate men should ever fail to prove heroic, the South's women would "call forth from among their own sex a leader for our armies to forego the pleasures of ease and feminine considerations and respond to the call of temporal requirements for the occasion like a Joan of Arc."[60] A soldier from the Army of Tennessee congratulated the women of Atlanta for their "constant and glorious patriotism and self-sacrificing devotion to our cause."[61] Even the Confederacy's beloved Stonewall Jackson noted that the South's women were "patriots in the truest sense of the word, and I more than admire them."[62] While women did not vote or (usually) shoulder muskets, southern men considered them a vital component of the nation, a fact that would become imperative in the immediate postwar efforts to commemorate the Confederacy.[63]

Tales of Confederate women's defiant, vituperative, and unfeminine behavior permeated the northern army and home front. Rather than merely chastising the unruly deeds of rebel women, these reports had the added effect of stirring resentment in the North both among and toward Union women, who many claimed were not as devoted as their southern counterparts.[64] Yet countless northern women had volunteered on behalf of the Union cause. Like Confederate women, when the war began tens of thousands rushed to organize informal soldiers' aid societies, where they sewed national and regimental flags for their troops. Coordinating their efforts through the U.S. Sanitary Commission, they produced clothing, bedding, jellies, and other goods to be distributed to the troops. They held grand bazaars like the one in Chicago in 1863, which raised more than $100,000 for soldier relief. Middle-class women in urban areas formed "Loyal Leagues" devoted to identifying disloyal elements of their communities. An estimated 21,000 women (out of a population of 22 million) served in hospitals as nurses, matrons, cooks, laundresses, seamstresses, and chamber-maids. And at least 400 donned the clothes of men and went off to the battlefields to fight.[65]

Despite their volunteer activities, the distance between the battlefront and the home front meant that northern women were often perceived by Union soldiers, the northern press, and even other women as indifferent to the war effort.[66] The very fact that they did not endure the tightening blockade meant they did not have to confine themselves to two meals a day or forego luxury clothing as some had urged. Moreover, unlike Confederate women, northern women had fewer opportunities to display acts of defiance against enemy soldiers.[67] When they did have contact with rebel forces, they too insulted enemy soldiers and boldly defended their cause.[68] And like Confederate she-devils, they relished battlefield relics; one woman later recalled that she had been thrilled to receive the sword of a Confederate soldier from the battle of Fair Oaks. She had been told that the saber had been "struck from the hand of a rebel colonel, while in the act of raising it to strike one of our officers." "Oh, how proud I felt of that beautiful silver-mounted trophy," she later wrote. She could not help but treasure the thought that as the rebel soldier "lay in the agonies of death . . . his splendid sword passed into my feeble hands."[69]

Loathing the enemy was not enough. Instead, loyal women were forced to wage a war on the home front against the stereotype that they were less than devoted patriots. In a well-circulated pamphlet titled "A Few Words on Behalf of the Loyal Women of the United States," an anonymous northern woman rebuked such nonsense. She dismissed the notion that Union women had not "shown passion enough," arguing that while northern ladies had been taught to demonstrate self-restraint, Confederate women were less educated and "more demonstrative." "Passionate utterance is no evidence of right feeling," she added. While northern women busily, if quietly, labored in their soldiers' aid societies or at collection centers of the U.S. Sanitary Commission for the cause of liberty, "the women of the South have no higher incentive than the determination to uphold their husbands in the attempt to perpetuate slavery." Was "passion" relevant, she wondered, when one's cause was wrong?[70] Such unwomanly, treasonous behavior was hardly something Union women should emulate. Like U.S. soldiers, Union women steadfastly believed theirs was the right cause, and they would continue to maintain this in the postwar years. Yet the perception that northern women had not been as devoted as Confederate women would continue to haunt them long after the war had ended.

If northerners looked upon Confederate women as barbaric and unwomanly, white southerners argued that the strongest evidence of Yankee savagery lay in the implementation of a hard-war policy.[71] Neither Lincoln nor his generals had commenced the war intending to inflict suffering on southern civilians or their property. Not only did few northerners initially believe that the Confederacy enjoyed widespread support, but targeting southern civilians was also anathema to the Union's war aim of restoring the country. Instead, throughout the first year of conflict, the U.S. government actively deployed a conciliatory policy that sought to spare white southerners from the hardships of war. But a series of Union defeats in the summer of 1862 convinced many northerners that only in abandoning conciliation could they achieve reunion.[72]

The hard-war strategy was most evident in Gen. William Tecumseh Sherman's march through Georgia and the Carolinas and Gen. Philip H. Sheridan's raids in the Shenandoah Valley in 1864.[73] Although both friendly and enemy armies wreaked havoc on the landscape, destroying railroads, fences, and fields, southern residents and soldiers watched as Union armies began to purposefully wage a war that included the destruction of any and all resources that might sustain an army in the field. As Union troops marched through Virginia, Tennessee, and Georgia, they seized crops and livestock and dismantled railroads in an effort to destroy Confederate morale. Even more egregious, according to Confederates, were Union bombardments of southern cities such as Fredericksburg, Vicksburg, Atlanta, Charleston, and Petersburg. Such barbaric attacks on civilians infuriated Confederates both in the field and on the home front, convincing them that the foe they fought was not abiding by the rules of civilized warfare. After all, churches and residences, not merely military infrastructure such as railroads, provided strategic targets for Union guns during each of these sieges. But more important, they believed that Union commanders had explicitly ordered the shelling of cities occupied primarily by women and children. Upon hearing that Petersburg had been fired upon, the *Charleston Mercury* ranted that the Union would resort to the "barbarous practice of shelling a city" occupied primarily by "defenceless [*sic*] women and children."[74] None "but the most dastardly race on the face of the earth would engage in a business so supremely contemptible, as well as inexpressibly villainous," declared one Richmond newspaper.[75] The Union policies only reinforced what many white southerners had believed for decades before the war, namely that northerners were a brutish, uncivilized, and barbaric people intent upon destroying all that was good about the South.

For Confederates, the most deplorable aspect of hard war was emancipation. White southerners had long believed that Republicans were intent on ending slavery, not simply preventing its spread west. The Confiscation Acts of 1861 and 1862, which authorized seizure of Confederate property, including slaves, had indicated as much, but the Emancipation Proclamation confirmed their worst fears.[76] Writing to Secretary of War James A. Seddon in January 1863, General Lee described the Emancipation Proclamation as a "savage and brutal policy . . . which leaves us no alternative but success or degradation worse than death."[77] Confederate clerk John B. Jones concurred, noting that the "Emancipation Proclamation, if not revoked, may convert the war into a most barbarous conflict."[78] And addressing the Confederate Congress that same month, Jefferson Davis denounced the proclamation as "the most execrable measure recorded in the history of guilty man."[79] The stakes were now higher than they had ever been: if the Confederacy was defeated, life would be radically different for all southerners, white and black, slave owner and nonslaveholder. By 1863, Confederate soldiers had even more reason to secure their independence than they had believed in 1861.[80]

More disturbing for many rebels was the entry of African American soldiers into combat.[81] Upon learning that Lincoln had demanded that the USCT be treated the same as white troops, one Confederate predicted that "the war will not be conducted in a civilized way hereafter."[82] The image of black troops only stirred white southerners' long-held fear of a race war, of armed black men roaming the land, raping white women and murdering white masters. From occupied New Orleans, Julia LaGrand noted that Union troops "preach openly to the negroes to arise and kill us." Such fears explain why some rebels proved exceedingly pleased with the murder of black prisoners of war at Fort Pillow and Petersburg's battle of the Crater.[83] Cities might be rebuilt, fields might be planted again, but the long-term effects of emancipation would not only be disastrous for the white South but also be permanent.

The hard-war policies of foraging, bombarding southern cities, and emancipation had the unintended effect of stirring a desire for retaliation and bolstering rebels' devotion to their nation. "If there is one degree of *hell* hotter than an other I think it will be retained for the Vandles who invade our homes, rob & destroy our property," one soldier advised his wife.[84] War weariness, strains of disaffection, class tension, doubts about slavery, and even fears of God's disfavor had taken their toll, causing some to question their government.[85] But even well into 1864, the Union's hard-war tactics tended to strengthen Confederate resolve. Whether a soldier hearing tales of his family's suffering on the home front or a woman encountering Union soldiers as they marched through South Carolina, hard-war tactics were likely to embolden white southerners' will to fight, reinforce their sense of themselves as a distinct people, and heighten the desire for an independent nation. Union tactics thus bound soldiers and civilians ever more tightly to the Confederate nation.[86]

For those who lived in the border regions, it was more difficult if not impossible to identify the enemy. With loyalties violently divided, one's minister, neighbor, or even brother might support the opposition. Although the border regions sent soldiers off to battlefields to fight under the regular armies, these locales experienced some of the harshest and most brutal atrocities of the war through guerrilla fighting. Guerrilla warfare was intense and sprawling. Spilling into parts of the Upper South, Deep South, trans-Mississippi West, and Midwest (well beyond the traditional notion of the Border States of Maryland, Delaware, Kentucky, and Missouri), guerrillas blurred the lines between friend and foe, civilians and combatants, even more than regular warfare.[87] Guerrilla troops— whether Unionist or rebel irregulars, bushwhackers, sanctioned partisan rangers like those led by John Singleton Mosby, lone gunmen, or outlaw gangs—attacked not only army supply lines and advancing troops but also civilians. They plundered towns, kidnapped alleged spies, and executed their avowed enemies under the cover of darkness. Confederate irregulars launched especially brutal attacks against African Americans who sought to enlist in the Union army. Perhaps the most infamous bushwhacking took place along the Missouri-Kansas border, where guerrilla chieftains William Quantrill, "Bloody Bill" Anderson, and George Todd led troops in pillaging, looting, terrorizing, and inflicting horrendous murders on Unionist civilians, then quickly disappeared into the countryside with the aid of the population sympathetic to the Confederates.[88]

In the border regions, guerrilla conflict muddied the waters, complicating the war's memory and prospects for reconciliation. Border residents often found it nearly impossible to come to any collective understanding of the conflict either among themselves or with those who lived in the major theaters of regular warfare. In the postwar years, some rebels would strive to forget the brutality of guerrilla warfare in an effort to refashion their image. Others proudly and defiantly remembered their role, insisting they had been legitimate soldiers and had nothing of which to be ashamed. Still others, both Unionists and rebels, clung to the memory as a marker of all they had endured.[89] The savage war of guerrillas would continue to pervade the public and private lives of those along the border well into the late nineteenth century.

For Unionists and Confederates living beyond the contested border, the treatment of prisoners of war engendered tremendous enmity. During the fighting, approximately 408,000 soldiers became prisoners, while 56,000 succumbed to the deadly conditions of their cells and makeshift compounds.[90] The treatment and horrid death of so many soldiers stirred embittered accusations and violent passions, especially after the system of prisoner exchange broke down in the wake of African American enlistments in 1863. Andersonville is infamous, but horrid accounts poured forth from the more than 150 prisons across both the North and South: of disease, starvation, rats, inadequate clothing, deplorable sanitary conditions, and guards who shot prisoners without provocation. No doubt many prisoners could have echoed what one Texas soldier said of his place of imprisonment when he declared that "if there was ever hell on Earth, Elmira prison was that hell."[91]

The degree to which the suffering was a result of intentional malice or a product of incompetence has been debated since the war.[92] But during the conflict, each side was sure that their foe was deliberately inflicting torture on prisoners. In 1864, the U.S. Sanitary Commission published a report charging that Confederates were employing cruelty and deprivations as part of a "predetermined plan, originating somewhere in the rebel counsels, for destroying and disabling the soldiers of their enemy." (Of course Confederate prisoners, the commission maintained, received generous treatment in Union hands.)[93] The northern press launched tirades in particular against Capt. Henry Wirz of Andersonville and Dick Turner of Richmond's Libby Prison for their alleged atrocities, while numerous eyewitness accounts from men who had survived these stockades appeared during the war. In June 1864, *Harper's Weekly* ran two illustrations of men appearing as nearly skeletons, thereby providing "indisputable proof" of Confederate authorities' "inhuman treatment" of Union prisoners in Richmond's Belle Isle. Prisons revealed the enemy in his most barbaric and brutal form.[94] It is no small wonder that the perceived inhumanity and atrocities committed against prisoners of war would prove to be one of the bitterest of memories for years to come.

FRANK LESLIE'S ILLUSTRATED NEWSPAPER

Entered according to the Act of Congress in the year 1864, by FRANK LESLIE, in the Clerk's Office of the District Court for the Southern District of New York.

No. 455—Vol. XVIII]   NEW YORK, JUNE 18, 1864.   [PRICE 10 CENTS, $4 00 YEARLY, 13 WEEKS $1 00.

The Campaign — Grant and Sherman — Richmond and Atlanta.

ANOTHER week of signal and uninterrupted successes has been added to the glorious record of our advancing armies, East and West. Grant thundering at the gates of Richmond, and Sherman sweeping down with his irresistible columns upon Atlanta, are the great historical facts of the day. The heart of every Unionist rejoices, while the chiefs, organs and oracles of the rebellion are amazed and confounded.

These treacherous guides of a deluded people are now beginning to realise their folly, and to hint at their hopeless situation. Their hitherto unfailing devices of audacious falsehoods and brazen deceptions have failed to account, to the satisfaction of their credulous followers, for the presence of Gen. Grant in front of Richmond and of Gen. Sherman at Atlanta. And why? Because the popular credulity of the South had been flattered with the promises of a crushing campaign through Maryland and Pennsylvania by Gen. Lee, and a sweeping invasion of Ohio by Gen. Jo. Johnston with an army of veterans 100,000 strong.

These royal promises, contrasted with the sorry performances of both Lee and Johnston, have demanded an explanation beyond the inventive faculties of the rebel leaders to make. But they have, nevertheless, tried, by the boldest misrepresentations and effrontery, to make it appear that Lee and Johnston are doing wonders towards the achievement of Southern independence. Thus, when a few weeks ago the people of Virginia inquired why Gen. Lee, instead of moving across the Potomac, was on the road to Richmond, with Gen. Grant close upon his flanks, they were answered that Gen. Lee is drawing the Yankees away from Washington. He will still entice them on to Richmond with a small force, so disposed as to appear a large army, while, with the main body

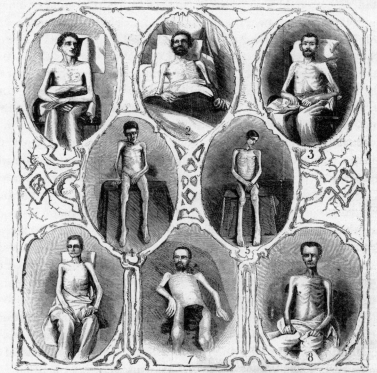

1. Private Lewis Klein, Co. A, 14th N. Y. Cav.   2. Private John Breinig, Co. G, 4th Ky. Cav.   3. Private George H. Wilde, Co. F, 8th Md.   4. Private Francis W. Beedle, Co. M, 8th Mich. Cav.   5. Private John Q. Rose, Co. —, 8th Ky.   6. Private Charles R. Woodworth, Co. G, 9th Mich. Cav.   7. Private L. H. Perham, Co. B, 2d W. Tenn. Cav.   8. Private Edward Cunningham, Co. F, 7th Ohio Cav.

UNION SOLDIERS AS THEY APPEARED ON THEIR RELEASE FROM THE REBEL PRISONS.—FROM PHOTOGRAPHS MADE BY ORDER OF CONGRESS.—SEE PAGE 199.

Union soldiers as they appeared on their release from rebel prisons.
This June 1864 edition of Frank Leslie's Illustrated Newspaper *depicting Union prisoners of war unleashed a torrent of anger among northerners.*
(Library of Congress)

If memories of prisoners of war conjured up resentment and animosity in the postwar years, the gallantry of battlefield fighting would prove to be one aspect of war on which many veterans would eventually agree. The first endeavor to commemorate a battleground occurred at Gettysburg just weeks after the battle ceased. One of the many thousands of visitors to the town in those first days was Pennsylvania governor Andrew G. Curtin, who was aghast at the number of unburied bodies and concerned by the temporary nature of the graves. In late July, representatives from the northern states who had lost men in the battle held an informal meeting to discuss the issue. All agreed, as army surgeon Theodore Dimon recounted, that it would be "practicable to have a piece of ground purchased for a burial place on or near the battlefield, to which the dead bodies of all our soldiers should be removed and there buried by regiments and states and their graves permanently marked." Gettysburg attorney David Wills conveyed the information to Governor Curtin, who agreed that a cemetery should be created on the hallowed ground. Working on behalf of Pennsylvania, Wills secured the purchase of several acres near the town's Evergreen Cemetery and the reinterments began.[95]

From October through March, crews labored to reinter 3,512 Union bodies in the burial ground. Uniting soldiers together in death, rather than returning them to their homes for burial as had been done in previous wars, was a radical concept born of necessity in a war that claimed more than 750,000 lives.[96] In designing the space, the Cemetery Association agreed that every state would receive equal placement and laid out the grounds so that each grave was of identical importance regardless of rank. All soldiers would be equal in death, among those who had fought on the side of right.[97] Charged with superintending the interments, Gettysburg physician Samuel Weaver meticulously examined every corpse to ensure that no rebel would lie beside an honorable Union soldier for eternity. The Confederate dead were instead left decomposing in mass shallow trench graves for years after the battle.[98] "None but loyal soldiers of the Union lie here," declared a December 1865 issue of the veterans' magazine *Hours at Home*. "This intermingling of States in the ashes of their dead," the periodical continued, "is itself a symbol and a prophecy of the reality and perpetuity of that Union which was here redeemed and sealed by so much precious blood." The cemetery would be known as the Soldiers' National Cemetery—the name itself invoking the exclusivity of the term "national," by which northerners meant those loyal to the Union.[99] In honoring the Union dead alone, the national cemetery at Gettysburg established a precedent for commemorating the war dead that would find full fruition after the war's guns finally fell silent.

Construction of the cemetery had only recently begun when, on November 19, 1863, nearly 20,000 people descended on the small Pennsylvania town to dedicate the first national cemetery. Like the southern Memorial Days that would commence three years later, the day's ceremony began with a military procession that wound from the center of town to the cemetery site. For two hours the principal orator of the era, Edward Everett, spoke laboriously, detailing the three-day battle and honoring the men who had fallen in one of the North's most triumphant victories. But there were four elements of his talk that would prove significant in the grander narrative of Civil War memory. First, Everett stressed that the field itself was memorable. "The spots where they stood and fell . . . Seminary Ridge, the Peach-Orchard, Cemetery, Culp, and Wolf Hill," would henceforth become "dear and famous." This land was sacred. Second, unlike most northern dedicatory addresses, he issued effusive praise to "the women of the loyal states" not only for nursing wounded soldiers, but also for their steadfast support on the home front. Third, he unreservedly denounced the war as a rebellion and condemned the South for initiating the war to preserve slavery. He reminded the crowd of the consequences of yielding to the rebels, namely "national suicide." Moreover, he noted the North's responsibility for ensuring that the "helpless colored population, thousands of whom are periling their lives in the ranks of our armies," were not returned to the horrors of slavery. Finally, and most important, he steadfastly believed that the war was first and foremost about re-Union. "The bonds that unite us as one People," he declared, "are of perennial force and energy, while the causes of alienation are imaginary, factitious, and transient. The heart of People, North and South, is for the Union."[100] While Lincoln's short address would become mythic, memorized by schoolchildren for generations and enshrined in stone throughout the nation, Everett's words, with the exception of his praise for northern women, foreshadowed more accurately how northerners would come to remember the war.

Efforts to secure the battlefield began at the same time as those to create a national cemetery, although the motives and visions differed from the start. Initiated by David McConaughy, another local attorney, the Gettysburg Battlefield Memorial Association (GBMA) was a private organization dedicated to protecting the land now sanctified by blood. In a letter dated August 13, 1863, McConaughy explained that immediately after the battle "the thought occurred to me that there could be no more fitting and expressive memorial of the heroic battle and signal triumph of our army . . . than the battle-field itself . . . preserved and perpetuated in the exact form and condition they presented during the battle." He had already purchased several significant portions of the field, including the heights of Cemetery Hill, the granite spur of Round Top, and a portion of Wolf's Hill. Calling on the "patriotic citizens of Pennsylvania" to subscribe by purchasing ten-dollar shares, he hoped to form an organization that would preserve the only battlefield on the free soil of the North.

The following year, on April 30, the GBMA was incorporated to "commemorate the heroic deeds, the struggles, and triumphs of [the Union's] brave defenders." "Let it be the shrine of loyalty and patriotism," declared the association, "whither in all times will come the sons of America, and the pilgrims of all lands, to view with wonder and veneration the sacred scenes of heroic struggles, in which were involved the life of the nation and the perpetuity of liberty." While the cemetery would honor those who had sacrificed their lives, the battlefield would serve as a memorial to both the living and the dead, preserving for eternity the Army of the Potomac's victory. With the war still raging to the south, the GBMA sought not only to protect the field now consecrated by blood but also to shape the lessons of the war for future generations.[101]

The battlefield was intended to serve as a site where visitors might come to better understand the war, but not everyone could travel to the nation's newest shrine. Thus by 1864, commercialized versions of the battle began to appear. Booklets, maps, photography collections, stereographs, and even sheet music became available for the American public. Baltimore's Sanitary Fair and Philadelphia's Great Central Fair both showcased and sold relics from the field. Such material objects were not trivial but intended to educate and connect those on the home front with those on the frontlines. Bringing a purchased print, image, or even minié ball found on the field into one's home was similar to collecting relics sent from soldiers to the home front. Both instances knit the home and battlefront more closely together in the great endeavor for the Union. On the other hand, enterprising merchants were well aware of the potential profit to be derived from such an emotional item.[102]

Militarily, Gettysburg may not have been as significant as the surrender of Vicksburg. But the battle had been resoundingly important for many in the North because it marked the Army of the Potomac's first clear victory over Lee and his Army of Northern Virginia. Here on the rolling hills of Pennsylvania, the Army of the Potomac had finally stopped Lee's momentum in the eastern theater generated by Fredericksburg and Chancellorsville. The outcome of the war remained uncertain, yet northerners felt compelled to commemorate so holy a plot of land that was within their domain. Eventually the battlefield would become a much more popular tourist attraction than the national cemetery, but both would permanently alter the landscape of the nineteenth century and thus serve as the most important physical reminders of the war. For future generations, these would be the places where victors and losers, veterans and tourists, would come to relive, experience, or learn about the nation's bloodiest conflict.

Just as white northerners began commemorating the Union dead at Gettysburg even before the war was over, African Americans initiated the first Emancipation Day celebrations in the winter of 1862–63.[103] Rejoicing in Lincoln's proclamation set to take effect on January 1, 1863, black Americans from the Midwest to the South heralded the act as confirmation that the national battle was indeed being fought for universal freedom. For them it would not be the battlefield that would loom as the principal site of commemoration, but rather the town and city streets on which they had been denied equal access as slaves. Throughout the holiday season in Mt. Pleasant, Iowa, a growing community of former slaves enjoyed a ball and sumptuous dinners and then went "marching through town all night whooping, dancing, and singing 'Kingdom Coming.'"[104] On New Year's Day, a day previously feared as one of uncertainty and horror because it marked the annual rental and sale of slaves in the South, freedmen and -women from the surrounding countryside arrived in Norfolk, Virginia, for an immense celebration. The occasion began with a spectacular procession led by black soldiers through the city's main avenues. Behind the freedom warriors marched civilians—men, women, and children, most on foot but many in wagons and carts. Demonstrating their intense revulsion of the rebel cause, two particularly daring black women proceeded to destroy a Confederate flag and subsequently to trample it, and later participants burned an effigy of Jefferson Davis. On the streets of Norfolk, black Virginians claimed their vision of a triumphant Union and a defeated Confederacy.[105]

Retaliation by local whites did not dim the celebration. Neither did the contingent nature of freedom. In 1863 Confederate defeat, and therefore slavery, was hardly a given. But this failed to diminish the faith many freedpeople held that history would be redemptive. The first Emancipation Day celebration and those in the following decades from Chicago to the Deep South defined the struggle for liberty among African Americans as the most important aspect of the war—the aspect most worth remembering.[106]

A HARMONIOUS REUNION

When veterans reunited on the bloody battlefields like Gettysburg in the 1880s and 1890s, some of their favorite memories would be those that stressed the fraternizing that occurred between armies. Although not nearly as ubiquitous as veterans would suggest, fraternization did happen on occasion. There are well-documented instances of an informal truce along the banks of the Rappahannock in December 1862 when soldiers from both sides tossed stones toward the enemies' bank while some of the most daring trekked across for visits with their foes.[107] A year later, a member of the 5th New York Cavalry stationed near Germania Ford noted that his men had become "quite familiar with Rebel pickets on the other side of the river," exchanging papers and swapping coffee for tobacco.[108] As the siege of Petersburg entered its ninth month, soldiers occasionally indulged in exchanges along the picket lines. "We had a truce in front of our Brigade this evening for a few minutes. I exchanged papers with a Yankee. Some of them gave our boys coffee, pocket knives, etc. The truce ended and both parties resumed firing," Confederate private James Hall scribbled in his diary.[109] Union nurse Cornelia Hancock likewise observed the rebels exchanging tobacco with soldiers in blue but knew that they would "shoot with vigor when ordered."[110]

As Hall and Hancock indicated, there was often a very practical rationale for this fraternization: a longing for goods to which the enemy had access. Union soldiers who craved tobacco were quite willing to trade northern newspapers and coffee with their foes. Recognizing that orders strictly forbade such contacts, some clever soldiers employed warning devices such as floating sailboats across the water to caution each other about approaching officers. Soldiers along picket lines likewise traded insults or profane jokes rather than goods. Even when these exchanges took place on friendly terms, seldom did they represent the fraternal camaraderie that veterans would recall in later years. Trade along the pickets did not signify the roots of reconciliation; rather, it was mere evidence of soldiers' desperation for tobacco, caffeine, or even lively banter.[111]

If such consorting with the enemy was not intended to promote reconciliationist sentiment, the wartime policies of President Lincoln and General Grant were. By the time frost reappeared in the fall of 1863, substantial portions of the Confederacy, including New Orleans, parts of Arkansas, and most of middle Tennessee, had come under Union control. Believing that the Union would soon be victorious, Lincoln began to formulate his policy for reconstructing the nation. He recognized, however, that process would be difficult because many northerners fiercely hated the rebels and wanted to see them punished, while others longed for a quick reunion. His December 8, 1863, proclamation previewed the policy he would adopt a year and a half later: he offered pardon and amnesty as well as the full restoration of rights "except as to slaves" to any rebels who took an oath of allegiance to the United States (high-ranking Confederate officers and government officials were omitted from this plan). In any given state, when the number of oath takers reached ten percent of the number who had voted in the 1860 election, the loyal constituency could establish a new state government that would be recognized by the president. Although some in the North believed his plan would facilitate a quick reunion, plenty of Democrats and Republicans offered sharp rebukes—the Democrats charging that the plan interfered with state rights, while Radical Republicans cried that it was much too lenient. Other proposals abounded, including the 1864 Wade-Davis Bill that would have required, among other things, an end to military resistance and a declaration of loyalty to the Union by half the population, so the heated disputes continued. Despite these points of contention, both Lincoln and congressional Republicans agreed on two things: winning the war was imperative, and slavery must be abolished to secure the Union.[112]

Grant's terms of surrender at Fort Donelson and Vicksburg were likewise intended to promote a harmonious reunion. Along the Cumberland River on February 16, 1862, Grant would first demonstrate the magnanimity toward the rebels that would become legendary at Appomattox. Asked if he intended to observe a traditional surrender ceremony, he declined: "The surrender is now a fact. We have the fort, the men, the guns. Why should we go through vain forms and mortify and injure the spirit of brave men, who, after all, are our own countrymen."[113] Sixteen months later his terms were equally generous. "Men who have shown much endurance and courage as those in Vicksburg," he wrote to Confederate general John C. Pemberton, "will always challenge the respect of an adversary, and I can assure you will be treated with all the respect due to prisoners of war."[114] Foreshadowing the policy he would employ with Lee, Grant provided the Confederate soldiers "paroles," which allowed them to travel home so long as they promised not to take up arms against the United States again and thereby relieving them of incarceration in northern prisoner camps. Defending his rationale against numerous complaints, he further explained: "The men had behaved so well that I did not want to humiliate them. I believed that consideration for their feelings would make them less dangerous foes during the continuance of hostilities, and better citizens after the war was over."[115] Grant, like Lincoln, fervently believed the Union would succeed and wanted the army to set the tone for a harmonious peace.

Lincoln and his commanders were joined by millions in their continued devotion to the nation. Throughout Illinois, Indiana, Ohio, New York, Massachusetts, Wisconsin, and California, Republicans rechristened themselves the "Union Party," abandoning the more radical principles of their recent past and claiming to become more bipartisan. The resulting fusion coalition refused to let anti-slavery alone define it. Declaring themselves, as opposed to the Democrats, the foremost devotees to the nation, Republicans could declare that the country was their party. In 1864, the national Republican convention assumed the banner of bipartisanship, renominating Lincoln as its presidential candidate and nominating former Democrat and Tennessee senator Andrew Johnson for vice president. The Union Party's primary goal was reunion.[116]

While the Democrats likewise agreed that saving the Union was imperative, adding emancipation to the war aims had intensified the divisiveness between the two parties and thus within the North.[117] Supported by a base of working-class northerners who feared competition with freedmen, the antiwar Copperheads railed against the Conscription Acts of 1863 and alleged Republican violations of civil liberties, and they blamed Lincoln's party for the faltering U.S. war effort. But even those Democrats who supported the war effort, the so called War Democrats, would use racism as their primary political weapon to wage a formidable presidential campaign in 1864. Democrats nominated George B. McClellan, former commander of the Army of the Potomac and a soldier favorite. Though widely regarded as a War Democrat, McClellan agreed to run on a peace platform, noting in late August that "if I am elected, I will recommend an immediate armistice and a call for a convention of all the states and insist upon exhausting all and every means to secure peace without further bloodshed."[118] But peace was not enough for many Democrats. Transforming Lincoln's Emancipation Proclamation into the "Miscegenation Proclamation" and calling on voters to reject "Abraham Africanus the First," the party exploited fears of racial amalgamation. By the early fall, it appeared that the Democrats might prevail, but news from the battlefield proved invaluable for the Republicans. On September 2, Sherman captured the key railroad city of Atlanta, and within weeks more favorable reports reached the north of Sheridan's triumphs in the Shenandoah Valley. On November 8, the northern public rejected the Democrats' peace and anti-miscegenation platform, resoundingly reelecting Lincoln. Fighting to save the Union would continue unabated.[119]

As 1864 gave way to 1865, those in both North and South recognized that the Confederacy was in desperate straits. In August 1864, Mobile Bay fell, closing the Confederacy's last port on the Gulf of Mexico east of the Mississippi River and thereby completing the Union's blockade. By early February, Sherman had captured Savannah and then turned north, leading his 60,000 men on a march of destruction across South Carolina. Outside Petersburg, General-in-Chief Grant, now accompanying the Army of the Potomac, held Lee's army in a siege that clearly could not last much longer. On February 3, three Confederate commissioners met with Lincoln, Grant, and Secretary of State William Seward aboard the *River Queen* near City Point to discuss peace. Lincoln made his terms clear: the restoration of national authority, no retreat on the slavery question, and the unconditional surrender and disbandment of all Confederate forces. Reflecting his intense desire for reunion, Lincoln promised generous terms of pardon for rebel leaders and their confiscated property. But Confederate president Davis had not authorized the commissioners to negotiate such terms, and so they returned to Richmond with no peace secured.[120]

Soon the ground began to thaw, and Confederate military surrender seemed increasingly likely. On March 27, Lincoln boarded the *River Queen* yet again, this time to meet with Grant, Sherman, and Rear Admiral David D. Porter. And again, he expressed his desire to end the war quickly and provide liberal terms of peace. "Let them surrender and go home," he stated, "they will not take up arms again. Let them go, officers, and all, let them have their horses to plow with, and, if you like, their guns to shoot crows with." In addition to these generous terms he demanded only that Confederates accept emancipation and swear loyalty to the United States. His principal agenda was restoring stability and civil government in the South. The president hoped that his top military commanders would recognize and concur with his deepest hope. "We want these people to return to their allegiance and submit to the laws," he noted. "Therefore, I say, give them the most liberal and honorable terms."[121]

Between these two meetings with his commanders, Lincoln voiced similar sentiments to the American public. On March 4, 1865, he delivered his second inaugural address. Even the mud-thronged streets that resulted from an incessant rain could not keep nearly 40,000 onlookers from the occasion. At mid-morning a procession began along Pennsylvania Avenue, as the crowds pushed forward for a glimpse of the volunteer firemen from various cities, Odd Fellows, but most especially the Union boys in blue. And for the first time, the crowd witnessed African American soldiers as four companies of the 45th USCT took their place in line. Though wet and overcast, the streets of Washington took on a joyous atmosphere. For unlike his inauguration four years earlier, the president and the nation had ample reason to be optimistic that peace—reunion—might be near.[122]

At precisely 11:40, the rain died away and the president stepped onto a temporary platform on the east front of the newly finished Capitol. Looking out over the sea of civilians and soldiers as the sun peaked through the clouds, he began his speech. Imparting a somber tone on what had heretofore been a celebratory day, his was not a triumphant oration. Rather, he reminded his fellow Americans that they were more alike than different, that both sides were complicit in the sins of slavery that had caused the war, and that God had his own divine purposes. In the final and most memorable passages from the speech, Lincoln set forth his vision of a reunited nation. He beseeched northerners to be forgiving and avoid harsh treatment of the defeated South. He asked that they reach deep within and find compassion for their foe. "With malice toward none; with charity for all . . . let us strive on to finish the work we are in; to bind up the nation's wounds . . . to do all which may achieve and cherish a just, and a lasting peace, among ourselves, and with all nations." Invoking the nineteenth-century meaning of "charity," Lincoln was asking Americans, northerners and southerners both, to love their enemies. Moreover, "malice toward none" meant exactly that—even Confederate military leaders, government officials, and soldiers, as well as civilians, were to be included in the president's exhortation. His postwar vision contained no retribution, no reprisals.[123]

Lincoln's hope for a reunited, reconciled nation was not, however, the predominant expression of northern attitudes in March 1865. The nation was weary of war, but many were not ready to open their arms and welcome the traitorous rebels back so easily. And yet this posed a problem for northerners. Had not the war been about restoring the Union? Had not more than 360,000 young men given their lives so that the nation might be reunited? Even if reunion of the states were achieved, did that necessitate reconciliation among those who had stared down the barrel of a rifle or watched as their brothers lay dying in agony? Neither were most Confederates willing to abandon their steadfast belief that they had been justified in their quest for southern independence. They might be vanquished on the field of battle, but the war had facilitated a deep and intense Confederate identity that would not be so easily subdued. Kate Foster, who had lost two brothers in the fighting, contemplated what might happen if the Confederate forces failed. "How can I ever love the Yankees as brothers when they made these deep and everlasting wounds in my heart?" she asked.[124] The military conflict might be nearing its end, but both sides remained adamant that theirs had been a moral and just cause.

Invasion, occupation, hard war, and emancipation had defined the last year and months of the war for soldiers, statesmen, and those on the home front. The sights and smells of smoldering buildings left in Sherman's path, the heated encounters of Union soldiers with Confederate women, and the sights of former slaves donning the U.S. blue—these would be the images seared into their memories most clearly as the Confederacy's hopes for independence dimmed. The bitterness and rancor engendered by four long years of fighting had reinforced white southerners' belief in their distinctiveness, a conviction that would not be easily subdued. In contrast, for freedmen and -women, the mixture of anticipation, uncertainty, and sheer joy of freedom would forever be linked in their minds to the war's last days.

Even before the fighting had ended, Unionists and Confederates, white and black, were already shaping the ways in which the conflict would be remembered. Northerners had waged a war for reunion. But did this mean forgetting the causes of the war, the costs of the war? Did it mean reconciliation? Confederates, on the other hand, needed to distance themselves from slavery's role in the conflict if they were to convince future generations that theirs had been a noble cause. But, ironically, as was often true in civil wars, the enemies shared an identical conviction. Both thought of themselves as the true Americans, men who had fought for liberty and their homes. Although their war goals would prevent reconciliation for years to come, this conception of themselves as Americans would eventually prove imperative for fostering a sense of reconciliation between 1880 and 1915, when interregional harmony was at its height. In the interim, many were left to wonder: how do you get from collecting enemy skulls to clasping hands with your former foe?

A MAGNANIMOUS PEACE?

April–May 1865

Routed from their trenches surrounding Petersburg and forced to abandon Richmond, Lee's ragged troops trudged west in early April 1865 hoping to find provisions and a route south. All along its path the army that had held the heights at Fredericksburg and stormed the ridges of Gettysburg left signs it was disintegrating—littering the roads with broken wagons, ambulances, artillery carriages, hundreds of discarded muskets, and haversacks. Thousands of stragglers dropped out of line, some simply collapsing along road beds, others wandering listlessly through Virginia's budding spring woods. But the signs were there for all to see. From his headquarters in Farmville, on the evening of Friday, April 7, Grant issued a note under a flag of truce inviting Lee to surrender.[1] After a series of exchanges between the commanding generals, on the cloudless morning of Palm Sunday, April 9, Lee decided to accept Grant's offer.

Dressed in his full-dress uniform replete with sash and jeweled sword, Lee and his two aides arrived first at the Wilbur McLean house, the site selected for the meeting. There they waited for thirty long minutes, until they heard horses approaching. Grant, still clad in his worn overcoat and mud-spattered pants because his headquarters wagon had failed to keep up in the mad rush to capture the rebel army, climbed the broad steps with his small party of officers and one reporter. In the home's parlor, the two commanders who had witnessed so much bloodshed since their first meeting at the Wilderness nearly a year prior shook hands.

There was some idle small talk before Lee reminded Grant of their purpose. Bending over the desk with a cigar in his mouth, Grant jotted down generous terms he was sure reflected Lincoln's wishes: officers and men could return to their homes "not to be disturbed by U.S. authority so long as they observe their paroles and the laws in force where they may reside." The arms, artillery, and public property of the army were to be turned over to the Union forces, but officers would be allowed to keep their personal sidearms and baggage. Lee asked for an addition. He explained to Grant that the Confederates had supplied their own cavalry and artillery horses, and he asked that they might be able to keep their mounts to return home and resume farming. Grant readily agreed. A grateful Lee assured him that this gesture would "have the best possible effect upon the men" and would "do much toward conciliating the people." Such a statement surely pleased Grant and all the Union soldiers, as this was what they had been struggling for four bloody years to accomplish. The generals spoke briefly about prisoner exchange and rations for the Confederates. Recognizing that passions among his men ran deep, Lee also asked Grant that the two armies be kept separate in order to prevent "unpleasant individual rencontres that may take place with a too free intercourse."[2] After the Confederate leader departed, Grant telegraphed Washington with a simple statement: "General Lee surrendered the Army of Northern Virginia this afternoon on terms proposed by myself."[3]

As reports of the surrender drifted north, cities from Washington to California erupted in celebrations, rejoicing that the rebellion had been quelled and the Union preserved. Black men and women on the home front and in the army's ranks celebrated the impending peace as well, eagerly anticipating what freedom might bring. The Union Cause had been triumphant, emancipation secured, and the rebellion destroyed. But questions still abounded. Unionists recognized that the final fulfillment of the Union Cause required bringing the misguided rebels back into the folds of the nation, but how were the victors to navigate the tension between ensuring that white southerners had truly abandoned their cause and encouraging them to rejoin the nation? Many Union soldiers and northern Democratic newspapers believed that following Lincoln and Grant's lead as magnanimous victors offered the best strategy. Others cautioned that stern punishment would be necessary for at least the rebel leaders. Yet even some Republicans began to consent to lenient terms. Perhaps the wounds of war might be healed quickly.

Six days later, the bullet of a southern sympathizer would call into question the magnanimous peace that had seemed so certain. Word of Lincoln's death unleashed a wave of disbelief, unmitigated sorrow, and utter fury across the North. "Before his death, peace was possible," proclaimed a resolution passed by the citizens of San Francisco. "All the atmosphere was filled with generous emotions and kind sympathy—but now peace means subjugation or annihilation!"[4] The assassination presented a terrible quandary: if the North carried retribution too far, the very goal of reunion might be undermined. And yet failing to make a show of force, of punishing someone, would similarly challenge the totality of Union victory. Many were left to wonder if Lincoln's death had forever vanquished the reconciliationist promise of Appomattox.[5]

In the midst of their celebrations of victory and tearful mourning, however, Unionists had vastly underestimated the tenacity of Confederate bitterness and insolence. On the same rain-soaked field where Grant secured the surrender of the most important rebel army, General Lee would help foster a romanticized and defensive memory of the Confederacy that would prove with time to be white southerners' most enduring act of defiance: the Lost Cause. Even Lincoln's death could not quell the Confederate spirit. Rather than quashing Confederate sentiment, Booth's bullet had shaped the course of Reconstruction, paving the way for the Radical Republicans and nurturing the rising momentum of the Confederate memory.

Ironically, the seeds of reconciliation would likewise be planted in the spring of 1865. Although rancorous feelings would reemerge between northerners and southerners in the months and years that followed, Grant and Lee set important precedents that would be resurrected with time to help fashion soldierly courage and honor as the basis for national reconciliation and healing.[6]

APPOMATTOX COURT HOUSE

When word of the surrender reached the Union lines, euphoria spread rampantly. "The excitement is beyond my description," Gen. Robert McAllister wrote his wife on the evening of April 9. "Why, officers and men were perfectly wild!" Shoes and hats were hurled to the skies amid the lusty cheers of a victorious army. Triumphant troops called for speeches, but these proved to be inaudible amidst the roar of huzzahs. Soldiers found every available star-spangled banner and waved them high and low, back and forth, while a salute of 100 guns rang through the damp spring air.[7] In the 1880s as he penned his memoir, Grant would recall that he had sent word at once for the salute to stop. "The Confederates were now our prisoners," he remembered, "and we did not want to exult over their downfall."[8] No contemporary diarists recalled this order; instead they wrote of the mad revelry that followed the news that the Union had finally been secured and that the men of the Armies of the Potomac, Shenandoah, and James had seen their last bloodshed.

Lying in camp that evening, the defeated Confederates struggled to make sense of the past four years. The only logic most could come to terms with was that they had been simply overwhelmed by the Union military machine. Capt. Henry Chambers of the 49th North Carolina certainly believed that the North's unending supply of troops was the reason for Union triumph. The "worthless fellows whom we have so often whipped, whose cowardly backs we have so often seen," he wrote on April 9, "have at last by sheer force of numbers, numbers swelled by contributions from almost every race and color on the face of the globe," managed to dominate the struggling, starving Confederates.[9] The rebel rank and file rushed to justify their defeat as the product of insurmountable Union resources rather than a failure of Confederate will, courage, or leadership. That night as the men gathered around their camp fires, the melancholy strains of "God Moves in Mysterious Ways" could be heard echoing across the hills.[10]

The soldiers were not alone in their rationale. Lee had muttered only a few words when he returned from the McLean House, but later that evening he asked one of his aides to draft a farewell order to the army that might be delivered before it disbanded. The first version of the order did not please Lee. In it he found several lines that might have kept harsh feelings alive.[11] On April 10, his revised address was read aloud. In General Orders No. 9 he lauded the loyalty, valor, and "unsurpassed courage and fortitude" of "the brave survivors of so many hard-fought battles."[12] He seemed to forget the staggering number of soldiers who had deserted or discarded their weapons since the flight from Richmond. Only ten days later, in a letter to Jefferson Davis, he admitted that his troops had been unreliable for months. But in his last order, Lee assured his men that the surrender was through no fault of their own. Instead, he insisted that the army had been "compelled to yield to overwhelming numbers and resources."[13]

Here, only a day after the surrender that was meant to foster reconciliation, the foremost Confederate hero set forth two of the central tenets of the Lost Cause: Confederate soldiers had been devoted, honorable, and chivalric; and the Confederacy had not been defeated on the field of battle but had been overwhelmed by the Union's forces and material.[14] In the coming years and decades, the order would achieve relic-like status, with countless individuals claiming to own original copies.[15] More important, because they were delivered by the foremost Confederate leader, the sentiments expressed in General Orders No. 9 proved imperative in helping to perpetuate the memory of the Confederacy and the men who had fought so desperately to ensure its survival.

Despite the mingling of officers who had known each other at West Point and Lee's efforts to diffuse tensions by striking the harsh words from his farewell order, George F. Williams, a correspondent traveling with the U.S. Fifth Corps, reported much virulent resistance among Confederate officers. According to Williams, the camps were filled with talk of Confederate officers seeking exile in Mexico, many having vowed they would never live under the U.S. flag and expressing their "determined hatred" toward the federal government. Many others feared that general officers would "die the death of felons at the hands of the common hangman," although Union soldiers assured them otherwise. "No one not actually on the ground would believe that such bitter hatred could be entertained by one section of a country toward the other. Our victories rankle in their minds, and the remembrance of our successes turns their hearts to gall," declared Williams. "The government has the hardest fight of all yet to come—to reconcile the two sections, smooth over past difficulties, as well as to prevent future misunderstandings." In stark contrast to the tales that would surface in years to come, Williams was under no illusion as to the vituperative and rancorous feelings present on the surrender field in mid-April.[16]

Confederate officers were not the only ones to harbor such harsh resentments even in the face of magnanimous surrender. Throughout Monday, many rank-and-file rebels became increasingly embittered by Yankee behavior. That morning several bluecoats approached the rebel camps for a closer look, and later in the afternoon Union officers began to ride among the tents. Even though Grant's senior officers had requested to visit with old friends, it is clear that some Union men simply relished the opportunity to parade triumphantly through their defeated foes' camp. Dr. Henry J. Millard of Massachusetts had gleefully written home of his pleasure in riding through Lee's army while they were still in possession of their arms.[17] Such was the fruit of victory, but it particularly galled one North Carolinian. "Our hearts have been today frequently stirred up upon seeing the conquering Yankee Officers riding about," he wrote. Along the picket lines, taunts from the Union soldiers became so malicious that even a rebel chaplain could not restrain himself from replying, disgusted that the "enemies seem to regard us as vastly inferior to themselves."[18] Capt. Henry Chambers could not contain the bitterness he felt toward the victors. He could only hope for some "terrible retribution" to "come upon this motly crew who have waged upon us so unjust, so barbarous a warfare!"[19] How could white southerners reunite with such barbarians?

Recognizing that such heated words could devolve into violent altercations, Union leadership tried to prevent escalating animosities. A few rebels noted that Grant had spared them as much mortification as possible. A private in the 31st Virginia was thankful that no salutes were fired near the Confederate lines even though they could hear the faint echo of cannon in the distance.[20] Most important, there were no disputes between the surrendered Confederates and Gen. Edward O. C. Ord's African American troops in the Army of the James. Perhaps recognizing this possibility, Ord had kept them in the camps behind their white comrades and sent them from the area before the formal surrender on April 12.[21] Even without the conflict that surely would have followed an encounter between the rebels and their former slaves, there was no call for reconciliation or mingling with the enemy among most of the enlisted men. While they willingly laid down their arms in deference to Lee, even Grant's generous terms did not soften the rancor most rank-and-file soldiers of the Army of Northern Virginia felt. Instead, they harbored deep animosities that would only fester in the coming months and years.

African American soldiers, however, would harbor different memories of Appomattox in the coming decades. Although most of the United States Colored Troops (USCT) remained as occupying forces in Richmond, seven regiments of approximately 2,000 men accompanied Grant in his pursuit of Lee. Indeed, Lee's last effort to break through the Federal lines was blocked in part by members of the 29th, 31st, and 116th USCT.[22] Although in the early 1900s members of the War Department would declare no significant action occurred on the surrender field, African American soldiers felt differently. In their telling, Union victory remained uncertain on the morning of April 9, but their actions had brought to an end the "last hour of the Slaveholders rebellion." A veteran of the 41st USCT noted not long after the surrender that it had been black soldiers' "remarkable courage" that made possible the "capturing of Lee's army."[23] As historian Elizabeth Varon points out, African Americans offered a counter-narrative to Lee's vision of overwhelming numbers expressed in his farewell address. The role of the USCT in the engagement at Appomattox proved a source of honor among African American veterans and civilians in their claims of both freedom and citizenship for generations.[24]

On Wednesday, April 12, Lee's army fell into their regimental formations one last time. Maj. Gen. John B. Gordon's Second Corps took the lead, marching down the muddy hill and across the shallow waters of the Appomattox. As they advanced up the stage road toward the courthouse, Brig. Gen. Joshua L. Chamberlain called the Federal columns to attention. Orders were given to "carry arms," and the Union soldiers raised their rifles to their shoulders in a sign of respect. A member of the 32nd Massachusetts explained how each southern unit proceeded: "The gallant but defeated foe advanced in front the length of our line, then faced us, stacked arms, laid colors and equipments on stack, then marched away to make room for another line." A soldier in the 155th Pennsylvania observed that it took nearly six hours for all the Confederates to stack their weapons. "Not an unkind word was spoken to them," he noted, adding that "some of their color bearers shed tears when they delivered up their colors."[25] A special correspondent stationed with the U.S. Fifth Corps was equally moved by the morose scene. "A more wretched and painful sight I have never witnessed," he wrote.[26]

A JUBILANT AND VICTORIOUS NORTH

Only a few individuals in Washington had learned of Lee's surrender on Sunday night, but by Monday morning the city buzzed with joyous excitement just as it had a week earlier. At dawn, 500 guns awakened the civilians from their slumber. Elation spread throughout the city. Men from the navy yard and arsenal formed an impromptu procession, marching through the city streets, playing triumphant music, and waving banners. At noon, a battery of artillery repaired to the grounds just south of city hall, firing celebratory rounds that shattered the windows of numerous homes in the area. Too energized to continue their work, the clerks of the Treasury Department abandoned their desks and headed to the White House, where they burst into a lively rendition of "The Star Spangled Banner." Soon others joined them, and shouts for the president to appear filled the brisk spring air. Lincoln presently emerged at a window amid a clamoring of huzzahs and waving of hats. "I am very greatly rejoiced that an occasion has occurred so pleasurable that the people can't restrain themselves," Lincoln told the gathering crowd. Observing the band that had accompanied the assembly, he asked that it play "Dixie." "I had heard that our adversaries over the way attempted to appropriate it," Lincoln began. "I insisted yesterday," he continued, "that we fairly captured it," and now, he declared, it belongs to the American people. The 1st regiment of the Quarter Master Volunteer band immediately struck up a lively rendition of the tune to the thunderous applause of all present. The president then proposed three rousing cheers for General Grant and his forces and three more for the Navy. With that, he retreated back into the Executive Mansion while the exuberant crowd proceeded to the War Department.[27]

As news of Lee's capitulation continued to wind its way north on Monday, April 10, citizens from Maine to California exulted in the triumphant news with torchlight parades, fireworks, and patriotic speeches.[28] Despite a heavy rain that fell throughout the day on Monday, great multitudes thronged New York's streets while cannons roared continuously. Bostonians rushed from their homes and businesses to greet each other with joyous congratulations and cordial hand shaking while trying to bedeck their residences and shops with flags and bunting.[29] In Trenton, New Jersey, both white and black alike rejoiced in song into the early dawn.[30] Union-occupied Nashville joined in the celebrations, as both chambers of the state legislature adjourned and business was suspended throughout the city on the 10th.[31] In Columbus, Ohio, preparations were underway for a grand celebration on Friday, April 14, that would be replete with a mock funeral for the Confederacy. Only the most devout Unionists (hence no Democrats) would be selected as pall bearers and orators for the occasion.[32] Union-occupied New Orleans joined in with illuminations and a grand celebration at Jackson Square, replete with Grant's name spelled out in gas-lit flames.[33]

Throughout the week, excitement continued to reign in Washington. On Wednesday, bonfires blazed and citizens persisted in their endeavors to launch rockets. That evening, thousands of people gathered on the lawn of the White House calling for the president to issue a few more words. Appearing at an upper window, he indulged the masses by speaking of his hopes "for a speedy return of peace." He reminded the crowd that he was not responsible for the victory, but that they should give a national thanksgiving both to God and to General Grant, his officers, and the brave men of his army. Most important, Lincoln took the opportunity to set forth his vision for a reunited nation—and defend his previous actions on the matter. He predicted that the reconstruction of the Union would be "fraught with great difficulty," noting that the people of the North disagreed as to the mode and manner of reconstruction. After a detailed defense of his policies in Louisiana and a rebuke of arguments about whether the seceding states were legally out of the Union, he observed that all agreed that a policy must be set forth on how to restore the rebellious states. "Let us all join in doing the acts necessary to restoring the proper political relations between the States and the Union," he intoned.[34] Lincoln, like Grant, had clearly issued a call for a speedy and peaceful reunion and reconciliation.

Celebrations of the Army of Northern Virginia's demise were not confined to the areas north of the Mason-Dixon Line. Throughout the Confederacy, white Unionists and African Americans reacted in much the same way as their northern counterparts. Freedmen and -women in Richmond had enjoyed a state of jubilation since the city fell on April 3.[35] Several miles from Appomattox, Fannie Berry watched along with her mistress as a white flag was hoisted in the village of Pamplin. Although Richmond had fallen the previous week, the news of Lee's surrender marked a day Berry would remember for the rest of her life. Throughout the small village, slaves burst into song for Appomattox, commemorating the moment at which they "knew dat dey were free."[36] A white Union soldier stationed in Lynchburg, Virginia, described the local African American population as "jubelant," offering to run for water or gifts of tobacco for every Yankee soldier.[37] Several days later, upon learning the news of Lee's surrender, nearly 3,000 freedmen and -women gathered in Charleston, South Carolina, to celebrate the end of the rebellion—and, more important, the end of slavery. One former slave, Samuel Dickerson, thanked the northern dignitaries in attendance, including the abolitionist William Lloyd Garrison, Senator Henry Wilson, and various Army and Navy officers, for all they had done to reunite his family. Referring to his two little daughters, who were by his side during the course of his emotional remarks, Dickerson said, "Through your instrumentality under the folds of the glorious flag which treason tried to triumph, you have restored them to me. We welcome and look upon you as saviors. We thank you for all you have done for us." A rousing round of cheers erupted at the end of his speech.[38] For Dickerson and other former slaves, Appomattox would harbor specific memories for African Americans in both the North and South. The surrender had reestablished not only the union of the nation, but also the union of families.

Even as both white and black Unionists celebrated the restoration of the nation, debates began to emerge over Grant's magnanimous policy. A soldier with the 84th Illinois recalled that the terms elicited "unaffected delight" among Sherman's men. "It is not in the heart of a true soldier, to feel vindictive, speak unkindly, or act ungenerously toward a valiant, yet vanquished foe," he noted. The true Union soldier admired the "unflinching resolution and stalwart courage of the rebel army" and desired that the "highest degree of clemency and magnanimity" be shown toward the mass of the rebel army. He believed that Union soldiers who had survived months and even years in the field had less bitterness toward the rebel soldiers than toward those in the North who had cried for peace "when it could only be attained by the dissolution of our glorious Union."[39] Though insisting that the rebel cause had been an unholy one, Union soldiers could empathize with the plight of their fellow soldiers.

Others who had endured the realities of battle found Grant's terms of surrender far too generous. William B. Stark of the 34th Massachusetts was angered that the rebels had been allowed to keep their personal property. "Most of us were opposed to it in spirit," he wrote, "to allow these Rebel Traitors horses and arms."[40] Declaring that there was "no truth or honor in a Rebel," Maj. William Watson, a surgeon with the 105th Pennsylvania, lamented that the "Army was greatly dissatisfied at the terms granted Lee."[41] On the home front, some northern politicians called for harsher punishment. Speaking only moments after Lincoln had offered his conciliatory speech on April 11, Republican senator James Harlan of Iowa declared that the Constitution specifically enumerated what constituted treason. "Those who hatched the treason should suffer the penalty," he declared to an assembly that voiced approval with vociferous huzzahs.[42]

Dismissing those who believed Grant's terms "not sufficiently exacting," New York lawyer and treasurer of the U.S. Sanitary Commission George Templeton Strong admitted in his diary that he had first thought Grant's terms too liberal. But upon reflection, he acknowledged that "Grant understands his business." In Strong's estimation, Grant's terms would do exactly as Lincoln hoped: bring the rebels back under the flag as a compliant and peaceable people. But perhaps more important, Strong—a staunch Unionist throughout the war—believed that the North should behave "as merciful as we *safely* can be." The punishment already inflicted on the South had been enough. "The death of their best (or worst) and bravest; the devastation, the breaking up of their social system, general destitution, the bitterest humiliation of the most arrogant of mankind, the most splendid and confident expectations disappointed, universal ruin, bereavement, and shame—these are among the terms of the sentence God has pronounced and is executing on rebellious slaveholders."[43] Maria Lydig Daly, the wife of a prominent New York City judge, concurred. She praised Grant's terms with the hope that the animosity that had held sway for so long would quickly pass. "May God comfort and change the hearts of our so long vindictive foes! They will have much to suffer for their folly and ambition," she wrote.[44] Such was the harvest the rebellious southerners had reaped.

If there was one issue that continued to enrage nearly all northerners, it was Confederate treatment of Union prisoners of war. With the fall of Richmond, reports flooded northern newspapers of the barbaric treatment Union prisoners had suffered. Northerners had long heard reports that Confederates had been unable to care for prisoners given their dire circumstances. But what most galled Unionists was the amount of food, clothing, and bedding sent by northerners to their loved ones that had been confiscated by greedy rebels.[45] Just days after Lee's surrender, *Frank Leslie's Illustrated Newspaper* featured an image of emaciated, starving Union soldiers rescued from a camp near Wilmington, North Carolina. "Southern Inhumanity," blazed the headline. According to the author, such wanton, needless murder of Union prisoners was more evidence of the "barbarism of slavery."[46]

Much of the wrath engendered by discussions of the prisoners was immediately directed at Jefferson Davis. Within days of the surrender Union general Benjamin Butler made a bitter speech about the harsh treatment of Union prisoners, vowing to hang Davis for the atrocities.[47] In New Orleans, Unionists prayed that Davis might die, one clergyman desiring to see the "rope adjusted around his neck."[48] The *New York Herald* condemned Davis as "both a scoundrel and a coward" and suspected few northerners would raise an eyebrow if he were captured and hanged in the streets of Richmond. "It is perfectly astonishing how bitter the feeling against the would-be President of the Confederate States of America," the *Herald* remarked.[49]

Calls to punish Lee drew a more mixed reaction, usually breaking down along partisan lines. The Republican *New York Times* explained that while northerners did not hold such feelings toward Lee as had been manifested toward Davis, they hoped he would be exiled and condemned to spend the remainder of his life "in a country where Washington never ruled and where free government is not as popular as it is here."[50] The problem, however, lay in Grant's surrender terms, which stated that Lee and his men were never to be disturbed by Federal authority as long as they observed their paroles and obeyed the laws.[51] "He is one of the guiltiest of all the rebel fiends," argued the staunchly Republican *Chicago Tribune*, "and could we do it lawfully, without a breach of our own national honor, we would hang him with patriotic pleasure."[52] On the other hand, the rebel chieftain found almost instant admiration among many Democrats. One Washington newspaper hoped that the federal government would secure peace by forgetting "the blood and toil of the past four memorial years" and keeping its promise to treat Lee magnanimously. According to the terms of agreement, Lee should be allowed to return to his home at Arlington. Although failing to mention that Lee's plantation had been transformed into a massive Union burial ground, the report noted that "it is his home . . . and the nation has pledged its faith to the great Captain that there he shall not be molested."[53]

Democratic newspapers similarly acknowledged the bravery and tenacity of Confederate soldiers. Washington's *Constitutional Union* argued that Grant's magnanimity at Appomattox was due primarily to the "heroic valor and generous fortitude of the Army of Virginia" and to "the spotless virtue of its unrivaled chief."[54] Fueling Confederates' arguments that they had not surrendered but had been overwhelmed by northern resources, the paper claimed that any army that had contended for so long against such insurmountable odds should command the utmost respect from the northern populace.[55] A New York daily called Lee's army the "bravest, best organized and most successful army of the rebellion" even if it did fight "for a hopeless cause."[56] Perhaps the *Philadelphia Inquirer* best expressed a popular opinion in the North among Democrats. The paper exulted in the triumph of the Union over "brave Rebels who took their lives in their hands in support of their treason."[57] Here the northern press would foreshadow the rhetoric of many Union veterans of the 1880s and 1890s in both condemning the rebel cause and acknowledging Confederate bravery. Such arguments did not detract from the Union victory. On the contrary, citing the enemy's bravery and tenacity only strengthened the Union's valor and accomplishment—it had managed to vanquish such a commendable foe.

Even as they debated the merits of Grant's terms, Unionists began to assess what the war had been about and what had been achieved. Foremost on the minds of most was the preservation of the Union—this was *the* most important outcome of the war.[58] "For four long years our armies had been battling for these glorious results," wrote Gen. Robert McAllister, but with the war over, "we could return to our homes with the proud satisfaction that it has been our privilege to live and take part in the struggle that has decided for all time to come that Republics are not a failure."[59] But commemorating Union triumph did not mean ignoring emancipation. On the contrary, Unionists laid full blame for the outbreak of war at the feet of the slaveholders, and therefore emancipation was almost always included as both a means and a fruit of victory in accounts by both soldiers and civilians. Taylor Peirce of the 22nd Iowa stationed in Morehead City, North Carolina, believed that the newly reunited nation was "about to enter a career of greatness and prosperity never equaled by any known on earth" after having being "purged of the heinous curse of Slavery."[60] William Rogers, chaplain of the 189th New York Volunteers, celebrated Appomattox as the deathbed of slavery. "Here culminated in utter failure the slaveholders' efforts to dismember and overthrow the free American Union," he declared.[61] Even the Democratic *New York Herald* observed that with the "violent death [rebels] have brought upon their institution of slavery, the cause, the argument and the party of a Southern confederacy cease to exist."[62] Emancipation had been not only a valuable tool in defeating the Confederacy, but in the minds of many white northerners who were by no means inclined toward racial equality it served as righteous retribution inflicted on those who had provoked the internecine war and assured that sectional discord would be no more.

A handful of abolitionists and Radical Republicans, however, did consider emancipation the most important product of war. The *Ohio State Journal* proudly noted the grand achievements of the war effort in this order: the end of slavery, a rebellion crushed, freedom, and the Union restored.[63] A Brooklyn, New York, publication declared that the "New Babylon whose corner-stone was to be 'slaves and the souls of men,' crumbles in ruins in the hands of its builders." In a gender-loaded analogy, the writer further gleefully quipped that "the South like a rebellious woman has attempted to ruin her husband's household, to destroy all family government. But four years of bitter chastisement, have cast the demon of Slavery out of her."[64]

There were equally those that emphasized the need for a generous and forgiving reconciliation. The *Louisville Daily Journal* invoked Lincoln's second inaugural when it asked that all wounds inflicted by the war "should be healed with the balm of national reunion and love." "Let the light of all embracing Peace envelop the whole broad land," wrote the columnist. Hoping for a speedy reconciliation, he observed that "they who were our brothers in the past are to be our brothers again." "As a free and mighty people, we shall dwell together in PEACE and UNION."[65] Others invoked family metaphors, including a northern minister who called for "a new wedding between the North and the South" in which the partners would "forget the discords of the past."[66] Even among those who espoused emancipation as the most important outcome of the war, there were voices who echoed Lincoln's call for a benevolent peace. Staunch abolitionist Henry Ward Beecher opposed expatriation, disenfranchisement, and, most especially, hangings from the "sour apple tree." He warned against "the terrible spectacle of retribution": "In mercy's name, has there not been suffering enough?" His congregation agreed, issuing a statement assuring the South that northerners had neither desire for glory over them nor revenge.[67]

This was not the reconciliationist rhetoric that would emerge in the 1880s and 1890s. That memory would be a compromise between Unionists and former Confederates, which necessitated silence on the divisive political issues that had caused the conflict as well as the results of the war. Appeals for a compassionate reunion were no compromise and could not be disentangled from the Union cause. They were based on the triumph of the North's war aims; as the victors, they would choose to be magnanimous to the defeated South. But the calls that rang out in the aftermath of Lee's surrender for "Americans in their hour of victory" to "be just, magnanimous, and generous to Americans in their hour of defeat" would serve as a foundation upon which reconciliation might one day be established.[68]

CONFEDERATE DEFIANCE

Most of Lee's men accepted that the surrender of the Army of Northern Virginia marked the end of the war. But not all of his soldiers complied. Determined to avoid submission, Maj. Gen. Fitzhugh Lee, the commanding officer's nephew, had left Appomattox on the morning of April 9 with Gen. Thomas Rosser and Gen. Thomas Munford and nearly all the cavalry, hoping to join with Joseph Johnston's forces to the south. The cavalrymen were not alone in their refusal to admit defeat. Perhaps as many as hundreds of other infantry broke rank and headed toward the James River despite the cease-fire, including repatriated prisoners who were especially fearful of returning to the Union prisons should the parole terms not hold.[69] Some, like Alfred S. Dorman of Georgia, remained defiant even after learning of Grant's terms, refusing to sign paroles and instead making their way home alone or in groups.[70] And others, even having signed the parole, spouted insolent thoughts; John Dooley thought that it was a "down right shame for people . . . to talk of giving up the glorious struggle and submitting to the ignominious bonds of Yankee slavery." Even if Lee's army had been defeated, "every southern heart must beat unsubdued [sic] and animated should each strong arm be to battle to the bitter end," he bravely remarked—in the confines of his diary.[71]

As gray-clad soldiers made their way home, many Confederate women recognized a direct link between the survival of their nation and the survival of their lives as they had known them, and they could scarcely contemplate surrender. On April 10, Assistant U.S. Secretary of War Charles Dana cheerfully reported to Secretary Edwin Stanton that Lee's surrender was beginning to have its desired effect. "Even the most malignant women now feel that the defeat is perfect and the rebellion finished," observed Dana.[72] But he clearly underestimated the devotion and stubbornness of rebel women. Throughout the week of April 10–14, Confederate women remained defiant and indignant. Many no doubt concurred with young Lizzie Alsop when she wished for retribution against the hated Yankees. "I pray God, that I may yet live to see his vengeance exercised against our enemies." She felt confident that "our brave, our noble army [would] rise up from the ashes of our burning homes, and yet avenge the death of our heroes slain."[73]

Such sentiments should not have surprised Union soldiers or the greater northern populace. Since early in the war, northerners had ranted about Confederate women's resolute devotion to the rebel cause. The surrender of the Confederacy's principal army had not diminished many women's devotion to their nation. On the contrary, it appeared to be making it stronger. Much was at stake. If they admitted defeat, life as they had known it before the war would forever be altered. For many this meant life without brothers, fathers, sons, husbands, and slaves. They had conferred too much for the cause to give up on their nation so quickly, prompting some to volunteer to fight themselves. "Even if the war-scarred veterans should fail in their noble efforts," cried several women in North Carolina, "the very women of the South should rise up to expel the hated invaders from the Soil."[74] They could not easily and instantly reject the cause for which their loved ones had died and for which they had lost their homes, communities, and slave-based culture. Instead, they needed to validate their cause and justify their sacrifice, so they held on to a faith in the Confederacy long after most of their menfolk had accepted defeat.

More important for the war's legacy, unlike the men of Lee's army, Confederate women had not had the opportunity to participate in a formal truce. They had not capitulated on the battlefield, they had not marched in long lines up the banks of the Appomattox to stack their arms, they had not received paroles, and they had not witnessed the magnanimous behavior of Grant's army. Women were denied the closure afforded to soldiers.[75] The killing might have ended, but in many other ways the war continued in April 1865 just as it had months earlier: women continued to tend to their sick and wounded, they continued to want for supplies, and they continued to loathe the Yankees who remained in the region. Having no guns to lay down, women would cling tenaciously to their Confederate identity and pride in their Lost Cause, thus forever shaping the gendered contours of Civil War memory.

Women, however, were far from the only ones who issued calls for sustained resistance. Southern sympathizers in Baltimore continued their defiant displays of Confederate patriotism, parading through the streets in their gray uniforms. The infuriated local Union commander of the city demanded that Grant order all rebel officers and soldiers paroled by Lee's surrender to report to the nearest provost marshal. There they would register their names and abandon their rebel uniforms.[76] Rumors swirled throughout the North that rebels were willingly taking the oath of allegiance, but such reports were either greatly exaggerated or too much was assumed from those who did take the oaths.[77] In Richmond, a Confederate clerk refused to take the oath because he still believed his country would survive. "The Confederacy is very ill," he wrote on April 14, "but I still haven't lost all hope."[78]

The flight of Jefferson Davis to Danville and then farther south through North Carolina gave evidence that at least some Confederates would continue to fight even without Lee's army. Edmund Ruffin felt confident that the cause for independence could still prove viable west of the Mississippi. Believing that all Confederate officers would have their property confiscated and face the death penalty as a traitor, he urged them all to go to Texas and fight there as their only refuge for safety.[79] William Glenn retracted his earlier sentiment that the war was over now that Lee had surrendered. Calculating the combined forces of Johnston and Nathan B. Forrest—and envisioning their ability to cross the Mississippi, Glenn too believed the Confederacy might yet survive. "An army of 50,000 men in Texas, with plenty of grass for horses and mountain ranges for defense could work miracles—if there was no dissension among leaders," he cautioned.[80] By April 14, throngs of refugees and straggling soldiers had flooded Charlotte, many of whom declared their intentions of pushing on to the trans-Mississippi. The Confederacy might have been defeated on the field of battle, but, as Unionists would come to learn, it would take more than a surrender to quell white southerners' deep attachment to their failed nation.

TOLLING OF THE BELLS

On Friday, April 14, a crowd of nearly 4,000 gathered in the Charleston harbor to watch an emotional Brev. Maj. Gen. Robert Anderson raise the American flag over Fort Sumter that he had been forced to lower four years earlier. Many of the jubilant crowd had boarded northern steamers only the day before to join this historic celebration, while numerous white and black Union soldiers, including the 54th Massachusetts, the famed African American regiment, took a break from their duties to attend the celebration. Following a hundred-round salute and a rousing rendition of "Victory at Last," Anderson entered the parade grounds and, precisely at noon, unfurled the tattered banner amid the deafening cheers of the multitude. As the flag was hoisted skyward, the surrounding forts that had inaugurated the rebellion now issued a salute of respect and rejoicing for the restoration of the Union.[81]

That evening, Anderson and scores of other northern dignitaries gathered at the Charleston Hotel for another round of celebrations. Called upon to give a toast, Anderson raised his glass to Abraham Lincoln. The president had been much maligned upon his election and had defied an attempted assassination in 1861, Anderson observed, but during four years of bloody war he had been able to secure the devotion of his people. Now he might "travel all over our country with millions of hands and hearts to sustain him." But 500 miles to the north and an hour later, not even the millions of hands and hearts of every northern citizen could save the dying president, who had been shot by John Wilkes Booth at Ford's Theater.[82] The next morning, the president was dead and Secretary of State William Seward lay terribly wounded by an accomplice's dagger.

Citizens could hardly believe the change that had occurred in a mere twenty-four hours. "From the loftiest pinnacle of our joy," observed a Detroit minister, "we are hurled down into the depths of heart-breaking anguish."[83] As the news raced along the telegraph wires from Washington to Baltimore, New York, Chicago, and farther west, people rushed to dismantle the red, white, and blue buntings of the previous week and instead draped their cities and homes with black mourning crape. Six days earlier stores and shops closed their doors out of sheer exultation. Now they did so in bereavement. Again the bells tolled, but now they pealed in sorrowful tones. Old and young, men and women, white and black openly wept in the capital's streets. In New York, Broadway and Wall Street wore the somber insignias of woe, while ships lowered their flags to half-mast in the harbor. Nearly every newspaper building, Republican and Democrat, was shrouded in black, while throngs of grief-stricken crowds gathered in front to read the bulletin boards for the latest news. Even in the poorer quarters of the city, people displayed twenty-five-cent flags adorned with a bit of black crape.[84]

News of Lincoln's death fell particularly hard among African-American communities. Lincoln had championed not only emancipation, but also the creation of USCT units, and now these men felt especially mournful. "With us of the U.S. Colored Army the death of Lincoln is indeed the loss of a friend. From him we have received our commission—and toward him we have even looked toward a Father," observed one lieutenant.[85] African Americans on the home front likewise found themselves utterly consumed by grief. Secretary of the Navy Gideon Welles observed several hundred freedmen standing in front of the White House "weeping and wailing in their loss." "This crowd did not appear to diminish through the whole of that cold, wet day," he wrote in his diary; "they seemed not to know what was to be their fate since their great benefactor was dead."[86] From St. Helena, South Carolina, teacher Laura Towne, a northerner, observed that the black families in her midst refused to believe the news, including one black minister who informed his congregation that if they knew the president was dead, they would mourn him. But he could not think it, so they would wait and see.[87]

Only a week earlier, northern papers and diarists had rejoiced in the magnanimous terms offered by Grant and the peacefulness of the surrender. But now, violence begot violence, prompting many Unionists to call for retribution—and many to unleash it on anyone who dared to celebrate the president's death.[88] On the night of the shooting, Washington erupted into a hotbed of hostility as rumors spread that Secretary Seward had also been assassinated and that General Grant had been struck down en route to Philadelphia. As word that paroled rebel soldiers had committed the crimes raced through the capital's streets, angry crowds vowed revenge on any and every white southerner, some threatening to visit the Old Capitol Prison to lynch all the rebel officers confined there.[89] Susan and Marion Constable of Baltimore were charged with treason and spent a week in jail for tearing down and allegedly burning a U.S. flag in the wake of the assassination.[90] In New York, those who dared whisper that it was a pity he had not been killed earlier were whisked off to jail. Even former first lady (and Virginian) Julia Tyler was not immune: a group of young Unionists arrived at her Staten Island home, where they stripped the rebel flag hanging in her parlor.[91]

Others fared much worse. Along Wall Street several men who spoke lightly of the assassination were instantly seized by onlookers and pummeled, one of them narrowly escaping death. Near Fifth Avenue, a man was tarred and feathered for not draping his house in mourning.[92] In Chicago, rumors swirled that three men had walked the streets shouting with glee upon hearing the news, only to be shot in their tracks. "The bodies lay there for some time," reported Pvt. Benjamin T. Smith, "as a warning to those who may entertain like centiments [sic]." In Westminster, Maryland, citizens angry at the disloyal expressions of newspaper editor Joseph Shaw sacked his plant on April 15, destroying his press and warning him to stay away. When he returned a week later, a group of citizens killed him.[93]

As word of the assassination reached the Union armies, cries of revenge rang out. "Imagination cannot paint the whirlwind of revengeful wrath that swept over the army," observed David Lane of the 17th Michigan. "The strong desire, openly expressed, to avenge his death by annihilating the people whose treason brings forth and nourishes such monsters. Woe to the armed Rebel, now and henceforth, who makes the least resistance," he warned.[94] Near Asheville, North Carolina, Henry Birdsall of the 11th Michigan Cavalry observed that Kirk's Raiders, a group of Unionist partisans, had "killed some of the rebs" despite an armistice.[95] In late April, a white Union soldier stationed in New Orleans informed his family that the U.S. Colored Troops had shot several Confederate revelers who were rejoicing in Lincoln's death. "That grinds the poor devils the worst of anything," he gleefully observed.[96] Throughout the nation, from New York to California, citizens were fired, beaten, arrested, and even killed for openly rejoicing over the tragedy.[97]

Those who had endorsed common brotherhood only days earlier or who had praised Grant and Lincoln's generous surrender terms now overwhelmingly called for uncompromising punishment and, in many instances, retribution. Retracting his own praise of Grant's generous terms, George Templeton Strong insisted that there should no longer be any talk of concession or conciliation. "Let us henceforth deal with rebels as they deserve," he declared.[98] Frederick Douglass warned northerners not to be "in too much haste in the work of restoration." "Let us not be in a hurry to clasp to our bosom that spirit which gave birth to Booth." Instead, he called for justice to the traitorous rebels and urged white northerners to look for loyalty rather than complexion in defining their new nation.[99] Sermons given throughout the North on Easter Sunday likewise called for more prompt retribution. The Reverend J. H. Mac El'Rey of Wooster, Ohio, assured his flock that reprisal was an undeniable principle of law endorsed by God. "Not to visit vengeance upon such traitors," he defiantly argued, "is to offend God and provoke His vengeance." "Unwavering, instituted punishment of the criminal is the only safeguard of society," he warned.[100] Speaking to a meeting of Massachusetts citizens in Washington, Gen. Benjamin Butler warned that the soul of the rebellion had not yet been subdued. He urged the nation to "take just retribution upon the authors of the rebellion and the aiders and abettors of the murder of Lincoln."[101] Gone were the calls for conciliation and in their place were pleas for punishment. The assassination had convinced all but a handful of northerners that the spirit of rebellion must be thoroughly crushed if the nation were ever to survive.

The assassination underscored what many northerners had long-believed: the South was innately evil. "The ferocious malignity of South-erners is indefinite and inexhaustible," noted one northern civilian upon learning of Lincoln's death.[102] The Reverend George Duffield of Detroit reminded his congregation of the South's "spirit of demoniac malignity." "The assassination of the President was but the culmination of this system of diabolical enterprise [rebellion], steadily, persistently, and Satanically pursued," he admonished.[103] Even the rebel chieftain Robert E. Lee was not immune from such accusations. At some point in the days after Appo-mattox, most likely after learning of the assassination, someone inscribed the word "Devil" on the outside of Lee's Richmond residence. Perhaps a Union soldier took it upon himself to mark the brick with chalk, or per-haps a Unionist resident had done so. Regardless, the graffiti was discov-ered on April 20 when Mathew Brady's crew arrived to photograph the de-feated general, and it was quickly removed before subsequent images were taken. No matter its origins, the epithet echoed much northern sentiment that held Lee and other rebel leaders responsible for the nation's loss.[104]

It was not just that Confederates were in concert with Satan, it was their horrid system of human bondage that had made them capable of such dastardly acts. "Slavery has done this deed," intoned the abolitionist Reverend William Potter from his pulpit in New Bedford, Massachusetts, on Easter Sunday. Slavery had corrupted the South, given birth to seces-sion, fomented treason, scattered families, destroyed homes, and starved prisoners, he informed his congregation. "Slavery," Potter bellowed, "which has eaten up the wealth of the country, and murdered your sons, or sent them to you as living skeletons—slavery, this fiend, has now slain your president. Slavery is the assassin."[105] The pages of *The Independent* rang with similar indictments. "The murder of the President is SLAVERY. The conspirator against the Republic is SLAVERY."[106] The assassination reminded northerners of the incredible gulf that remained between them and their slaveholding enemy.[107] As one Union soldier noted, "Slavery has divested them of every principle of humanity."[108]

Indicative of this was the fact that most northerners did not single out Booth and his accomplices as the sole perpetrators of the crime. Instead, government officials such as Secretary Stanton, ministers, and much of the northern population tended to argue that all slaveholders were some-how responsible.[109] The list of atrocities committed by slaveholders in the defense of slavery were innumerable: the caning of Sumner, the Fugitive Slave Act, the hanging of John Brown, secession, firing on Fort Sumter, and the battlefield deaths of more than 360,000 Union men. Lincoln's

Someone had inscribed the word "devil" on Robert E. Lee's Richmond residence in April 1865 (barely visible five bricks above the chair). Photographer Mathew Brady's crew noticed and removed the marking before subsequent photographs were taken. (Library of Congress)

murder, it appeared, was merely the culmination of all these crimes. As one Baltimore resident observed, the assassination was "characteristic of the spirit which has laminated [sic] the Rebellion from the beginning."[110]

Along this line of reasoning, some white northerners believed that the best form of revenge would be in raising the position of the newly freed slaves to citizens or, more specifically, to voters who would support the Republican Party. This would surely "shut out from power forever the leaders of the rebellion," declared one northern minister.[111] Others employed Lincoln's death to praise the African American soldiers and civilians who had helped the Union to secure victory, arguing that they deserved "the equal rights of the government they helped maintain."[112] Still others were more forthright in their desire for former bondsmen to be the bearers of revenge against the white South. "I would be in favor of letting the niggers go in now and make a clean shucking of the South," wrote a fuming soldier of the 22nd Iowa. "I am in favour of having the South Settled with a better breed of dogs and therefore let the negroes take it. For I believe they are as much better than the Southern Whites that they might bear the same comparison to them that the Jews did to the Gentiles."[113]

Although some Unionists firmly believed that every Confederate soldier from Lee down to the "humblest camp-follower" deserved to swing from a rope, most reserved such punishments only for the leaders.[114] A Vermont woman informed her son who was still in the field with Sherman's army that she hoped measures would soon be taken to punish the rebel leaders. "I hope they will get Jeff Davis and hang him just where they hung John Brown," she seethed, ending her fiery letter with a staunch "Death to traitors."[115] The ignorant masses in the South, on the other hand, should be pardoned.[116] Diarist Maria Lydig Daly of New York had heard that most of the men in the South—even those who supported the Union—had been forced into the Confederate army for fear of retaliation against their families. Such individuals should not be subjected to the same punishment as those of the slave oligarchy who had orchestrated secession and the subsequent bloodbath. The Reverend John Chester agreed, urging that "conciliatory measures be shown in abundance to [the] poor deluded followers, who have long since seen their folly, and for many months have longed to hear the tramp of that army which should free them from their oppressors."[117]

President Andrew Johnson concurred. Prior to the assassination he had proclaimed that "treason must be made odious, and the traitor must be punished and impoverished." In his new role as chief executive, he tempered his calls for retribution, adding that "leniency, conciliation, and amnesty" should be directed toward the "thousands whom they [the leaders] have misled and deceived." He informed members of Congress that while he was willing to act with "the utmost magnanimity towards the common rebels," those who were leaders "must be severely punished." Similarly, he told a clergyman who begged him to be forgiving that "mercy to individuals is not always mercy to States."[118] Confining their vengeance to southern leaders meant not only punishing those responsible for the bloodletting, but also justified reconciliation with the poor, deluded masses.

Debates about how to deal with the rebels were put on hold on for Lincoln's funeral. President Johnson declared Wednesday, April 19, a national day of mourning to coincide with the state funeral. Bells pealed throughout the North, while sanctuaries overflowed with mourners who came to hear their ministers eulogize the slain president. All of official Washington, with the exception of Mary Lincoln and her son Tad, gathered to attend the president's funeral at the White House. When the services concluded, thousands of Union soldiers, federal employees, church groups, and businessmen escorted his remains to the Capitol, while thousands more gathered on the sidewalks, windows, and rooftops to witness the hearse pass. Although unintended, the procession had been led by African American soldiers. The 22nd U.S. Colored Infantry had been unable to reach its slated spot at the rear of the column because of the crowds and instead came to lead the march, perhaps fitting for those who saw emancipation as Lincoln's greatest legacy. Upon reaching the Capitol, the president's body lay in state where it remained throughout the next day as immense crowds somberly filed past the open coffin.[119]

Exactly a week after Lincoln's visit to Ford's Theater, his remains, along with those of his son Willie, began their long trip home to Springfield, following nearly the reverse route Lincoln had taken in 1861. Along the way, the funeral train wound through six states, stopping eleven times for additional public funerals. In each city, thousands of onlookers, both white and black, took part, though not without some controversy. In New York City, several African American soldiers joined the procession with signs of "Abraham Lincoln, Our Emancipator," fastened to their breasts. The group, however, was accompanied by a police force because the city council had opposed their participation. Despite this, one newspaper reported that when the troops marched up Fifth Avenue "they were greeted with every mark of respect and consideration from the denizens of that fashionable neighborhood." This display, noted the paper, proved that a "revolution has been effected in the hearts of the people."[120]

After New York, the funeral train traveled westward to Cleveland, Indianapolis, and Chicago, the outpouring of grief exceeding all expectations. At night, citizens lit bonfires and torches along the tracks to illuminate the path of the black-cloaked train, while during the day citizens erected arches to greet the somber cortege. The longest serial funeral in history covered more than 1,654 miles during twelve days before Lincoln's body was finally entombed, albeit in a temporary vault, in the Illinois prairie on May 4. During this two-week period, approximately 1 million people personally viewed the body, while another 7 million participated in the memorial services in some fashion. The sense of near universal mourning shared among northerners evoked an American nationalism that precluded southerners. The Union armies might have secured the reunion of divergent sections of the country. But Lincoln's funeral had unified the North, enshrined emancipation as an accomplishment, added a purifying conclusion to the war, and underscored the limits of reconciliation.[121]

Eclipsed by the northern outpouring of grief, a meeting between General Sherman and General Johnston at Durham Station, North Carolina, on April 17 went nearly unnoticed in the northern newspapers. Although he had just learned of the assassination, Sherman agreed to terms far more lenient than had Grant eight days earlier.[122] When news of his surrender terms reached Washington, Secretary of War Stanton became incensed. Denouncing the general as a traitor for such excessively generous terms in the wake of Lincoln's assassination, Stanton pledged to have Sherman arrested. The northern public, too, flew into an outrage. "People feel very indignant they wont stand such terms with rebels," wrote one Vermont woman.[123] Trying to calm the secretary, President Johnson dispatched Grant to North Carolina with instructions that Sherman repudiate the agreement and instead issue the same terms as had been submitted to Lee.[124] On April 26, Johnston formally surrendered the largest of the Confederate forces, and again the soldiers in Sherman's ranks rushed to celebrate the end of the war. Yet many Radicals felt reassured by the secretary's reproach of Sherman and believed that perhaps the new administration would advance their cause.[125]

PUNISHING REBELDOM

Genuinely fearing the retaliation preached in northern sermons and newspapers, many Confederates took a pragmatic approach; contrition, they believed, would serve them well.[126] Sarah Morgan reported that Union-occupied New Orleans had been decked in funerary black, even by men who hated Lincoln with all their souls. They hastily tied black crape to their homes, she disclosed, under fear of confiscation or imprisonment.[127] In Farmville, Virginia, the Common Council issued a statement calling the assassination "a great national calamity" and resolved to obey commanding general John I. Curtin's order to observe the obsequies on April 19. A Union clerk confirmed that the town's citizens showed up en masse for the services.[128] In perhaps the most blatant case of false sentiments, a rebel gunboat in New Orleans sailed past the city in broad daylight in late April with the Stars and Stripes at half mast. But as soon as the gunboat had passed the United States fleet, the crew hauled down the Stars and Stripes and raised their own colors. According to one Union soldier, "Then the fun commenced." The Union gunboat, the *Hollyhock*, gave chase and ran the rebel boat ashore several miles south of the city. Only one man and a boy were captured, but fourteen more turned themselves in the next day.[129]

In the far reaches of the Confederacy, namely Texas, diarists and newspapers had no reasons to hide their true feelings. "It is certainly a matter of congratulation that Lincoln is dead because the world is happily rid of a monster that disgraced the form of humanity," reported a Marshall newspaper.[130] In Tyler, Kate Stone was equally delighted to learn that Booth had rid the world of a tyrant. "What torrents of blood Lincoln has caused to flow, and how Seward aided him in his bloody work," she coolly noted. "I cannot be sorry for their fate," she continued. "They deserve it. They have reaped their just reward."[131] Most Confederates, it appeared, did not legitimately mourn Lincoln's death.[132]

But the recalcitrance of some Confederates went beyond mere words. Throughout late April, at least a handful of rebel forces refused to surrender. In northern Virginia, Confederate partisan John S. Mosby met with Union commanders and offered condolences for Lincoln's death but remained defiant that he would not surrender. On April 21, Mosby finally realized he would have to disband the rangers who had menaced U.S. forces for the past two years, and the next day nearly 200 of his men sought paroles under the Appomattox terms. Mosby refused to do the same, however, knowing now that the federal government had offered a reward of $2,000 for his capture.[133] Writing from Texas, Junius Bragg, a member of Gen. Edmund Kirby Smith's command, informed his wife that he was not in favor of submission. "When thoughts of submission come into our minds," he cautioned, "we should think of Yankee Masters, a ruined country, Negro equality and the mortification of defeat, and fight on a little longer."[134] Admitting defeat was tantamount to social anarchy for most of the white South.

Perhaps such sentiments led Lee to give his first public interview only ten days after the assassination. On April 24, reporter Thomas Cook of the *New York Herald* visited Lee at his Richmond residence, hoping, as he wrote, "to get some clear light for the solution of the new complications growing out of the murder of President Lincoln." Admitting that he paraphrased the general, Cook recounted that Lee took special pains to note that he was a paroled prisoner, not a politician, and "was ready to make any sacrifice . . . that would tend to the restoration of peace and tranquility in the country." He described the assassination as deplorable and assured Cook that the Confederacy had not sanctioned such a heinous crime. Moreover, Lee observed that the "best men of the South" were pleased with the abolition of slavery (a far cry from the sentiments expressed in 1861).[135] This was the Lee of myth: Lee the reconciler who immediately set about trying to heal the wounds of war; a Lee that Lincoln would have warmly embraced.[136]

Lee's subsequent remarks in the interview, however, were not nearly so reconciliationist and were hardly apologetic. Instead, he insisted that surrender had not quashed the doctrine of state rights and that the war could not be considered an issue of treason: it was a Constitutional dispute. Like other Confederates, he adamantly refused to denounce the South's decision to wage war, and he defended Davis by arguing that the former president should be accorded leniency because he had been a reluctant secessionist. For northerners concerned about the plight of the freedmen, Lee's remark that "the negroes must be disposed of" could not have boded well. But in a more anti-conciliatory bent, Cook described Lee's veiled warning to the North: treat the South with moderation and liberality. If not, the South's sons who were "the country's bone and sinew, its intelligence and enterprise, its hope for the future," would expatriate themselves to Mexico, Brazil, and Canada. But more important, Cook noted that Lee maintained the South might yet still wield "a great deal of vitality and strength." If arbitrary or vindictive policies were adopted by the victors, the South would gladly take up arms again and could "protract the struggle for an indefinite period."[137] The North, and not the defeated Confederacy, thus remained liable for ensuring peace. In refusing to repudiate the Confederate cause and warning the North to exhibit moderation, Lee added to the Lost Cause message of his farewell address at Appomattox three weeks prior: the South's cause had been just, and though they had been overwhelmed on the battlefield, Confederates would retaliate with even more force if pushed. Neither battlefield defeat nor Lincoln's assassination would force Confederates to deny the justness of their cause.

Anxious to witness Confederate contrition, northerners became increasingly infuriated. Touring Richmond in late April, George Templeton Strong and Judge Charles Daly of New York observed both rebel women's continued defiance and the increasingly hostile feelings among Union officers toward their former enemies.[138] Secretary of War Stanton was irate to hear reports of rebel soldiers donning their uniforms in the loyal states and perceived such actions as a fresh act of hostility toward the government.[139] Richmond Unionist John M. Humphreys was no less vexed that rebel editors continued to print their traitorous rags. "Each one of the editors are by common justice and right no longer even citizens or property holders in Our Country they having been potent in getting up the rebellion and strengthening it," he asserted.[140] Even Union soldiers who had participated in the so-called magnanimous surrender ceremonies became increasingly incensed. "The sight of the greyback uniform and buttons seems to irritate our officers, whose feeling against Rebeldom has become bitterly intensified," Strong observed. "They now seem to regard rebels as mortal enemies, unscrupulous, malignant, faithless, and unfit for any treatment but stern repression."[141] Clearly this was a tremendous change in attitude from that which had appeared on the surrender field at Appomattox only two weeks earlier.

Lee's farewell order to his troops especially galled northerners. On April 27, two days before his interview with the *Herald* appeared, the *New York Times* published the order "so that our readers may see what encouragement paroled rebel officers have had from their chief, to bear themselves insolently and defiantly, on their release."[142] Unionists responded with fury. A letter to the editor of the *Times* was indignant that the loyal press had not responded more prominently to the "insolent General Order No. 9." Pointing out that having surrendered his army Lee had no right to issue a general order, the reader asserted that "Lee deserves more condemnation that any other traitor who has upheld the bloody rebellion." He hoped that "loyal men would always mention his name simply as a traitor and murderer." Another reader declared Lee "chief of the traitors who have attempted assassination of the nation, and who have assassinated our beloved President." Having been granted clemency and pardon by Grant, Lee had responded with "insolence and defiance and a public declaration to his followers that the attempted assassination of this nation was a '*duty faithfully performed for their country*.'" "A generous clemency can win no peace from a spirit as this," declared the author.[143]

Even if Lee remained free on his parole, northerners felt increasingly relieved to learn that some of those involved in the assassination had been captured. By April 24, alleged conspirators Samuel Arnold, Michael O'Laughlen, Edman Spangler, Lewis Powell, George Atzerodt, Samuel Mudd, and Mary Surratt were all in federal custody. Two days later, David Herold surrendered and Booth was mortally wounded by Federal troops near Port Royal, Virginia. With Booth dead and the others awaiting trial in Washington, much of the fear that had gripped the city for nearly two weeks began to dissipate.[144] But President Johnson and his administration, especially Secretary Stanton and Judge Advocate General Joseph Holt, remained convinced that Booth and his "hirelings" had not acted alone.[145] On May 2, Johnson issued a proclamation declaring that the "atrocious murder of the late President" and the attempted assassination of Seward "were incited, concerted, and procured by and between Jefferson Davis . . . Jacob Thompson, Clement C. Clay, Beverly Tucker, George N. Sanders, William C. Cleary and other rebels and traitors against the Government of the United States harbored in Canada." Offering rewards ranging from $100,000 for the arrest of Davis to $10,000 for the arrest of Cleary, late clerk of Clay, the Johnson administration left no doubt that it intended to punish the Confederate leadership for its heinous acts.[146] Protected by the surrender terms and conspicuously absent from the list were the names of any Confederate military leaders, including Lee.

On May 9, the trial against Booth's eight alleged co-conspirators began in Washington amid a flurry of national interest. The following day, the military commission formally charged the prisoners with "maliciously, unlawfully, and traitorously . . . combining, confederating, and conspiring together" with Booth, Davis, and others to kill Lincoln, Johnson, Seward, and Grant.[147] The timing of the 4th Michigan Cavalry 700 miles to the south on that very day could not have been better. In a secluded section of southern Georgia, the troops caught up with Davis and his party, which now included his wife, Varina, his children, several aides, slaves, and a handful of armed soldiers. In desperation, Davis attempted to escape on foot, but the cavalry men quickly captured him disguised in his wife's shawl. Suspected of complicity in the assassination, the Confederate president soon joined the recently captured Alabama senator Clement Clay on his way to imprisonment at Fortress Monroe in Hampton Roads, Virginia.[148] News of Davis's capture—and especially tales of his effeminate disguise—sent rejoicings throughout the North.[149]

Still reeling from the assassination, many were likewise thrilled to learn that some Confederate leaders were being sought after for their crimes of treason. In early May, Grant issued instructions for the arrest of all Virginia men still in arms and "all other particularly obnoxious leaders in the state."[150] But chief-of-staff General Henry Halleck wondered if these arrests might hinder the reunion process. "All classes are offering to take the amnesty oath," he wrote the general-in-chief, "and those excluded from its benefit are nevertheless taking it and making petitions for pardon." He noted that many of Lee's officers had come forward to take the oath, while rumors abounded that the rebel chieftain might follow suit. "Should he do this the whole population with few exceptions will follow his example," Halleck maintained. In short, he believed that "it would be unfortunate to check by unnecessary arrests this general desire for amnesty."[151] Grant concurred, replying that while much of the North might oppose allowing Lee amnesty, such would doubtless "have the best possible effect toward restoring good feelings of peace in the South."[152] Reunion, of course, had always been the goal of the Union Cause.

But these merciful feelings seemed only to apply to military leaders. Throughout May, Federal forces arrested and imprisoned at least twelve Confederate officeholders, including several southern governors, Vice President Alexander Stephens, Assistant Secretary of War John Campbell, Postmaster General John H. Reagan, and Senator Benjamin Harvey Hill, while Lee and his men remained free on their paroles.[153] The men who had waged war on the field of battle went unmolested while civilian leaders were imprisoned for their transgressions. There appeared to be a clear line between civilian and military wartime experiences that would continue for decades.[154]

While Grant's reconciliationist leanings and the military paroles might have deterred the Union army from arresting rebel generals, they did not prevent federal courts from indicting these men. In the May session of the district court in Norfolk, Virginia, the grand jury issued indictments against thirty-four Confederate leaders. Included on the list were some of the South's most famous military personalities—Jubal A. Early (whom Lee had relieved of his command in March 1865 and who refused to seek a parole or amnesty), Richard Ewell (captured at Sailor's Creek prior to Appomattox and imprisoned at Fort Warren), Fitzhugh Lee (who had refused to surrender at Appomattox), James Longstreet, and, the most celebrated of all, Robert E. Lee himself.[155]

The arrests and indictments convinced many white southerners that their interests would be best protected outside the United States. In the wake of military defeat, countless Confederates like Sarah Morgan had scribbled impassioned diary passages threatening to abandon their native land. Though opposed by Lee, these were not idle threats for many. Determined not to bare the humiliation and horror they were sure would accompany Yankee subjugation of the region, thousands fled the country.[156] Belligerent and bitter, several families from the Lower South fled to Brazil, by 1865 the only slaveholding nation in the western hemisphere, when Emperor Dom Pedro II held out the offer of subsidies and tax breaks in an effort to improve his nation's cotton production.[157] For Confederate leaders, however, the stakes were much higher. In the wake of the May indictments and arrests of office holders, many rightfully feared that they would be subjected to trials for treason. Recognizing that the only punishment for treason was execution, many elected to expatriate themselves.[158] Confederates not facing indictments, imprisonment, or trials for treason found such ideas to be ludicrous, including Eliza Andrews. "The men are all talking about going to Mexico and Brazil," she wrote in her diary; "if all emigrate who say they are going to, we shall have a nation made up of women, negroes, and Yankees."[159] No doubt sarcastic, Andrews's quip nevertheless implied that the reunited nation would be devoid of Confederate men. Perhaps ironically, it would be the Confederate women who would be the most ardent resisters to national reconciliation.

THE GRAND REVIEW

On May 23 and 24 the conspirators' trial paused while the nation celebrated its heroes in a spectacularly impressive Grand Review of nearly 150,000 troops. White and black, men and women, old and young crowded the streets, windows, balconies, and roofs along Pennsylvania Avenue cheering the troops and waving small flags. Throughout the capital, banners carried inscriptions such as "The public schools of Washington welcome the heroes of the republic," "Honor to the Brave," "Welcome Brave Soldiers," "Defenders of the Country," and "Union and Freedom forever." One of the largest of the banners had been prominently displayed over the western portico of the Capitol bearing the inscription "The only national debt we can never pay is the debt we owe to the victorious Union soldiers."[160] Just as they had rushed to send off their troops four years earlier to save the Union, now the home front greeted its veterans with an enthusiastic homecoming.

Even if they had all been responsible for victory, the Union armies exhibited their divergent personalities during the national pageant. On the first day, Gen. George G. Meade's well-clad eastern Army of the Potomac marched in precise lines up Pennsylvania Avenue for one final review before President Johnson, his cabinet, General-in-Chief Grant, members of the Supreme Court and Congress, state governors, and the general public.

Gen. Henry W. Slocum (Army of Georgia) and staff marching down Pennsylvania Avenue during the Grand Review on May 24, 1865. (Library of Congress)

The following day, Sherman's western armies took to the streets, show-casing their bravado and swagger in a manner substantially different from the eastern soldiers. Having spent the last few months living off the land and away from supply lines, they were not nearly as well dressed as the Army of the Potomac. Straggling along behind them were many of the freedmen and -women who had followed Sherman's men north; they were leading mules and horses loaded with plunder gathered along the army's march through Georgia and the Carolinas. Upon reaching the re-viewing stand of the president and other dignitaries, the men whooped and hollered, raising cheers until both Johnson and Grant acknowledged them.[161]

With the exception of the black pioneers who marched with Sherman's men, the parade was entirely white. No USCT soldiers marched on either day.[162] But significantly, several reporters commented on the absence of black troops. Some wondered if the exclusion had been to "spare the sensitive feelings of the rebels." Newspapers such as the *New York Times* and William Lloyd Garrison's *Liberator* refuted these claims, noting that the black soldiers were absent for the same reason as were many white troops: soldiers whose enlistments had not expired, including members of the USCT who had been in service for little more than two years, remained on active duty in the far reaches of Texas or in Union-occupied cities. "Our Generals are more just than to refuse due honor to any soldier, white or black, who has battled nobly for the cause of the Union," observed *The Liberator*.[163] As with Lincoln's death, in the Grand Review African American leaders saw the overlap of white and black memories of the war.

Perhaps more important, although not surprising, was the absence of Confederate troops from the review. If the war, and thus the parade, had truly been about celebrating reunion, should not the surrendered rebel soldiers have marched alongside their countrymen? Conversely, as the defeated foe, should they not have been paraded through the streets as captives? Both may seem absurd suggestions, but the question of how to handle the defeated rebels remained highly volatile during the review, as evidenced by Sherman's refusal to shake hands with Stanton because of their differences over the surrender terms offered to Johnston.[164] The Grand Review, like the burial of U.S. war dead in national cemeteries, was devoted exclusively to honoring those who had fought to preserve the Union.[165] Thus the review embodied the question of reunion and reconciliation that would vex the nation for decades: how could the nation be reunited and remembered without aggravating the wounds that had caused a civil war while simultaneously celebrating the Union triumph?

The review offered one more poignant reminder: the savior of the Union was not there to receive his victorious armies. Even though Washington had been decked out in celebratory red, white, and blue bunting, flags remained at half-staff and black ribbons reminded all of Lincoln's assassination. Seated next to President Johnson and other dignitaries, Secretary of the Navy Gideon Welles lamented Lincoln's absence. "All felt this," he sadly wrote. A Baltimore newspaper recalled the Union soldiers' affection for "Father Abraham." The president, "who called the men composing the splendid pageant now passing home from their peaceful firesides to protect the Government he had sworn to support would have been most glad and happy to have bidden them kindly greeting on their return." Echoing calls from the pulpit only a month earlier, the newspaper reminded its readers who had committed the dastardly act: "What has Secession and

Slavery to answer for?"[166] Later that summer, poet Henry Howard Brownell invoked the Grand Review and the soldiers' sense of loss that Lincoln was not there to review them:

> And our boys had fondly thought,
>   To-day in marching by,
> From the ground so dearly bought,
>   And the fields so bravely fought,
> To have met their Father's eye.
>
> But they may not see him in place,
>   Nor their ranks be seen of him;
> We look for the well-know face,
>   And the splendor is strangely dim.

But for Brownell, the soldiers need not be discouraged:

> Perished?—who was it said
>   Our leader has passed away?
> Dead? Our President dead?
>   He has not died for a day!

Instead, the memory of the slain president lived on in the memory of his soldiers who had secured the Union:

> We looked on a cold, still brow,
>   But Lincoln could yet survive;
> He was never more alive,
>   Never nearer than now.[167]

For Brownell and other northerners, the Grand Review was a bittersweet symbol of the past two months. Triumphantly, the boys in blue marched through the capital heralding the twin victories for the North: preservation of the Union and its happy byproduct, universal freedom. The Union cause had prevailed. Yet the absence of Lincoln foretold much about the way in which the war would be remembered. The Union veterans would not be the only symbol of the Cause Victorious.[168] Instead, the assassination had ensured that Lincoln, too, would become a potent if contested symbol of northern victory. As one northern woman observed, Lincoln's memory "will ever be sacred among liberty-loving people, and his deeds of kindness stand as monuments to his great worth for after generations to emulate."[169]

MOURNING AND CELEBRATION
IN THE WAKE OF WAR

1865–1869

On the morning of June 11, 1865, several Union officers accompanied by a large party of civilians climbed aboard a train in Washington bound for the old battlefield at Manassas. It was far different from the affair for which crowds had gathered in 1861 to witness the first great battle of the war. Now, four years later, these officers and civilians had come to dedicate two monuments, one on the field of the first battle of Bull Run and another on the field where the second battle was fought. Planned and erected only the previous week by troops from the 22nd Corps stationed at nearby Fairfax Courthouse, the monuments were unimposing, plain structures of red sandstone. But the dedications that day reflected the tone and message of more elaborate monument dedications that would follow in the months and years to come.[1]

Here on the field of the war's first battle and the first monument dedication after the war, Union soldiers and Washington's elite sang out in praise of Union victory. Echoing the sermons preached in the wake of Lincoln's assassination, the Reverend John Pierpont's hymn pointed to slavery as the cause of both the war and the president's death, rejoiced that Union soldiers had secured freedom, and condemned the rebel dead.[2] Just as would be the case at countless other Union monument and cemetery dedications, there was no hint of the reconciliationist tone that would become so frequent on battlefields in the coming decades. Instead, on the field

Members of the 22nd Corps built and dedicated one of the first postwar memorials on the battlefield at Bull Run during the summer of 1865. (Library of Congress)

where U.S. forces had twice been defeated by rebel armies, Union veterans and civilians reclaimed the space. They left no doubt that they were the victors, commemorating in stone the Union soldiers who had so bravely ensured that slavery would never again tear the nation asunder.

A week later, rumors began to circulate that local rebels had defaced the monument. While some northern papers expressed hope that it was not true, they noted there was strong reason to believe the reports. "The temper of people in that part of Virginia is not a whit more loyal than it was six months ago," observed the *New York Times*.[3] The story was soon contradicted, and Union soldiers were glad to learn that the original story was untrue. Had it not been, they warned in no uncertain terms, "some of our soldiers would have taken terrible revenge for such an insult."[4]

But what would have happened if Union soldiers had embarked on a vengeful retaliation? Would sectional conflict have flared up again? In the first years after Appomattox, Unionists continued to confront the dilemma of whether reunion necessitated gestures of reconciliation. Was punishment a necessary precursor to a reunited nation? Would more deaths, those of the Lincoln conspirators or leaders such as Jefferson Davis, be required to make sure the rebellion was thoroughly suppressed? What should or could be done to stifle the Confederate sentiment that appeared to linger on even after defeat?

As army and government leaders wrestled with these issues, mourning and death continued to shape sectional animosities and memories of the war. Unionists might not agree on how to proceed with binding up the nation's wounds, but they did adamantly refuse to allow former rebels within the confines of the new "national" cemeteries. These sanctified places would be reserved for loyal Americans who had been true to the Union cause. Former Confederates responded in kind. Humiliated by the continued presence of Union troops, infuriated by the end of slavery, angered by the neglect of Confederate graves, and emboldened by lenient federal policies intended to nurture national healing, former Confederates audaciously defended the sacrifice of their soldiers in cities of the dead. At cemetery dedications and Memorial Day services, they found a viable and tenacious way in which to maintain their continued defiance, create an identity separate from that of the North, and cultivate the Lost Cause.

African Americans' earliest memories of the war were shaped by a more complicated relationship between mourning and celebration. Black Americans north and south, too, mourned the loss of their soldiers at cemetery dedications and Union Memorial Days. Yet Emancipation Day, Juneteenth, Evacuation Day, and July Fourth ceremonies proved to be more festive occasions. In elaborate parades and public celebrations, they honored USCT soldiers and provided opportunities for all African Americans to rejoice in emancipation and the promise of equal citizenship. Whether solemn observances at cemeteries or grand processions marking the end of slavery, between 1865 and 1869 it became readily apparent that no single vision of the war could encompass the range of meanings and understandings such a vast American public found in the conflict.

HONORING THE UNION DEAD

As the soldiers of the U.S. Army mustered out during the summer of 1865, most marched home to a hero's welcome. From major cities to the smallest village, joyous citizens received their victorious men with celebrations at the local train depot, feted them with fine dinners, and cheered them in parades.[5] For nearly 360,000 Union families, however, this would be impossible, their sons, brothers, husbands, and other loved ones having lost their lives in the four bloody years of fighting. The bodies of most of these men had not been returned home, nor did they reside in the newly created national cemeteries such as those in Gettysburg and Arlington; instead, they remained in unidentified mass graves on southern battlefields.[6]

Fearing that the temporary headboards offering some identification might soon be lost to weather and outraged by reports of Union grave desecration by recalcitrant rebels, the northern public clamored for more honorable and more respectable sepulchers for these saviors of the Union. In early June 1865, Quartermaster General Montgomery C. Meigs issued orders sending Capt. James M. Moore, an assistant quartermaster, to the battlefields of the Wilderness and Spotsylvania to reinter and remark the graves of those killed in the previous year's battles. Bearing twenty wagon loads of coffins, Captain Moore's crew, including soldiers of the USCT not yet mustered out of service, tended to more than 1,500 Union graves. Over the course of three weeks, the men re-sodded the existing graves, painted headboards, and laid out two cemeteries enclosed by fences for those whose remains had not been properly interred at the time of battle. Similar efforts prevailed in the western theater, where Chaplain William Earnshaw commenced identifying and reinterring soldiers' remains near Murfreesboro, Tennessee, in the Stones River National Cemetery. But just as had been the case in Virginia, there was no effort to systematically collect all the Union dead and inter them in one or more central cemeteries. That would have to wait.[7]

Indicative of how salient the prisoner of war issue remained, however, was the immediate effort to tend to graves at the Confederacy's most notorious prison. In early July, Moore was relieved of his work in Virginia and sent to Andersonville. Between February 1864 and the end of the war, some 45,000 Union prisoners of war had suffered under especially brutal conditions in the Georgia sun, at least 13,363 of them paying with their lives. The shocking images of the skeletal survivors and stories of the unfathomable conditions sent northerners into a near frenzied state. With the war over, they beseeched the government to honor these noble heroes. Working (often acrimoniously) alongside the former Union nurse Clara Barton, who now ran the Office of Missing Soldiers, Moore's team of clerks, painters, letterers, and carpenters coped with the same unbearably stifling heat that had claimed the lives of so many prisoners. Within weeks they had established a fifty-acre cemetery that closely resembled that in Gettysburg, composed of subdivided sections, walks, a board fence, and a flagstaff in the center. On August 17, even as the prison's commandant, Henry Wirz, stood trial, the graves were formally dedicated as a national cemetery. The prison, however, had been untouched. It would be left as "a monument to the inhumanity unparalleled in the annals of war."[8]

Just as Union troops moved to provide respectable resting places for individual soldiers in the aftermath of war, they also continued to erect monuments to their fallen brethren on battlefields. In Manassas, Chambersburg, and elsewhere that summer, orators paid tribute to the

sacrifices and heroics of U.S. soldiers, and many heralded the war's two results: preservation of the Union and the end of slavery.[9] Dedicating the soldiers' monument in Gettysburg on July 4, 1865, Maj. Gen. O. O. Howard,
who had commanded the 11th Corps during the battle and was now commissioner of the Freedmen's Bureau, reminded the somber crowd that the
memorial they were dedicating was raised to the American soldier and his
"unceasing herald of labor, suffering, union, liberty, and sacrifice." "The
maimed bodies, the multitude of graves, the historic fields, the monumen-
tal stones like this we are laying to-day," he noted, "are only meager memorials of the soldiers' work." Invoking Abraham Lincoln's dedication of the
cemetery in November 1863, Howard intoned that these men had not died
in vain. Instead, their sacrifices had brought about African Americans'
concept of what Lincoln had called for, a "new birth of freedom."[10] The
monument would serve as a perpetual reminder that the preservation of
the Union and universal freedom could not be disentangled from the soldiers' sacrifice.[11]

Speakers were more diverse when it came to dealing with former rebels.
Some seemed to call for speedy reconciliation. In remarks read at the
Gettysburg monument dedication, President Andrew Johnson (perhaps
not surprisingly) believed that white southerners would soon exhibit "such
loyalty and patriotism as were never seen nor felt [in the South] before."[12]
Others unabashedly condemned the rebel cause. A hymn penned by the
Reverend John Pierpont and sung at the Bull Run monument dedication in June had exhorted that northerners were content to let both "rebel
bones and memories rot."[13]

Regardless of their position on the former rebels, Unionists would not
let the remains of their loyal soldiers molder unacknowledged. In the
spring of 1866, Congress finally provided the financial support for gathering all the remains of Union soldiers still reposing in the former Confederacy. This massive reinterment project would send crews across the South
to scout for grave sites and organize cemeteries for Union soldiers similar to those that had been created during the war in Gettysburg, Arlington, Chattanooga, Knoxville, and Stones River.[14] As early as February, officers and work crews began arriving in Richmond to gather the remains
of northern prisoners who had been buried at Hollywood and Oakwood
Cemeteries and at Belle Isle. These cemeteries would be premised first and
foremost on the Union, and unlike Gettysburg and Antietam (which had
been organized initially by several northern states), they would explicitly
not be arranged by state. Instead, like Gen. George H. Thomas after the
battle of Chattanooga, the Union Burial Corps elected to "mix them all up,"

no doubt "sick of state's rights."[15] The corps laid out the grounds so that each grave was of equal importance and provided individual headstones for all remains. By 1871, 303,536 Union soldiers had been reinterred in seventy-four national cemeteries.[16]

These national cemeteries were not to be for white soldiers alone. In a radical departure from the antebellum period in which racially integrated cemeteries were rare, the burial corps routinely included black soldiers in the memorial grounds.[17] The cemetery in City Point, Virginia, contained more than 1,300 USCT burials, that in Arlington had more than 400 USCT soldiers (as well as the remains of 3,235 refugee runaway slaves or "contrabands"), and even Gettysburg served as the final resting place for one black soldier, Henry Gooden.[18] At some of the national cemeteries, USCT veterans were buried in separate portions of the field, but at others they mingled freely in death with white soldiers as they had not in life.[19]

If national cemeteries failed to discriminate between white and black, the divide between blue and gray remained. There appears to have been virtually no dissent within the U.S. Army ranks to interring only loyal soldiers; northerners clearly understood that providing proper burials implied bestowing honor on the dead. If the Union dead served as reminders of the nation's sacrifice and suffering, how could loyal Americans rightfully include the Confederate dead among their ranks?[20] Many likely agreed with a Union woman visiting the national cemetery at Arlington in 1866 who hoped that "no rebel will ever set his accursed foot within those sacred precincts."[21] National cemeteries were sacred ground for the loyal, Union dead alone.[22]

Even as some Unionists continued to push for Lincoln's and later Johnson's vision of reconciliation, in the immediate aftermath of war white northerners, southern Unionists, and African Americans were hardly willing to praise Confederate soldiers' bravery and courage as they stood at the graves of those whom the rebels had slain. Reconciliation would not emerge from mutual respect and mourning for slain soldiers. On the contrary, sectionalism would thrive in the cities of the dead for decades to come.

DEATH SENTENCE

Three days after the Fourth of July, photographers captured one of the last stark images of the war: four limp bodies of the Lincoln assassination conspirators dangling from the ropes in the Old Arsenal Penitentiary. Included among them was Mary Surratt, the first white woman ever executed by the United States. Many were shocked by such a sight, but others

The dangling bodies of four of the Lincoln conspirators, including Mary Surratt, served as a powerful warning to the defeated South in July 1865. (Library of Congress)

praised the president for meting out severe punishments. "President Johnson is moving in the right direction now," observed Tennessee governor William "Parson" Brownlow's Knoxville newspaper. Finally, the president was "carrying out his maxim that 'traitors must be punished and treason made odious.'" "He hung four rebels in one day in Washington," proclaimed the paper, "and among them *Madam Surratt*, a female rebel." Although the press did not indicate as much, it is not hard to imagine that Surratt was a surrogate for all the rebel women who had so defiantly snubbed, spit upon, and otherwise harassed Union troops during the war.[23]

Next to Lincoln's murder, the subject of prisoners of war elicited the most rancorous responses among Unionists. Tales of Confederate atrocities toward Union prisoners had filtered north throughout the war, but those that enraged people the most were the tales from Andersonville. With the war over, they now clamored for punishment against those who had perpetuated the inhumanity. In May, Union forces arrested Capt. Henry Wirz, commandant of the camp. For three months he stood trial facing the testimony of more than 160 witnesses, most of whom were former Union prisoners. As the trial lingered on, Wirz's health deteriorated to the point that he was barely able to rise from the couch where he rested. He elicited no sympathy, and, not surprisingly, was found guilty and sentenced to hang. As they had done during the war, U.S. officials attempted to connect Davis to the prison camp atrocities, offering Wirz amnesty in exchange for testimony incriminating the former Confederate president. He refused, vowing that Davis "had no connection with me as to what was done at Andersonville."[24] On November 10, northern spectators gathered around the same scaffold that had claimed the lives of Booth's conspirators just a few months prior. Amid cries of "remember Andersonville," Wirz met his death before an exultant crowd. And just like the conspirators, his postmortem image circulated throughout the North as proof of his demise.

Almost as reprehensible to northern sensibilities as the slaying of their president and the atrocities committed against prisoners of war were the brutalities of rebel guerrilla forces. Nearly all of those who remained in the field after Lee and Johnston's surrenders were granted paroles, including John S. Mosby's Virginia partisans and Jeff Thompson's men in Arkansas. Those captured before the surrenders or considered to be the most notorious characters, however, faced formal legal proceedings. Henry Magruder, of John Hunt Morgan's command in Kentucky, was hanged in Louisville in late October. One of the most notorious guerrillas was Champ Ferguson, a Kentucky native whose most atrocious killing occurred in Saltville, Virginia, in October 1864, when his band scoured the field after the battle and executed wounded Union soldiers. They killed both blacks and whites, but appeared to especially target African American soldiers. He was captured in May and his trial received nearly as much national attention as had Wirz's. Found guilty and sentenced to die in Nashville, Ferguson climbed the gallows on October 20 as more than 300 residents and members of the 16th USCT watched. Asked if he had any final words, Ferguson remained defiant and recalcitrant to the end. He nodded toward his coffin and proclaimed, "When I am dead I want my body placed in this box, delivered to my wife . . . in White County and be buried in pure, Rebel soil." His was a path far removed from that which his eastern compatriot, John S. Mosby, would take decades after the war.[25]

These death sentences had not quelled the calls for Jefferson Davis's execution. The Reverend Mr. Burton of Hartford had been especially successful in swelling his summertime congregation through his powerful sermons calling for the execution of Davis and "all his principal men." Speaking to a packed sanctuary in late August, Burton argued that the hot passions of April had cooled and northerners overwhelmingly harbored neither hate nor malice toward the defeated South. But Davis must still hang. "They would release him if they could," he observed, "if they could forget the dead . . . if their bells of victory were not drowned by their bells of mourning; if they could forget their country." Northerners could not forget; Davis could not be spared. Davis's conviction and execution, Burton argued, "will do more for the stability of the country, and for the cause of public order, than almost any dozen great acts of the last for years."[26] By late summer, Burton, Judge Advocate General Joseph Holt, and others had become convinced that Union victory could be fully realized only if southern leaders such as Davis were punished for their crimes.[27] The memory of the Union dead, as Burton observed, was far too powerful to allow northerners to forget.

But as had been the case since the war, not all Unionists felt so vehemently and instead pushed for a speedy reconciliation free of harsh or punitive measures. Prominent abolitionist the Reverend Henry Ward Beecher, remained firm in the convictions he had expressed since Appomattox that Davis need not hang. Ample blood had already been shed, he believed, and the nation was strong enough to forego any manifestation of revenge or retaliation.[28] Gerritt Smith, an abolitionist who had been instrumental in John Brown's 1859 raid on Harpers Ferry, likewise advocated a mild policy toward white southerners. While he believed the South guilty of treason, he maintained that the United States had acknowledged the Confederacy as a de facto government and thus the rules of war applied. White southerners were a defeated foe, not traitors to be hanged. Moreover, he argued, the North had been equally complicit in the horrific system of slavery, so why should the South alone be punished?[29] At least some northern Democrats warned that Republican fanaticism calling for more contrition on the part of white southerners threatened perpetual war.[30] *The Old Guard*, a Democratic, fiercely white-supremacist monthly magazine published in New York, observed that with the rebellion ended, the southern states would naturally gravitate to their old positions in the Union. "No armies are needed," the magazine noted, "no efforts whatever; the secession ordinances repealed and re-union is complete, if no obstacles are placed in the way. President Johnson has only to appoint federal officers in the South, and the Union is restored."[31] In late June, even the Republican-leaning *New York Times* concurred that punishment was not necessary. Rather, the paper attributed the "progress of pacification" in the South to Grant's "great magnanimity" at Appomattox, Sherman's similar terms at Durham Station, the generosity of the president's amnesty, and most important, to "the liberal and fraternal spirit in which the North ... has stretched wide open its arms to greet again the repentant South."[32]

Others joined politicians and activists in their calls for a lenient peace and a speedy reconciliation. Businessmen such as John Travers of New York hoped to renew amicable relations with the South. Writing to an antebellum business partner in Virginia, Travers supposed that "time will obliterate all feeling of dislike caused by the ungenerous unnecessary war" and hoped that they might renew their associations as smoothly as possible.[33] In December 1865, John W. Garrett, president of the Baltimore & Ohio Railroad, called for building a railroad through the Shenandoah Valley. Not only would the railroad help Virginia recover quickly from the war, but it would also "accomplish much in the restoration of kindly feelings ... assure mutual interest ... [and] aid in binding in iron bands those great commonwealths to the union of our fathers."[34] Families divided by war also sought to navigate the postwar world of reunion and some measure of reconciliation, as was the case with the Ellets of Washington, D.C., and the Cabells of Virginia. Despite protestations from her paternal uncle, a Unionist, that it was too soon to forgive her Confederate relatives for the past four years, Mary Ellet headed to Virginia in late July determined to renew relations with her mother's family. Apparently her trip did serve to bridge the internecine division, as she quickly began a flirtation with her cousin, William Daniel Cabell of Lynchburg, which resulted in marriage two years later.[35]

In the immediate postwar years, northerners sometimes used the terms "reunion" and "reconciliation" interchangeably. But many took great effort to distinguish between the two. Rebuking an address by Massachusetts senator Charles Sumner that questioned white southern loyalty in January 1866, the moderate Republican senator Edgar Cowan of Pennsylvania observed that unlike the radical senator from Massachusetts, he was for "reconciliation." While the nation might have been reunited at Appomattox, Cowan desired a "Union by consent, not by force." "I would like to make friends of all the people with whom we have been at enmity heretofore." Parading the exceptional cases of white southern ill-behavior before the country, he insisted, would only excite angry passions more than they already were.[36] President Johnson agreed. The war had accomplished the goal of reunion, he noted, but its aftermath proved "the auspicious time to commence the work of reconciliation," to meet former Confederates "in the spirit of charity and forgiveness, and to conquer them even more effectually by the magnanimity of the nation than by the force of arms."[37] Intending to reunite the nation as peacefully and smoothly as possible,

Unionists, whether Republican or Democrat, radical or moderate, could hardly believe how their reconciliationist efforts served instead to embolden former rebels in their spirited defense of the Lost Cause.

LOYALTY IS ONLY LIP DEEP

Less than three weeks after Lincoln's remains were entombed in Springfield, President Johnson began to retreat from his bombastic vows to punish the rebels. With Congress adjourned until December, he initiated his own conciliatory vision of a restored Union. On May 29, he issued two proclamations detailing how the remaining seven states without reconstruction governments could return to the Union. He offered amnesty and pardons with the restoration of all property rights (excepting slaves) to participants of the rebellion so long as they took an oath pledging loyalty to the Union and endorsed emancipation. Fourteen classes of people were exempt from the pardon, most important among them Confederate officials, those who had broken prior amnesty oaths, those who had attended West Point or Annapolis, and those who owned taxable property worth more than $20,000. Of special note was the exemption of persons "who had mistreated prisoners of war or were under arrest for other military crimes," which included the Lincoln assassination conspirators, Davis, and others already in custody. Those individuals would have to apply personally to the president for pardon.[38]

Why this seemingly sudden shift to moderation by Johnson? A combination of personal grievances and political ambitions probably sparked the change. As the most powerful man in the nation he now had the southern elite, a group whom he had always envied, groveling at his feet. Johnson relished former slaveholders beseeching him for amnesty and particularly enjoyed the pleas from attractive southern wives who appeared sufficiently contrite. Simultaneously, he worried that emancipation would unleash anarchy in the South, and he fervently believed that only planters could maintain control over the black population. If barred from a political role in southern society, the region's antebellum leaders would be unable to exert such influence. Perhaps most important, the support of white southerners necessary for his own reelection as president shaped Johnson's response. Heeding the advice of Secretary of State Seward, Johnson came to believe that lenient terms toward the rebels might help create an alliance among conservatives and moderates that could thwart the Radical Republicans in the next presidential election.[39]

A convention of former slaves meeting in Alexandria, Virginia, in mid-

August knew better. In an address to the loyal citizens of the United States, the freedmen recounted the myriad of ways in which they had aided the Union war effort. They had flocked to Union lines, served as scouts and spies, dug trenches, driven teams, aided escaped prisoners of war, and fought under the star-spangled banner at Fort Wagner, Milliken's Bend, and Petersburg. But now the war was over, and yet their former masters— former foes—appeared to be regaining power. "Four-fifths of our enemies are pardoned or amnestied, and the other fifth are being pardoned," they observed. Rather than protecting the civil rights of African Americans who had been devoted to the Union cause, Johnson had left the former slaves "entirely at the mercy of these subjugated but unconverted rebels." "We know these men—know them well," they wrote, "and we assure you that, with the majority of them, loyalty is only lip-deep, and that their professions of loyalty are used as a cover to the cherished design of getting restored to their former relations with the Federal Government."[40] These freedmen understood perhaps better than white northerners the depth of Confederates' attachment to their defunct nation and the political and social ramifications likely to follow such a deep-seated devotion.

Throughout the summer and fall of 1865, white southerners began to exhibit a combination of stoic resolve, self-pity, and defiance.[41] The self-pity was most evident in southern whites' insistence that they were the true victims of war. In letters and diaries, former Confederates lamented all that they had lost and blamed the North's hard-war policies for inflict-ing such unnecessary and brutal damage to the region. Richmond's Lucy Fletcher, for one, seethed at the presence of "the people who for 4 years have been slaying our brethren, and desolating our land, burning and rav-aging our homes insulting and robbing our defenceless women and grey haired men."[42] Even Robert E. Lee, still facing an indictment for treason, believed that northern officers and their soldiers had wantonly destroyed civilian property and inflicted unnecessary suffering on noncombatants.[43]

Beyond Union occupation, the aspect of defeat white southerners found most demeaning was the emancipation of nearly 4 million slaves. Not only did white southerners have to rebuild their economic system, but they also faced complex psychological challenges in a world without the scaffold-ing of slavery to ensure their social hierarchies. Throughout the summer, former slaveholders found themselves awash in a mixture of self-pity and anger as their slaves left.[44] In the pages of her diary, teenager Sallie Strick-ler of Madison County, Virginia, simultaneously defended slavery, reeled in anger at the Union "liberators," and questioned her identity in a post-emancipation South. "It grinds me sorely to think of our being *compelled* to give up our best-beloved institution," she wrote in May. "I truly believe that African slavery is right. I love it & all the South loves it. It suits us & I do not see how we can do without it." But like countless others, what vexed her most was the way slavery had ended. "It humiliates me, more than language can tell, to think of our being forced, ay forced, to give up what we love. So well! And that by Yankees!"[45] Robert Garlick Hill Kean agreed. "The *abolition of slavery* immediately, and by military order, is the most marked feature of this conquest of the South," he concluded in early June. "Manumission after this fashion will be regarded hereafter," Kean predicted, "as the greatest social crime ever committed on the earth."[46] Even a nonslaveholder described emancipation as "d—d robbery and nothin' else."[47]

Ironically, the protection of slavery had prompted the southern states to leave the Union, and thus emancipation had made reunion possible. Yet as would become increasingly clear throughout Reconstruction, emancipation and the accompanying racial uncertainty complicated reconciliation more than any other issue.

One aspect of the new status of black men that especially galled white southerners was the presence of black occupying troops. Fear of slave insurrections had been a constant part of southern life as long as most could remember. Now, black men sanctioned by the federal government carried guns and occupied southern cities. White southerners feared they would incite the 4 million freedpeople to unleash a race war throughout the region. All this reminded white southerners of the extent of their defeat and served as a powerful symbol of the magnitude of social disruption engendered by the war, simultaneously enraging and horrifying them. Former Confederates hurled insults at black troops, violently attacked them, and accused them of plundering their homes. In Texas and Louisiana at least a few whites disguised themselves as USCT troops and committed crimes against other whites. Humiliation combined with an intense racism fueled a bitter resentment toward both freedmen and Yankees that would prove to be an incredibly daunting obstacle to reconciliation.[48]

Despite the presence of both white and black Union troops, white southerners remained determined to restore as much of the antebellum social and political order as possible. Encouraged by Johnson's lenient amnesty policies and fierce stance against black civil and political rights, white southerners quickly crafted the so-called black codes. Enacted by states throughout the region during the summer and fall of 1865, the laws masqueraded as attempts to define the rights and responsibilities of freedmen. In reality, the statutes sought to stabilize the black labor force and define the relationship between southern whites and blacks (for instance, in their restrictions against black men testifying against whites in court or prohibitions of interracial marriage).[49] Black codes were an attempt to restore the antebellum status quo as much as possible. But they were equally part of the larger pattern of Confederate defiance that reverberated throughout the region in the immediate postwar period. Just as white southerners continued to sing anti-Union ditties, wear their rebel gray (sans insignia), and defy occupying troops, they implemented black codes in defiance of Union victory.

In letters, diaries, and newspapers throughout the summer and fall of 1865, Confederate civilians and soldiers widely admitted that they were "subjugated," "whipped," and "conquered." Even northern observers repeatedly remarked on the use of these phrases by former rebels.[50] But to acknowledge being whipped was hardly an admission of guilt or rejection of the cause for which they had fought. Instead, these statements served two purposes. First, such rhetoric was part of a strategy of acquiescence that white southerners hoped would convince the North that they had no intention of furthering the conflict and therefore should be treated with leniency.[51] Second, building on Lee's farewell address to his troops at Appomattox, former rebels' insistence that they had been "whipped" implied that they not been defeated so much as overwhelmed by superior numbers and resources. "Heroically the South struggled against adverse fate," Texan Sallie McNeill concluded, "and endured all ills, 'till exhausted and 'overpowered' by numbers, she surrendered her gallant little army, and the Confederacy was *no more*."[52] Such an explanation offered an excuse for battlefield defeat while maintaining the heroism of Confederate soldiers. In fact, it implied that Confederate soldiers were even more valiant and laudable than their foes because they had waged a battle they were likely to lose from the beginning.

Tantamount to this rejection of shame were two other budding elements of the Lost Cause, each inextricably wrapped up with the other and each offering a defense of the Confederacy that would become cardinal tenets of the white southern apologia in the postwar era. First, despite their calls for an independent slaveholding republic in 1861, most defeated Confederates immediately and instantly rallied to deny that the South had seceded to protect slavery. Confederate vice president Alexander Stephens, who had insisted in 1861 that slavery was the "cornerstone" of the new nation, quickly changed positions. "The slavery question had but little influence with the masses," he wrote in June 1865 from his prison cell at Fort

Warren. "Many even of the large slave-holders, to my personal knowledge, were willing from the first years of the war to give up that institution for peace on recognition of the doctrine of ultimate Sovereignty of the separate States." Second, it was not slavery that drove white southerners to secede, Stephens claimed; rather, their motive had been "to maintain and perpetuate the principles of the Constitution, even out of the Union when they could no longer maintain them in it."[53] In Richmond, another former rebel informed northern reporter John Richard Dennett that few in the South had owned slaves and therefore slavery could hardly have been the cause for the conflict. Instead, it had been the unjust tyranny of the North that had brought on the war. "The North has repeatedly violated the constitutional guaranties of slavery. Yes, sir, we had a most perfect right to secede, and we have been slaughtered by the thousands for attempting to exercise it. And yet it is the fashion to call us traitors." Hardly apologetic or submissive, he paused to add that "the people of the South are not going to stand that."[54]

Like countless other Confederates, these men espoused two of the most important ideologies of the Lost Cause: slavery was not the source of the conflict, and secession had been a constitutional right. Arguing that the Union had been a compact from which the states were free to withdraw, white southerners maintained that they were not traitors.[55] This would be crucial in determining how Confederates elected to remember the war: free from the label of treason, they felt entitled to honor their cause and the sacrifice of their soldiers as honorable, worthy, just, and purely American.

EMANCIPATION DAYS

On January 1, 1866, Emancipation Day celebrations unfolded throughout the nation as they had since 1863. Near Fort Monroe, where Jefferson Davis remained imprisoned, thousands of African Americans gathered at the schoolhouse for a procession composed of local organizations, men, women, and children. Banners with inscriptions such as "Abraham Lincoln, The Liberator and Friend of Our Race," were festooned in red, white, and blue along the schoolhouse walls as the crowd listened attentively to the various speakers. In Petersburg, several thousand freedmen and -women joined in a procession that extended for a nearly a mile before the crowd gathered for songs and general jubilation. In Richmond, 4,000 African Americans assembled at a local church where the 24th Massachusetts supplied the music. The services opened with the singing of a poem:

Oh! Praise and tanks, the Lord he come
To get the people free,
And massa tink it day of doom
And we of jubilee.

In stark comparison to the observances for Union soldiers that northerners had observed in Gettysburg and Manassas the previous year, Emancipation Days tended to be cheerful occasions described by many as a day
of jubilee. As one northern reporter observed, "Freedmen joyously spent
the day and . . . the emancipation era was in all the region felicitously and
auspiciously inaugurated."[56]

Even with the festive nature of the day, there remained a serious tone
of the work yet to be accomplished. The Richmond orator reminded his
audience that when the war began, the federal government had not intended to free them. Instead, emancipation had served as a strategy to
secure the perpetuity of the Constitution. Nevertheless, they were free and
must now strive to harness that freedom through hard work, education,
and faith. Most important, they must work to secure suffrage. Speaking to
the overflowing crowd at Quinn's Chapel in Chicago, the Reverend R. De-
Baptist sounded a similar tone. He, too, reminded his congregation that
emancipation had not come easily. For years, abolitionists such as William
Lloyd Garrison had battled not only slavery but also the northern public.
Eventually, the North had changed courses during the war, the battle had
been fought, and slavery was forever abolished. But like others, DeBaptist
reminded his audience that the struggle was not over. The black race was
the only one that had remained true to the country during the war; every
other race had traitors. Rebellion was not dead, it was only vanquished
and ready to rise again. It was for the safety of the Union, he argued, that
the black man be given the franchise.[57]

New Year's Day was not the only occasion on which newly freedmen
and -women celebrated emancipation. Just as former Confederates would
select different days to observe Memorial Day, African Americans and
their abolitionist allies elected to hold their celebrations on days mean-
ingful to them. Those in East Texas celebrated Juneteenth to honor the
day they first learned of their freedom on June 19, 1865, more than two
months after Appomattox.[58] In Des Moines, Iowa, black residents commemorated August 1, combining their antebellum celebrations of the 1834
abolition of slavery in the British West Indies with U.S. emancipation.[59]
African Americans in Washington, D.C., selected April 19, the anniversary
of the abolition of slavery in the District of Columbia, for their commemo-

ration. Banners and flags adorned the Capitol and other public buildings that bright spring day as cannons roared in merriment. According to one observer, every black resident of the city had flocked to the streets to watch the procession led by black soldiers, marching with silken sashes, glittering bayonets, and their battle-torn regimental colors. Behind them, wrote one witness to the affair, "thousands of contrabands" marched, "redeemed by the blood of their brothers—this is the procession of the emancipated race." "What a sight for Washington!" she exclaimed. "There is not a city in the South where such a demonstration could be a greater triumph."[60] When the procession paused in front of the White House, President Johnson offered a short address in which he claimed to be one of the best friends of the black man (less than a month after vetoing the Civil Rights Act).[61] But his attempts to excite the distrust of African Americans against Congress were not lost on the crowd. Instead, they listened quietly and then resumed their march to the Capitol. There, the long procession of black veterans gave three cheers for the House of Representatives followed by three cheers for the Senate. Such shouts, observed one reporter, "went up as only emancipated men can give." "*That* was the reply of the colored people to the President," he continued. "They know their friends, *and they know their enemies.*"[62]

Among more hostile enemies, Emancipation celebrations in the South jeopardized the safety of African Americans. Such was the case on a similar occasion, the Evacuation Day ceremony sponsored by Richmond's black residents on April 3, 1866, to mark the fall of the Confederate capital. Much like Emancipation Days, the event was to include a parade of ex-slaves taking to the streets to celebrate their newfound freedom. When white residents learned of the planned festivities, they reacted viscerally, vowing to "prevent any demonstration by the negroes." One Richmond newspaper editor proclaimed that April 3 was no time for merriment but rather "a day of gloom and calamity to be remembered with a shudder of horror by all who saw it, whether it be the Federal soldier, or the resident, whether white or black." Although the city's black residents published a notice stating that they did not intend to celebrate the failure of the Confederacy but to commemorate their liberation, their efforts did not prevent violence. Just days before the ceremony, an unknown (but presumably white) person burned the Second African Baptist Church, a freedman's school, and the meeting location for those planning the event.[63]

Despite the church razing and rumors that effigies of Jefferson Davis and Robert E. Lee were to be burned (as had been done in Norfolk in 1863), and despite threats by whites that they would rather "wade through blood" before allowing the celebration, the festivities took place with only one minor incident and no bloodshed. Gathering at the fairgrounds to the northwest of the city, approximately 1,000 to 1,500 black men, many dressed in uniform and carrying muskets, marched while several hundred more rode horses down the city's streets. As the procession wound down Broad Street to Capitol Square, a crowd of 15,000 spectators cheered them along. White Richmonders did little to stop the event but warned that black people who had abandoned their work "to engage in the jubilee" would "not be employed again by their old masters."[64]

Some white northerners defended the Evacuation Day ceremony as the right of loyal men and women. White southerners would have to bear "with the best grace they can" such celebrations, noted the *New York Times*. "The future will necessarily be full of painful reminiscences of their gigantic crime in the rebellion," observed the paper, but quickly added, "We do not see that they have any right whatever to take offense at the negroes' celebration of their day of freedom."[65] The *Boston Advertiser* concurred, arguing that the celebration was the privilege of those who sought to mark "the downfall of treason and the establishment of the constitution."[66]

Less than a week later, on April 9, black residents from southern Virginia assembled to celebrate the surrender of Lee's army. Along the North Carolina border, freedmen and -women in Mecklenburg County took to the streets that day, pointing out that "if Lee had never been beaten ... the [emancipation] proclamation would have been to no avail."[67] In Hampton, black veterans played a central role in the day's festivities, marching through the streets shouldering the guns they had carried in battle. Seething with anger, someone attacked the procession, and later that night white mobs scoured the town. "Are we to be forbidden to hold national celebrations in our own country, lest we offend the enemy?" asked an indignant Republican newspaper.[68] Like Emancipation and Evacuation Days, Surrender Day ceremonies marked a pivotal moment in the process of claiming freedom and the full meaning of citizenship.[69]

Though they might differ by date or name, emancipation celebrations offered a wide variety of speeches, sermons, and testimonies. Almost universally, however, they featured the reading of the Emancipation Proclamation. Every year, those who gathered listened to the pronouncement of slavery's end in the Confederate states—and the exclusion of emancipation in the Border States and Union-occupied portions of the South. Despite this constant reminder of the proclamation's limits, many African Americans heralded its author as the "Great Emancipator." In cheers from the crowd and banners carrying his image, they memorialized Lincoln as the man who "stretched out his long arm and smote the monster on the head with his Emancipation hammer, such a blow as none but Abe could strike."[70] But others were quick to remind the crowds that Lincoln should not reap such high praise. After all, they reasoned, as late as August 1862, he had declared that if he "could save the Union without freeing any slave I would do it, and if I could save it by freeing all the slaves I would do it; and if I could save it by freeing some and leaving others alone I would also do that." Thus, Confederates' unwillingness to surrender, not Lincoln, had forced emancipation. "Davis is our modern Pharaoh, and through the hardness of his heart, God wrought our freedom," declared J. Carey of Iowa in 1866.[71]

Freedom was not the only thing on the minds of African Americans on such occasions. The centrality of black soldiers in the processions served as a reminder that USCT troops had not only been present at Appomattox, but that they had also participated in defeating Robert E. Lee.[72] In their estimation, reunion was still uncertain on Palm Sunday, April 1865, but they had played a central role in securing northern victory. Highlighting the USCT's role in quelling the rebellion allowed African Americans to offer a powerful contradiction of the Lost Cause image of heroic Confederate forces overwhelmed by northern resources and manpower. In the African American memory, the virtue of the northern cause, coupled with black troops' devotion, had secured Union victory. Righteous in the eyes of providence, their cause had prevailed.[73] White Unionists might have demurred from setting aside a holiday that celebrated the end of the war or the vanquishing of the enemy, but the black citizens of Hampton would not.[74] For many African Americans the war would be much more than merely the "War of the Rebellion." Instead, for them it had been the "Slavery War," the "Freedom War."[75]

THE CONFEDERATE DEAD

If freedom celebrations and occupation troops were enough to rouse the ire of former rebels, the presence of the Union Burial Corps tending to the graves of U.S. soldiers ignited their passions. The well-tended, neatly organized Union cemeteries stood in stark contrast to the vast number of Confederate skeletons and bones that lay exposed and bleaching on the fields of Shiloh, the trenches of Petersburg, and on other battlefields.[76] The real issue, however, was the underlying message of these new "national cemeteries" (as they had been designated by Congress). The care rendered to only the Union dead led white southerners to believe that the federal government intended to subjugate the Confederate South rather than place the region on an equal footing within the Union. Here was no gesture of reconciliation, no forgetting and forgiving. Instead, providing national cemeteries for the northern dead confirmed that these soldiers had given their lives for a noble cause, while Confederate soldiers had died in vain.[77] Perhaps more important, national cemeteries and monuments to the U.S. soldiers on southern soil served as constant reminders of Union victory. Silently resting in their sepulchers, the Union dead would prove to be a permanent occupying force in the South.

In the spring of 1866, Confederate women rushed to the defense of their dead.[78] Transforming their soldiers' aid societies into Ladies' Memorial Associations (LMAS), women from Richmond, Vicksburg, Chattanooga, Memphis, Augusta, Charleston, and countless other places in between sought to create their own national cemeteries—Confederate national cemeteries.[79] Like the Union cities of the dead, Confederates treated each grave with equal importance, designated a separate location for the unidentifiable remains, and frequently left a central space where a monument might later be erected. But in a distinct departure from most Union cemeteries, they grouped Confederate soldiers from the same state together.[80] States' rights would remain alive and well in Confederate burial grounds.

The LMAs quickly realized, however, that the cost of disinterring and reinterring thousands—in places such as Richmond tens of thousands— of remains would be astronomical.[81] Women in these communities simply could not afford to reinter so many bodies or purchase land for cemeteries without the aid of a unified South. Members of Richmond's Hollywood Memorial Association (HMA) sent an appeal addressed to "the Women of the South," reminding their "southern sisters" that the South remained united even if the Confederate war effort had failed. "The end we propose is the *cause of the South* . . . the permanent protection and adornment" of at least 13,000 Confederate dead interred in Hollywood Cemetery. The South remained "one family," they observed; "the southern heart [still] throbs with one impulse." Calling on all former Confederates, LMAs in Fredericksburg, Richmond, Franklin, Perryville, and "other places where great battles were fought" likewise appealed to every state in the South for funds so that the "names and graves of your noble sons are saved from oblivion."[82] In response, donations poured into LMAs from all corners of the former Confederacy.[83] For the women of the LMAs and the individuals who sent them money, the end of the war had failed to sever their cultural and emotional ties to the former slave states.

But these cemeteries would prove to be much more than places for the dead to slumber. If the U.S. Burial Corps had forever altered the southern landscape by creating national cemeteries for the Union dead, former Confederates would do likewise, creating their own permanent, enduring memorials to their slain soldiers. Within the walls of these cities of the dead, white southerners had created a literal space where the Confederate cause might live on indefinitely. Many no doubt agreed with the HMA when it hoped that its "Mausoleum, to the Martyrs of the South" might become the "'Mecca' of the South—to which, annually, shall come from every Southern State, Pilgrim widows and Orphans, Fathers and Mothers, Brothers and Sisters, relatives and friends, bringing their tribute of flowers, bedewed with Southern tears!" For generations to come, Hollywood Cemetery would be one "of the Holiest and most sublime features in the History of the Southern Cause."[84] Ever cognizant of the fact that rebel dead had been excluded from the U.S. national cemeteries, one Virginian declared upon visiting the soldiers' cemetery at the University of Virginia that "these are not the 'nation's dead,' they are 'our dead.'"[85] Unlike many of their soldiers, Confederate nationalism was far from dead. As one white southerner observed in 1866, "The South is now united by a band of graves—a tie that can never be sundered."[86]

Establishing Confederate cemeteries motivated women to organize LMAs, but their most visible and popular activity was the annual celebration of Memorial Days, which began in 1866.[87] Held in the spring as a sign of renewal and rebirth, communities chose dates that held special resonance for them rather than settling on a universal date (as the North would do). Petersburg's LMA elected to observe June 9, the date on which, two years prior, the "grey haired sires and beardless youths" of the home guard defended the city until Lee's troops could arrive.[88] The women of the HMA agreed on May 31, the anniversary of the day Richmonders first heard the cannons of war. Farther south, groups such as the Ladies of Columbia, South Carolina, and those of Augusta, Georgia, selected April 26 to mark Johnston's surrender to Sherman.[89] Notably, none of the groups—including the Appomattox LMA—chose to observe April 9, suggesting that the day most associated with the death of the Confederacy was far more painful than the death of the men who gave their lives for the cause.[90]

Regardless of date, Memorial Days tended to follow similar patterns. The women of the LMAs gathered on the days preceding the event to make evergreen and floral arrangements and requested that young men or boys do any physical work such as remounding of the graves. On Memorial Day, hundreds and even thousands of citizens gathered at some central location in town, usually a church or town hall, and then marched in procession to the cemetery where the women and children decorated the graves with flowers and evergreens. Subsequently, former Confederate military or civic leaders chosen by the LMAs delivered prayers, poems, and speeches.

If the occasions had merely involved mourning loved ones, the victorious North might not have noticed. After all, mourning was a sacred aspect of Victorian culture. But it quickly became apparent that Memorial Days were more than mere sentimental occasions.[91] The fact that LMAs in several Virginia communities elected to hold their services on May 10, the anniversary of Stonewall Jackson's death, underscored the degree to which the day was intended to enshrine the Lost Cause as immortal. From Richmond to Lexington, residences exhibited photographs and likenesses of the general draped in mourning, while businesses posted signs such as "Closed in honor of Stonewall Jackson and other Confederate dead." At the cemeteries, speakers boasted of Jackson's piety, heroics, undying devotion to the cause, and the terror he struck in the hearts of the enemy. Central to their adulation of Jackson was the fact that he had never surrendered.[92] Like Jackson, Confederate soldiers who had died in service remained undefeated. They had known the Confederacy as an independent nation; they had never surrendered. They had died free from the clutches of the U.S. government, free from the alleged horrors of Reconstruction. Such sentiment was doubtless on the mind of the ever-recalcitrant and dramatic Sallie Strickler after she returned from services in Charlottesville, Virginia, in May 1866. "I almost wish I was dead, & in the grave with them when I think of our state of degradation," she lamented.[93]

At the May 10 services as well as at others, speakers elaborated on the ever-increasing Lost Cause sentiment. They invoked the superior-numbers explanation for defeat, honoring the dead warriors who had given their lives to protect southern homes and hearths. Most likewise praised the sacrifices of civilians, especially women, reminding the crowd that the depravity and suffering inflicted by cruel Yankees had created an enduring bond among former Confederates. More than a few of the 1866 services evoked a militaristic tone. At Richmond's Oakwood Cemetery in early May, former general Raleigh E. Colston praised the loyalty of the enlisted men to the Lost Cause, after which 200 Confederate survivors saluted him with a rebel yell. Replicating the freed slaves Evacuation Day procession a month earlier, on May 31 twenty-three military companies (wearing their uniforms without military insignia or buttons as the law required) marched to Grace Church before heading to Hollywood Cemetery.[94] Most important, speakers universally insisted that white southerners had been just in their cause. Not one offered apology or remorse. Rather, as a Virginia newspaper reported, "Proudly, defiantly, we proclaim our love for the dead soldiers of the Confederate armies." White southerners would obey the laws of the victors, but the federal government would "never control the affections, sentiments, and sympathies of the Southern people."[95]

In continuing to invoke the "Spirit of '76," white southerners were well aware that they trod on dangerous ground so soon after defeat and while Union forces still occupied their communities. Indeed, the services did excite the ire of many northerners. On Monday, May 28, only a month after the first Confederate Memorial Days (and before the more elaborate ceremony at Richmond's Hollywood Cemetery), Representative Thomas Williams of Pennsylvania offered a resolution in Congress calling for President Johnson to make good on his promise "that treason should be made odious." Williams had heard numerous reports that "the memories of the traitor dead have been hallowed and consecrated by local public entertainments and treasonable utterances in honor of their crime." Most egregious, however, were rumors that these services had "not only been tolerated by the national authorities, but in some instances approved by closing the public offices on the occasion of floral processions to their graves, while the privilege of paying like honors to the martyred dead of the armies of the Union who perished in the holy work of punishing the treason of those who are thus honored . . . has been denied to the loyal people of those communities by the local authorities." Such displays, he insisted, were "calculated to make loyalty odious and treason honorable, and to obstruct, if not entirely prevent, the growth of such a feeling as is essential to any cordial or permanent reunion of these States."[96]

Others joined Williams in warning of the dastardly consequences Confederate Memorial Days were generating. The *New York Times* cautioned northerners that the "Southern spirit" was continuing to grow "with wonderful rapidity." "Its most fruitful feeders," it noted, "are the Memorial Associations." The paper reminded its readers that these seemingly "noble" Memorial Days provided forums for ex-Confederate men to make speeches, "wherein [they] adroitly inculcat[e] hatred of the North." "These memorial days have now become painfully frequent, and on every one of them recruits are gathered to the Democratic banner," it fumed. The *Chicago Tribune* agreed, denouncing the Ladies for strewing flowers on the graves of the Confederate dead, charging that these women sought "to keep alive the political feeling of hostility to the Union."[97] Northerners understood that reunion with their former enemies had been their primary war aim and thus had been relatively lenient in doling out punishments. But they hardly expected former Confederates to honor their traitorous cause in such public displays. Reconciliation might be a goal of reunion, but it was not intended to be reciprocal. The victorious North anticipated dictating the terms of reconciliation to the defeated South.[98]

Former Confederates thought otherwise. For them, reconciliation demanded mutual forgiveness, more lenient treatment by the North, and an adherence to the Constitution. Some suggested that the best way to achieve reconciliation was not through legislation but by talking of other things, engaging in intersectional commerce, and even inviting northerners to live among them.[99] Others offered only vaguely veiled threats in pursuit of a southern version of sectional accord. In the fall of 1866, John Baldwin of Staunton, Virginia, observed that the continued imprisonment of Jefferson Davis preempted "all real reconciliation between the North and South." If Davis were to die in captivity, he warned, "his name will become the watchword of Southern hate!"[100] Taking up his pen as a political philosopher, Robert E. Lee argued that if the war had confirmed the inviolability of the Union, then "it naturally follows . . . that the existence and rights of a state by the constitution are as indestructible as the union itself." In his estimation, reunion meant that all political rights should be restored to the South.[101] The following spring, the Virginia General Assembly cautioned that with the Union restored, attempts by Congress to enfranchise former slaves or fasten "the yoke of negro supremacy upon the necks of hereditary freemen" would forever forestall harmonious relations between the sections. As "free American citizens in a free American state," these former Confederates expected to be treated as equal members of the Union under the Constitution.[102] Having acquiesced to reunion, they expected reconciliation to be a two-way street.

Even as they defined reconciliation on their own terms, white southerners consciously framed their Memorial Day services' blatant displays of Confederate patriotism within the domestic sphere of women in an effort to avoid cries of treason from northerners. As both newspapers and orators throughout the South universally noted, Memorial Day was "under the direction of the Ladies"—they selected the date, chose the orators, invited groups to participate in the procession, and even picked the musical selections.[103] "The mothers and daughters of Virginia are the chief mourners and actors in these touching obsequies," Maj. Uriel Wright reminded those attending Winchester's first service on June 6. Because the day's activities had been born in the heart of women, he argued, it could only be interpreted as true and pure. According to his reasoning, these women certainly could not be viewed as traitorous—they were simply exhibiting the qualities nineteenth-century Victorian ideology attributed to women:

sentiment, emotion, and devotion to one's menfolk. In fact, Wright declared that southern white women "were not political casuists." They had not paused "to enquire whether the teachings of Jefferson, Madison, or Mason furnished the true interpretation of the Constitution, and correctly marked the boundaries of State and Federal powers." If women were not political, then by extension their actions could not be construed as such. Memorial activities, clearly within the province of female mourning (and hence the domestic sphere), therefore should pose no threat to sectional reunion. But in so vigorously denying the political nature of women, Wright and other male speakers only served to underscore the very political nature of the LMAs and their memorial work.[104]

It is easy to overlook what a bold and daring move this was on the part of former Confederates. Only a year earlier, rebel women had been required to sign loyalty oaths to acquire government rations or marriage licenses. As the North reeled in anger following Lincoln's assassination, women had not been exempt from suspicion or punishment. Many had been arrested for treasonous speech and, most famously, Mary Surratt had been hanged. Of course the backlash against Johnson and his administration for her death had been overwhelming.[105] Former Confederates were well aware of this and no doubt recognized that highlighting women's apolitical nature would serve them well. It was therefore under the direction of the LMAs that Memorial Days provided legitimate venues for ex-Confederate veterans to march into towns, for thousands of white southerners to gather in a central location, and for former generals and political figures to praise the Confederate cause in a public forum. Protected by their gender, white women were able to escape charges of treason during Reconstruction for which men, as "political-beings," would have been found guilty. By allowing white women to take center stage at memorial activities, men could both express their bitterness toward Yankees and assure the federal government of their loyalty.[106]

Although white southerners' couched their memorial services in the "gentle and tender hands" of women, such displays only heightened the sense among some Unionists that something needed to change. Former Confederate soldiers parading through the streets, orations filled with bombastic claims about the South's cause, southern whites' treatment of freedmen, and President Johnson's moderate policies toward the South all prompted the Republican-dominated Congress to begin passing the Reconstruction Acts in March 1867. Together these acts denied all former Confederates political power, instituted martial law, directed southern states to provide freedmen with political rights, including access to the ballot box, and laid out the means by which civil governments might be restored.[107]

In the months following the Reconstruction Acts, Union authorities began restricting expressions of Confederate sentiment throughout the South. In Raleigh, North Carolina, occupying troops ensured that the local LMAs abstained from organizing a procession on Memorial Day. Members of the association later recalled that "indeed the threat was made that if the Ladies' Memorial Association, chiefly women and children in mourning, did form a procession, it would be fired on without further warning." The LMAs throughout the state were thus prohibited for five years from marching in processions to cemeteries, although small groups of women quietly made their way to the burial grounds to lay wreaths and flowers under the watchful eye of Federal soldiers. The Union commander in Memphis likewise refused to allow any processions, speeches, or public demonstrations for that city's 1867 Memorial Day.[108] While there appears to have been no official crackdown on memorial services in Virginia, nearly all of the state's LMAs elected to dispense with official processions and orations.[109] Yet in Richmond, businesses still closed as if for the Sabbath and nearly 60,000 people, mostly women and children, turned out to place flowers on the graves at Hollywood Cemetery. The significance of this overwhelming feminine presence was not lost on James Henry Gardner of Richmond. Witnessing the day's activities, he noted that even without the parades and speeches, if the affair "had not been under the control of the Ladies," then a "thousand bayonets would have bristled to prevent the celebration."[110]

UNION MEMORIAL DAY

Confederates were not the only ones who felt compelled to honor their war dead with Memorial Day observances. The origins of the national (Union) Memorial Day are highly disputed. Some accounts suggest that commemoration began at Gettysburg in May 1864 when a soldier's widow and another soldier's mother happened upon each other placing flowers on the graves. Some point to services at Charleston's Race Course cemetery led primarily by black South Carolinians and their abolitionist allies on May 1, 1865, as the first commemoration. Others suggest the practice began among veterans in Waterloo, New York, in May 1866. Still others contend that the wife of a Union general, John A. Logan, witnessed such activities in Petersburg and suggested that northern soldiers implement the practice for their own fallen. Whatever the origin, in the spring of 1868

General Logan, commander-in-chief of the Grand Army of the Republic (GAR), the northern veterans' association, called for the first nationally observed Memorial Day. Released as General Order No. 11, Logan called on GAR posts throughout the country to organize ceremonies on May 30 at which they might strew with flowers or otherwise decorate "the graves of comrades who died in defense of their country during the late rebellion."[111]

Claiming Memorial Day as a southern institution, many former Confederates were incensed. The outspoken *Southern Opinion* seethed that the "memorial tributes paid the Federal dead is [*sic*] a miserable mockery and burlesque upon a holy and sacred institution, peculiar to Southern people, and appropriately due only to the Confederate dead."[112] And at least some northerners agreed. The Philadelphia *Sunday Dispatch* rebuked the GAR for modeling its celebration after the treasonous "rebel practice" and shuddered to think that tributes to the Union's noble dead should mimic those honoring rebels. The *New York Times* concurred, reminding its readers that the "ladies of the South instituted" Memorial Day to "keep alive the rancors of hate" and "to annoy the Yankees." "Now the Grand Army of the Republic, in retaliation, and from no worthier motive, have determined to annoy them by adopting their plan of commemoration. The motives of both are unworthy," the writer exclaimed. Such services seemed to engender sectional animosity rather than reconciliation.[113]

Despite the protests, on Sunday, May 30, 1868, U.S. veterans across the nation followed Logan's orders and initiated memorial services in 183 national cemeteries in twenty-seven states, including southern states such as Virginia, North Carolina, and Tennessee.[114] The occasion was remarkably similar to those organized by Confederates: crowds gathered at the cemetery (either on their own or via a procession), decorated graves with flowers and evergreens, and listened to orators discuss the merits of soldiers' patriotism and virtue. There were, however, three key differences between the celebrations of Confederate and Federal Memorial Days. First, Union Memorial Day took place on a single day (rather than the myriad of dates chosen by former Confederates). Second, it was supported by the federal government.[115] Third, whereas the Confederate practice had begun and remained under the auspices of women, Union services were the province of men, most often military men. While Unionist women attended Memorial Days, took part in the processions, and placed flowers on the graves, they played no role in organizing the events. Nor did Union orators generally pay tribute to women's wartime sacrifices and devotion to the cause, as was common rhetoric at Confederate exercises. As the victors, Union soldiers were primarily responsible for honoring their war dead.

Unlike ex-Confederate soldiers, Federals saw no reason to turn over their tributes to the feminine sphere.[116]

Like their Confederate counterparts, Union Memorial Days were replete with political and patriotic meaning. In Cincinnati in 1868, 3,000 citizens gathered at the newly erected Soldiers' Monument for the city's first Memorial Day. Earlier that morning, a procession that included the police force, carriages bearing the city council, a detachment of 100 U.S. regular soldiers, 200 members of the German Veteran Society, and nearly 400 GAR men wound its way through the streets to the cemetery. There, Gen. Henry L. Burnett of Ohio gave the oration. "We are met to-day . . . to strew flowers upon and fittingly decorate the graves of those who died in defence of their country," he began. He described the war as a "conflict between the idea that man should be free, against the idea that man should be enslaved." "In response to this and subsequent calls by their chief," he observed, "they came, millions of men, to fight for the rights of man, and that the nation might live and be free."[117] In neighboring Portland, Indiana, Gen. John C. P. Shanks offered similar remarks. The men in blue had "voluntarily entered that greatest of human struggles . . . to save our common country and institutions of freedom from destruction." All realized that "the perpetuation of slavery in America" had been "the rallying-ground, for forces to carry out the nefarious work" of attempting "to utterly overthrow the Government of our fathers."[118] As with the monument dedications in Gettysburg and Manassas in 1865, many of the first services tended to emphasize both the preservation of the Union and its happy byproduct, emancipation.[119]

In the border regions where many Unionists had been slaveholders, emancipation was not nearly so universally celebrated. In Frankfort, Kentucky, Col. Jonathan Mason Brown informed the crowd of 1,000 that the slain soldiers resting in their midst "were willing to die that the Nation might live," but he made no mention of slavery as the cause of war or emancipation as an accomplishment.[120] Yet in Louisville, Col. Charles A. Gill unabashedly rejoiced that slavery was no more. The dead had not died in vain, he assured the attendees: "The war for the Union was not a failure," he proclaimed. Rather, it was "a victory, glorious, grand and brilliant for the Union, liberty, and equality. The Union was restored, the shackles were broken from the hands, the manacles removed from the feet, and the brand of the slave obliterated from the brows of four million bondsmen."[121] In Lexington, Professor Robert Graham neglected to mention anything about slavery to the thousands of white Kentuckians gathered for the service. But after these ceremonies concluded, African Americans assembled to decorate the graves of their soldiers. Black men composing Post No. 5 of the GAR headed the procession, followed by a group of discharged USCT soldiers, African American women, and carriages containing the speakers. At the cemetery, the Reverend W. L. Muir reminded the crowd that "these men fought for your freedom, and not only you, but your children after you, and you should come here to do them honor." "We are now a free people," he rejoiced. Gen. James S. Brisbin seconded Muir's remarks, observing that "you owe these dead men much; and on each recurring anniversary . . . come here and strew flowers on the graves of your heroes."[122]

The prominence of so many African Americans at Union Memorial Days, especially in the South, allowed former Confederates to both dismiss and rebuke the services. Of the 3,000 people who attended the 1868 services at the national cemetery along Williamsburg Road in Richmond, the *Daily Dispatch* estimated that only 400 were white. Moreover, the presence of so many former slaves seemed to confirm former Confederates' suspicions that the day lacked the respectability of their services. The newspaper appeared to take a special glee in observing that "the solemnity of the exercises" at the national cemetery "was much marred by the cries of cake, lemonade, and peanut-vendors, who made the most noisy efforts to dispose of their wares." And if pointing out the alliance of white and black attendees at the Federal celebration was not enough to condemn the occasion, the southern press reminded former Confederates that the Union cemeteries stood in stark contrast to their own. Funded by Congress with neat wooden headboards painted white in precise rows, "this cemetery is a beautiful spot," observed the correspondent.[123]

Although many former Confederates made no effort to conceal their enmity, at least some Unionist orators made a special effort to invoke themes of reconciliation that would became more pronounced by the 1890s.[124] A speaker in Lexington, Kentucky, encouraged the crowd to "go forth from this place in the spirit of kindness, free from hatred and all uncharitableness, but with the love of country and humanity invigorated."[125] But just as would be the case at the close of the century, Union veterans set forth the clear conditions for this reconciliation. As a Colonel Curtis of Erie, Pennsylvania, remarked in 1868, "When the angry passions which have been engendered in the recent conflict shall have passed away; when the States lately in revolt shall be made to understand their own true interest . . . the people of these very States will then rejoice with us in our nationality, our common country, and the prospect of glorious destiny."[126] But that time had not yet come.

An incident at Arlington National Cemetery's 1869 Memorial Day services made it abundantly clear that reunion and reconciliation remained two very different things. Even as the orator pleaded for a brotherly reunion between "this great united people," a patrol of Union veterans stood guard over the thirty Confederate graves within the enclosure to prevent visitors from honoring the rebel remains. When a woman threw a small bouquet on one of the graves, the commanding lieutenant rushed to the spot, grabbed the flowers, and trampled them beneath his feet. As onlookers gathered around, the infuriated commander threatened them with a bayonet, shouting "D—n you, get away from here, every one of you, or I'll make you." Public response to the episode in the North was mixed. Some thought that the guard had acted too harshly, thereby creating an unnecessary controversy. But others were more sympathetic. Members of the GAR Post No. 1 supported the guard's actions, passing a resolution observing that while they bore no malice toward the Confederate dead, they would not tolerate the decoration of their graves "and thereby taint the character of those who sacrificed their lives that their country might live." Writing to Supreme Court chief justice Salmon P. Chase, who had publicly proposed a conciliatory policy toward the South, one Unionist noted that while veterans might be ready to forgive former Confederates, "we will never consent by public national tribute to obliterate the wide gulf which lies between the objects, motives and principles for which we fought, and our comrades died."[127] Reunion seemed certain, but reconciliation would have to wait.

The dying may have ended in 1865, but death and mourning would continue to shape the contours of Civil War memory, setting the parameters of reunion and, to some degree, of reconciliation. Efforts to provide sepulchers for the battlefield dead of both sides through national cemeteries—both Union and Confederate—tended to exacerbate sectional tensions rather than heal the nation's wounds.[128] Such efforts did not diminish as the years passed; rather, they tended to gain in popularity. By 1869, 336 cities and towns in thirty-one states had organized Union Memorial Day services. Four years later, New York's legislature designated May 30 a legal holiday, and by 1890 every northern state had followed suit.[129] And just as former Confederates used Memorial Day to defend their cause, so Unionists continued to espouse the successes of theirs: the preservation of the Union and the end of slavery and its poisoning effect on America's future.

UNION AND EMANCIPATION

1865–1880s

Although Memorial Day services had quickly become an annual observance honoring the Union dead, northern veterans seethed at the burgeoning Lost Cause with its distorted and reimagined renderings of the
Confederacy. "It must never be forgotten," warned former U.S. congressman and director of the Gettysburg Battlefield Memorial Association
Edward McPherson in 1889, "that the force which was the deciding one
between combatants so nearly equally matched, was the strength of our
cause, and the moral weakness of their cause." Speaking at the Michigan
state monument dedication at Gettysburg, he reminded those in attendance that "we fought for Union and liberty [and] they fought for disunion
and slavery. Nothing can gloss over this difference." "The Rebellion," he
intoned, "had not a redeeming feature. It was wholly bad."[1] Addressing
the same group, Capt. Clinton Spencer of the 1st Michigan acknowledged
that he harbored no feelings of bitterness or revenge toward the former
rebels. But, he maintained, "We claim it to be our solemn duty, here above
this hallowed dust to proclaim and reiterate, that disloyalty to the old flag
was, is and always will be, TREASON, *deep, dark, and damnable.*" "What
lesson would it teach the sons of the North and South if we say the other
side simply erred in their construction of the Constitution?" he asked.[2]
Too much was at stake to allow former Confederates to control the war's
meaning and legacy.

It was not merely that Union veterans hoped to diminish the credibility
of the Lost Cause. In the years following Appomattox, many U.S. veterans

began to worry that the northern public's appreciation of their service and sacrifice was steadily eroding. Throughout the 1870s and 1880s, veterans had lamented the pathetic turnout at Memorial Day observances, and, despite the increasing number of memoirs and short stories about the war rolling off the presses, many sensed a prevailing attitude among the northern populace that veterans should accept that the war was over and move on with their lives. "Have the four hundred thousand Union soldiers who 'died that our nation might live,' been restored to life and health, and home and happiness?" asked the *Soldiers' Tribune* in 1888. "Has the weeping mother who sent her darling and only son to defend the flag had him safely returned to her? Have the dependent and orphaned children whose brave father was miserably starved to death in Andersonville prison pen, again been given his fostering love and care?" the paper demanded. Veterans had every right, asserted the newspaper, to remember the war and remind the nation of their sacrifices.[3]

As the *Tribune* well knew, the relationship between Union veterans and northern civilians was fraught with a tension unheard of in the South. Amid debates about federal soldiers' homes, the intensely partisan issue of pensions, and the economic boom in the North that convinced many that anyone who could not make something of himself deserved to fail, the northern public increasingly stereotyped veterans as grasping pensioners, alcoholic dependents, or even wayward tramps. Moreover, unlike the South, where virtually all white military age men had served in the Confederate armies, a slight majority of men in the North had not served. Fighting had not been the predominant wartime experience for most northern men, nor had the war been the defining moment in their lives. Together, these factors ensured that Union veterans were not as universally revered within their society as were Confederate veterans within theirs. Northern veterans would have to wage a sustained fight to preserve the memory of their cause.[4]

Contrary to historians' descriptions of the period between 1865 and the mid-1880s as one of "hibernation" in Civil War memory, these years proved pivotal for both sides to cultivate, advance, and protect their interpretations of the war.[5] Through Memorial Days, monument dedications, regimental histories, memoirs, the Grand Army of the Republic, women's auxiliaries, as well as on battlefields such as Gettysburg, U.S. veterans worked tirelessly to assure that the Union memory would neither be forgotten nor eclipsed by that of their former foes. Too many lives had been lost for them to do otherwise.

While preservation of the Union was preeminent among veterans' memories, they had not forgotten the centrality of slavery to the war. Along with some of the northern populace, they continued to maintain former Confederates' responsibility in igniting the war and were insistent that the disruptive politics of slavery had led to disunion. Such sentiments were not reserved for white veterans alone.[6] Though they might disagree on emphasis, throughout the postwar decades black and increasingly white U.S. veterans agreed that Union and emancipation served as the dual legacy of their victory. In the process, they guaranteed that a reconciliationist interpretation would not come to dominate the landscape of Civil War memory.

THE WAR FOR THE UNION WAS RIGHT

By 1870, the nation looked vastly different than it had only five years earlier. With the passage of the Thirteenth, Fourteenth, and Fifteenth Amendments to the Constitution, slavery had been abolished; African American men had attained the right to vote; and several had been elected to state and federal legislative seats. The former rebellious states had all been restored to the Union, and most of the occupying troops had been removed from the South. Amid these political changes, Union soldiers had returned to their homes, fields, factories, and shops, taking with them a multitude of memories of the war: the indescribable terrors of battle, the trauma of watching comrades die, the acrid smells of gunpowder and decaying corpses, the bitterness and humiliation of time in prison, and the pain of the surgeon's table. Yet the question remained: how would their individual and personal understandings of the war be preserved for future generations? How would they make sure that their war not be forgotten?

In the first two years after Appomattox and Durham Station, scores of U.S. veterans began to pen regimental histories in the name of the Union Cause. Written for members of the unit and their families in the immediate aftermath of the fighting, regimental histories provide one of the best collective renderings of what the war meant for the veterans as they returned to their civilian lives.[7] And overwhelmingly, soldiers heralded Union as their primary objective. Harris H. Beecher, historian for the 114th New York, sounded a familiar theme when he wrote that the "weather-beaten men, and the lost ones they represent, are not the defenders merely, but the saviors of the Republic." "Think, oh! think of what they have done," he wrote. "Think of the ark of constitutional liberty they have aided to rescue from assault. Think of the Union they have helped to preserve, with all its blessings, all its memories, and all its hopes."[8]

John F. Chase of the 5th Maine Battery received forty-eight shrapnel wounds at Gettysburg, two of which required that his right arm be amputated and destroyed his left eye. A member of the GAR, he was one of many Union veterans who would recount his story and remind audiences of the war's costs. (Gettysburg National Military Park-T-2788)

Veterans and their communities inscribed their understanding of the war on the landscape as well. The first soldiers' monuments had been dedicated during and immediately after the war on battlefields at Stones River and Bull Run. During the next fifteen years, the pace of monument construction intensified, providing both memorials to the fallen and re-minders to future generations of the war's meaning. From Maine to Wis-consin, communities dedicated monuments featuring obelisks, soldiers at rest, and the national symbol—the eagle. Regardless of their form, most contained simple inscriptions such as "in memory of our soldiers" or "to our heroic dead." But countless monuments elaborated on the specifics of that cause, offering poignant thanks to the soldiers "who served in defense of the Union" or to those who had fallen "in the war for the suppression of the Rebellion of 1861."[9]

Gettysburg proved to be the most popular location for regimental and state memorials for veterans of the Army of the Potomac. Since the war, the Gettysburg Battlefield Memorial Association (GBMA) had been work-ing to improve the field for tourists, rebuilding Union works, placing wooden placards on key battlefield locations, and arranging several dozen condemned cannons on the landscape.[10] In the late 1870s, veterans began

proposing monuments on the field of battle (as opposed to in the cemetery). The first of these appeared on August 1, 1878, when Brig. Gen.
Strong Vincent's men dedicated a tablet on the southern slope of Little
Round Top where their commander had fallen mortally wounded. The
following year, the 2nd Massachusetts erected a monument to the men
of their brigade who had died in Spangler's Meadow.[11] Anticipating the
twenty-fifth anniversary of the battle, efforts intensified in 1884 when the
legislatures of loyal states began providing funds for each unit that had
fought at Gettysburg. Within two years, more than a hundred tablets and
monuments had been dedicated. As one guidebook observed, the field was
quickly becoming a "National Mecca." "The more the field is decorated
with these works of art," the author believed, "the more powerful becomes
the impulse of the traveler and patriot to visit or revisit the field of glory."[12]

The monument frenzy at Gettysburg certainly provided compelling
reasons for tourists to visit the field, local merchants with more customers,
and monument companies with seemingly unending business.[13] But more
important, the monuments allowed the veterans of the Army of the Potomac to memorialize their first decisive victory in the war. After a series of
humiliating defeats along the Peninsula, at Fredericksburg, and at Chancellorsville (and a string of unsuccessful commanders), in July 1863 the
largest U.S. army had finally whipped Lee's seemingly invincible army,
sending it back into Virginia. For the Army of the Potomac veterans, the
battle was the beginning of the inevitable victory over treason.[14] In countless monument dedications, veterans heralded Gettysburg as the death
knell of efforts to sunder the Union. John S. Strang of the 104th New York
observed that the battle was historic in that it "marked the beginning of
the overthrow of treason and rebellion."[15] A. M. Mills concurred, noting
simply that "the rebellion that was inaugurated at Charleston in 1861 culminated at Gettysburg in 1863."[16] This was not the Gettysburg that would
later be described as the "Mecca of American Reconciliation."[17] Instead,
the marble, granite, and bronze statuary of the 1870s and 1880s and the
dedicatory services at their unveilings served as poignant reminders that
Gettysburg was an exclusively Union memorial park.[18]

Monuments and battlefields memorialized the Union Cause, but soldiers understood that their wartime experience had by nature been vastly
different from those who had remained on the home front. Civilians could
not begin to fathom what it meant to be a veteran. They had never been
on a firing line, or heard the wretched screams of men whose limbs were
being torn from their bodies, or survived bitterly cold nights on picket
duty, or witnessed their comrades being shredded by shrapnel. Only fel-

low soldiers could comprehend all they had endured and sacrificed in the name of the nasty business of war.[19] Recognizing the importance of shared experiences, soldiers hoped that organizations might provide men with like-companionship and allow them to preserve their memories.

Following the American Revolution, officers had organized the elite Society of Cincinnati, but the Civil War provided the impetus for the first large-scale organization of veterans from all ranks. In the months after Appomattox, dozens of fraternal organizations sprang up in the North. The Military Order of the Loyal Legion of the United States (MOLLUS) organized in Philadelphia in April 1865. Modeled after the Society of Cincinnati, it was open to Civil War officers and their oldest male descendants. The association spread slowly at first, forming branches in only six states by 1875, but by 1891 it could claim membership in more than fourteen states. In part, its growth was inhibited by the organization of competing groups. Thousands of veterans elected to instead join associations alongside the men with whom they had fought. The 3rd Army Corps Union, initiated as a type of burial insurance program for officers, held its first reunion in May 1865. Other societies soon followed, including the Society of the Army of the Tennessee (1865), the Society of the Army of the Cumberland (1868), and the Society of the Army of the Potomac (1869).[20] Still other veterans relished simply attending the annual reunions of individual regiments or brigades.

The largest and most prominent of the veterans' organizations, however, proved to be the Grand Army of the Republic (GAR), founded in 1866. As with Memorial Day, the origins of the association are shrouded in dispute. The story propounded by the GAR claims that the group was the brainchild of former Union surgeon Dr. Benjamin Franklin Stephenson and his fellow veterans in Decatur, Illinois, who wished to form a brotherhood among the veterans dedicated to fraternity and relief. The account embraced by most scholars, however, argues that Stephenson hoped that his new veterans' association would further the political ambitions of two Illinois Republicans, Governor Richard Oglesby and Gen. John A. Logan. Regardless of its genesis, throughout the spring of 1866, organizers traversed the Midwest enrolling more than 180,000 veterans. Interest soon spread throughout the North, and that November the association held its first encampment in Indianapolis. By 1868, the society claimed to have more than 240,000 members.[21]

Like many Confederate groups, including the Ladies' Memorial Associations, the late 1870s proved a difficult period for the GAR. Amid the economic dislocation incurred by the Panic of 1873, increasing immigra-

Members of the 87th Pennsylvania gathered for a reunion in 1869.
(Gettysburg National Military Park-T-2792-B)

tion, labor disputes, and the political corruption that captured the country's attention, GAR membership plummeted to a low of 25,000 and posts folded.[22] The 1880s, however, brought renewed enthusiasm as the nation recovered from the panic and older, more prosperous veterans had the time and inclination to devote to the association. Perhaps the greatest impetus for expansion came when the GAR began to more aggressively pursue pensions in 1881.[23] Other associations organized as well during these years, including the Union Veteran Legion (1884), the Union Veterans' Union (1886), and more specialized groups such as the National Association of Naval Veterans and the Union Ex-Prisoners of War. Accompanying this revival of interest in veterans' organizations was the development of auxiliary organizations, including the Sons of Veterans of the United States (1881), later called simply the Sons of Union Veterans. But the GAR remained the most wide-reaching and influential. By 1890 the association could claim a high of 409,489 comrades.[24] Despite these high numbers, a large percentage of Union veterans, perhaps even most, never joined any of these organizations.[25]

The men who flocked to the Grand Army did so in large part because of its goals, reflected in their motto "Fraternity, Charity, and Loyalty." Many found their escapism in the local post's club room, which provided ever-expanding relic collections, well-stocked libraries, and an oasis from the monotony of everyday life. The opportunity to visit one of the burgeoning Gilded Age cities during a national encampment attracted many men, while still others found enticing the singing, storytelling, and reminiscing of campfires. As Gen. William T. Sherman observed in 1888, campfires tended "to irradiate the gloom of ordinary humdrum existence." But the social aspect was not the only attraction. Veterans remained devoted to caring for their less fortunate comrades and their dependents. At the local level, posts raised charitable funds through fairs and lotteries, helped the unemployed find work, and provided funerals for members whose families could not afford the expense. They successfully pushed for state-sponsored soldiers' homes, agitated for land grants for loyal soldiers and their families, secured preferential hiring of veterans in government jobs, and lobbied for ever-more inclusive federal pensions.[26]

In all these endeavors, GAR members never strayed from the third component of their motto: loyalty. At monument dedications, Memorial Days, and national encampments; in arguing for service pensions; and in the pages of their unofficial newspaper the *National Tribune*, they entreated the nation to remember that they had been loyal to the Constitution and had saved the Union.[27] GAR members from every corner of the nation repeatedly and ardently pointed out that their cause had been the only righteous one. "Your career in arms was to combat and conquer a treason the most hideous and a rebellion the most dangerous in the history of the world," a GAR comrade informed his Boston-based post in 1868.[28] Ten years later, General Sherman similarly declared, "We of the National Union army were right, and our adversaries wrong." "No special pleading, no excuses, no personal motives, however pure and specious, can change this verdict of the war." Speaking to a group of Indiana GAR members in 1886, Maj. Charles L. Holstein proclaimed that "the war for the Union was a conflict between right and wrong—between truth and error. The Union soldier stood embattled on the side of right and truth. The Confederate soldier was arrayed on the side of wrong and error."[29] Perhaps GAR commander-in-chief William Warner put it most succinctly: "We were eternally right . . . and they were eternally wrong."[30] This was the crux of the matter: the Union cause had been just, the Confederate cause wrong.

Despite protestations by former abolitionists like Frederick Douglass that emancipation was being forgotten by the white North, for many veterans the task of saving the Union could not be separated from issues of slavery.[31] In 1865 and 1866, numerous regimentals condemned white southerners for instigating a war to protect slavery. Typical was M. D. Gage, chaplain of the 12th Indiana, who blamed "the mischievous doctrine of State Rights, inculcated by Calhoun and a large class of extremists who succeeded him" for luring "those States from their allegiance to the Constitution and laws of the Union, to engage in the Utopian scheme of founding a Southern Confederacy, based upon the declared right of capital to own the labor of the subject African race."[32] Recalling Appomattox, the regimental chaplain of the 189th New York celebrated the "failure the slaveholders' efforts to dismember and overthrow the free American Union, for the purpose of rearing upon its ruins a slaveholding aristocracy."[33] "The cause of the great War of the Rebellion against the United States will have to be attributed to slavery," concluded Ulysses S. Grant in his memoirs.[34] Even among white northerners who had not initially opposed slavery, by the postwar years many agreed that white southerners' resolute defense of the institution had prompted secession and therefore war. Though they might conflate the terms, for many Unionists slaveholders, not slavery, had been the real enemy.[35]

Conceding that most white northerners had not marched off in 1861 determined to end slavery, Union orators and regimental historians frequently retraced the process by which the Union army came to prosecute an emancipationist war. In 1865, Wales Wood of the 95th Illinois observed that while some white northerners might choose to believe the war had been about ending slavery from the beginning, the Emancipation Proclamation "was proclaimed only as a *war measure* to hurt traitors and kill rebellion."[36] Nearly twenty years later at Memorial Day services in Arlington National Cemetery, former Union officer William H. Lambert offered a similar explanation. "Our people sprang to arms, not for conquest . . . not to accomplish moral reform, not to abolish slavery—the curse of the land, that disgrace of the century—but to preserve the Republic." "To save the Union was the single purpose of the people," he maintained. But "what statesmen had prophesied, what ourselves had surmised, we learned in the hard school of war—the perpetuity of the Union could be secured only through the freedom of the slave."[37] Cpl. James Tanner of New York, who wore two artificial feet after "having been deprived of his natural members by a cannon ball" at Second Bull Run, likewise pointed to the evolution of emancipation as a war aim. "We did not go in to free the slaves," he informed Indiana veterans in 1886, "but God's almighty hand urged us on to that."[38] Recounting a conversation with Otto von Bismarck, Grant recalled informing the German chancellor that the war had been fought not just to save Union, "but destroy slavery." Fighting to preserve the republic had precipitated the war, but, observed the former general, "we all felt, even those who did not object to slaves, that slavery must be destroyed. . . . We were fighting an enemy with whom we could not make a peace. We had to destroy him. No convention, no treaty was possible—only destruction."[39] Emancipation had been an unplanned yet providential war measure.

Numerous Union veterans explained the transformation of soldier to liberator as a product of witnessing white southerners' brutal treatment of their slaves. An Indiana soldier recounted observing a slave owner, mounted on horseback, dragging his captured slave by a rope tied around his neck. Enraged, members of his regiment intervened, cutting the slave free, pulling the master from his mount, and kicking him "for his insolence and his barbarous treatment of his slave." In his 1886 history of the 7th Pennsylvania Cavalry, Joseph G. Vale conceded that "the political complexion of all [the regiment's] companies, except one, was that of decided Democrats, and but little antislavery sentiment was heard in the regiment." That changed when a party of mounted men entered their camp searching for an escaped slave. When one of the regiment's black cooks bolted from a tent, men chased after him, indiscriminately firing their weapons until subdued by the soldiers. "The entire political sentiment of the regiment was changed by the incident," Vale wrote, "and henceforth it was one of the strongest anti-slavery regiments in the service."[40]

While most U.S. veterans continued to champion preservation of the Union as their foremost war aim and accomplishment, many celebrated the fact that their triumph had ended slavery. In countless Memorial Day speeches, monument dedications, and regimental histories, they rejoiced that the "foul blot of slavery" had been removed from the nation's shores, thereby allowing the nation to fulfill its promises of liberty and global power.[41] In areas where abolition had been especially strong such as New England, monuments often elaborated on that legacy. Such was the case with the Manchester, New Hampshire, memorial dedicated in 1878 just a year after the final Union troops had been removed from the South. Featuring a bronze solider at rest, the monument was dedicated to the men of the city "who gave their services in the war which preserved the Union of the States and secured equal rights to all under the Constitution."[42] With each passing year, it seemed that more and more white veterans were celebrating emancipation as both a fruit of Union victory and proof that morality was on the side of the North.[43]

As emancipation gained importance in the pantheon of Union accomplishments, the meaning of "liberty" began to evolve. In the antebellum years, "liberty" had largely connoted the freedom of white men to do as they pleased, but increasingly in the memory of many northern veterans "liberty" came to embrace emancipation.[44] In celebrating the Union army's centrality to emancipation, veterans argued that the liberation of others was an essential aspect—indeed a justification for—American war more generally. This did not mean, however, that they were willing to extend civil rights to the newly freed African Americans or that they supported a revolution of race in the defeated South.[45] Many veterans made it perfectly clear that ending slavery was necessary, even commendable; but anything that pushed beyond freedom—including suffrage and equality before the law—violated the principles for which they fought.

Building upon one of the memory strains that had appeared immediately after Lincoln's assassination, celebrations of the war president frequently invoked emancipation as one of the Union Cause's central accomplishments (rather than a necessary way to hurt the enemy and happy by-product of the conflict). Addressing a MOLLUS meeting, Brig. Gen. Samuel Fallows observed that Lincoln "knew after the first shot against Sumter that freedom and union would ultimately have the grip of life. . . . With the Union, slavery had ultimately nothing to hope."[46] Former Union officer Henry Harnden agreed when he asked, "Did not the sin of slavery bring this nation to the verge of ruin, and did not the righteous act of Abraham Lincoln, in emancipating the slaves, exalt it?"[47] Lincoln, as the commander-in-chief, had transformed the United States Army from mere saviors of the Union to liberators of the enslaved.

Nowhere was this more evident than in efforts to memorialize Lincoln in bronze and marble. In 1867, shortly after passing the Reconstruction Acts that called for an amendment to the Constitution to protect equal rights and ensure black male suffrage, Congress incorporated the National Lincoln Monument Association. Though sponsored by leading Republicans, the monument was to be publicly funded by "the loyal people of the United States of all classes, without distinction as to race or color," and quickly gained the support of Frederick Douglass, who was appointed to its board of managers.[48] The association hired Clark Mills, best known for his monument to Andrew Jackson in Washington's Lafayette Park, to design a colossal memorial that would stand just east of the Capitol.

Charged with creating a monument that would commemorate "the great charter of emancipation and universal liberty in America," Mills's design was ambitious. His model depicted six equestrian statues of generals "whose valor contributed to the preservation of the Union" around the base; a tier of twenty-one statues of statesmen, philanthropists, the common soldier, and a female nurse; allegorical figures representing Justice, Liberty, and Equality; an elaborate cycle featuring the progress from slavery to freedom; and, crowning the top, a seated Lincoln signing the Emancipation Proclamation.[49] Ultimately, the grandiose plan never generated enough support, financial or otherwise, and it was abandoned. Regardless, the proposed monument was more than a monument to Lincoln alone. Instead, it was a war memorial intended to celebrate what the U.S. army, Lincoln, and other loyal citizens (including former slaves and women) had secured: preservation of the Union and emancipation.[50]

Even as Mills's project was abandoned, Unionists did not discard hopes of erecting monuments to their late chieftain.[51] Perhaps the most famous—and controversial—of the early monuments was the Freedmen's Memorial placed in Washington's Lincoln Park on April 14, 1876.[52] Unveiled by President Grant, Thomas Ball's sculpture featured a standing Lincoln who in one hand clutched the Emancipation Proclamation while his other hand extended over a kneeling slave.[53] The orator of the day, Frederick Douglass, made no direct reference about the slave figure's subservient posture to the crowd of white and black dignitaries. Instead, he candidly observed that Lincoln was "the white man's President" ready "to deny, postpone, and sacrifice the rights of humanity in the colored people, to promote the welfare of the white people of his country." He astutely recognized that most white Unionists did not celebrate Lincoln—or emancipation—for the same reasons as did the freedmen. As had been the case during the war, for most loyal whites, emancipation had served first and foremost as a means of preserving the Union. "For while Abraham Lincoln saved you a country," Douglass informed the white members of the audience, "he delivered us from bondage."[54]

Beyond Douglass's objections to the monument, there was yet another limitation of Ball's memorial: it removed the soldiers, both black and white, from the story of emancipation and freedom. Unlike Mills's aspiring design, the war was entirely absent. During the war, Lincoln had been regarded as the soldiers' president, making special efforts to visit the wounded men in Washington's hospitals and mingling with those in camp when he could. In the 1864 election, seventy-five percent of military personnel had voted for him, and thousands had been among the crowds gathered to hear his second inaugural.[55] But did Ball's design mean that the memories of emancipation and the hard-won battles of Union soldiers would take divergent courses in the popular imagination? Would the memories of the president and his soldiers become increasingly disconnected? Would Lincoln alone be remembered for ending slavery? If the broader public understood Lincoln to be solely responsible for emancipation, what did that mean for Union veterans' understanding of their contribution? Would it compel them to make ever more forceful claims to their role in ending slavery as a threat to the nation? Only time would tell.

Many Unionists might have been quite content to allow Lincoln alone to don the banner of "great emancipator." Throughout the North, those who had been indifferent or outright opposed to abolition refused to acknowledge, much less celebrate, their role as liberators. Not surprisingly, memories of freeing the slaves were unlikely to appear in border regions where many Unionists had been pro-slavery. In Kentucky, Missouri, and elsewhere, slaveholding Unionists had offered their loyalty to the Union with the understanding that the federal government would protect slavery, not destroy it. Kentuckians etched such sentiments into the landscape. The first Union monument erected south of the Mason-Dixon in a public space (rather than in cemeteries or on battlefields) was unveiled in Vanceburg, Kentucky, in 1884. Perhaps in response to the eleven Confederate monuments that had been dedicated in the ostensibly loyal state to that point, the Unionists of Lewis County made their sentiments known, inscribing their monument: "The war for the Union was right, everlastingly right, and the war against the Union was wrong, forever wrong." Absent was any commentary on slavery.[56] In Kentucky and elsewhere along the border regions, the emancipationist memory never proved a viable memory for most whites.[57] But for countless other Union veterans, both white and black, there was much to celebrate in emancipation. As one white Union veteran rejoiced in 1866, the "black stain upon our Nation's past record, Slavery, is blotted out in the conflict."[58]

COMRADES OF EVERY CLIME AND CREED

Just as white U.S. soldiers were welcomed home in the summer and fall of 1865, so too were the veterans of the USCT. The most famed regiment of all, the 54th Massachusetts, received no less than a grand public reception upon its return to Boston in September 1865. Retracing the path they had marched in the spring of 1863, the men marched past the statehouse, where they were reviewed by Governor John Andrew, and then on to the Common. There, the former commander, Gen. Edward N. Hallowell, addressed the men, reminding them that the whole nation had watched as they marched out of the city two years earlier. From Massachusetts to Florida, they had bravely defended their colors, brought them safely home, and proved themselves to be good soldiers. Now, he beseeched them to be equally devoted as citizens, to "show themselves to be men, without respect to their color or condition," and to prove themselves entitled to the privileges of citizenship.[59] In a *New York Tribune* editorial, Horace Greeley observed, "The demonstrations of respect were rather more than have usually been awarded to returning regiments, even in Massachusetts, which cherishes her soldiers with an unforgetting affection." He supposed that reason for the reception was not surprising. "It is not too much to say that if this Massachusetts Fifty-fourth had faltered when its trial came, two hundred thousand colored troops for whom it was a pioneer would never have been put into the field, or would not have been put in for another year, which would have been equivalent to protracting the war into 1866," he wrote. "But it did not falter."[60] Like Hallowell, he believed that the regiment had secured a special place in the memory of not only its home state, but also in that of the nation.

Like their white comrades, African American veterans recognized that Union—with or without slavery—had motivated most white soldiers in the first years of the war. Emancipation had evolved as a war measure, indeed, a vital means to gain victory. The historian for the 59th USCT recognized that the war might have ended with slavery intact, if not for Confederate intractability. "These great changes in the condition of the colored race were the result of events and convictions providentially forced upon the country from time to time, as the rebels, with a madness never equaled, stubbornly resisted our well-meant endeavor to save the Union, save slavery too," he wrote.[61] Black veterans and their white officers also understood that their enlistment had been a hard-fought battle. "In the earlier days of the war, when men came forward in greater numbers than were wanted by the Government, the idea of putting arms into the hands of the colored man was not, probably, seriously entertained by his most devoted friend," noted the 7th USCT regimental. "But later, when reverses came," continued the historian, "when the battle-lists grew longer and longer, and every village throughout the land was in mourning . . . the project of arming the negro was seriously thought of and discussed."[62] Speaking to a GAR post, USCT veteran and historian George Washington

Williams similarly observed that only military necessity had compelled the government to enlist black men and fight for emancipation. "It was not that the country was willing to loose the yoke of bondage which had galled the Negroes neck. It was not that the country had come to see the wrong of slavery, but it was that emancipation was a necessity. It was only emancipation and the advent of the Negro soldier that brought victory to our national arms."[63] Union, he acknowledged, was the principal cause and reason for the northern war effort.

Whereas most white men recollected that they had fought for Union first and emancipation second, African Americans tended to reverse the order.[64] Black men, asserted Sgt. Maj. Christian Fleetwood, had enlisted "to assist in abolishing slavery and to save the country from ruin."[65] However essential freedom had been, black veterans never forgot their role in saving the Union.[66] Speaking to the all-black Tucker Post in Newark, the Reverend Charles Dickerson declared that African Americans "fought for a chance to save the Union. We urged our way to the field of battle amid showers of stones flung by the hands of prejudice." A commander of an all-black GAR post in New York explained why soldiers' graves must be decorated on Memorial Day. The dead must be honored, he maintained, as a "token of our love and patriotism of our Union."[67] Without Union, emancipation would be meaningless.

Like their white counterparts, black veterans found that associations might best serve their interests. In 1866, USCT veterans from across the country formed the Colored Soldiers' and Sailors' League in the hopes of furthering their quest for suffrage.[68] After the passage of the Fifteenth Amendment, other organizations focused more explicitly on fostering the memory of black veterans. During the summer of 1875, a group met in Charleston, South Carolina, to organize an association for all honorably discharged black Union soldiers who had served at least one year. Four years later, the Colored Veterans Association of Washington County invited "all colored soldiers" from Pennsylvania, Ohio, and West Virginia to join them in a grand reunion. And just as white units and communities raised money to erect monuments to their war heroes across the North, by 1887 the Colored Soldiers' and Sailors' League was endeavoring to secure a monument to black veterans in the nation's capital.[69]

USCT veterans, however, were not relegated to black-only associations. For many white Union veterans, membership in the ranks of the GAR appeared only fitting for the veterans of the USCT who had helped advance the Union cause. At the fourth national encampment of the GAR in 1870, commander-in-chief John A. Logan welcomed the survivors of the "glorious and successful struggle on behalf of liberty and independence for *all* men." "We realize that no particular race or sect belongs to the glory of our victories," he observed, "but that in the Union Army were found comrades of every clime and creed."[70] Not only was the GAR the nation's largest veterans' organization, but it also sustained an interracial association during the emergence and height of segregation. Any honorably discharged Union veteran, regardless of race, was welcomed into the order's folds. USCT soldiers had been included in the national cemeteries, and so too were they welcome in the GAR.[71]

From Boston to Denver and in thousands of small towns north and south of the Mason-Dixon Line, black veterans joined the ever-swelling ranks of the Grand Army. In urban areas with a significant number of African American veterans, many chose to form all-black posts that endured well into the twentieth century. While African Americans sometimes created black posts to suit their own purposes (much like the all-black church), racial exclusivity did not preclude interracial cooperation. Black and white posts marched as one in processions at national encampments, observed Memorial Days at national cemeteries together, and attended their comrades' funerals. White veterans were frequent guests at black posts meetings, while black members held state and occasionally national offices.[72]

African Americans were also admitted into integrated posts. Although post records fail to explain why some posts welcomed black members and others did not, wartime experience and geography likely played crucial roles in determining the presence of integrated posts. Black veterans joined predominantly white posts in western cities such as Denver and Minneapolis or small towns like Franklin, Indiana, where there were often not enough black veterans to form all-black posts. White Midwesterners had been among the most virulently racist and staunchest opponents of emancipation in 1862–63, but in the postwar years many were surprisingly willing to accept black veterans into their posts. It is plausible that white veterans from the Western armies who had marched alongside USCT regiments proved more hospitable to their black comrades than their mid-Atlantic counterparts in the Army of the Potomac (which only had a handful of black units). But such generalizations did not always prove true. George W. Patterson of Iowa struggled for three years, in three different attempts, to join his local GAR before being admitted in 1890. That same decade, seven black veterans from Newton, Iowa, were likewise denied membership in a white post. Former slaveholding states, perhaps not surprisingly, proved even less welcoming to such posts. In the South, only a handful of integrated posts existed.[73]

But in hundreds of predominantly white posts, men like Robert A. Pinn, a black attorney from Ohio and a Medal of Honor winner, were among thousands of "colored comrades" who participated fully in every facet of GAR life. They attended meetings, performed the mundane work of the post, and even held elected offices, such as guard and color-bearer. In keeping with John Logan's appeal that loyal Union veterans of all races, religions, and social classes be welcomed into the fold, GAR records rarely indicated the extent of the interracial fellowship.[74]

Whether in integrated or colored posts, African American GAR members and their associates served as a constant reminder of the black freedom struggle. All-black units often named their posts after antislavery crusaders such as the Robert Gould Shaw, Charles Sumner, John Brown, and Frederick Douglass. At campfires and national encampments, in regimental histories of white units, and in the pages of the *National Tribune*, black and white veterans recounted the heroic charges of black regiments at Petersburg, Fort Wagner, Olustee, and Port Hudson as well as the atrocities of Fort Pillow. White officers of USCT units proved especially prone to praise their black troops. Refusing to engage in a rewriting of history, they told of the prejudice both they and their African American soldiers had faced from friend and foe alike. "White troops threatened to desert if the plan should be really carried out," recalled Thomas Jefferson Morgan. "Those who entered the service were stigmatized as 'nigger officers,' and negro soldiers were hooted at and mistreated by white troops." But, he explained, "The conduct of the American slave, during and since the war, has wrought an extraordinary change in public sentiment regarding the capabilities of the race. The manly qualities of the negro soldiers evinced in camp, on the march and in battle, won for them golden opinions and made their freedom a necessity, and their citizenship a certainty."[75] Beyond the post room, the larger community could read the names of black veterans as recorded in newspaper obituaries or carved in monuments to Union soldiers in Cleveland, Ohio, and Hartford, Connecticut, and also hear them mentioned in the solemn observations of the northern war dead.[76]

While black GAR members might gather at the graves of their comrades on Memorial Day, freedom celebrations offered a more festive occasion to remember the war. Along with civilians, an all-black GAR post near Atchison, Kansas, organized a picnic celebrating the anniversary of the preliminary Emancipation Proclamation in September 1884. The jovial day included refreshments, a sham battle, and a torchlight parade led by two bands.[77] The twenty-fifth anniversary of the proclamation brought about a tremendous celebration in Norfolk, Virginia, on January 1, 1888. The Cailloux Post No. 2 and Shaw Post No. 5 GAR marched alongside various other civic societies in a procession that included the Car of Liberty as the chief feature of the occasion. Perched atop the wagon sat Belle Wiley as the Goddess of Liberty, wrapped in the U.S. flag and surrounded by children representing each state of the Union. After parading through the city's streets, the procession halted and the several hundred participants sang "America."[78] In Southside Virginia, African Americans continued to hold festivities on April 9, the day Lee surrendered to Grant at Appomattox. "We do it," observed one participant, "because we held that our real deliverance was accomplished by the 'surrender.' If Lee had never been beaten and the Confederacy never crushed, the proclamation would have been of no avail."[79] Even though black GAR members were neither the organizers nor the sole participants of freedom celebrations, the gathering crowds still recognized that freedom and Union were not mutually exclusive.

White GAR members, however, had no such festive occasions to mark the end of the war. Speaking to a GAR post in Philadelphia on Memorial Day 1879, William H. Lambert observed, "No day of rejoicing and gladness is set apart whose annual recurrence celebrates the close of the war — the deliverance of the Nation. This day, consecrated not to exultation over vanquished enemies, but to the honor of our dead, is the only memorial we observe."[80] For the first three decades after the war, there was no equivalent of the Fourth of July for white Unionists.[81] There would be nothing like D-Day or Pearl Harbor Day commemorated by later American veterans. African American GAR members and their communities felt otherwise. Indeed, they had much to celebrate. Black and white GAR comrades might find common ground fulfilling their motto of charity, fraternity, and loyalty, but their rituals for remembering the war would diverge upon this point. If white GAR posts had celebrated Appomattox Day or Durham Station Day in the same way that they observed Memorial Day, gestures of reconciliation with Confederate veterans might have turned out quite differently. Instead, they gathered on May 30, a day not associated with any great battle or military triumph, but rather reserved for somber reflections over the graves of their comrades.

In the North, Union men took the lead in orchestrating Memorial Days. After all, their cause had been victorious; there was no need for men to hide behind the apolitical skirts of women as ex-Confederates did when memorializing their dead. But Union women were active participants in these events. The GAR routinely called upon all "loyal" women and children to decorate soldiers' graves and included young girls in symbolic roles in the ceremonies. At the 1874 services in Gloversville, New York, the Canby Post invited fifty-two young ladies—all dressed in white and carrying a small national banner—to decorate the cemetery.[82] Women, too, helped dedicate monuments in their communities. During the summer of 1868, the ladies of Chambersburg, Pennsylvania, held a strawberry and floral festival to raise proceeds for a monument to the Franklin County soldiers "who fell fighting against treason."[83] Union men were not the only ones honoring and celebrating their victorious cause.

Neither were soldiers' reunions exclusively male affairs. Both widows and wives of Union soldiers joined in the commemorations by attending GAR and other army reunions. Bessie Green of Massachusetts was among the many women and children who cheerfully attended a regimental reunion in the early fall of 1871. She was especially moved that the veterans provided transportation for the regiment's widows and orphans—a service most regiments were unable to afford. "The widows are delightful," she told a friend; "they come down and cry, and then they go and enjoy themselves a while, and then retire and shed a few tears, they can't help it you know." The guests feasted on a picnic of chowder, crackers, coffee, and tea as well as the many other goodies the ladies had brought in their baskets. And though the widows refrained from dancing after dinner, the orphans joined in the merriment.[84] Emily Gillespie, a farm wife from Iowa, was likewise thrilled to attend the reunion of the 12th Iowa Co. F in the summer of 1880. "Twas very good indeed," she remarked.[85]

Socializing at soldiers' reunions allowed some women the opportunity to escape the monotony of everyday life and celebrate Union victory, but others found the war's memory an indelible part of their daily lives. Peace had not meant the end of suffering for hundreds of thousands of Union veterans. During the war, tens of thousands of Union soldiers had at least one limb amputated, making any labor on the farm or in the factory nearly impossible. Others found themselves permanently disabled from gunshot wounds or camp diseases, some suffering bouts of chronic diarrhea for the remainder of their lives. Countless wives and daughters nursed their

Camp U. S. Grant, GAR reunion at Gettysburg, August 1885.
(Gettysburg National Military Park-T-2076)

loved ones in the privacy of their homes, but others sought to alleviate the widespread suffering through more formal networks.[86] Women of New York's wartime Ladies' Union Relief Association (LURA) continued their efforts to relieve maimed and impoverished veterans well after the fighting had ceased. Hoping to alleviate some of their pain, in December 1865 the ladies delivered baskets of poultry, pies, and other delicacies to 250 "crippled and suffering heroes" at David's Island Hospital. Countless other associations formed in communities throughout the North and Midwest. As late as 1882, Caroline Briggs, a sixty-year-old widow in Massachusetts, noted that she spent much of her time caring for poor, convalescent veterans. "There is plenty to do," she wrote. "The help that they do need is constant watching, advice, and . . . being taught to take care of themselves— that is the last thing many of them think of; to eat, drink, and sleep makes up the measure of their lives."[87]

Soldiers' families were often equally in desperate straits. By 1869, LURA had expanded its charity to the families of more than 300 Union heroes who had given their lives in the late struggle. While the association lauded efforts to raise monuments to the Union soldiers, in the 1870s it beseeched the northern public to pay tribute to widows and orphans, "the soldier's sacred legacy to the Republic." With the lapse of time, LURA president

Mrs. John A. Kennedy noted, public interest had diminished while the association's work had only intensified.[88] Confederate women showed their continued devotion to the Lost Cause primarily by honoring the dead, but the federal government and northern men provided for the U.S. fallen. Union women's first tributes to their cause therefore tended to focus on the welfare of the living—the "brave men who fought in the war for the Union" and their families.[89]

As female associations dedicated to education and social activities gained popularity in the post-bellum North, some female relatives of GAR members hoped to elaborate on their wartime loyalty by establishing more formal ties to the veterans' organization.[90] In 1869, the women of Portland, Maine, requested an official affiliation with the local Bosworth Post. It may have been such an action that prompted the GAR to take up the matter of women at their fourth annual convention in 1870, noting a general desire "to acknowledge the mothers, wives, daughters, sisters, and widows of comrades."[91] The following year, the subject was again discussed but to no avail. When the proposal arose again in 1879, the GAR adamantly declared that women would never be allowed to join its ranks.[92] Even though local posts might recognize the devotion of Union women to the war's memory, the national GAR maintained that it was to be an organization devoted to and populated exclusively by men who had fought. While women certainly made sacrifices on the home front and in other capacities as nurses and spies, only men had served as citizen soldiers. Women might be welcomed at Memorial Days and monument dedications, but it had been men who had endured the harsh realities of camp and the field of battle. They, not women, were best suited to control the war's memory.[93]

Despite refusals by the GAR to include women in its folds, women of the Massachusetts relief associations decided to form the first statewide organization of northern women. At a meeting of approximately sixty ladies in 1879, they agreed to form "a secret association" for which "all loyal women" would be eligible. Adopting the name Woman's Relief Corps (WRC), they set out to enlist all the local Soldiers' Aid Societies and relief associations in the state. In 1880, the women of New Hampshire joined their ranks. Two years later, Connecticut's associations united with them.[94] By 1883, as the GAR experienced its own growth spurt, the men took notice and reconsidered their previous objections. Recognizing that "federal assistance and state infrastructure were grossly inadequate for dealing with the tens of thousands of veterans," Commander Paul Van Der Voort invited all the various ladies' organizations to form a national order that might unite to assist the GAR in its charity work. Designated as "auxiliaries" to the men's posts, the women would serve in separate and subordinate associations, required to affiliate with and take the name of their nearest GAR post. Within months, twenty-six different women's associations from sixteen states formed under the banner of the WRC—the nomenclature of "relief" suggesting women's primary role in Union memory.[95]

Although the official auxiliary to the GAR, the WRC insisted that its corps be open to any loyal woman regardless of her kinship to a Union veteran (a proposal heartily endorsed by Van Der Voort). But how would patriotism and loyalty be measured? Should not a woman who had served as a nurse, whether or not the daughter or wife of a Union soldier, be allowed to show her continued patriotism? And what about the woman who had folded away her wedding garments and sent her sweetheart off to war before they could wed? "Not *all* loyal men were soldiers," observed national WRC president E. Florence Barker in 1884, "not every loyal woman a soldier's wife." Recognizing that a woman might be a devoted and loyal citizen regardless of her status as a wife or daughter was a progressive view for the time. In an era when women were increasingly attending college, working outside the home, and joining in reform efforts such as temperance, ideas regarding women as dependents still held sway. The restraints of coverture (a legal doctrine that held upon marriage a woman's legal rights, such as the right to own property or sign contracts, were subsumed by those of her husband) might be lessening, but "respectable" women were still expected to find their primary identity as the wives and daughters of men. The WRC thus offered a striking tension between dependence and independence in its subordination to the men's organization while still maintaining that individual members might be independently loyal citizens.[96]

Numerous widows and daughters fiercely objected to such liberal membership terms, electing instead to form their own societies. Founded in 1885, the Ladies' Aid Society served as an auxiliary to the Sons of Union Veterans. Its members included the mothers, wives, sisters, daughters, and granddaughters of Union veterans or members of the Sons. That same year, several grammar school girls in Massillon, Ohio, established the Daughters of the Union, open only to daughters and granddaughters of honorably discharged Union veterans. A year later, the Ladies of the GAR (LGAR) organized in Chicago, admitting women of "good moral character" who were the wives or blood kin of an honorably discharged Union veteran. Each of these groups devoted itself to perpetuating the memory of the men who had fought—and in many cases died—for the "maintenance of our free government."[97] Like the WRC, they assisted various GAR posts with Memorial Days, cared for invalid veterans and their dependents, lobbied for soldiers' homes, and generally helped craft "a positive memory of the Union cause."[98] Yet the hereditary societies' kinship basis of membership signaled that only their role as dependents solidified their devotion to the nation.

The WRC's insistence that membership be open to any loyal woman meant that its ranks, like those of the GAR, would be open to women of color. Throughout the northern states from Boston to Topeka, African American women belonged to the interracial organization most often as auxiliaries to all-black GAR posts. Before the end of Reconstruction, a small number of black women had worked alongside white women in state departments. Like white WRC corps, African American corps helped provide charity to the veterans of their communities in an era before social welfare and played a pivotal role in Memorial Day. But in sharp contrast to their male counterparts, the southern corps were definitively segregated by race. By the 1890s, as the number of northern women who moved south increased, concern abounded that an integrated membership would jeopardize their social standing in southern communities. Although a minority of white and black members from the North objected, southern white members advocated for a white-only clause and launched a campaign to segregate all relief corps in the region (meaning that the corps remained "detached" from the state-level departments). White WRC members felt the same pressure as Union veterans in the southern states to abide by both social and de jure segregation. But without the bonds of wartime comradeship that compelled the veterans to maintain an interracial society, the women of the WRC succumbed to the powerful force of the color line.[99]

For all the women who joined war-related associations, whether white or black, a family member of a soldier or not, honoring the loyalty of the Union cause was paramount. Each emphatically refuted the memories perpetuated by Confederate LMAs, casting the war as one between right and wrong, between the righteous and unholy. "Treason is treason, living or dead," declared Elizabeth D'Arcy Kinne, fourth national WRC president. "Our boys in blue were loyal and true. We cannot say that of the other side."[100] Chief among the auxiliary's objectives was to encourage "true allegiance to the United States of America" and "discountenance whatever tends to weaken loyalty" by teaching the next generation the "lessons of patriotism." Neither had the women forgotten slavery or its role in the conflict. As one member noted, their duty was to honor the "heroes whose valor and self-sacrifice saved this nation from secession and slavery."[101]

Women, like their male counterparts, endorsed a patriotism that vindicated the Union war effort and condemned that of the disloyal, slaveholding South.

THE BLOODY SHIRT

GAR members of both races were enlivened by former Confederates' vigorous attempts to rewrite their history and enshrine the Lost Cause. Efforts by white southerners to remove the role of slavery in the conflict, to cast the war as merely over constitutional issues, and to deny that they had committed treason infuriated many GAR posts. Abraham Gilbert Mills, a New York businessman and commander of the Lafayette Post GAR, declared former Confederates "enemies of the Union and of law and order."[102] Vehemently rejecting the Lost Cause, another GAR speaker was amazed that "they who brought about the war now . . . strive to cover the crime of treason with a varnish of patriotism, so that they who sought to destroy the Government might go down in history hand in hand with its defenders."[103] Many Union veterans simply could not fathom this blatant effort to rewrite history. "It is a marvelous delusion that inspires the vanishing generation of traitors to monumentalize their own infamy," observed a Minnesota GAR member.[104] "Neither the living nor the dead of a great and holy cause can be confounded with those who fell in the wretched struggle to destroy a nation or erect a system of government false to the great principles of liberty," asserted Massachusetts native Charles Devens.[105] Most Union veterans were not yet willing to let go of the South's culpability in fomenting such a horrific and costly war or eager to appease their recent foe.[106]

The lingering effects of the Union Cause went well beyond monument dedications and GAR orations. From the beginning of Reconstruction, the northern memory of the war had shaped national politics.[107] On the floor of Congress in 1866–67, Radical Republican Thaddeus Stevens nearly exhausted himself in his vigorous waving of the "bloody shirt." Animated by a combination of retribution against the South and desire for black civil rights, he repeatedly and continually railed against the "murderers" of the South. "Do not, I pray you, admit those who have slaughtered half a million of our countrymen until their clothes are dried, and until they are reclad. I do not wish to sit side by side with men whose garments smell of the blood of my kindred." Presidential Reconstruction, he and other Radical Republicans argued, was insufficient reparation for the crimes committed by the South.[108]

In waving the "bloody shirt," those like Stevens sought not only to establish war guilt as a justification for congressional Reconstruction, but also to foster a political base in which men "voted as they fought." In 1868, during the first presidential election after Lincoln's assassination and Johnson's impeachment, memories of the war again took center stage. Democratic candidate Horatio Seymour built his campaign around the evils of Reconstruction and a desire to forge reconciliation. Ulysses S. Grant would adopt "Let Us Have Peace" as his campaign slogan, but many of his supporters harkened to the divisive memories of the war to generate support.[109] George Williams Curtis penned a public letter intended to rally veteran Union troops to the ballot box on behalf of their former commander. "Grant will enter the White House next year as surely as he entered Richmond three years ago," he wrote, "and against the same opposition." Curtis implored voters—the veterans—to remember "the bloody years from Sumter to Appomattox, to reflect [on] who and what made those years," and then "bring the rebellion at the polls, as it had already brought it in the field, to 'unconditional surrender.'" Having claimed credit for saving the Union, the Republican Party was determined to control it. Although the campaign had been fraught with horrific violence in the South carried on in part by the Ku Klux Klan, on Election Day Grant nearly swept the Electoral College with twenty-six states to Seymour's six.[110] By the closing decades of the century, the Republican Party had become the most prominent national institution devoted to remembering the war.[111]

Four years later, the memory of the war still proved to be an equally powerful backdrop to national politics. Appalled by the scandals and corruption of Grant's first term, many of his detractors had grown increasingly frustrated with the former general's presidential prowess. They fumed over his attempts to annex Santo Domingo (despite strong protests from party leaders), and lamented his indifferent attitude toward civil service and tariff reform. Amid all this, discouraging news about the progress of Reconstruction continued to stream into Washington. Alienated and in search of a new path, a disaffected wing of the party led by Charles Sumner and Carl Schurz bolted to form the Liberal Republican Party.[112]

At their convention in Cincinnati, the group selected *New York Tribune* owner and editor Horace Greeley to run against Grant. Believing that a coalition of the nation's "best men," including white southerners, might lead the country in the right direction, the former abolitionist but now moderate called for northerners and southerners to join forces, to "clasp hands across the bloody chasm." Return the South to "home rule," Greeley urged, by restoring the citizenship rights to ex-Confederates. Enlivened by the opportunity to unseat the hated Grant, Democrats allied themselves with the new party, nominating Greeley on their own ticket. Despite the Liberal Republicans' two-pronged platform calling for an end to corruption and achieving reconciliation, most northerners appeared neither willing nor ready to abandon their victorious general. The results overwhelmingly validated Grant, who defeated Greeley by a landslide in the popular vote (56 percent to 44 percent) and an even larger Electoral College majority (286 to 66).[113] Reconciliation, it seemed, would have to wait.

After the official end of Reconstruction following the Compromise of 1877, a raucous debate over the selection of the doorkeeper for the House of Representatives revealed that sectionalist rhetoric had not receded in the political arena.[114] In April 1878, the former Union general Benjamin Butler, a Republican member of Congress, nominated Brig. Gen. James Shields, a "true Union, maimed soldier," for the position. What might have otherwise been a routine appointment quickly became bogged down in the politics of Civil War memory. Congressman Samuel S. Cox of New York and his Democratic colleagues, who controlled the House, seized the issue, contending that Butler was using Shields (who claimed to not be interested in the position) to exploit bitter and painful war memories. If Democrats rejected Shields, they would be cast yet again as an anti-Union, pro-southern party while Republicans would reap the political prize. During a weekend caucus, the Democrats tried a different tactic. Angling for a reconciliationist posture, they nominated Charles William Field, a native Kentuckian and Confederate major general who had survived a severe hip wound at Second Manassas. "The war is over," noted Cox; the two sections were "one and inseparable, why may we not come together in a spirit of fraternity, the gray along with the blue?" Outraged, Butler rejected Field. In selecting the doorkeeper, he insisted that the House "show that [we] prefer courage and brave conduct when shown on the battlefield in behalf of patriotism, loyalty to the flag, to the Government, rather than the same traits devoted to treason and rebellion." After more than two weeks of debate, the Democrats triumphed, electing Field to the position. But dozens of letters to Butler and the Republican press congratulated the former general on his commitment to the memory of loyal Union men, thanking him, in the words of one, for "skinning the Confederates" during the debates.[115]

Even with all the "bloody shirt" rhetoric, it is essential not to exaggerate the unity among Union veterans. Political issues in particular deeply divided old soldiers. The election of 1888, often touted as the pinnacle of veterans' electoral influence, featured GAR member Benjamin Harrison and incumbent president Grover Cleveland. The president was no favorite among many veterans, having hired a substitute to take his place in the war and proposing a return of captured battle flags to Confederates. Yet voting patterns in Indiana (Harrison's home state) reveal that veterans failed to vote with one mind: GAR members voted two-to-one for Harrison, but Indiana veterans who did not belong to the association tended to be more evenly divided between the candidates. While the GAR, Republican Party, and even pension agents strove relentlessly to promote unanimity among Union veterans, this was far from the case.[116]

The memories of prison horror, however, plagued contemporary politics as no other issue could. Throughout the late 1860s and into the 1890s, the northern press continued to print inflammatory images and stories of rebel atrocities in prison camps while Union veterans began to publish provocative and damning prison narratives, join associations such as the Union War Prisoners' Association, and listen to survivors speak at reunions or GAR encampments. In all these venues, ex-prisoners of war elaborated on the unfathomable conditions that had shaped their war experience, reminding the North of the "barbarous atrocity of those who sought to destroy the Union." During the congressional election of 1867, *Harper's Weekly* implored its readers that those "who love freedom, will vote for the Republican," while those "who secretly wish . . . the Andersonville pen had succeeded, will vote for his Democratic opponent." Democrats, in the eyes of many northerners, were perhaps only slightly less traitorous than southern rebels.[117] In the presidential election of 1868, Republicans amplified their attacks on southern prisons as part of their "bloody shirt" rhetoric. An anonymous author summed up much of the northern sentiment regarding Andersonville: "I should like to see a picture of that stockade, and on the left the United States Cemetery, with the Stars and Stripes flying over those poor boys' graves. I do believe," the author declared, "it could clinch the nail in the political coffin of Seymour and Blair."[118] Along with the Union dead, prisoners of war proved to provide political capital for decades after Appomattox, reinforcing the relationship between northern morality and the Republican agenda.[119]

In hopes of proving the barbarities of northern prison camps and the insurmountable odds faced by Lee's men, northern veterans had been anxiously awaiting the publication of the federal government's *War of the Rebellion: A Compilation of the Official Records of the Union and Confederate Armies*. Efforts to collect and print the significant reports, correspondence, and telegrams produced during the war had emerged as early as 1863 but had become virtually moribund during Reconstruction. In 1874, Congressman James A. Garfield, a former Union general, renewed calls for congressional funding to support the War Department's "publication of the official records of the war of the rebellion, both of the Union and Confederate armies." Garfield's motivations are unclear. Perhaps he was hoping to ease sectional tensions by presenting the facts from both sides. Alternatively, veterans' groups such as the GAR and Loyal Legion may have been pressuring legislators for an "official" account to combat Lost Cause arguments or for attractive, printed relics of their battlefield past. Regardless, throughout the 1870s and 1880s the War Department strove to make the project as nonpartisan and nonpolitical as possible. The curator, Capt. Robert N. Scott, a Union veteran charged with organizing the project in 1877, tried to include both sides by reaching out to the Southern Historical Society for assistance in acquiring records and hiring former Confederate general Marcus J. Wright to purchase material. For decades, an army of clerks and copyists, both male and female, labored to organize the more than fifty tons of paper. The first volume appeared in 1881 and the last of the 128 volumes finally rolled off the presses in 1901.[120]

Frustrated with the slow pace of the *Official Records'* publication, some of the most prestigious Union generals began to record their personal experiences and memories of the war to both preserve the memory of their cause and to battle the ever-growing Lost Cause. Gen. William Tecumseh Sherman's two-volume *Memoirs* appeared in 1875. In 1888, Phillip H. Sheridan published his memoirs, relating his "participation in our great struggle for national existence, human liberty, and political equality." Dedicated to his "comrades in arms during the War of the Rebellion," he left it as "a heritage to my children, and as a source of information for the future historian."[121] But by far the most anticipated and widely read were those of Ulysses S. Grant, the Union's preeminent war hero.

As fate would have it, the very day Grant accepted a book contract with the Century Publishing Company he was diagnosed with throat cancer. Throughout the next nine months he suffered from an incessant cough, lost weight, and was unable to eat, walk, or converse. Yet he persisted in his task. Drawing upon the thousands of battle reports he had written during the war, he exhibited the same determination as he had on the field. Between September 1884 and his death on July 23, 1885, the *Personal Memoirs* consumed nearly all his time.[122] Posthumously published in December 1885, the two-volume set eventually sold more than 300,000 copies.[123]

Determination to finish the manuscript alone did not compel him to write through the intense pain. As Lost Cause leaders such as Jubal Early increasingly called into question Grant's generalship, labeled him a bloody butcher, and disparaged the ability of his soldiers (all the while extolling his former foe, Robert E. Lee, as a demigod), the dying general vowed to defend his reputation and the Union Cause. On this matter Grant was of a like mind with Union regimentals, Memorial Day speakers, and the GAR (of which he became a dues-paying member by 1877). He categorically rejected the Lost Cause and maintained the moral superiority of the Union's own cause. Reflecting on Appomattox, he observed that he had not felt like rejoicing "at the downfall of a foe who had fought so long and valiantly, and suffered so much for a cause, . . . though that cause was, I believe, one of the worst for which a people ever fought, and one for which there was the least excuse."[124] Not only did he hold the Confederate cause in contempt, but he also found the South's most beloved hero, Lee, lacking. Grant praised Lee's behavior at Appomattox yet disparaged his defensive strategy in the Overland Campaign that only served to prolong the war. And he heartily rebuked Lee's claim that the Confederacy had merely been overwhelmed by superior numbers.[125]

Grant and his memoirs have frequently been celebrated for their reconciliationist tone. In one repeatedly quoted passage, he noted, "I feel that we are on the eve of a new era, when there is to be great harmony between the Federal and Confederate. I cannot stay to be a living witness to the correctness of this prophecy; but I feel it within me that it is to be so."[126] Grant named former Confederate general and close prewar friend James Longstreet as surveyor of customs of the port of New Orleans and former guerrilla John S. Mosby as U.S. consul to Hong Kong. Who can overlook his 1868 presidential campaign slogan, "Let Us Have Peace"? But Grant's vision of reconciliation was to be one on northern terms. "I would not have the anniversaries of our victories celebrated, nor those of our defeats made fast days and spent in humiliation and prayer; but I would like to see truthful history written," he noted; "such history will do full credit to the courage, endurance, and ability of the American citizen, no matter what section of the country, he hailed from, or in what ranks he fought." But then he added his most important message: "The justice of the cause which in the end prevailed, will, I doubt not, come to be acknowledged by every citizen in the land, in time."[127] For Grant, like the soldiers who had followed him into the trenches of Vicksburg and the thickets at the Wilderness, who had overwhelmingly voted for him in the 1868 and 1872 presidential elections, the South was wrong and the North was right.

Unionists' efforts to ensure that their cause would not be forgotten enlivened former Confederates. As they watched the federal government establish national cemeteries across the South and witnessed the celebrations of freedom by African Americans, white southerners lashed back, justifying secession and war as a constitutional right while defending their defeat as a product of overwhelming northern manpower. Former Confederates reacted with furor that their surrender at Appomattox had resulted in what they saw as the atrocities of Reconstruction. They denounced the war that preserved the Union and produced emancipation as unconstitutional, unjust, and barbaric. For many veterans and civilians on both sides, the battleground of Civil War memory remained contested long after the gunfire had ceased.

THE LOST CAUSE

1867–1890

For more than three years, George N. Dexter of Georgia had read newspaper accounts of GAR encampments and U.S. veterans' reunions. A former quartermaster in the 3rd Georgia, he had thought often of a similar meeting with his former comrades—a time when they might gather to clasp each other's hands, renew friendships, and discuss the struggles and sufferings they had faced in camp and on the field of battle. But like many other former Confederates, he had been reluctant to pursue such a meeting during Reconstruction. "Surrounded as we were by political confusion, and questioning in radicalism, negro-rule, military despotism and the many other evils of the times," he observed, such a reunion might prove more injurious than good.[1] But in 1870 circumstances appeared to be changing. In July, Georgia had been readmitted to the Union. Two years later, the Redeemers, conservative Democrats, regained control of the state, violently forcing African Americans from their offices. By 1874, the time seemed ripe for a Confederate reunion.

On a balmy late July evening, former members of the regiment met for the first time since 1865 at the fairgrounds in Union Point, Georgia. Opening the occasion, Capt. Charles H. Andrews assured the group that they had not met "to revive angry discussion, or to conjure up sectional hatred." Instead, hinting at reconciliation, he observed that former Confederates "never were degraded enough to hate a foe, who dared to defend his side of the question." Yet Lost Cause sentiment pervaded his message. The cause for which they had fought had been just: "In olden time we were patriots enough to be jealous of our rights in the government, and we were manly enough to endeavor to defend them," he declared. Invoking the superior numbers argument, he reminded the veterans that they had only surrendered when Lee said they should return to their homes and fight no more. But after nearly a decade, the men thought the moment right to gather again in order that they might perpetuate their valor and "keep green memories of the past war." Later that night, torch light beacons illuminated the camp as the veterans waltzed with their ladies to joyous music recalling all that had been dear to them under the Confederate flag.[2] Like their Union counterparts, they had not forgotten—and they would not forget.

In the years since 1865, the southern spirit had continued to thrive.[3] Through the southern press, LMAs, regimental histories, the creation of survivors' associations, and eventually the United Confederate Veterans in 1889, former Confederates defended the justness of their cause and took solace in the heroics of their soldiers. At monument unveilings and Memorial Day observances, they offered up the increasingly familiar chorus: Confederate soldiers had fought honorably and bravely. The South had not been defeated, they claimed, but overwhelmed by insurmountable odds (and therefore had been destined to lose). They heralded Robert E. Lee as the epitome of a southern gentleman and the greatest military leader of the war. Some denied slavery as a cause of the war, but most asserted that, catalyst or not, it had been sanctioned by the Constitution and Providence. Above all, they insisted that secession had been constitutional, that their cause had been just.[4]

Borne as a justification for defeat in the days after Appomattox, the Lost Cause proved to be much more than a romanticized image of an unsuccessful war. Gaining strength in the late 1860s through the 1880s as a reaction and rebuke to both Reconstruction policies and the Union memory of the war, the Lost Cause helped foster a separate sectional identity, an extension of Confederate nationalism that would encourage resistance and defiance for years to come.

GREEN IN MY MEMORY

Like their northern counterparts, in the years immediately following the war, former Confederates began unveiling stone memorials to their cause. In the spring of 1866, an association of officers and cavalry of the late Army of Northern Virginia organized to erect a marble bust at the grave of Gen. J. E. B. Stuart. Two years later, Captain Whipple's Company (Leon

Hunters) of the 5th Texas Regiment dedicated a monument of white marble to their captain in Richmond's Oakwood Cemetery. At least one monument was established by a foreigner. In 1875, a British admirer donated a life-size statue of Stonewall Jackson that was placed on the statehouse lawn in Richmond. But overwhelmingly, in the South, LMAs were the primary impetus behind Confederate memorials in the 1860s and 1870s. From the imposing stone pyramid erected by Richmond's Hollywood Memorial Association (HMA) in 1869 to the more common funerary obelisks unveiled in cemeteries throughout the South, middle- and upper-class women of the LMAs publicly claimed that monument building was clearly an extension of the feminine sphere into the public domain.[5]

Not only did women take the lead in monument building in the South, but the geography of monument placement also differed markedly from that of the North. Throughout the first two decades after the war, Unionists found no limits to where they might erect their marble memorials. Northern communities busily dotted their town squares, courthouse lawns, cemeteries, and even battlefields with stone tributes to the Union Cause. But under the auspices of mourning that had compelled the Ladies to initiate the Lost Cause, white southerners tended to confine their monuments to the cemeteries where their dead slumbered. As one might expect amid the rebel sepulchers, memorial inscriptions focused on the dead. The Hollywood Cemetery's ninety-foot pyramid, for example, was inscribed "To the Confederate Dead" and "Numini et patriae asto" (In eternal memory of those who stood for God and country).[6] Here was no justification or explanation of defeat. Defiantly, in limestone and marble, the inscription perpetuated Confederate nationalism. Appomattox had not ended white southerners' loyalty to the Confederacy. From Virginia to Alabama, the LMAs' efforts to alter the southern landscape were indeed powerful, political statements in the midst of Reconstruction and in the presence of federal occupying forces.

While the LMAs helped enshrine the Lost Cause on the southern landscape, many veterans eagerly set about to record their memories of the war. A handful of Confederate regiments published histories as early as 1866 to defend their failed war effort.[7] A few individuals likewise hoped to offer a corrective to the Unionist message pouring from northern presses. Edward Porter Alexander, an artillery commander and member of Lee's staff, began collecting battle reports and other reminiscences of his corps immediately after the war. Writing to Alexander in the fall of 1866, his comrade Dudley McIver Du Bose encouraged the undertaking. "We did as much hard fighting, marching, and suffering as any men ever did for the cause of Constitutional liberty," he wrote. "Future historians and future generations will acknowledge it and give us due credit, if they can only get at the true facts." If Union veterans sought to explain their contributions and elaborate on the meaning of their victorious cause, former Confederates were equally determined to honor and defend their failed cause.[8]

Although the number of regimental histories was relatively small, a handful of periodicals appeared in these years to vindicate the southern cause. Former Confederate general Daniel Harvey Hill's *The Land We Love* (1866) and Albert Taylor Bledsoe's *Southern Review* (1867) both espoused sustained defenses of the Lost Cause.[9] One of the most vocal public opponents of so-called Radical Reconstruction, however, was a new weekly Richmond newspaper, the *Southern Opinion*. Established by avowed secessionist H. Rives Pollard, wartime editor of the *Richmond Daily Examiner*, only three months after the Reconstruction Acts, the paper regularly printed weekly indictments of the Republican government and the freedmen.[10] He advised the people of the South to "comply in good feeling with the requirements of the military bill" and vowed that his paper would not obstruct the military "in any of its operations through our influence."

Pollard's express purpose, however, was to foster an independent, distinctive southern identity. The paper's masthead, for example, noted: "My Country—May she always be right; but right or wrong—My Country." While the South might be "politically dead," reasoned Pollard, it was not "socially or intellectually dead." Here was a central component of the burgeoning Lost Cause: the South would not seek political independence from the Union, but through a concerted effort it might create a cultural, regional identity that could not be squelched by the North's military resources. Echoing much of the LMAs' sentiment, Pollard repeatedly encouraged former Confederates to "foster in the hearts of our children the memories of a century of political and mental triumphs," and preserve the heroism and endurance of their cause.[11] The flames of Confederate nationalism would continue to burn bright as future generations of white southerners claimed loyalty not as citizens of the Confederacy, but simply as "southerners" (implicitly white by definition). In the vernacular of the Lost Cause, "southerner" had replaced "Confederate."

It was Rives's brother, Edward A. Pollard, who has been credited with coining the term "Lost Cause." An outspoken secessionist by 1859, during the war he assisted his brother as an editor of the *Richmond Daily Examiner*. He also found time to pen a three-volume history of the war even as it raged around him, as well as a book recounting his experiences as prisoner of war for eight months. In 1866, he published *The Lost Cause: A New*

Southern History of the War of the Confederates distilled from his four-volume *Southern History of the War*.[12] In this and other works, Pollard elaborated on many of the themes his brother published in the *Southern Opinion*, articulating a defense of the southern cause and a fiery rebuke of the Union. Pollard lauded Lee as one of the most virtuous of all generals but vigorously berated Grant's military record. He argued that Confederates could never have won given their material disadvantages. Even as Congress and President Johnson debated the terms of Reconstruction, Pollard was espousing several of the chief components of the Lost Cause: the white South had not fought for slavery nor was the system inhumane; Lee was a substantially better general than Grant; and the South had not been defeated but merely overwhelmed by superior manpower and resources. If Unionists were determined to promote their cause as righteous and just, former Confederates remained even more determined to counter such arguments.

While the Pollards rallied to the defense of the Lost Cause in fiery rhetoric, Lee publicly counseled white southerners to remain silent and avoid controversy in the name of peace.[13] In the immediate aftermath of Appomattox, he appeared to be the conciliatory statesmen, having laid down his sword and turned his attentions instead to his new duties as president of Washington College. From his home in Lexington, Virginia, he outwardly claimed to harbor no animosity toward the North, repeatedly maintaining that he had "avoided all discussion of political questions since the cessation of hostilities." Summoned before the congressional Joint Committee on Reconstruction in February 1866, he declared he was not acquainted with the sentiments of Virginia's secessionists, insisting that he "had but little communication with politicians." The following year, he turned down calls to run for governor, noting that his election "would be injurious to Virginia." Still hoping to regain his property at Arlington (now surrounded by Federal graves), Lee surmised that "it [would be] better even now to proceed quietly . . . & to exercise as much patience as possible."[14] In claiming to be above partisan discord—even apolitical like the LMAS—Lee only elevated his already esteemed position within the Lost Cause.

Unlike the LMAS, Lee adamantly avoided efforts to venerate the war. Though besieged with requests from the Ladies to attend Memorial Day services, time and again the Confederate chieftain politely demurred, observing only that "the graves of the Confederate dead will always be green in my memory." When asked to support a monument to his former lieutenant Stonewall Jackson in 1866, Lee declined, stating that neither the students at Washington College nor Shenandoah Valley residents could afford to contribute to such a project.[15] And in 1869 when the Gettysburg Battlefield Memorial Association requested he attend a meeting of former officers engaged in the battle, he replied in no uncertain terms: "My engagements will not permit me to be present. I believe, if there, I could not add anything material to the information existing on the subject. I think it wiser moreover not to keep open the sores of war, but to follow the examples of those nations who endeavored to obliterate the marks of civil strife, to commit to oblivion the feelings it engendered." (His nephew Fitzhugh Lee likewise declined to attend, observing that "if the nation is to continue as a whole, it is better to forget and forgive rather than perpetuate in granite proofs of its civil wars.")[16]

Yet as with many Confederate veterans, Lee's private sentiments often stood at odds with his public persona. Cautioning Jefferson Davis and Jubal Early to avoid "epithets or remarks calculated to execute bitterness or animosity between different sections of the country," Lee admitted that he "understood [such] feelings."[17] For him conciliation was a pragmatic tactic rather than an end in itself: he believed that cooperation would allow white southerners to regain control of the South more swiftly than would hostility and discord.[18] But when Congressional Reconstruction placed the South under military rule, and constitutional amendments enfranchised African Americans, Lee could no longer contain his animus. Throughout these years, much of his private correspondences and political treatises radiated a controlled fury. In draft essays that were never published he seethed about "a national civilization which rots the life of a people to the core" and railed against the cruel Reconstruction measures implemented by "unprincipled men who look for nothing but the retention of place & power in their hands."[19] "The avowed objects of the war, 'the restoration of the Union with all the dignity, equality & rights of the States *unimpaired*,' have not been fulfilled," he hotly asserted. "The certain part seems to be that though the war is ended, peace is not restored to the country."[20]

Lee's growing bitterness toward Radical Republicans finally convinced him to more publicly denounce northern policies by championing the maliciously racist and anti-Reconstruction platform of the Democratic Party in 1868. In August, he agreed to attend a meeting of former Confederate officers at White Sulphur Springs, West Virginia, where former Union general and Democrat Williams S. Rosecrans hoped to convince him to campaign against Grant, the Republican presidential nominee, in the upcoming election. But Lee offered his own vision of national healing. In a public statement he signed along with more than twenty other former

Confederate leaders at the meeting, Lee refused to dismiss slavery or secession as morally wrong; rather, the statement argued that these were
"questions . . . decided by the war." It condemned Radical policies, specifically black suffrage, for the "oppressive misrule" of northern occupation
since Appomattox and declared that "this old irritation would have passed
away, and the wounds inflicted by the war would have been in great measure healed" in the absence of such harsh measures.[21] Two years later, Lee's
disgust proved only to have increased. Speaking with Jefferson Davis's
former aide-de-camp William Preston Johnston (who had spent several
months imprisoned at Fort Delaware after being captured with Davis),
he reviled the "vindictiveness of the Yankees, of which he had no conception before the war."[22] Despite his initial posture of accommodation and
moderation, like most former Confederates, Lee continued to harbor deep
resentments toward the Yankees and pointedly refused to denounce the
Confederate cause.

If Lee was the most celebrated Confederate soldier, he was far from the
only one honored by the South for his sacrifice and commitment. Whereas
in the North at least some Union veterans were treated with disdain or
simply forgotten, almost all Confederate veterans were welcomed back
into their communities as heroes. In part this was a product of the nearly
universal experience of military service in the South; most white men of
military age had served in the Confederate armies. One could not walk
through any southern community in the years after the war without encountering a veteran. But equally important, Confederate veterans did not
find themselves embroiled in the partisan wrangling over pensions and
federal soldiers' homes as did Union veterans. Though some Confederate
veterans earned the scorn of civilians for failing to fit back into society or
joining the ranks of the Republican Party (as James Longstreet did), most
were held up as dedicated, honorable men who had fought for a valiant
cause.[23]

WE MUST VINDICATE THAT CAUSE

Even as their most vaunted hero rejected reveling in the past, Confederate veterans, like their Union counterparts, recognized that associations
might further their memory of the war. But to openly organize such groups
during Reconstruction would tread too closely on perilous ground. Groups
such as the Ku Klux Klan, which initially formed as a Confederate social
club in 1866, were never concerned explicitly with commemorating the
Confederate cause and instead used their organizations to instigate a reign

of terror against southern Republicans both white and black.[24] Only a handful of veterans dared come together publicly to form clubs, such as that established by officers of the 3rd North Carolina or the Confederate Soldier's Association of Pickens County, South Carolina.[25] Instead, during the early years of Reconstruction, the Confederate memorial movement remained firmly under the control of the South's middle- and upper-class white women and their allies in the press.[26]

Between 1868 and 1870, however, several factors converged that appeared to lessen the strictures of Reconstruction and therefore the necessity of women's control of the Lost Cause. First, having rewritten their constitutions and approved the Fourteenth Amendment, the states of the former Confederacy were readmitted to the Union. As Democrats regained control of the states, federal troops were removed. Second, a substantial portion of northerners began to show less interest in southern affairs as issues such as immigration, labor, and the Indian wars occupied their minds.[27] Taken together, these circumstances allowed southern white men to seek a larger role for themselves within the Confederate memorialization effort. Across the region, veterans gathered in groups such as the short-lived Confederate Survivors' Association of South Carolina, the Confederate Relief and Historical Association of Memphis, and the Southern Historical Society (sHs), all formed in 1869.[28]

By far, the most important factor shaping Confederate efforts to memorialize their cause was the death of the South's preeminent hero. On October 12, 1870, Robert E. Lee died at his home in Lexington. News of his death unleashed a deep wave of mourning throughout the South not experienced since the surrender at Appomattox. From Maryland to Texas, private residences covered their doors with black mourning cloth or hung photographs of the late general in their windows while statehouses and businesses closed their doors and lowered flags to half-staff. In many ways reminiscent of 1865 and 1866, this period of deep mourning inspired former Confederates to honor their past. But with the immediate threat of Union troops removed in many parts of the South and some vestiges of reunion apparent, southern white men were not content simply to follow women's lead in memorializing Lee. They had agreed that it was both politically and socially expedient for women to command the memorial movement in the first years after the war, but Confederate veterans saw Lee's death as the first real opportunity to glorify their war effort and honor their own martial spirit—to breathe new life into the Lost Cause.[29]

Since 1862, Lee and his Army of Northern Virginia had stood at the center of Confederate nationalism, but after his death others seized his image as the incarnation of the Confederate cause. In the newspaper tributes and funeral eulogies that followed, he was described simultaneously as a Christian gentleman, chivalric knight, ideal patriot, and invincible military genius. Ministers related anecdotes of his religious life and compared him to saints. Just as northern preachers had with Lincoln, their southern counterparts likened Lee to Moses—a man who had led his people but failed to reach the Promised Land. White southerners deified him, turning him into a flawless icon of all that was good and righteous about the Old South and the Confederacy.[30]

In the wake of Lee's death, a flurry of associations formed to provide some lasting tribute to the former Confederate commander. The very day of his passing, a group of ex-Confederates under the leadership of the Reverend William N. Pendleton, former chief of artillery in the Army of Northern Virginia, met in Lexington to form the Lee Memorial Association. Their express purpose was to erect an equestrian statue on the college grounds, a bust in the chapel, and a recumbent statue on Lee's tomb. The women of the Hollywood Memorial Association, claiming to be the guardians of Confederate memory, likewise wasted no time in initiating their own organization to memorialize Lee in Richmond.[31] But it was the former Confederate lieutenant general Jubal A. Early who was most dogmatic in his efforts to seize control of Lee's memory.[32]

An irreligious and often profane man known by many to be eccentric, Early graduated eighteenth in his class at West Point and served in the Seminole and Mexican Wars, but spent most of his antebellum career practicing law in Lynchburg, Virginia. During the war he steadily rose to the rank of colonel and then lieutenant general as one of Lee's corps commanders. After a failed campaign in the Shenandoah Valley during the fall of 1864, Lee relieved Early of his command in March 1865, citing negative public opinion regarding the faltering general. Having missed Appomattox, Early traveled to Texas where he hoped to join a Confederate force still refusing to surrender before heading to Cuba, Mexico, and eventually Canada in a self-imposed exile. In Toronto, he penned *A Memoir of the Last Year of the War for Independence* (1867), returning to the United States in 1869.[33]

Despite the fact that Lee had removed him from command, Early remained an ardent admirer of his general and wanted to honor him in grand fashion. Acting with haste to preempt the efforts of both Pendleton's group and the HMA, Early invited veterans to meet during the Virginia state fair on November 3 and 4 to form two complementary organizations: one to sponsor a monument, the Lee Monument Association, and another to perpetuate the veterans' legacy, the Association of the Army of Northern Virginia (AANVA).[34]

The desire of Early and other veterans to gain control of the Confederate movement was indicative of complex gendered meanings of the war and its aftermath. Veterans' organizations and efforts to enshrine Lee served as outlets for all Confederate men to reclaim their honor and manhood.[35] With battlefield defeat and the implementation of Reconstruction, ex-Confederate men had not only been denied much of their previous wealth and political positions, but also felt humiliated by their loss to northern soldiers, the emancipation of their slaves, their impoverished financial conditions, and Republican control of state and local politics. Their honor, their manhood, had been called into question. In an effort to counter this emasculated image, Early insisted that it be "those who had fought for the same cause to which General Lee had devoted himself"—and not the ladies of the Hollywood Memorial Association—who should take the lead in erecting a monument to their chieftain. (The ladies would be invited to "lend their assistance and cooperation" in collecting money, Early assured them.) He implored all former Confederate soldiers and sailors to tell the world that they were not "ashamed of the principles for which Lee fought and Jackson died."[36] Approximately 150 veterans from across the state heralded his call, electing Early president of both the AANVA and Lee Monument Association. Describing himself as "the senior in rank of all the officers of the Army of Northern Virginia now living in the State," Early crowned himself as the spokesman for all things Confederate and quickly became one of the most vocal proponents of the Lost Cause.[37]

Acknowledging the success of the Virginians in revitalizing interest in the Confederate past and conceding that New Orleans was not the SHS's most suitable home (Louisiana remained under Republican control at a time when other southern states had been "redeemed" by Democrats), the leaders of the nearly defunct society elected to join forces with Early and the AANVA. In 1873, the SHS voted to move its headquarters to Richmond and elected Early as its new president committed to maintaining its original goal of preserving "all authentic Southern records" of the war. Meeting at White Sulphur Springs, West Virginia, on August 14, the newly elected fifty-four delegates included such prominent wartime figures as Fitzhugh Lee, George Pickett, Raphael Semmes, Wade Hampton, and Jefferson Davis.[38]

As central figure of the two-day gathering, Early was selected to deliver the keynote address. Taking the stage dressed in his Confederate uniform, replete with cuff links featuring the rebel flag, he attacked the northern histories of the war that he described as falsehoods and "monstrous fabrication[s]." "The history of our war has not been written," he observed, "and it devolves upon the survivors of those who participated in that war, to furnish the authentic materials of history." "We must vindicate that cause, rekindle and strengthen the faith and spirit of the living, and do justice to the memory of our fallen comrades," he counseled.[39] No ex-Confederate should be willing to have history penned by his enemies. The duty of Lee's soldiers had not ended at Appomattox, he implored. Memory was at stake, and it was the veterans who needed to preserve it.

As Early indicated, central to this preservation was an emphasis on vindication. It was not enough merely to honor their fallen soldiers or pay tribute to the South's heroes.[40] If northerners were intent on castigating the southern cause as an attempt to destroy the Constitution and extend slavery, white southerners needed to prove that they had not been "arrayed on the side of wrong and error."[41] "Never was a cause apparently less understood or more maligned," Judge J. A. P. Campbell lamented in 1874.[42] The legitimacy of white southern control hung in the balance. "If we cannot justify the South in the act of Secession," observed former Confederate general Clement A. Evans, "we will go down in History solely as brave, impulsive but rash people who attempted in an illegal manner to overthrow the Union of our Country."[43] It was imperative that the survivors exonerate themselves from charges of treason and rebellion. To do so, they needed to embrace their past, not repudiate it.

No Confederate proved better suited to provide a positive image of the South than did the recently departed Robert E. Lee. Through hundreds of lectures, books, and the SHS's publication the *Southern Historical Society Papers* (*SHSP*), which began in 1876 and continued into 1959, Lee became the apotheosis of the Lost Cause.[44] Lee offered an antidote to northern depictions of an immoral, unconstitutional cause: he had been torn between the loyalty to his nation and his state. Repeatedly pointing to Lee's insistence that the Union had been a voluntary compact of the states, Lost Cause writers such as J. William Jones stressed that Lee could have anticipated "no greater calamity for the country than a dissolution of the Union," but he had stood by his neighbors and defended his state. Such could not be regarded as treason, they argued. Geography, his accident of birth, had compelled him to side with the Confederacy. Moreover, as the son of Revolutionary War hero "Light Horse Harry" Lee and a member of George Washington's family by marriage, Lee's genealogy assured that he of all people would not want to destroy the Union unless he felt it beyond repair.[45]

Implicit in their veneration of Lee was a sustained emphasis on the wartime theme of sheer Yankee numbers and resources (though certainly not superior determination, ability, or morality). Recalling Lee's farewell address at Appomattox, Lost Cause proponents repeatedly and doggedly stressed the strength of northern manpower, arguing that the Confederates' sustained effort was even more gallant in the face of such odds. Lee's Army of Northern Virginia "had been gradually worn down by the combined agencies of numbers, steam-power, railroads, mechanism, and all the resources of physical science," Early argued. Northern generals like George B. McClellan, he informed the South Carolina Survivors' Association in 1871, repeatedly falsified "the truth of history" by inflating Lee's strength "in order to excuse their manifold failures, and to conceal the inferiority of their troops in all the elements of manhood."[46]

Lee's image was not the only thing at stake. Those who adopted the overwhelming-numbers explanation sought to venerate the military prowess of all southern white men. *Our Living and Our Dead*, the official organ of North Carolina's SHS branch published by artillery colonel Stephen D. Pool, declared in 1873 that it would show "beyond controversy . . . that the soldiers, of the Confederate Armies accomplished more in proportion to their numbers, and the resources at their command, than was ever before accomplished by the same number of men similarly opposed."[47] Confederates' willingness to fight even when outnumbered and outgunned served as testimony to southern courage, manhood, and fortitude. They were not only relieved of any humiliation caused by defeat, but they were rendered the best fighting men in the world.[48]

Even brute force could not deter such an invincible military genius as Lee, argued former Confederates. "Lee was never really beaten," shouted Gen. John B. Gordon to a packed room of veterans in Richmond. "Overpowered, foiled in his efforts, he might be, but never defeated."[49] For those who might question the results at Gettysburg, Lee's image-molders had an answer: James Longstreet. Several factors encouraged Early and others to attack Longstreet, Lee's senior subordinate throughout the war. Not only had Longstreet publicly questioned Lee's competence, but he had also deserted the South since the war by becoming a Republican and urging white southerners to accommodate themselves to Reconstruction. Clearly, politics motivated the Virginians to launch a full-frontal assault on Longstreet. In speeches and on the pages of the *SHSP*, Fitzhugh Lee and others castigated Longstreet for being late on the second day at Gettysburg. More bluntly, J. William Jones observed that the South would have "won Gettysburg, and Independence, but for the failure of *one man*." The Longstreet-lost-at-Gettysburg rationale proved appealing to white southerners because it simultaneously offered the hope that success had been possible and provided a scapegoat for the South's failure.[50]

Defending Confederate soldiers as heroic and brave even though defeated on the battlefield was one thing. Absolving white southerners of fomenting a war to overthrow the Constitution and protect slavery required a more concerted effort. Most former Confederates recognized that to concede they had fought to establish a slaveholding nation would only undermine their status in a world increasingly opposed to enslavement. Yet the more Unionists championed their war as one that had saved the Union and freed the slaves, the more former Confederates contended otherwise. By describing slavery as merely "incidental" to the war, the Lost Cause sought a legal and constitutional justification of the southern cause. In March 1861, for example, Confederate vice president Alexander H. Stephens had argued that slavery "was the immediate cause of the late rupture and present revolution." But in his two-volume, 1,455-page *Constitutional View of the Late War Between the States* (1867 and 1870), he averred that the war had nothing to do with the "policy or impolicy of African subordination." The war "was not a contest between the advocates or opponents of that Peculiar Institution"; rather, slavery was but a "minor issue."[51]

To say that former Confederates contended slavery had nothing to do with the war is overly simplistic.[52] The relationship between slavery and the war's causation was more complicated than simple amnesia. Some outright defended the institution, noting that it had been protected by the Constitution. According to the regimental history of the 6th Georgia, soldiers had marched off to fight for "the safety, protection, and perpetuation of their political rights and institutions," prominently among them "the Right of local State Sovereignty, and the Institution of Slavery," which had been declared "a local institution and in no way subject to Federal interference." "Its stability was regarded as more imperiled and more uncertain than at any time during its existence upon this continent," observed the author.[53] Writing in 1866, the historian for the 3rd Louisiana accused New England "fanaticism" of inciting the war. "The first aim and object of this foul spirit was the eradication of slavery on this continent, an interference with the peculiar institutions of one section by the powerful arm of the opposing section." "As years passed by, feelings of hatred and enmity first engendered, grew in intensity and bitterness," recounted the historian, "until all compromise was rejected and the sword was unsheathed to settle the differences which existed."[54]

In an effort to counter Union claims of moral superiority regarding emancipation, other white southerners argued that economic reasons, not morality, had dissuaded northerners from embracing slavery.[55] Veteran Edward McCrady took this logic a step further. Slavery was "a burden imposed upon us by former generations of the world," he charged, "a burden increased upon us by the falsely-pretended philanthropic legislation of Northern states."[56] Whereas Lincoln's second inaugural held the entire nation responsible for the sin of slavery, he argued that northerners were more complicit in its continuation than were southerners.

Even if a "burden," white southerners scarcely forgot their peculiar institution. Throughout the postwar years they insisted that they had done much to civilize the heathen race and told tales of happy, content, and faithful slaves (as chapters 7 and 8 will further detail). Some proudly boasted that slavery both cultivated and reflected the region's exceptional character. Speaking before a group of former Confederates in 1871, South Carolinian William King Easley reminded his audience that both George Washington and Robert E. Lee had been "slaveholders and sons of slaveholders." Could slavery have been a pernicious system, he asked, if it "could produce such men as Washington and Lee?" On the contrary, he argued, slavery had been responsible for the nobility of the South.[57]

In a posthumously published essay, Jubal Early offered one of the most thorough defenses of slavery. Written more in the style of a legal brief than a polemic, as befitted a lawyer turned soldier, he began by meticulously tracing the institution's history to ancient civilizations. Having established that the Bible condoned enslavement, he challenged the contention that it was antithetical to the spirit of Christianity. "If slavery was contrary to the principle of the religion and morality taught by the Saviour, why should he have abstained from announcing the first in unmistakable terms, and have resorted to an indirect way of enunciating a great moral truth, which could be found out only after long centuries of profound ignorance on the subject," he asked. The notion that slavery was immoral was a recent phenomenon, he concluded, and an unsound one at that. If Christ had allowed slavery to go undisturbed, and it had endured for centuries after, by what rationale did nineteenth-century Americans claim its immorality? Slavery's extermination by the war was not proof that Providence was against the southern people for being slaveholders, Early reasoned. Even had they fought to preserve slavery, white southerners were not morally suspect or out of step with the precepts of Christianity.[58]

Most white southerners, however, avoided the topic of slavery or insisted that it was but one of many rights and responsibilities that fell to the states. Building upon the arguments of 1861 and repeated at countless Memorial Day services, Lost Cause advocates maintained that the union had been a compact of sovereign states from which every state had the right to withdraw. As William Preston Johnston noted in 1879, "The idea of self-government and resistance to centralization [and] . . . constitutional liberty" had inspired southern men to leave the Union and pick up their guns in self-defense.[59] In speeches and regimental histories, white southerners denied culpability for igniting the war, claiming instead to have sought every peaceful means to avert bloodshed. The "long, fierce and terrible war," they charged, had been "by the United States for subjugation."[60] The Yankees, not Confederates, had been guilty of the "disapprobation of wrong and tyranny."[61] White southerners had merely been "patriots defending our rights, and vindicating the true principles of the government founded by our fathers."[62] Southerners had not provoked the war, they maintained; rather, it had been the meddlesome, invading North that had violated the principles of the Constitution by attacking the expansion of slavery and other state rights. Most important, if secession had been a constitutional right, then those who supported it could not have been rebels or traitors.

Yet another central tenet of the Lost Cause removed all politics and even constitutional questions from the war's causation. Many Confederate veterans insisted that they had fought as the truest Americans in defense of hearth and home. "The resistance made by the South was not merely an attempt to preserve political institutions, but to perpetuate a social organization inherited through a thousand generations—the sanctity of marriage, the inviolability of the family, the faith in truth, honor, and virtue, the protection of the home," maintained Bradley T. Johnson, a Maryland Confederate, at a monument dedication in 1891. "Historically the position of the South was impregnable," he argued.[63] Theirs had been a defensive war in response to the Yankee vandals who had invaded the region—destroyed their farms and cities, freed their slaves, and persecuted their women and children.[64] Focused on protecting homes and families, the southern cause was moral, righteous, and virtuous. Claims of such chivalric conduct were not only imperative to vindication, but they also heralded defeated Confederates as the better men. Every argument espoused by the Lost Cause was buttressed by claims of moral superiority: the legal explanation for secession, the gallant Confederate soldiers who had been doomed before overwhelming odds, and the defenses of slavery. To think otherwise was tantamount to accepting the Yankee argument that "might makes right."[65]

For the Lost Cause it was not enough to defend the Confederacy as righteous and explain the South's defeat. Instead, both publicly and privately white southerners recalled the unjust Union Cause to boost their own version of the past. They accused Unionists of fomenting the horrific bloodshed. And they sneered at claims that northerners had fought principally to free the slaves, arguing that such fabrications were merely a ploy by Republicans to garner votes. Unionists might highlight the contemptible Confederate cause in their Memorial Day addresses and GAR post meetings, but white southerners responded in kind.

Former Confederates were willing to acknowledge their losses. The trial by war had extinguished slavery, settled the question of secession, and repudiated the Confederate debt. But they refused to concede that they had sinned and therefore felt no need to repent. "Repentance is a result of conscious guilt," noted a Memphis newspaper in 1870, "which no man in the South, whose heart was in the late war, entertains." They had left the union because they believed they had a right to go. Having fought bravely and failed, they returned to the union seeking peace. "But we come not as inferiors or guilty supplicants, but as brave, high-minded Americans, in all respects the equals of our conquerors."[66] Reunion they were willing to embrace. Reconciliation might be another matter.

THE FOULEST POLITICAL CRIME
THE WORLD HAS EVER WITNESSED

Lost Cause celebrations not only sought to vindicate the Confederate past; they also provided a forum for critiquing the present. In 1866, assaults on Reconstruction had been shrouded in mourning at Confederate Memorial Day services. But in the wake of the Reconstruction Acts of March 1867 and the Fourteenth and Fifteenth Amendments, which disenfranchised former Confederates and brought black men into political power, Lost Cause orators and writers no longer felt compelled to mask their contempt behind the veil of bereavement. Convinced that Reconstruction had been a terrible mistake meant primarily to increase white southerners' suffering and strip them of all power, at monument dedications, veterans' gatherings, and in the pages of periodicals, many openly challenged the "injustice" of Union occupation and black suffrage.[67]

Lee's October 1870 death proved to be an especially powerful rallying call against continued northern intrusion into southern affairs in New Orleans. By that fall, evidence of "radical" Reconstruction abounded in Louisiana: a Republican governor and biracial state legislature controlled the state, African American men served on juries and on New Orleans's police force, black children attended public schools, and former slaves expected service in the city's restaurants and theaters. A well-armed black militia, under the command of Lee's former lieutenant James Longstreet, drilled on city streets and public squares. But Lee's death provided an opportunity for conservative whites to challenge the biracial Republican regime and reestablish white supremacy. Pointing out that some Republicans, including the state's African American lieutenant governor, Oscar J. Dunn, had mourned the fallen chieftain by draping their homes in mourning cloth, the conservatives began publicly asserting their "universally loved" hero's loyalty to the Lost Cause.

Yet instead of stressing reconciliation, on the day of Lee's memorial service, more than 3,000 white southerners, including former Confederate generals P. G. T. Beauregard, John B. Hood, and Braxton Bragg, listened to orators defend secession, the Confederacy, and white supremacy. Conservative newspapers echoed the message, condemning the city for failing to lower the flags to half-mast in honor of Lee. The "men now in power," asserted one paper, "are strangers to the motives and principles that actuated the conduct of General Lee." "His life," claimed the editor, "was a standing protest against the dishonor and degradation which they have heaped upon the American name."[68] Throughout the region, Lee came to symbolize the chivalry and honor of the South so lacking in the corrupt Republican Reconstruction governments of carpetbaggers, scalawags, and freedmen.[69]

In the years following Lee's death, Lost Cause denunciations of Reconstruction continued to increase. Speaking before the SHS in 1873, Jefferson Davis declared that the South had been more cheated than conquered by the declarations of the president, Congress, and generals. "There never would have been a surrender had we anticipated what followed," he boldly declared. Former cavalry general Wade Hampton likened Reconstruction to a "ship of state cut loose by mutinous hands from the safe moorings established by our forefathers." William King Easley proclaimed that the end of the war represented "the overthrow of the constitution," while yet another South Carolinian described Reconstruction as the "period of revengeful hatred." The ever-loquacious Jubal Early condemned Reconstruction as the "foulest political crime the world has ever witnessed." Under Republican rule, the autonomy of eleven free and sovereign states had been subjected to the "rule of an ignorant and inferior race, utterly incapable of understanding the first principles of government," and controlled by carpetbaggers—"a vile herd of alien adventurers, swindles, and thieves."[70] If northerners argued that secession had been unconstitutional, Lost Cause leaders responded that Reconstruction had been an utterly contemptible overthrow of constitutional liberty.

Justifications of slavery were likewise more than ex post facto defenses of the institution. They were also intended to counter Reconstruction demands and reestablish antebellum social relations. Rooting racial hierarchies in nature, history, and divine providence affirmed that Republicans' calls for equality were not only unconstitutional but unnatural. Basic inequality "is as old as nature and wide as the world," insisted Easley.[71]

As white southerners grew more and more irate with Reconstruction policies, Ulysses S. Grant proved to be a favorite target for Lost Cause advocates. Speaking before the South Carolina Survivor's Association in 1871, Early rebuked Grant as a bloody butcher who hurled an unlimited supply of unfortunate soldiers against Lee's humble forces. Absent was any discussion of the "magnanimous" surrenders Grant had overseen at Fort Donelson, Vicksburg, or Appomattox. Instead, Early found in Grant only "the most ordinary brute courage" and the "control of unlimited numbers and means."[72] Former Confederate major general Dabney H. Maury conceded that Grant had been a successful general but harangued him for the "recklessness with which he dashed men to death." Maury held special contempt for Grant's role in stopping the prisoner-of-war exchange, designating it "the most cruel act of his plan of attrition." "No parallel can be found for this double crime against humanity," Dabney wrote. Above all, he disavowed Grant's leadership during Reconstruction. His presidency had been little more than a "sad spectacle of States overthrown and constitution and laws set aside by the man who had sworn to protect them, and all the rights of the people subordinated to the one prime object of placing a centralized power in the hands of him who was incapable of statesmanship broader than the bounds of his own personal convenience or pecuniary profit."[73] As white southern women would again argue in the 1930s, the connections between Grant's brutal generalship and his imposition of Republican rule on the defeated South went hand in hand.[74]

Not all former Confederates agreed. Testifying before Congress, former Confederate general John B. Gordon recalled the "liberal, generous, magnanimous policy" of Grant at Appomattox.[75] Reconstruction, he observed, had been a betrayal of Grant's magnanimous policy. Capt. D. N. Sanders had not forgotten the magnanimity of Grant and his soldiers. "Never did that army pay you a higher compliment, or do themselves a greater honor, than by their conduct and words on that occasion," he reminded veterans at the 3rd Georgia's 1874 reunion. Yet seemingly forgetting that Grant had been both a military man and politician, Sanders argued that if the policies of Reconstruction had been left to the soldiers rather than to the politicians, "complete harmony [might have been] restored before the end of a single year." He implored his men to always cherish the banner of their loved "lost cause," yet encouraged his brethren to embrace the "grand old flag of the Union." This sentiment was not lost on a special guest at the reunion, Sidney Herbert, editor of the *Troy Messenger* (Alabama) and a former major in the Union Army. Raising his glass in a toast to the Confederate dead, he quoted the Union's Gen. Joshua L. Chamberlain, observing the fraternal feelings that appeared to be increasing between the former foes. "We never hated them, except that they struck at the old flag," he noted. "Fellow-soldiers, this is a tribute of praise that we who wore the Blue, and who fully tested your fidelity, your courage, and your perseverance, pay to your dead comrades."[76] For some veterans, the memory of Grant and his army's magnanimous gestures at Appomattox would prove to be fertile ground for reconciliation in the years to come.

Yet others could not ignore the alleged unjustness of the Union war effort and the perceived atrocities of northern occupation. Scrambling to his feet after Herbert's toast, Col. Claiborne Snead recounted the "unjust humiliation" and suffering of Reconstruction. The most pronounced Lost Cause speech of the reunion, however, was that given by C. A. Winn. In defiant tones, he lamented that the war had not been fought for any principle and had not settled any issue. Its result had demonstrated only one fact: "namely that 600,000 so-called rebels, however intrepid, brave and self-sacrificing, could not whip in the open field 2,000,000 of white men, well-armed and equipped." "We were not *rebels* in the war," he declared; rather, "the enemy were usurpers and their course since the war demonstrates the truth of this assertion."[77] Contrary to the contention that in the 1870s most white southerners rejected the anti-northern tenor of Early and his group, preferring instead to quietly decorate graves, regimental and state-level reunions offered their fair share of sectional animus.[78]

Confederate memory went beyond simply rebuking federal policies. If the northern memory of the war had influenced politics through waving the "bloody shirt" and as a justification for congressional Reconstruction, former Confederates likewise recognized that national political clout rested on wartime memories, chief among them the "slanderous" accounts of rebel barbarity toward prisoners of war. Beginning in the late 1860s, ex-Confederate prison survivors not only refuted northern allegations, but they also levied their own indictments. In bitter recriminations, they argued that northern prisons such as Point Lookout, Camp Douglas, and Elmira should be "placed by the side of the exaggerations about Libby, Belle Isle, Tyler, and Andersonville."[79] But the most sustained and shrill of the defenses came from the pages of the *Southern Historical Society Papers* during the presidential election year of 1876. In January, Maine congressman James Blaine condemned a pending bill that would have conferred amnesty to Jefferson Davis. The rebel president, argued Blaine, was unworthy of amnesty because "he was the author, knowingly, deliberately, guiltily, and willfully, of the gigantic murders and crimes at Andersonville."[80] Responding to Blaine, in March the *SHSP* devoted an entire issue, more than 200 pages, to "The Treatment of Prisoners during the War between the States." Though admitting that there had been "a vast amount of suffering and fearful mortality among the Federal prisoners at the South," the *SHSP* asserted that conditions were far worse for Confederate prisoners. The editor defended the scarcity of rations for Union prisoners, noting that it was no fault of the Confederacy's but a result of the Union blockade. Such could not be said of northern prisons, the editor argued. In a land "flowing with plenty, our poor fellows . . . were famished with hunger." "Our men died by the thousands from causes which the Federal authorities *could* have prevented."[81] The *SHSP*'s claims of higher mortality rates and worse conditions in Union prisons were gross exaggerations, yet the political implications of the debate were clearly evident.

Waving the "gray shirt" was even more effective in state-level politics, perhaps nowhere more than South Carolina. Hoping to reclaim the governor's mansion from the Republicans, in 1876, Democrats backing former Confederate cavalry general Wade Hampton invoked the memory of the Lost Cause to restore conservative control.[82] To rally white voters, many of whom had not voted since the war, Hampton embarked on a tour of the state that fall accompanied by hundreds, if not thousands, of armed and mounted local rifle clubs composed primarily of Confederate veterans. From the upcountry town of Anderson to the colonial city of Charleston, throngs of frenzied spectators turned out for torch light processions where they cheered Hampton's "Red Shirts." For many former Confederates the marches, thunder of cannons and fireworks, and the exuberant crowds recalled the spirit of 1861 when the boys were marching off to war. "South Carolina white men," wrote a Spartanburg journalist, "were going into this fight with more determination and desperation of purpose than they went into the Confederate war."[83]

Though fraud and brutality certainly aided Hampton's narrow victory, the martial display of ex-Confederates riding alongside their former cavalry chief helped secure white unity at the polls. Here the Lost Cause was

much more than a nostalgic longing for the past. It was a call to arms, a re-
vived Confederate nationalism that heralded a united resistance to federal
intrusion into state affairs. Vindication of the Confederate cause would not
be found on the battlefields of war but in the determined and successful
fight to overthrow the chains of Reconstruction.[84]

Even as Hampton's Red Shirts embarked on their triumphant tour of
South Carolina, the fate of Reconstruction hinged on the presidential election of 1876. If the winner, with the support of southern white men, turned
out to be Democrat Samuel J. Tilden, the last remnants of Union troops
in the South would be removed, and with them the ever-present reminder
of Confederate defeat. If Republican (and Union general) Rutherford B.
Hayes were to win, the fate of Reconstruction would remain uncertain.
In the end, the amnesty bill did not pass, Davis was not pardoned, Hayes
won the presidency in a contested election, and in a backroom compromise Union troops were removed from the South.

Like its Union counterpart, Confederate memory served as a powerful call to political action. But where the Union Cause ultimately sought
a reunited nation free of sectional animosity, the Lost Cause fostered a
distinctive and separate southern identity determined to resist interference by the federal government. "If we would really serve this country—
this whole country—this American nation," Col. Edward McCrady Jr. exhorted the AANVA in 1886, "so far from suppressing our love for our own
section, let us cultivate it above all others, and so love it that we shall keep
it worthy of the confederation of which it is a part."[85] Having finally triumphed over Reconstruction, white southerners expected to be treated
as full members of the Union. But they likewise appeared more, not less,
anxious to hold onto their sacred Confederate past.[86]

NOT CALCULATED TO INSPIRE LOYALTY

During the first decade after the war, the occasional regimental and brigade reunion had allowed veterans from Virginia to Texas the opportunity
to fraternize with their comrades and reminisce on the most trying time of
their lives.[87] But just as the ranks of the LMAs and the GAR faltered in the
years surrounding the Panic of 1873, Confederate veterans too found it difficult to sustain membership in their associations.[88] As the economy began
to rebound by the late 1870s and early 1880s, and after the bitterness of
Reconstruction slowly faded with the removal of the last Union troops
from the South and the return of the remaining statehouses to Democratic
control, rank-and-file ex-Confederates formed permanent associations

and held reunions with increasing frequency. In 1877, the Association of the Army of Tennessee joined the AANVA as another army-wide veterans' organization akin to the Union's Society of the Army of the Cumberland, Society of the Army of the Tennessee, and Society of the Army of the Potomac.[89] The following years saw the inauguration of the Confederate Survivor's Association of Augusta, Georgia, as well as the reunions of Terry's Rangers in San Antonio, Rosser's Cavalry Brigade and Artillery in Maryland, and Govan's Brigade in Little Rock.[90] By the mid-1880s, Confederate veterans from every corner of the South found ample opportunities to join with their former comrades at annual reunions.

Throughout the region, these years witnessed a swell in nostalgia for the Lost Cause. No longer couched in the feminine sphere of mourning, interest in (state-level) soldier' pensions, the death of Jefferson Davis, the beginnings of industrialization, integration into the national economy and mass culture, gender anxieties, and racial tensions all contributed to the development of a regional celebration that honored white southerners' self-sacrifice and honor. But two inexplicably linked factors also helped stimulate popular interest in the Lost Cause at the grassroots level. First, the generation of veterans and women who had experienced the war as young adults were now coming into their own, running businesses and rearing children. They had the financial resources and time to participate in such endeavors. Second, and related to the first, they desperately needed their offspring to understand their devotion to the Confederate cause even though it had failed. When asked, "Why are the old Confederates gathering together again? and what are they going to *get out of it*?" Thomas Munford reminded a crowd of Virginia veterans in the mid-1880s that the answer lay with the next generation: "To our children and their children's children, let it be our pride to teach them, as is done in every land where patriotism and self-sacrificing spirits are honored and esteemed, that the Confederates shed their blood for their Mother, Virginia, defending a cause she knew to be just and right."[91]

Historians have described the Lost Cause of the 1880s as one premised on celebrating the experience and camaraderie of battle rather than on sectional politics. But even after Reconstruction, expressions of the southern spirit and defenses of the cause were ubiquitous at Confederate reunions.[92] Amid stages festooned with Confederate battle flags from Maryland to Florida, veterans recalled the heroics of battle, but they also gave blistering defenses of their cause. Speaking before a reunion of the Army of Tennessee in 1882, Gen. Thomas R. Markham assured the veterans that their fallen had not died in vain. Men die, he noted, but principles live. "The principles of constitutional right and individual liberty, of State sovereignty, and local self-government, for which our men warred and died, find assertion and advocacy throughout the land."[93] Observing that professions of loyalty abounded at an ex-Confederate reunion in Rogersville, Tennessee, a St. Louis newspaper felt certain such pronouncements rang hollow. "The sentiments expressed," concluded the paper, "were not calculated to inspire loyalty to the Union."[94] The cause might have been lost, but the Lost Cause was alive and well.

One 1881 reunion especially raised the ire of northerners. On August 10, approximately 4,000 Missouri Confederates gathered in Dallas to celebrate the twentieth anniversary of the battle of Wilson's Creek. According to northern newspapers, the principal address by the Reverend General L. M. Lewis was itself a ranting, roaring affair lacking both patriotism and scholarship. The remarks of Capt. W. H. Grigsby, however, proved beyond the pale. Grigsby opened by boasting that he had ridden with Quantrill and had been with Bill Anderson when he was shot off his horse. But his words were not to be celebrations of the raiders' courage and heroism. Instead, he quickly turned to contemporary times. In fiery language, he praised Governor Oran M. Roberts of Texas for refusing to call upon his state to sympathize with President James A. Garfield, who lay dying from an assassin's bullet. Bolstered by applause, Grigsby shouted that he felt no sympathy for the former Union general in his misfortune.[95] From the audience some advised him to temper his words and not "mingle confusion with his talk," but Grigsby continued. "Ever since I knew anything about constitutional law, ever since I knew of the Confederate Government and of State rights, I have always been a secessionist," he avowed. And he was still. "Should ever war again commence let us be found in the front rank battling against Garfield and all that crew," he cried.[96]

From New York to California, newspapers railed against the die-hard rebel and his anti-Union sentiments. Some labeled him as one of the "Confederate lunatics" who were as "red-hot and reckless as ever." Others wondered how many white southerners shared his sentiments—and how quickly those who did might pass from the earth. Such unreconstructed rebels inhibited the path toward an era of good feeling between the North and South that was both possible and desirable. "They will all disappear in time," one paper remarked, optimistically noting that the next generation would know little of the southern cause. Others were not so sure that Confederate sentiment was—or ever would be—on the decline. "It wouldn't be a bad idea to discontinue the reunions," advised one Missouri newspaper.[97]

Despite such incidents, rare though they might be, former Confederates adamantly defended their reunions, castigating instead those of their former foes. "How different the confederate reunion from the federal," observed an Arkansas newspaper. "Ours are purely social, theirs purely political. Ours have a gentle, mellowing influence over the passions; theirs excite and frenzy the worst passions of our nature and stir up and keep alive hatred, malice, and uncharitableness."[98] Twenty years after the first shots rang out from Charleston Harbor, sectional feelings lingered. The war may have settled questions of secession and slavery, but veterans' of both sides refused to concede that their cause was unjust or unrighteous.

Veterans' reunions, Memorial Days, and the countless memoirs and regimentals that rolled off the presses recounted Confederates' suffering and defended their political cause. But many white southerners sought more enduring reminders of their struggle. Since the late 1860s a handful of monuments had been erected by LMAs in Confederate cemeteries across the region. Beginning in the late 1870s and accelerating in the 1880s, however, the style and placement of these monuments began to change— began to look more like the Union monuments erected since 1865. Ladies' groups supported by veterans associations no longer felt compelled to secure their memorials behind cemetery walls. Instead, monuments occupied a more public, literally a more central place, on courthouse lawns and town squares. No longer shrouded in mourning, communities abandoned the funerary designs of the 1860s, selecting instead (often from a catalog) a marble or bronze Confederate soldier standing at ease.[99]

As with Memorial Days, monument dedications often began with a procession that included little girls donning white dresses, other children carrying Confederate flags, numerous militia units, and, of course, the local Confederate veterans. When the parade reached the site of the monument, spectators gathered to hear orators praise the heroics and courage of southern soldiers (and generally that of women on the home front as well), reaffirming that they had fought for constitutional liberty. Then, with some sort of flourish—perhaps the sound of a bugle—a special guest would pull the chords unveiling the bronze or marble soldier to a thunderous applause.[100]

As monuments to Confederates increasingly dotted the southern landscape, veteran societies began to call for a general association of Confederate veterans akin to the GAR. Some, like the Richmond-based Lee Camp, achieved its goal of a statewide confederation by 1887, as did veterans in both Tennessee and Georgia. But a handful of veterans, led primarily by a group in Louisiana, pursued the formation of a national Confederate veterans' association. In June 1889, veterans from Louisiana, Tennessee,

Members of the R. E. Lee Camp of Confederate veterans gathered for a reunion in Richmond during the early 1900s. Reunions of Confederate veterans began much later than their Union counterparts. (Virginia Historical Society)

and Mississippi met in New Orleans, where they adopted a constitution and anointed themselves the United Confederate Veterans (UCV). Like the GAR, the UCV instituted a hierarchical, martial structure: the highest officer was called commander, officers were designated by rank, geographical departments were established, and local organizations were called camps. From every corner of the former Confederacy, veterans rushed to form camps and establish state-level organizations.[101]

Former Confederate general John B. Gordon represented the veterans as the first commander of the UCV. A native of Georgia, Gordon had practiced law throughout the antebellum years. During the war, he had advanced steadily through the ranks, eventually serving as major general (although he would later claim to have been promoted to lieutenant general). After the war, he proved to be a staunch opponent of Reconstruction, rejecting equality for freedmen, reportedly joining forces with the Ku Klux Klan, and helping to restore Georgia to Democratic rule. Foreshadowing his reconciliationist inclinations, his activities were not confined to the South. Instead, during Horace Greeley's 1872 run for the White House against President Grant, Gordon traveled to northern states like Indiana where he preached the gospel of white supremacy. In 1873, he was elected to the U.S. Senate, and six years later he became the first former Confederate to preside over the chamber. Seduced by an offer from the Georgia-Pacific Railroad, he resigned his seat in 1880, but his passion for politics trumped his business calling. In 1886, he was elected governor of Georgia, and in 1891 he returned to the U.S. Senate.[102] A dynamic speaker, contemporaries considered him one of the most descriptive and provocative orators of his time. Gordon's demeanor, background, and beliefs made him a compelling choice for commander of the UCV.[103] Although a proponent of the New South, Gordon's defense of the South's antebellum racial and political order served as an extension of the message promoted by Early and the SHS two decades earlier.[104]

During his fourteen-year tenure as commander of the UCV (from 1890 until his death in 1904), Gordon began offering a more reconciliationist stance. Especially important to this message was his description of Appomattox. In countless speeches, he remarked on the "magnanimous spirit" of the surrender.[105] But it was not merely such rhetoric that hinted at regional reconciliation. Gordon had chaired a joint GAR–ex-Confederate committee charged with raising funds for a Confederate home in Richmond, and before he became commander of the UCV he had discussed the possibility of forming a Blue-Gray organization of veterans with a northern general.[106]

Perhaps such positions led some Union veterans to believe that former Confederates—or at least the next generation—might see the error of their ways. "Before the middle of the twentieth century, two hundred millions of happy Americans will look back with horror and scorn upon the incredible baseness of a rebellion in the interest of human slavery," remarked a Minnesota veteran in 1891. "The grandsons of the Confederates will go forth in storm and darkness to tear down the marble shafts which are now rising in the South," he predicted, "and grind to tongueless dust the momentoes [sic] of confessed and pardoned crime." He could not have been more wrong.[107]

In the years between 1866 and the early 1890s, the Lost Cause proved to be a powerful and effective rationale for former Confederates to reclaim social and political power. By resolutely defending secession as constitutional, insisting that they had fought to defend their homes only to be overwhelmed by the northern resources, and denouncing Republican Reconstruction governments as the true usurpers of liberty, white southerners claimed the moral high ground. Although Confederate veterans did not have an organization comparable to the GAR until 1889, the Lost Cause had proved unbelievably successful in rallying white southerners to the cause of self-rule. Yet there was also evidence of the range of feelings that existed among former Confederates. Some were willing as early as 1874, even before all the occupying Union forces had been removed from the South, to extend their hands across the bloody chasm in the name of reunion. Others, like Jubal Early and W. H. Grigsby, refused to consider such gestures. Some acknowledged slavery as a cause of the war; others adamantly denounced such blasphemy.

Even with this range of expression, the Lost Cause was not about shouldering rifles again or continuing the fight for an independent Confederate nation. Instead, most white southerners would have agreed with William C. P. Breckinridge. "The formulation of a separate Confederacy has forever passed away," he declared before the AANVA in 1892. "It would now be an anomaly; it would not receive the support of those who survive that war." But, he cautioned, "How far the matters involved in that controversy passed away in that surrender may become a matter of dispute."[108] The Lost Cause offered another type of war, one that sought to conquer the hearts and minds of the coming generations—one that would guarantee that Confederates' children, grandchildren, and their progeny would know that the cause for southern independence had been true and righteous, and that they would continue to identify with the South as a region if not a separate country. Not willing to let their cause die with the war generation, white southerners ensured that the Lost Cause would alternatively complicate, promote, and hinder reconciliation well into the twentieth century.

OUR FRIENDS, THE ENEMY

1880s–Early 1900s

By the summer of 1881, news of the Luray Caverns in Virginia's famed Shenandoah Valley had spread throughout the East Coast. Only three years after its discovery, tales of the cave's magnificent stalactites and stalagmites, along with sketches that appeared in *Harper's Weekly*, had led scientists, journalists, and visitors from near and far to proclaim its splendor. Union general David H. Strother professed that it surpassed all other grottoes in the "richness and profusion of its ornamentation" and was especially spectacular "when illuminated by the electric light recently introduced." "These effects are beyond the reach of descriptive art," he declared, "and must be seen to be fully understood and appreciated." Hundreds of curious visitors devoured these accounts and began to flood the small farming town to see what was being touted as one of the world's geological wonders. The Union veterans of Carlisle, Pennsylvania, were no exception — but theirs was not to be a sightseeing adventure alone.[1]

In June, the Carlisle GAR post wrote to the prominent men of Luray proposing an excursion of the ladies and gentlemen of Pennsylvania's Cumberland Valley to the caverns where they might meet the local survivors of the Confederate army. There was no need for "ostentatious show" or "expensive reception"; rather, they merely desired a "friendly handshaking." "We will furnish a band of music," the post gladly wrote. "If you think favorably of meeting us there, with as many comrades as you can conveniently muster, we should be pleased to form the new acquaintances."[2] Luray's local paper agreed, beseeching Confederate veterans to come together demonstrating "to these men who fought as bravely for what they thought right as did we of the South for what we thought right, that we have also as much of the feeling of amity and forgiveness as have they."[3]

On July 21, twenty years after they met on the battlefield of Manassas, the former enemies met for one of the first Blue-Gray reunions. Predating the much larger affairs that would follow in the coming years, early that day nearly 2,000 Confederate veterans from the Shenandoah Valley gathered at the newly opened Luray train station to greet the 600 Pennsylvanians. In language that would prove representative of Blue-Gray reunions for decades to come, Lt. Andrew Broaddus, Confederate veteran and editor of the local paper, called upon the veterans of both sides to forget the war, reminding them "that only cowards bear malice, and that brave men forgive." While partisan leaders continued to employ political issues to "keep down the cry of peace that comes from every section," he hoped that this meeting would do much to end such sectional animosities. GAR post commander Judge R. M. Henderson concurred with Broaddus, but added that the veterans should "forget everything except the lessons of the past." Veterans might gather on the former fields of battle to ceremoniously shake hands over the proverbial bloody chasm, but, as Henderson observed, they would not surrender their cause.[4]

Throughout the 1880s and 1890s, such affairs helped convince Americans on both sides of the Mason-Dixon Line that the horrors of war and the upheavals of Reconstruction were behind them. The creation of the first national military parks, popular magazines, plays, and even political campaigns encouraged northerners and southerners to embrace their former foes in the spirit of brotherly love and American progress. In recent years, historians have interpreted these gestures as evidence of a new national memory of reconciliation that triumphed over earlier memories of the war.[5] Forgotten was the Union Cause with its emphasis on preserving the republic and ending slavery, they argue. Buried were the disputes over the war's causation or accusations of wrong versus right. Instead, northerners appeared to buy into the Lost Cause sentiments that extolled the battlefield bravery and valor of all (white) soldiers. Reconciliation, these scholars contend, offered both a whitewashed memory of the war and vision of sectional healing on Confederate terms.[6]

This vision of sectional harmony premised on amnesia about the war's causes, however, was not a category by which most veterans elected to remember the war. As they had done since the 1860s, the majority adamantly defended their own cause as righteous and just while refuting that of their opponent as without merit. Yet this fierce need to protect sectional memories of the war was not at odds or inconsistent with their cries for reconciliation. On the contrary, both Union and Confederate veterans favored national unity—albeit on their own terms.[7] Even as U.S. veterans continued to grapple with animus toward their former enemy, for them the triumph of reunion *was* the Union cause, and gestures of reconciliation served as evidence of the reunited nation. For ex-Confederates, reconciliationist sentiments helped convince them that they were back on equal footing in the Union, and claims that they had fought against a worthy enemy only bolstered the courage of their soldiers. Perhaps more important, rather than reconciliationist gestures fostering a memory of the war that erased the causes and consequences of the conflict, Blue-Gray lovefests often had the unintended consequence of fostering a deeper attachment to the respective Union and Lost Causes. While they might occasionally meet in the spirit of reconciliation, neither Union nor Confederate veterans were willing to forget—much less forgive—all that had happened. True, heart-felt reconciliation was rare indeed.

THE BLUE AND THE GRAY

With the sectional and racial bitterness of Reconstruction seemingly behind them, Americans rushed forward into a period of unprecedented economic boom and bust. The tremendous growth of the industrial sector during the 1880s marked an era of big business led by so-called robber barons, whose opulent homes along Fifth Avenue highlighted the increasing disparity between the rich and poor. While some Americans clamored to view the first skyscrapers, ride on streetcars to their new homes in the suburbs, buy the latest gadgets from mail order catalogs, or shop in opulent department stores, others struggled simply to exist in the slums of ever-expanding cities. Labor strife, Populist revolt, political corruption, unbridled materialism, social Darwinism, state-sanctioned segregation, and the height of lynching were hallmarks of this period. But so too were reform efforts instigated by the likes of Jane Addams's Hull House, the quest for women's rights, and the conservation movement that would preserve wondrous national spaces such as Yellowstone.

Yet life did offer some respite from twelve-hour working days. In working-class neighborhoods, men gathered for a beer at the local saloon during their precious hours away from the factory. Spectator sports such as boxing and baseball captured the popular imagination with the likes of John L. Sullivan and the Cincinnati Red Stockings. Among the middle and upper classes, college football found a growing audience, despite its propensity for brutal and sometimes fatal injuries. (Even former guerrilla fighter John S. Mosby objected to the sport following the death of a University of Virginia student.) Some elected to spend their leisure time at vaudeville shows, Chautauqua lectures, or a day at Coney Island. Still others found appeal in the burgeoning number of women's clubs or fraternal organizations such as the Masons, Odd Fellows, and Knights of the Pythias.[8]

Amid all these changes, interest in the Civil War reached a fevered pitch. Virtually moribund in the 1870s, the ranks of the GAR swelled to more than 350,000 by the mid-1880s just as Confederate veterans began to rally members to their growing societies. Monument companies from Georgia to Vermont thrived on the burgeoning requests for memorials to fill town squares, courthouse lawns, and sacred battlefield sites. Gettysburg continued in its transformation from scarred battlefield to genteel tourist attraction with the addition of a new railroad and a hotel constructed at the medicinal springs. For those who could not make their way to such hallowed fields, paintings, sculptures, and stereoscopes provided a tangible connection to the war. But perhaps no sector peddled the memory of the war more vigorously and more successfully than did the publishing industry. Throughout the Gilded Age, a plethora of soldiers' memoirs, wartime diaries, regimental histories, serials, fictional accounts, battlefield guidebooks, and travelogues burst forth from the popular press highlighting the bravery and honor of both Union and Confederate soldiers.[9]

Appalled by the "heedlessly imperfect, and strongly partisan histories" of the war published to date, in March 1877, newspaper editor Alexander K. McClure began soliciting accounts from both Union and Confederate participants for a series in the *Philadelphia Weekly Times*. Acknowledging that a war "so costly in blood and treasure, and reaching almost every household with its sore bereavements" was bound to "inflame the bitterest passions and resentments," he hoped that by inviting famous generals and lesser-known staff officers of both sides (as well as a handful of civilians) to contribute essays, the "truth of history" might be ascertained. Two years later, he selected fifty-six of the articles to appear under the title *Annals of the War*, a massive 800-page book.[10]

Though some of the authors embraced McClure's reconciliationist mission, others highlighted the lingering sectional bitterness and disputed memories of the war. Former Confederate general Joseph E. Johnston used the occasion to pointedly refute line after line of William T. Sherman's *Memoirs*. Seeking to explain why "traces of bitter feeling" still existed in the South, Confederate general John D. Imboden's article attacked his former adversary Union general David Hunter, charging him with wanton destruction and savage behavior in the 1864 Shenandoah Valley campaign. Confederate contributors were not the only ones bent on settling old scores and correcting false claims by their former foes. Frustrated with the extent to which Confederates seemed to be writing the history, Union colonel William Brooke-Rawle observed that "we begin to distrust the memory of those days, and almost to question the general belief that the battle of Gettysburg was a victory for Union arms." Gen. Robert S. Northcott turned to the ever-contentious discussion of prisoners of war. Contrary to southern accounts of Federal officers violating the prisoner-exchange agreement, he argued that the obstructions to the exchange system came from Jefferson Davis. "The Confederate Government either did not understand the usages of civilized warfare, or else violated them willfully," he wrote. Robert Ould, the Confederacy's chief of the Bureau of Exchange, countered, arguing that blame for halting the exchanges lay with Grant, Butler, and other northern culprits. Still other articles helped fuel debates among former comrades, perhaps none more so than the question of Longstreet's performance at Gettysburg. More than fostering reconciliation, at least some of the articles that appeared in the *Annals* had the opposite effect—a fact not lost on McClure. Controversy, after all, was sure to elicit interest and boost sales.[11]

By the early 1880s, attempts at a reconciliationist message proved more successful. In 1881, when the first volume of the government's *Official Records of the War of the Rebellion* finally appeared, it garnered positive responses from many former Confederates. The indefatigable Lost Cause warrior J. William Jones, editor of the *SHSP*, objected to the word "rebellion" in the title, observing that it "conveys a reproach upon the Southern part of the re-united country" and its use might "stir up bad blood, and revive bitter memories." But even he noted that the government officials had been "very competent" in their duties and "fair in their treatment of Confederate as well as Federal reports and documents." By 1901 when the series had been printed in its entirety, white southerners could proclaim it an "invaluable memorial . . . the value of which in vindicating the truth of history cannot be overestimated."[12]

The Louisville-based *Southern Bivouac* began publication in 1882. Filled with soldiers' reminiscences and battle sketches, the magazine reflected its border-state origins. While committed to honoring the Confederate past, during its first three years the editors moved beyond the *SHSP*'s Lost Cause message, instead heralding a more pragmatic reconciliationist tone. The "good and brave deeds" of the war, wrote editor William N. McDonald, constituted a "precious heritage for our common country." Hoping to further such reconciliationist spirit, the periodical offered joint subscriptions with a Boston GAR monthly and by 1883 boasted of numerous Union veteran subscribers. "We never miss reading a single number," wrote an admiring excerpt from the Manchester (New Hampshire) *Union*, "to say that we thoroughly enjoy reading the 'other side' when so acceptably presented, is the simple truth. . . . The *Southern Bivouac* ought to find thousands of readers among the boys who wore the blue, as well as those who wore the gray."[13]

Despite its initial emphasis on reconciliation, the *Southern Bivouac* continued to promote a Confederate interpretation of the war. It would be left to another to take the reins as the leading Blue-Gray magazine. In November 1884, the first issue of *Century Magazine*'s serial *Battles and Leaders of the Civil War* appeared. Editors Robert Underwood Johnson and Clarence C. Buel had commissioned first-hand accounts from the highest-ranking living officers on both sides, including Union generals Grant, Sherman, McClellan, and Rosecrans as well as Confederate generals Johnston, Beauregard, Hood, Mosby, and Longstreet. Only a handful such as Sheridan and Early refused. The editors hoped to avoid controversy by omitting the "political questions," and they meticulously corroborated each essay with the War Department's *Official Records*. Conspicuously absent was any commentary on the causes and consequences of the war. Excluded were tales of combat horrors and the savagery of battle. Neither did the finger-pointing that had riddled *Annals* appear because of the editors' strict injunction that contributors avoid politics. Instead, readers found lavishly illustrated accounts of battlefield glory, valor, and heroism equally dispersed among Union and Confederate soldiers. Indeed, a growing audience of both veterans and the larger public appeared eager for such an account, clamoring to purchase copies that allowed them both to read about and visualize the war. Within six months the series circulation had nearly doubled from 127,000 to 225,000. Enlivened by its success, in 1888 the *Century* reproduced the series in an expanded four-volume set.[14]

Repeatedly and unabashedly, Johnson and Buel declared that they hoped the series might diffuse sectional tensions and promote reconciliation by "bringing about a better understanding between the soldiers who were opposed in that conflict."[15] "On the whole 'Battles and Leaders of the Civil War,'" Johnson asserted, "is a monument to American bravery, persistence and resourcefulness, and has the additional distinction of having struck the keynote of national unity through tolerance and the promotion of good will. We rightly judged that articles celebrating the skill and valor of both sides would hasten the elimination of sectional prejudices and contribute toward reuniting the country by the cultivation of mutual respect."[16] But such high ideals alone surely did not account for their message. Commercial presses were driven first and foremost by profit, and publishers recognized that appealing to the sentiments of both sections might sell more copies than those that touted an explicitly Union or Confederate memory. By avoiding contentious issues such as the war's causes and consequences (and even to a significant degree debates regarding prisoners of war), the editors and their veteran authors sterilized the war. As the title suggested, the series stripped the war of its horrors and perhaps even significance, distilling it down to a sanitized—and sellable— account of famous battles and their leaders.

While the *Century*'s canvassers spread out across the nation to sell subscriptions, Confederate veteran camps and GAR posts began to gather with their former enemies on battlefields and in cities north and south.[17] But there had been glimmerings of reconciliationist sentiment since the American centennial celebrations of 1875–76. The editor of *Scribner's* had beseeched northerners and southerners to see to it "that the Centennial heals all old wounds, reconciles all old differences, and furnishes the occasion for such a reunion of the great American nationality as shall make our celebration an expression of fraternal good will among all sections and all states."[18] Many veterans heeded his call. In April 1875, Confederate veterans from South Carolina and Virginia joined those from Massachusetts at the anniversary of the battle of Bunker Hill as the strains of "Auld Lang Syne" and "Dixie" mingled with the "shouts of a reunited and heartily reconciled people."[19] In the border region of Chattanooga, Tennessee, where the former foes called one another neighbor, Union and Confederate veterans gathered for a service in 1876, prompting the local newspaper to proclaim that "Chattanooga knows no North, no South, no East, no West," but only "one indivisible country."[20]

Twenty years after the Civil War and, perhaps more important, nearly a decade after Reconstruction, more veterans appeared ready to recall the most exciting and traumatic moments of their lives. Their reasons for doing so were diverse. Some longed to revisit the grounds where they had fought, while others relished the opportunity to travel to some distant city. Some found comfort in reunions with their former foes that they could not find among civilians who had never endured the war's trial by fire. Even if they had faced each other from opposite sides of the field, these men shared a powerful bond in the horrific moments they had survived. Others reasoned that the men who had shot at them might help them better understand their own experiences and help heal any lingering wounds. "I think that a better feeling would be engendered and demagoguism more thoroughly rebuked both north and south by frequent similar friendly greetings and sincerity of expression," wrote a New York veteran after visiting Richmond's Lee Camp in 1892.[21]

Regardless of their rationale for attending, the parameters of such Blue-Gray meetings were clear: veterans mutually (if silently) agreed not to discuss the causes or consequences of the war. Instead, they limited their reminiscences to the military campaigns between April 1861 and April 1865. They commiserated on the severity of camp life and marches—and repeatedly, almost ad nauseam, they commend each other for their bravery on the field of battle. "The events recorded are proofs that between the brave men, who for four long years faced and fought each other with a heroism without parallel, there exists no animosity," observed one typical publication.[22]

Such rhetoric was not merely reconciliationist in nature. For Union veterans this was not simply a means of appeasing or consoling their vanquished foe; rather, it served to bolster their own triumph. "The gallantry of the defense must be measured by the bravery and persistence of the assault," noted one member of Congress.[23] Neither was this sentiment lost on former Confederates. "What is the chief glory of the great army of the North?" asked the late Confederate secretary of the Treasury. "Is it not the military genius and valor of the men they defeated? Was it not great glory for Grant that it was Lee who surrendered his sword to him?"[24] Praising the valor and courage of their enemy served to boost Union veterans' claims of bravery and triumph. And yet such language simultaneously reinforced Lost Cause claims of northern numerical superiority. Continually assured by their former foes that they had fought courageously and valiantly, how could they attribute defeat to anything beyond northern resources? For both the victors and the losers, having a worthy adversary made the war's outcome more honorable.

It is imperative to remember that even as Blue-Gray meetings occurred with increasing frequency, they remained the exception rather than the norm.[25] Veterans from Philadelphia, Chicago, or Boston might travel south to meet with their former foes or welcome their southern brethren north once or twice a year. But the majority of veterans' time was spent in their own posts and camps where they cultivated the Union and Lost Causes that dominated their respective memories. Given the infrequent and celebratory nature of Blue-Gray reunions, the public displays and re-ports of reconciliationist gestures generated wide coverage by the press and the veterans.

As reports of the Blue-Gray reunions increasingly filled the pages of the nation's newspapers, men from both sides contended that soldiers, not politicians or those too young to have fought, were best suited to bind up the nation's wounds. Those who had sacrificed so much on the bloody fields and had endured the horrific sights and sounds of combat knew the cost—and benefits—of a peaceful reunion more than any others. Those who had shouldered the rifles and marched into the fiery face of death had suffered equally (if not for equal causes), and they were best equipped to lead the nation toward reconciliation. "Federal and Confederate, have laid aside both their arms and their bitterness, and having fought their differences out like *men*, now greet each other as fellow-*countrymen*, and point with pride to a common flag as the aegis of our liberties," proclaimed one Union general.[26] Consciously or not, veterans revealed the gendered nature of reconciliation. Wars were masculine, and despite the allegorical female figure of peace, reconciliation would likewise thrive in the mas-culine settings of camp halls, veterans' reunions, and former battlefields. As chapter 8 explores, women would find it exceedingly difficult to find a place within the male world of reconciliation.

While veterans increasingly reveled in memories of battlefield gallantry, they simultaneously began to invoke their dead comrades as symbols of a reunited and reconciled nation. With a timely bit of amnesia, many ap-peared to forget the bitter rancor that had surrounded the establishment of Federal and Confederate national cemeteries in 1865 and 1866. When members of the 2nd Rhode Island gathered to dedicate their monument at Gettysburg in 1886, Gen. Horatio Rogers recalled the field in the battle's aftermath: "Stricken men lay in myriads about us. Blue uniforms and gray were commingled there, the wearers having joined other ranks where those colors ceased to have significance."[27] Instead of the dead serving as reminders of the Union or Confederate cause, Rogers called upon his listeners to acknowledge the mutual sacrifice of both sides. Several years later, Governor Roswell P. Flower of New York observed that time had fur-thered this unity. Willfully forgetting that Union and Confederate veter-ans had been deliberately interred in separate cemeteries, Flower noted that "the same green sod covers the grave of Union soldier and Confed-erate soldier, and the firm texture which nature has woven over the dead bodies of those who were once in mortal conflict here, is symbolic of that close feeling of affection, sympathy, and respect which now binds together the people of the North and South."[28] Elsewhere, Union veterans invited Confederates to join in Memorial Day services and vice versa (albeit without their rebel flags and gray uniforms).[29] And in cemeteries where both the blue and gray slumbered, such as Chicago's Oakwood Cemetery that contained the graves of Confederate prisoners of war, it was increasingly common to find flowers strewn on all graves.[30] Heralding this newfound reconciliation, a New Jersey paper wondered: "Why should not those yet above the ground be friends, since those beneath it are at peace?"[31]

Perhaps no death proved more symbolic of the reunited nation than that of Ulysses S. Grant. On July 23, 1885, the retired general and former president's valiant fight against throat cancer ended. A week and a half later, Americans throughout the nation gathered to observe memorial services for the greatest of all Union heroes. But all eyes would be on New York, the site of the largest state funeral since Lincoln's. On August 8, a million and a half people lined the city's streets to witness the elaborate funeral procession that accompanied the fallen commander to his temporary tomb at Riverside Park. Among the 60,000 participants were 18,000 Union veterans, representing the GAR, Societies of the Army of the Potomac, the Army of the Cumberland, and the Army of the Tennessee. But this pageantry of woe was not for Union veterans alone. Instead, at the request of Grant's son Fred, President Grover Cleveland and Maj. Gen. Winfield Scott Hancock consciously framed the obsequies as a testament to reconciliation, inviting two ex-Confederate generals, Joseph Johnston and Simon B. Buckner, to serve as pallbearers alongside Union generals William T. Sherman and Philip H. Sheridan.[32] Confederate units represented by two companies of the First Virginia Regiment likewise found a prominent place in the procession, as did ex-Confederate soldiers residing in New York. Gen. Fitzhugh Lee, an ex-Confederate cavalry officer, nephew of Robert E. Lee, and Democratic candidate for governor in Virginia, accepted Hancock's invitation to act as an aide during the ceremonies, notwithstanding the criticisms he received from die-hard Confederates such as Jubal Early. "I accept the position," wrote Lee, "because by so doing I can testify my respect for the memory of a great soldier and thus return, as far as I can, the generous feelings he has expressed toward the soldiers of the South."[33]

In stark contrast to Lincoln's death, which had served to heighten sectional animosities, or that of Robert E. Lee, which had helped to enshrine the Lost Cause, eulogies and obituaries from across the nation heralded Grant's funeral as evidence that reconciliation had triumphed. Fitzhugh Lee suggested that the inclusion of ex-Confederates in the procession served as testimony that "the North and South are reunited forever." "If the War Did Not End in 1865," declared one headline the day after the funeral, "It Certainly Ended Yesterday."[34] In the pronouncements of former Confederates, this reconciliation had begun with Grant's magnanimous behavior at Appomattox. "We of the South," observed a New Orleans newspaper, "forget the stern General who hurled his terrible masses upon the ranks of our fathers and brothers, whose storm of shot and shell mowed down our friends like wheat before the gleaner, remembering only the manly soldier, who in the hour of triumph, displayed the knightly chivalry that robs defeat of its bitterest pang." Absent was any commentary on "Negro rule" or the "dark days of Reconstruction" under Grant's presidency. Instead, many white southerners stressed Grant's leniency and mercy in their hour of peril in the name of reconciliation.[35]

In the wake of Grant's death, this forgetting blossomed into the myth of Appomattox. Electing to overlook the rancor and humiliation of the day, Confederate veterans reimagined the surrender's fraternal camaraderie and the instantaneous termination of sectional animosities. "As my command, in worn-out shoes and ragged uniforms, but with proud mien, moved to the designated point to stack their arms and surrender their cherished battle-flags, they challenged the admiration of the brave victors," UCV commander John B. Gordon remembered. Recalling Union general Joshua Chamberlain as one of the "knightliest soldiers of the Federal army," Gordon remembered how the "veterans in blue gave a soldierly salute to those vanquished heroes—a token of respect from Americans to Americans."[36] Chamberlain likewise recollected his respect for the defeated rebel soldiers: "We could not look into those brave, bronzed faces, and those battered flags we had met on so many fields where glorious manhood lent a glory to the earth that bore it and think of personal hate and mean revenge."[37] In the memories of both sides, Union armies had provided rations for starving Confederate troops, Lee's sword had been magnanimously returned by Grant, and Union soldiers had saluted their fallen foes at the surrender parade.[38] According to this legend, Appomattox was a special place, for there peace had been secured among not Union and Confederate soldiers, but American soldiers.

It was this "Americanness" that proved an especially vital element of reconciliation. At nearly every Blue-Gray reunion, speakers from both sides lauded the "American traits" of courage and honor to dedicate the fields where "American met American" in bloody struggle.[39] During the war both northerners and southerners had conceived of themselves as the true Americans perpetuating the founding fathers' legacy. Both had maintained that they were Americans, either of the United States or the Confederate States (it was their foe whom they described as decidedly un-American). But three decades later, focusing on their common "American" heritage allowed veterans and politicians to avoid the divisive political issues of the conflict while commemorating the best of white northern and southern society.

Emphasizing the valor of both Union and Confederate soldiers also fostered a belief in American exceptionalism. "Here charges which none but American soldiers could have made were met and repulsed as none but American troops could have done," remarked a Union veteran of Gettysburg.[40] The very process of reconciliation served as testimony of America's greatness. When a Chicago-based GAR post dedicated a monument to Confederate prisoners of war—a Lost Cause monument on northern soil—in 1895, former Confederate general Wade Hampton remarked that such a scene "could not be witnessed in any country but our own." Though the same men had stood facing each other in battle only years earlier, they now "proudly claim Federal and Confederate soldiers as Americans, men who have given to the world as noble examples of courage and devotion to duty as can be found enrolled on the page of history."[41] In what other nation, torn asunder by violent civil war, could a people reunite with such rapidity? Neglecting to remember the bloodletting that continued by guerrillas in the border regions after 1865, not to mention the murders of African Americans throughout Reconstruction, white Union and Confederate veterans crafted a memory of an easy peace that sanctified not only their history, but also their future.

If veterans were the chief unifying symbol and the focus of most reconciliationist pageantry, business interests likewise formed a powerful coalition dedicated to eliminating sectional rancor. Speaking at the 1880 Atlanta Cotton Exposition, former Massachusetts cotton mill executive (and Free-Soil Party member) Edward Atkinson urged citizens of the two sections to visit each other to further their economic development. In doing so, they would "become convinced that in their mutual inter-dependence is the foundation of their true union."[42] The exposition's Atlanta-based director, Hannibal Kimball, another businessman who remained a civilian during the war, believed that the exposition itself would help in "obliterating from the minds and hearts of the people all the remains of sectionalism, and in opening up a knowledge of the South to capital, labor, invention, and commerce."[43] But veterans too championed renewed business ties. "We invite you to invade us again," noted former Confederate general Stephen Lee at Chicago in 1895, "not this time with your bayonets, but with your business. Let the voice of your commercial traveler be heard in our land, the flying columns of your goods push into our furthermost strongholds, and the smile of the tourists make glad the [rest] places of our health resorts."[44]

Northerners and southerners recognized that a commercially unified nation would be well positioned to take its place on the world stage. The Gilded Age's rapid industrialization, technological advances such as steamship travel, and the official closing of the frontier had increased the appeal of foreign markets and colonies. By 1890, the federal government had already become involved in affairs in distant lands ranging from Samoa to the Hawaiian Islands. And for years, tales of Spanish atrocities against the Cubans had enlivened the bellicose posturing of imperialists. Together, Americans might become a world power.[45] With the "Union preserved; the nationality established; slavery destroyed," declared one northern periodical, "we are to be henceforth one people with one flag" and therefore able to "ignore the past and set our faces toward the future, to work out together our manifest destiny."[46] Some individuals embraced these sentiments at face value. But countless others recognized that employing the language of reconciliation ennobled their financial and political objectives with a grander meaning.

Such frequent refrains calling on Americans to look forward and not to the past underscored the extent to which reconciliation was an arduous undertaking. The conscious and concerted efforts by veterans, boosters, and politicians in arenas well beyond Blue-Gray reunions to wipe out sectionalism testified to the extent of bitterness that remained in the 1880s and 1890s. Reconciliation, they realized, often had to be crafted, cajoled, and compromised. It did not simply flow from the common bond of an American heritage, like-minded goals, or even race (as the next chapter discusses). Instead, reconciliation was often hard work.

While many worked diligently to foster a strong American nation, northerners and southerners held their own interpretations of reconciliation. For northerners, the triumph of reunion and reconciliation *was* the Union cause. Northern soldiers had fought to preserve the principles established by the founding fathers that set the United States apart from other nations. They had fought to prevent secession, to restore the Constitution as the supreme law of the land. They had fought to reunite a nation shattered by slavery. And they had won. "The Union has been maintained. We are one people in fact. . . . Should we not be in feeling?" asked veterans of the Army of the Potomac as early as 1875. It was reunion, after all, which allowed northerners to embrace reconciliation. "We at the North," declared a Cincinnati newspaper, "can afford to be liberal, inasmuch as we were the victors in the armed contest."[47] Just as Grant could offer generous and magnanimous terms at Appomattox, twenty years and more after the war the triumphant North would be willing to forgive the errant southerners for their mistakes. Mercy was in the hands of the victors.

Yet even decades after the war, U.S. veterans continued to grapple with the paradoxical feelings of a longing for national unity and lingering sectional rancor.[48] When a GAR comrade proposed making April 9 a national holiday to celebrate the Confederate surrender at Appomattox and emancipation of the slaves during the 1892 national encampment, a heated debate ensued. "Let us not perpetuate the humiliating spectacle of our descendants rejoicing over the brave men who went down in honorable battle and surrendered to us," counseled Washington Gardner of Michigan. "We fought for the Nation, not for the North, and we want the Nation undivided in sentiment and loyal to a common flag from the gulf to the lakes and from Maine to California," he declared.[49] But this did not mean that Union veterans had forgotten the transgressions of their former foes. "Though we, as citizens, hold former soldiers of the South as our dearest friends, it is another matter when we don the blue," Gen. John W. Noble declared amid discussions for a Blue-Gray reunion. He would never consent to sharing dignity or a place of honor with Confederate veterans at a parade or any other ceremony. "It would be admitting that the United States had made its strides forward since the Civil War because of the rebellion, and forgetting the fact that we have risen in spite of the internecine struggle. We must continue to assert that right triumphed," he avowed. "That cannot be buried."[50] Northerners might forgive, but they would not forget. There would never cease to be "right and wrong" in the war. Here was no reconciliation based on acquiescence to the Lost Cause.[51]

In embracing a vision of a reunited America, Confederate veterans were buying into—consciously or not—at least part of the Union cause. Of course most refused to concede anything of the sort. Instead, former Confederates interpreted Blue-Gray reunions and like gestures as evidence that their cause had been vindicated. Speaking before the AANVA in 1895, Clement Evans celebrated the fact that sectional strife had been buried and true peace had been established. Yet even as he seemingly eschewed sectionalism, Evans carefully elucidated how the Union as now celebrated had been crafted primarily by southerners. "Your Union, my countrymen, developed into its present form, your Constitution, which is the palladium of your rights as States or as people, and all the privileges you enjoy in this free Commonwealth are due at least in equal measure to the energy, the valor, the wisdom and the patriotism of Southern men," he argued.[52] George L. Christian pushed this logic even further. "It is just in proportion as we are true and loyal to the cause of the South, that we will be true and faithful citizens of our country to-day," he declared, "because the principles for which the Confederate soldiers fought, are the only ones on which constitutional liberty can ever rest in this, or any other country."[53] In their rendering, the Lost Cause was the American Cause. Even if Confederates had failed to establish a separate government, the principles of individual liberty, state sovereignty, and anti-centralization still lived.[54] When Union veterans suggested otherwise, ex-Confederates were simultaneously outraged, appalled, and more determined than ever to prove their cause had been just.

EVERLASTINGLY AND ETERNALLY WRONG

For those who believed that the pageantry of Grant's funeral symbolized a reunited and even reconciled nation, events of the spring and summer of 1887 quickly revealed otherwise. Two years earlier, Grover Cleveland had become the first Democrat, and first nonveteran, to occupy the White House since the war. Elected in large part by the solid South, Cleveland had doled out cabinet offices, diplomatic postings, and even Supreme Court appointments to numerous ex-Confederates such as Lucius Q. C. Lamar. Given this atmosphere, in April 1887, U.S. Army Adj. Gen. R. C. Drum suggested that the more than 550 flags captured from Confederates during the war be returned to their respective states. "Over twenty years have elapsed since the termination of the late war," Drum wrote the secretary of war. "Many of the prominent leaders, civil and military, of the late Confederate States are now honored representatives of the people in national councils." Should not the War Department return the flags? Cleveland concurred, authorizing the adjutant general to write southern governors and arrange the flags' return.[55]

As word spread that the battle flags were to be returned, indignation among the GAR ran rampant. "May God palsy the hand that wrote the order," thundered Lucius Fairchild, the one-armed commander-in-chief of the GAR at a meeting in New York. "May God palsy the brain that conceived it, and may God palsy the tongue that dictated it." In all his travels to GAR posts, Fairchild had never heard anything but kindly words expressed toward former rebels, he noted, and he in turn had tried to encourage this feeling. But the president's directive had changed this. If the order remained, he felt confident that 350,000 GAR men would "rise as one man in solemn protest against any such disposition of the trophies won at such fearful sacrifice of blood." Leaping to their feet amid shouts of "hurrah," those present heartily endorsed his blistering attack.[56] So did Federal veterans across the nation. The governors of Ohio, Iowa, Nebraska, and New York joined GAR departments from Wisconsin and elsewhere in denouncing the order. A Kansas newspaper reeled in anger, observing that the Lost Cause already appeared to be eclipsing the Union Cause. "Gradually, but steadily and surely, the soldiers of the Union are being robbed of every honor they won," the paper lamented. Confederate veterans seemed privy to any government position they desired, and ex-rebels represented the United States in foreign capitals. "It is beginning to be a question difficult to determine whether it was Ulysses S. Grant or Robert E. Lee who surrendered at Appomattox," quipped one newspaper. Returning the captured flags to the late rebel states only confirmed this.[57] "All were unanimous," declared a Milwaukee newspaper, "that as an effort to bring the South and North 'closer together,' it was the most foolish thing that could have been done."[58] Inundated with letters labeling him a "viper," "traitor," and "skulker" (referencing Cleveland's hiring of a substitute during the war), the president rescinded his authorization in mid-June.[59]

The timing of this renewed sectional acrimony could not have been worse for one of the most anticipated Blue-Gray reunions to date. Earlier in the spring, Confederate veterans of Gen. George E. Pickett's division agreed to meet with some of their former adversaries in Gen. Alexander S. Webb's Philadelphia brigade at Gettysburg—the first Blue-Gray meeting on the hallowed field. But tensions among the veterans nearly thwarted the reunion. Some Virginians openly questioned the loyalty of their brethren who agreed to attend. Debates among Union veterans were more visceral. When several northerners proposed returning three Confederate flags to Pickett's men as a gesture of reconciliation, former general Benjamin F. Butler argued that the flag was "an 'archive,' an evidence of victory," that should not be returned. Reports that the rebels would place a memorial behind Union lines, at the so-called High Water Mark of the Confederacy, however, caused a ruckus among northerners. John Bachelder of the Gettysburg Battlefield Memorial Association received "bushels of letters" opposing any such memorial, while Governor Joseph B. Foracker threatened to use the Ohio National Guard "to prevent such sacrilege."[60] Not surprisingly, Fairchild adamantly denounced the reunion. Given such animosity, the Virginians unanimously agreed not to attend. Only an open letter from the Philadelphia Brigade Association and a concession to mark the spot reached by Pickett's men during their now famous charge convinced them otherwise.[61]

On July 2, 1887, nearly 500 Philadelphia Brigade veterans and their families arrived in Gettysburg to welcome some 200 former foes. In the sweltering heat, the veterans listened to countless speeches extolling the greatness and glory of all Americans exhibited on the hallowed field. LaSalle Corbell Pickett, widow of General Pickett, became the central attraction of the day, hosting a reception on the ground over which her husband's division had charged and signing autographs for Union and Confederate veterans alike. The *New York Times* rejoiced in the day's camaraderie, while other northern papers pointed to the reunion as evidence that the bitter sectionalism espoused by Fairchild was confined to a minority. Southern newspapers likewise celebrated the good feelings. As a Confederate veteran wrote to a New Orleans paper, "Henceforth and forever southern chivalry and northern valor shall stand shoulder to shoulder in defense of one common country."[62]

The approaching silver anniversary of the battle in 1888, however, revealed that not all Union veterans embraced the Philadelphia Brigade's spirit of reconciliation. Many lamented that Pickett's charge was eclipsing the Union victory on the field, while others grew increasingly angry that the victory's cost was being forgotten amid the Blue-Gray lovefest. One Union veteran counseled former Confederates that "the hallowed field of Gettysburg is no place to vaunt treason and glorify rebellion." He was perfectly content that the ex-rebels "stay at home and gnaw the file of discontent in obscurity."[63] And stay home they did. While nearly 20,000 Union veterans and their families crowded the field in 1888 to dedicate monuments and rejoice in their most famous triumph, most Confederates elected not to attend. Even LaSalle Pickett sent her regrets. Northerners hostile to national reconciliation rejoiced. Addressing a GAR post atop Little Round Top, Gen. J. P. S. Gobin declared that he for one was "tired of this gush and pretense for the glorification of the veteran simply because he wore a gray uniform with a Southern flag printed on his badge. That badge meant treason and rebellion in 1861, and what it meant then it means now." "I want it to be distinctly understood, now and for all time," he bellowed, "that the men who wore the gray were everlastingly and eternally wrong."[64]

Later that year, even the Philadelphia Brigade's commitment to reconciliation would be tested. Hoping to expand on the good feelings of the 1887 reunion, the Virginians invited the Philadelphians to visit Richmond in October to help dedicate a monument to Pickett. Those Union veterans who had opposed the Gettysburg ceremonies failed to understand what would compel the Philadelphia Brigade to participate in such rites. Some Virginians likewise objected to the invitation, citing the debacle over placing a monument to Pickett at Gettysburg. And as some predicted, the dedication became highly politicized when the quest for an orator proved exceedingly difficult. The military parade, however, reverberated with explosive tension. Several prominent Virginia veterans' groups refused to send delegations because they objected to the participation of both the Philadelphia Brigade and the Philip Kearney GAR Post 10 (made up of Union veterans who resided in Virginia). On the morning of the parade, when the Philadelphia Brigade witnessed the Virginians lining up beneath the Confederate ensign, the U.S. veterans pointedly refused to participate. Pointing to the Stars and Stripes that they carried, one Union soldier explained that they had borrowed the flag under the condition that it "not be used in procession with a 'rebel' flag." Former Confederate and Richmond mayor J. Taylor Ellyson managed to save the day, offering a compromise: the Philadelphia Brigade would not march with their borrowed flag, but neither would the Stars and Bars be displayed. Instead, Union and Confederate veterans would march under the U.S. flag that belonged to the Lee Camp of Confederate Veterans. The procession and dedication proceeded without further controversy, but the Confederate veterans would not soon forget the insult.[65]

Such acerbic sectionalism compelled Union veterans Henry Van Ness Boynton and Ferdinand Van DerVeer to call for the preservation of another battlefield, one that would be established on the premise of national reconciliation. In their telling, the idea occurred to the two Army of the Cumberland veterans as they traversed the former battlefield of Chickamauga that same summer, electing to remember the silver anniversary of their army's bloodiest battle. In August, Boynton, a lieutenant colonel in the 35th Ohio Infantry during the battle, penned a series of articles in a Midwestern newspaper, imploring his former comrades to preserve the notable field. "Why should it not, as well as the Eastern fields, be marked by monuments, and its lines accurately preserved for history?" Chickamauga was exceptional, he claimed. "There was no more magnificent fighting during the war than both armies did there." Hoping to move beyond the sectional bitterness that still seemed to hold sway at Gettysburg, he suggested that at Chickamauga "both sides might well unite in preserving the field where both, in a military sense, won such renown."[66]

In September, Boynton and Van DerVeer presented their idea at the annual meeting of the Society of the Army of the Cumberland. The veterans found the notion compelling and appointed a committee to report back the following year. Enlivened by the support, Boynton worked tirelessly on his propaganda campaign. As the Washington correspondent for the *Cincinnati Commercial Gazette*, he continued to send articles to Ohio. But he also reached out to former Confederates, requesting individual officers to support the endeavor and entreating the *Southern Historical Society Papers* to publish his appeal. Gettysburg had been established exclusively by (and many argued for) northerners. Only the position of the Army of the Potomac had been marked, while the marble, granite, and bronze statuary erected on the field in the 1870s and 1880s served as poignant reminders that Gettysburg was an exclusively Union memorial park.[67] Chickamauga would be different. Not only would it honor both a Confederate and Union victory, but, men like Boynton hoped, it would be funded and directed by the national government rather than a private corporation or a handful of states. Moreover, its location in two former Confederate states was sure to garner support from southern congressmen. This park, unlike Gettysburg, would honor Union and Confederate veterans "with equal satisfaction."[68]

On September 19, 1889, the intersectional Chickamauga Memorial Association held its first official meeting at Chattanooga. Gathered under a large tent, more than 12,000 veterans listened intently to speeches by Union general William Rosecrans and former Confederate general John B. Gordon, who emphasized unity and lauded the idea for a national park at Chickamauga as a symbol of the nation's healed wounds.[69] Heralded by his comrades as the man responsible for the proposed park, Boynton likewise took the stage that day. Like the others, he reminded his audience of Chickamauga's importance, of its astronomical casualty rate, and the heroics of its assaults—assaults far more daring and commendable than Pickett's Charge at Gettysburg. "There is no other field of the war which more fully illustrates the indomitable courage and all the varied qualities of the American veteran," he asserted. Here the lines of both armies would be equally marked along with monuments from each of the states who had sons in the fight. "We meet here, surviving veterans of that field," he declared, "under one flag, citizens of one country, to celebrate and take measures to perpetuate the memory of the fighting which will cause Chickamauga to take first rank among the battles of the world."[70]

Like his fellow veterans, Boynton sought a spirit of sectional cooperation and comradeship. This was indeed a significant part of the impetus behind the park movement. But such did not mean that he had forgotten why they had waged such a bloody battle twenty-six years earlier. "I yield to no man an iota of my convictions," he firmly stated. "They are as dear

1st Massachusetts monument at Gettysburg immediately after being raised. When it was dedicated in July 1886, Gettysburg remained almost exclusively a Union memorial park. (Gettysburg National Military Park-T-1969)

to me, as clear in my mind, as when we fought for them." He had not forgotten the Union cause. Neither did he expect the Confederates to forget theirs. He insisted that these were differences that need not be discussed. Questions of politics and blame did not belong. Such might threaten the very premise of national reconciliation that was central to the proposed park. Instead, the park project should emphasize "American fighting" and "the achievements of American manhood" performed by each side on the field at Chickamauga.[71] This was to be a national park established on the premise of sectional harmony.[72] On August 20, 1890, President Benjamin Harrison, a former Union general, signed the bill into law establishing the nation's first military park.[73]

The reconciliationist spirit may have prompted the park, but it did nothing to suppress the growing Lost Cause. Instead, during the same years that reconciliationist sentiment peaked on the national stage, enthusiasm for all things Confederate soared. The UCV had formed only in 1889, but by 1896, 850 camps claimed membership. Three years later, it could boast more than 1,200 camps from each of the eleven Confederate states as well as posts in Illinois, Missouri, and California. At the height of its membership in 1903, there would be 1,523 camps and approximately 80,000 members.[74]

With a constituency stretching from Texas to Virginia and beyond, the UCV sought a periodical to keep its ever-growing base informed. In 1894, the *Confederate Veteran*, a monthly magazine established the previous year by former Confederate soldier S. A. Cunningham, fulfilled that need. The *Confederate Veteran* proved to be a far different sort of publication than the *Southern Historical Society Papers*. Markedly cheaper than the *SHSP* (initially fifty cents per issue as compared to three dollars), the *Veteran* was much more accessible to a mass audience. But perhaps more important, where the *SHSP* had been filled with lengthy articles on military and constitutional issues, the *Veteran* offered briefer, illustrated stories about both the war and efforts to commemorate it. As Cunningham observed, it was published more for those "who were not in the War, since its contents will make them more patriotic and prouder of their ancestry."[75] Veterans, their wives, and children penned pieces about troops and leaders, but they also contributed articles about monument dedications, reminiscences of old soldiers, essay contests for children, veterans' obituaries, as well as news of the UCV and its corollary organizations, the United Daughters of the Confederacy (formed in 1894) and the United Sons of Confederate Veterans (formed in 1896 and later called the Sons of Confederate Veterans). By December 1894, circulation surpassed 7,000, and by 1902 a reported

22,000 copies were being delivered to the homes and businesses of Confederate veterans and their families, making it the largest southern-based periodical. In the pages of the *Veteran* (which continued publication until 1932, when the Great Depression finally ended its proud run) and amid the flurry of monuments that seemed to spring forth from the ground, the Confederate cause flourished.[76] The Lost Cause was hardly lost—it gloried in its heyday.

During the 1860s and 1870s, Confederate memory had evolved as a response to the Union Cause and Reconstruction. By the last two decades of the century the divisive Reconstruction policies had been largely swept under the rug, but reconciliationist gestures ensured that memories of the war would still be on display. With every parade of Union veterans, every handshake across the bloody chasm, and every reference to the noble Union cause, former Confederates responded in kind—cultivating, nurturing, and guarding their own memory of the conflict.

Robert E. Lee had long served as the epitome of the Lost Cause, but never was this more apparent—and more repugnant to northerners—than when Richmonders unveiled a large equestrian statue to their hero in 1890. Even before the unveiling, rumors had swirled through the North that southerners intended to ban the U.S. flag in favor of state flags and the Confederate banner. Celebrating secession, the states were to be arranged in the procession by the order in which they seceded. Incensed, one New York newspaper proposed that Congress ban all monuments to rebel leaders and the display of the Confederate flag. Union veterans from Palestine, Illinois, hastened a telegram to President Harrison earnestly protesting such a flagrant display of defiance. Quoting Andrew Johnson, they declared that "treason must be made odious." The Indianapolis *Journal* concurred. The demonstration in Richmond, it noted, "is to be deplored because it will tend to restore the old South, and to make the generation now coming into control of the South adherents of the lost cause of the Confederacy rather than American patriots."[77] The GAR balked: when compared to Grant and other Union generals, it said, Lee had accomplished nothing to warrant the preposterous memorial. "That he was a military genius," the GAR observed, "nobody, except one poisoned with the virus of rebellion, will claim."[78] For at least some northerners, one could not be both a Lost Cause advocate and a loyal American.

Such outcries did not prevent the largest Confederate crowd to date from gathering. That May, more than 100,000 people from all parts of the South traveled to Richmond, where they were greeted by miles of bunting, portraits of Washington and Lee, and thousands of waving Confederate *and* American flags. The parade of nearly 20,000 marched west out of the city, past Lee's former residence on Franklin Street, accompanied by bands playing "Dixie" and other southern tunes. At the lead as chief marshal was former Confederate general and Virginia governor Fitzhugh Lee. Behind him more than forty other officers, including Joseph Johnston, James Longstreet, Jubal Early, and John Gordon, as well as the governors of every former Confederate state, rode or marched alongside the rank-and-file veterans. Addressing the concerns expressed by northern papers, the *New York Times* observed, "On no occasion has there been more of genuine loyalty and devotion to the Union than displayed to-day." The monument was not meant to incite rebellion by honoring Lee. Indeed, the paper editorialized, Lee had been brave and honorable: "His memory is, therefore, a possession of the American people."[79]

Yet unlike the battlefield dedications or even the unveiling of Grant's Monument at New York in 1897, this was not an intersectional occasion.[80] Secretary of the Navy Benjamin F. Tracy refused to allow the Marine Band to participate, and the 7th New York Regiment, who had hosted a Richmond regiment during the centennial, declined to attend.[81] In a testament to the divergent attitudes of the generations, the older men—those who had served in the Union ranks—were less amenable to attending than were younger men. Not only would the occasion be held a day prior to national Memorial Day, but many of the veterans felt that there would be much more involved "in the undertaking than a mere pleasure excursion." Recognizing Lee as a great military man was one thing, but, as one officer noted, northern men should never forget that his achievements were obtained while fighting in a rebellion against the national government. Perhaps more important, those who rejected the invitation did so because they could not be "assured that the sentiments expressed by the orators of the day on that occasion will not be diametrically opposed to the genius of the union of States." "We cannot afford to give even moral support or countenance to any sentiment which shall seem to uphold the 'lost cause,'" they maintained.[82] This would be a Confederate-only affair. For white southerners, the Lost Cause was the primary memory of the war and they would not shirk from embracing it.

As much as they objected to the Lee Monument, efforts to venerate Jefferson Davis caused an unbridled furor among Union veterans.[83] Many had long despised the Confederate president whom they held responsible above all others for igniting the war and the unbelievable horrors of prisoner-of-war camps. But his unexpected death in New Orleans in December 1889 and the massive funeral that followed unleashed a torrent of vitriol. "At last Jeff Davis is dead," rejoiced the *Grand Army Record*; "we are finding no fault with the Lord on that account."[84] The *National Tribune* likewise exulted in his demise. Not only had he led the cold-blooded plot to "drench a prosperous and peaceful land with fraternal gore," but since Appomattox he had continued to utter his wickedness. He could not have died too soon. Other U.S. veterans were outraged by the elaborate, state-like funeral that attracted more than 20,000 grief-stricken white southerners. After learning that approximately forty GAR members marched behind the Confederate cavalry in the funeral procession, the national encampment court-martialed and removed the Department of Mississippi, Alabama, and Louisiana commander Jacob Gray.[85] The Elwood Hill Post of Indiana implored the loyal people of the nation to protest in unmeasured terms the demonstrations in honor of the arch traitor. The rebel flag draped over Davis's remains could only be construed as calculated to honor treason and dishonor loyalty, they declared.[86]

The Elwood Hill Post's outrage over Davis's rebel flag-draped coffin captured the intense hatred many Union veterans still felt toward the Confederate ensign. Speaking for countless others, George M. Finch of the Ohio MOLLUS castigated the Confederate flag as "a treasonable emblem" flown in "insulting defiance."[87] Like a veteran of the 64th New York Infantry, many Union men felt that even though the Stars and Stripes flew proudly over the reunited nation, "the flag of treason should be suppressed, for the reason that it is a constant menace to perpetual peace."[88] Given the mounting animosity generated by the banner, in 1891 the GAR's commander-in-chief issued an order declaring that any member who recognized that "emblem of traitors and disloyalty" by marching or appearing alongside it was untrue to his obligations as a member of the Grand Army.[89] A true, proud Union veteran would never march under the flag of treason—even in the name of reconciliation.

Even more than they detested Confederate monuments and the rebel flag, Union veterans abhorred the thought that white southerners were winning the textbook battle raging in classrooms across the nation. No doubt still fulminating from the flag flap, at the national GAR encampment in 1888 Lucius Fairchild accused several publishers of glossing over the causes of the war and neglecting to differentiate between "right" and "wrong." These pro-Confederate histories justified secession, upheld the theory that the Union was a voluntary compact of states, attacked Lincoln as a warmonger, and charged that Union armies had been composed of immigrant mercenaries—all the while avoiding the word "rebellion" and upholding Confederate leaders as bastions of virtue, patriotism, and loyalty.[90] "There is no more injustice and no more injury being done than by some of the text books that are being used, which hold up Stonewall Jackson and Robert E. Lee as the exemplars of American valor," declared John Vanderslice of Pennsylvania.[91] To combat such distortions, in 1891 the GAR established a committee charged with monitoring school history texts. Educating the next generation would be critical to their mission of Fraternity, Charity, and Loyalty.[92]

In 1894, the GAR took special aim at Ellis's *Complete History of the United States*, a text being used in several northern public schools. "Its tone is biased in favor of treason and the cause of the South," observed Posts 2 and 19 of Philadelphia in a circular addressed to the entire GAR. While the text omitted the names of many Union heroes, it "persistently and conspicuously depicts in strong colors the achievements of the rebel commanders and their armies." Nowhere did the word "rebellion" or "treason" appear. By omitting the war's causes, the GAR men believed that this "insidious work . . . vilely belittles and aims to detract from the fidelity, courage, and patriotic work performed by the soldiers of the Union armies." Most problematic, however, was the text's refusal to pronounce the South wrong. Such neutrality was unthinkable. No true history could portray the two causes as equally just and honorable. As the GAR saw it, the Union Cause was the *only* righteous cause. If the nation and its ideals were to survive, future generations must be taught the truth.[93]

Confederates were no less weary of the pro-northern propaganda they feared would be used to sully their memory among future generations. "The shrewd, calculating and wealthy Northerners realized the importance of trying to impress the rising generation with the justice of their cause," observed former Confederate George L. Christian, "and to that end they soon flooded our schools with histories, containing their version of the contest, and in many of these 'all the blame' is laid on the South."[94] "Too much history has already been written for us—too little has been written by ourselves, and for the justification of our people," added Capt. Francis W. Dawson at a reunion of Maryland soldiers in 1887. "It is, then, but meet and right that, on such an occasion as this, the truth shall be told, and the whole truth, even if it hurt the feelings of 'our friends, the enemy.'"[95]

Only a year after the GAR deputized a committee to supervise school texts, the UCV followed suit, forming a historical committee to condemn all "untrue" history books. Headed by Gen. Stephen Lee of Mississippi, throughout the 1890s the group protested nearly every northern-written account of the war. In 1895, the UCV petitioned southern legislatures and school boards to adopt only texts approved by the committee. The state history committee of Virginia heeded the committee's advice, demanding that school texts declare secession legal and insist that Confederate soldiers were neither rebels nor traitors. Under such strictures, they convinced the state board of education to drop Barnes's *A Brief History of the United States* in favor of works by southern writers Susan P. Lee and J. William Jones.[96]

Instilling a reverence for the Confederacy among future generations was not confined to schoolrooms. Memorial Days, monuments located in the center of southern towns, and veterans' reunions all provided ample opportunities to educate children on the Lost Cause. But plenty of instructing went on in less formal occasions as well. Certainly many veterans elected not to talk about the horrors they had seen or even the causes of the war, but others reminisced at family gatherings and conversations with their children and grandchildren. Countless white southerners could no doubt relate to Katherine Du Pre Lumpkin's observation that she was "reared in a home where the Confederacy is revered as a cause, holy and imperishable."[97]

It was not just that white southerners sought to defend and explain their actions to their children; some adamantly decried the immorality of the Union Cause. The North's "cause seems to me as bad as it well could be," declared the ever-contentious George L. Christian before the Grand Army of Confederate Veterans of Virginia in 1898. "The determination of a mere numerical majority to enforce a bond, which they themselves had flagrantly violated, to impose their own arbitrary will, their idea of national greatness, upon a distinct, independent, determined and almost unanimous people. The North fought for an empire which was not and never had been hers." Invoking language that had been standard during the war, Christian reminded his audience of the "outrage inflicted upon this defenseless people by the mercenary hordes of the North, permitted and encouraged by the remorseless cruelty and unquenchable ambition of some of their leaders."[98] The Reverend J. W. Stevens, chaplain of Hood's Texas Brigade, likewise failed to find any valor or common brotherhood with Union men. Confederates had fought for the constitutional principles of their forefathers. They had fought a purely defensive war against "the onslaught of an insolent, invading host, whose battle cry was devastation and hatred, and whose line of march was marked by the smoke of devastated homes and burned towns and cities."[99] How could any sensible person fail to see that the South's cause was honorable while that of the Yankees was without moral worth?

Other former Confederates could not abide even the sight of Union veterans, much less imagine cooperating in the Blue-Gray lovefest. Confederate general Lafayette McLaws seethed at the mere presence of his former foes, especially in the South. Thirty years after Appomattox, he was indignant that "these Bummers" had established GAR posts throughout the former Confederacy "with total disregard of the proprieties and decencies of life and respect due to the feelings of those among whom they are living." They "proceed to glorify themselves for the victories they assisted," and then, he noted, they had the "barefaced audacity" to request that white southerners join them in decorating the graves of both armies. To "join in such mockery" would degrade him, insult the dead, and deride the Confederate cause.[100]

Speaking before a group of Florida veterans, the Honorable John S. Beard explained why former Confederates fought so tenaciously to defend and promote their cause. "Such persistent efforts have been made to fasten upon the South the stigma, and to impress posterity with the conviction, that the Southern States were in rebellion and that the Southern patriots were traitors," he observed.[101] Here he touched upon a truth that historians of Civil War memory have largely overlooked: Confederate veterans would not have had to be so vocal if Union veterans were not constantly declaring that *they* had fought the righteous cause, that the moral worth was on *their* side. If true reconciliation had occurred—reconciliation in which both sides agreed to remain silent on the causes of the war—these fierce debates would not have existed. Indeed, many veterans on both sides tried to embrace reconciliation. But doing so did not mean forgetting. On the contrary, gestures of reconciliation reminded both Confederate and Union veterans how fiercely they needed to protect their own memories of the war.

THE MASON AND DIXON LINE
HAS BEEN WIPED OFF THE MAP

By the mid-1880s, Americans could find ample evidence of the reconciliationist spirit well beyond the expected venues of Blue-Gray reunions. In contrast to many Memorial Day speeches or the attitudes expressed at GAR and UCV meetings, popular culture proved an overwhelmingly fruitful source of reconciliationist sentiment. Plays like *The Blue and the Gray* (1884), Bronson Howard's *Shenandoah* (1889), and Augustus Thomas's *Alabama* (1891) brought the story of a reconciled North-South to the stage. Novels and popular songs recounted romantic renderings of the plantation South and fierce military battles. Even the *Ladies' Home Journal* burst forth with pro-Southern sentiment, praising the South as the "heart of America." The region remained a place where "men and women are guided in their action by wholesome sentiment, where people live righteously, where the best of our customs are perpetuated, [and] our own language is spoken by all."[102] Perhaps no metaphor heralded the conciliatory process more than that of romantic love threatened by sectional discord. The formula for countless plays and novels rested on a gendered framework in which once rebellious southern women ultimately became the compliant wives of northern men. Seemingly depoliticizing the war and its aftermath, the romance of reunion suggested that sentiment was the most important factor for healing the sectional divide.[103]

On the political stage, like the Liberal Republicans of 1872 and former Union general Winfield Scott Hancock's 1880 Democratic presidential campaign, the new Populist Party urged Americans to transcend the war's sectional passions.[104] Insisting on a policy of forgetfulness, Populists lambasted newspapers and magazines that printed sentimental tales of the war, arguing that such stories only kept the American people divided.[105] In 1891, Leonidas Polk, president of the Southern Alliance, reminded voters that the modern struggle was unlike that of twenty-five years ago: "The gigantic struggle of today is between the classes and masses." "In the appalling presence of such an issue," he advised, "buried and forgotten forever be the prejudices, animosities, and estrangements of that unfortunate war."[106] The following year, the party attempted to harness the symbolism of a reunited nation by selecting Union general James B. Weaver and one-legged Confederate veteran James G. Field as its presidential ticket.[107] Four years later, Union veteran and Republican presidential candidate William McKinley borrowed from the Populists' playbook—but with much more success. Rather than urging voters to forget the war, McKinley's campaign mobilized the war's memory to emphasize a renewed nationalism premised on sectional reconciliation. Speaking before a group of Confederate veterans in October 1896, McKinley averred, "Let us remember now and in all the future that we are Americans, and what is good for Ohio is good for Virginia."[108]

There were other less partisan and unexpected signs of reconciliation. In 1895, Indianapolis newspaper editor and pension attorney Philander H. Fitzgerald suggested that Union veterans might again march on Georgia. This time, however, they would do so in peace. Seeking a place where veterans could find relief from the chilling Midwestern winters and rich soils to pursue farming, Fitzgerald purchased 100,000 acres in southern Georgia for a soldiers' colony to be named after himself. Within a few years, a reported 10,000 GAR men and their families resided in the town of Fitzgerald only miles from the spot where Jefferson Davis had been captured in 1865. A Union veteran who had walked from Illinois recalled that he had first marched through the state with Sherman thirty years prior. Had anyone told him he would one day return in peace, he would have been insulted. "But the times have changed," he noted. "The bitterness engendered by the war is fast dying out and here I am right in the heart of rebeldom and intend to stay here." Indeed, the very layout of the town was meant to model reconciliation. Streets along the eastern half of the town were named after Union officers and those to the west were named after Confederate leaders, a spacious park was christened the Blue and Gray Park, and the mammoth Lee-Grant Hotel stood in the center of town. GAR and UCV posts found ample members in the town, as did a Blue-Gray association. For years, aging veterans of both sides could be found throwing horseshoes and recounting war stories in a vacant lot. "This colony is one more link," observed a Kansas newspaper, "in the chain which binds together the gray and the blue."[109] These chains, however, were tenuous. At Fitzgerald, Union veterans and their Confederate neighbors clashed about how best to commemorate the war and disagreed over descriptions of the two sides in textbooks. And the divisive memory of prisoners of war was never far from mind when the Union veterans made their yearly pilgrimage to Andersonville.[110]

Even within the pages of the *Blue and Gray: The Patriotic American Magazine*, challenges to the reconciliationist message could be fierce. First published in 1892, the magazine regularly featured memoirs from veterans of both sides alongside editorials and correspondence promoting reconciliation. But a letter from a Kansas pension agent served as a stark reminder that beneath the veneer of reconciliationist sentiment, lingering sectional animosity ran deep. He lashed out at former rebels' "ungrateful and damnable treachery, treason, and virulent abuse of power" to attack the pension laws. Their use of such phrases as "paupers—mendicants—hirelings—and sand baggers of the treasury" to describe Union pensioners led him to wonder "if or whether the time has come for it to be patriotic to mingle the Blue and Gray in honorable connection and thereby allow the cause we sacrificed health, means, opportunity, and life for to become obliterated & swall[ow]ed into the subterranean abysses of eternity by a hord of cowardly ingrate traitors to our government."[111]

The dedication of the Richmond Soldiers' and Sailors' Monument on May 30, 1894, sparked an especially tense national debate over the limits of reconciliation. In the course of his dedicatory address, Confederate private-turned-reverend Robert C. Cave spoke the standard lines about soldiers' bravery and devotion common at every monument dedication, be it Union or Confederate. But he went further that day, delivering what many northern writers described as a eulogy for the Confederacy. Appomattox had not been a divine verdict against the South, he argued; instead it had been the triumph of the physically strong. Going beyond the traditional Lost Cause message of overwhelming northern resources, he intoned that "brute force cannot settle questions of right and wrong." "The South was in the right," he maintained, noting that "the cause was just; that the men who took up arms in her defense were patriots." And yet he still went further, suggesting that indeed southerners had been more devoted to the Union than had northerners and denouncing the character, motives, and actions of the North. "Against the South was arrayed the power of the North, dominated by the spirit of Puritanism, which . . . worships itself and is unable to perceive any goodness apart from itself, and from the time of Oliver Cromwell to the time of Abraham Lincoln has never hesitated to trample upon the rights of others in order to effect its own ends."[112] When he was finished, newspapers reported, the crowd leapt to its feet in thunderous applause.[113]

As news of Cave's remarks made its way north, a storm of denunciation flowed from every corner of the nation. From newspapers in Milwaukee, Philadelphia, and Portland, Oregon, came headlines of "Unreconstructed Rebel" and "The Rebel Yell is Heard: Treason Preached at Richmond's Monument Unveiling." The *Washington Post* declared Cave's statements out of place in this "era of reconciliation," reminding white southerners that Union soldiers had recognized the "valor, the devotion, and the fine manhood of the Confederates" and tried to spare "them every possible humiliation in their defeat." Surely the South would denounce such brazenly treasonous speech, the paper observed.[114] A handful of southern papers did dismiss Cave's remarks as ill-gotten and hardly representative of the South, but many others either reprinted his speech without any commentary or explicitly endorsed him.[115] And each time they did, northern papers responded in turn. With each salvo, the conflict continued to escalate.

The real battle, however, erupted not between the newspapers but among the veterans. Two years earlier, the Columbia Post GAR of Chicago had traveled to Richmond, where they enjoyed the "the hospitality and generous welcome" of the Lee Camp of Confederate Veterans.[116] But hearing of Cave's oration in 1894, they were outraged. The post informed the Lee Camp that on the very day Cave had delivered his oration, they had joined with Confederate veterans in Chicago to decorate the graves of Confederate prisoners of war without mentioning the cause of the conflict or its final settlement. Certainly, they felt, the Lee Camp that had so graciously hosted them would not endorse such statements. "If the sentiments uttered by Rev. Cave . . . and which 'tremendous applause' from the audience assembled there, be the true sentiments of the average ex-Confederate veteran," they noted, "then will it indeed be hard to ever heal the breach between 'brothers of one land,' engendered by that awful conflict, and the generous action of our Union veterans seems truly wasted." Invoking reconciliationist sentiment as a way to combat the Lost Cause rhetoric, the Union veterans noted, "While anxious to look with pleasure upon these reunions in your sunny South land, we cannot but regret such disloyal sentiments as these, and *must protest* in the name of the fallen of both sides."[117]

Upon receiving the letter, the Lee Camp was at first unsure as to how to respond. Some favored tabling the discussion in order to avoid a national controversy, while others remained indignant by the perceived insults. But continued newspaper coverage stirred the debate, with one southern paper referring to the Chicago GAR post as "a lot of hoodlums, cattle, and vulgarians." Soon other Confederate organizations began to rally behind Cave. The Southern Women's Historical Society of St. Louis sent the reverend their "heartfelt thanks," while the Pickett Camp of the UCV voted to remove the photograph of a Federal officer from its camp walls.[118]

Finally, in July, the Lee Camp responded to the Columbia Post. Shocked by the post's letter, the Confederate veterans observed that while they did not suspect "any purpose on your part to provoke sectional controversy or add fuel to the dying embers of sectional hate . . . such seems to be its natural tendency." The Lee Camp failed to understand how Cave's words could be interpreted as "disloyal" and affirmed his contention that Appomattox had settled the military questions but not the Constitutional ones. "Physical might cannot determine the question of legal or moral right," they observed. They noted that both sides had erected monuments to their respective causes, and that they too had laid flowers on the graves of their former foes. But most important, the camp noted that Cave had not spoken at a Blue-Gray reunion or a monument unveiling at a battlefield in which both sides were meant to be honored. Instead, "his oration was delivered at the unveiling of a monument to the private soldiers and sailors who died in behalf of the Southern cause, in resistance to an armed invasion of their native land, and in defense . . . of their personal liberties and constitutional rights." It was therefore right that "he should also refer to and vindicate 'the cause for which they fell.'"[119]

This was the crux of the matter. Former Confederates believed that they were free to observe, defend, and memorialize their cause when speaking to other white southerners. For them, the Lost Cause was the primary memory of the war. The same held true for Union veterans. They might gladly welcome former foes to their city, recite the obligatory language about brave and courageous "American" soldiers, and even gather to place flowers on the graves of the enemy dead. But gestures of reconciliation did not lessen the devotion to their respective causes. Instead, every time veterans marched in a joint Memorial Day procession or united with their former enemies in reunion revelry, they were reminded of what they had fought for so many years prior.

No reunion captured the tension between reconciliationist sentiment and the fierce need to protect both the Union and Lost Causes more than the 1895 dedication of Chickamauga and Chattanooga National Military Park. In mid-September, crowds began flocking to Chattanooga for the dedication of the nation's first national military park. Thousands of Union veterans made their way south from Louisville, where they had attended the annual GAR encampment—the first ever south of the Ohio River. Others, both Union and Confederate, came from every direction on the compass, by rail, wagon, and carriage. Flags were unfurled in the breeze, and colorful bunting decorated the homes and businesses of every town along the route. "This bubbling spirit of pleasure and exuberant feeling of patriotism seems to have penetrated every community in this section," observed a journalist from Atlanta, transforming the surrounding countryside into "one solid streak of red, white and blue."[120] Having spent the better part of the previous year upgrading roads and securing accommodations, food, and care for their guests, Chattanooga welcomed the expected crowd of 50,000 with open arms.[121]

Not everyone looked forward to the impending Blue-Gray lovefest. "I am in for a rather conspicuous part in the Chattanooga Park dedication—though I did my best to dodge it," Senator Edward Cary Walthall, a former Confederate general from the Army of Tennessee, wrote to a friend. "I am a poor hand at Blue and Gray *gush*, but the occasion will require a little of that," he confessed. "My idea is to do enough in that direction to save my distance, but to set the Confederate before the world, briefly, as eating no dirt but still bowing to the inevitable—but raising his head afterward and keeping it up ever since—& to show too, that a Southern soldier & a Mississippian took the lead in bringing about the state of things that makes the justification possible." "Have I said the Confederate stuff *stiff* enough & not too much so?" he wondered.[122] Clearly, he recognized the precarious balancing act required of him. How would he find the right tone—the right mix of "gush"—without denouncing his own cause?

Despite Walthall's reservations, the spirit of reconciliation pervaded the three-day celebration. Unionists and former Confederates greeted each other with warm embraces, marched together under the Stars and Stripes in great processions, and heralded the bravery and honor of their former foes. In his keynote address, Vice President Adlai E. Stevenson reminded the crowds that this day was truly auspicious. Thirty-two years after the great battle, the honored survivors had gathered once more on the heights. "They meet, not in deadly conflict," he noted, "but as brothers—under one flag, fellow-citizens of a common country."[123] Reporters from across the nation echoed these sentiments. "The Mason and Dixon line has been wiped off the map," observed a Los Angeles newspaper. "The friendly, brotherly feeling that has been displayed here this week . . . proves that the bitter sectionalism that so long divided the Union no longer exists." "There is no 'North and South,'" declared the reporter. On this blood-stained field, the aging warriors had "signed a compact by which the last vestige of venom caused by the civil war was blotted out."[124]

But even on this occasion orchestrated to consecrate the battlefield in the name of reconciliation, Union veterans refused to forget that there had been a right cause and a wrong cause. Col. Henry M. Duffield of Michigan was not opposed to honoring Confederates for their bravery, but he adamantly refused to acknowledge that their cause had been just. "Upon this field hallowed by the bravery and sanctified by the blood of the men who saved the Union," he implored, "no mawkish sentiment should confuse the right or palliate the wrong." Some day, he believed, the South would recognize that "the cause of secession was wrong and the cause of the Union was right."[125] Gen. Charles F. Manderson, a senator from Nebraska, perhaps expressed such sentiments most succinctly. Paraphrasing Ulysses S. Grant after Appomattox, he asserted that "we, who fought to save, were forever right and they, who fought to destroy, were eternally wrong."[126]

For Union veterans and the northern public, the dedication of the park, replete with former Confederates marching under the Stars and Stripes, was no less than a vindication of the Union Cause. It seems small wonder that they would herald the reconciliationist spirit of the day. Not only did their former enemies now assure them of their allegiance to the United States, but the veterans of both sides revealed that they could work together to preserve a field once drenched with their blood. This was no capitulation to the Lost Cause. A *New York Times* headline stated the feeling most succinctly: "The Spirit of Union Predominant."[127]

At least some former Confederates recognized that homages to the Union Cause implicitly called the Lost Cause into question. A year prior to the park's dedication, Alexander P. Stewart, the Confederate member of the park commission, had strenuously objected to a proposed inscription on the 2nd Minnesota Volunteer Infantry's monument. Wishing to paraphrase Andrew Jackson's famous quote, the regiment had requested that "The Union, it must and shall be preserved," be inscribed upon their monument. But Stewart complained that the inscription was "a violation of both the letter and spirit" of regulations that stipulated against any commentary on the moral cause of the war. In the spirit of reconciliation, veterans and their monuments were supposed to refrain from any judgment on who was right and who was wrong. As Louisiana's state commission observed, such an inscription would only serve to "keep open rapidly healing sores."[128]

The Union Cause was not the only cause that would be remembered and even celebrated during the dedication. The most ostentatious display of the Lost Cause, indeed of continuing sectional rancor, came from the one-armed Confederate colonel who was now Alabama's governor, William C. Oates. His address began with an account of the battle of Chickamauga replete with references to his "humble" but "conspicuous" role in it. But he soon shifted tone. As he had done in countless other speeches over the years, he turned to an exposition on the causes of the war filled with venom and acrimony. Like the Reverend Cave the preceding year, he condemned the North for its Puritan ancestry and suggested that the southern cavalier represented a substantially superior culture. The Puritans and their "aggressive fanaticism," he intoned, had "caused an ocean of tears to be shed, drenched the land in blood and sacrificed the lives of a million men and untold millions of treasure." In his estimation, northern fanatics were responsible for the war and its bloodletting, not honorable southerners. "Let the blasphemous mouths of the bloody-shirt shriekers be closed and the truth be told," he exclaimed, "and our cause and the heroism which sustained it for four immortal years will illuminate the brightest chapter of the true history of that great conflict." Expecting the usual Blue-Gray rhetoric, the veterans must have been stunned into rapt silence.[129]

Antagonistic denunciations of the Union Cause were not uncommon at Confederate-only occasions (as Cave's remarks had revealed), yet seldom did speakers employ such discordant language at Blue-Gray reunions, especially at such events on the national stage. Oates's divisive remarks were more than a rejection of the reconciliatory language—they were a rejection of the Union Cause. As soon as the recalcitrant rebel made his way back to his seat, several northern governors leapt at the opportunity to respond. Vermont governor Urban A. Woodbury took the stage first. Assuring the veterans that he harbored no ill will toward those who had worn the gray, he observed that he was willing to admit that Confederates had fought for what they believed right. "But," he proclaimed, "we cannot teach our children but that they were wrong." Incensed, Governor Peter Turney of Tennessee, a former Confederate colonel, strode to the podium, offering what appeared at first to be a more reconciliatory tone. "We fought this fight together. This is our common country," he bellowed. But he would not denounce his cause. "I was on the losing side. I believed I was right." "It has been said that our children should be taught that we were wrong," he observed. "I stand before you as one who does all in his power to persuade his children . . . that their father was no traitor, that he acted from an honest conviction . . . and expects to stand by his convictions." With that, the Confederate veterans in the audience erupted in applause.[130] Just as Union veterans accepted the sentimental gush of reconciliation on their own terms, so would former Confederates. Veterans might be willing to commend their former foes for bravery and courage, but they would not go so far as to concede that their cause had been wrong. Reconciliationist sentiment had its limits.

Five years after the dedication, strife again threatened a Blue-Gray reunion. Meeting in Atlanta for a joint reunion of the survivors who had fought around the city in July 1864, GAR commander Albert Shaw informed the crowd that the Confederacy had passed into history and there it should remain. He argued that the Confederate flag should be furled for all occasions except reunions, and he scorned efforts to keep the "memories of bitterness of the war alive in the breasts of young Southerners." Construing Shaw's remarks as tantamount to a declaration that southern children were being taught that their fathers were wrong, UCV commander John B. Gordon strode to the platform for a vigorous rejoinder. He was proud of the fact that he had fought for the Confederacy, he declared in no uncertain terms. Though he "loved Shaw devotedly," he wanted to give him notice that he and every southern man would be "untrue to their manhood and Christianity" if they did not teach their children that "the dying generation contended for a righteous cause." After an eruption of applause from the Confederate veterans, Shaw rose and calmly acknowledged that he would allow for a difference in opinion. According to newspaper reports, he and Gordon then shook hands and listened to the remainder of the speeches with their arms resting on the other's shoulder.[131] Clearly these men did not agree on how to remember the war, yet they both recognized the importance of embracing the rituals of reconciliation.

Even as sectional hostility boiled beneath the surface, many veterans continued to attend events orchestrated to celebrate reconciliation. Following the model of Union and Confederate cooperation at Chickamauga and Chattanooga, four more battlefields were authorized as national parks: Antietam (1890), Shiloh (1894), Gettysburg (1895), and Vicksburg (1899). Aging solders persisted in organizing reunions with their former foes and gathered for dedication ceremonies that highlighted the reunited and reconciled nation. And speakers continued to espouse the "American brotherhood" that held such a predominant place at the 1895 dedication.[132]

More than a few, however, could do without the brotherly handshaking. "I don't like these blue and gray reunions," Col. R. J. Harding, the president of Hood's Texas Brigade Association, declared on June 28, 1905; "something unpleasant always happens." But Harding had a simple solution to the problem: "The quickest way to stop sectional feeling is to let each other alone. We are as far apart in what we fought for as we ever were, that is," he quipped, "as far as Boston is from heaven." No one wished for more strife and dissensions, he assured his comrades, but neither had they ever given up their view of the war.[133]

It was for this reason that despite numerous proposals over the years, the GAR and UCV would never meet for a joint national encampment. "To find a common ground upon which the survivors of the bitter struggle can meet is not easy," observed one journalist.[134] Union and Confederate veterans could come together for ritualistic performances that many participated in even if they did not fully believe in the "lovefest" message when there was no real work to be done or real meaning to consider. But discussions about how to honor one's comrades, efforts to secure pensions, or debates regarding school textbooks could not possibly be addressed at joint conventions. While veterans of both sides served as the nation's chief symbol of reconciliation, many continued to grapple with the tension between their stated desire to move beyond past differences and their inability to forget old antagonisms.[135]

Despite extensive efforts to cultivate reconciliation, veterans' insistence on enshrining the righteousness of their own cause (and in many instances questioning the morality of their former foes) ensured that the larger public would be equally unable to overlook the lingering bitterness.[136] Those who controlled the political parties, popular press, and play houses frequently called for sectional harmony in the name of patriotism, commercial interests, political goals, and global dominance. But the millions of Americans who lived with veterans, attended Memorial Day services, witnessed dedications, or accompanied the aging soldiers to reunions often heard a very different message. Veterans occupied most southern governors' mansions, filled the seats of Congress, and captured the White House for much of the Gilded Age. Veterans' influence had not waned by the 1890s. It was at its peak.[137] Even for those who had come of age after 1865, throughout the late nineteenth century it remained clear that for many veterans the war's bitterness and resentment had not yet completely receded. Reconciliation might be wonderfully successful in establishing national military parks, but everyone understood that it had its limits. The war had been too bloody, too long, and too costly for most Americans to surrender sacred convictions about its meaning, much less to forget.

SLAVERY, RACE,
AND RECONCILIATION

1880s–1890s

For three warm autumn days, tens of thousands had enjoyed the reconciliationist spirit of the Chickamauga and Chattanooga park dedication.
But all such occasions must come to an end, and such was the case on September 20, 1895, when the veterans of the Army of the Potomac and their
former foes from the Army of Northern Virginia met under a great canvas
tent at Orchard Knob. For most of the evening, the men and their guests
enjoyed the typical speeches commending the honor and bravery of soldiers from both sides who had fought on the fields.[1] When Alabama governor William C. Oates climbed to the stage, however, the reconciliationist
feelings quickly dissipated. The Yankees and their "aggressive fanaticism,"
he shouted, had "caused an ocean of tears to be shed, drenched the land in
blood and sacrificed the lives of a million men and untold millions of treasure." But his critique did not stop there. Instead, he invoked one of the
issues sure to dispel any fraternal spirit. Slavery, he argued, had long been
the Pandora's Box of American politics. It had been a lawful state institution and the responsibility for its continuance belonged to the states alone.
In the tradition of the Lost Cause, he described a land of benevolent masters and faithful slaves. The South had not provoked the war, he assured
his audience. Rather, it had been Lincoln and his "band of fanatics" who
had incited "the slaves to insurrection, arson, and indiscriminate murder
of white people," and who had martyred such figures as John Brown. He

challenged the notion that abolition had been one of the grand objects of the northern soldier. In race-baiting language, he asserted that such was the revisionist interpretation of the Radicals. "You could not more deeply offend a Union soldier than tell him he was fighting for the freedom of the negroes," he shouted. Wrapping up his diatribe, he informed the veterans that the white South, "awakened to common danger-not about slavery alone, but that their ancient and well defined right to govern their own internal affairs in their own way would be denied and destroyed . . . under the guise of law and constitutional administration." Having endured enough, the Union veterans jumped to their feet in protest. No Confederate would slander the hallowed Union Cause.[2]

Oates had not taken the stage that evening to intentionally provoke his former foes, but rather to provide a rebuttal and corrective to the denunciations of the Lost Cause that former Confederates had endured throughout the dedication. "The principle these men [Confederates] fought for meant the perpetuation of human slavery," Democratic governor John P. Altgeld of Illinois had declared the previous day; "they were fighting for a condition against which the humanity of the age protested."[3] Union general John N. Palmer had likewise informed those who donned both blue and gray uniforms that African slavery had been "the root of sectional bitterness." Not only had U.S. veterans refused to forget that slaveholders had precipitated the war, but many also highlighted their role in emancipation. Union victory had guaranteed that "the flag of our country became at once the emblem of freedom and the symbol of National power," observed Palmer.[4] In a bit of revisionist history, or selective memory at the least, Altgeld went so far as to suggest that most U.S. soldiers had been motivated from the outset by abolitionist sentiment. "More than a million of men [sic] in all came down from the North, shouting as they marched, 'This Union forever and equal rights for all,'" he proclaimed.[5] And some exceptional figures, such as Maj. Gen. O. O. Howard, the one-armed former commissioner of the Freedmen's Bureau, recognized the long-term implications of emancipation, pointing out that "black men are advancing; the schools are almost universal; his home is being improved."[6] Even at the Chickamauga dedication where both Union and Confederate veterans gathered to consecrate the field in the name of reconciliation, slavery had not been forgotten. If anything, its memory remained a powerful, divisive force.

While some influential voices, such as the publishers of *Battles and Leaders*, elected to remain silent on the issues of slavery in an effort to foster positive relations between white northerners and southerners, in other instances debates about slavery proved to be among the most powerful obstacles to reconciliation. Since the Constitutional convention, the slavery question had aroused consternation, vigorous debate, and of course civil war.[7] Thirty years after the war, the debate had not subsided. As the nineteenth century gave way to the twentieth, white and black Unionists as well as former Confederates contended with slavery—and subsequently race relations during Reconstruction—as they attempted to navigate the shoals of Civil War memory. Even the Spanish-American War, long championed as evidence that the white North and South had reunited to fight a foreign, non-white foe, would not thoroughly bind up the nation's wounds.

EMANCIPATION AND RECONCILIATION

By the last decades of the nineteenth century, white southerners, many of whom had come of age after emancipation, took up the banner of white supremacy in an effort to reverse what they saw as the tragedies of Reconstruction. In 1890, Mississippi became the first state to disenfranchise African Americans by a constitutional convention. Five years later, Louisiana and South Carolina were preparing to follow Mississippi's lead, and it appeared likely that every other southern state would do the same. But it was not black officeholders and suffrage alone that angered white southerners. The mobility of African Americans, a growing black middle class, and the imagined threat black men posed to white women brought the white South to a near frenzy. When the Supreme Court declared Congress's 1875 civil rights law banning racial segregation in transportation and public accommodations unconstitutional in 1883, several states called for all railroads to be segregated by race, and by 1895 every state of the former Confederacy except Virginia and North Carolina required that passenger cars be segregated. The next year, the U.S. Supreme Court supported state-sanctioned segregation of all public facilities and transportation in *Plessy v. Ferguson*. Where disenfranchisement and segregation efforts proved to be inadequate measures to keep southern blacks in their subservient position, white southerners turned to the extra-legal method of lynching.[8]

Observing the surge of Blue-Gray reunions and battlefield dedications within a context of state-sanctioned segregation, disenfranchisement, and lynching, many historians have argued that this newfound sectional camaraderie was based in large part on a shared commitment to a whitewashed memory of the war. Reconciliation, they argue, had a "Southern base," premised on the Republicans' abandonment of African Americans, a nationalized white supremacy, and a "tacit forgetfulness" about the role of blacks and emancipation in the war's outcome.[9] But this logic overlooks crucial factors. First, segregation did not cause the rise of reconciliationist sentiment. Meetings between Union and Confederate veterans began as early as the 1870s, and state-sanctioned segregation began a decade later. Second, most white northerners had always believed in white supremacy. Although the later part of the nineteenth century witnessed an emphasis on Anglo-Saxon superiority supported by scientific racism and social Darwinism, most white Unionists had believed in 1861, as they did in 1865 and into the postwar years, that they were socially, culturally, physically, and mentally superior to African Americans.[10] Most continued to believe this in the 1890s. They did not need to attend battlefield dedications with their former foes to be convinced of their racial superiority. Third, in addition to their racial attitudes, Republicans' ideologies of labor, political economy, and federalism encouraged them to abandon Reconstruction and left black southerners to the whims of Redeemer governments.[11] Fourth, and most important, central to historians' argument that racism informed reconciliation is the contention that, by the late nineteenth century, white Unionists had forgotten that slaveholders fomented the war and that four years of fighting by Union armies had brought emancipation. Union veterans had forgotten neither.

Throughout the century's closing decades, white Union veterans continued to castigate rebel leaders for instigating the "slaveholders' rebellion." Addressing a crowd of Midwestern veterans at the dedication of the Michigan state monument at Gettysburg in June 1889, Gen. L. S. Trowbridge declared that the war had been between "two conflicting civilizations." On one side had been "the defenders of the institution of slavery" who had "drawn their sword, not to cut the disease from the body politic, but to murder the State, and establish a vast empire with slavery as its chief cornerstone." On the other side stood "the great free north girding its loins for one more struggle for human liberty."[12] An 1896 booklet honoring those resting in Arlington National Cemetery declared that they had "died upon the battlefields around their country's capital in its defense when it was menaced and attacked by foes upholding a slaveholders' rebellion."[13] One particularly vexed veteran observed that Lee "was a breeder of human cattle, and was ready like other Virginians to shed human blood for the 'liberty' of human slavery."[14] And one Pennsylvania veteran put it most succinctly: "The primary cause of the Civil War was the bondage of the black man."[15] Despite white southerners' protests to the contrary, Union veterans understood that the war had been caused by secession, and the South had seceded first and foremost to protect slaveholding interests.

In fact, white Unionists' memory of emancipation as a central war measure only seemed to increase with the passing of time.[16] "We had in our civil war the unparalleled spectacle of a vast army of men fighting for another race than their own," declared the Reverend Myron Hanes at a Chicago Memorial Day service in 1895.[17] Weeks later during New York Day at Gettysburg, one orator insisted that "the cause which was substantially decided here was the cause of freedom, and justice." "We may never forget that, behind the cause of the Union, was the cause of unpaid labor, of bartered manhood, of a traffic which dealt in human hearts."[18] Dedicating Indiana's monument at Andersonville in 1908, Governor J. Frank Hanly paid tribute to the men who had died to save the Union and "died to save from whip and lash 'the naked back of unpaid toil,' to end the traffic in human flesh and blood." "They died to give freedom to the slave," he noted, "that the freedom of the free might be secure."[19] Even *Laney's Gettysburg* battlefield guide, produced ostensibly for both northern and southern tourists, closed its narration by declaring that "the battle was ended, and the cause of freedom upheld."[20]

Not surprisingly, an emphasis on emancipation was especially pronounced at dedications on Antietam National Battlefield. Recalling Lincoln's decision to issue the preliminary Emancipation Proclamation in the wake of the September 17, 1862, battle, speakers at monument dedications in the 1890s and early 1900s routinely invoked freedom as one of the principal successes of the Union war effort. "On this field died human slavery," observed New Jersey governor Franklin Murphy.[21] Addressing the men of the GAR in 1903, President Theodore Roosevelt concurred. After the Union army had driven Lee back across the Potomac, Lincoln had published that "immortal paper . . . the paper which decided the Civil War," he noted. "From that time onward the causes of Union and Freedom, of national greatness and individual liberty, were one and the same."[22] In a bit of revisionist memory, two years later, Governor Thomas Marshall recalled slavery as a "national sin," noting that "now as then" Hoosiers stood "for the equality of all men before the law, for the striking of gyves from off the slave whether he be white or black."[23] And in language that would have surely suited Frederick Douglass, in 1906, Dr. S. M. Whistler of the 130th Pennsylvania declared that freeing the slaves "has thrown upon the American people a weight of responsibility second to no other question." "The negro cannot be relegated to his former condition," he warned.[24] Union veterans firmly believed that they had fought on the side of morality—they had removed the stain of slaveholding from the nation's shores.

Although most white Union veterans had not marched off to war in 1861 or even 1863 determined to end slavery, in the decades after the war emancipation had become entrenched as a central achievement of Union victory. In large part, this was because it increasingly carried a redemptive value. By the end of the nineteenth century, slavery was generally seen as morally reprehensible and had been eliminated in the western hemisphere. Moreover, Union veterans, now firmly into middle age, claimed responsibility for the triumph of the free labor ideology. The rise of the industrial power, the settlement of the American West by white families (along with the triumph over Indians), and the constant stream of immigrants into the nation's ports affirmed that the Union war aims had not only been vindicated, but were also morally superior.[25] Though most Lost Cause proponents attempted to erase slavery as the catalyst for war, Unionists heralded its demise ever more forcefully.

While condemnations of the slaveholders' rebellion continued, the common rebel soldier often proved an antidote to the slave oligarchy argument—and a path to reconciliation. Recounting a popular wartime theme in the North, Union veterans observed that the poor class of white southerners had been mere puppets of the slave oligarchy who exploited them to fight the war. "In the presence of bonded black laborers they were regarded a superfluous class, and therefore a *cheap war material*," wrote James A. Mowris of the 117th New York as early as 1866. "To what extent, the leaders of the rebellion were actuated by their contempt of the class which would constitute the rank and file of their army, is difficult to say," he concluded.[26] Twenty and thirty years later, his sentiment endured. If the poor, ignorant masses of Confederates had been duped by the slaveholding oligarchy, they could be forgiven even if their cause could not.

This logic allowed some Union veterans to prove remarkably capable of embracing both emancipation and reconciliation. The Council of Nine GAR of Birdsboro, Pennsylvania, for example billed their 1891 Memorial Day as a solemn and reverent observation of "the men who died to keep the Union whole, and unshackled four million held in bondage." Post secretary H. G. Hunter included the program, replete with this description, in a very cordial letter sent to the Lee Camp of Richmond. A veteran of Chancellorsville and Gettysburg, Hunter praised the ex-Confederates as "among the bravest and most reliable in this country" and complimented the camp for their work in relieving their distressed comrades. "May the light of Peace continue to shine in our country many centuries," he wrote.[27] Here was a Union veteran who simultaneously acknowledged the bravery of his former foes and attended a Memorial Day service where the abolition of slavery was heralded as one of the twin accomplishments of the Union army. He unabashedly included the day's program in his correspondence to the Confederate veterans, making no attempt to explain or otherwise excuse the reference to emancipation. Reconciliation and emancipation were not mutually exclusive.

Four years after the formal end of Reconstruction, President James A. Garfield offered the nation a vision of reconciliation that heartily embraced not only emancipation, but also equal rights. At his March 1881 inaugural, the former Union general spoke passionately about the Civil War's twin legacies of reunion and emancipation. Union victory, he told the crowd of 50,000, had provided a magnificent opportunity. "The elevation of the negro race from slavery to the full rights of citizenship is the most important political change we have known since the adoption of the Constitution," he declared. "It has liberated the master as well as the slave from a relation which wronged and enfeebled both." As former slaves in the audience wept, Garfield surged on, noting that the "emancipated race has already made remarkable progress," and promising that he would do everything in his power to extend suffrage to all men. But this was not a simple repudiation of the white South. Instead, striking a reconciliationist tone, he implored Americans to forget section, race, and partisanship. Fifty years hence, he observed, "our children will not be divided in their opinions concerning our controversies. They will surely bless their fathers—and their fathers' God—that the Union was preserved, that slavery was overthrown, and that both races were made equal before the law." "We may hasten," he concluded, "or we may retard, but we can not prevent the final reconciliation."[28] This was not reconciliation absent any discussion of slavery and race.

A similar pattern of embracing both emancipation and reconciliation could increasingly be found in the pages of middle-class magazines. The same *Century Magazine* responsible for publishing one of the most important conduits of reconciliation, *Battles and Leaders*, continued to include articles on slavery as a cause of the war, the necessity of emancipation, and the contributions of the USCT. Described by one of its editors as "national and antislavery in its views," in 1887 the monthly praised Charles Sumner's "moral fearlessness" regarding abolition and included a six-page story on the black troops at Petersburg who "commanded admiration and respect of every beholder on that day." A biographical series about Abraham Lincoln maintained that southerners had initiated the rebellion to defend slavery.[29]

But so, too, did the monthly include continued evidence of former Confederates espousing reconciliation. Even more important, the journal was likewise sympathetic to the southern view evidenced in a story by James Lane Allen. Having suffered the war and Reconstruction, Allen, a native Kentuckian, fondly recalled the days of old: contented loyal slaves, kind masters, and slave mistresses who served as "the real practical philanthropists of the negro race."[30] Including both antislavery and white southern perspectives was invaluable to national healing, reasoned editor Richard Watson Gilder. "It is of no particular utility to the South to have a Southern periodical manifest hospitality to Southern ideas," he observed. "But it is of great use that a Northern periodical should be so hospitable to Southern writers and Southern opinion . . . even when they are not altogether palatable to our Northern readers, among whom, of course is our greatest audience."[31] In allowing southern writers a wider readership, northerners hoped they might find some common ground on which to move forward in a reunited nation.

Remembering emancipation did not preclude reconciliationist tendencies, in part because white northerners need not be racial liberals or civil rights advocates to remember that Union victory had ended slavery. Moral outrage about the institution of slavery did not have to be the centerpiece of recalling emancipation. Veterans and the loyal white citizenry could celebrate emancipation as something that punished the old slaveholding oligarchy, helped restore the Union, and prevented future dissension without lauding it as a humanitarian act.[32]

Nor did acknowledging the bravery and devotion of the USCT negate ideas about African Americans' racial inferiority. Speaking before the Vermont Commandery of the Loyal Legion in 1893, Lt. Col. E. Henry Powell of the 10th USCT observed that "the Negro soldier . . . was an unbidden and unwelcomed guest" to the army ranks. "The soldiers had no ambition for such companionship," he recalled, but "during the dark days of 1863, when the rebellion struck high noon, his welcome grew apace . . . [and] troops white and black fought side by side like brothers." "It was demonstrated that the negro had in the war of which he was the prime cause, a most important work to perform."[33] Here was no enlightened sense of black and white soldiers as comrades; rather, USCT soldiers provided a pragmatic means of winning the war. Similarly, in *Century* magazine, Henry Goddard Thomas commended his black troops at Petersburg for "exhibiting fighting qualities that I never saw surpassed in the war." Yet he stereotypically recounted the "joyous negro guffaw always breaking out about the campfire" and described the "picturesque scene" just prior to battle, the "dark men, with their white eyes and teeth and full red lips crouching over a smoldering camp-fire."[34] Prejudice and praise for the gallantry of USCT soldiers could—and did—coexist.

Even amid such attitudes, the GAR continued to welcome African American members in both all-black and integrated posts to join their white brethren at monument dedications and encampments. When the bronze figure of Victory was hoisted atop the New York state monument at Gettysburg in 1893, more than 7,000 New York veterans as well as thousands more from other states attended the dedication festivities. Selected to deliver a sermon and prayer prior to the dedicatory addresses was the Reverend W. B. Derrick, a USCT veteran.[35] Among those participating in a grand review of veterans in Kansas City in 1891 were more than 200 African American veterans.[36] Though segregated into their own units, four years later, colored veterans proudly marched with their white comrades in a rousing parade in Guthrie, Oklahoma.[37]

Race-based controversies did arise in some of the more than 300 GAR posts throughout the former Confederacy. In the late 1880s and 1890s, white veterans in Texas, Alabama, South Carolina, Georgia, Mississippi, and Louisiana proposed either denying the establishment of all-black posts altogether or creating racially segregated departments within their respective states. In each instance, the national GAR's policy protested that "no honorably discharged veteran should be discriminated against on account of the color of his skin." Only Texas and Alabama succeeded in banning black veterans.[38] But these states proved the exception, not the rule. Numerous white veterans, both in the South and throughout the nation, voiced their objections to the discriminatory practices.[39] "During the fierce struggle for the life of the nation," the national encampment declared in 1891, "we stood shoulder to shoulder as comrades tried. It is too late to divide now on the color line."[40]

Determining whether USCT veterans participated in Blue-Gray reunions such as the Chickamauga and Chattanooga dedication is more difficult. Numerous African American newspapers reported on the ceremony, even labeling it "the grandest affair in the whole history of Tennessee," and it is clear that African Americans joined in the festivities.[41] White and black schoolchildren from Chattanooga marched in the procession on September 20, and according to one newspaper "hundreds of the black men and sons of the black men, whose bright charter was written out of the ashes and embers of blood of those years of heartbreak" attended the services.[42] It seems likely that African American members of the GAR, including those in the all-black Chattanooga Post, were among those men.[43] Only days earlier, black GAR members had been welcomed at the national encampment in Louisville, where they "were treated with special consideration" despite reports of the color line being drawn in Kentucky.[44] It would not be a stretch to believe that some of these men might have accompanied their comrades south to Chickamauga. Regardless of the USCT's presence, white Union veterans had not forgotten that their victory emancipated 4 million enslaved men and women.

Rather than reconciliationist memories overtaking the emancipationist memory of the war, for many white Union veterans a conciliatory posture was possible only because the source of sectional conflict had been resolved through Union victory. "Slavery forever abolished and our nation saved," observed the 14th New Jersey's historian. "Our beloved country, healed of its wounds, to-day stands among other powers a free and independent nation forever."[45] The "sentiments of fraternity between North and South" were the result of the destruction of slavery, observed C. L. Sumbardo before a MOLLUS meeting in 1891.[46] Slavery had caused the war, and victorious Union armies had ensured that slavery would never again tear the nation asunder. It was not a silence about slavery but the absence of the institution that was essential for reconciliation. The Union—reunion—was possible only because slavery had been forever eliminated. With its death, a reunited America might rightfully take its place on the world stage.

CONFEDERATES AND SLAVERY

As William C. Oates's response at Chickamauga revealed, Union veterans' commemoration of emancipation enraged and enlivened former Confederates. Responding to the nefarious misrepresentations by northern textbooks in 1899, Dr. Hunter McGuire warned Virginia veterans that such histories were intent on arguing that "the Southern soldier, however brave, was actuated by no higher motive than the desire to retain the money value of slave property." "They rightly believe that the world, once convinced of this, will hold us degraded rather than worthy of honor, and that our children, instead of reverencing their fathers, will be secretly if not openly ashamed," he declared.[47] "We are not willing to be handed down to the coming generation as a race of slave-drivers and traitors," avowed another.[48] Lost Cause proponents seemingly had no choice but to refute the ill-founded and absurd northern memories of slavery and emancipation.

Yet the Lost Cause position on slavery and the war remained far from unified. Just as Jubal Early and others had acknowledged slavery's role in the conflict during the 1860s and 1870s, Oates was not alone among former Confederates in his refusal to avoid the topic more than three decades after Appomattox. During the 1890s, frequent orators John W. Daniel and John H. Reagan both identified slavery as the conflict's catalyst.[49] In a 1901 speech titled "Origins of the American Civil War," Confederate cavalry officer Thomas Rosser observed, "The Southern states legalized African slavery, and although it was also recognized and protected under the Constitution of the general government, the northern states excluded it and the people in the northern states were repugnant to it, and this geographical division of sentiment developed a political antipathy which destroyed the political amity between the states North and South."[50] Former guerrilla John S. Mosby minced no words. "In the retrospect slavery seems such a monstrous thing that some of us are now trying to prove that slavery was not the cause of the war," he wrote another white southerner. "The Confederate soldiers were slaveholders; what did the 95 percent fight for? I answer that the 5 percent & the 95 percent all fought for the same thing—for their country. It was our country & we fought for it, & we didn't care if it was right or wrong."[51]

At reunions of Kentucky's Orphan Brigade between 1887 and 1895, speakers spoke unabashedly about the role of slavery. Col. John W. Caldwell observed that the perpetuation of slavery was "the direct cause of the war." He refused to condone or defend the institution, but he did point out that the North was as culpable as the South for its maintenance. What worried him most were the implications of federally mandated emancipation. "In destroying, without compensation, the accumulated wealth of a century, invested in that institution and protected by the Constitution, the Government set a dangerous precedent, that may be invoked in the next decade or two to justify confiscation upon a much broader and larger scale," he warned.[52]

Most white southerners did not publicly share these views. Instead, northerners' contention throughout the 1880s and 1890s that the South had provoked the war to protect slavery served to fuel the state rights argument. "No man ever saw a Virginia soldier who was fighting for slavery," argued frequent Lost Cause speaker George L. Christian.[53] In Jefferson Davis's two-volume *Rise and Fall of the Confederate Government*, published in 1881, the former president declared slavery a property right and repudiated arguments suggesting it had been the cause of the war.[54] Textbooks, the *Confederate Veteran*, the shsp, and countless orators all routinely included denunciations of slavery as the source of conflict. Most white southerners had not owned slaves, they observed. Why, they asked, would nonslaveholders march off to war in the name of an institution they had no stake in preserving?[55]

If white southerners were split as to whether the war had been prompted by the slavery question, they were equally conflicted about where northerners stood on the issue. Many attacked what they perceived to be the exaggerated assertions of emancipationist sentiment in the Union ranks. "The Southern states did not secede to preserve slavery," observed one former Confederate, "nor did the Northern states invade the South for the purpose of abolishing slavery, as has been so often falsely stated."[56] War-hungry northerners, not white southerners, were to blame, reasoned Hunter McGuire. "We were called upon to resist an invasion of soldiers, armed and sent into our country by the concurrent purposes of several fairly distinct parties then and now existing in the North," he argued. "They came seeking our injury and their own profit."[57] Distinguishing between slavery and the slave power (a point many northerners would have concurred with in 1861), former Confederate general Bradley T. Johnson noted that "the Southern race ruled the continent from 1775 to 1860, and it became evident that it would rule it forever as long as the same conditions existed." "Slavery was the source of political power," he conceded, "and it was selected as the point of attack."[58] Under this logic, the fight to end slavery was replaced with the contention that white southerners had been forced to fight merely to protect their homes. Like others, he held a small group of abolitionist rabble-rouses accountable. The introduction to his book on Maryland Confederates blamed the war on those "detested abolitionists, who for a generation had been stirring up 'battle and murder and sudden death' through midnight insurrection, and arson, and rape, and had been killing Marylanders, who pursued their property into the Northern States." Abolitionists had been the provocateurs, not Confederates.[59]

Some former Confederates pushed the blame even further, arguing that emancipation, not slavery, was the true crime of the era. "Against his will, [the freedman] has been turned loose in America, to do the best he can, in the contest with the strongest race that ever lived," observed Johnson at the dedication of restored White House of the Confederacy in 1896. "Nothing was ever devised so cruel, as forcing on these children, the power and responsibility of the ballot. It requires powers they have not got; it subjects them to tests they cannot stand, and will cause untold misery to them in the future." Johnson summed up the legacy of the war, declaring in no uncertain terms that "the great crime of the century was the emancipation of the Negroes."[60] Though they might not agree on slavery's relationship to the war, most white southerners concurred that white northerners' claims of moral superiority were gross distortions.

In a stark departure from this logic, as well as their sentiments in 1865, numerous other Confederate orators maintained they were glad slavery had ended. "It is an inestimable blessing, not only to the whole country, but *especially to us of the South*, that the war ended in the removal of the incubus of slavery," declared former brigadier general R. E. Colston.[61] At a reunion of the Orphan Brigade, the Honorable Ira Julian exalted that the Confederates had "lost the institution of slavery, and we are all glad of it."[62] More than a few suggested that white southerners would have eventually abandoned the institution and that the region was better off without it.[63] Some invoked the sentiment in a fashion akin to their former foes; with slavery removed the source of sectional tension would likewise vanish. "We are glad that the slave has been set free," noted former Confederate major C. S. Stringfellow at the Annual Reunion of the Pegram Battalion Association in 1886. "We rejoice to night in the integrity of the Union cemented as it is in the best blood of the North and South."[64]

Though they might deny slavery as a cause, white southerners spent an exhaustive amount of energy rationalizing their peculiar institution. White southerners had been defending slavery as a divinely ordained social system with benefits to both black and white even before abolitionists began their attacks in the 1830s. And their defensiveness continued in the 1880s and 1890s, exacerbated by defeat and Union memories of emancipation.[65] "Our opponents have published tons of literature giving the dark side of slavery," wrote a Louisville resident to the *Confederate Veteran* in 1893. "We have little telling of its bright side." Hoping to counteract the influence and misrepresentation of *Uncle Tom's Cabin*, he encouraged editor S. A. Cunningham to include more positive accounts of "the corn shuckings, the quiltings, the barbeques, the big meetings, the weddings, etc., showing that the slaves enjoyed life and were not eternally skulking in dark corners dodging the whip of the overseer, or quaking with terror at the bay of the blood hound."[66] Cunningham complied, printing countless reminiscences by former slaveholders. Depictions of happy, contented slaves likewise filled the pages of the plantation literature penned by Joel Chandler Harris and Thomas Nelson Page. Written in dialect, the wildly popular stories recounted tales of southern gentlemen, beautiful ladies, and of course numerous "Mammies" and "Uncles," all living harmoniously in the pastoral Old South. Not content with published accounts of loyal slaves, in 1896 Capt. Samuel White, a Confederate veteran, financed a modest monument to faithful slaves in rural Fort Mill, South Carolina.[67]

Slaves were not merely happy and well cared for, argued the Lost Cause, but most had been faithful to both their owners and the Confederate nation. "They were quite as loyal to the Confederacy as their masters, and to them we are indebted for the fact that the war lasted four years," remarked one periodical in 1880. The Fort Mill monument praised the "faithful slaves, who, loyal to a sacred trust, toiled for the support of the army . . . and with sterling fidelity guarded our defenseless homes, women, and children, during the struggle for the principles of our 'Confederate States of America.'"[68] Though it rarely mentioned black Union troops, the *Confederate Veteran* oozed with tributes to black "veterans," the body servants and other enslaved men who it claimed had willingly assisted the Confederate war effort. Conveniently forgetting that these men had been forced to accompany the rebel armies, former Confederates invited them to veterans' reunions and Memorial Days, using such occasions to laud them with praise.[69] Accounts of loyal "Confederate" body servants helped to sustain the illusion of the happy and content slave and would eventually give rise to the myth of "black Confederates" in the late twentieth century.[70] For the time being, memories of loyal, faithful slaves would serve as a model for the "proper" postwar racial order in the age of Jim Crow, disenfranchisement, and lynching—a fact that would become increasingly clear in the coming decades.[71]

The image of the faithful slave was not restricted to the South. White northerners also found both comfort and intrigue in tales about loyal African Americans pouring forth from the pens of the plantation school and appearing in the pages of popular magazines like *Scribner's* and *Lippincott's* or on the theater stage. In the antebellum years countless white northerners had enjoyed minstrel shows and objected not so much to slavery as to the power and influence of slaveholders. In the postbellum years, many playwrights and authors returned to romanticized and comical portrayals of slaves in the name of reconciliation. Plantation stories such as those written by Joel Chandler Harris, Thomas Nelson Page, and even George Pickett's widow, LaSalle, allowed southern whites to present a view of harmonious and orderly race relations to their northern counterparts. Tales written in dialect likewise suggested that African Americans remained at a primitive stage of development, thereby allowing northern whites a justification for ignoring the plight of black southerners. As the nineteenth century gave way to the twentieth, these images would become even more popular, none more so than the figure of Mammy.[72]

Embracing the "faithful darky," however, did not mean that white northerners had forgotten that slavery had caused the war, nor that the Union army had facilitated the institution's demise. Humans are inherently complicated, contradictory, and conflicted, untroubled by logical inconsistencies and amazingly capable of compartmentalization.[73] The same white northerners who might have read *Uncle Tom's Cabin* in 1852 and been appalled at the brutality of enslavement might in 1892 read a story by Thomas Nelson Page and relish the romantic tale of the plantation South. For some, such stories offered an escape from the Gilded Age's rampant industrialization, labor disputes, immigration debates, and financial panics. A nostalgia for the agrarian past where race relations seemed more certain fueled the popularity of the Old South and its "old time negroes"—a sentiment expressed often among those who had come of age after the war. Perhaps most important, the assurance that slavery would never blight the land again freed many to celebrate the fictional, romanticized slave.

Even as white northerners read tales of Uncle Remus and Mammy, Union veterans' insistence on celebrating emancipation at monument dedications and Memorial Day services meant that forgetting slavery was not an option for white southerners.[74] In the textbook debates, Memorial Day services, veterans' reunions, monument dedications, and postwar fiction slavery was ever present. Race may not have facilitated reconciliation, but it certainly informed white southerners' memory of the war. Defending slavery and reimagining slaves as happy and loyal became essential to former Confederates' version of the past. Despite their protestations to the contrary, they guaranteed as much as did their northern counterparts that the issue of slavery remained integral to the war's memory.

AFRICAN AMERICANS' MEMORIES

Throughout the 1880s and 1890s, Emancipation Days and Memorial Days regularly drew crowds of hundreds and even thousands of African American men, women, and children in cities both north and south. Memorial Days, in particular, revealed mixed feelings among African Americans. On one hand, the day evoked a great sense of pride within black communities highlighting the sacrifice of USCT soldiers. At least in the North, the occasion frequently brought white and black Unionists together at the same services. On the other hand, Memorial Day too often evoked resentment. In the South, the color line meant that the day was increasingly dominated by African Americans as white Republicans and Unionists refused to attend. In some cases, southern GAR circles held racially segregated ceremonies. In other instances, black GAR and WRC posts were alone called upon to tend the tens of thousands of northern war dead slumbering in southern cemeteries, something many simply did not have the resources to do. In still other cases, the taunting of black soldiers by white southerners or the placement of a black post at the rear of a northern parade served as a visceral reminder of prejudice and disappointment.[75]

Emancipation Days, however, remained almost exclusively African American affairs meant to foster unity among freedpeople and their children. Marking the seventeenth anniversary of Lincoln's preliminary Emancipation Proclamation on September 22, 1880, the largest crowd to date met in Springfield, Illinois, for a magnificent parade replete with representatives from the colored Republican party clubs. That same day, Lafayette, Indiana's black citizens gathered at the fairgrounds to hear an address by Col. R. P. Dehart. On June 19, 1884, approximately 500–800 African Americans assembled in Parsons, Kansas, for a round of speeches and a picnic.[76]

New restrictions on black militias that accompanied Jim Crow had forced more subdued affairs in some parts of the South, yet elsewhere they continued unabated. On Juneteenth, great processions and speechmaking were the order of the day in communities throughout Texas.[77] South Carolinians celebrated January 1, one speaker noting the day's "double meaning." During slavery New Year's Day "was a day of horrors—a day of uncertainty," recalled Thomas E. Miller, "the day upon which sales of negroes were universally made . . . the day upon which husbands were separated from wives, and mothers from children." But by the 1880s, Emancipation Days had become universally celebrated throughout the state.[78] Even in Vicksburg, rapidly experiencing the stark color line of segregation, excursion trains brought hundreds of black Mississippians together for ceremonies in September 1885.[79] Whether above or below the Mason-Dixon Line, the days often proved to be a mixture of conciliation, defiance, capitulation, and resolve. Some speakers focused on honoring black heroes, some expounded on black visions of progress, and still others addressed issues such as emigration, ensuring that the war's memory extended well beyond the temporal boundaries of 1861–65.[80]

The diversity of days celebrated concerned at least some African American leaders, who hoped for a more unified, imposing occasion like national Memorial Day. The idea for a single national holiday originated with George W. Williams, a former slave and black leader in Richmond, Virginia, during the silver anniversary of the war's end.[81] Working alongside newspaper editor John Mitchell Jr., Williams called for a Grand National Celebration of Freedom set for October 15–17, 1890, in Richmond that might arouse a renewed interest in the occasion. "It is a deplorable consideration when one thinks of how ungrateful and unthankful the colored citizens have been that they have failed to establish a National Thanksgiving Day . . . for that inestimable blessing (freedom) for which our forefathers prayed for more than 200 years," lamented an advertisement. Organizers of the event, to be held for three days at the Virginia Exposition Grounds, encouraged former slaves to bring old costumes and apparel, spinning wheels, and other implements used during slavery that they would be willing to sell. Old plantation songs and hymns would be sung, and speakers from every state in the Union would address the crowd. "Among the many noted and important features of this occasion," promised the advertisement, "will be the largest gathering of the colored soldiers just as they appeared in the Union Army who will give a sham battle, which of itself will be of vast interest."[82]

Although the Reverend J. Anderson Taylor, addressing the assembly, maintained that they had not been called together to discuss any political points, much of the three-day occasion belied his contention. In his opening remarks, Taylor reminded the crowd of the necessity in selecting a single day to commemorate their freedom and embrace the pride of their race. "We want race pride. Don't love everybody better than you do yourselves," he cautioned. "Nobody will ever recognize you unless you recognize yourself." John Mercer Langston, a former slave and the first African American from Virginia elected to Congress (and whose seat there had been challenged), observed that they had gathered in the state capital a free people. "They say this is a white man's government," he observed. "I am here to tell you that this is a black man's government as well." Some, such as George T. Downing, more implicitly drew the connection between the war's outcome and contemporary politics. The Republican Party no longer served black interests, he warned. Others stood steadfastly behind the party of Lincoln. Just as politics ran through Confederate Memorial Days, it likewise infused emancipation celebrations.[83]

The following day, October 16, had been reserved for a spectacular parade. Every black-owned business in the city had been festooned with flags and bunting for what one white reporter described as the largest procession ever staged by African Americans in the former Confederate capital. For more than two miles, militia companies, civic societies, and GAR posts wound through the city while more than 10,000 spectators lined the streets. Banners carried by the marchers declared a spirit of racial uplift, one proudly boasting "In 1860 slaves; in 1890 bankers." Other marchers used the procession to announce their preference for a national emancipation day, cheering for April 9 or other dates while passing City Hall. As the *Richmond Planet* observed, it was indeed a "gala day," celebrating all that had been achieved since 1861.[84]

The matter for which they had all gathered, selecting a national day to celebrate, was taken up on the final day of the convention. The 200 delegates made various suggestions: April 3, to commemorate the fall of Richmond; April 9, to celebrate Appomattox, "for the day of the downfall of the Confederacy was the day of the uprising of the Negro"; and September 22, to honor Lincoln's preliminary proclamation. At least a few submitted that commemorating the ratification of the Fourteenth and Fifteenth Amendments would be best. Some argued that matters of weather and time off from work should be considered. Surely a celebration in early fall was preferable to one in the dead of winter, some asserted. Others suggested that taking a day off in autumn would be nearly impossible in the Deep South because of the cotton harvest. Eventually, the delegates settled on January 1, the day Lincoln's proclamation took effect in 1863.[85]

Determining the long-term influence of the convention is difficult. January 1 never became a national holiday dedicated to emancipation, nor the only day selected by African Americans to celebrate freedom. Yet there is some evidence to suggest more communities elected to mark New Year's Day with emancipation ceremonies in the years that followed. In 1891, for example, the cities of Minneapolis, Fort Worth, Jacksonville, Raleigh, Alexandria, and even small towns like Lexington, North Carolina, all observed celebrations on January 1.[86] By the end of the century, a Virginia newspaper remarked, "We are glad to see the increasing and worthy observance of this important anniversary." But it is impossible to determine whether this was a direct effect of the Richmond meeting.[87]

The convention called by Williams did, however, serve as a reminder that freedom celebrations remained an important component of not only African American civic rituals, but also Civil War memory. Like national and Confederate Memorial Days, Emancipation Days were infused with political activism and often centered on instilling the next generation with a sense of pride in the war's legacy.[88] In a letter to the "colored people of the United States" written in December 1890, the Reverend J. Anderson Taylor implored them to remember that the object of a national emancipation day was to keep the memory of freedom "fresh in the memory of the present generations and handed down to others yet unborn."[89] Twenty years later, the Calhoun Colored School in Alabama reported that it marked the day by having old people sing slavery songs and recall stories of their days in bondage.[90] Like their white counterparts who had survived the war, former slaves understood that memory was a powerful weapon.

Apart from Emancipation celebrations and Memorial Days, African American veterans continued to hold their own reunions in the 1880s and 1890s. In Texas, where white GAR members had succeeded in banning black membership, USCT veterans organized independent reunions such as that held in Fort Worth in 1895.[91] In locales where all-black GAR posts existed, black members attended festivities not unlike those of their white comrades. Members of the First and Second regiments of the colored volunteers of Kansas who gathered for a reunion in Leavenworth, Kansas, enjoyed a full day of activities, including an afternoon street parade followed by an evening campfire and speaker.[92] No doubt the William L. Garrison Post 207 and Thaddeus Stevens Post 255 of New York and Brooklyn enjoyed themselves immensely during their reunion at the Old Iron Pier dancing pavilion at Coney Island.[93]

While Emancipation Day ceremonies focused on celebrating freedom and the continued struggle for equal rights, not surprisingly African American veterans' reunions more emphatically focused on the role of the black soldier both during and after the war. In August 1887, the 54th and 55th Infantry and 5th Cavalry regiments of Massachusetts hosted a wildly successful reunion at Boston's Tremont Temple. On the reunion's second day, the veterans issued a statement underscoring "the magnitude of the work done by the colored soldiers in assisting to quell the rebellion and preserve the Union." But recognizing that the battle they had waged was not finished, they went further, condemning the deplorable conditions that black southerners still faced. They had been subjected to mob violence, deprived of their right to vote, and in the GAR's Department of the Gulf denied the opportunity to obtain a charter for an all-black post.[94] In 1865 and 1866, African American veterans believed that their service had been integral to saving the Union, and therefore they and their race were entitled to the full benefits of citizenship. Thirty years later these sentiments had only deepened.

Perhaps nothing acknowledged the bravery and sacrifice of black soldiers more than Augustus Saint-Gaudens's stunning Robert Gould Shaw Memorial. On a rainy Boston Memorial Day in 1897, immense crowds gathered to witness the parade and dedication of the monument honoring the white colonel "and the brave black men who comprised his followers." Marching alongside their white officers, the aging black survivors of the 54th and 55th Massachusetts Infantries and 5th Cavalry wound their way down Beacon Street to a site directly across from the golden-domed Massachusetts State House. There they halted to unveil the memorial—a magnificent bronze relief, featuring Shaw astride his horse leading his black volunteers out of Boston and toward their futile charge at Battery Wagner in July 1863.[95]

Touted by some of the nation's leading periodicals as an unsurpassed memorial, it beseeched all who looked upon it to remember that black men had fought to preserve the Union and end human bondage. The inscription on the marble surround said nothing about slavery or emancipation, but simply declared, "Together they gave to the nation and the world undying proof that Americans of African descent possess the pride, courage, and devotion of patriotic soldiers."[96] The monument and its dedication revealed a commemorative moment that celebrated both black and white participants in the war. But they also suggested the various meanings both white and black speakers and attendees could bring to and take away from a single event.

After the unveiling, U.S. ships in the harbor and a battery in the Common fired salutes while the dampened crowd sloshed to the Boston Music Hall to hear the day's speeches. In the packed hall, Governor Roger Wolcott reminded the audience, many of whom were among the famous antislavery element of the city, that the blood-stained ramparts at Fort Wagner had witnessed a race called to manhood. "On that day the world learned to know that whatever the color of the skin the blood in the veins of the colored man is red, with the lustrous hue of manhood and humanity," he noted.[97] William James, the Harvard philosopher and brother of an officer who had fallen at the battle of Fort Wagner, took the stage next to deliver the day's principal oration, illuminating several important strands of the Union Cause.[98] Like countless white U.S. veterans, he asserted that the war had been prompted by "the fanatics of slavery." Though still "exclusively a white man's war," in 1862, Shaw had agreed to take command of the first black regiment in the North. "Should colored troops be tried and not succeed, confusion would grow worse confounded," James observed. After recounting the regiment's history and their gallant but unsuccessful charge against Fort Wagner, he implored his listeners to differentiate between the war's meaning and the gallantry of soldiers. Alluding to the reconciliationist sentiment sweeping the country and Lost Cause contentions that Confederate soldiers had been heroic, he reminded them that "moral service" must be distinguished from mere "fortitude." Monuments should be built to "civic courage," not merely to "battle instinct," he cautioned—the kind of civic courage exhibited by Shaw and his men. "What Shaw and his comrades stand for and show us is that in such an emergency Americans of all complexions and conditions can go forth like brothers, and meet death cheerfully if need be," he noted, "in order that this [experiment in liberty] of our native land shall not become a failure on earth."[99]

The day's final speech had been reserved for Booker T. Washington, the president of Tuskegee Institute. A young slave child in Virginia during the war, in 1895 he had gained national fame at the Cotton States and International Exposition in Atlanta for a speech his critics remembered as a capitulation to white supremacy and his defenders recalled as part of his strategy for economic and educational uplift for black southerners. Climbing to the stage amid the choral strains of "The Battle Hymn of the Republic," he first paid tribute to Shaw as a nearly Christ-like figure and recalled the efforts of former governor John Andrew and abolitionist George L. Stearns to recruit black troops. Then he turned his attention to the black veterans of Battery Wagner, sixty-five of whom sat upon the stage. "To you who fought so valiantly in the ranks," he observed, "the scarred and scattered remnant of the 54th regiment, who with empty sleeve and wanting leg, have honored this occasion with your presence, to you your commander is not dead." In a dramatic moment, Sgt. William H. Carney rose to his feet gripping the regiment's U.S. flag. "I have never seen or experienced anything which equalled this," Washington later recalled. "For a number of minutes, the audience seemed to entirely lose control of itself."[100]

Washington may have been startled by the exuberant reaction to Carney, but those in the audience surely were not. Most were likely well aware that he was the first African American to be awarded the Medal of Honor for rescuing his regiment's colors, despite a bullet wound to his hip. A widely reproduced (if inaccurate) lithograph by Kurz and Allison of the assault on Battery Wagner depicted Carney baring the flag next to a mortally wounded Shaw. The frontispiece to the regimental history for the 54th featured a portrait of Carney standing with the rescued flag. By 1890, a Sons of Veterans post bore his name. And at countless Fourth of July celebrations, he had recounted the story of his daring bravery. "As the color-bearer became disabled," he remembered, "I threw away my gun and seized the colors, making my way to the head of the column." If Shaw was to be martyred for his death, Carney was celebrated for his bravery and determined effort that "the old flag never touched the ground."[101]

Sgt. William Carney, a member of the 54th USCT, frequently gave speeches recounting his heroic efforts to save the regimental colors at the battle of Battery Wagner. (Library of Congress)

Once the audience had settled, Washington continued. Though gathered to pay tribute to Shaw and his soldiers, Washington understood the occasion celebrated much more than the bravery and courage of these men on the field of glory. Like USCT veterans and Frederick Douglass, he believed that the battle begun during the war was not yet finished. Drawing upon his "Atlanta Compromise" speech, he urged black education both in industrial schools like Tuskegee and in colleges, and he touted the success of black men and women in the thirty years since Appomattox. In a message he would return to frequently, he assured the families of all Union soldiers—whether black or white—that their loved ones' sacrifices had not been in vain. The real monument to the Union soldiers, he declared, "the greater monument," was being slowly built in the South "in the struggles and sacrifices of a race to justify all that had been done and suffered for it." Union victory had meant so much more than ensuring that the republic was never again torn apart.[102]

Even as he praised the Union Cause, Washington returned to another theme of his Atlanta speech and urged racial reconciliation. "The black man who cannot let love and sympathy out to the white man, is but half free," he observed. "The white man, who would close the shop or the factory against the black man seeking an opportunity to earn an honest living, is but half free." He counseled not just racial but also sectional reconciliation. "My heart goes out to those who wore gray as well as to those clothed in blue," he confessed, "to those who returned defeated, to destitute homes, to face blasted hopes and [a] shattered political and industrial system." Only true, heartfelt reconciliation among both sections and races, he believed, could set the nation on the path to finding "the full measure of the fruit of Fort Wagner." "What these heroic souls of the 54th regiment began," he advised, "we must complete."[103]

Though the Shaw Memorial was the lone monument to black soldiers built during the nineteenth century, it was far from the only tribute to these men and their cause. During the 1880s and 1890s the black press expanded substantially, and both newspapers and religious periodicals helped articulate African American memories of the war. Editors urged local communities to observe the Fourth of July, Emancipation Day celebrations, and other black memorials. "Every man, woman, and child with one-eighth of negro blood in his veins should deck themselves in their very best attire and show their appreciation for the birthday of their American liberty," insisted a typical article. Newspapers regularly ran features about slavery and the Civil War, emphasizing the role of black soldiers. "No class of soldiers (and there were many) fought more bravely in the late war than did those of color," proclaimed the *Washington Bee*. Black newspapers rallied to the defense of black soldiers' widows in their efforts to secure pensions. And they often included stories on heroes such as John Brown, Frederick Douglass, Charles Sumner, Ulysses S. Grant, and Abraham Lincoln.[104]

So too did African American newspapers regularly challenge the Lost Cause.[105] Among the most vocal editors was John Mitchell Jr., owner of the Richmond *Planet*. When the Richmond city council proposed an appropriation for the Lee monument dedication in 1890, Mitchell, one of three black councilmen, became indignant. He refused to support the effort, observing that those who wore the "clinking chains of slavery" should not be forced to vote on the issue.[106] Reflecting upon the affair, he offered a response in keeping with many white northerners: a monument to the rebel chieftain would hand down "to generations unborn a legacy of treason and blood." "It serves to reopen the wound of war and cause to drift further apart the two sections." In raising monuments to its leaders, the South, he maintained, "goes too far in its adulation, and while doing them no good, do their respective sections much harm."[107]

Other African American newspapers offered similar reactions. The *New York Age* conceded that Lee was "one of the greatest generals of modern times" but hastened to note that "he was a traitor." A Springfield, Illinois, paper acknowledged that "he had many virtues which are worthy of emulation," but it could not tolerate the accompanying rebel flag, "that ensign of treason." A Baltimore newspaper noted that the entire occasion had served as "an opportunity to justify the southern people in rebelling against the U.S. Government and to flaunt the Confederate flag in the face of the loyal people of the nation." This was not only an insult to loyal Americans, but also a "stigma on Gen. Lee's record as commander of the Confederate Army."[108] A group of black Richmonders offered a different solution: a monument to General Grant, who had "compelled the capital of the Confederacy to surrender." They freely admitted, however, that no white Virginians would contribute to the fund.[109]

Despite such sentiment, the *Washington Bee* reported with scorn that a colored militia had requested to participate in the Lee monument procession. "It is a mockery to the memory of those many thousand Union heroes that fell in defense of liberty," scolded the paper. Invoking the image of the lynch mob, the paper continued in vehement rant: "Every Negro that participated in those ceremonies ought to have a rope around his neck and swung to the tail of the horse upon which the dead ex-Confederate is mounted."[110] Mitchell's *Planet* responded that no such application had been made and no black militia companies had participated in the ceremonies (even if black men had labored to erect the monument).[111] One can only imagine Mitchell's reaction to a *New York Times* story, noting that "four or five old colored men who followed the army" had attended the dedication to pay their respects to the Confederate cause. According to the reporter, Jubal Early introduced two of his former slaves to Congressman Charles T. O'Ferrall, remarking that "these are respectable darkies; none of your scalawag niggers."[112] According to Early, these were black men who knew their place, "faithful slaves" who had not abandoned their white masters to flee to the Union lines, donned the hated Yankee blue, or attempted to corrupt southern politics.[113] Foreshadowing the debates that would challenge reconciliation in the early twentieth century, Early's remarks intimately connected the war and its aftermath—Reconstruction.

Even as white southerners simultaneously erased slavery as a cause of the war and romanticized the institution, black leaders could not come to a consensus on the meaning of slavery's legacy. Some attempted to distance themselves from slavery, maintaining that African American history had begun after emancipation. Prominent African Methodist Episcopal Church member Theophilus Gould Steward spurned the notion that the "dark and hideous" past could serve as a source of unity and pride. "Our history is something to be ashamed of," he observed. "Men do not like to be referred to slavery now." The Reverend Emanuel K. Love agreed. "I need not consume much time in speaking of [the past]," he noted at a Savannah Emancipation Day service in 1888. "The present and future concern us most. Slavery with all of its inhuman hardships, wounds, bruises, cowhides, bullwhips, patrols and every course which the damnable system of slavery in this country had, are forever gone."[114] Others disagreed, insisting that remembering a history of slavery would serve not only to prove how far African Americans had come since bondage, but also to counter the increasingly distorted recollections of white southerners.[115]

Making the memory of slavery and the war even more complicated, not all black leaders rejected reconciliation. Booker T. Washington had not only taken this position publicly at the Shaw Memorial dedication, but he also privately donated funds to a Confederate soldiers' home in Alabama.[116] Other black spokesmen championed not necessarily Blue-Gray, but white-black, reconciliation. Even before Reconstruction ended, African American leaders in Raleigh, North Carolina, had begun constructing a common past with whites. In 1869, Charles Hunter called for white and black residents to join together on July 4. Three years later, he invited white officials ranging from radical Republicans to conservative Democrats to participate in Emancipation Day ceremonies (no such partnership occurred). In 1877 and 1878, Zebulon Vance became the first Democratic governor to speak at Emancipation Day, praising the hard work and achievement of black citizens. Ten years later, Governors Thomas Michael Holt of North Carolina and E. A Perry of Florida spoke at celebrations in their respective states, scorning white violence and offering instead a paternalistic vision of black-white relations. Even on occasions that remained overwhelmingly black, speakers in Raleigh often assured whites that they harbored no ill will toward former slaveholders and praised efforts by whites on behalf of the black population. Contrasting harshly with black commemorations that stressed the revolutionary nature of emancipation, Raleigh's black leaders highlighted white-black relations stretching from slavery to the present that might bind the races together in a common memory. Together, black and white had traversed the transition from slavery to freedom, assuring advancement for all.[117]

Some took this accommodationist memory a step further. At least a handful of black speakers and authors invoked the figure of the faithful slave, ever ready to protect white women and children while their masters were away on the battlefield. During the war, enslaved men and women understood that Union victory meant their liberation and that defeat meant their continued enslavement, observed Booker T. Washington. But "when the suggestion and temptation came to burn the home and massacre wife and children during the absence of the master during battle," he noted, slaves had "chosen the better part, and for four long years protect[ed] and support[ed] the helpless, defenceless ones entrusted to their care."[118] Because of their fealty, some like Washington argued, African Americans had proven their worthiness for the full rights of citizenship.[119] Although it failed to serve its intended purpose and may even have backfired by feeding into white depictions of the "faithful slave," the rationale behind such arguments was clear. In this scenario, southern black leaders simultaneously inverted the citizenship arguments usually reserved for black Union soldiers and embraced the loyal-slave tenet of the Lost Cause. This message, of course, did not sit well with countless African Americans, proving the extent to which they failed to agree on slavery's legacy and responded in a variety of ways to white southerners' attempts to rewrite the past.[120]

At the other end of the spectrum, some black veterans and their allies rejected any instance of clasping hands with former rebels. When an all-black GAR post from Pittsburgh received an invitation from the UCV requesting aid for indigent rebel soldiers, they tabled it without discussion.[121] In 1895, the integrated W. B. Smart and Ward posts of the GAR joined the William H. Carney Sons of Union Veterans camp in protesting the dedication of the Confederate monument in Chicago as well as "all such displays of honor to zealous yet traitorously misguided men."[122] Perhaps no one excoriated the Lost Cause and reconciliation more than Frederick Douglass before his death in February 1895. He repeatedly assailed northerners' adoration of Confederate commanders, especially Robert E. Lee. But above all, Douglass feared that the "North [would] turn away from the ghastly scene of war and the past [and] let bygones be bygones." He explicitly "did not want national reunion; he wanted racial justice, promised in law, demonstrated in practice, and preserved in memory."[123] Race and reconciliation remained as equally contentious within black memories of the war as they did within white during the last decades of the nineteenth century.

A SPLENDID LITTLE WAR TO REUNITE THE NATION

In the spring of 1898, Theodore Roosevelt, William Randolph Hearst, and other militarists finally got their "splendid little war."[124] For years, tales of Spanish atrocities against the Cubans had enlivened the bellicose posturing of imperial-minded Americans. Couched in the rhetoric of a humanitarian effort to free Cubans from their colonial oppressor, imperialists well understood that expelling Spain from the Caribbean would open naval bases and foreign markets and extend U.S. power around the globe. When the battleship *Maine* mysteriously exploded in Havana Harbor on February 15, 1898, killing 260 Americans, the drumbeat for war grew louder, and Congress joined the cacophony of newspapers in their cries for recourse. President William McKinley, the last Civil War veteran to occupy the White House, was not yet convinced. "I have been through one war," he famously wrote a friend. "I have seen the dead piled up, and I do not want to see another." But on April 20, he acquiesced, authorizing Congress to declare war on Spain in the name of Cuban independence.[125]

McKinley was not alone in his hesitation. Throughout the 1890s, soldiers' reunions and memorial dedications had focused on the grandeur and valor of battle, but veterans had not forgotten the grim and ghastly cost of war. With the images, sounds, and smells of war seared in their memories, and with their missing limbs or consumptive coughs as constant reminders, many hoped to avoid any future combat. Throughout the spring, letters from both Union and Confederate veterans flooded Washington, many lamenting the need for more bloodshed. Yet even as they looked forward to another war with trepidation, some recognized that it might prove useful beyond the stated purpose of liberating the Cubans.[126] For Confederate veterans in particular, a war with a foreign foe offered them an opportunity to prove their allegiance and fidelity to the United States. "The loyalty of ex-Confederates to our government has for years been made a subject of criticism," wrote a veteran of Hood's Texas Brigade, offering to raise a regiment of former Confederates. "All we ask is an opportunity to let our actions speak for our loyalty."[127] "I do want you to know and appreciate," wrote another to McKinley, "what a true Southerner and Mississippian is and with what loyalty they *can* and *will* support the *Union now* and *forever*."[128]

Not all former Confederates felt so anxious to prove they were reconciled to the old flag. "We have not yet offered our services for the 'Spanish War,'" quipped one former rebel, "thinking that as the President has such a *large* army of *'Pensioners'* we will just let them adjust the little matter with Spain, and so *earn their pay* and, *support*."[129] S. A. Cunningham, editor of the *Confederate Veteran*, warned that many white southerners abhorred the thought of donning a blue uniform and suggested that the U.S. Army might adopt brown uniforms to appease southern sensitivities. "The fraternity may be complete between the North and South, but it will not occur through anything that is humiliating to the people of the latter section," he warned, adding simply: "Personal honor is above country."[130] Although the army did not adopt brown uniforms, it took note of lingering sectional animosity and elected to route trains carrying soldiers of the 71st New York south to Florida around rather than through Richmond, the former Confederate capital.[131]

McKinley and others recognized that the war (which lasted only four months and claimed the lives of 460 Americans in battle and another 5,200 of disease) was perfectly positioned to capitalize on existing reconciliationist sentiment and end sectional bitterness.[132] This would be a war fought by a united, a reunited, nation.[133] To this end, McKinley appointed both Union and Confederate veterans to key positions. Most prominent among the white southerners was sixty-three-year-old Fitzhugh Lee, a former Confederate cavalry general and governor of Virginia currently serving as consul in Havana. Given his experience, McKinley selected Lee as a major general of volunteers. Chosen more for political reasons than experience, Joseph Wheeler, a West Point graduate, former Confederate cavalry leader, and Democratic congressman from Alabama, received the same commission. Along with former Confederates from the ranks and their sons who had not yet won glory on the battlefield, Lee and Wheeler joined forces with their former enemy under the Stars and Stripes.[134] White southern men fought valiantly and bravely on the Cuban fields, contradicting images of an emasculated South that had poured off northern presses since Jefferson Davis's alleged capture in a dress.[135] Newspapers gushed that the Mason-Dixon Line had been obliterated by the war, while white southerners in Atlanta and Vicksburg celebrated July 4 for the first time since 1860.[136] "This war with Spain is worth all it will cost in blood and treasure," declared Union veteran S. W. Fordyce, for "the confidence it begets between the ex-soldiers of both armies, as well as the fraternal feeling it will create between the people of all the states."[137]

For white southerners, the war did more than foster reconciliation. It also vindicated the Lost Cause. The words "traitor" and "rebel" no longer applied, they maintained. "It is a source of no small pride that the whole country has at last learned its true value the depth and fervor of Southern patriotism," observed former Confederate general Stephen D. Lee. Lest anyone believe that the Spanish-American War was an aberration, white southerners insisted otherwise. The same stirrings of patriotism that prompted them to fight in 1776, in 1812, in the Mexican War—even in the "great struggle between the States"—had motivated them now. In each instance, they had fought for principles that were constitutional and

Col. William Jennings Bryan (left) and Maj. Gen. Fitzhugh Lee at Cuba Libre, Jacksonville, Florida, September 1898. President William McKinley selected Lee, a former Confederate cavalry general, to serve as a major general of volunteers in the Spanish-American War. (Virginia Historical Society)

unequivocally American. They had fought in 1861 as they did in 1898 (in the name of Cubans) for the principle of self-government and liberty.[138] Surely no one could argue that the Lost Cause was immoral when presented in such terms. By highlighting their own fight for "liberty" (as opposed to Union veterans' claims to freeing the slaves), white southerners could simultaneously claim loyalty to the U.S. flag and to their Confederate heritage.[139] But most important, the war with Spain allowed former Confederates to accomplish on an international stage what the Lost Cause had been claiming for years: a vindication of southern honor, manhood, and loyalty.[140]

Black men likewise looked to Cuba as another opportunity to prove their patriotism and masculinity. Just as they had tied their Civil War service to a demand for political rights, in 1898 many African Americans hoped their participation might help turn back the growing tide of disenfranchisement and segregation. "Our fathers labored . . . fought . . . and died to perpetuate this country and leave a heritage to us," argued the *Iowa State Bystander*. Harkening back to the years 1863–65, the paper continued: "Let us be men and show loyalty and we shall be rewarded."[141] Not all were so enthusiastic. *Richmond Planet* editor John Mitchell Jr.

insisted that black men should fight only if they could do so under black officers with the ranks of colonel or major—a departure from the white officers of the USCT. "No officers, no fight," demanded Mitchell. "We'll wait the change."[142]

Many white southerners would have been content to let them wait. Responding to President McKinley's call for colored troops, the *New Orleans Times-Democrat* insisted upon the "inexpediency" of enlisting African Americans, urging the president to "allow the white folks to handle this war without their assistance."[143] Invoking the Civil War's memory, Mitchell responded that this was the same advice given to Lincoln. Even Robert E. Lee had "recommended that the Confederates arm these same Negroes, and use them to fight against the United States." But the results were clear: "Lincoln enlisted these Negroes and won. Mr. Jefferson Davis would not enlist these Negroes and lost." "History repeats itself," warned Mitchell.[144] Other Unionists joined in recalling the Civil War service of African Americans during the current conflict. It seems hardly coincidental that in early July, Col. Thomas Wentworth Higginson published a lengthy article detailing the valorous history and contributions of his 1st South Carolina Volunteers, the "First Black Regiment."[145] The heroics of USCT soldiers had not—and should not—be forgotten.

Black soldiers assigned to "pacify" Indians in the American West, the so-called Buffalo Soldiers, were among the first to be mobilized in 1898 (especially because many white military leaders believed them physiognomically suited to fight in the tropics).[146] During the short war more than 10,000 African Americans served, many to much acclaim. News of the Ninth and Tenth Cavalry's heroics alongside Roosevelt's Rough Riders on San Juan Hill, under the overall command of former Confederate Joseph Wheeler, filled newspapers throughout the nation.[147] As he had praised the 54th Massachusetts at the Shaw Memorial, Booker T. Washington frequently lauded the service of black soldiers during the Spanish-American War. Addressing his largest audience ever at the Chicago Peace Jubilee celebrating the end of the war in mid-October, Washington recalled the heroic sacrifice of African American men in the nation's wars. From Crispus Attucks to black men who fought with Andrew Jackson at the Battle of New Orleans; the brave colored troops at Forts Wagner and Pillow to the heroism of the black regiments who had stormed El Caney and Santiago—in all these victories, black men had fought for their nation. With that, he looked up to President McKinley sitting in a box and, to an eruption of applause and waving handkerchiefs, thanked him for recognizing black men in his appointments during the war. After the audience had once more settled, Washington noted that there remained one more victory for Americans to win. "We have succeeded in every conflict except in the effort to conquer ourselves in the blotting out of racial prejudices," he observed. "We can celebrate the era of peace in no more effectual way than by a firm resolve on the part of Northern men and Southern men, black men and white men, that the trenches we have together dug around Santiago shall be the eternal burial places for all that separates us in our business and civil relations."[148] Here was Washington again offering the ultimate reconciliationist message—trying to unite the nation in sectional and racial peace, not in purposeful forgetting, but in an acknowledgment of the sacrifice and devotion black men had always shown to the United States.[149]

Though he hoped otherwise, Washington well understood that the service of the African American soldiers had not prevented white southerners from charging black soldiers with riots, ignoring segregation laws, and other unruly behavior.[150] Nor had it deterred white mobs on the home front from continuing to hang, shoot, and burn black men—the massacre in Wilmington, North Carolina, in November 1898 being the most outrageous example. But these issues were not confined to the continental United States. Lewis H. Douglass, a veteran of the 54th Massachusetts and son of the late Frederick Douglass, could not help but see a pattern of postwar racial violence playing itself out on the world stage. In his estimation, America's imperialist ambitions meant "the extension of race hate and cruelty, barbarous lynchings and gross injustice" around the globe among people of color.[151]

Reaction among white southerners reinforced Douglass's prediction. With the prospect of "colored people" in Cuba and the Philippines being brought under the American flag, the notion of Anglo-Saxon superiority soared.[152] White northerners embraced Anglo-Saxonism at the turn of the century, but white southerners employed it in the name of Civil War memory.[153] While some white southerners warned that a U.S. presence in the Philippines was little more than a reprise of Reconstruction that would turn Americans into carpetbaggers, others found in international affairs affirmation of Reconstruction's horrors.[154] At their annual reunion in May 1899, the UCV observed that both the recent war and the Supreme Court had confirmed white southerners' efforts to remove the "specter of misrule from our borders" by restoring "the more educated and capable race" to power in the South. "The reception given our benevolent intentions in the Philippines is . . . likely to inspire a wholesome respect for the matter of governing people of another blood which have started late in the race of civilization," the UCV noted in 1899. The "difficulties of the race problem abroad" confirmed that white northerners had been wrong about African American suffrage and political rights. "We are not likely in the future," commented the veterans, "to hear so much about the right of men who have not yet learned to govern themselves, to govern others by their votes."[155] Reconstruction had been at best misguided if not arbitrarily cruel, and white southerners had not forgotten. In the decades to come, the memory of Reconstruction would increasingly hinder sectional reconciliation.[156]

For now, another pattern emerged. Just as the memory of the dead had fiercely animated sectionalism in 1865 and 1866, in 1898 the dead became the chief symbol of a reunited nation. Once again, the blood of the North and South flowed. Yet this time it did so not in the name of contending sections, but beneath the same flag. When newspapers learned that one of the first war deaths was Worth Bagley, a sailor from North Carolina and son of a Confederate veteran, they raved with reconciliationist sentiment. "There is no north and no south . . . we are all Worth Bagley's countrymen," proclaimed the New York Tribune.[157] From Tennessee came the story of two fathers, one a Union veteran, the other a Confederate, meeting at the graves of their sons who had fallen on San Juan Hill. Men who had once fought against each other now mingled their tears over sons who had sacrificed their lives on the same altar of patriotism.[158] Invoking the "new birth" Abraham Lincoln had spoken of at Gettysburg, countless orators suggested that a new nation might be born from the Spanish-American War dead. "The last hateful memory that could divide our country is buried with them," observed Stephen D. Lee at the UCV national convention. "About their graves kneels a new nation, loving all her children everywhere the same."[159]

At the Atlanta Peace Jubilee on December 14, 1898, President McKinley likewise embraced the war dead as a symbol of the reunited nation. In part a gesture of reconciliation and in part a bid for southern support of overseas expansion (a majority of southern senators were refusing to ratify the peace treaty with Spain), he proposed that the federal government should assist in caring for the graves of *all* who had fallen in the Civil War.[160] "Sectional lines no longer mar the United States," the president asserted. "Sectional feeling no longer holds back the love we bear each other." Invoking the Union Cause as much as reconciliation, he rejoiced that the most recent war had proven that "the Union is once more the common atlas of our love and loyalty, our devotion and sacrifice." "The time has now come in the evolution of sentiment and feeling under the providence of God," he declared, "when in the spirit of fraternity we should share with you in the care of the graves of the Confederate soldiers."[161] With his announcement, old men who had fought for the South leapt to their feet in applause, waving their hats madly in the air.[162]

Hoping to capitalize on such sentiment, a southern congressman and senator proposed bills that would open the National Soldiers' Homes and provide pensions to both Union and Confederate veterans. If the government was willing to care for the graves of Confederate dead, it should be no less willing to care for the disabled and impoverished living.[163] But most Union veterans found the idea of Confederate pensions insulting.[164] The editor of the GAR's *National Tribune* conceded that he did not have a problem honoring graves of those "who were deluded and deceived into joining the rebellion." "They are Americans and our countrymen," he observed, and helping them to tend the places where their fallen slept was an "act of brotherly sympathy." (It did not mean, he added, that there would be no distinction between the Union and rebel grave. The Union grave would always be worthy of an honor unavailable to the rebel.) Placing rebel survivors on the pension rolls or admitting them to the Soldiers' Home, however, would be "subversive of every principle upon which the war for the preservation of the Union was waged."[165]

Many Confederate veterans agreed, albeit for different reasons. UCV camps and the southern press immediately issued statements denouncing pensions for former Confederates, the admission of Confederate veterans to retired soldiers' homes, and even the care of Confederate dead by the national government. Veterans from Nashville concluded that accepting a pension was tantamount to "placing a money value on the patriotism of those who were willing to give their all, and their lives . . . in defense of their Southern country." Another southern publication suggested that Union soldiers were less heroic than Confederates because they had accepted government assistance.[166] And after a spirited debate at the UCV's annual reunion in May 1899, the veterans voted to politely decline the president's offer with the exception of those Confederate graves located in the North. The care of the South's dead was a "sacred trust, dear to the hearts of Southern women." "We believe that we can safely let it there remain."[167]

To accept aid for either the living or the dead from the federal government would be a concession, a failing of the honor and pride among those who had fought and died for the South. The legality of secession might have been settled in a trial by battle on the field at Appomattox, but the spirit of states' rights and southern independence was alive and well.[168]

The Spanish-American War had been promoted and celebrated as a moment of national reconciliation, but for former Confederates it served primarily to embolden their defense of the valorous Lost Cause and underscore the injustice of Reconstruction.

Even as former Confederates rejected federal pensions and cemetery aid, the color line appeared more readily apparent at Memorial Days in the wake of the Spanish-American War. For years, in many national cemeteries located in the former Confederacy, African Americans had alone attended to the Union dead.[169] But at the 1899 Memorial Day, white leaders of South Carolina's GAR posts observed that the African Americans who had so long observed the day in the national cemetery in Florence had failed to decorate the graves. Galvanized by the spirit of reconciliation during the recent war, white GAR members called for the formation of a Florence Blue and Gray Memorial Association organized to sponsor Memorial Day services and decorate the graves of both Union and Confederate soldiers. Perhaps most significant, the group elected to bar African Americans from the observances. This was to be a white-only affair, purging the memory of African American Union soldiers.[170] Yet the actions of this GAR post did not mean that most of their fellow Union veterans had forgotten that the war had been about slavery.

Three years after the Spanish-American War, Indianapolis unveiled one of the most impressive Civil War monuments in the country. On a bright mid-May day in 1902, more than 50,000 people, including 15,000 veterans in town for the annual GAR encampment, gathered to dedicate the elaborate memorial that encompassed nearly an entire city block at the very heart of the Indiana capital. The monument was an impressive site. Reaching more than 284 feet into the sky, it was replete with cascading fountains, bronze candelabras, sculptures of each military branch, and twelve bronze bison heads, and it was crowned by the figure of Victory. But it was the large stone groupings of Peace and War that stood out the most. Designed and sculpted by the German artists Bruno Schmitz and Rudolph Schwarz, the east side of the monument depicted War, represented by shooting infantry, charging cavalry, and artillery. The goddess of war dominated the center, while Columbia held the Stars and Stripes high in the air as she trampled the Confederate flag. Below, more figures recalled the sacrifices made by the dying soldier. On the west, Peace reigned. Here, returning soldiers celebrated their triumph while Liberty held forth the flag and the angel of peace carried both the wreath of victory and an olive branch. But Peace meant much more than a cease-fire. At the lower right, a freed slave lifted his shattered chains toward Liberty.[171] The monument expressed the vision of emancipation held by many whites: a black man seated submissively, beginning to rise yet not asking for equality.[172] Nevertheless, the largest Civil War monument ever built was hardly a reconciliationist message that called for forgetting slavery.

Although Americans had come together in the common defense of the nation in 1898, they had not done so merely by agreeing to remain silent on the memory of slavery. In fact, many had difficulties agreeing on how best to remember the nation's most divisive legacy. For some African Americans, finding a common history with their white neighbors was imperative. Others fiercely challenged the burgeoning reconciliationist narrative. Neither had many white Union veterans sought reconciliation based upon a whitewashed memory of the war, as historians have argued. They had not capitulated to the Lost Cause. In refusing to do so, they forced white southerners to defend their actions and their peculiar institution. The repeated protestations by former Confederates only underscored just how central slavery remained even thirty years later. As one century gave way to the next, slavery and emancipation persisted in competing memories of the war.

WOMEN AND RECONCILIATION

1880s–1910s

At two o'clock on July 21, 1911, the skies above northern Virginia opened and the rain came in torrents. For miles, mud-clogged roads and swollen creeks stranded automobiles, including five that were part of President William Howard Taft's entourage bound for Manassas. Bedraggled, mud-spattered, and nearly two hours late, the president had come to attend the closing exercises of the Manassas Peace Jubilee and Reunion, a week-long festival celebrating the fiftieth anniversary of the Civil War's first major battle. Every day that week had witnessed stirring ceremonies, yet the crowning event was the much anticipated clasping of hands among the veterans of the blue and gray. At noon, a thin line of aging Confederate and Union veterans advanced toward each other across Henry House Hill with halting steps and outstretched hands. For more than five minutes, the men clasped hands, posed for the cameras, and vowed eternal friendship.[1]

As was typical at Blue-Gray reunions, women attended along with their husbands and fathers, but their only official roles on this day of fraternal handshaking were symbolic and supportive.[2] Few in the late nineteenth or early twentieth century paused to consider this male-centered culture of reconciliation.[3] After all, reconciliationist sentiment had largely been premised on the shared experience of combat. Of course it would be the veterans who gathered to reminisce about the horrid marches and gallant charges they had both experienced. Efforts to establish the national military parks had been orchestrated in the male-bastions of Congress; the battlefields had been marked and preserved by the men who had fought

On July 21, 1911, President William Howard Taft addressed the fiftieth reunion of the battle of Manassas/Bull Run. Overwhelmingly, veterans dominated reunions. Women played only symbolic roles, such as the forty-eight young women—far too young to remember the war—dressed all in white representing the states of the Union featured just beneath the American flag. (Library of Congress)

on those fields; and the dedicatory addresses delivered by male officers and politicians. Without the fraternal bonds of soldiering or political and financial incentives, women found little reason to commiserate with their counterparts across the Mason-Dixon Line. Northern and southern women might join together in the name of temperance, but remembering the war remained a whole other issue entirely. Unlike the veterans, Confederate groups like the Ladies' Memorial Associations (LMAs) and the United Daughters of the Confederacy (UDC) rarely found any common ground with their northern counterparts, the Woman's Relief Corps (WRC) and Ladies of the GAR (LGAR).

It was not merely that women did not facilitate reconciliation; it seemed in many instances that southern white women actively sought to hinder the lovefest propounded by veterans. Returning home to Pennsylvania after the jubilee, Union veteran James E. Maddox seethed with indignation. The Manassas women, he charged, had spoken curtly and refused water to the troopers of the 15th Cavalry "because they wore the uniform of the United States army." Amid the blue-gray cluster of men greeting each other and (appearing) to forget the wrongs of days past, the southern women had maintained an icy attitude. "Our women will never forgive the North," one Confederate veteran seemed to proudly explain. "They are as bitter today as they were when the civil war was declared."[4]

Isabel Worrell Ball, president of the WRC Department of the Potomac, believed southern white women to be not only bitter, but fiercely disloyal and corrupting. Upon arriving in Manassas, she had been appalled to observe Confederate battle flags as well as the Stars and Bars fluttering alongside Old Glory from nearly every storefront and home. "To the United Daughters of the Confederacy is due the cunning arrangement of the decorations on all these Blue Gray occasions," she charged. But Union men were not without recrimination. To her utter horror she had witnessed GAR men wearing Confederate flags alongside the American flag. Some had even gone so far as to remove their GAR badges and Loyal Legion buttons to don the rebel flag. "They dare not do otherwise," she added without explanation. Union women, however, would never stoop to such a "surrender of principles." "In my blood runs the same hot hatred of treason's emblem that sent my father forth in defense of the Nation's honor," she declared, "and beloved of him, as I was, he would have laid me dead at his feet had I dared to place over his loyal old heart the despised emblem of the rebellious South."[5] In the fifty years since the war, veterans seemed to have found reasons to shake hands with their former foes in the name of reconciliation, but the women—of both sides—would not be so quick to join forces.

Ball's exasperation no doubt came from her frustration with the tenacious sectionalism of the UDC. Though numerically more active than their Confederate counterparts, Union women proved decidedly less visible within commemorations. This was in part because Union veterans failed to see their women as essential to either the war or its memory. But it was equally an artifact of the cause they sought to remember. Like their veterans, black and white northern women celebrated reunion—and frequently emancipation—as a vindication of the Union Cause. Although they fiercely objected to the Lost Cause, their mission of encouraging American patriotism necessitated that they reach out to white southerners.

Alternatively, southern white women proved to be even more recalcitrant than their fathers in resisting the reconciliationist gush. And they appeared to be gaining ever more influence over Civil War memory. Praised by their men for their unflagging loyalty to the Lost Cause, they remained intent on vindicating the Confederate cause and keeping its memory alive among future generations. More tenaciously and persistently than the veterans, southern white women attacked negative images of both the Confederacy and slavery. Perhaps most astonishing, in the early 1900s, the Daughters claimed space for their cause in the very epicenters of the Union Cause: in Washington, D.C., at the gates of Andersonville prison, and in Arlington National Cemetery. Under their watch, the Lost Cause was ever so slowly beginning to overshadow the Union Cause.

THE MOTHERS OF MEN

In the years after Appomattox, Confederate veterans seemed unable to refrain from gushing about their loyal, devoted, and sacrificing women. Laudatory accounts filled southern newspapers, Memorial Day addresses, and monument dedications praising above all else Confederate women's tenacious and feisty defense of the cause. During the war, argued Mississippi governor James Vardaman in 1907, Confederate women "were at home doing greater deeds than even Lee or Grant." "The greatest battles were fought by the mothers of men," he declared.[6] Theirs had been a far different experience from that of their Union counterparts. "Northern women had no special care or discomfort," exhorted Capt. Francis W. Dawson before a group of Confederate veterans in Baltimore in 1882. "They were in no danger themselves. There was no Milroy, no Butler, no Hunter, no Sheridan, no Sherman, to taunt and upbraid them, to strip them of their most precious mementoes, to steal or scatter their scanty store of provisions and burn their homes over their head." All Confederate women, he declared, "are beyond the reach of comparison, and stand nobly, supremely alone, without peer or rival."[7] Confederate women were not only essential, they were also exceptional.

Many southern white men no doubt believed what they said about their women. Yet there were also deeper, if not necessarily conscious, motives for white southern men to place women at the very heart of the Confederate cause. White southerners insisted that they had fought in defense of hearth and home rather than a war for some abstract principle like the Union. They had waged a defensive war against those who had invaded their land—threatened their homes, freed their slaves, and harassed their women and children.[8] Certainly northerners would have done the same. The Confederate objective was not "about politics, or slavery, or even constitutional principles." Focused on the family and home, the southern cause was moral, righteous, and virtuous—it was domestic.[9]

In striking contrast to their former foes, northern men were nearly silent on the role of Union women.[10] In the immediate aftermath of war, a few publications had celebrated the angelic qualities of female hospital workers and the tireless loyalty of Union women on the home front. But by the 1880s, representations of Union women had become relatively infrequent.[11] Unlike their southern counterparts, acknowledgments from Union veterans of women's contributions, at least public ones, were rare. Few Memorial Day speeches by northern veterans made any reference to women. Orators routinely focused on the bravery and "patriotic zeal" of soldiers, the triumph of the Union, and (in some cases) celebrated emancipation, but the trials and labors of women were largely absent from the addresses. The same held true among black veterans, who rarely recognized the role black women had played as laundresses, nurses, and cooks.[12] References to women at Union monument dedications, in regimental histories, or even among memoirs of generals such as Ulysses S. Grant were conspicuously absent. Where Confederate veterans rallied to build monuments to their southern women on every statehouse lawn in the South (a clearly public space), no memorials honoring all Union women were erected.[13] Only when celebrating specific nurses or directly addressing the women of the WRC or LGAR did Union veterans appear inclined to heap praise on the war contributions of Union women.

During the war, the distance between the battlefront and the home front meant that Union soldiers and the northern press often perceived northern women as indifferent to the war effort. Many of these sentiments gained credence in the postwar years. Men had fought to save the Union and, many added, to emancipate the slaves. But the Union women's "relief" on the home front had not been essential to either. Seldom subject to wartime invasions and unlikely to be caught in crossfire (with the notable exceptions of the border regions), white northern women seemed to have experienced very little of the conflict. The Union Cause was not seen as necessarily part of women's sphere. Only the nurses and sanitary workers who had been on the frontlines and risked their lives for the cause received acknowledgment from veterans. For example, Rossiter Johnson's 1896 *Campfire and Battle-field* included a chapter on women of the Sanitary and Christian Commissions, noting that "many of them lost their lives, directly or indirectly, in the consequence of their labors."[14] The following year, the Department of Kansas GAR set aside July 19 as Mother Bickerdyke Day to honor not just her but "all that noble band of American heroines—THE ARMY NURSES."[15] But in the eyes of many Union veterans, most northern women were tangential to both the Union war effort and its memorialization.[16]

Aware that they were becoming increasingly invisible, and no doubt animated by the wartime perception that northern women had been less committed to the war than Confederate women, some women worked tirelessly to ensure that they would not be forgotten. "Let us remember that from the soldier alone came not all the sacrifice," urged WRC president Florence Barker in 1884. "Many a brave woman's duty in the hospital—yes, in the march and in the field—would compare in deeds of valor with that of the soldier," she declared.[17] Such sentiments led the WRC to campaign for federal pensions for all army nurses, which they finally achieved in 1892.[18] Other northern women took up their pens, such as former Sanitary Commission leader Mary Livermore, who published her memoirs in 1887. "The consecrated and organized work of women, who strengthened the sinews of the nation with their unflagging loyalty," had not yet been "fully narrated," she observed.[19]

If the divergence of Union and Confederate women as the objects of commemoration was a product of perceptions about their respective causes, it was equally a response to women's role in shaping the war's memory. Where Confederate Memorial Days had begun and remained under the auspices of southern white women (in large part to guard against charges of treason), Union celebrations were the province of men and the federal government. The victorious Union army had interred its slain soldiers, not northern women. For the first twenty years after the war, Union women attended Federal Memorial Days, but their role was limited to procuring floral arrangements rather than organizing the affair. Men's organizations likewise had been the primary impetus behind most monuments and memorials to their cause as well as efforts to preserve battlefields like Gettysburg. Union commemorative efforts had been almost exclusively dominated by men.

Having no political reason to take the lead in memorialization, northern women's postwar efforts tended to be extensions of their wartime charity and relief work. In every city, town, and hamlet, declared the WRC president at the second national gathering, loyal northern women could be found ministering to wounded soldiers just as they had done during the war. "When our soldiers had accomplished their work," she observed, they had "returned to their homes, laid down their arms, returned to the State authorities their precious flags . . . and become private citizens." But unlike their soldier counterparts, the women of the Relief Corps had "not mustered out."[20] Their work continued. Devoted in large part to aiding needy veterans, widows, and orphans, the war-related efforts of the WRC and LGAR may have been far less noticeable than those of their southern counterparts, whose principal focus concerned staging Memorial Days and erecting monuments.[21]

Equally important were demographics. The war had been a defining experience or memory for virtually all white southerners because 75 to 85 percent of white southern men of military age had served in the Confederate armies. In the North, however, a slight majority of the population did not serve. And as immigration increased in the last decades of the nineteenth century, the percentage dropped even more.[22] Although northern women were numerically more active in memorialization than their southern sisters, Union veterans' wives and daughters represented a far smaller percentage of the northern population than did Confederate wives and daughters in the South. Northern women who engaged in memorial work were in many ways simply less visible than their southern counterparts.

There is yet another possible explanation for northern women's inconspicuous role in Union memory: defeat may have been easier to share than victory. If Union veterans had enough difficulty securing a positive image of themselves within a northern populace that increasingly came to see them as pension-grubbing dependents, why would they want to share their glory with a female public whom they believed had contributed relatively little to the cause?[23] After all, the GAR had resisted including women in auxiliary societies until 1883.

Confederate men, on the other hand, consistently praised their unreconstructed women as actors in Civil War commemorations. In the wake of war, these veterans recalled, southern women had been first at the grave, helping to soothe defeat and fostering an eternal devotion to the Lost Cause. "Southern women were the most ardent of original secessionists, the most hopeful and indefatigable of belligerents," declared one newspaper editor in 1867, "and to-day their submission is the most tardy and reluctant."[24] Six years later, speaking before the SHS at White Sulphur Springs, West Virginia, Jefferson Davis similarly extolled not only the wartime devotion of all Confederate women, but also their continued resistance to northern forces. While southern men had been forced to yield the principles for which they had struggled, Davis declared that he had never seen a reconstructed southern woman. Their devotion would be paramount, he argued, as they would teach the next generation to maintain and perpetuate all that had been lost.[25]

Many white southerners understood that women might be especially well suited to keep the flames of sectionalism alive. Just as had been the case with the LMAS' mourning rituals in 1866 and 1867, both southern and northern men might dismiss southern white women's defiance as mere emotion. Women might prattle on about the horrors of Yankee troops, the righteousness of secession, and the unjustness of Reconstruction, but surely their bombastic and unreconstructed sentiments were benign. They were merely the sentimental and silly rants of women, lacking all reason and thought. Such could not possibly jeopardize sectional reconciliation. Conversely, white northerners could tolerate (though not necessarily embrace) a Lost Cause that emphasized devoted, if emotional, women. This domesticated romantic rendering of the Confederacy simultaneously feminized the region and its cause. In some instances, sympathizing with poor, self-sacrificing (and nonpolitical) southern women offered white northerners a more acceptable path toward reconciliation than did alliances with southern white men. Not surprisingly, the widely repeated formula in much postwar literature heralded the domestic union between a northern man and southern woman—acknowledging the economic dominance of the North but conceding the feminine virtue of the South.[26]

Perhaps most important, extolling southern white women's continued hostility to the North throughout the 1880s and into the early 1900s allowed ex-Confederates to both embrace and repudiate the sectionalist rhetoric. When men like Davis commended women's untiring devotion to the Confederacy, they were giving credence to such sentiments. Men might be forced to conceal their bitterness in the name of Blue-Gray gush, but women were not. Southern white women's visceral loyalty to the Lost Cause allowed ex-Confederate men to simultaneously espouse the contradictory impulses of sectional animosity and a desire for a reunited nation.[27]

Assured of their special place within the Confederate cause, southern white women became increasingly determined that it was their imperative to protect and promote its memory. Even the passing of the war generation would not dissuade their efforts. On the contrary, it only seemed to encourage their fierce attachment to the Lost Cause. But as much as veterans' ideas influenced women's place within commemorations, both northern and southern women held very strong ideas about their respective roles in Civil War memory, their relationship to one another, and reconciliation.

THERE'D BE HAIR PULLING SURE

In the 1880s, as veterans began planning their much-celebrated Blue-Gray reunions, two women, one northern and one southern, embarked on their own grand reconciliatory mission. Crisscrossing the South by horse, buggy, train, and foot under the banner of the Woman's Christian Temperance Union (WCTU), Frances E. Willard and Sallie F. Chapin understood that convincing southern women to join the northern-based (and northern-dominated) organization would be no easy task. It had been the southerner Chapin who first called for sectional reconciliation in the name of temperance at the national WCTU convention in 1881. Pleading for support, she insisted there be "No North, No South," only women of the nation standing "Firm in one Cause." During the next few years, the two traveled thousands of miles across the nation, frequently joining up at Chapin's home in Charleston, to spread the message of temperance.[28]

Some historians have suggested that women's groups that were not affiliated with the Civil War, such as the WCTU, helped to facilitate sectional reconciliation.[29] But encouraging a united front of southern and northern women, both white and black, in the battle against alcohol did not mean that women agreed on the causes or consequences of the war. Sallie Chapin was no exception. She had neither forgotten nor was she willing to abandon the Lost Cause. Her ties to the Confederacy were plentiful: her brother James had served as a leader in the South Carolina secession convention, another brother died during the war, and her husband (though born in Massachusetts) had served in the 5th South Carolina Cavalry. For her part, Chapin had presided over the Charleston Soldiers' Relief Society and volunteered in the hospitals. Like so many other Confederate women, her devotion to the failed nation had not ended at Appomattox, first evident when she joined the ranks of the local LMA. In 1872, she turned to her pen to continue her fight. Her novel, *Fitz-Hugh St. Clair: The South Carolina Rebel Boy*, told the story of a brave southern man who married a northern girl. But Chapin's novel was premised on vengeance, not reconciliation—revenge against the evil Yankees who had burdened the South with slavery only to later unleash the horrors of emancipation and Reconstruction. In it she lambasted critics who suggested that the South should graciously accept defeat. "Why, if we should keep silence, while our children are being taught that their hero-fathers were 'fiends, brutes, thieves and murders,' the very stones would cry out against us," Chapin fumed. "One day the world will acknowledge," she boldly declared in standard Lost Cause rhetoric, that the Confederacy had crumbled "because We were Outnumbered! Not Outbraved!"[30]

Even as Chapin embarked on her national campaign to rid the country of alcohol, she remained a self-proclaimed unreconstructed rebel. At the 1881 national WCTU convention, she described the southern delegates as a "crowd of regular rebels" and declared that white southern women were "still full of fight." Six years later in the pages of the *Union Signal*, the WCTU's national newspaper, she ardently insisted that "the cause which drew from its scabbard the sword of Robert E. Lee, and took the life blood of Stonewall Jackson will never be apologized for by any true Southern heart, nor would any high-minded Northerner expect it." "I am not one of the apologizing kind," she asserted. "Principles are immortal."[31] Her sentiments were well apparent to Willard and other northern women of the organization. Pointing to *Fitz-Hugh St. Clair*, WCTU secretary Anna Gordon observed that Chapin was "a *thorough* rebel," though conceding that "her kindness to us could not be exceeded."[32]

Both Chapin and Willard well understood that promoting a united front of both northern and southern women was essential for prohibition to succeed.[33] But this was hardly the same as a reconciliationist memory of the war. In fact, rather than a champion of national reconciliation, Chapin relied upon—even emphasized—her sectional identity to convince southern white women that the ranks of the WCTU were an acceptable outlet for their energies (as opposed to the "radical" woman's rights movement that emerged from the abolitionists).[34] Women north and south could certainly agree that alcohol was poisonous to society, but the war remained a whole other issue entirely. Nothing in their fight for temperance necessitated that Union or Confederate women abandon their interpretation of the war.[35]

The same held true for another set of friends, the widows of Ulysses S. Grant and Jefferson Davis. The informal meeting of Julia Grant and Varina Davis near West Point in 1893 was lauded by northern papers (though not those in the South) as more evidence that sectional animosity had all but vanished. "Celebrated Women Meet," crooned the *New York Times*, adding the next day that their acquaintance "Promises to Ripen into a Warm Friendship." Over the next few years, the two women did become friends. Residing only twenty blocks apart in New York City, they increasingly enjoyed each other's company during carriage rides and dinners. In 1897, Julia invited Varina and her daughter Winnie to attend the dedication of the Grant memorial as her special guests, yet another reconciliationist gesture celebrated by the northern press. But this friendship was not as unlikely as it might appear. The women had much in common: both were from slaveholding families (Grant from Missouri, Davis from Mississippi), both had been controversial first ladies, and they shared the same social temperament.[36]

Their friendship aside, many of Varina Davis's public comments and writings served to inflame rather than dampen sectional hostilities. In the

1890 biography of her late husband as well as countless letters to newspapers, she defended secession, argued that the only inalienable allegiance was to one's state, and provoked an outpouring of consternation from northern veterans for her portrayal of Gen. Nelson A. Mile's treatment of Davis while he was imprisoned at Fort Monroe. In one of her fiercest letters, penned only days after she attended the unveiling of the Grant Memorial, she lambasted the GAR's textbook committee for its insinuation that white southerners had been treasonous. "When Gen. Grant's former foes came long distances to march with reverent mien to his place of rest they did not do it as convicted and confessed traitors whose crime has been condoned, nor did the Grand Army heroes receive them as such," she wrote in a letter published by the *Chicago Daily Tribune*. "If, then, I have interpreted this manifestation of a reunited country right, how can the recommendations of the Grand Army committee be adopted by generous, fair-minded, and honorable men?" In the same letter in which she had sternly defended the Confederate cause, Davis concluded by imploring the veterans of both blue and gray to refrain from their acrimonious reviews, cease emblazing their flags with the battles fought in the fratricidal war, and render each other the praise due to an honorable foe. In her estimation, it was veterans who blocked the road to reconciliation.[37]

Like Chapin and Davis, most women committed to commemorating the war were much more resistant to reconciliation than even the veterans. For their part, southern white women did not simply resign themselves to the anti-reconciliationist role prescribed by their men. They recognized that their Confederate identity had allowed them to venture into the public sphere first through soldiers' aid societies and later through LMAs where they gained a sense of themselves as patriots performing vital civic duties for their communities and the larger South. Emboldened by the new public outlet available to them, many southern white women ardently embraced the image of the unreconstructed she-rebel to continue expanding their sphere of influence even as men increasingly celebrated the era of reconciliation. But no group relied upon their Confederate identity or found greater influence in their opposition to the Blue-Gray gush more than the United Daughters of the Confederacy.[38]

On September 10, 1894, an assembly of women led by Caroline Meriwether Goodlett and Anna Davenport Raines gathered in Nashville, Tennessee, to organize a national federation of all southern women dedicated to promoting the Lost Cause. An outgrowth of LMAs and other Confederate memorial societies that had been active since 1866, the Daughters directed most of their efforts toward raising funds for Confederate monuments, sponsoring Memorial Days, caring for indignant Confederate widows, sponsoring essay contests and fellowships for southern students, and maintaining Confederate museums and relic collections. A hereditary association (much like the Daughters of the American Revolution [DAR] and the LGAR,) the UDC admitted only the relatives of those devoted to the southern cause: Confederate veterans' female kin, women who had served the Confederacy, and the documented descendants of both these groups. The UDC grew rapidly in membership and influence; during its first year alone, twenty chapters were chartered. Within three years that number had swelled to 138 chapters. By 1912, the Daughters listed more than 800 chapters and 45,000 members in their memorial army.[39]

A wide range of women joined the Daughters between 1894 and 1919. Many belonged to a variety of women's organizations, including the LMAS, DAR, Colonial Dames, WCTU, Young Women's Christian Association (YWCA), and a host of other benevolent and literary societies. Some were suffragists; others were fiercely anti-suffrage. They represented a wide swath of religious denominations, including Episcopalians, Methodists, Baptists, Jews, and Catholics, and they included both the most elite and solidly middle class among their members. Perhaps most important, the majority of UDC members had been born after 1850, meaning that the oldest among them experienced the war as children. But many of the most ardent supporters of the Lost Cause by the 1890s and early 1900s had no personal memory of the war.[40] Instead, their lives had been shaped by their experiences as children or young adults during or since Reconstruction.

Founded during the height of reconciliationist pageantry, the Daughters intended in large part to provide an antidote to the Blue-Gray gush. "I am pained to see and realize that so many of our people have accepted and are preaching the Creed that there is no North or South, but one nation," Raines wrote Goodlett in April 1894. For several months, as the two corresponded to plan their organization, Raines could not contain her disgust of sectional reconciliation. "No true Southerner can ever embrace this new religion," she insisted, "and those WHO DO should be ostracized by the 'Daughters of the Confederacy.'"[41] Like the LMAS decades earlier, the Daughters refused to relinquish an attachment to their cause.[42]

Though not specifically stated in their founding documents, vindicating the Confederate generation proved to be the UDC's paramount objective. Proving that their parents and grandparents had been justified in secession and war guided the Daughters' textbook and memorial campaigns.[43] "Our duty is clearly defined," declared Mildred Rutherford, chairman of the UDC's Historical Committee in 1899. "To strive to vindicate, by a truthful statement of facts we can prove, the heroism of our fallen comrades and surviving Veterans, it should be our privilege and is certainly their right."[44] Mary Overman, president of the North Carolina Division, echoed these sentiments. The "promulgation and preservation of the truth" should be the "earnest effort" of every UDC member, she beseeched. "It will be the one thing eternal in our organization—preserve the truth—in that lies the vindication of our brave men and faithful women of the South."[45] Enlivened by the nefarious teachings of northerners who argued that secession had not been constitutional and that Confederates had fought for slavery, Helen DeBerniere Wills, president of the Leonidas Polk Chapter called upon all the Daughters to create children's auxiliaries such as the Children of the Confederacy to further "vindicate the South and her heroes, and place before the world a narrative of facts instead of the falsehoods which have been hitherto disseminated."[46] With a concerted effort on the part of the UDC, future generations would understand the motives of their ancestors. Indeed, they would uphold them as exemplars of honor, virtue, and defenders of constitutional right.

Contemporary issues of gender, class, and race influenced the popularity and enthusiasm for the UDC as much as, if not more than, memories of the past. Just as LMAs had embraced the name "ladies" in 1866–67 to reclaim their position as ranking members of society in the wake of emancipation, the Daughters, too, hoped to reclaim what they perceived to have been lost. In their minds, Confederate defeat and Reconstruction had denied them the privilege of living in a world in which women were placed on a pedestal. In juxtaposition to northern women, they imagined that the war's outcome had denied them access to a life much different than the one they lived—one filled with economic uncertainty and black southerners who did not seem to know their proper place. Their loving tributes to so-called faithful slaves, their glorifications of all that was the antebellum South, and their vicious denouncements of Yankees and the "horrors of Reconstruction" all suggested that the Confederate cause was not all that had been lost. Within the ranks of the Daughters, a white southern woman could reclaim the class status of a southern lady.

Defining southern identity in relation to the Confederate past extended well beyond the UDC's membership rolls. Indeed, the Daughters and affiliated groups such as the Confederate Memorial Literary Society (CMLS) helped inculcate a sense of who was—and by extension who was not—a "legitimate" southerner.[47] Through their textbook campaigns, efforts to create the Confederate Museum in Richmond, and various public celebrations of the Confederacy, these women encouraged communities to demonstrate pride in their white southern heritage in an effort to quell the political, social, and cultural changes unleashed by the war, emancipation, Reconstruction, and the industrializing society around them.[48] "We are unreconstructed rebels, we cling to our Southern ideals and individuality," declared Mary P. Fowle, president of a Washington, North Carolina, chapter. "We are so loyal, so true to the old South, I fear we do not look with eyes too loving on the ways of the new South."[49]

Women's commitment to honoring the Union Cause likewise compelled tens of thousands of northern and Unionist women to enlist in the ranks of various war-related associations. By 1898, 25,000 women belonged to the LGAR. Two years later the Daughters of the Union claimed 1,000 inductees while the Ladies' Aid Society reported 8,000 members. The WRC, however, continued to prove the most popular of all, having grown from 10,000 members in 1884 to more than 118,000 by the turn of the century. Every state except Alabama boasted at least a handful of local corps, with membership strongest in New England and the Midwest.[50]

Like the UDC, the women who joined the WRC were a diverse group. Its members tended to belong to any number of women's associations, including the WCTU, YWCA, DAR, and other benevolent associations. Some demanded women's right to vote, some called for equal rights for all citizens, and others believed that women's superior moral nature mandated they assume a greater public role to improve society. Their ranks included ethnic groups such as a contingent of German speakers in New York, a small number of Native Americans, white and black women who joined together in associations in every part of the country (although most southern women's auxiliaries insisted upon segregated corps), and increasingly white southern women married to Union veterans.[51]

In a striking departure from the UDC, many of the WRC's most active members had been born before or during the 1840s. Not only did this mean that they had experienced the war as women in their twenties and early thirties, but it also indicated that WRC members tended to be older than UDC women. Overwhelmingly, national presidents were the wives of Union veterans or, in the case of Sarah E. Fuller, widows who watched their husbands march south never to return.[52] They were likely to have directly assisted in the war effort, as was the case for Kate Brownlee Sherwood, the wife of a Union general who had served as president of a Soldiers' Memorial Association. A young Illinois teacher when the war erupted, Susan Augusta Pike Sanders, the ninth annual president, had defiantly displayed Old Glory in her classroom despite the strong Copperhead sentiment in her town, and she joined a relief society to support her four brothers and nine cousins who had marched off to fight for the Union.[53] The memory of these women was one founded primarily on the war—not its aftermath.

For all of their diversity, Unionist women could be as equally disdainful of reconciliationist gestures as their southern counterparts. In 1880, former abolitionist Lydia Maria Child wrote that she was especially pleased with former Union general James Garfield's emphasis "on the assertion that there was a right and wrong in the War of the Rebellion." Slavery had been wrong, she maintained, and "the means they took to sustain and extend it were bad." "I have been disgusted, and somewhat discouraged, by the 'mush of concession' that has passed current under the name of magnanimity. The tendency to speak of both sides as equally in the right, because they both fought bravely, is utterly wrong in principle and demoralizing in its influence."[54] In 1887, the founder of the LGAR wrote President Cleveland that his offer to return captured battle flags to the rebels revealed him "untrue to the cause of freedom, country, and God."[55] That same year at the WRC's fifth national convention, Elizabeth D'Arcy Kinne of California fiercely objected to a suggestion that the women decorate the graves of Confederates on Memorial Day. "Treason is treason, living or dead," declared the national president. "Our boys in blue were loyal and true. We cannot say that of the other side, and while we are willing to forgive and forget the past," she continued, "never while life shall last, will we of the WRC honor and love the gray."[56]

Abbie C. Fowler, a member of the Phil Kearny Relief Corps in Richmond, Virginia, agreed completely. By the spring of 1896, the forty women who made up her corps were struggling simply to provide a fitting Memorial Day without assistance from the North. They were the only corps in the former Confederate capital (the colored corps having disbanded), and Fowler described the group's difficulty in attracting regular attendees. Most of the local GAR men, she noted, had married southern women who were less than enthusiastic about the corps's mission. "Sometimes we think that we, and we alone," she wrote in a letter to the *National Tribune*, "are left to keep up the respectability of the Union cause." Former Confederates had plenty of "patriotism" for their "Southern country," she noted with not a little sarcasm. While the WRC and local GAR lacked the means even for a humble parade on Memorial Day, "some of our Northern boys, belonging to bands, military companies, cavalry, etc., have gone with the immense crowds that turn out in all their splendor to do honor to those who died fighting against the Union. They march under that, by us, despised Confederate flag."[57]

Even as Fowler insisted that the nation never forget the difference between right and wrong, like the GAR, she and other Unionist women celebrated reunion as a vindication of the Union cause.[58] "The Grand Army is steadily cultivating a friendly spirit and disseminating the ideas of National unity," she concluded her letter (though she could not help adding that while the Confederate veterans were very nice to the WRC women at such reunions, most other times they had little interaction).[59] The clasping of hands among the Blue and Gray was to be celebrated because it stood as the most discernible evidence that the North's quest to reunite the country had prevailed. Reunion was the embodiment of the Union Cause. And women had a special role to play in reunion. "The perpetuity of this government depends on the patriotism of her women," observed Annie Wittenmyer, WRC president, in 1890.[60]

Nowhere was women's special role more on display than in the WRC's patriotic instruction campaign. As federal pensions and soldiers' homes took the place of women tending to invalid veterans and still battling wartime stereotypes that depicted northern women as less devoted to their cause than their Confederate counterparts, the WRC increasingly devoted itself to cultivating patriotism. Like the UDC, the WRC women believed that they were especially well suited to impart the next generation with a love of country. Working alongside the veterans, they hoped to place American flags in every schoolhouse, encouraged the observance of national Memorial Day, spread the practice of schoolchildren "pledging allegiance" to the Stars and Stripes (the pledge was minted in 1892 in honor of the 400th anniversary of Columbus's first voyage to the New World), and called for legislation to ban the desecration of the flag. Instilling the young with a deep and abiding patriotism was essential, they argued, in a period witnessing mass immigration, violent struggles between labor and capital, and the rise of socialism among the lower classes.[61] But in committing themselves to the patriotic education of the next generation, WRC members would reaffirm Union women's chief contribution to the war effort as they saw it—their loyalty.

The WRC's patriotic focus was not only national in scope; it was also aimed in large part at white southerners. Textbook campaigns, funds to support Memorial Day observances, and the pledge of allegiance all targeted the South as much as the North. This does not mean, however, that the WRC was championing a reconciliationist memory of the war devoid of blame.[62] In fact, quite the opposite held true: the WRC believed that its patriotic instruction campaign was crucial to combatting the Lost Cause and the increasingly harmful effects of Confederate women's groups. In

1894, Hollen E. Day, a native of New York who had recently moved to Missouri, bemoaned the outpourings of rebel sentiments seeping from the mouths of the Show Me State's women. "The elements of disloyalty in our State have combined in the Woman's Southern Historical Society and the Post Bellum Club, whose avowed purpose is to teach our Southern youth that the war for the Union was wrong and that secession was right," she stormed. But among the worst offenders was the newly established UDC. Although she could concede that their effort to establish a home for Confederate soldiers was a worthy cause, she despaired that the Daughters "never spare an opportunity to cast aspersions upon the Union cause, and yet, do not hesitate to put their hands in the pockets of the Grand Army to help sustain their home."[63]

The patriotic campaign appeared to be helping. That same year, Hattie Loring of San Antonio reported the presence of many ex-Confederates at the Texas WRC convention, among them "hundreds of school children, the children of rebel parents," and a company of twenty-three young ladies (all daughters of Confederates) who demonstrated the flag drill adorned in red, white, and blue. Four years earlier such a sight would not have been witnessed, she cheerfully noted. "We know that our work is being felt," she added, "and that we are teaching Loyalty, not only to the ones who fought against our flag, but to the rising generation."[64] Throughout the next two decades, the women continued to devote themselves to cultivating patriotism to the United States, hoping to remove the attachment to the late Confederate States. Yet the Relief Corps's work was hardly complete. In 1911, the patriotic instructor for Illinois warned that five southern states had designated the birthdays of Lee and Davis as legal holidays. "Does it not behoove us to work with diligence to combat this danger, and to use every effort to make clear and plain the dividing line between treason and loyalty?" she asked. "Make the Flag Salute and its meaning familiar to every child, for in them lies the hope of the Nation," she warned.[65]

Despite the WRC's earnest efforts to convince them otherwise, many white southern women failed to understand American patriotism and their fealty to the Confederate past as mutually exclusive. For most UDC members, it seemed only natural to salute the Confederate Stars and Bars at the same meeting where they saluted the Stars and Stripes. They could likewise support the WRC's schoolhouse flag campaign (even as they pressured school boards to adopt pro-southern textbooks and pushed for Confederate flags and pictures of Confederate leaders to adorn the same classrooms).[66] As white southerners had been insisting since 1861, the Daughters believed that they were true Americans. *They*—not northerners—were the true heirs and defenders of Revolutionary principles. This tenacious belief helps explain in part why so many members of the UDC were simultaneously members of the DAR.[67]

There were some more militant UDC members who resolutely resisted identifying themselves as members of the United States, including Adelia A. Dunovant, historian of the Texas Division. In "applying the term 'nation' to the United States," she declared in 1901, the UDC would be repudiating their objective to vindicate "the men of the Confederacy who fought and died in defense of the constitutional right of State sovereignty." While she rejected the term "nation" because it invalidated the principle of state rights, even Dunovant declared herself an American. For most UDC members, however, the Americanism of the Lost Cause meant that white southerners could be simultaneously loyal Americans and faithful Confederates.[68] Pledging allegiance to the *American* flag did not mean that the Daughters had repudiated the Confederate cause or that they overwhelmingly embraced the Blue-Gray gush of reconciliation.

If, in nineteenth-century parlance, women were the "fairer sex," why did they so adamantly resist the gestures of reconciliation that many (though not all) men seemed willing to at least occasionally embrace? There are several possibilities. First, both Union and Confederate veterans had shared the experience of combat. Despite their fierce ideological differences, consciously or not, veterans often believed that their former foes better understood what it meant to shoulder a rifle, suffer the screams of their comrades crying out in pain, or endure a winter sleeping on the bitterly frozen ground.[69] But without the fraternal bonds of soldiering, women emphasized what they perceived as their regionally distinctive wartime contributions. Southern women understood, and their men continued to remind them, that they had suffered far more than their northern counterparts and devoted more of themselves to their cause—even if it had failed. They had been martyrs to their cause just as much as southern white men. Union women simply could not abide by what they perceived as such nonsense.[70]

Second, northern and southern women found few compelling reasons to lock hands with their counterparts across the Mason-Dixon Line. Men had a litany of practical rationales for encouraging a reunited, reconciled nation, from the United States' global ambitions to domestic politics. But there was nothing at stake if women, as ostensibly nonpolitical beings, harbored a deep and abiding disdain for their former foes. An increasing number of women were demanding the vote through the National American Woman's Suffrage Association, but they had yet to achieve their

Group portrait of the Woman's Relief Corps of Gunnison, Colorado, c. 1890.
(Denver Public Library)

goals of electoral participation and political recognition by mainstream America. Largely barred from the business and political world, women were free to embrace bitterness without jeopardizing financial or partisan opportunities. They could air their true feelings without fear of the consequences. The fact that they were never censured—and often praised—for such sentiment by their respective veterans suggests that perhaps these were equally the true feelings of many men. Gestures of reconciliation might be required in legislative halls and former battlefields but not in the spaces occupied by women.

A third possibility arises from the generational difference between the most active members of the WRC and those of the UDC. Constrained by its 1883 rules admitting only women who had personally supported the Union Cause, state and national Relief Corps leaders were older than many of the UDC officers. WRC leaders were more likely to have experienced the war as young women, to have sent their husbands and sons off to the frontlines. Alternatively, many of the most active Daughters had been young girls during conflict or had been born after Appomattox. The ever-outspoken UDC member Mildred Lewis Rutherford, for example, had been born in 1851 and therefore experienced the war as a teenager. Unlike the veterans,

Unionist and Confederate women might have found very little over which to commiserate.

The very nature of women's Civil War societies was perhaps the most important factor shaping their resistance to the Blue-Gray gush. How could the Daughters actively pursue their primary mission of honoring the Confederate past and instilling a "southern" sense of pride in their youth if they joined forces with northern women?[71] As the ever-passionate Adelia A. Dunovant observed, if white southern women failed to recognize the sovereignty of the states or work to vindicate the "earth's noblest heroes, the men of the Confederacy," they would "destroy the very basis upon which our association of United Daughters of the Confederacy stands."[72] The same held true for Union women of the WRC and LGAR. How would they celebrate their chief contribution—their loyalty to the nation—alongside the UDC?

The difficulties of reconciliation between Union and Confederate veterans were serious enough, explained one Union veteran in 1903. But women's associations proved even more likely to "nurse the old fight." "The women," he noted, "are said to be the most implacable foes. Why, if you got the GAR Relief Corps with the Daughters of the Confederacy together there'd be hair pulling sure." Though he likely overstated the degree of animosity between the groups, the notion that there was little sisterly feeling between women of the North and South was well founded.[73] There would be no grand reunions of Blue-Gray women, no newspaper stories heralding the efforts of the WRC and UDC to unite the nation. Only on non-war-related issues would northern and southern women find common ground.

THE CROSS OF HUMAN SLAVERY

Like their male counterparts in the GAR, well into the twentieth century countless Unionist women celebrated emancipation as central to Union victory.[74] Addressing the annual reunion in 1888, national president Annie Wittenmyer celebrated the veterans who had not only "redeemed the country from treason," but also "with their sharp swift swords sundered the chains that bound in human slavery four millions of God's people."[75] Six years later, national president Sarah C. Mink likewise urged northerners to keep the spirit of Memorial Day true by honoring only those "heroes whose valor and self-sacrifice saved this nation from secession and slavery."[76] The 1895 national encampment of the GAR and WRC held in Louisville was dripping with reconciliationist rhetoric. But even here

Kate Brownlee Sherwood, a leading figure in the Relief Corps, condemned those who had fought under "the cross of human slavery."[77] And at the dedication for a memorial at Andersonville prison in 1911, Belle C. Harris observed that "today we raise our hearts in gladness that we have a country glorious in human liberty."[78]

Just as with the veterans, refusing to forget slavery's centrality to the Union Cause did not translate into unequivocal acceptance of black women within the corps. Despite objections by many black and white members, WRC leaders gave in to pressure for racial segregation at the state level in the South. But efforts to segregate African Americans within the national WRC failed, as did the national president's 1906 effort to ban black women altogether.[79] In fact, black women remained an integral part of the association well into the twentieth century. Between 1891 and 1905, every national convention of the WRC discussed black membership in the South and means for encouraging new chapters (even as it sought to increase the number of southern white members). Motivated in large part by their commitment to the veterans, women of the black corps frequently aided the local GAR posts with Federal Memorial Day.[80] The WRC likewise helped numerous needy African American veterans' families, who, though entitled to federal pensions, often found navigating the federal bureaucracy an impossible task. Personal motives may also have prompted some women to join the WRC. Within the ranks of the corps, some southern black women found valuable networks of women who had experience with securing pensions for their veteran kin.[81]

Some also found a civic space for themselves alongside white women. Such was the case for Julia Mason Layton. Born into slavery, by 1911, she held the office of assistant national inspector. That year, her travels took her to Virginia, North Carolina, South Carolina, Florida, Georgia, and Tennessee in search of colored corps, a journey that was beyond perilous. Forbidden from riding in the same coach as white people, she was forced to travel in the Jim Crow cars with convicts. Neither was she allowed to wait in the ladies' room at the depot. Instead, she was required to remain outside for the train. Fearful for her life, she spent one terrifying night with her "left hand in the hand of God" and a six-shooter in her right. But she nevertheless thanked the national president for appointing her to the task of visiting the much-neglected colored corps of the South. "You listened to their mute appeal," she noted, "and I trust that you may see the day when they are numbered among the best workers of the Woman's Relief Corps."[82]

Other African American women were inspired to join the ranks of the

Corps to honor the black Civil War experience—and perhaps counter the Lost Cause. In 1892, the Callioux Corps of Norfolk, Virginia, collected money to build a monument to black soldiers who slumbered in the African American section of a local cemetery.[83] Susie King Taylor, a former slave, wartime nurse, and active member of the Massachusetts WRC, highlighted the contributions of black soldiers to the war in her 1902 reminiscences. Though she wondered if the war had been in vain given that black southerners were burned, tortured, denied fair trials, and murdered across the South for imaginary crimes, she implored her readers not to forget that terrible war. "We do not, as the black race, properly appreciate the old veterans, white or black, as we ought to," she wrote. "My heart burns within me, at this want of appreciation. There are only a few of them left now, so let us all, as the ranks close, take a deeper interest also, and remember that it was through the efforts of these veterans that they and we older ones enjoy our liberty today."[84]

Like the tension between Union and Confederate veterans, the WRC's insistence on commemorating emancipation prodded southern white women to defend their peculiar institution. Some, like Jefferson Davis's widow, Varina, joined the ranks of Jubal Early and William C. Oates, pointing out that slave property had been protected by the Constitution. "The abolition of slavery," she wrote in language more forthright than her late husband's in 1890, "was a gigantic wrong to the owners of negro slaves." They had been freed without compensation to their masters, plunging many white southerners into abject poverty. "But the South does not brand those who did so as traitors or rogues," she sarcastically noted. One is left only to wonder if she and her friend Julia Dent Grant, also the daughter of a slaveholder, ever dared broach the subject.[85]

Most UDC members, however, fiercely rejected the idea that their noble Confederates had fought to preserve slavery. Rather than avoiding discussions of slavery, like many other white southerners, Daughters and LMA members turned northerners' argument on its head by insisting that the North's alleged commitment to abolition was disingenuous. In the restored White House of the Confederacy, known simply as the Confederate Museum, the Georgia Room displayed a book titled *The History of Slavery in Massachusetts*. The CMLS collected newspaper clippings announcing the discovery of a slave dungeon in Philadelphia and decried Harriet Beecher Stowe as a fraud.[86]

Other Confederate women argued that the period before emancipation and Reconstruction had been a golden era of race relations. Conveniently forgetting the number of freedmen and -women who fled to Union lines during the war, they told stories of the happy slaves who were part of the southern family.[87] Mildred Lewis Rutherford, historian general of the UDC between 1911 and 1916, insisted that slaves "were the happiest set of people on the face of the globe." "We never called them slaves," she noted; "they were our people, our negroes, part of our very homes." They had been content in slavery—happier than after emancipation, she maintained. "I need only to call to mind what happened after they were free that made Thad Stevens's 'Exodus Order' necessary to tear them from their old owners," she observed. "I need only to call to mind the many mammies who stayed to nurse 'Ole Master's' children to the third and fourth generations."[88] Confederate soldiers had not fought to keep these loyal men and women in servitude, argued women like Rutherford; they had fought to protect them from the Yankee vandals and the uncertainty of freedom.

Depictions of the faithful slave were omnipresent in the New South: in tributes to "faithful old mammies" that filled the *Confederate Veteran*, in the plantation literature of Joel Chandler Harris and Thomas Nelson Page, and even on boxes of pancake mix.[89] But the Daughters devoted a good bit of their effort to fostering the image. "Preserve as history sketches not only of the old mammy of the South," instructed Mildred Rutherford, "but of the many faithful slaves to whose care the women and children were confided when our brave men were at the front and of those true to their former owners after the war closed."[90] In these essays shared at annual and chapter meetings, members emphasized the idealized plantation past with its harmonious master-slave relations. There had never been "a peasantry so happy . . . as the negro slaves of America," wrote a Daughter from Tennessee.[91]

Not content with literary tributes to their so-called faithful servants, in 1904 some members of the UDC began pressing for a national faithful slave monument. Such a monument would "prove that the people of the South who owned slaves valued and respected their good qualities as no one else ever did or will do," advised UDC member Mary M. Solari, but it would simultaneously influence "for good the present and coming generations" of black southerners.[92] In commemorating those African Americans who knew their place in society, did not question the authority of white men, and did not need segregated railroad coaches or streetcars to inform them that they were inferior in both mind and body, white southerners hoped to provide a model for New South race relations. Black southerners could either conform to white images of the submissive "old-time negro" or be subject to white violence.[93]

Other UDC members fiercely objected to anything that honored African Americans. "This is not the time for erecting monuments to the old slave—if there ever will be a time," protested Mrs. W. Carleton Adams of Memphis. In language that some UDC members would replicate with increasing frequency in the following years, she turned her attention not to a memory of the war, but to Reconstruction. Invoking the image of the black rapist, she asked why such a monument should be erected "when there is not a state in the South not mourning for some beautiful woman whose life has been strangled out by some black fiend." Instead of raising a "black monument to mar any Southern city," she wrote in a letter printed in the *Confederate Veteran*, "secure an authentic list of the Southern homes desecrated by the freedman during the past forty years." Only "when the southern home is as safe with the black man as with the white man," she concluded, should white southerners consider a monument to former slaves.[94]

Even as the Daughters continued to debate the merits of a faithful slave monument, another dispute centered on the memory of slavery erupted within their ranks. In January 1902, UDC officers in Lexington, Kentucky, petitioned the local opera house to cease booking the popular traveling production of *Uncle Tom's Cabin*. Both the show and the novel on which it was based, they claimed, conveyed a false conception of the institution, seizing "upon imaginary or isolated cases of cruelty to slaves and magnify[ing] them." "It is an insult to the South," declared Henrietta Morgan Duke, wife of Confederate general Basil Duke and representative of a Louisville UDC chapter. Another declared the performance a baneful influence on the coming generation of children who "may see it and gain the wrong idea of the South . . . their grandfathers fought and died for."[95] The Daughters' quest was in keeping with their mission to vindicate white southerners as kind and benevolent slaveholders. Yet they also acknowledged another motive for their protest: the show could "have no other effect than that of arraying the vicious among the young generation of Negroes against the white people, breed dissentions and conflicts, encouraging animosity, riots, criminals assaults and lynchings."[96] From Wilmington, North Carolina, to Tacoma, Washington, Daughters waged public-relations battles warning of the play's slanderous content and potential to foster race prejudices. But Kentucky's UDC chapters took a decidedly political approach, turning to the General Assembly for legislation that would ban the drama throughout the Bluegrass State.[97]

African Americans refused to sit idly by. Instead, they embraced the UDC's arguments and launched a counter-protest against a stage version of Thomas Dixon's *The Clansman*, which portrayed the alleged "negro domination" of Reconstruction. Dixon's "nefarious" play, argued L. M. Hagood, a black minister from Lexington, glorified the Klan, and his books were "a thousand times more baneful" than *Uncle Tom's Cabin*. "Are we not trying to forget the Civil War," he asked. "Are we not trying to mollify its wounds? Why force these old stories open for filthy lucre?" Embracing the Daughters' logic, he insisted that Dixon's play would "inflame the ignorant and dissolute blacks and whites and awaken the bitter memories of hatred days that ought to be forgotten." Beyond Kentucky's borders, Lewis Douglass, Union veteran and son of the famous abolitionist, lambasted the Daughters for their efforts, as did WRC member Susie King Taylor. Pointing out the hypocritical nature of the UDC's protest, King wondered if "these Confederate Daughters ever send petitions to prohibit the atrocious lynching and wholesale murdering and torture of the negro? Do you ever hear of them fearing this would have a bad effect on the children?" Despite such protests, *The Clansman* appeared as scheduled.[98]

The Kentucky Daughters, however, had been successful in their undertaking. In March 1906, the legislature passed the Uncle Tom's Cabin Law, which made the production of "any play that is based upon antagonism alleged formerly to exist, between master and slave, or that excites race prejudice," a crime punishable by fines and imprisonment. Under the guise of conservative womanhood, Lexington's UDC women had exerted tremendous political influence to silence a historical memory that contradicted the Lost Cause. Yet Kentucky's African Americans were not without a victory. While the law had come too late to prevent *The Clansman*, black leaders invoked the law a decade later when D. W. Griffith's film version of the play, *The Birth of a Nation*, was scheduled to be shown in Lexington.[99]

Just as among Confederate veterans, discussions of slavery occupied a central place in the Daughters' memory. But perhaps more important, both the faithful slave monument and *Uncle Tom's Cabin* debates revealed that by the early 1900s, the UDC's gaze had begun shifting from the war to Reconstruction. As would become increasingly apparent in the next decades, the memory of Reconstruction would allow the Daughters to even more forcefully reject symbols of national reconciliation in favor of their southern identity, heritage, and race.

RABID AND DISLOYAL FIRE EATERS

As the Daughters well knew, no war memory was more fraught with bitterness and more likely to revive sectional passions than the prisoner-of-war issue. Yet this did not prevent them from proposing a monument to Henry Wirz, commander of the infamous Andersonville prison. Since the

GAR had taken over the site in 1870, numerous Union monuments had been erected, all of which "inscribed a false presentation of Wirtz [sic]," the Daughters insisted. "We have nothing there to refute the lies and slanders proclaimed in marble on all sides," declared Sara Hull, president of the Georgia Division in 1905, "nothing to bear witness to the Truth, and to the brave testimony of Wirtz and the men who died with him."[100] Determined to protest the northern memory inscribed on the southern landscape, the UDC initiated a national fundraising campaign to build a monument that would clear Wirz of the "false charges."[101]

As news of the monument reached Union veterans and the WRC, sectional tensions reached a fevered pitch. Throughout the planning process, numerous disputes ensued, including where to the place the monument (it would not be allowed in the memorial park; that was owned by the WRC) and what the inscription might read.[102] But for northern opponents, there was one issue that needed no debate: it was southern women who were stirring the sectional embers. "The veterans of the Confederate Army are not, to any appreciable degree, interested in this movement," noted the GAR at its 1906 encampment. Instead, its impetus and force was to be found chiefly among the "women of the South."[103] Union veterans warned that the monument "would do more to interrupt the flow of good feeling between the North and the South, and would roll back more effectively the waves of reconciliation than any other one matter of which the mind of man could conceive."[104] James Tanner, a former GAR commander-in-chief and Union corporal who had lost both legs below the knee at Second Manassas, deprecated the UDC's efforts as without an "atom of truth" and wholly despicable. How could they even consider raising a monument to such a character, Tanner asked. When Wirz graced the corridors of hell, he observed, "the devil recognized that his only competitor was there."[105] The Union Veteran Legion likewise condemned the monument as an effort on the part of the Daughters to "make treason famous and loyalty to the Union a crime, reviving between the sections the embers of a bitterness which all patriots have long hoped to see completely extinguished."[106] And the WRC's national committee on the Andersonville Prison Park reviled the thought of such a memorial. "The building of this monument is to be deplored by all who would cherish the virtues of pure patriotism, 'with charity for all and malice toward none,'" they pronounced.[107]

Isabel Worrell Ball, a pioneer woman journalist raised in Kansas and president of the Washington, D.C.–based WRC Department of the Potomac, was perhaps the most outspoken critic of the memorial.[108] The Wirz monument would be the "crowning infamy of an organization of women which does more to keep alive the fires of sectionalism than anything else in the world," she declared. As the owners of the Prison Park, the WRC had worked tirelessly to ensure that it would not offend white southerners, even those who thought the South right and the North wrong "in that great war for human liberty." When some southern white women objected to the signs erected by the WRC in the grounds, the Corps had removed them to promote peace and "a better feeling between North and South." Not one remained in place today. But, she warned, should the UDC persist in their efforts to place the Wirz monument at the gate of the prison, "every placard that we took from the grounds will be put back and there will be others more significant placed there." If the Daughters sought justness for Wirz, Ball avowed justice for the thousands of men who died in the loathsome pen now resting in unknown graves.[109]

Reconciliation, however, clearly was not the objective of the Daughters. Responding to the GAR, Alice Baxter of the Georgia Division insisted that UDC women "do not desire to stir up bitterness but we are unwilling for the South to remain under false charges."[110] The UDC was committed first and foremost to vigilantly protecting the memory of the Confederacy—whatever the cost.

Although the vitriol directed at the monument caused friction among the Daughters and delayed the selection of the shaft's final site, it only served to galvanize support for the UDC from southern men. "God bless our southern ladies," wrote Lemuel M. Park in a letter to the *Atlanta Constitution*. "Their instinct is unerring and they know the humble hero of the ranks as well as the brave general of the hosts."[111] Writing to the *SHSP*, Confederate veteran J. R. Gibbons declared that white southerners would stand for many things, but when northerners say "anything about our women," it "gets all of the fuz turned the wrong way." Gibbons found Tanner's attack especially odious considering he had expressed such love for his fellow foes at a Blue-Gray reunion only a few years prior. "We cannot understand how Corporal Tanner expects us old fellows in Gray to love and hobnob with him when he attacks our women in this way." Regardless of the Union veterans' opposition to the monument, Gibbons observed, the "ladies of the South are going to erect one, and it will be built just as tall as it will be possible for them to get the money to build it, and they will inscribe upon it the truth, the whole truth, and nothing but the truth."[112]

While the culture of reconciliation encouraged veterans to leave their past differences behind and come together under the banner of fraternity, the Daughters would be under no such obligation. Just as Confederate men had relied upon the feminine sphere of mourning to shield them from charges of treason at Memorial Days in 1866 and 1867, in the early 1900s they continued to hide behind the skirts of women. In defending the Daughters, white southern men were doing more than protecting their women: they were encouraging the women's sectional animosities under the guise of chivalry.[113]

On May 12, 1909, the Daughters finally unveiled the Wirz monument in downtown Andersonville, a short distance from the park and national cemetery, the obelisk standing as an unrepentant and defiant symbol of the Lost Cause. In stark juxtaposition to the dedication of northern monuments in Andersonville, there was no indication of forgiveness or humility from the mouths of speakers. Neither did the monument's text offer a mollifying memory of the war or prison camps. Instead, continuing the Lost Cause pattern of inverting northern arguments, the monument and its dedication insisted that Wirz was "the last victim of a misdirected popular clamor." In rhetoric that recalled the war's aftermath rather than conciliatory images of battlefield glory, the monument's text insisted that Wirz had been "arrested in time of peace, while under protection of a parole, tried by a military commission of a service to which he did not belong and condemned to ignominious death on charges of excessive cruelty."[114] Wirz, the Confederate "martyr," offered a striking contrast to the North's retributive policies, a notion the Daughters would revive with increasing frequency in the decades to come.

If the Daughters had built the Wirz monument in the name of vindicating the South, their general convention held in Washington, D.C., in 1912 was intended to show the nation that the UDC was nevertheless a devoted, patriotic organization committed to sectional reconciliation (albeit on southern terms). The UDC heralded the convention as the first held outside the South (though it really meant that the meeting was the first held in the North, as the group had met in San Francisco in 1905) and was elated by President Taft's reception at the White House. Invited to hold their largest sessions in Memorial Continental Hall, the DAR's national headquarters, the nearly 2,000 attendees were overwhelmingly pleased by their reception. Virginia Clay Clopton, a suffragist and Daughter from Alabama, observed that the UDC was grateful to have held its convention in the nation's capital because it allowed them to prove to non-southerners "that our object is not to keep alive the fire of sectionalism." "The emblems of the Confederacy will ever be engraven upon our hearts," she noted, yet "we rejoice now that Americans are a people of one God, enjoying one faith, one hope, one love."[115] As was almost universally the case with the UDC, Clopton welcomed sectional reconciliation but recognized that her identity as a southern woman was grounded solidly in a defense of the Confederate past.

Members of the UDC were especially delighted with President Taft's address to the delegates. His brief comments began with the familiar reconciliationist refrain: both North and South shared in the pride of a common courage and glorious sacrifice. Yet his subsequent remarks must have astonished many Union veterans. The physical evidence of war had lingered far longer in the South than in the North, he noted, and the impoverishment of the South had served as a constant reminder of the region's defeat. "Hence, those of us at the North who have been sometimes impatient at a little flash now and then of the old sectional antagonism are unreasonable in our failure to appreciate these marked differences," he confessed. But he did not stop here. While Republican presidents had labored since the war to bind up the sectional wounds, he believed that circumstances had rendered it difficult for the Grand Old Party to heal the nation. The incoming Democratic administration of Woodrow Wilson, with its southern support, would be able to make even greater strides than any Republican president ever had in the name of national unity.[116]

Taft's remarks highlighted a subtle but discernible shift in the national memory of the war. Only thirteen years old when the war began, his was not a veteran's memory but that of the next generation. He, like many of the Daughters, had come of age during Reconstruction and thus his interpretation of the war was in many ways shaped by its aftermath more than by the battlefield conflict of 1861–65. Clearly, he understood the partisan nature of memory and recognized that it still held a powerful grip on the nation. But perhaps more important, though his words were doubtless intended to assuage the lingering sectional bitterness, his allusion to Reconstruction was not lost on the Daughters. In the years to come, they too would find themselves reviving memories of the postwar years more than those prior to Appomattox in the name of the Lost Cause.

Despite the cordial welcome the Daughters received from the president and the numerous teas and receptions held in their honor, not all Washingtonians were delighted to host the southerners. Some DAR chapters were indignant that the UDC had been invited to use their national headquarters, calling the display of the Confederate flag in the hall a "desecration."[117] A letter to a Brooklyn newspaper castigated the UDC as "rabid and disloyal fire eaters." Although a few patriotic members of the Daughters had protested, the author noted, a faction had insisted upon decorating the capital city with the stars and bars, "the emblem of slavery, secession, treason, and bitterness." But, the author rejoiced, this action had left the

Daughters hopelessly divided. "The bitter split in the UDC ranks is hailed everywhere as marking the dawn of an era in the history of our reunited country," he proclaimed.[118]

The UDC's most fierce critic was the indefatigable Isabel Worrel Ball. The fighting men of both sides had embraced peace and harmony, she noted in the pages of the *National Tribune*. Those who had followed Lee and Jackson, Grant and Sherman accepted that the war had ended. But "the women of the South do not know the war is over," she declared. Invited to the national capital and treated with the utmost hospitality, the Daughters had "insolently flaunted . . . the flag representing sectional strife and bitterness" that "Lee gladly left with Grant at Appomattox." While there were hundreds of "high-bred, law-abiding, Flag-loving women" among the Daughters, they were overshadowed by the "howlers of the UDC" who were a "menace to the South," sowing "seeds of treason where the lilies of peace are trying to take root." It was now clear, she maintained, why the Georgia Division selected "the beast Wirz for a 'gallant' and 'heroic' example of Southern chivalry."[119]

The UDC had not succeeded in building their monument to Wirz within the national cemetery at Andersonville, but their efforts would be more fruitful and spectacular at Arlington National Cemetery. During the Atlanta Peace Jubilee in 1898, McKinley had proposed that the federal government assist in the care of Confederate graves. The following year, the UCV followed up on this offer, requesting that Congress allow the remains of Confederate soldiers still scattered around the nation's capital to be interred at Arlington. By 1906, not only had reinterment of Confederate dead begun in Arlington (albeit in a separate section—they would not be buried alongside the Union dead), but McKinley's offer became a reality when Congress authorized the government to assume obligation for tending the graves of more than 30,000 southern soldiers who had died in Union hospitals and prison camps.[120] True to their anti-reconciliationist stances, Confederate women's associations scoffed at the plan. Janet Weaver Randolph, a UDC leader from Richmond, suggested that the Confederate remains be brought back to Richmond as the LMAs had done in the 1870s for southern soldiers buried at Gettysburg. The North Carolina Division of the UDC favored this plan, asking its senators to introduce a bill ensuring that each state would be given the privilege of caring for its own dead. Katie Behan, president of the Confederate Southern Memorial Association (an alliance of LMA groups), railed that the veterans had not consulted southern women in the matter, protesting in part because the federal government would forbid the erection of monuments to ex-

Confederates in Arlington. To support her claim, she recounted an effort by a Philadelphia chapter of the UDC in the late 1890s to erect a monument to the unknown Confederate dead in a national cemetery. But the local GAR post, along with the national commander-in-chief, had rebuffed the effort, insisting that traitors did not deserve to rest next to the Union dead. Given such hostility, Behan believed, Confederates had no place in U.S. national cemeteries.[121]

Despite the earnest protests by these women, in June 1900 Congress passed the act, and reinterments began the following year.[122] The UDC, however, would not be content with the mere reburial of Confederates in a cemetery once reserved exclusively for loyal Union soldiers. Instead, the Daughters pressed their demand for a monument to the Confederate dead, a request granted by Secretary of War William Howard Taft in 1906.[123] The significance of building a Confederate monument on the land once owned by Robert E. Lee, in a national cemetery and directly across the Potomac River from the White House, was not lost on the Daughters.[124] This would have to be a magnificent and imposing memorial.

Six years and several thousand dollars later, the Daughters gathered to lay the cornerstone for their monument. Billed as a celebration of Blue and Gray, a handful of Union veterans had joined their more numerous Confederate counterparts and the Daughters for the ceremony (perhaps not surprisingly, there is no indication that any WRC members attended). In addition to an address by President Taft, the featured speaker of the day was three-time presidential candidate William Jennings Bryan, who simultaneously praised the UDC and alluded to slavery as the cause of the war.[125] The most notable orator, however, was James R. Tanner, the former GAR commander-in-chief who had attacked the UDC's building of the Wirz monument. When UCV member Col. Hilary Herbert extemporaneously called him to the stage, a murmur of disapproval rippled through the crowd. But a hush descended as Tanner, leaning heavily on his cane to support his artificial feet, pleaded for an end to sectional animosities. In carefully chosen words, he praised the Daughters for honoring their dead, yet he did not surrender to the Lost Cause. Instead, invoking the Union Cause, he reminded the crowd that "we have settled some things forever and founded a republic that shall endure forever." More pointedly, he addressed the UDC. "To you of the younger generation," he noted, turning toward the Daughters, "I appeal for the establishment of true community of feeling between the North and South." Johnny Reb and the Old-time Yank had found peace, he observed; now it was up to the next generation to maintain sectional harmony—not provoke more discord.[126]

In June 1914, the United Daughters of the Confederacy dedicated a monument to the Confederate dead in Arlington National Cemetery. (Library of Congress)

Unveiled two years later on June 4, 1914 (Jefferson Davis's birthday), the monument was touted throughout the nation as evidence of the reconciled nation. Veterans of both the Union and Confederacy placed wreaths on the graves of their former foes; GAR commander-in-chief Washington Gardner as well as UCV commander-in-chief Bennett Young addressed the crowd, as did Col. Robert E. Lee, grandson of the Confederate hero. (Again conspicuously absent was the WRC.) Embracing the unofficial theme of reconciliation, President Wilson declared the monument as an "emblem of a reunited people." Reviving the notion of American exceptionalism so often present at Blue-Gray affairs, Wilson observed that only in a democracy could such a peace be found. But the time had come to let go of the past and look to the future, he urged. Just as he finished his words, a violent thunderstorm unleashed torrents of wind and rain, prompting a mad dash to the automobiles and trolley cars.[127] The next day, in a headline befitting the dedication within a cemetery, a Nebraska magazine declared simply: "Sectionalism is Dead."[128]

The Daughters considered the Arlington Confederate Monument one of their most important achievements and a symbol of their allegiance as patriotic Americans. But like the Wirz monument, it simultaneously served as a symbol of defiance. Designed by Moses Ezekiel, a Confederate veteran and sculptor who resided in Rome, the monument featured the bronze figure of a woman, representing the South, her head crowned with olive leaves and a laurel wreath in an extended hand. In the other hand rested the plow stock and sickle, signifying the South's agricultural past. The circular pedestal below included the coat of arms for each Confederate state (plus Maryland) as well as a frieze depicting thirty-two life-size reliefs of soldiers, women and children on the home front, and faithful slaves—with a slave dutifully following his master off to war and a "mammy" holding a white child.[129] As one of the monument's inscriptions read: "Victrix Causa Diis Placuit Sed Victa Caton" (The Victorious Cause was Pleasing to the Gods, But the Lost Cause to Cato).[130] The intention of the monument, Ezekiel explained, was that it might serve as "a monument to peace without forgetting the sacrifices of the South, and emphasizing the fact that they were fighting for a constitutional right, and not to uphold slavery."[131] In presenting the monument as a "gift" to the United States, UDC president Daisy McLaurin Stevens paid homage to the Confederate soldiers and spoke of reunification. But she also stressed the theme of self-government.[132] Here, on ground where Lee's slaves had once toiled now hallowed by the victorious Union dead, the Daughters had managed to erect a monument that honored state rights and insisted that white southerners had not fought in defense of slavery. In doing so, they believed they had made a tremendous stride toward vindicating the Confederate cause. Under the Daughters' watchful eyes, reconciliation would happen only on terms they dictated and accepted.[133]

In 1916, Ed Rogers, a GAR veteran living in South Carolina, looked forward to attending the upcoming national encampment of the UCV and SCV. He anticipated that the Confederate veterans would welcome him but worried about the reaction of the southern women. "*Most*," he wrote fellow veteran Charles W. Cowtan, "are still very vindictive. For them there are no heroes no patriots but those who wore the gray." In recent years, they had done their best to transform Washington into a southern city, with its southern banquets, balls, receptions, and statesmen, and they had succeeded in erecting the "finest and most costly monument in Arlington." A memorial to the Confederate dead was one thing, he noted, but now the women had proposed a statue to Jefferson Davis in Washington. "*This is too much*," he insisted. "If anything will throw a damper on this proposed re-union it will be the attitude—not of the C.S.A. veterans, but of the women, and the young folks who have been taught that the highest

UDC president Daisy McLaurin Stevens addressing those gathered for the dedication of the Confederate monument in Arlington Cemetery, June 1914. (Library of Congress)

social standing is found only in the ranks of those hailing from their much vaunted 'Southland.'"[134]

Like many other northerners, Rogers recognized that the women of the UDC, more so than the veterans, continued to fan the flames of sectionalism a half-century after Appomattox. For their part, the Daughters were proud of this legacy. After all, it had been their mission to teach the next generation about the principles, courage, and heroism of their forefathers and mothers. Just as the WRC dedicated itself to instilling patriotism in the hearts of all Americans, so the UDC prided itself on fostering a deep attachment to the Confederate past. Encouraged by their men and undaunted by attacks from the GAR or Isabel Worrell Ball, the Daughters remained faithful to their mission to absolve Confederate men of failure— to prove that they were above all else American patriots.[135] And by all accounts, they were succeeding.

A NEW GENERATION

1913–1939

In July 1913, Gettysburg once again claimed the nation's attention. Fifty years after having faced each other in the war's largest battle, more than 53,000 aging Union and Confederate veterans gathered again amid the sweltering summer heat in the name of reconciliation. For four days, a crowd of nearly 100,000 spectators and press correspondents from all over the nation and Europe watched as the old warriors fraternized in the great tent city camp. But as with every reunion on the field since 1887, the great climactic moment took place along the famed stone wall. At 3:00 P.M. on July 3, almost exactly fifty years to the minute of Pickett's charge, crowds swarmed to watch approximately 500 Confederate survivors march in double-column, without arms, across the field toward their former foes. After climbing the final steep ascent, the seventy-plus-year-old southern men clasped hands with smiling northern veterans across the wall.[1]

Almost everyone reveled in the reconciliationist spirit of the day. In language reminiscent of the 1895 Chickamauga dedication, Confederate veteran and Virginia governor William H. Mann declared, "There is no North and no South, no rebels and no Yanks. All is one great nation."[2] Speaker of the House Champ Clark, a teenager during the battle, intoned that all Americans should be equally proud to claim the men who had stormed the slippery slopes of Gettysburg alongside Pickett as well as the "unconquerable men in blue" who had defended the "heights in the face of fierce assaults." "It was not Southern valor, or Northern valor," he asserted. "It was, thank God, American valor."[3] Echoing the celebration's orators, newspapers from coast to coast exulted that the Gettysburg reunion proved the "death of sectionalism" and the obliteration of the Mason-Dixon Line.[4] By Gettysburg's golden anniversary, such sentiments had become standard fare amid the pageantry of reconciliation.

A few, however, resolutely rejected the Blue-Gray lovefest. In the months prior to the reunion, several members of the Richmond-based Lee Camp of Confederate Veterans had launched a determined protest against the semi-centennial celebration. "I do not see how any man who came back in April of 1865 to smoking ruins and desolated fields, who fought for existence through six bitter years of reconstruction and remembers the wormwood of those days can celebrate side by side with the victors in our defeat in the most important battle of the war," charged St. George T. C. Bryan. Dr. Landon R. Mason concurred, observing that such reunions could never accomplish a true healing of old wounds. "They only effect a superficial healing of the sore, leaving beneath the surface the smarting, irritating pus," he declared. "I, for one, cannot go to Gettysburg where the Grand Army will celebrate with festival the battle which broke the back-bone of the Confederacy while we recall it only with tears of deep sorrow."[5] The editor of the *Confederate Veteran* outright refused to call the gathering a "reunion" and noted that the "best soldier-veterans are repulsed by it on each side."[6] Even among those who made the trek to Gettysburg, not all were awash in the reconciliationist gush. When the son of Confederate major Robert Randolph Henry began disparaging Lincoln at a local hotel, a Union veteran jumped to his feet to defend the martyred president, precipitating a raucous fight that left eight men suffering from stab wounds.[7]

Several black leaders likewise criticized the celebration. "A Reunion of Whom?" asked the editor of the *Washington Bee*. "Only of those who fought for the preservation of Union and the extinction of human slavery?" No, he continued, it was "for those who fought to destroy the Union and perpetuate slavery."[8] In his estimation, locking hands with former Confederates was essentially the same as an endorsement of Jim Crow. He was only partially correct. Organizers had invited soldiers of the USCT, and at least 300 black veterans attended. They were, however, housed along a separate street within the tent camp.[9] White Union veterans had not agreed to forget slavery in the name of national unity even if they forced their former comrades to accept second-rate and separate accommodations. Civil rights and slavery remained two different issues. Black leaders were forced to continue carving out their own spaces to celebrate emancipation and its promise of equal rights.

The pageantry of reconciliation, built primarily on the shared military

Confederate veterans attending the fiftieth reunion at Gettysburg in 1913. Not all veterans relished the Blue-Gray lovefest. (Gettysburg National Military Park-T-2692)

experiences of white veterans, had reached a high point between 1890 and 1915. But the time for such sentiments was quickly passing. By 1920, fewer than 15 percent of the war's survivors were still alive, and most of those were age seventy-five or older. For those who were still so inclined, the GAR and UCV remained active, holding their national encampments and annual reunions for comradeship, observing Memorial Days, and continuing their work of educating the next generation.[10] Yet reconciliation remained tenuous. So long as the war generation survived, so would vestiges of sectional rancor and animosity.

The veterans had long understood that with their passing the Civil War would be relegated to the pages of history and its memory conceded to the next generation. By the early twentieth century, the northern cause of Union and emancipation remained integral to many Americans' understanding of the war—celebrated most impressively and permanently in the Lincoln Memorial. In other ways, the Union Cause's very success forced it to recede into the background, as a reunited people pledged allegiance to the Stars and Stripes and championed the "American Cause" of liberty and freedom during the Great War. The Lost Cause was another story. Still struggling to vindicate their cause, the next generation of white southerners, led by a small but vocal group of women in the UDC, turned to a more explicitly racist memory centered on Reconstruction. As they did so, they steadfastly rejected the reconciliationist sentiment in their effort to maintain control of and finally dominate the war's legacy. Though most white Americans never adopted the Daughters' more radical views, a reconciliationist memory premised on diminishing the role of slavery and emancipation in the nation's greatest conflict emerged in the national memory.

SECTIONAL FEELING

As horse-drawn hacks gave way to motorized cars and people turned to motion pictures instead of the local play house for the latest dramas, fewer and fewer old men attended the Blue-Gray reunions. But still some came, tottering to the grand semi-centennial anniversaries at Manassas and Gettysburg or to more intimate meetings among only a handful of survivors. There were countless other confirmations of fraternal feelings between North and South. In 1905, Congress finally settled the battle flag issue when it authorized the return of any captured Confederate flags still in the possession of the federal government.[11] The following year, the National Veterans' Association of the Blue and the Gray and their Sons was established in Atlanta to unite "in the spirit of brotherly love the survivors of the armies of Grant and Lee."[12] Northerner Charles Francis Adams II, a Union cavalry veteran and son of the U.S. minister to Britain during the Civil War, championed Robert E. Lee, most famously in his "Lee Centennial" address delivered at Washington and Lee University in 1907. Standing before Lee's recumbent statue on the very altar of the Lost Cause, Adams declared the Confederate general a "great man,—great in defeat . . . well-nigh the highest type of human development."[13] Motivated by such

GAR parade through Campus Martius Park in Detroit, September 1914. While Union and Confederate veterans occasionally came together for Blue-Gray reunions, most of their time was spent with their own comrades. (Library of Congress)

an outpouring of reconciliationist sentiment, in 1912 a congressman from North Carolina suggested constructing a Lincoln-Lee-Grant memorial in Washington.[14] A year later, another House member proposed a memorial bridge known as the Grant-Lee Bridge to span the Potomac River between the site selected for the Lincoln memorial and Arlington, Lee's former home turned hallowed Union ground.[15]

Despite these gestures, tension between the reconciliationist spirit and sectional memories of the war remained strong.[16] When word spread in 1909 that Congress was considering allowing a monument to Lee in full Confederate uniform and insignia to be placed in Statuary Hall of the House of Representatives, the New York branch of MOLLUS responded with indignation. "The attitude of Union veterans has been one of kindly forbearance," noted MOLLUS member Thomas Sturgis, holding that "much should be forgiven, conceded, and overlooked on the part of the defeated." But he could not abide by efforts to "make Washington the Westminster Abbey for rebel generals and admirals." "Every man who loves his country should voice a most earnest, if not indignant protest," he admonished. "The time has come when silence would mean cowardice."[17] Nearly a half-century after the war, many veterans of both sides refused to abandon their deep attachment to the cause for which they had fought.[18]

If white Union soldiers refused to forget that they had been both righ-

teous and victorious, neither had time made them forget the role of slave-holders and slavery in the conflict.[19] The triumphant Union armies had "buried for all time rebellion, treason, slavery, and the degradation of human labor," declared Frank O. Cole of New Jersey at the 1915 national encampment.[20] "When the cause of the rebellion was checked on the field of Gettysburg, the Union Army was not only dealing a death blow to slavocracy," maintained Robert W. McBride, Department Commander of the Indiana GAR in the wake of the Great War, "but was also preserving for the future a great Nation which was to deliver the death blow to the Prussian spirit of world domination."[21]

Union veterans expressed these sentiments so adamantly because they recognized that their cause was being diluted if not wholly forgotten. The growing commercial interests that censured anything vaguely anti-Confederate, the proposed appropriation of public moneys for a statue to Lee, and the recent inscription on Spanish-American War veteran Joseph Wheeler's tombstone in Arlington National Cemetery that paid heed to his Confederate service all seemed to confirm a diminishing appreciation of the Union Cause. Members of the New York MOLLUS pointed to the increase in population (largely through immigration) and the birth of new generations as the reason for this forgetfulness. "If those to whom the War of the Rebellion is history only, including our own young generations, do not learn from *us* the conceptions of true patriotism, we shall fail in one of our highest and noblest duties," they warned. This was precisely the reason for all the monuments, the battlefield parks, and the textbook campaigns.

It was up to the veterans and their women's auxiliaries to ensure that the principles of national allegiance, the line between loyalty and disloyalty, would be perpetuated for all time.[22]

Perhaps the veterans likewise recognized a great irony: the very success of the Union Cause had led to its steady demise in the memory of the war.[23] With the union secured, the term "Unionist" disappeared from common rhetoric, and the principal symbol of the Union Cause—the Stars and Stripes—now belonged to all Americans. Encouraged by groups devoted to the Union Cause such as the WRC, former Confederates and their descendants now pledged allegiance to the U.S. flag—albeit one that continued to add more stars as the nation admitted new states into the fold. The United States of 1861 or even 1865 was not the United States of 1915. Suspended in time, however, the Confederate cause and its symbols continued to stand apart, inseparable from the war. With the passing of years, it would seem to many that the Lost Cause was the only memory of the war as the Union Cause became more and more amorphous and obscure.

THE WAR OF RECONSTRUCTION

Throughout the early 1900s, black communities continued to hold Emancipation Days and, in Richmond, an Evacuation Day ceremony, even as these occasions focused less on partisan politics and more on racial uplift, emphasizing Booker T. Washington's message of industry, education, and morality.[24] But as the semi-centennial of emancipation approached, calls for a large-scale celebration began to reverberate. In 1908, both Booker T. Washington and President Taft called for a national event in 1913 celebrating Lincoln's edict. W. E. B. Du Bois, editor of *The Crisis*, the magazine of the National Association for the Advancement of Colored People (NAACP), along with a black Spanish-American War veteran, testified before Congress in favor of a $250,000 appropriation to fund an emancipation exposition. But the proposal died in the House in 1912.[25]

Clearly, Congress believed that a federally funded, national semi-centennial celebration of emancipation was not in order. Others agreed. "What is more desirable," declared a *New York Times* editorial, "is the strengthening of the bonds which unite the North and South." White northerners should remember, the author cautioned, that it had been a comparatively short period since "the most pitiful era in our history, the Reconstruction era." Any national attempt to celebrate the fiftieth anniversary of emancipation would only hasten white southerners to recall "bitter memories of those evil days."[26] Here, fifty years after the war, a

Black GAR veteran participating in a Memorial Day parade in New York City, May 30, 1912. (Library of Congress)

whitewashed memory of the Civil War premised on sectional reconciliation was beginning to take root.

Even without federal support, several exhibitions celebrating fifty years of freedom were held in cities such as Philadelphia, Chicago, Louisville, Milwaukee, and Atlantic City between 1913 and 1915. But the largest and most popular was the National Emancipation Exposition, organized in New York City by Du Bois and other civic leaders between October 22 and 31, 1913. Aided by an appropriation of $25,000 from the state of New York, the gala affair featured paintings, sculptures, music, and exhibits on manufacturing and agricultural industry. Charts advising people on sanitary conditions were intermingled with displays on dressmaking and clanking models of cotton mills. The central attraction, however, was the *Star of Ethiopia* pageant written by Du Bois. First presented on opening night to an audience of more than 5,000 African Americans, the three-hour performance was a magnificent tribute to black history from prehistoric African societies to emancipation and its aftermath, "the gift of freedom." The memory of the Civil War remained central in the final episode, as John Brown, Abraham Lincoln, and Frederick Douglass all made appearances along with marching black soldiers.[27]

While Du Bois was busy celebrating emancipation, a handful of white southerners became convinced that the reunited nation might welcome a grand celebration commemorating the fiftieth anniversary of Appomattox. In the spring of 1913, a Richmond merchants' association proposed a peace jubilee to be held in their city two years later.[28] No place was better suited, they noted, for the "last great reunion which the veterans of either the North or South will have" as the "spot where the final scene of four years drama was enacted."[29] But Richmond's Confederate societies were not so enthusiastic about an occasion that would celebrate the death knell of their cause. The women of the CMLS protested not only the "so-called peace jubilee" to be held on the anniversary of April 9, "the saddest day in the history of the South," but also the suggestion that the GAR be invited to participate.[30] The Lee Camp of Confederate Veterans followed, adopting resolutions that bitterly condemned any celebration "which has for its purpose the commemoration of the downfall of the Confederacy and the commingling of the Grand Army of the Republic and the United Confederate Veterans in the capital of the Confederacy."[31] Even Virginia governor William H. Mann, who had so heartily endorsed reconciliation at the Gettysburg reunion, opposed the celebration. "The Gettysburg reunion was an entirely different affair," he maintained. "The spirit of Gettysburg was of friendship and kindly relations," not a celebration of one side's victory or defeat. "Any reunion which celebrated the fall and burning of Richmond would be woefully inappropriate."[32]

Determined to recognize the golden anniversary, two years later a small contingent of Confederate veterans from Manassas again floated the idea of a Blue-Gray "jubilee" at Appomattox. And again it was vehemently rejected. The women of the CMLS joined by the several local UDC chapters, intoned that any "true southerner" could not possibly consider supporting such an event, especially "at Appomattox, the sepulcher of the dead hopes of the Confederacy." J. Taylor Ellyson, a Confederate veteran and lieutenant governor of Virginia, insisted that a reunion on the surrender grounds could have only "sad memories" for the Confederate soldiers and do nothing to promote good feelings between the former foes.[33] An editorial in the *Richmond News Leader* perhaps best summarized Lost Cause advocates' feelings about Appomattox: "The South would ask the North to remember that if this is the half-century of the amnesty proclamation and the disbandment of the armies, it is also the half-century of the surrender of Lee and of the movement for the enfranchisement of blacks."[34] Foreshadowing a fierce debate over commemorating Appomattox that would erupt in the 1930s, Richmond's Lost Cause supporters could not disentangle Confederate defeat from the origins of Reconstruction and African American political power.[35]

This was not the Lost Cause of the 1860s and 1870s or even the 1890s. In those years, white southerners had cultivated a public memory of the Confederacy that sought to present the war and its outcome in the best possible terms. They had focused overwhelmingly on the heroics of their soldiers and the sacrifices of women on the home front. A few Lost Cause orators such as Jubal Early and William Oates had defended slavery, and many white southerners had touted the so-called faithful slaves. But overwhelmingly, in the latter half of the nineteenth century, Confederate groups were not concerned with race primarily because they simply assumed white supremacy.[36]

By the early twentieth century, however, much had changed. Not only was the war generation rapidly passing, but race relations throughout the country had become more explosive. African Americans began more systemically to fight disenfranchisement, lynching, and segregation through the Niagara Movement in 1905. Three years later, states throughout the nation, not just those in the former Confederacy, had begun disenfranchising African Americans, and in a two-month period in the summer of 1908 alone, there were twenty-five lynchings. By August, tempers reached a boiling point in Lincoln's hometown of Springfield, Illinois, when a mob's demand for the surrender of a black man accused of assaulting a white woman unleashed a horrific two-day race riot.[37] Reeling from the race war, on the centennial of Lincoln's birth, February 12, 1909, a group of interracial leaders issued a call to organize what became the NAACP. Observing that on January 1 (Emancipation Day), Georgia had become the last southern state to disenfranchise black men, they invoked Lincoln's memory to reignite the fight for political and civil liberty.[38]

If African American leaders turned to the war to invigorate their cause, Confederate groups likewise invoked the war's memory to shore up the cause of white supremacy. By the early 1900s, the UDC (assisted by the Sons of Confederate Veterans) had succeeded in placing Confederate flags, portraits of leaders such as Lee, and pro-Confederate textbooks in nearly every southern classroom. They sponsored essay contests for schoolchildren and encouraged descendants of Confederates between the ages of six and sixteen to join the Children of the Confederacy.[39] Using the memory of the war, the Daughters' campaign of indoctrination emphasized the inferiority of African Americans and the benevolence of slavery. Confederate memory had become explicitly wrapped up in southern race relations.

Central to this story, however, was Lost Cause proponents' decision to end the wartime narrative not with Appomattox but with the overthrow of Reconstruction. With increasing frequency, articles in the *Confederate Veteran* recalled the period of 1865–77 in such bellicose language as "the nightmare after the death of the Confederacy" or a "worse persecution than war."[40] If Confederate defeat had managed to bind together white southerners, their unique (if painful) experience of Reconstruction bound them even tighter. Writers heralded those who had survived the dark days of "negro rule" and praised the heroics of groups like the Klan for reclaiming "home rule."[41] Mildred Lewis Rutherford, who had come of age during the war and Reconstruction, implored her UDC sisters to provide the magazine with historical sketches that explained "the story of the Freedman's Bureau, of the Ku Klux Klan (why a necessity)," and of Reconstruction generally.[42] In celebrating those who had taken up arms against black equality, white southerners attempted to mitigate the humiliation inflicted by Union victory. Here was not only a story of redemption rather than defeat, but also a historical foundation for Jim Crow.[43]

This shift toward more inflammatory discussions of Reconstruction did not occur solely among members of the Confederate organizations—nor was it confined to white southerners. Blistering accounts of Reconstruction were especially prominent among the generation that had come of age after the war. In his seven-volume history of the United States (1893–1906), James Ford Rhodes, an industrialist turned historian born in Cleveland, argued that slavery was the sole cause of the war but maintained that Reconstruction had been an immense mistake.[44] In 1907, Columbia University professor William A. Dunning denounced the "negro rule" of Reconstruction as having ruined the South, thus paving the way for an entire school of scholarship that would carry his name.[45] The ever-popular southern author Thomas Nelson Page decried Reconstruction as "a crime, a blunder . . . a cool, deliberate, calculated act violative of the terms on which the South had surrendered and disbanded her broken armies."[46] Reconstruction, such authors argued, had been a colossal mistake. Thomas Dixon agreed. A young man during Reconstruction in North Carolina, the dynamic Baptist preacher was outraged by the popular stage productions of *Uncle Tom's Cabin*. In 1901, he took up his pen in response. His first novel, *The Leopard's Spots*, was an instant best seller, reviving several of Harriet Beecher Stowe's characters, including the infamous Simon Legree, to portray the horrors of Reconstruction. Dixon produced a second novel, *The Clansman* (1905), which proved even more popular. Ten years later, coinciding with the semi-centennial of Appomat-

Veterans from North Carolina during the 1917 United Confederate Veterans'
annual reunion in Washington, D.C. (Library of Congress)

tox, filmmaker D. W. Griffith brought Dixon's story to the big screen in *The Birth of a Nation*.[47]

Like Dixon's novels, the motion picture version acknowledged the bravery of both Union and Confederate soldiers. But where veterans' reunions had often tried to avoid the causes and consequences of the war, Griffith's film had no problem doing so. In his telling, abolitionists—not Lincoln, whom he admired—had ignited the war. More important, the film highlighted what Griffith considered the atrocities of Reconstruction: the U.S. army unleashed renegade black soldiers on the South while Radical Republicans accompanied by black politicians took over southern legislatures. Central to the plot was the final scene in which the Ku Klux Klan prevented a young white heroine from being raped by a black assailant. White southern men might have lost on the battlefield, but they had won the postwar battles that the North had caused.[48]

Amid this atmosphere, a group of black men from Virginia once more suggested that Congress might provide monetary support for a semicentennial celebration of emancipation. During the summer of 1914, the

Negro Historical and Industrial Association, led by lawyer Giles B. Jackson, appealed to Congress for an appropriation of $55,000 for an exposition celebrating freedom in the former Confederate capital. In presenting their request, Senator Thomas S. Martin of Virginia argued that the black race had "accomplished a great deal" in their fifty years of freedom. An exposition supported by Congress would showcase the progress in industry and education achieved by former slaves and their descendants. A racial liberal, Martin noted that "the white people of the South are as anxious to see the negro advance in all legitimate lines as are the people of the North or the people of the country anywhere." In the relatively brief discussion that followed, a senator from Illinois requested that the appropriation be made in the name of black people throughout the nation, not just the South, and a senator from Mississippi observed that the "white man has done more than the negro has done for himself," but he conceded that the appropriation would no doubt pass.[49]

It was Senator Frank White of Alabama, however, who elicited the Lost Cause—with its growing emphasis on Reconstruction—to support the measure. White southerners were grateful, he argued, for all that slaves had done to support the Confederate cause. "When all the colored man had to do to obtain his freedom was to cross the line and take up arms against our section, he stood by our side and fought our battles with us," he argued. Invoking the faithful slave, he described how "loyal" black men had camped with Confederates at night, marched with them during the day, guarded white southern women and children, and carried their dead masters back to their wives. White argued that it had been Reconstruction that caused the strife in southern race relations. If Lincoln had lived, white and black southerners "would have continued to live together in peace." Instead, Radical Republicans had thrust upon the newly freed men "political responsibilities" they were "unable to carry." "In this way he was made to compete in an unequal struggle with the white man, and this caused the only estrangement between the races in the South," White maintained. The celebration should be funded, he concluded, to honor the black men and women who had so devoted themselves to the Confederate Cause.[50] White left no doubt about the ever-increasing centrality of race and Reconstruction to the Confederate memory.

For three weeks in July 1915, only a month after the grand ucv reunion, the "National Negro Exposition" ran at the state fairgrounds in Richmond. Endorsed by President Wilson in a national proclamation, the fair included exhibits by black educational institutions and industry from at least ten southern states. Beyond these showcases, the midway offered a spectacular array of entertainment including Wild West Shows, vaudeville performances, minstrel singers, and a roller-skating act.[51] During the fair's second week, the planners included a pantomimic pageant titled *Answer to the Birth of the Nation*, which featured 300 black schoolchildren performing scenes from African American history, including the arrival of the first slaves at Jamestown in 1619 and closing with freedmen beginning on the road of opportunity.[52]

Despite the president's endorsement and the congressional allocation, black newspapers throughout the nation condemned the affair as a "rank failure." Few people had attended and the majority of African Americans had refused to support it, they observed, in large part because of both the accommodationist tone and bad management on Giles B. Jackson's part. The appropriation had been given to Jackson, observed a Saint Paul newspaper, because "he is of the antebellum type so loved by the South . . . [who knows] how to bow and kowtow before his 'white frens' and got his coin." A Utah paper agreed, noting that the lack of interest generated by black people should serve as a lesson to white southern men that the old-time "Negro, of whom he is so especially fond," was not the type to foster such enterprises.[53] Instead of gathering for a Lost Cause–inspired emancipation celebration, many black Americans joined the NAACP in fighting Griffith's white southern version of the war and its aftermath, *The Birth of a Nation*, which premiered that same year.[54]

Several GAR posts and state departments likewise denounced the film. Grand Army members in Montana adopted resolutions condemning it and sent for an interview with the governor, while the Department of Oregon petitioned Congress to ban the picture it deemed likely to damage "the wholesome spirit of democracy throughout the country." C. A. Meek, commander-in-chief of the Department of Kansas, went straight to the governor with his objections. Quoting from the GAR's official organ, the *National Tribune*, Meek explained why Union veterans were so outraged: "It is as vile and treacherous, as poisonous to the minds of the rising generation as anything can be. It degrades the war for the Union and the exalted courage of the men who fought to save the nation into a shameful lust of conquest, with only the most debased of mankind engaging in it."[55] Though the film might portray reconciliation between white Union and Confederate soldiers in the name of white supremacy, at least some GAR members vehemently objected to any such memory of the war.[56]

Regardless of the denunciations by Union veterans and the vigorous protests of the NAACP in several U.S. cities, white audiences flocked to witness the nation achieve a rebirth—a reunion—quite different from the one that had been celebrated by war veterans in recent years. Confederate societies in particular extolled the film, offering screenings during a UCV national reunion in Birmingham. One member hailed the motion picture for showing the country that "there was really more distress in the South during the War of Reconstruction than in the Civil War."[57] Mrs. S. E. F. Rose, a Confederated Southern Memorial Association (CSMA) member from Mississippi, observed that "the silent language of the photo drama has proved more powerful than all else in bringing about a realization of 'things as they were' during Reconstruction."[58] *The Birth of a Nation* was implicitly connected to the rise of the second Klan in the 1920s, but, perhaps more important, the film and its response revealed a subtle yet powerful shift in the national rhetoric of reconciliation.[59] In theaters throughout the country, the story of heroic veterans clasping hands on former battlefields had been replaced by an emphasis on the horrors of Reconstruction and the race war that followed in its wake.

Most Americans, however, found their attention captured by another war. When fighting erupted in Europe in the summer of 1914, President Wilson pushed for a policy of nonintervention. But after the British ocean liner *Lusitania*, whose passengers included 128 Americans, was sunk by a German submarine in May 1915, calls for U.S. involvement in the war mounted. Two years later, the United States declared war for the second time since the Civil War. Again, soldiers from the North and South rushed to defend the Stars and Stripes. And as they had done during the Spanish-American War, civilians and soldiers alike heralded the prowess of the American soldier who hailed from North, South, East, and West.

Women's auxiliaries and memorial societies, too, rushed to the new cause. Members of the WRC cooperated with the Council of National Defense and the Red Cross to support troops in the field and attached patriotic sentiment to domestic labors such as conserving food and other supplies.[60] In nearly every southern town, UDC chapters paused from their monument fund-raising and turned their attentions to war relief. Food conservation efforts, selling liberty bonds, and fund-raising drives to supply American military hospitals in France occupied the time of women north and south. For a brief moment it appeared that war—not peace—might lend itself to national reconciliation between the women's organizations. At its 1917 national convention, the UDC passed a resolution requiring members to stand with their right hands over their hearts during the national anthem and whenever a U.S. flag passed in review.[61] Even more astounding, at the urging of Congress (notably all male with the exception of Representative Jeannette Rankin of Montana), in 1917 the women of the WRC and UDC joined together for the first time to provide three Tiffany stained-glass windows in the newly built national headquarters of the Red Cross. During the next few years, the two women's associations would each furnish a window, and together they provided the funds for the central window that was dedicated on May 18, 1923.[62]

More than fostering reconciliation, like the southern white men who fought in the trenches of France, southern white women's efforts during the Great War served primarily as a vindication of southern patriotism. As UDC President-General Cordelia Odenheimer noted, cooperating with national organizations like the Red Cross would help to show "as indisputable fact" that the "patriotism of the South is second to that of no other section of the country."[63] But perhaps more important, the First World War helped revive white southern women's interest in the Civil War. Though they devoted themselves to Red Cross work, their original objectives were not forgotten. They continued to care for aging veterans, assist needy widows, and provide scholarships for the descendants of loyal Confederates. Their usual essay contests continued as well, but the UDC also added a Soldier's Prize to recognize the best essay composed by a Daughter about a southern-born staff officer in the Great War. They established new committees, such as the World War Record Committee devoted to recording "every lineal descendent of a Confederate Veteran who served in the World War," bestowed a medal similar to the Cross of Honor upon World War I veterans who were descendants of Confederate soldiers, and offered a Hero Scholarship to aid such men.[64] Even during an era of heightened nationalism, an independent strain of southern sectionalism remained strong among the Daughters.

SONS AND DAUGHTERS

As the ranks of the GAR became thinner, surviving members recognized that the Union Cause was receding ever more in the nation's memory. Not only had their cause increasingly been absorbed into the American Cause of the Spanish-American War and the World War, but the veterans had little hope that the Sons of Union Veterans (SUV) would step forward to preserve their memory.[65] For decades, the SUV had failed to mobilize the next generation, having reached a high of 54,000 members in 1891 before dropping to fewer than 26,000 in 1900. At national meetings, leaders continually lamented the low enrollments. Some suggested that it was the result of too many young boys who quickly lost interest; others thought that there were not enough rituals to keep them enthusiastic.[66] By 1918, however, there was a clear reason. "The world's war has in large measure diverted the minds of the sons from the war in which their fathers fought a half century ago to the war of to-day, in which their sons are fighting," concluded the GAR's commander-in-chief, Lewis Pilcher.[67] After 1919, men who had fought in the World War, many the sons and grandsons of Civil War veterans, had their own powerful patriotic organization in the American Legion. But unlike the GAR, African American soldiers were admitted into its ranks only on a segregated basis and barred completely from conventions as late as 1927.[68] Integrated posts for World War veterans would have to wait.

Their own ranks thinned by death, the UCV likewise had wanted their male heirs, the Sons of Confederate Veterans (SCV), to accept control of the Lost Cause. Formed in 1896 as an official auxiliary to the UCV (unlike the Daughters who remained an independent organization), by 1904 the SCV and veterans had worked out an agreement whereby the Sons enjoyed rights at UCV business meetings, could serve as Veterans' escorts in parades, and were permitted to wear the Confederate gray (without military rank). But even with all these provisions, the SCV struggled to maintain its membership base. In 1903, the group could claim 16,000 members in 427 camps, but in 1905 only 42 delegates attended the annual reunion (membership numbers are unavailable). "The future of the United Sons of Confederate Veterans," Commander Thomas M. Owen wrote in 1907, "is not bright with any special promise."[69] Fifteen years later, Commander-in-chief Walter L. Hopkins continued to beseech the Sons to help fill the ranks, noting that "one of the greatest needs of our organization today is an increased membership."[70] Like the SUV, however, many Confederate sons found themselves drawn to other organizations, including the American Legion.

While the Sons groups declined, women's Civil War associations saw steady growth. In 1894, the WRC counted 139,081 women among its ranks, and by 1911 that number had risen to more than 164,000.[71] Yet by the late 1910s the WRC recognized that its 1883 insistence on admitting only women who had personally supported the Union Cause would naturally lead to its extinction, as was becoming increasingly evident among the ranks of the GAR. To prevent a rising attrition rate, after the Great War the WRC began to admit the female relatives of a new generation of veterans. "We are gaining many new members from the ranks of mothers, wives and sisters of the men who offered their lives, if need be, for the freedom of the world," national secretary Eliza Brown-Daggett reported in 1920, the membership having risen to 188,368.[72] Perhaps this sentiment enticed many African American women to remain among the most dedicated WRC members. As late as 1933, five all-black corps remained active in both Kentucky and Virginia, one in Florida, and two each in North Carolina and South Carolina.[73]

In spite of its hefty membership numbers, over the years the WRC had drifted away from its sole emphasis on the Union Cause. The women continued to espouse patriotic instruction, but their message became more diffuse—less centered on convincing white southern children to pledge allegiance and more focused on other causes. In the 1880s, the WRC joined the GAR in reviling Mormons for the "horrors of polygamy" and opposed "the further importation of Chinese women, for the purposes of prostitution."[74] By the early twentieth century, it had united with the DAR in approving legal constraints preventing immigrants from learning their native languages in schools or speaking them in public. In 1916, the WRC endorsed a national woman's suffrage amendment.[75] And after the Great War, it admitted all "loyal" women into their ranks. In each of these endeavors, commemorating the Union Cause receded more and more from the women's efforts.

The UDC likewise continued to grow rapidly. While fewer in absolute numbers, the UDC represented a higher percentage of the southern white population than their northern counterparts. By 1919, the Daughters claimed nearly 64,000 members and 1,161 chapters extending from Atlanta to Los Angeles.[76] Women had been active in Confederate memorialization since the 1860s, but they flocked to the Daughters in such unprecedented numbers in part because doing so provided a popular social outlet for middle-class women. By joining the UDC, women expanded their communities to include not just like-minded women from their own neighborhoods, cities, and state, but women from across the region and nation.[77] But the racially charged atmosphere of the 1910s and 1920s probably also contributed to the organization's steady growth. Middle- and upper-class southern white women involved themselves in contemporary political and social issues of their day by commemorating their Confederate (i.e., white) heritage. Just as the LMAs had provided a platform for ex-Confederates to condemn federal policies at Memorial Day celebrations during Reconstruction, in the early 1900s members of the Daughters looked to the region's past as a means to shape race and gender relations in the New South.[78]

As the descendant organizations came to the forefront in the 1920s and 1930s, Civil War memory—and especially the Lost Cause—became increasingly feminized. Not only did this indicate that the war had become less central to society, but among white southerners it also indicated a swelling hostility to the reconciliationist spirit.[79]

A MAGNIFICENT MARBLE MEMORIAL

In the spring of 1922, Washington, D.C., was once again festooned in flags of red, white, and blue. And again, hundreds of Union veterans descended on the city, this time to dedicate one of the largest and most impressive equestrian monuments in the world. Begun twenty years earlier, Henry Merwin Shrady's magnificent memorial to Ulysses S. Grant was an imposing site. Grant and his horse served as the central figure of the 252-foot-long memorial; to the north and south of the equestrian statue were large groupings of cavalry and artillery charging into battle. Situated prominently at the west foot of Capitol Hill in the aptly named Union Square, the memorial offered no allegorical figures of peace, no laurel wreaths of victory. Neither did it commemorate Grant the president. Instead, the quiet determined look of Grant atop his massive steed, the tense muscles of the thirteen horses, and the steely-eyed look of the Union soldiers evoked the harsh reality of war's carnage. The memorial would serve as a perpetual reminder of the Union victory secured by Grant and his soldiers.[80]

In striking contrast to the monument, the dedication on April 27, the 100th anniversary of Grant's birth, was awash in messages of peace and reconciliation. The ceremonies began with a military parade of 10,000, including U.S. regulars, veterans of the Spanish-American War and the Great War, and cadets from the military academies marching from the White House down Pennsylvania Avenue—the same route as the 1865 Grand Review. The immense crowd had enthusiastically applauded and waved flags throughout the procession. But it reserved its loudest cheers for the white-haired Union veterans marching in slow, measured step alongside a handful of Confederate veterans, many pointing with wonder as a GAR man and former rebel marched hand in hand. The dedicatory addresses likewise overflowed with homages to peace and unity, paying special tribute to Grant's proclivity for magnanimity and his famous words "Let Us Have Peace." In a stirring eulogy, Secretary of War John W. Weeks observed that Grant had done much to unite the nation at the close of the war, "giving hope to a gallant people who had fought for and lost a cause." And newspapers made much of the huge floral tributes from both the GAR and UCV that graced the base of the monument. The only reference to slavery—or even war—came from Vice President Calvin Coolidge.

"There is no substitute for a militant freedom," he cautioned. "The only alternative is submission and slavery." Oblivious to the disparity in their words and the monument behind them, the orators all paid tribute to one central fact: Grant stood at the base of the nation's capitol as an emblem of the triumphant Union war.[81]

If the Grant monument served as a memorial to the military leader who had secured the Union, northern veterans hoped that renewed calls for a Lincoln Memorial in 1909 would likewise connect their commander-in-chief to the Union war effort. At least a few congressmen too young to have fought in the war concurred, suggesting that the memorial should explicitly tie Lincoln to the victory his soldiers had secured on the battlefield.[82] But others insisted that the most appropriate Lincoln memorial would emphasize not war but peace.[83] "We should not be reminded so much of the physical and awful struggle between neighbors and brothers of a half century ago," insisted Congressman Frank Nye of Minnesota.[84] Like Nye, many of those who had come of age after the war called instead for a "universal" work, one that would highlight the timeless appeal of Lincoln's humanity. Sanitized of the blood, agony, and sacrifice of war, they envisioned a memorial much different than that being erected to Grant—one that would transcend the conflict.

Though explicit connections to the carnage of war might be avoided, the Union Cause remained paramount to the proposed Lincoln memorial. Architect Henry Bacon's colossal design featured a Parthenon-inspired rectangular hall surrounded by thirty-six Doric columns walls, one for each state in the Union in 1865. The names of the forty-eight states at the time of the dedication were to be carved into the top of the frieze. Lincoln's connection to the battlefield and his soldiers would ring out in the engraved words of his Gettysburg Address, imploring the nation never to forget what the "brave men, living and dead," had fought to protect. And the inscription above Daniel Chester French's seated statue would declare simply and most crucially that Lincoln had "Saved the Union."[85] This would be much more than just a monument to a man—it would be a memorial to U.S. soldiers, sailors, and their cause.

The place of emancipation in the monument was more tenuous. Before the design had been selected, several African Americans had written to the Lincoln Memorial Commission, observing that emancipation should form a central component of the design. William H. Davis of Washington, the son of slave parents and the stenographer for the National Negro Business League, urged the commission to consider a great plaza between the Capitol and Union Station, where a Temple of Justice would house the

Supreme Court. Amid his ambitious plan that included a series of lawns replete with national emblems such as the eagle, he proposed a statue representing "emancipation" in tribute to Lincoln, "Freedom's Foremost Friend." A. R. White of Wisconsin offered a much simpler proposal: an Egyptian-style pyramid dedicated to "the emancipator . . . of the black race," while a Richmond man had hoped that the national memorial to Lincoln would be more utilitarian in its scope. There were already too many marble statues in the country, he observed, offering that the establishment of a colored school in the South would be a more fitting tribute to Great Emancipator.[86]

Subjected to lynchings, race riots, and innumerable less violent but no less detrimental forms of oppression, however, some African Americans had begun to question their abiding affection for Lincoln and the unfulfilled promises of emancipation. Reviving Frederick Douglass's critiques that Lincoln had not been radical enough, Archibald Grimké, an African American lawyer born into slavery, accused the war president of being timid and lacking moral feeling toward the slaves. Lincoln's "devotion to the Constitution with its slave clauses amounted almost to idolatry," he wrote in *The American Missionary*, "and kept him hesitant and conservative in respect to the subject of slavery during the first two years of the war of the Rebellion." Had Lincoln been able to save the Union without freeing a single slave, he would have, Grimké reminded his readers. Hubert Harrison, a native of the West Indies who moved to the United States in 1900, concurred. In a four-part series he penned for the *Negro World* in 1911, Harrison declared that Lincoln had been no abolitionist, favored making slavery perpetual in 1861, refused to pay USCT soldiers the same as their white comrades, and issued the Emancipation Proclamation not to abolish slavery but to cripple the rebel armies. Here was no "Great Emancipator," he argued.[87]

Some white planners of the memorial agreed that celebrating Lincoln for emancipation was unwise, albeit for different reasons. Royal Cortissoz, art critic and author of the inscription above the statue, cautioned that discussions of slavery should be avoided in the name of reconciliation. "By emphasizing his saving the union you appeal to both sections," he wrote in 1919. "By saying nothing about slavery you avoid the rubbing of old sores."[88] Instead, the designers allowed Lincoln the only words on emancipation; his descriptions of the war as divine retribution for slavery's offense that might bring forth a "new birth of freedom" from the Gettysburg Address and the Second Inaugural were carved into the walls. The only other allusion to universal freedom came in the form of Jules Guerin's so-called emancipation mural depicting the shackles of bondage falling from slaves as the angel of truth bestowed them with freedom and liberty.[89] Although a minor part of the memorial, these oblique references to slavery ensured that a tenuous if fragile connection between Lincoln and emancipation remained.[90] And in the years to come, they would prove the backdrop to more forceful statements about equality and civil rights.

By the spring of 1922, the last touches had been completed on the marble temple and the formal dedication set for May 30. Throughout the morning, steady streams of pedestrians and automobiles scrambled to get as close to the monument as possible, gathering as far as the eye could see along the new reflecting pool. They watched eagerly as the guests of honor arrived, including foreign dignitaries, members of Congress, Supreme Court justices, and a feeble Robert Todd Lincoln. But for the dwindling group of northern veterans set to witness the dedication, the selection of Memorial Day could not have been more fitting. Earlier that morning, the GAR had held its annual services in Arlington National Cemetery honoring the nation's dead. Back across the Potomac, veterans opened the dedication ceremonies by presenting the symbols of the army and navy at the foot of the memorial.[91]

Though some congressmen and planners had hoped to elevate Lincoln above the blood and fighting of battle, for GAR commander-in-chief Lewis S. Pilcher and the Union soldiers he represented, Lincoln could never be separated from the Union war. "They died bravely when needed to make real Lincoln's ideals," he told the crowd of more than 50,000, pronouncing the memorial "the crowning glory of the lives of Lincoln's soldiers, sailors, and marines."[92] Others agreed, observing the close tie between the aging veterans and the man they had come to enshrine. In his remarks, President Warren G. Harding observed that Lincoln "loved 'his boys' in the army, and would have reveled in the great part they played in more than a half century of the pursuit of peace and concord restored."[93] In 1865, many northerners had recognized that Lincoln's death served as a symbol of all the Union deaths during the war. Fifty-seven years later, this sentiment still held resonance. For years to come, one newspaper reporter commented, the memorial would serve as "the mecca of a nation come to honor the soldier dead through Lincoln, the greatest martyr to their beloved cause."[94]

As had been the case at Chickamauga, the Grant Memorial, and numerous other national dedications, the day's speeches overflowed with reconciliation sentiments. And like these other occasions, the reconciliation celebrated was more precisely a vindication of the Union Cause.

Dedication of the Lincoln Memorial, May 30, 1922. (Library of Congress)

Supreme Court chief justice and former president William Howard Taft, the chairman of the memorial commission, observed that the memorial marked the final restoration of "brotherly love" between the North and South.[95] In the prayer of dedication, GAR chaplain Bishop Samuel Fallows gave thanks that the "wrath of war has been stilled, that brother no longer strives against brother," and that the whole nation had come to realize the greatness of Lincoln.[96] Accepting the monument on behalf of the American people, President Harding likewise noted that it served as a testament to the national feeling cemented by Lincoln. Looking out upon the crowd, he declared that Lincoln's heart would have rejoiced to see the Union and Confederate veterans sitting side by side, "each with common pride and all of them with common confidence in the future of this reunited republic."[97]

If the dedication was heralded for its unity between Blue and Gray, some had hoped that it might likewise serve as an emblem of unity among white and black. Recognizing the centrality of emancipation to Lincoln's memory, the memorial commission invited Dr. Robert Moton, successor to Booker T. Washington as president of Tuskegee Institute, to provide the keynote address. In response, however, Moton drafted a zealous plea for racial justice rather than a tribute to national unity. His original text openly criticized the federal government, calling the memorial a "hollow mockery, a symbol of hypocrisy." Borrowing Lincoln's famous words, he implored the nation to "strive to finish the work which he so nobly began, to make America the symbol for equal justice and equal opportunity for all."[98]

But the commission refused to allow any speech that rang of militant protest. Instead, in language reminiscent of Washington's 1895 Atlanta Exposition speech, Moton underscored African Americans' devotion as loyal citizens, marveled at the progress of interracial cooperation, and focused on Lincoln as a symbol of national unity. He refused, however, to remove all vestiges of tension, speaking of America's dual heritage of freedom and slavery. While Lincoln had died to save the Union, Moton insisted that his greatness lay in emancipation. "In the hour of the Nation's utter peril, he put his trust in God and spoke the word that gave freedom to a race and vindicated the honor of a nation conceived in liberty and dedicated to the proposition that all men are created equal."[99] Like the USCT veterans of the 1860s, some of whom sat on the stage beneath Lincoln's marble gaze, for Moton emancipation preceded Union in the war's accomplishments.

Moton's speech was not alone in belying the unity the ceremony was intended to convey. Prior to the dedication, several African Americans, including prominent real estate broker Whitefield McKinlay and secretary-treasurer of Howard University Emmett J. Scott, had refused to be seated in the segregated section and abruptly left. J. LeCount Chestnut, a *Chicago Tribune* reporter, concluded that this incident proved the Lincoln Memorial to be a mockery. "The spoils have gone to the conquered instead of the conquerors when rampant segregation is rife in the seating of members of the Race," he wrote.[100] In Chestnut's estimation, the Lost Cause had overwhelmed the Union Cause. The promises of emancipation—of the legacy of the Civil War—had been unfulfilled in the name of sectional reunion.

But the vast majority of white Union veterans never saw it this way. Many, no doubt, agreed with President Harding's insistence that the Union was the paramount cause. "The supreme chapter in history is not emancipation, though that achievement would have exalted Lincoln throughout all the ages." "Emancipation," he observed, "was a means to a great end—maintained unity and nationality. Here was the great purpose, here the towering hope, here the supreme faith."[101] Harding's message had not entirely excluded the memory of slavery or emancipation; his address was awash in references to freedom and liberty. But this twentieth-century president, born seven months after Lincoln's assassination, reflected what many white Union soldiers had believed in 1861–65: the war had been first and foremost a fight to ensure the republic's survival. In the intervening fifty years, numerous white veterans had recalled the twin legacies of Union and emancipation, some increasingly giving near equal weight to both. But for many of them, race and slavery had been separate issues. White U.S. veterans understood that slavery had caused the internecine war and therefore could celebrate emancipation because it had removed that deadly source of sectional conflict, even if they did not favor civil and political equality for African Americans.[102] For these veterans, celebrating Lincoln amid a segregated audience seemed hardly hypocritical.

Just as important, Harding's comments both reflected the cyclical nature of Civil War memory and suggested the emergence of a new pattern. White Americans who had come of age within a segregationist society—and well after slavery had threatened to tear the nation asunder—could more easily recall a war absolved of cause. As the veterans' generation gave way to the next, a reconciliationist memory premised on diminishing the role of slavery and emancipation in the nation's greatest conflict emerged.[103] But the temple to Lincoln proved to be a brilliant merging of the old and the new, of the veterans and the next generation. In varying degrees, this magnificent marble memorial paid tribute to the sacrifice of Union soldiers, celebrated emancipation, and heralded the unity of the states. And yet as the younger generation had hoped, the memorial transcended the war. In the years and decades to come, it would prove to be not only one of the most visited and photographed of all Civil War memorials, but also one of the most important podiums for messages of freedom, liberty, and unity—the resounding hope of Lincoln.

Less than a month after the Lincoln Memorial dedication, Confederate associations met in Richmond for the thirty-second reunion of the ucv. Led by Mildred Rutherford, the History Committee recommended a pamphlet to be used in the South's schools charging Lincoln as personally responsible for "deliberately conceiving and instigating the war between the states."[104] "The sentiment has been so aroused that perverted Yankee histories will no longer be used to instruct our children," the report declared. Instead, the "school children of the South will know that the South was right, eternally and everlastingly right, in fighting for principles upon which our glorious country was founded." Amid a great swell of cheers, many still smiting from the Lincoln Memorial that stared directly across the river at Lee's Arlington mansion, the ucv and udc adopted the resolution by acclamation.[105]

As news of the resolution spread, a storm of protest erupted across the nation. Henry B. Rankin, an eighty-five-year-old Illinois lawyer who had studied in Lincoln's office, publicly denounced the charge as a "lie."[106] Grand Army Departments from New Jersey to Minnesota condemned the resolution as "libelous, untruthful, and without foundation in fact," while the national encampment offered resolutions proposing retaliation by the soldiers of the North against the Confederate veterans.[107] Mary Logan, the president of the Dames of the Loyal Legion and widow of GAR founder John Logan, said the UCV's claims were a "perversion of facts" and urged all patriotic societies to seek the suppression of any such histories.[108] The black press concurred, labeling Rutherford a "rattle-brained southern woman" whose aim was to poison the minds of the rising generation of southerners "with a view of intensifying sectional animosity and racial antipathy."[109]

The resolution might have been issued in the wake of the Lincoln Memorial, but its sentiments were not new. Southern animus toward the war president had persisted for years. In 1911, the University of Florida fired a professor for teaching his students that Lincoln had been a greater man than Jefferson Davis.[110] Scores of books and articles written by Mildred Rutherford, Lyon Gardiner Tyler, and others insisted that Lincoln had been an irreligious brute responsible for the South's despair. Tyler, the son of former president John Tyler and the president of the College of William and Mary (1888–1919), argued that for too long white southerners had believed that Lincoln's assassination had resulted in the atrocities of Reconstruction. In fact, Lincoln, with his "abolition policy . . . was the true parent of reconstruction, legislative robbery, negro supremacy over their masters, cheating at polls, rape of white women, lynching and the acts of the Ku Klux Klan," he wrote.[111] In a letter to the *Confederate Veteran*, Mrs. M. P. Shepard offered a similar denouncement of the Union president. The most egregious of all Lincoln's many insults, she noted, was his "emancipation of six millions of slaves, his exciting them to insurrection, his placing guns in the hands of negroes to murder their former masters," and his extension of the ballot to "ignorant negroes who had no more knowledge of the rights of suffrage than so many mules."[112] During World War I, a series of widely published pamphlets wondered if the "unspeakable inhumanities" of the German government were not equivalent to those let loose by Lincoln's Emancipation Proclamation.[113] As was becoming increasingly the case among many keepers of the Confederate flame, the memory of the war—and even Lincoln—could not be separated from that of race and Reconstruction.

Reaction to the UCV's 1922 resolution, however, suggested that the sympathies of many white southerners were changing. Newspapers throughout the former Confederate states expressed indignation at the attacks on Lincoln.[114] The Missouri UCV went on record denouncing the resolution, observing that the gray army had fought valiantly for the Lost Cause and criticism of the dead president would avail them nothing. The nation was now united, it maintained, "and all true Americans have the same reverence for Lincoln, the Great American."[115] Confederate widow Helen Dortch Longstreet condemned the "Lincoln slur" as a ploy by the southern textbook trust, exhorting that the South never had "a knightlier friend than Lincoln." A Virginian and son of a Confederate soldier, Wythe Leigh Kingsolving penned a letter to the *New York Times* defending Lincoln. The war president had tried to avert many evils, desired to pay slave owners for their slaves, and was "the best friend in the North the South ever had," Kingsolving wrote. But his highest praise for Lincoln, like that of many white southerners, revolved around Reconstruction. "Had Lincoln lived," he insisted, "the terrible inequities of the 'carpetbag era,' would never have been permitted."[116] Recognizing that the national UCV leadership appeared out of step with many white southerners, within days the group's commander-in-chief issued a statement explaining that the resolution had been passed amid confusion and deploring that it had aroused any ill feeling.[117]

There was other evidence that Lincoln's name was being held in increasingly high regard in the South. Despite the efforts of Rutherford and the UDC, schools throughout Dixie housed busts of Lincoln, and southern schoolchildren were required to recite the Gettysburg Address just as their northern counterparts had been doing for years. On the Senate floor in 1928, fifty-six-year-old Democratic leader Senator Joseph Taylor Robinson of Arkansas eulogized Lincoln on his birthday. That same year, the Virginia Assembly adopted a resolution to adjourn in honor of the Union president's birthday. Again, the most ardent Confederate supporters rose in protest, the UDC demanding that the assembly "expunge this blot on the historical record." But the Richmond newspapers applauded the assembly's action. "However clear or beclouded Lincoln's title to greatness be," the *Times-Dispatch* editorialized, "it is conceded by all that his fame is second to none in the annals of this country."[118]

Mainstream white southerners might be more willing to accept Lincoln, but the UDC offered one last rejoinder to the Great Emancipator's sacralization. Less than a year after the Lincoln Memorial dedication, the Daughters proposed a monument to the "Faithful Colored Mammy of the Southland," to be placed along Massachusetts Avenue in Washington, D.C.[119] Contrary to the African Americans who had rebelled against slavery, aided Union troops, and served in the Union army or even the message of Moton's revised speech, the UDC hoped to pay tribute to the "loyal," feminine, and asexual surrogate-mother image of the mammy.[120] And it was nearly successful. While a Senate bill appropriating $200,000 for the memorial remained in committee, the black press launched a vigorous campaign against the monument. Was it not a mockery to erect a monument to the "faithful mammy" in the era of Jim Crow, disenfranchisement, and lynchings, newspapers asked? Several national associations including the WRC likewise denounced the plan. At the Relief Corps's annual convention, members resolved that "agitation for a monument in the District to the colored mammy of the South is a 'sickly sentimental proposition' and the [WRC] 'forever protests against it.'" Expending the money on bettering the conditions of "Mammy's" children would be a far more appropriate use of the money, the WRC maintained.[121]

Recognizing the memorial's potential to reduce the history of slavery to the mammy figure, Chandler Owen of *The Messenger* penned his own powerful protest. Like Civil War memorialists, he worried about the next generation. "We want the children of this generation to abhor and forget those days when the white madam had leisure and the black mammy had labor," he exhorted. If anyone should be celebrated in the nation's capital, it should be the black soldiers of the Civil War. "We favor [a monument] to the 200,000 Negro soldiers who fought to wipe out slavery and to unfurl the flag of freedom," he stormed. "We favor a salute to these men who helped save the Union, who indeed were a great factor in crushing out the iniquitous viper—slavery—which had vitiated the entire American atmosphere with its venomous and poisonous breath." A monument to the runaway slaves "who had the courage to dash to freedom," to black artists, inventors, or scholars—any of these would be preferable to one that recalled "Southern whites' good times" during slavery.[122] By challenging the mammy figure with that of a black Union soldier, Owen offered the very antithesis of the nostalgic and faithful female: black men who shouldered rifles in the name of democracy and citizenship.[123] The monument to USCT soldiers would have to wait another half-century, but the mammy memorial would never be built.

Despite its failure to erect the monument, the UDC found more and more white southern women flocking to its cause, reaching a membership of more than 100,000 members by 1924.[124] With their ever-expanding numbers and continued emphasis on the postwar years, the Daughters continued to raise the ire of Union memorial groups. "You must stand ever ready to combat the baneful influence of that other group of women, the Daughters of the Southern Confederacy," former GAR commander J. W. Willett warned in the Federated Patriotic Societies in 1930. Another past GAR commander agreed. "It should be one of the purposes of these affiliated organizations to protect the country from what I warn you is its worst enemy—the Daughters of the Confederacy."[125] While other Civil War memorial groups faded more quickly with each passing year, the Daughters proved to be an indomitable group with plenty of fight still left in them.

PEACE MEMORIAL

By the Great Depression, the great majority of the war generation had died, leaving only the octogenarians tottering to their meeting halls.[126] With the passing of time and veterans, there was ample evidence that the reconciliationist pageantry of the late nineteenth and early twentieth centuries likewise appeared to be waning. In 1931, the UCV rejected an invitation from the governor of Kentucky and the GAR to partake in exercises commemorating the life of Abraham Lincoln. UCV commander-in-chief Gen. C. A. DeSaussure unabashedly declined to participate, saying that Lincoln had never been a friend to the South. The Daughters and women of the CSMA heartily endorsed his actions, congratulating DeSaussure for refusing to join in the tribute to a man "whose name will ever bear a stigma for the crucifixion of the South." Later that same year, the Georgia members of the CSMA rejoiced that "southern patriotism is not dead" when they managed to prevent an effort to make Lincoln's birthday a holiday in their state.[127]

And yet among the general public there were still vestiges of the reconciliatory attitude, especially when such sentiment could help line the pockets of individuals, communities, and corporations. In lamenting the lack of tourism to the small town of Appomattox, the local newspaper reminded its readers of the "nobility of character of Gen. Lee, never more glorious than in defeat, and the generosity of General Grant" in victory. Amid the economic turmoil of the Depression, local residents were willing to sing the praises of both generals if veterans of either side would open their pocketbooks and visit the impoverished farming community.[128] National companies likewise tried to sell reconciliation, as was the case with the Old Union Beer Lager. When prohibition was repealed in 1933, the Houston-based company advertised the "Re-birth of the Union." The beer, "known for generations to all Southerners," was now available again. "Don't forget," the advertisement noted. "In Union there is strength!"[129]

The federal government similarly thought that the time was appropriate for a national monument celebrating reunion. In 1926, a congressional commission recommended the erection of a central Peace Monument and the reconstruction of the dismantled McLean House at Appomattox.[130] Five years later, the War Department invited any American architect of standing and reputation to submit a design for this monument and a landscape treatment of the proposed site. In keeping with the reconciliationist spirit, the announcement stressed that the memorial should not focus on the conflict, but rather should "symbolize an undivided Nation and a lasting peace." "If this is accomplished," the announcement continued, "those engaged in the tremendous conflict will be fittingly honored and the requirements of the act of Congress will be carried out."[131] After reviewing 186 applications submitted by architects from throughout the country, the jury, chaired by Virginian William C. Noland, came to a unanimous decision. The winning design featured two pylons of either granite or marble banded with laurel at the top and rising from a base symbolizing the nation's founding. Adorned with the seal of "our undivided nation," one side of the monument would bear the likeness of Grant and the other that of Lee, perhaps with an inscription such as "Duty—the most sublime word in our language." As the designers explained, the memorial would thus "symbolize an undivided nation and a lasting peace."[132]

In April 1932, as word spread that the monument design had been selected, Confederate groups once again rallied around their old flag. Penning a powerful missive to Brig. Gen. L. H. Bash of the War Department, the ucv's DeSaussure warned that the monument would no doubt "foster the very result which their specification endeavors to avoid." "Who can view this monument without opening afresh the memory of the circumstances which gave rise to its erection, the hot, burning antagonisms, the fierce desire to kill, the death of fathers, husbands, brothers, the privations, the sufferings, the oppressions of those times, the memory of which the 70 years have done so much to obliterate," he asked. Why, he wondered, was it necessary to revisit those wounds, to awake those "unholy and painful recollections of all that roused the worst passions of human nature?" Why not, he asked, "let the dead past bury its dead?"[133]

Though Bash reassured the ucv that the monument would be a "beautiful and dignified memorial to the ideals of both sides" and entirely devoid of sectionalism, the real issue appeared to be that Confederate veterans and their descendants were not prepared to commemorate the final defeat of their cause.[134] DeSaussure acknowledged that the War Department had already memorialized the war at national military parks from Gettysburg to Vicksburg. At each of these sites, the battlefields and their monuments represented struggles between opposing armies—with "equal intention, equal determination, equal purpose, equal beliefs in themselves and equal hope." Veterans and their descendants could visit Shiloh or Fredericksburg to revel in the heroic fighting of *both* sides without acknowledging the final outcome of the war. Even on those fields that were clearly Union triumphs, such as Gettysburg, Confederate veterans could boast of their heroism and bravery through monuments to specific regiments.[135]

But unlike other battlefields, Appomattox marked the death of the Confederate cause. As DeSaussure observed, a single, federally sponsored monument at the surrender grounds would commemorate "the realization of blasted hope, sacrifice for naught, and the humiliation and failure" of the entire South.[136] How could Confederates deny the defeat of their cause at Appomattox? While the Lost Cause embodied Confederates' conviction that defeat had been a result of the Union's overwhelming numbers of men and resources, white southerners recognized that the so-called Peace Monument would stand as a constant reminder to white Virginians—to all former Confederates and their descendants—that however heroic, their fight had been in vain. Contrary to proclamations that "both armies were victorious at Appomattox," Confederate societies bitterly opposed a monument that permanently commemorated in stone Union victory and southern defeat, especially on Virginia's hallowed ground.[137]

More important than military defeat, memories of Reconstruction dominated white southern opposition. Peter J. White of Richmond believed that Appomattox marked "the advent of the carpetbagger, the scalawag, and a horde of harpies too numerous to mention, the disenfranchisement of the whites, the enfranchisement of the blacks, and the horrors of 'reconstruction.'" "What sort of peace was there after Appomattox?" he asked.[138] DeSaussure observed that rather than peace, the ten years following Appomattox had seen "carpet bag rule and bayonet oppression."[139] Instead of a monument at Appomattox, he proposed erecting tributes to "the termination of the horrible 're-construction,'" period, when "we drove out the carpet bag marauders in South Carolina, or similar periods in Louisiana, Mississippi, and Tennessee with their accompaniments of oppression, subjection to our former slaves, disenfranchisements, rule of negro bayonets, etc."[140] Reconciliationist sentiment had been predicated upon a focus on soldiers' heroics *and* a silence on issues of causation and postwar consequences. The proposed Appomattox monument by its very nature could not help but destroy this fragile compromise.

Perhaps not surprisingly, the most virulent and frequent attacks against the Peace Monument came from the UDC. Not only had Confederate women resolutely resisted any reconciliationist efforts that were not on their terms, they were likewise not afraid to take on those who challenged their authority on the past. Even as the debates about the Peace Monument intensified, the Daughters were waging a battle with African American leaders over the so-called Faithful Slave monument at Harper's Ferry.[141] Because they believed that southern white women had inaugurated the Lost Cause through Memorial Days and Confederate cemeteries in the 1860s, they sought to continue shaping Confederate memory. They would not concede to serve merely as secondary participants, and thus they saw no reason not to confront the federal government and defend their jurisdiction over the Confederate past.[142] As women of the UDC became the most vocal defenders of Confederate memory in the 1930s, Confederate memorialization reflected their more pro-southern, anti-northern, and anti-reconciliatory stance on the war.

Like Confederate men, the UDC employed the rhetoric of Reconstruction to launch their attacks, yet they did so in an explicitly gendered way. In an open letter to the Daughters in the fall of 1932, Mary Davidson Carter of Upperville, Virginia, recommended that women read Claude Bower's *The Tragic Era: The Revolution after Lincoln* (1929). In his narrative popular among Confederate groups, he explained how the South had been "placed under Negro and Carpetbag Rule, while Davis, Lee, and all the worth-while were denied the rights of citizenship."[143] Bower's work, she said, would remind the UDC of the peril their mothers and grandmothers had faced. Like many white southerners, Carter believed that Reconstruction had been responsible for the rise of the "new negro crime"— black men raping white women.[144] Quoting another author, Carter wrote, "Before the Klan appeared . . . no white woman dared venture out in the black belt unprotected." And, of course, Grant had supported all of this "by Federal Bayonets." She asked the Daughters if they were willing to stand by and allow Lee to be forever linked with Grant—the man who "brought untold disaster to the South"—"or are we going to show the country and the world, that no monument that insults the name of our great Confederate leader shall be erected on Virginia soil?"[145]

It seems hardly coincidental that Carter's letter describing black men's uncontrollable desire to rape white women came in the summer and fall of 1932 during the appeals of the so-called Scottsboro boys, nine teenaged

African American boys accused of gang-raping two white women in Alabama.[146] With the case splashed across the nations' newspapers each day, many white southerners made explicit connections between it and Reconstruction. (Moreover, to many white southerners, Franklin Delano Roosevelt's New Deal looked like Yankee meddling once more.)[147] An editorial in the local Scottsboro paper implied that Reconstruction might begin anew when it reported that the involvement of the "New York defenders" was "the most dangerous movement launched in the South in many years."[148] The *New York Times* informed its readers that "the memory of the reconstruction period . . . is a vivid and haunting one" to many in Alabama.[149] Most tellingly, several white women whose names appeared on the affidavit admitted that "they did not care what happened to the Negroes so long as they were killed, because if they were freed the South would not be safe for white women."[150]

Consciously or not, Confederate women's groups made associations between the proposed peace monument and the Scottsboro case. One Richmond, Virginia, association collected clippings about the case in a scrapbook dedicated primarily to Confederate activities. Throughout the summer and fall of 1932, the women attached newspaper articles about the NAACP's efforts to hinder the Scottsboro case and Alabama "treating its negro population too kindly" next to articles about UDC essay contests and monument dedications.[151] Carter, too, must have been making such connections. Ostensibly talking about Reconstruction, she warned the Daughters that "all over the South white women armed themselves in self-defense." "The spectacle of negro police leading white girls to jail was not unusual in Montgomery," she wrote.[152] Clearly women such as Carter envisioned a race war abetted by northern involvement, a second Reconstruction. The Daughters thus harkened back to images of "Yankee aggression," "black betrayal," and the alleged rape of white women by black men in Reconstruction to galvanize protest against the Peace Monument. With the Scottsboro trials drawing constant media attention, surely all could see that Grant and his Reconstruction policies were still having dire consequences for southern white women.

Carter's message proved to be overwhelmingly successful in such an atmosphere. By the fall of 1932, the CSMA and other UDC chapters had joined her vitriolic protest.[153] The women of the CSMA went on record protesting the Appomattox memorial as "an insult to General Lee and to every southern soldier who fought and died for the Confederate cause." As they saw it, the federal government was attempting to humiliate and insult the South.[154] A Mrs. Lamar of Georgia denounced the "infamous association of Lee, the soul of honor, with Grant the tool of interests, the victim of drink, and the head of the infamous policies of the Tragic Era." The project, she bitterly argued, "should be abandoned as cruel to the memory of the great Lee and certain to put new emphasis on the bitterness that resulted from the war and its *hideous aftermath*."[155] The attacks launched by Carter and the Daughters, therefore, occurred in an atmosphere of a more visceral and blatantly racist defense of the Confederacy—one that was framed in explicitly gendered terms and one that found little room for reconciliationist sentiment. For the Daughters, Appomattox did not mean peace but instead the opening of a whole new war.[156]

In the fall of 1933, most Americans found their attention drawn to President Roosevelt's National Recovery Administration, the hurricanes that repeatedly slammed into the Gulf and Atlantic coasts, efforts to repeal prohibition, and the World Series between the New York Giants and the Washington Senators. But letters from Confederate groups about the Appomattox monument continued to fill the War Department's mailbox.[157] And the verbal lashings persisted as well. At the annual meeting of the Confederate associations in Atlanta, Dr. William R. Dancy, commander-in-chief of the scv, deplored the project as both an insult to Lee and a monument "designed to memorialize the subjugation of the South."[158] Using sectionalist rhetoric to defend his address in the weeks that followed, he declared that his primary objection was that it would do more to rekindle the feelings of discord between the regions than any other action. "The war is nearly seventy years past, animosity has subsided," Dancy declared, "why again arouse it by placing in the South a monument memorializing the most horrible features of the conflict?"[159]

Not all white southerners supported his stance. Throughout 1932 and 1933 white southerners from North Carolina to New Orleans denounced Dancy, the scv, and the Daughters for instigating more intersectional acrimony than did the proposed monument.[160] The most dynamic support for the Peace Monument came from Virginius Dabney, a prominent Virginia journalist and historian. Grandson of a Confederate veteran, Dabney nevertheless fiercely maintained that nothing about the plan could offend the South. In editorials printed in the *New York Herald Tribune*, *New York Times*, and the *Richmond Times-Dispatch* he dismissed notions that it was a "diabolical plot originating in the brain of some official of the Grand Army of the Republic" or a scheme hatched by the War Department to humiliate the South. He took special aim at Confederate women's organizations, maintaining that their views were "out of harmony with those of most southerners." He likewise disparaged Confederate and Union veterans for their recent refusal to attend one last Blue-Gray reunion. Although he believed that veterans on both sides might go to their graves "unreconciled" and "unreconstructed," he was yet hopeful that sectional animosities were becoming increasingly less important to the average American. "There are still die-hards on both sides of the Potomac," he admitted, but thankfully "their ranks are thinning steadily." Most important, he felt confident that "the erection of a 'peace monument' at Appomattox, signifying the end of hostilities and the rise of a united nation, should aid measurably in wiping out unreasoning enmity between the sections."[161] Reunion and reconciliation might emerge as one and the same through the proposed memorial.

But such moderate voices would not prevail. On August 10, 1933, the military parks were transferred, from the War Department to the National Park Service (NPS) in the Department of Interior as part of President Roosevelt's efforts to reorganize the federal bureaucracy. Two months later, the NPS announced that it had no intention of erecting the peace monument so long as there was any opposition in the South. The park service was not inclined to engage in such battles. By February 1934, newspapers were reporting that the monument had been abandoned by the Virginians who had first proposed it. "Old Soldiers Win Fight," heralded the New York Times, pointing to the "wave of protests from Confederate organizations of women primarily, but backed by a thin gray line," as the culprit. Former UCV commander William McKee Evans declared that he was pleased at the news. "All Confederate leaders with whom I have talked opposed that monument depicting Grant and Lee," he maintained, as such would be "an insult to General Lee and to every Southern soldier who fought and died for the Confederate cause."[162]

Attentions now returned to the proposals that had been floated more than forty years earlier to create a battlefield park at the site.[163] There was not a single voice of dissent from the Confederate organizations. Perhaps the notion of a national battlefield appeased the veterans who could point to one last heroic stand. Or maybe the Daughters found the plans to re-create the McLean House in line with their own recent efforts at building preservation. But almost certainly, unlike a monument whose message would endure indefinitely in stone, the restored home might be an inoffensive historical site open to interpretation. On August 13, 1935, President Roosevelt approved the creation of a national historical park at Appomattox with its chief goal the restoration of the McLean House.[164]

The fierce fight that unfolded between the War Department and Confederate sympathizers in the 1930s—and the ultimate victory of the Confederate contingent over the federal government—suggested that among the most vocal white southerners, the memory of the war was no longer as important as the memory of defeat and what followed in its wake. More important, it revealed that the UDC with its anti-reconciliationist bent and commitment to white supremacy had come to dominate much of the Lost Cause. Perhaps the pageantry of reconciliation had run its course.

BEYOND THE VETERANS

While Mary Carter and the Daughters worked tirelessly against the Appomattox monument, resistance to reconciliationist gestures remained evident among the veterans. Throughout the 1920s and 1930s, both Confederate and Union veterans renewed calls for a joint GAR-UCV encampment. And each time they were defeated. "The South has never admitted that it was wrong or expressed regret for what it did," observed one GAR officer. "We can't fall in line with it until it does." Confederate veterans were no less anxious to spend their national encampment in the presence of their former foes. "If we all met together," observed former Confederate M. J. Bonner in 1935, "war would be renewed." The commander-in-chief of the UCV, Rice A. Pierce, put it more succinctly: when the GAR insisted former Confederates march with their flag furled, he informed a reporter, "I introduced a resolution telling them to go to hell." Much to the surprise of the American public, many of whom believed that the quarrels of the past should be left to the past, not once would the chief veterans' organizations ever join together for a national meeting. Neither side was willing to forget what it had fought to preserve, even in the name of sectional reconciliation.[165]

Seventy-five years after the battle of Gettysburg, there was one last gasp of reconciliationist sentiment—one last gesture of peace among the veterans. Their ranks nearly depleted, 1,400 Union veterans and 500 Confederate veterans now in their nineties gathered for the Last Reunion of the Blue and the Gray to dedicate the Eternal Light Peace Memorial. Broadcast live to the country on the radio, President Roosevelt described Gettysburg as a shrine of American liberty and reminded his listeners that Lincoln's wisdom was timeless. And again, as they had done so many times in the past, newspaper editorials waxed nostalgic that the occasion bore witness to a nation united in peace. But the winds of war were stirring again. Paraphrasing the Union Cause so long championed by northern veterans, one editorial reminded readers that in a world again threatened with war, "the meaning of Gettysburg is that no sacrifice is too great for the preservation of a united Nation and the defense of its priceless guarantees of individual freedom."[166] The Union Cause had not been forgotten.

Yet the once mighty Grand Army was passing.[167] When the GAR held its last encampment in 1949 at Indianapolis, only six members were present. Seven years later, the lone surviving GAR member, Albert Woolson, died and the Grand Army was finally no more.[168] The UCV saw its ranks exhausted even more quickly. With only about 35,000 Confederate veterans still alive in 1932, the *Confederate Veteran* observed that "it seems the thin gray line has reached the breaking point and cannot be stretched further."[169] Those that survived held their final reunion in 1950.[170] It remained to be seen, however, whether the Union Cause and Lost Cause would survive the veterans.

It was increasingly left to their descendants to perpetuate the war's legacy. With the Sons groups struggling to attain membership, Union and Confederate women managed to maintain the most viable organizations dedicated to carry on the war's memories. Having reached a peak membership of more than 100,000 members in 1924, by 1939 the UDC still carried more than 38,000 women on its rolls. Seven years later, the WRC could claim more than 200,000 members, and in 1962 it was finally incorporated by Congress to perpetuate the memory of the "men who saved the Union in 1861 to 1865."[171]

Perhaps no Confederate descendant was more instrumental in shaping the memory of the South's most celebrated hero than Douglas Southall Freeman. The longtime editor of the *Richmond News Leader* and holder of a Ph.D. in history from Johns Hopkins University was born in Lynchburg, Virginia, in 1886. Freeman's father, a veteran of the Army of Northern Virginia, served as national commander-in-chief of the UCV in 1925, and young Freeman came of age attending Confederate reunions and witnessing such memorable occasions as the reinterment of Jefferson Davis in Hollywood Cemetery and a reenactment of the battle of the Crater. By 1915, he had edited two collections of Confederate documents—*A Calendar of Confederate Papers* and *Lee's Dispatches*—and gained a significant following as a popular speaker and an authority on the Confederate past. But it was his multivolume work, *R. E. Lee: A Biography* (1934–35), that solidified his reputation.[172]

In *R. E. Lee*, Freeman reinforced themes espoused by Jubal Early and others after the war. He insisted that Confederate defeat was a result of superior northern materiel and numbers, and he lauded praise on the heroic soldiers of the Army of Northern Virginia who had devoted their all to the cause. He reaffirmed, with impressive scholarly trappings, Lee's canonization (along with his right-hand man, Stonewall Jackson) as the Confederacy's most gifted general. There was no one, Freeman wrote, "who so embodies the glamour, the genius, and the graces with which the South has idealized a hideous war." Deftly weaving thousands of small details—such quotidian things as the weather and Lee's conversations—into its narrative, the four-volume series received incredible acclaim from all parts of the nation and garnered the Pulitzer Prize in biography in 1935. "You rise from the completed work," wrote a reviewer for the *New York Times*, "with the conviction that here is Lee's monument. Granite, bronze, or marble cannot so visibly . . . present either the man or the soldier to the mind's eye." Critics praised Freeman for his masterful storytelling and his ability to reveal Lee "as the man he was rather than as we would like to have had him," capable of military mistakes and with human flaws. With the national popularity of author and subject rising, Freeman crisscrossed the nation giving lectures on the Confederate general. By the time his second multivolume work, *Lee's Lieutenants: A Study in Command*, was published in 1942–44, Freeman had succeeded in situating the rebel commander alongside Lincoln as one of the two most celebrated figures of the war.[173]

With the American people increasingly receptive to the Lost Cause, in 1939 Hollywood producer David O. Selznick released his lavish screen version of Margaret Mitchell's best-selling novel, *Gone with the Wind*, which eclipsed *The Birth of a Nation* as the most memorable and profitable cinematic portrayal of the Civil War. During the first six years after its release, more than 120 million Americans, essentially every adult in the country, saw the film. In some places, demand for tickets was so great that theaters doubled their prices or added second and even third showings to accommodate the crowds. Still immersed in the Great Depression and about to enter the Second World War, Americans could not get enough of the romantic epic depicting white southern resolve in the face of defeat.[174]

Whereas Griffith's 1915 film had offered a vision of North-South reconciliation premised on white supremacy, *Gone with the Wind* was a staunchly Lost Cause interpretation of the past. In the "land of Cavaliers and Cotton fields . . . Knights and Fair Ladies," white southerners had loved their slaves—and their slaves had loved them. They had not gone to war to protect slavery; rather, northerners had been the villainous aggressors, invading the South, burning southern cities, and threatening to rape white southern women. Though outnumbered and overwhelmed, Confederate soldiers like Ashley Wilkes fought on valiantly until defeat. They returned home to find their cities and farm in ruins, only to be doubly devastated by the tyrannical hand of the federal government during Reconstruction.[175]

By all accounts *Gone with the Wind* appeared to be a triumphant vindication of the Lost Cause. But few recognized that it proved so immensely popular with audiences regardless of region in large part because the Union had triumphed—and because reunion had succeeded. The threat of white southerners rebelling against the federal government had been secured seventy-four years earlier at Appomattox. In the intervening years, the North and South had been reunited under the banner of Americans. What was the harm in embracing a nostalgic interpretation of a *failed* Confederacy? It was equally significant that the film's central character was a woman (even though the fiery, hot-tempered Scarlett O'Hara defied the Lost Cause vision of the sacrificing, patriotic Confederate woman). Just as Confederate veterans had believed women might be especially well suited to keep the flames of sectionalism alive because they occupied an "apolitical" and nonthreatening space, so Scarlett's defiance and resistance might be chalked up to women's silly emotional outbursts. Firmly situated in the hands of the UDC by the late 1930s, the Lost Cause had been feminized—a fact that *Gone with the Wind* captured all too well.

If the Confederate cause proved benign in part because it resided in the hands of white southern women, however feisty they might be, the film remained mute on slavery as a cause of the war. Instead, it depicted the reciprocal loyalty between white masters and their slaves, between Scarlett and Mammy or Big Sam that might have been lifted straight from the pages of the *Confederate Veteran*.[176] White Americans who had come of age within a segregationist society—years after slavery had threatened to tear the nation apart—could more easily embrace an interpretation of the war that ignored slavery than could Unionists of the war generation. With fewer and fewer surviving Union veterans able to voice their consternation, a vision of a reconciled nation premised on forgetting slavery finally became possible with the help of the silver screen.

Even as *Gone with the Wind* celebrated the "old-time negro" of the antebellum South, African Americans continued to claim their own memory of the Civil War. In 1935, W. E. B. Du Bois published *Black Reconstruction in America, 1860–1880*. Vehemently denouncing the Dunning School's portrayal of Reconstruction as a "diabolical" time to be "remembered, shuddered at, and execrated," Du Bois also rejected the notion that it had been an unqualified mistake. Instead, the Harvard-educated professor highlighted newly free slaves as the chief actors and reclaimed the period as one of African American progress and potential.[177] Du Bois was not alone in his efforts. Between 1936 and 1938, ex-slaves interviewed by the Federal Writers' Project of the Works Progress Administration recounted a version of slavery much different from that of pleasant plantations or faithful servants and told of their own contributions to the Union war effort. Some recalled the joys of seeing U.S. troops arriving in the South, and others remembered their arrival as "scandalous days." And in stark contrast to UDC descriptions of Reconstruction, some recounted the horrific violence of lynchings and beatings enacted against black men and women in the postwar years.[178]

On April 9, 1939, exactly seventy-four years to the day that Lee surrendered at Appomattox, Marian Anderson climbed the steps of the Lincoln Memorial. Denied by the Daughters of the American Revolution and the color bar the right to perform at Constitution Hall in Washington, an act that aroused the consternation of First Lady Eleanor Roosevelt and the nation, the celebrated contralto delivered a magnificent open-air concert to a crowd of more than 75,000 people beneath the shadow of the Great Emancipator. Through her performance, Anderson managed to forge a link between Lincoln and the burgeoning civil rights movement— a link that Robert Moton had been prevented from making at the 1922 dedication.[179] From Du Bois to Anderson and in Emancipation Day ceremonies throughout the nation, African Americans continued to offer up a counter-memory of the Civil War and Reconstruction that stood at odds with the white South and, increasingly, the white North. Reunion may have triumphed by 1939, but a whitewashed reconciliationist memory of the war had not.

EPILOGUE

As the nation prepared to commemorate the 100th anniversary of its greatest war in 1961, many hoped it would do so in the spirit of reconciliation. "The war did not divide us," insisted retired Maj. Gen. Ulysses S. Grant III. "Rather, it united us, in spite of a long period of bitterness, and made us the greatest and most powerful nation the world had ever seen." Nearly a century after his grandfather had accepted Lee's surrender at Appomattox, Grant urged American families to partake in the commemorative festivities in the name of reunion and reconciliation. Indeed, many Americans were swept up in centennial fever. Under the guidance of the federally sponsored Civil War Centennial Commission (CWCC), grand reenactments of battles such as First Manassas, exhibitions of war relics, new historical markers, and elaborate parades were to mark the years. The four-year affair would be a national pageant showcasing the bravery, courage, and devotion of both the Blue and the Gray, celebrating the valor and patriotism of *American* soldiers amid the uncertainty of the Cold War.[1]

As it had at countless anniversaries and reunions before, however, the spirit of reconciliation proved elusive during the centennial. The idea of a national commission to honor the war was anathema to some white southerners who worried that the impending commemoration would force them to minimize their Confederate heritage in the name of national consensus. Building on the Lost Cause tradition emphasized by Mary Carter and other UDC members in the 1930s, others recognized that the war's memory could be used to address contemporary racial issues. The U.S. Supreme Court's decision in *Brown v. Board of Education* (1954) and President Dwight D. Eisenhower's intervention during the Little Rock desegregation stand-off (1957) had convinced some white southerners that the Civil War's memory might promote white unity as the region again came under attack from federal intrusion. Commemorating Jefferson Davis's inauguration with a week-long historical pageant in Montgomery, Alabama, in 1961, the site of the 1955–56 bus boycott, for example, offered a platform on which to defend the "southern way of life" and promote solidarity among the region's white residents. The South was facing the same attacks it had in 1861, observed a local newspaper: "We the people of a democracy should stand up and fight as our forefathers did so we can lick this ever present battle with the federal government as it continues to usurp rights delegated to the states."[2] Just as Confederate veterans had done in the 1870s and 1880s, white southerners employed the war's memory in the name of contemporary social and political issues.

Hoping to promote a national consensus on the war, the cwcc reassured white southerners that it had no intention of imposing a northern, liberal agenda on the South.[3] White southerners would be free to commemorate the war as they saw fit. No event suggested more about the commission's acquiescence to white southern demands than the 1961 dispute over Madeline A. Williams. When the cwcc held its annual meeting at a hotel in Charleston, South Carolina, Williams, a black member of New Jersey's state commission, was denied entry. Insisting it had no influence over a state's racial codes, the cwcc—a federal agency created in the spirit of national cohesion—refused to intervene. The story quickly garnered national front-page news, forcing the new president, John F. Kennedy, to publicly criticize the national commission. Eventually the delegates reconvened at Charleston's desegregated U.S. Navy Yard, but the damage to the commission's image and the centennial had been done.[4]

Other mishaps and negative publicity soon followed. Anticipating the anniversary of the preliminary Emancipation Proclamation in 1962, Martin Luther King Jr. sent an open letter to the president appealing for a national rededication of the principles of Lincoln's declaration. But unwilling to alienate southern Democrats prior to the fall's congressional elections, Kennedy ignored the request. Still, southern state commissions worried that a planned ceremony at the Lincoln memorial on September 22 would be used as a platform to promote civil rights, and many threatened not only to boycott the ceremony but also to secede from all observances of the centennial. Any commemoration of emancipation, they warned, was nothing but "propaganda . . . to reopen the wounds of war." Always hoping to avoid confrontations over such divisive issues, the cwcc offered a tenuous compromise, proposing that independent groups would be the primary sponsors of the ceremony and racial divisions would be minimized.[5]

The centennial brought into stark relief a Civil War memory that high-lighted regional reconciliation and patriotism to the exclusion of stories of slavery and emancipation. Aided by the continued overwhelming success of *Gone with the Wind*, by the 1960s a whitewashed vision of reconcilia-tion had finally taken center stage.

But just as had been the case for the previous century and a half, this memory of the war would not go unchallenged. Instead, in the midst of the civil rights movement, African Americans found themselves in a stronger position to contest the Lost Cause and other white-only interpretations of the war. Black magazines such as *Jet* published scores of articles not only about the failures of the cwcc but also the contribution of uscт soldiers.[6] In 1963, Martin Luther King Jr. delivered his famous "I Have a Dream" speech at the Lincoln Memorial, alluding to the Emancipation Proclama-tion and reminding the crowd that "one hundred years later, the Negro still is not free." The national NAACP warned its local chapters that the centennial might strike a blow at the movement toward equality. Others explicitly denounced the white-only vision of reconciliation promoted by the commission. "The Civil War we hear about today is a fight of brave brother against brother, with both separately but equally righteous in their causes," complained black historian Dorothy Sterling in March 1961. Sounding much like a Union soldier, be he white or black, she counseled that "there was an underlying issue in the war—slavery. The leaders of the Confederacy were fighting to perpetuate a slaveholding, slave breeding, slave driving society."[7]

Fifty years later, amid the sesquicentennial, the issue of reconciliation resurfaced, this time under the mantra of inclusiveness. Congressional bills calling for a national commission between 2009 and 2011 advocated a memory of the war that would recognize "all people affected by the Civil War," be they northern or southern, white or black.[8] But debates surround-ing the war's cause, legacy, and meaning remained so infused with ten-sion that the sesquicentennial was commemorated without a national commission. The National Park Service developed programming, the *New York Times* and *Washington Post* ran regular features on the war, universi-ties and museums showcased special exhibits, several anniversary-related shows appeared on television, and publishers such as the University of North Carolina Press issued new titles to coincide with the anniversary. But overwhelmingly, sesquicentennial events were left to heritage soci-eties, local organizations, and state commissions.

Some states, weary of the racial controversies that troubled the centennial (and strapped for cash amid the recession), were reluctant to establish commissions. Others created what might at best be described as quasi-sesquicentennial agencies. Alabama, for example, combined its sesquicentennial events into a larger "Becoming Alabama" initiative that planned to commemorate the Creek War and civil rights movement alongside the Civil War. Still others established well-funded and ambitious agencies. Virginia's commission was supported by a generous funding of nearly $17 million from the state legislature. By the summer of 2012, this commission had launched a project to digitize Civil War collections that remained in private hands and staged several successful public symposia on the causes of the war, the African American experience, and military strategy, among others.[9] Scattered among state agencies and a host of other local organizations, the sesquicentennial remained a relatively low-key affair.

If the war's 150th anniversary has proven more subdued than the 100th commemoration, divisiveness and competing memories have not disappeared. Earlier demarcations between Lost Cause proponents, Emancipationists, and Union Cause advocates in some cases remain. In other instances, new lines of division have become increasingly apparent. The divide between scholars and the general public is especially notable on the topic of the war's causation. Overwhelmingly, professional historians agree that slavery caused the war. The same is not true among popular audiences.[10] A substantial portion of the American public, even those who reside outside the South, remain reluctant to concede that slavery had anything to do with the war.[11] Instead, people offer tariff disputes, state rights, or constitutional issues as the fundamental cause. Paradoxically, popular audiences are more comfortable with the participation of African American soldiers and the notion that Union soldiers fought to end slavery. The Academy Award–winning movie *Glory* (1989) and Ken Burns's documentary *The Civil War* (1990), among others, have conveyed both to the popular consciousness. Why, we still need to ask ourselves, do most Americans, especially whites, deny the centrality of slavery to secession and the war, while also (wrongly) insisting that the Union war effort was mainly intended to destroy slavery?

The Lost Cause has found a more ambivalent place in the sesquicentennial. Local organizations and heritage societies like the Sons of Confederate Veterans, for example, have demonstrated the persistence of Confederate mythology. Scoffing at calls for "commemoration not celebration" as "political correctness" in December 2010, revelers in antebellum dress staged a secession ball in Charleston, South Carolina, to celebrate the state's withdrawal from the Union.[12] Two months later, on February 19, 2011, crowds gathered in Montgomery, Alabama, to witness the scv re-enact Jefferson Davis's inauguration, an occasion that seemed eerily reminiscent of the 1961 affair. Central to the celebration was a procession of Confederate reenactors and women in hoopskirts: they started at the spot where slaves were once sold, marched past the place where Rosa Parks boarded a public bus in 1955 sparking the Montgomery boycott, traversed the site where Martin Luther King Jr. culminated the historic Selma-to-Montgomery march, and ended at the capitol steps where Governor George Wallace had proclaimed "segregation forever" in 1963.[13]

It was apparent, however, that in the twenty-first century many Americans had come to reject Confederate symbols that were intimately connected to a slaveholding, white-supremacist past, such as the battle flag. The commemorative events in South Carolina and Alabama in 2010 and 2011 attracted national protests from the NAACP and other groups and also provided fodder for national news agencies.[14] Meanwhile, the state governments refused to sponsor these events, and elected officials in Alabama avoided the Jefferson Davis inauguration festivities altogether.[15] Other southern politicians likewise rejected racially divisive attempts to celebrate the Confederate past. In February 2011, Mississippi governor Haley Barbour declined to sign a bill supported by the scv that would have placed Confederate general Nathan Bedford Forrest, an antebellum slave trader and the first Grand Wizard of the Ku Klux Klan, on a license plate.[16] A Lost Cause interpretation of the war that was mainstream in the 1950s and 1960s had become increasingly marginalized.[17]

What about the Union Cause? Where has it fit in the sesquicentennial? Although emancipation has taken a more prominent role in the 150th anniversary than it did in the 1960s, many Americans might still suggest that the Union Cause has all but disappeared. But if we understand reunion as the Union Cause, this memory of the war was clearly evident in President Barack Obama's April 11, 2011, proclamation commemorating the war's onset. "When the guns fell silent and the fate of our Nation was secured, blue and gray would unite under one flag and the institution of slavery would forever be abolished from our land," he noted. The struggle to extend equal rights to all citizens would continue into the postwar period with the Reconstruction Amendments and well into the twentieth century. "We are the United States of America," he declared; "we have been tested, we have repaired the Union, and we have emerged stronger."[18] Although his speechwriters likely did not realize it, this was not reconciliationist pageantry, nor were there any nods to the Lost Cause. Instead, it was the Union Cause as the veterans understood it: North and South re-united under the Constitution and slavery banished never to threaten the Union again.

So far, the sesquicentennial has left us with a mixed legacy with which to judge reconciliation. Countless journalists, event organizers, and other public figures have resurrected the images of the Blue-Gray lovefests. There was no right or wrong cause, they argue; northerners and south-erners both believed they were right. For others, the commemorations provided evidence that a North-South divide remained. "New events sometimes make me wonder if we have forgotten the bitter lessons of that war—or whether we never quite stopped fighting it," observed syndicated columnist Clarence Page. "You need look no further than our electoral map to see how the red state/blue state divide over politics, parties and values largely follows the old North/South divide."[19] Have the wounds ever really healed? Has the nation ever truly experienced reconciliation?

It is too soon to tell exactly what the sesquicentennial's overall impact will be on the course of Civil War memory. But several issues remain clear. First, reunion and reconciliation were related albeit never quite the same phenomena. The Union war aim of reuniting the nation happened. The imprecise nature of reconciliation makes it more difficult to determine if and to what extent it ever occurred. Along these lines, reconciliation never was, nor has it ever been, the predominant memory of the war. Try as they may, those from the war generation to the present have never succeeded in finding a memory of the war that absolved all parties of blame and was palatable to most Americans, be they white or black, northern or south-ern, men or women. Finally, it is clear that despite the fears of Frederick Douglass, Jubal Early, and others, the Civil War is far from forgotten. In-deed, it seems likely that for decades and perhaps generations to come, Americans will continue to grapple with questions of the war's memory, of what to commemorate and what to condemn.

NOTES

1. According to Robert Toplin, an estimated 13.9 million Americans watched the first episode of Burns's documentary. Approximately 40 million watched one or more episodes (Toplin, *Ken Burns's The Civil War*, xv–xxvi).

2. *Winchester (Va.) Times*, November 6, 1889; *Chicago Defender*, September 21, 1929.

3. There is a vast scholarly literature on memory studies, which explores the difference between history and memory, revealing the extent to which the past has been "invented." Scholars in the fields of history, sociology, and cultural theory have applied this analysis to events such as commemorations of the Alamo, the Holocaust, and the Enola Gay. See for example Hobsbawm and Ranger, *Invention of Tradition*; Thelen, *Memory and American History*; Gillis, *Commemorations*; Winter, *Sites of Memory*; Connerton, *How Societies Remember*; Linenthal, *Sacred Ground*; and Kammen, *Mystic Chords of Memory*.

4. Scholars have differentiated between formal history and collective memory. In the words of Barry Schwartz (*Lincoln and the Forge of National Memory*, 8–9), "Collective memory refers simultaneously to what is in the minds of individuals and to emergent conceptions of the past crystallized into symbolic structures." In other words, the ways in which people think about and understand the past are shaped by the societies and cultures in which they occur. While collective memory shapes how individuals think about the past, it is not a literal memory for many people. Instead, it can embrace events occurring before an individual was born. For more on collective memory, see Halbwachs, *Collective Memory*; Nora, "Between History and Memory"; and Anderson, *Imagined Communities*.

5. As historian W. Fitzhugh Brundage has observed, "Because power is central to the propagation of a version of history, changes in the relative power that groups enjoy invariably has consequences for what and how they remember" (Brundage, *Southern Past*, 8).

6. Douglass, quoted in Blight, *Beyond the Battlefield*, 96.

7. Early, *Proceedings of the Southern Historical Convention*.

8. For the argument that the war's memory was frequently about "necessary forgetting," see Blight, *Race and Reunion*, 5, 7, 9, 31, 44; Madison, "Civil War Memories," 198–230; Poole, "Memory and the Abolitionist Heritage," 202.

9. For an example of a contemporary distinguishing between reunion and reconciliation, see *Valley Virginian*, November 13, 1867.

10. *Chicago Tribune*, July 19, 1872.

11. *Valley Spirit* (Chambersburg, Pa.), June 28, 1865.

12. Edward Blum argues that national reconciliation required the "forgiveness" of white southerners (Blum, *Reforging*, 15).

13. For historians who have emphasized reunion and reconciliation, see Buck, *Road to Reunion, 1865–1900*; Blight, *Race and Reunion*, 2–5, 65, 265; Silber, *Romance of Reunion*; Smith, *Golden Age of Battlefield Preservation*; Woodward, *Origins of the New South*, 43–50; Fellman, *Making of Robert E. Lee*, 304; Campbell, *When Sherman Marched North*, 105. For those who have highlighted the complexities of reconciliation

and the persistence of sectional animosities, see Neff, *Honoring the Civil War Dead*; Reardon, *Pickett's Charge*; Blair, *Cities of the Dead*; Waugh, *U. S. Grant*; Gallagher, *Causes Won, Lost, and Forgotten*; Gallagher, *Union War*; Gannon, *Won Cause*; Coski, *Confederate Battle Flag*, 67; O'Leary, *To Die For*, 121–28; Marten, *Sing Not War*, 273; McConnell, *Glorious Contentment*, 189–91; Cloyd, *Haunted by Atrocity*; and Harris, "Across the Bloody Chasm."

14. No scholarly study of Civil War memory and reconciliation has shaped the field more than David W. Blight's award-winning *Race and Reunion*. Central to his thesis, and those of many scholars who have followed, is the contention that white northerners and southerners reconciled their war wounds through shared ideas about white supremacy (Blight, *Race and Reunion*, 65). Even before Blight, numerous scholars argued that reconciliation had marginalized slavery and emancipation. See, for example, Buck, *Road to Reunion*; Linenthal, *Sacred Ground*, 91; Silber, *Romance of Reunion*; and Foster, *Ghosts*, 194.

15. McCook, *Address before the Society of the Army of the Cumberland*, 8–9; *Memorial Day with the Canby Post*, 16, HL; Gallagher, *Union War*.

16. For scholars who have focused on African American memories of the Civil War, see Clark, *Defining Moments*; Gannon, *Won Cause*; Jeffrey, *Abolitionists Remember*; Kachun, *Festivals of Freedom*; Shaffer, *After the Glory*; Blair, *Cities of the Dead*; Blight, *Race and Reunion*; Savage, *Standing Soldiers*; Schwalm, *Emancipation's Diaspora*, 219–63; and Van Zelm, "Virginia Women."

17. The Lost Cause has enjoyed tremendous scholarly attention. See among others, Foster, *Ghosts*; Wilson, *Baptized in Blood*; Gallagher and Nolan, *Myth of the Lost Cause*, 1–34; Gallagher, *Causes Won*; Woodward, *Strange Career of Jim Crow*; Osterweis, *Myth of the Lost Cause*; Blair, *Cities of the Dead*; Brundage, *Southern Past*; Coski, *Confederate Battle Flag*; Fahs and Waugh, *Memory of the Civil War*; Cox, *Dixie's Daughters*; Bonner, *Colors and Blood*; Blight, *Race and Reunion*; Hale, *Making Whiteness*, 47–49, 79–80; Savage, *Standing Soldiers*; Janney, *Burying the Dead*; Gardner, *Blood and Irony*; Goldfield, *Still Fighting*; Poole, *Never Surrender*; and Marshall, *Creating a Confederate Kentucky*.

18. For historians who have argued that the white South largely defined the war's memory, see Silber, *Romance of Reunion*; Blight, *Race and Reunion*; Campbell, *When Sherman Marched North*, 105; and Fellman, *Making of Robert E. Lee*, 304.

19. In recent years, historians have begun to emphasize the Union Cause. For several excellent examples, see Gallagher, *Union War*; Neff, *Honoring*; Waugh, *U. S. Grant*; Gallagher, *Causes Won*; and Gannon, *Won Cause*.

20. Blight organizes his study around three overall "visions" of Civil War memory: the reconciliationist vision, white supremacist vision, and emancipationist vision (Blight, *Race and Reunion*, 2). In his study of representations of the Civil War in paintings, sculpture, and film, Gallagher focuses on four interpretative traditions: the Lost Cause, Union Cause, Emancipation Cause, and Reconciliation Cause (Gallagher, *Causes Won*, 2). Numerous other historians have followed their lead employing some, if not all, of these categories of memory.

21. *Washington Post*, July 1, 1913.

1. Jackson, *Southern Women of the Second American Revolution*, vi, 113 (quoting *Richmond Whig*).

2. For a discussion of what the term Yankee meant to white southerners, see Phillips, *Diehard Rebels*, 47.

3. *Illinois Daily State Journal*, July 31, 1861.

4. For a discussion of each side's depiction of the enemy, see Mitchell, *Civil War Soldiers*, 24–55, 90–147.

5. There is an extensive literature on what caused the Civil War. For some of the more comprehensive arguments, see Potter, *Impending Crisis*; Holt, *Political Crisis of the 1850s*; Freehling, *Road to Disunion*; Varon, *Disunion!*; Dew, *Apostles of Disunion*.

6. In the past twenty years numerous historians have sought to explain why Civil War soldiers enlisted and why they continued to fight. One of the central debates in this literature is whether or not soldiers were motivated by ideology. For those that argue ideology was not important, see Barton, *Goodmen*; Linderman, *Embattled Courage*; and Robertson, *Soldiers Blue and Gray*. For discussion of how ideology mattered, see McPherson, *For Cause and Comrades*, and Mitchell, *Civil War Soldiers*. For other historians who focus on why Union soldiers fought, see Hess, *Liberty, Virtue, and Progress*; Hess, *Union Soldier in Battle*; and Woodworth, *Nothing but Victory*.

7. Saxon DeWolf to sister, October 18, 1861, quoted in McPherson, *For Cause and Comrades*, 18.

8. Varon, *Disunion!*; Fleche, *Revolution of 1861*; Quigley, *Shifting Grounds*.

9. Ohio lawyer quoted in McPherson, *For Cause and Comrades*, 19.

10. Union regimentals published between the summer of 1865 and 1866 described Union and liberty as their primary reasons for fighting (Gallagher, *Union War*).

11. Because "Union" does not hold the same resonance today that it did in the nineteenth century, some scholars have argued that such an abstract term could not possibly have motivated more than 2 million men to fight. For example, Chandra Manning observes that "preservation of the Union, though important, was not enough, unless accompanied by the ending of slavery." "No lesser outcome could make the trauma of the war worthwhile," she notes (Manning, *What This Cruel War Was Over*, 153). Reid Mitchell notes that "it is unhistoric for us to claim that the Civil War, the War for the Union, really was a war for freedom, when most who fought cared so little about the rights of black people" (Mitchell, *Civil War Soldiers*, 131). For historians who emphasize that contemporary Americans do not understand the notion of "Union," see Waugh, *U. S. Grant*, 188; Gallagher, *Causes Won*; and Gallagher, *Union War*.

12. Chandra Manning argues that Union soldiers' interactions with slaves and slaveholders induced them to push for emancipation as early as 1861. "Union soldiers, in the first year of the war, became the first major group after black Americans and abolitionists to call for an end to slavery," she notes (Manning, *What This Cruel War Was Over*, 51).

13. For a discussion of the free labor ideology, see Foner, *Free Soil, Free Labor*.

14. Gara, "Slavery and the Slave Power," 6.

15. "Message to Congress in Special Session," July 4, 1861, Basler, *Collected Works of Lincoln*, 4:437.

16. Hess, *Union Soldier in Battle*, 101–2; Hess, *Liberty, Virtue, and Progress*, 78–80; Mitchell, *Civil War Soldiers*, 109–17; Grimsley, *Hard Hand of War*, 8–11.

17. William Blair similarly argues that Congress and Lincoln recognized that confiscation policies in general (not just that of freeing slaves) might jeopardize reunion (Blair, "Friend or Foe," 40–41).

18. Brasher, *Peninsula Campaign*. Sheehan-Dean, *Why Confederates Fought*, 3, argues that Virginia was able to enlist nearly 90 percent of its white population between the ages of 15 and 50 in large part because of slave labor on the home front.

19. Brasher, *Peninsula Campaign*, 27–49. Slaves began flocking to Union lines as early as the spring and summer of 1861. This factor combined with northern desires to deny Confederates slave manpower prompted Federal officials to institute the Confiscation Acts in August 1861 and July 1862, which first authorized the seizure of property—including slaves—that was used for the purpose of insurrection and subsequently granted freedom to slaves in rebellious states whose owners supported the Confederacy. Along with the Emancipation Proclamation, these acts had the combined effect of providing refuge for slaves who made their way to Union lines, thus enticing hundreds of thousands of African Americans to flee their masters by 1865. Mark Grimsley expressly argues that emancipation was not a military necessity; rather, it was driven by the strength of the antislavery movement combined and Lincoln's personal animosity to slavery. He argues that the Union military situation of 1862 allowed Lincoln to push for emancipation (*Hard Hand of War*, 120–41).

20. United States Colored Troops did relatively little fighting until the summer of 1864. Nevertheless, they freed white soldiers to do more fighting by providing much of the manual labor such as constructing field works.

21. Gallagher, *Union War*, chap. 3; Glatthaar, *Forged in Battle*, 29–30; McPherson, *For Cause and Comrades*, 120–24. For argument that emancipation was a military strategy, see Mitchell, *Civil War Soldiers*, 127.

22. Quoted in Grimsley, *Hard Hand of War*, 120–21.

23. Indiana colonel quoted in McPherson, *Battle Cry*, 558–59.

24. Manning, *What This Cruel War Was Over*, 89–91; McPherson, *Battle Cry*, 354, 494–96, 505–10, 557–60; McPherson, *For Cause and Comrades*, 123; Mitchell, *Civil War Soldiers*, 126. Many Democrats, especially the so-called Copperheads, were worried that emancipation had become a Republican war aim. But most Republicans and most Democrats always viewed Union as the goal and emancipation as a major means to attain that goal, not a war aim.

25. Gallagher, *Union War*, 75–118. Some Union soldiers were intensely angry about emancipation. See Grimsley, *Hard Hand of War*, 137; Manning, *What This Cruel War Was Over*, 89–90.

26. A study by Kenneth H. Williams and Russell Harris contends that there were 109,201 Kentucky men in Union service. There is little doubt that the nearly 24,000 black men who joined the ranks of the U.S. Army from the Commonwealth of Kentucky (41 percent of the 1860 black male population) did not join to fight for slavery in the Union. The 72,275 white volunteers constituted 29 percent of white males ages 18–59 in 1860 (Williams and Harris, "Kentucky in 1860: A Statistical Overview," 743–64).

27. Marshall, *Creating a Confederate Kentucky*, 23–38.

28. Mitchell, *Civil War Soldiers*, 121; Manning, *What This Cruel War Was Over*, 50; Glatthaar, *Forged in Battle*. As Manning notes, "Hostility to slavery did not necessarily mean support for racial equality. In fact, Union soldiers strove mightily to keep the issues of slavery and black rights separate."

29. Gallagher, *Union War*, chap. 3.

30. Clark, *Iron-Hearted Regiment*, 85.

31. De Forest, *Random Sketches*, 204–5.

32. John Lee Holt to wife, May 2, 1862, Holt, *I Wrote You Word*, 79.

33. For discussion of Confederates comparing themselves to the revolutionaries of 1776, see Thomas, *Confederacy as a Revolutionary Experience*, 44–46; Mitchell, *Civil War Soldiers*, 1–2, 12, 20, 23, 24; McPherson, *For Cause and Comrades*, 20–22; Quigley, *Shifting Grounds*, 78, 148–49; Fleche, *Revolution of 1861*, 11–12, 81. Both Quigley and Fleche likewise argue that Confederates understood themselves to be part of the revolutionary age, drawing inspiration from the nationalist movements in Europe.

34. Joseph T. Glatthaar has recently shown that "southerners who resided in slave-holding households turned out in disproportionate numbers to fight in Virginia, comprising four out of every nine men" (Glatthaar, *General Lee's Army*, 30).

35. Glatthaar, *General Lee's Army*, 29–42; Sheehan-Dean, *Why Confederates Fought*, 17–19, 31–35. Sheehan-Dean notes that "volunteers perceived the war from the start as one that revolved around slavery."

36. For historians who have discussed Confederate nationalism, see Sheehan-Dean, *Why Confederates Fought*, 9–10, 59–62, 70–71; Gallagher, *Confederate War*, 63–111; Rubin, *Shattered Nation*, 2–7; Campbell, *When Sherman Marched North*, 12–13, 15, 71–74, 91–98, 101–4; Faust, *Creation of Confederate Nationalism*; Beringer et al., *Why the South Lost the Civil War*; Foster, *Ghosts*, 36–62; Neff, *Honoring the Civil War Dead*, 10–12; Quigley, *Shifting Grounds*; Clampitt, *Confederate Heartland*; Brundage, "White Women and the Politics of Historical Memory," 115. Arguments for and against Confederate nationalism abound. Emory Thomas argues that nationalism flowed from the formation of national institutions such as the Confederate government or state-sponsored industries. When these institutions fail to be maintained, nationalism floundered. Conversely, Drew Faust contends that common elements in the culture of the South, namely religion, provided the foundation for nationalism. Elites such as government officials and the clergy used these features of southern distinctiveness to construct a national identity. Beringer, Hattaway, Jones, and Still understand nationalism to be an ideology based on perceived southern distinctiveness that proved fragile and insecure from its inception. They situate Confederate "cohesiveness" in southern churches, slavery, and state rights, but conclude that only slavery truly separated the sections. The authors argue that when southerners' allegiance to slavery failed, they lacked any ground for distinctiveness. More recently, Paul Quigley has argued that Confederate nationalism must be understood as an ever-evolving, often conflicted process that found roots in the late 1840s. For a discussion of northern nationalism and the role of citizen's voluntary organizations fostering nationalism, see Lawson, *Patriot Fires*.

37. Graham quoted in Gallagher, *Confederate War*, 91.

38. For historians who have stressed white southern discontent with the Confederacy and challenges to the southern nation posed by slaves and southern Unionists, see

for example Faust, *Mothers of Invention*, 238–47; Freehling, *South vs. South*; McCurry, *Confederate Reckoning*.

39. Mitchell, *Civil War Soldiers*, 23.

40. Jones quoted in McPherson, "Antebellum Southern Exceptionalism," 418–33.

41. This is an example of the Thomas Theorem. In 1928, sociologist W. I. Thomas noted, "If men define situations as real, they are real in their consequences" (Thomas and Thomas, *Child in America*, 571–72). For historians who have argued for "two civilizations," see Nevins, *Ordeal of the Union*; Genovese, *Political Economy of Slavery*; and Barton, *Goodmen*. For historians who argue that the regions were more alike than different, see Govan, "Americans below the Potomac," 19–39; Edmund Morgan, "Puritan Ethic." For middle positions, see Potter, *Impending Crisis*; Ayers, *In the Presence of Mine Enemies*; and Quigley, *Shifting Grounds*.

42. McPherson, *Battle Cry*, 39–41; Phillips, *Diehard Rebels*, 42–46; Foner, *Free Soil*; Grant, *North over South*; Mitchell, *Civil War Soldiers*, 90–147; Varon, *Disunion!*, 131–35.

43. Quigley, *Shifting Grounds*, 183. For a discussion on how soldiers surmounted the Sixth Commandment ("Thou shall not kill"), see Faust, *This Republic of Suffering*, 32–60.

44. As quoted in Mitchell, *Civil War Soldiers*, 25.

45. Cimprich, *Fort Pillow*, 90–91; *New York Daily Tribune*, April 16, 1864; *Cleveland Morning Leader*, May 6, 1864. Cimprich notes that some radical Republican newspapers blamed the U.S. Army's unequal treatment of USCT soldiers for the massacre, while some Democratic papers suggested that cowardly black troops had caused the defeat.

46. As quoted in Glatthaar, *General Lee's Army*, 154–55.

47. Jackson quoted in Glatthaar, *General Lee's Army*, 150–51.

48. Lee quoted in Pryor, *Reading the Man*, 307.

49. Mitchell, *Civil War Soldiers*, 24–36; Glatthaar, *General Lee's Army*, 150–63; Phillips, *Diehard Rebels*, 40–75; Holzer, "With Malice Toward Both," 109–36.

50. Printed in Phillips, *Diehard Rebels*, 55.

51. Printed in Phillips, *Diehard Rebels*, 56–57.

52. "The Evidence of Southern Civilization," *New York Times*, April 7, 1862; *Lowell (Mass.) Daily Citizen and News*, March 11, 1863; Diary of Mollie Dorsey Sanford, March 1862, NAWLD.

53. *Daily Evening Bulletin* (San Francisco), July 26, 1862. F.F.V. refers to the "First Families of Virginia," socially prominent Virginia families descended from the colonial elite (though not necessarily the first settlers).

54. Peirce, *Dear Catherine, Dear Taylor*, 385 (Taylor Peirce to Catherine Peirce, April 17, 1865).

55. Emily Aylett to Alice and Etta Aylett, July 27, 1864, Aylett Family Papers, VHS; Lucy Muse Walton Fletcher Diary, June 7, 1864, DU; Pember, *Southern Woman's Story*, xv.

56. Lizzie Alsop diary, July 14, 1862, Wynne Family Papers, VHS.

57. LeConte, *When the World Ended*, 60, 66.

58. Spears and Pettit, *Civil War Letters of Arabella Spears*, 1:155.

59. Historians Drew Gilpin Faust and Stephanie McCurry have both argued that wartime sacrifices of loved ones, food, and the lack of men on the home front to sustain the system of slavery led southern white women to contest the government (Faust, *Mothers of Invention*; McCurry, *Confederate Reckoning*). For other accounts of Confederate women, see Rable, *Civil Wars*; Campbell, *When Sherman Marched North*; Ott, *Confederate Daughters*; Clinton and Silber, *Divided Houses*; and Gallagher, *Confederate War*, 75–80.

60. Jackson, *Southern Women of the Second American Revolution*, iv.

61. As quoted in Gallagher, *Confederate War*, 79–80.

62. *Southern Opinion* (Richmond), October 12, 1867, emphasis added.

63. For women who disguised themselves as male soldiers, see Leonard, *All the Daring of a Soldier*.

64. Silber, *Daughters*, 1–3. Confederate women, too, found their patriotism under scrutiny, especially late in the war (Silber, *Gender and the Sectional Conflict*, 45). But no evidence suggests that Confederate men ever compared them to their northern counterparts in respect to patriotic devotion.

65. Schultz, *Women at the Front*, 20; Silber, *Gender and the Sectional Conflict*, 42–43; Giesberg, *Army at Home*, 124. For other accounts of northern women, see Silber, *Daughters of the Union*; Attie, *Patriotic Toil*; Gallman, *North Fights the Civil War*, 110–18, 122–24, 152–55; and Lawson, *Patriot Fires*, 14–39.

66. Nina Silber argues in both *Daughters of the Union* and *Gender and the Sectional Conflict* that the difference in the respective causes accounted for the perceived importance of women in each section. "Confederate soldiers fought for 'home,'" she notes, and "Union men very clearly—and more self-consciously—fought for 'country'" (*Gender and the Sectional Conflict*, 13). I believe Confederate soldiers likewise fought for their nation, albeit a nation that only lasted four years. I agree with her that the domestic obligation to protect northern women was less immediate for Union soldiers. But this was because of where the fighting occurred, not a reflection of either side's cause.

67. Of course, Unionist women in the border regions would have had more interaction with enemy soldiers. Unionist women likewise ranted against the Copperheads, or Peace Democrats, in their midst.

68. For an example, see Peter, *A Union Woman in Civil War Kentucky*, xix, 30–31, 41. Perhaps the most iconic example of a defiant Union woman was Barbara Frietchie of Frederick, Maryland, who boldly waved an American flag when Stonewall Jackson's troops occupied her city. Immortalized in John Greenleaf Whittier's 1863 *Atlantic Monthly* ballad, Frietchie allegedly told the rebel troops to "shoot if you must this old gray head, but spare your country's flag." The ballad was a sensation in the North, widely reprinted in newspapers and made the subject of numerous illustrations. Though the authenticity of the incident is debatable, the popularity of "Barbara Frietchie" underscored the degree to which Union women could be as fiercely devoted to their nation as Confederate women (Fahs, *Imagined Civil War*, 124).

69. Edmonds, *Nurse and Spy in the Union Army*, 189. In 1861, Edmonds disguised herself as a male, used the alias of Pvt. Franklin Thompson, and served with the 2nd Michigan Infantry. After battling malaria for several months, in the spring of 1863 she left her military duty. But rather than risk execution for desertion once she had recov-

ered, she served as a female nurse in a Washington hospital. Her 1865 memoir did not disclose that she was Private Thompson, though she did recount disguising herself as a man for spying missions. (Blanton and Cook, *They Fought Like Demons*, 9, 98–99, 157).

70. "A few words in behalf of the loyal women of the United States." Giesberg identifies the author as Caroline Kirkland (Giesberg, *Army at Home*, 124–25).

71. Historians have differentiated between total war and hard war. For those who argue against a Union policy of total war, see Neely, "Was the Civil War a Total War?" 27; Grimsley, *Hard Hand of War*, 2–5; Campbell, *When Sherman Marched North*, 55–56. For argument that the Union did employ total war, see Janda, "Shutting the Gates of Mercy."

72. Grimsley, *Hard Hand of War*, 2–3.

73. Union troops had begun using such tactics as early as mid-1862 (Sheehan-Dean, *Why Confederates Fought*, 77–78; Blair, "Barbarians at Fredericksburg's Gates," 142–70; Grimsley, *Hard Hand of War*, 142–43).

74. Walker, *Private Journal of Georgia Freeman Walker*, 106; *Charleston Mercury*, June 23, 1864.

75. *Richmond Enquirer*, July 4, 1864, reprinted in the *New York Times*, July 7, 1864.

76. Grimsley, *Hard Hand of War*, 120–41; Sheehan-Dean, *Why Confederates Fought*, 5, 76–77, 98; Blair, "Barbarians at the Gate," 142–70; Phillips, *Diehard Rebels*, 66–68. The First Confiscation Act (signed by Lincoln on August 6, 1861) stipulated that owners of slaves engaged in military service for the Confederacy (such as digging trenches or acting as teamsters) forfeited their ownership in said slaves. The Second Confiscation Act (passed on July 17, 1862) stated in part that any slave who escaped from a rebel owner could not be returned to his or her master.

77. Dowdey and Manarin, *Wartime Papers of R. E. Lee*, 388–90, Lee to Seddon, January 10, 1863.

78. Jones, *Rebel War Clerk's*, January 15, 1863. Jones was referring to the Confederate policy of not exchanging USCT prisoners of war, but rather insisting that former slaves be returned to bondage and their officers charged with inciting servile insurrection. Confederates' refusal to exchange black troops thus dissolved the cartel (Trudeau, *Like Men of War*, 60–61).

79. Davis quoted in Cooper, *Jefferson Davis*, 439.

80. For an excellent discussion of how Confederate motivations changed over time, see Sheehan-Dean, *Why Confederates Fought*.

81. For two excellent accounts of the USCT, see Trudeau, *Like Men of War*, and Glatthaar, *Forged in Battle*.

82. As quoted in Phillips, *Diehard Rebels*, 67.

83. LeGrand, *Journal of Julia LeGrand*, 94 (diary entry January 20, 1863); Cimprich, *Fort Pillow*, 87, 94–96.

84. As quoted in Glatthaar, *General Lee's Army*, 153.

85. For several historians who argue that internal divisions plagued the Confederacy, see Beringer et al., *Why the South Lost*; McCurry, *Confederate Reckoning*; Faust, *Mothers of Invention*, 238–47; Freehling, *South vs. the South*; Whites, *Civil War as a Crisis*, 13; and Hahn, *Roots of Southern Populism*. For the best refutation of this argument, see Gallagher, *Confederate War*, 15–59.

86. Sheehan-Dean, *Why Confederates Fought*, 106–10; Campbell, *When Sherman Marched North*; Quigley, *Shifting Grounds*, 184.

87. For an excellent account of Confederate guerrilla fighters, see Sutherland, *Savage Conflict*.

88. For more on the violence along the Kansas-Missouri border, see Neely, *Border between Them*. For a wonderful account of the James brothers and their devotion to the Confederacy even after Appomattox, see Stiles, *Jesse James*.

89. Sutherland argues that former Confederates tried to forget the savage nature of guerrilla warfare in the postwar period in an effort to rehabilitate their image (Sutherland, *Savage Conflict*, 278–79).

90. Robertson, *Soldiers Blue and Gray*, 190.

91. As quoted in Robertson, *Soldiers Blue and Gray*, 205.

92. Much of the Lost Cause literature would argue that Union prisons were in fact much crueler than Confederate prisons because the North had the resources to provide for prisoners while the blockade prevented the South from doing so. In his 2005 book *While in the Hands of the Enemy*, Charles W. Sanders Jr. argues that leaders on both sides deliberately ordered the mistreatment of prisoners. For a challenge to the interpretation that Union officials were deliberately cruel to prisoners, see Gillispie, *Andersonvilles of the North*.

93. U.S. Sanitary Commission, *Narrative of Privations*, 68.

94. Mitchell, *Civil War Soldiers*, 53.

95. Dimon quoted in Neff, *Honoring the Civil War Dead*, 110. For a more thorough account of how the Gettysburg National Cemetery developed, see Neff, *Honoring the Civil War Dead*, 109–11; Kinsel, "'From These Honored Dead,'" 112–30.

96. For a discussion of burial practices and the advent of the national cemetery system, see Neff, *Honoring the Civil War Dead*; Faust, *This Republic of Suffering*; and Blair, *Cities of the Dead*. Historians have long claimed the number of war dead at 620,000. For the argument that the number of war dead is probably closer to 752,000, see Hacker, "Census Based Count."

97. Kinsel, "From These Honored Dead," 111–23; Neff, *Honoring the Civil War Dead*, 109–16. Thousands of families had descended upon the town to claim their loved ones, thus explaining why only 3,512 Union soldiers were buried in the cemetery. The Gettysburg Cemetery Association was a semi-public organization in that Pennsylvania held title to the land, but the cemetery was managed by a corporation authorized by the state's legislature. The board consisted of eighteen trustees representing the northern states whose soldiers fought in the battle. The states agreed to contribute funds proportional to their congressional representation (Kinsel, "From These Honored Dead," 116–18).

98. For discussion, by Gen. George Meade among others, of whether the Confederate dead should receive interments, see Neff, *Honoring the Civil War Dead*, 114–15.

99. *Hours at Home* as quoted in Neff, *Honoring the Civil War Dead*, 115.

100. Kinsel, "From These Honored Dead," 90–110; Everett, *Address of Hon. Edward Everett*, 60, 63, 69–71, 79–82.

101. *Gettysburg Battle-field Memorial Association: Announcement*; *Philadelphia*

Press, September 4 and 29, 1863; Neff, *Honoring the Civil War Dead*, 211; Kinsel, "From These Honored Dead," 151–62 (incorporation language quoted in Kinsel); Weeks, *Gettysburg*, 18.

102. Weeks, *Gettysburg*, 13–17.

103. Historian Leslie Schwalm points out that Emancipation Day celebrations had occurred in the upper Midwest since at least 1857 when a group of African Americans in Muscatine, Iowa, observed the anniversary of the 1834 abolition of slavery in the British West Indies. In this and subsequent festival days, they condemned slavery's persistence in the United States (Schwalm, *Emancipation's Diaspora*, 225–26).

104. Quoted in Schwalm, *Emancipation's Diaspora*, 227.

105. Clark, *Defining Moments*, 13–19.

106. Clark, *Defining Moments*, 13–19.

107. Gallagher, *Causes Won*, 108; Rable, *Fredericksburg*, 146–47.

108. Boudrye, *Historic Records of the Fifth New York Cavalry*, 88. (This book originally went to press in November 1865 [p. 114n1]. I am therefore electing to use it as a contemporary source.)

109. Hall, *Diary of a Confederate Soldier*, 128 (diary entry March 23, 1865). Hall had only recently been released from Camp Lookout. He had been captured following the battle of Gettysburg and imprisoned until February 10, 1865. He rejoined his regiment on March 16 near Petersburg.

110. Hancock, *Letters of a Civil War Nurse*, 102 (diary entry June 10, 1864).

111. Mitchell, *Civil War Soldiers*, 37.

112. Foner, *Reconstruction*, 35–76; McPherson, *Battle Cry*, 698–717. For the remainder of the war, Lincoln and congressional Republicans quibbled over whether secession was illegal and thus who controlled the process of readmittance. Lincoln maintained that secession was illegal and therefore the states had never left the Union. Therefore he controlled their readmission. Republicans, especially Thaddeus Stevens and Charles Sumner, insisted that they had ceased to exist as states and therefore would assume the status of territories. If this were the case, Congress would be solely responsible for readmission. Lincoln, nevertheless, pushed forward with his policy sanctioning Unionist state governments in Tennessee, Louisiana, Arkansas, and Virginia.

113. As quoted in Waugh, *Grant*, 54.

114. Grant to John Pemberton, July 3, 1863, *PUSG*, 8:455.

115. As quoted in Waugh, *Grant*, 65. For an excellent discussion of Grant and his surrender policies, see Waugh, *Grant*, 53, 64–66.

116. Lawson, *Patriot Fires*, 79–82. Lawson notes that the metamorphosis from Republican toward the Union Party occurred on the state level relatively early. The Ohio Union movement, for example, appeared in the fall of 1861. Although some Democrats did join the party ranks, most of its adherents were Republicans.

117. When emancipation became a salient issue in 1862, Democrats split into war and antiwar (or peace) factions. War Democrats, such as Gen. George B. McClellan, supported the goal of reunion through military victory but opposed emancipation. The Peace Democrats, or Copperheads, also opposed emancipation but called for reunion through negotiations rather than on the battlefield. As James McPherson notes, "War

and Peace Democrats would maintain a shifting, uneasy, and sometimes divided coalition, but on one issue they remained united: opposition to emancipation" (McPherson, *Battle Cry*, 506).

118. McClellan quoted in McPherson, *Battle Cry*, 771.

119. McPherson, *Battle Cry*, 770–91; Waugh, *Grant*, 93–95. Lincoln won in a landslide with 212 electoral votes (to McClellan's 21) and 55 percent of the popular vote.

120. McPherson, *Battle Cry*, 821–25; Campbell, *When Sherman Marched North*.

121. Waugh, *Grant*, 96–97; Lincoln quoted in Gallagher, "End and New Beginning," 41.

122. For the best analysis of Lincoln's second inaugural address, see White, *Lincoln's Greatest Speech*.

123. White, *Lincoln's Greatest Speech*, 39–42, 165–79.

124. Quoted in Ott, *Confederate Daughters*, 56 (diary entry July 14, 1864).

CHAPTER 2

1. Catton, *Stillness at Appomattox*, 369–80; McPherson, *Battle Cry*, 847–48. Confederate chaplain William Wiatt estimated that at least 25,000 to 30,000 men deserted before reaching Appomattox (Wiatt, *Confederate Chaplain*, 237 [diary entry April 9, 1865]).

2. McPherson, *Battle Cry*, 848–50; McPherson, *Ordeal by Fire*, 482; Grant to Maj. Gen. George Meade, April 9, 1865, *PUSG*, 14:377–78; Catton, *Never Call Retreat*, 454.

3. Grant, *Personal Memoirs*, 2:633.

4. Quoted in Searcher, *Farewell to Lincoln*, 40.

5. Schwartz, *Abraham Lincoln*, 23, 43. Merrill Peterson argues that Lincoln's memory can best be categorized into five images: Savior of the Union, Emancipator, Man of the People, Self-Made Man, and First American. This work does not seek to dispute those categories; rather, I am interested primarily in the connections between Lincoln's memory and that of the war, hence my focus on Savior of the Union and Emancipator (Peterson, *Lincoln in American Memory*).

6. Both participants of the war and historians have vastly underestimated the amount of bitterness and rancor that existed in early April 1865.

7. McAllister, *Civil War Letters*, 607–8 (letter to wife Ellen, April 9, 1865).

8. Grant, *Personal Memoirs*, 2:633.

9. Chambers, *Diary of Captain Henry A. Chambers*, 262 (diary entry April 9, 1865).

10. Wiatt, *Confederate Chaplain*, 238 (diary entry April 9, 1865).

11. The language of the original draft has long been unknown and much sought after (Freeman, *R. E. Lee*, 4:153–55). In 2005, the alleged missing draft was sold for $84,000 by Christie's in New York. According to this copy, the excised paragraph read: "God willing, the surviving south, still there, strikes for the right cause for which so many sacrifices have already been made, for which doubtless many will yet be required. But remember when for always, the heart of every man will be strengthened by the recollection of friends left through necessity, in hands of the hated foe and one day by the help of God, we will return to retrieve the loved ones and unfold to the breeze from our own blue hills, the glorious flag of our young republic which has been baptized by fire

and shell for four long sad years. Farewell my friends. We leave you to God & with sad hearts bid adieu to home, friends & kindred, aged and sever even stronger ties, thinking all sacrifices light in comparison with the noblest cause for which sword was ever drawn—God will defend the right" (Christie's, lot number 252, sale 1587, sold December 15, 2005, http://www.christies.com/lotfinder/LotDetailsPrintable.aspx?intObjectID =4643670, accessed May 30, 2012).

12. Dowdey, *Wartime Papers of R. E. Lee*, 934–35.

13. Marvel, *Lee's Last Retreat*, 189.

14. Gallagher, *Confederate War*, 12.

15. In a September 27, 1887, letter from Charles Marshall published in the *SHSP*, he noted that after he had made corrections to the original, "other copies were then made for transmission to the corps commanders and the staff of the army. All these copies were signed by the general, and a good many persons sent other copies which they had made or procured, and obtained his signature. In this way many copies of the order had the general's name signed as if they were originals, some of which I have seen" (*SHSP*, 4:747).

16. *New York Times*, April 19, 1865.

17. Henry J. Millard to Sister Hattie, April 26, 1865, Henry J. Millard letters, MHS.

18. Wiatt, *Confederate Chaplain*, 238 (diary entry April 11, 1865); Marvel, *Lee's Last Retreat*, 185.

19. Chambers, *Diary of Captain Henry A. Chambers*, 262 (diary entry April 9, 1865).

20. Hall, *Diary of a Confederate Soldier*, 136 (diary entry April 10, 1865).

21. Marvel, *Lee's Last Retreat*, 185.

22. Calkins, *Appomattox Campaign*, 181–83; Varon, "'Last Hour.'"

23. *Christian Recorder*, July 29, 1865.

24. Varon, "'Last Hour.'"

25. Quoted in National Park Service, *Appomattox Court House*, 80.

26. *New York Times*, April 19, 1865.

27. *Boston Herald*, April 11, 1865; *Baltimore Sun*, April 11, 1865.

28. *Daily Evening Bulletin* (San Francisco), April 12, 1865.

29. *New York Times*, April 11, 1865; *Boston Herald*, April 11, 1865.

30. *Trenton State Gazette*, April 11, 1865.

31. *Daily Ohio Statesmen*, April 12, 1865.

32. *Ohio State Journal*, April 11, 1865.

33. *New Orleans Times*, April 16, 1865.

34. *Pittsfield (Mass.) Sun*, April 13, 1865; *Baltimore Sun*, April 12, 1865.

35. Garidel, *Exile in Richmond*, 369 (diary entry April 4, 1865).

36. Fanny Berry interview, WPA Slave Narrative Project, Virginia Narratives, Volume 17, accessed through "Born in Slavery: Slaves Narratives from the Federal Writers' Project, 1936–1938," http://memory.loc.gov/ammem/snhtml. Varon, "'Last Hours'"; Litwack, *Been in the Storm*, 171–72. For information on the WPA slave narratives, including their shortcomings as sources, see Bay, *White Image in the Black Mind*, 115–16.

37. William B. Stark Diary, April 12, 1865, MHS.

38. *Charleston Courier*, April 17, 1865; Hawks, *Woman Doctor's Civil War*, 132 (diary entry April 15, 1865).

39. Simmons, *History of the 84th Reg't*, 252–53. I have elected only to use regimentals published in the immediate postwar period to gage reaction to events of April 1865. This regimental was published in 1866.

40. William B. Stark Diary, April 11, 1865, MHS.

41. Watson, *Letters of a Civil War Surgeon*, 93–94 (letters from April 18 and 27, 1865).

42. *Baltimore Sun*, April 12, 1865.

43. Strong, *Diary of George Templeton Strong*, 3:578–82 (diary entries April 10 and 11, 1865).

44. Daly, *Diary of a Union Lady*, 352 (diary entry April 10, 1865).

45. *New York Herald*, April 13, 1865.

46. *Frank Leslie's Illustrated Newspaper*, no. 498, vol. 20, April 15, 1865.

47. Hubbs, *Voices from Company D*, 372 (diary entry April 14, 1865). See also *Boston Herald*, April 11, 1865, for more on Butler's speech.

48. *New Orleans Times*, April 16, 1865.

49. *New York Herald*, April 13, 1865.

50. *New York Times*, April 11, 1865.

51. Catton, *Never Call Retreat*, 454.

52. *Chicago Tribune*, April 14, 1865.

53. *Constitutional Union*, April 11, 1865.

54. *Constitutional Union*, April 11, 1865.

55. *Constitutional Union*, April 11, 1865.

56. *New York Herald*, April 10, 1865. The Republican *New York Times* similarly observed that Lee "surrendered an army never surpassed in bravery, in suffering, in persistence in a bad cause" (quoted in *Baltimore Sun*, April 11, 1865).

57. *Philadelphia Inquirer*, April 11, 1865. For another example, see also the *Ohio State Journal*, April 14, 1865.

58. For the argument that during and immediately after the war, union was the United States' paramount cause, see Gallagher, *Union War*.

59. McAllister, *Civil War Letters*, 607–8.

60. Peirce and Peirce, *Dear Catherine, Dear Taylor*, 383 (Taylor Peirce to Catherine Peirce, April 16, 1865).

61. Rogers, *History*, 108.

62. *New York Herald*, April 12, 1865.

63. *Ohio State Journal*, April 14, 1865.

64. "The End of the War," *Circular*, April 10, 1865.

65. *Louisville Daily Journal*, April 11, 1865.

66. "The End of the War," *Circular*, April 10, 1865.

67. *Charleston Courier*, April 18, 1865.

68. *New York News* quoted in the *Baltimore Sun*, April 11, 1865. The *Sun* noted that the *News* was an "anti-war," Democratic newspaper.

69. Freeman, *R. E. Lee*, 4:130; Marvel, *Lee's Last Retreat*, 178–79.

70. Lynch, *Dorman-Marshbourne Letters*, 103.

71. Dooley, *John Dooley*, 185, 195.

72. Asst. Sec. Dana to Sec. Stanton, April 10, 1865, *OR*, series 1, vol. 46.

73. Lizzie Alsop Diary, April 12, 1865, Wynne Family Papers, VHS.

74. Dooley, *John Dooley*, 185, 195. Women had voiced similar calls for action during the war.

75. Campbell, *When Sherman Marched North*, 102.

76. Brig. Gen. W. W. Morris to Lt. Gen. Grant, April 12, 1865, *OR*, series 1, vol. 46.

77. *New York Herald*, April 13, 1865; *Philadelphia Inquirer*, April 15, 1865.

78. Garidel, *Exile in Richmond*, 378 (diary entry April 14, 1865).

79. Ruffin, *Ruffin Diary*, 3:850–51 (diary entry April 17, 1865).

80. Marks and Schatz, *Between North and South*, 191 (diary entry April 11, 1865).

81. *Charleston Courier*, April 15, 1865; *New York Times*, April 18, 1865; *New York Observer and Chronicle*, April 20, 1865; Neff, *Honoring the Civil War Dead*, 66–67.

82. Anderson quoted in Neff, *Honoring the Civil War Dead*, 67; *Charleston Courier*, April 15, 1865.

83. Duffield, *Nation's Wail*, 3.

84. Strong, *Diary of George Templeton Strong*, 3:585 (diary entry April 16, 1865).

85. Quoted in Glatthaar, *Forged in Battle*, 209. Glatthaar notes that some USCT soldiers interpreted Lincoln's death like that of Moses: he had led them to the promised land but, his job finished, he had not accompanied them into peace.

86. Welles quoted in Leonard, *Lincoln's Avengers*, 10.

87. Towne, *Letters and Diary of Laura M. Towne*, 159–62 (diary entries April 23 and 29, 1865). For other accounts of African Americans' reactions, see Blum, *Reforging*, 21; Blight, *Race and Reunion*, 30, 68.

88. Neff, *Honoring the Civil War Dead*, 81, 95.

89. Hubbs, *Voices from Company D*, 572 (diary entry April 15, 1865); Diary of Annie G. Dudley Davis, April 15, 1865, HL.

90. Case against Susan and Marion Constable, April 26, 1865, Union Provost Marshal's File, M416, Roll 56, NARA.

91. Searcher, *Farewell to Lincoln*, 39–40.

92. Daly, *Diary of a Union Lady*, 354–57 (diary entries April 19, 25, 1865); Strong, *Diary of George Templeton Strong*, 3:583–86 (diary entries April 15–16, 1865).

93. Smith, *Private Smith's Journal* (diary entry April 15, 1865); Turner, *Beware*, 50. Many historians have claimed that no lives were lost in the wake of Lincoln's assassination; see, for example, Peterson, *Lincoln in American Memory*, 7.

94. Lane, *Soldier's Diary*, 261–62 (diary entry April 19, 1865).

95. Henry A. Birdsall Diary, Southern Historical Collection, University of North Carolina at Chapel Hill, April 25, 1865. Thanks to Evan Jones for sharing this citation with me.

96. Manley Ebenezer Rice to Elizabeth Jane Day Rice, General Hospital, Fort Gaines, Ala., April 30, 1865, Manley Ebenezer Rice Papers, HL.

97. *Chicago Tribune*, April 17, 1865; Barclay & Co., *Terrible Tragedy at Washington*, 113; Turner, *Beware*, 50; Searcher, *Farewell to Lincoln*, 37–41. Many historians have claimed that no lives were lost in the wake of Lincoln's assassination. See for example Peterson, *Lincoln in American Memory*, 7.

98. Strong, *Diary of George Templeton Strong*, 3:583–4 (diary entry April 15, 1865).

99. Blassingame, *Douglass Papers*, 4:76–77.

100. Mac El'Rey, *Substance of Two Discourses*, 21–22.

101. *Liberator*, April 28, 1865.

102. Strong, *Diary of George Templeton Strong*, 3:582 (diary entry April 15, 1865).

103. Duffield, *Nation's Wail*, 10. For another similar example, see Potter, *National Tragedy*, 3–4.

104. The "devil" graffiti was discovered during the Center for Civil War Photography's Image of War Seminar in Richmond, October 2005 (Gorman, "Lee the 'Devil' Discovered," 1, 3–4).

105. Potter, *National Tragedy*, 8–9.

106. *Independent . . . Devoted to the Consideration of Politics, Social, and Economic Tendencies, History, Literature, and the Arts*, April 27, 1865.

107. For other examples of slavery as responsible for the assassination see Duffield, *Nation's Wail*, 9; Butler, *Martyr President*, 7.

108. Peirce and Peirce, *Dear Catherine, Dear Taylor*, 384 (letter April 17, 1865).

109. Leonard, *Lincoln's Avengers*, 10. Thomas Reed Turner and David B. Chesebrough both note that most ministers failed to mention Booth by name precisely because they equated the assassination as a crime perpetrated by the entire South (Turner, *Beware*, 80–81; Chesebrough, *No Sorrow*, 41). Many northern diaries and newspapers, however, do name Booth.

110. David Hunter Strotter, Baltimore, to Lewis, April 17, 1865, Brock Collection, HL.

111. Clark, *Order of Services*, 19.

112. Potter, *National Tragedy*, 10–11.

113. Peirce and Peirce, *Dear Catherine, Dear Taylor*, 385 (Taylor Peirce to Catherine Peirce, April 17, 1865).

114. Dexter, *What Ought to Be Done*, 25–33.

115. Mary Mellish [Mother] to George H. Mellish, April 19, 1865, Papers of George H. Mellish, HL.

116. Chesebrough, *No Sorrow*, 57. For example of one such sermon, see Potter, *National Tragedy*, 10.

117. Chester, *Lesson of the Hour*, 10; Daly, *Diary of a Union Lady*, 357 (diary entry April 25, 1865).

118. Graf and Haskins, *Andrew Johnson Papers*, 8:612–13; *Southern Recorder* (Milledgeville, Ga.), May 2, 1865, extracted from the *New York Post*, April 18, 1865.

119. For detailed accounts of the Washington funeral and the funeral train, see Neff, *Honoring the Civil War Dead*, 74–83; Peterson, *Lincoln in American Memory*, 14–21; Schwartz, *Abraham Lincoln*, 48–57.

120. Daly, *Diary of a Union Lady*, 358 (diary entry April 26, 1865); *Chicago Tribune*, April 30, 1865.

121. Diary of Annie G. Dudley Davis, April 19, 1865, HL; Neff, *Honoring the Civil War Dead*, 74–83. "In part," Neff argues, "because of the close proximity to the war, Lincoln's death called the nation itself into question. . . . It was his death that catalyzed the American nation" (69). Elsewhere he argues that the commemoration of war dead, both soldiers and Lincoln, served to underscore the divisiveness of the sections rather than reconciliation.

122. Woodworth, *Nothing but Victory*, 635; Simpson et al., *Advice after Appomattox*,

xxiv. Confederate soldiers would be allowed to march to their respective state capitals, stack their weapons at state arsenals, and return home after promising to no longer wage war on the United States. President Andrew Johnson was to recognize the existing, that is rebellious, state governments so long as their members took an oath of future loyalty to the United States. In short, the terms would restore *status quo antebellum* with the exception of slavery.

123. Mary Mellish [Mother] to George H. Mellish, April 26, 1865, Papers of George H. Mellish, HL.

124. Woodworth, *Nothing but Victory*, 636–37; Holberton, *Homeward Bound*, 37–38; Bailey, *Class and Tennessee's Confederate Generation*, 107. At Durham Station, Grant allowed Sherman to renegotiate the surrender confining the discussion to military matters; but again, the terms were more generous than those conferred upon the Army of Northern Virginia. Not only would officers be allowed to keep their sidearms and men their mounts, but approximately twenty percent of the men were permitted to retain their rifles for protection and hunting on their long way home to Alabama, Tennessee, Georgia, and beyond. For an account of Unionist retaliation against returning Confederates in eastern Tennessee, see Marten, *Sing Not War*, 42.

125. Simpson et al., *Advice after Appomattox*, xxiv; Trudeau, *Out of the Storm*, 237–42.

126. There is an abundance of primary source evidence indicating that many rebels believed Lincoln's death would be more harmful than good for the South. See for example Dawson, *Civil War Diary of Sarah Morgan*, 607 (diary entry April 19, 1865); Chadick, "Civil War Days in Huntsville" (diary entry April 15, 1865); Marcus, *Memoirs of American Jews*, 3:341 (Emma Mordecai diary, April 21, 1865); Edmondston, *Journal of a Secesh Lady*, 692–708 (diary entry April 23, 1865).

127. Dawson, *Civil War Diary of Sarah Morgan*, 608 (diary entry April 22, 1865).

128. Calkins, *Final Bivouac*, 69.

129. Manley Ebenezer Rice to Elizabeth Jane Day Rice, General Hospital, Fort Gaines, Ala., April 30, 1865, Manley Ebenezer Rice Papers, HL.

130. *Texas Republican* (Marshall, Tex.), April 28, 1865.

131. Stone, *Brokenburn*, 333 (diary entry April 28, 1865). For other accounts of Confederate women celebrating Lincoln's death, see LeConte, *Diary of Emma LeConte*, 65 (diary entry April 21, 1865).

132. Neff, *Honoring the Civil War Dead*, 96.

133. Bonan, *Edge of Mosby's Sword*, 153–55; Ramage, *Gray Ghost*, 266–67.

134. Letter from Junius Newport Bragg to Anna Josephine Goddard Bragg, April 23, 1865, in *Letters of a Confederate Surgeon 1861–65*, NAWLD.

135. *New York Herald*, April 29, 1865. Statements such as these have been interpreted by historians to craft the Lee-of-legend who advocated the immediate abandonment of all opposition to the United States, insisted that the questions of dispute had been settled, and urged acquiescence to the victorious North (Nolan, *Lee Considered*, 137).

136. On Robert E. Lee, see Gallagher, *Lee the Soldier*. For historians who have emphasized Lee the reconciler, see especially Freeman, *R. E. Lee*, 4:219; Smith, *Lee and Grant*, 302.

137. *New York Herald*, April 29, 1865.

138. Daly, *Diary of a Union Lady*, 359 (diary entry April 30, 1865).

139. *New York Herald*, April 26, 1865.

140. John M. Humphreys to Governor Pierpont, April 27, 1865, Francis Pierpont Papers, Brock Collection, HL.

141. Strong, *Diary of George Templeton Strong*, 3:592–93 (diary entries April 23–24, 1865).

142. *New York Times*, April 27, 1865.

143. *New York Times*, April 30, 1865.

144. Leonard, *Lincoln's Avengers*, 38, 59.

145. Leonard, *Lincoln's Avengers*, 63–65.

146. Andrew Johnson Proclamation, May 2, 1865, The American Presidency Project, http://www.presidency.ucsb.edu/ws/index.php?pid=72356&st=davis&st1.

147. Leonard, *Lincoln's Avengers*, 70.

148. *New York Times*, May 14, 1865; Leonard, *Lincoln's Avengers*, 75–76.

149. For an excellent analysis of the gendered interpretation of Davis's capture, see Silber, *Romance of Reunion*, 29–37.

150. *OR*, 1:46, Part 3, 1082 (Grant to Halleck, May 4, 1865).

151. *OR*, 2:8, 534 (Halleck to Grant, May 5, 1865).

152. *OR*, 2:8, 535–36 (Grant to Halleck, May 6, 1865).

153. *OR*, 2:8, 550–664. Reagan was not pardoned until April 1867 (M1003, NARA, Roll 54).

154. The distinction between civilian and military leaders was due in part to the surrender terms signed by both Lee and Johnston. But it was likely also an unspoken recognition that soldiers were acting on behalf of the state while cabinet members and legislators were active leaders, creating the laws and directing the armies.

155. Federal Records, U.S. Circuit Court, Virginia District, *U.S. v. Jefferson Davis*, MOC. Mass-printed for the explicit purpose of charging Confederate leaders who had once sworn loyalty to the United States, the indictments were nearly identical. Each accused the given individual with "being moved and seduced by the instigation of the devil, wickedly devising and intending the peace and tranquility of the United States of America to disturb, and the Government . . . to subvert, move and incite rebellion and war against the United States." The details of each individual's efforts were filled in by hand.

156. Some historians estimate that as many as 10,000 Confederates migrated from the South, primarily to Latin America, between 1865 and 1885. Most southern migrants, however, relocated within the United States, opting to move west or even north for employment (Dawsey and Dawsey, *Confederados*, 13).

157. Dawsey and Dawsey, *Confederados*; Harter, *Lost Colony of the Confederacy*.

158. Confederate generals Joe Shelby, John B. Magruder, Edmund Kirby Smith, and Sterling Price, world famous oceanographer Matthew Fontaine Maury, and several governors headed to Mexico at the prompting of Emperor Maximilian. Still others, like Jubal Early and George Pickett (facing an indictment for war crimes on account of executing Union soldiers), fled to Canada. John C. Breckinridge, the former U.S. vice

president who became a Confederate general and the Confederacy's secretary of war, took his chances first in Cuba and subsequently in Canada and Great Britain.

159. Andrews, *War-Time Journal of a Georgia Girl*, 184 (diary entry April 25, 1865).

160. *New York Times*, May 24, 1865; Royster, *Destructive War*, 406.

161. Grant, *Personal Memoirs*, 2:655; McConnell, *Glorious Contentment*, 6–8. At least a few eastern troops complained that the crowd appeared to enjoy the rowdy bummers more than the disciplined Army of the Potomac.

162. Several scholars have made much of this, claiming that the exclusion of these soldiers serves as evidence that northerners were not prepared to acknowledge the sacrifice and citizenship of African American troops who made up ten percent of the army by 1865. For historians who have argued that the USCT were purposefully excluded from the Grand Review, see McConnell, *Glorious Contentment*, 8; and Holberton, *Homeward Bound*, 28.

163. *New York Times*, May 26, 1865; *Liberator*, June 2, 1865; Gallagher, *Union War*, 7–32.

164. McConnell, *Glorious Contentment*, 8.

165. Neff, *Honoring the Civil War Dead*.

166. Welles, *Diary of Gideon Welles*, 2:310; *Baltimore American and Commercial Advertiser*, May 25, 1865.

167. Brownell, "Abraham Lincoln," *War Lyrics and Other Poems*, 111–38. As Merrill Peterson points out, this poem was first published in the *Atlantic Monthly*, October 1865.

168. Here I borrow John Neff's term for the victorious Union cause.

169. *Christian Recorder*, May 27, 1865.

CHAPTER 3

1. *New York Times*, June 12, 1865; *Daily National Republican* (Washington, D.C.), June 12, 1865; *Harper's Weekly*, July 1, 1865.

2. *New York Times*, June 12 and 13, 1865; *Independent*, June 22, 1865.

3. *New York Times*, June 16, 1865.

4. *Flag of Our Union*, July 8, 1865. This story appeared in several newspapers.

5. Holberton, *Homeward Bound*, 78–79. Holberton notes that in some instances, such as Davenport, Iowa, soldiers received "less than enthusiastic" welcomes. For an excellent account of the Union armies disbanding, see Marten, *Sing Not War*, 33–73.

6. There is a considerable literature on Civil War dead. See, for example, Blair, *Cities of the Dead*; Neff, *Honoring the Civil War Dead*; Faust, *This Republic of Suffering*; and Schantz, *Awaiting the Heavenly Country*.

7. Faust, *This Republic of Suffering*, 214–17; *Chicago Tribune*, June 30, 1865; *New York Times*, June 12 and July 4, 1865; Neff, *Honoring the Civil War Dead*, 127; Blair, *Cities of the Dead*, 52–53.

8. Faust, *This Republic of Suffering*, 215–17; *New York Times*, August 25, 1865; of the 13,363 graves at Andersonville, 12,912 were identified. The remainder were marked "Unidentified." For more about Wirz's trial, see Cloyd, *Haunted by Atrocity*, 36–37.

9. There were several other monuments and services that summer, including the dedication of a memorial to Luther Ladd and Addison Whitney, two of the first casualties of war in the summer of 1861. The monument was erected in Lowell, Massachusetts, in June 1865. Circus entertainer Dan Rice likewise erected a monument to Union soldiers that summer in Girard, Pennsylvania.

10. Soldiers' National Memorial Cemetery, *Oration of Major-General O. O. Howard and Speech of His Excellency A. G. Curtin*; *New York Times*, July 6 and 10, 1865; *Chicago Tribune*, July 6, 1865. Much of the historiography on Civil War memory has suggested that the Union Cause and Emancipationist Cause were two separate interpretations of the war.

11. Unable to attend because of ill health, President Johnson sent his comments, which (perhaps surprisingly) likewise addressed the issue of freedom. "In your joy tomorrow, I trust you will not forget the thousands of whites, as well as blacks, whom the war has emancipated, who will hail this Fourth of July with a delight which no previous Declaration of Independence ever gave them," he observed (Bartlett, *Soldiers' national cemetery at Gettysburg*, 63). For another example of this emphasis on slavery, see the Reverend John Pierpont's hymn sung at the Bull Run dedication in 1861, published in *The Independent*, June 22, 1865.

12. Bartlett, *Soldiers' National Cemetery at Gettysburg*.

13. *Independent*, June 22, 1865.

14. On April 13, 1866, Congress passed an act to "preserve from desecration the graves of the soldiers of the United States that fell in battled or died of disease in the field and in hospital during the war of rebellion." On February 22, 1867, Congress passed legislation that formally linked these resting places under the National Cemetery System (Neff, *Honoring the Civil War Dead*, 131).

15. When asked by a chaplain after the battle of Chattanooga whether the dead should be arranged by state as at Gettysburg, Thomas allegedly quipped, "No, No, mix them all up. I'm sick of state's rights" (quoted in Catton, *This Hallowed Ground*, 302).

16. *New York Daily News*, April 5, October 12, 1866; Faust, *Riddle of Death*, 17–18; Faust, *This Republic of Suffering*, 236; Blair, *Cities of the Dead*, 52–53; Neff, *Honoring the Civil War Dead*, 125–67; Blight, *Race and Reunion*, 68–70.

17. Of the seventy-four national cemeteries, at least sixty-two contained the remains of USCT soldiers (Neff, *Honoring the Civil War Dead*, 133).

18. Neff, *Honoring the Civil War Dead*, 133. Gooden died in 1876.

19. Neff, *Honoring the Civil War Dead*, 133; Faust, *This Republic of Suffering*, 236.

20. As Neff points out, "No Confederates who died while under arms opposing the Union were interred in any of the national cemeteries. Only those who died in Union custody—while prisoner of war or in Union hospitals—were interred in the grounds that eventually became part of that system." There were cases, however, where "smaller Confederate plots or individual graves were contained within the walled national cemetery, although almost always relegated to a separate corner of the field" (Neff, *Honoring the Civil War Dead*, 132, 134).

21. Quoted in Massey, *Bonnet Brigades*, 329.

22. Some Confederate prisoners or soldiers who had died in northern hospitals were interred in national cemeteries, including thirty Confederates buried at Arlington. But

overwhelmingly, national cemeteries were reserved only for loyal U.S. soldiers. As chapter 9 discusses, the first change to this policy occurred in 1900 when Congress authorized a separate section for the burial of Confederate dead in Arlington National Cemetery. In 1906, Congress approved legislation allowing the federal government to assume the obligation of tending to the graves of approximately 30,000 Confederate soldiers who had died in northern prison camps and hospitals (Neff, *Honoring the Civil War Dead*, 224; Blair, *Cities of the Dead*, 179–93; *Daily Phoenix* [Columbia, S.C.], August 1, 1869).

23. *Brownlow's Knoxville Whig*, July 12, 1865.

24. *Appleton's Annual Cyclopedia*, 6:188. On the trial of Wirz, see Cloyd, *Haunted by Atrocity*, 34–37.

25. Sutherland, *Savage Conflict*, 82–83, 229–30, 273; John McCue Court Martial Files, RG 153, entry 15, MM 2302, NARA; S. C. E. McCue to U. S. Grant, July 10, 1865, McCue and Martin Family Papers, UVA; Grant endorsement, October 24, 1865, *PUSG*, 15:604–5; *New York Times*, October 24 and 25, 1865; Mays, *Cumberland Blood*, 1–5, 126–45. For the most thorough account of guerrilla warfare, see Sutherland, *Savage Conflict*.

26. *New York Times*, August 28, 1865. The paper included testimonies from several men noting that Burton had represented the views of "quite a number of able-bodied gentlemen."

27. Leonard, *Lincoln's Avengers*, 148. For more radical leaning Republicans like Stanton and Sumner, this meant enfranchising the freedmen. For more on Holt, see Leonard, *Lincoln's Forgotten Ally*.

28. *New York Times*, August 28, 1865.

29. Smith detailed further reasons why the South should not be punished, including the fact that the South believed it was righteous in seceding and that there had been enough bloodshed. *New York Times*, June 9, 1865.

30. *Valley Spirit* (Chambersburg, Pa.), August 9, 1865.

31. "Union-Disunion-Reunion," *Old Guard*, June 1865, vol. 3, no. 6, 241–45. The magazine's cover noted that it was "devoted to the principles of 1776 and 1787." It ran from January 1863 through December 1867.

32. *New York Times*, June 23, 1865.

33. John Travers of New York to F. B. Dean, December 13, 1865, Misc. Files, Brock Collection, HL.

34. *Valley Virginian*, December 20, 1865.

35. Taylor, *Divided Family*, 153–89; Alfred Ellet to Mary Ellet from Union Grove, Ill., July 13, 1865, Cabell and Ellet Family Papers, UVA.

36. *Valley Spirit* (Chambersburg, Pa.), January 10, 1866.

37. *Keowee (S.C.) Courier*, April 6, 1867.

38. Foner, *Reconstruction*, 182–84; Trefousse, *Andrew Johnson*, 216–17.

39. Fellman, Gordon, and Sutherland, *This Terrible War*, 302; Foner, *Reconstruction*, 191.

40. *New York Times*, August 13, 1865.

41. This is not to say that there had been a "moment of possibility" in April or May when the relations between North and South during Reconstruction might have been

different. Contrary to reports by John Richard Dennett and northern reporters such as Whitelaw Reid, John Townsend Trowbridge, and others, that there was a period before Johnson's proclamation when Confederates had been willing to accept any provisions established by the federal government, most evidence suggests that there was continuity in white southerners' mood. They simply were more willing to express it as the summer progressed (Perman, *Reunion*, 19, 40; Dennett, *South as It Is*; Trowbridge, *Desolate South*; Reid, *After the War*).

42. Lucy Muse Walton Fletcher diary, April 12, 1865, DU.

43. Gallagher, *Lee and His Army*, 257.

44. Rubin, *Shattered Nation*, 233.

45. Sarah Ann Graves Strickler Fife diary, May 16, 1865, UVA.

46. Kean, *Inside the Confederate Government*, 208–10.

47. Nonslaveholder quoted in Campbell, *When Sherman Marched North*, 99–100.

48. Litwack, *Been in the Storm*, 268–69; Glatthaar, *Forged in Battle*, 214–17; Campbell, *When Sherman Marched North*, 99; Ott, *Confederate Daughters*, 67.

49. Foner, *Reconstruction*, 199–201, 208–9; Summers, *Dangerous Stir*, 61–62.

50. For several examples of northern commentators, see Annie G. Dudley Davis diary, June 11, 1865, HL; William Henry Redman diary, May 2, 1865, UVA; Reid, *After the War*, 24; Trowbridge, *Desolate South*, 593; Dennett, *South as It Is*, 19.

51. Perman, *Reunion*, 28–30.

52. McNeill, *Uncompromising Diary of Sallie McNeill*, 123–25 (diary entry November 10, 1865), emphasis in original.

53. Stephens, *Recollections of Alexander H. Stephens*, 166, 171 (diary entry June 5, 1865).

54. Dennett, *South as It Is*, 19–21.

55. Nolan, "Anatomy of the Myth," in Gallagher and Nolan, *Myth of the Lost Cause*, 18–19.

56. *Independent*, January 14, 1866.

57. *Chicago Tribune*, January 3, 1866.

58. Clark, *Defining Moments*, 25.

59. Schwalm, *Emancipation's Diaspora*, 225, 228.

60. "A Woman in Washington," *Independent*, April 26, 1866.

61. Congress passed the act on April 9, 1866.

62. "Washington Correspondence," *Independent*, April 26, 1866.

63. *Lynchburg News*, March 30, April 5, 1866; *Richmond Dispatch*, March 26, 1866; Blair, *Cities of the Dead*, 35–42; Clark, *Defining Moments*, 25, 54.

64. The minor event of the day occurred when a single gunshot was fired in the crowd, but the perpetrator was immediately arrested and no one was struck by the shot. Two weeks later, however, violence erupted in Norfolk, Virginia, when the city's black residents held a procession in honor of the Civil Rights bill. Two white people were killed and several wounded while one black youth was bayoneted in the stomach and several more injured (Van Zelm, "Virginia Women," 75; *Lynchburg News*, April 5, 1866; *Richmond Times*, April 18, 1866; Blair, *Cities of the Dead*, 35–42; Clark, *Defining Moments*, 54).

65. *New York Times*, April 4, 1866.

66. *Boston Advertiser*, quoted in Blair, *Cities*, 40.

67. Quoted in Varon, "'Last Hour,'" 14.

68. Quoted in Blair, *Cities*, 23–24.

69. By the 1890s, these days would often fall under the title of Emancipation Days. For a debate among Richmond's black residents regarding which date to observe, see the *Richmond Planet*, October 11, 1890.

70. Quoted in Schwalm, *Emancipation's Diaspora*, 231.

71. Schwalm, *Emancipation's Diaspora*, 231–32, Carey quoted p. 232.

72. Seven USCT regiments, with a total of nearly 2,000 soldiers, were present at Appomattox. The 29th, 31st, and 116th regiments had participated in blocking the last rebel attempt to break through the lines, while four others waited in the wings (Calkins, *Battles of Appomattox Station*, 88–90).

73. Varon, "'Last Hour,'" 14.

74. There were some celebrations of April 9 by white Unionists, especially in 1867 and 1868. These are discussed in chapter 4.

75. Clark, *Defining Moments*, 15. Despite threats from whites, there was very little violence at the Evacuation Day and Surrender Day ceremonies. But on April 16, 1866, when freedmen and -women gathered in Norfolk for a procession to mark the passage of the civil rights bill, a shootout left two white people dead, one black youth stabbed in the stomach, and countless others wounded (Blair, *Cities*, 41–42).

76. *Evening Telegraph* (Philadelphia), March 27, 1866; *Edgefield Advertiser*, May 23, 1866. For discussion of Union burial practices and exclusion of Confederates from National Cemeteries, see Neff, *Honoring the Civil War Dead*, 112–29.

77. Blair, *Cities of the Dead*, 52–54; Faust, *Riddle of Death*, 18.

78. Women in Winchester, Virginia, had formed a Ladies' Memorial Association in May 1865. Most LMAs, however, did not organize until the spring of 1866 (Janney, *Burying the Dead*, chap. 2).

79. *Southern Opinion* (Richmond), August 29, 1868. Like most of the wartime associations, LMAs were organized by women at the community level and operated independently of one another. But such local origins did not prevent the groups from interacting or supporting each other's efforts.

80. Although organized and administered at the local level, every LMA intended to care for the remains of all Confederate soldiers in their midst, not just those from the local community or even state.

81. Janney, *Burying the Dead*, Appendix A; Faust, *This Republic of Suffering*, 244. Within five Virginia communities alone, women of the Ladies' Memorial Associations reinterred the remains of more than 72,520 Confederates, nearly 28 percent of the 260,000 Confederate soldiers who perished in the war.

82. HMA, *To the Women of the South*.

83. HMA, *To the Women of the South*; *Petersburg (Va.) Daily-Index Appeal*, March 30, 1867; Petersburg Ladies' Memorial Association minutes, LOV; *Ladies Memorial Association of Montgomery, Alabama, 1860–1870*, Pamphlet Collection, MOC; *Montgomery Mail*, March 18, 1866.

84. "Letter to the Women of Virginia," c. 1866 (with envelope addressed to Mrs. Charles T. Barney), HMA correspondence, MOC.

85. *Daily Richmond Examiner*, May 10, 1866.

86. *Richmond Dispatch*, May 11, 1866.

87. Although some historians tend to refer to the southern observance as "Decoration Day," most of the earliest references by LMAs and southern communities refer to "Memorial Day." By the late 1880s and 1890s, the term "Decoration Day" could be found to designate both northern and southern observances. For example, in 1884, the civic leaders of Winchester, Virginia, dubbed National Memorial Day "Decoration Day," and strongly encouraged the townspeople to participate. They reserved the term Memorial Day exclusively for their Confederate services.

88. The observance by Nora Davidson's schoolchildren is often heralded as the first Memorial Day in the South and is frequently cited as the inspiration for the national Memorial Day (Davidson, *Cullings from the Confederacy*, 155–60).

89. Janney, *Burying the Dead*, chap. 2; Whites, *Crisis in Gender*, 160.

90. The Appomattox LMA settled on May 10, the anniversary of Jackson's death, as their Memorial Day (Schroeder, *Confederate Cemetery at Appomattox*, 24).

91. For discussion of mourning rituals during the nineteenth century, see Loughridge and Campbell, *Women in Mourning*; Douglas, *Feminization of American Culture*, 200–226; and Faust, *This Republic of Suffering*. For the argument that Memorial Days were political, see Janney, *Burying the Dead*; Blair, *Cities of the Dead*; and Faust, *This Republic of Suffering*, 247–48.

92. *Daily Richmond Examiner*, May 11, 1866; Blair, *Cities of the Dead*, 58. For an examination of attempts to enshrine and remember Jackson, see Hettle, *Inventing Stonewall Jackson*.

93. Sarah Ann Graves Strickler Fife diary, May 10, 1866, UVA. Sallie had attended the May 10, 1866, services in Charlottesville, Virginia.

94. *Richmond Times*, May 12, June 1, 1866.

95. *Richmond Times*, May 12, 1866.

96. U.S. Congress, House, *Congressional Globe*, 39th Cong., 1st sess., May 28, 1866, 755; Neff, *Honoring the Civil War Dead*, 146. The resolution called for Johnson "to inform this house whether any of the military or civil employés of this government, within the State of Georgia, or any of the other rebel States, have in any way countenanced or assisted in the rendition of public honors to any of the traitors, either living or dead." It was decided in the affirmative on June 4, 1866.

97. *New York Times*, May 21, June 18, 1866. The *Chicago Tribune* is quoted in the *New York Times*.

98. Blair, *Cities of the Dead*, 50.

99. *Valley Virginian*, February 6, 1867. The Virginia General Assembly invited "to this Commonwealth as permanent residents and citizens thereof the people of the North and West, irrespective of their political opinions, for the purpose of developing its wealth and repairing its waste places, pledging that our people will receive them in the spirit of kindness and welcome" (Resolutions of the Virginia General Assembly, Brock Collection, Misc. Collections, Box 289, HL).

100. *Daily Phoenix* (Columbia, S.C.), May 31, 1866; *Valley Virginian*, September 12, 1866.

101. Robert E. Lee to John Dalberg Acton, December 15, 1866, quoted in Freeman, *R. E. Lee*, 4:304–5.

102. Resolutions of the Virginia General Assembly, Brock Collection, Misc. Collections, Box 289, HL.

103. For several examples see *Richmond Times*, May 11, 1866; *Daily News and Herald* (Savannah, Ga.), Saturday, May 19, 1866; and *Petersburg (Va.) Daily Index*, June 11, 1867, June 10, 1868.

104. *Winchester (Va.) Times*, June 13, 1866. For discussion of antebellum southern white women and politics, see Varon, *We Mean to Be Counted*, 71–168.

105. Leonard, *Lincoln's Avengers*, 142–43.

106. Rubin, *Shattered Nation*, 208, 218–29. Rubin describes this as "political ventriloquism."

107. The first of the acts stipulated the terms by which the southern states might re-enter the union: each of the eleven Confederate states, excluding Tennessee, would be required to write a new constitution that provided for manhood suffrage approved by a majority of voters and to ratify the Fourteenth Amendment. Equally important, the act divided the region into five military districts whose commanders could utilize the army to protect life and property (Foner, *Reconstruction*, 271–80).

108. Blair, *Cities of the Dead*, 62–63; Neff, *Honoring the Civil War Dead*, 150; CSMA, *History of the Confederate Memorial Associations of the South*, 233.

109. Janney, *Burying the Dead*, 73. John Neff observes that the extent of restrictions placed on memorial activities is difficult to assess possibly because "they had been communicated by military officers through means other than formal orders, for example, through intimidation" (Neff, *Honoring the Civil War Dead*, 153).

110. *Richmond Times*, June 1, 1867; *Richmond Whig*, June 1, 1867; *Richmond Dispatch*, June 1, 1867; *New York Times*, June 3, 1867; Henry Clay Brock diary, May 30, 1867, VHS; Blair, *Cities of the Dead*, 64; James H. Gardner to Mary Gardner Florence, June, 1, 1867, James Henry Gardner Papers, VHS.

111. Neff, *Honoring the Civil War Dead*, 136–40; Blight, *Race and Reunion*, 68–71; Blair, *Cities of the Dead*, 69–76; McConnell, *Glorious Contentment*, 16, 183–84; Moore, *Memorial Ceremonies*; GAR, *Journal of the Forty-first National Encampment* (1907), 67.

112. *Southern Opinion* (Richmond), May 30, June 6, 1868.

113. The *Sunday Dispatch* (Philadelphia) quoted in *Southern Opinion* (Richmond), June 6, 1868; *New York Times*, June 5, 1868. David Blight argues that "the process of dealing with the dead" helped foster a reconciliationist vision (Blight, *Race and Reunion*, 2).

114. Neff notes that some GAR posts scheduled their services for Saturday, May 29, to avoid violating the Sabbath (Neff, *Honoring the Civil War Dead*, 137).

115. Moore, *Memorial Ceremonies*. William Blair argues that Union Decoration Days were distinctive (Blair, *Cities of the Dead*, 70).

116. For discussion of northern women and children in supporting roles at Union Memorial Days, see Silber, *Romance of Reunion*, 59.

117. Moore, *Memorial Ceremonies*, 423–25.

118. Moore, *Memorial Ceremonies*, 524–25.

119. Blight notes that "the emancipationist legacy [was] very much a part of early Memorial Day rhetoric" (Blight, *Race and Reunion*, 73).

120. Moore, *Memorial Ceremonies*, 542–43. Brown, like others, did refer to the "freedom" of the nation, but never directly to slavery.

121. Moore, *Memorial Ceremonies*, 557–59.

122. Moore, *Memorial Ceremonies*, 551–53.

123. *Richmond Daily Dispatch*, June 1, 1868; Blair, *Cities of the Dead*, 72.

124. Blight argues that many Union Memorial Day speeches in the late 1860s flowed with reconciliationist sentiment (Blight, *Race and Reunion*, 73).

125. Moore, *Memorial Ceremonies*, 549.

126. Moore, *Memorial Ceremonies*, 344.

127. *Evening Telegraph* (Philadelphia), May 28, 1869; *Charleston Daily News*, June 3, August 1, 1869; *Valley Virginian*, June 3, 1869; Blair, *Cities of the Dead*, 73–74; letter to Chase quoted in Blair, p. 74. The Confederates buried within Arlington had died in prison or while being treated in Washington hospitals. The refusal to allow women to decorate the Confederate graves prompted calls in the South for the LMAs to reclaim the remains of all Confederates still interred in the North (*Charleston Daily News*, August 1, 1869). For more on this see Janney, *Burying the Dead*, chap. 4.

128. For argument that the Lost Cause and memorial activities served to foster a separate, southern identity, see Blair, *Cities of the Dead*; Rubin, *Shattered Nation*; and Janney, *Burying the Dead*. For argument that Memorial Days were agents of reconciliation, see Buck, *Road to Reunion*, 119–20, and Foster, *Ghosts*, 44.

129. Blight, *Race and Reunion*, 71.

CHAPTER 4

1. *Michigan at Gettysburg*, 49–50. Edward McPherson was a lawyer in the Lancaster practice of Thaddeus Stevens prior to the war. In 1858, he was elected as a congressman from Pennsylvania and served until 1863 (he was not reelected in 1862). He later served as clerk of the House of Representatives. His farm west of Gettysburg was the site of much of the first day's fighting on July 1, 1863.

2. *Michigan at Gettysburg*, 72–73, emphasis in original.

3. *Soldiers' Tribune* quoted in Marten, *Sing Not War*, 246.

4. Marten, *Sing Not War*, 19–21, 245–49. Marten is careful to note that the veterans who suffered from physical disabilities, mental handicaps, and poverty may not have been a majority; nevertheless, the experience of minority often came to dominate public perception.

5. Linderman, *Embattled Courage*, 266–75; Foster, *Ghosts*, 47–48. Blight describes this period as one in which soldiers' memory was more "in a stage of incubation . . . stored and unsettled, more festering than sleeping" (Blight, *Race and Reunion*, 150).

6. Gannon, *Won Cause*. While racism affected black veterans, it did not preclude the cooperation and comradeship among men who had fought so desperately to put down the rebellion.

7. Between 1863 and 1866, Union veterans published sixty-eight regimental his-

tories. As Gary W. Gallagher has noted, these early regimentals represented a diverse cross-section of the Union armies including units who saw action in every theater of the war and those from seventeen different loyal states (plus the Colorado territory) (Gallagher, *Union War*, 65–66; Luebke, "Union Regimental Histories, 1865–1866," 1–6). I would like to thank both Gary Gallagher and Peter Luebke for their extensive help and advice about the importance of these early regimentals.

8. Beecher, *Record of the 114th Regiment, N.Y.S.V.*, 504–5. The preface was signed by Beecher in January 1866, indicating that the regimental was probably written in 1865.

9. Baruch and Beckman, *Civil War Union Monuments*, 122, 142. Text of the Marietta, Ohio, monument (dedicated 1875) found at Ohio Civil War Monuments, http://library.cincymuseum.org/starweb/civilwar/servlet.starweb, accessed July 18, 2010. A survey of Baruch and Beckman, the most complete collection of listings of Union monuments, suggests that monuments to the Union Cause predominated.

10. Weeks, *Gettysburg*, 21; Marten, *Sing Not War*, 133–35. Weeks offers the most complete narrative of the transformation of Gettysburg from battlefield to military park.

11. Vanderslice, *Gettysburg: A History*, 211. Strong Vincent was a colonel during the fighting on July 2 at Little Round Top. He was promoted the next day to brigadier general. The first monument was erected by the Strong Vincent Grand Army of the Republic (GAR) Post of Erie, Pennsylvania. For a searchable database of the monuments at Gettysburg, see http://www.virtualgettysburg.com/exhibit/monuments, accessed July 19, 2010.

12. Wert, *Complete Hand-book*, 5.

13. Weeks, *Gettysburg*, 61.

14. Harris, "Across the Bloody Chasm," 101.

15. New York State Monuments Commission, *New York Monuments Commission for the Battlefields*, 2:750.

16. New York State Monuments Commission, *New York Monument Commission for the Battlefields*, 2:832. For more on this, see Harris, "Across the Bloody Chasm," chap. 2.

17. Minnigh, *Battlefield of Gettysburg and National Military Park* (1895). Numerous historians have elaborated on the theme of Gettysburg as a site of reconciliation. See for example Linenthal, *Sacred Ground*, 90–91, and Smith, *Golden Age*, 2, 145–78.

18. The first Confederate monument was erected by the 1st (2nd) Maryland in 1886.

19. Marten, *Sing Not War*, 28, 246; Frederickson, *Inner Civil War*, 166–80.

20. Neff, *Honoring the Civil War Dead*, 134; Davies, *Patriotism on Parade*, 28–30; Marten, *Sing Not War*, 11–12. Some enlisted men were admitted to these groups, but the members were overwhelmingly officers.

21. Davies, *Patriotism on Parade*, 31–33, 74; McConnell, *Glorious Contentment*, 24–25.

22. Janney, *Burying the Dead*, 130–31; Davies, *Patriotism on Parade*, 34–36; Blight, *Race and Reunion*, 157.

23. On Union veterans and pensions, see Marten, *Sing Not War*, 200–233; McConnell, *Glorious Contentment*, 148–62; Logue, *To Appomattox and Beyond*, 80–100; and Skocpol, *Protecting Soldiers and Mothers*, 102–51.

24. Davies, *Patriotism on Parade*, 35–37, 74. The Union Veteran Legion at one point had its own junior organization known as the Loyal Guard.

25. Logue, *To Appomattox and Beyond*, 132.

26. Davies, *Patriotism on Parade*, 119–21, 139–55, Sherman quoted on p. 121; McConnell, *Glorious Contentment*, 125–52, 170–80. For the most comprehensive treatment of the GAR and their efforts to secure pensions, see Skocpol, *Protecting Soldiers and Mothers*.

27. For example, in 1868, Brevet Maj. Gen. J. Watts de Peyster assured members of a Boston-based post that "you were the saviours [*sic*] of the country" (*Reunion of Post Phil Kearny*, 1868, 10).

28. *Reunion of Post Phil Kearny*, 1868, 11.

29. GAR, Dept. of Indiana, *Journal of the Seventh Annual Session* (1886), 148.

30. Warner quoted in McConnell, *Glorious Contentment*, 190.

31. Gallagher, *Union War*, 75–118; Hunt, 20–41. There has been an extensive debate within the scholarly literature as to the significance of emancipation as a war goal of Union soldiers. Ira Berlin, Barbara J. Fields, Steven F. Miller, Joseph P. Reidy, and Leslie S. Rowland of the Freedom Project credit slaves for forcing the war for Union into a war for freedom. Chandra Manning counters, offering white Union soldiers as the earliest and most vocal proponents of emancipation. For works on this debate, see Berlin et al., *Slaves No More*, 4; Manning, *What This Cruel War Was Over*, 11, 13, 152–53; and Brasher, *Peninsula Campaign*.

32. Gage, *From Vicksburg to Raleigh*, 15.

33. Rogers, *History of the One Hundred and Eighty-ninth Regiment*, 108. Numerous regimentals employed the term "slave holders' rebellion." See for example Mowris, *History of the One Hundred and Seventeenth Regiment*, vi.

34. Grant, *Personal Memoirs*, 2:659.

35. For an excellent discussion of how the victory over "slavery" as opposed to victory over "slaveholders" became a feel-good and morally superior claim, see Robert Penn Warren's discussion of the "Treasury of Virtue" (Warren, *Legacy of the Civil War*, 54, 59–66).

36. Wood, *History of the Ninety-fifth Regiment*, 62–63, emphasis in original. On the difference between slavery and slaveholders, see Gara, "Slavery and the Slave Power," 5–18.

37. Lambert, *Memorial Day Oration*, 7–8.

38. GAR, Dept. of Indiana, *Journal of the Seventh Annual Session* (1886), 148.

39. *PUSG*, 28:409–10.

40. Hunt, *Good Men*, 21, 25–33, quotations pp. 30–31. There were certainly dissenters. Some white U.S. veterans recalled that liberating the slaves might lead to a race war in the South. See for example Merrill, *Campaigns of the First Maine*, 376.

41. Lucas, *History of the 99th Indiana*, 167.

42. Baruch and Beckman, *Civil War Union Monuments*, 112.

43. A survey of regimental histories, monument dedications, GAR speeches, and Memorial Day addresses suggests that the frequency of celebrating emancipation intensified rather than diminished between 1865 and 1900.

44. For a discussion of how the meaning of "liberty" changed during the course of

the war, see Gallagher, *Union War*, chap. 3. For examples of Lincoln suggesting definitions for "liberty," see Basler et al., *Collected Works of Abraham Lincoln*, 7:301.

45. For a similar argument, see Hunt, *Goodmen*, 5.

46. Military Order of the Loyal Legion, *War Papers Read Before the Commandery of
the State of Wisconsin*, 2:377–78.

47. Military Order of the Loyal Legion, *War Papers Read Before the Commandery of
the State of Wisconsin*, 3:102.

48. Fundraising appeal quoted in Savage, *Standing Soldiers*, 103. Douglass requested that the Colored People's Educational Monument Association turn over its
money to the Washington-based group (NLMA, *National Lincoln Monument Association: Incorporated by act of Congress, March 30, 1867*).

49. The twenty-one figures were to include "Stanton, Seward, Chase, George H.
Stewart (Christian Commission), Dr. Bellows (Sanitary Commission—eastern), J. E.
Yateman (Sanitary Commission—western); 'the loyal pulpit' represented by Henry
Ward Beecher and Bishop Simpson" (NLMA, *Organization and Design*). For a more
detailed description of the monument's design, see Savage, *Standing Soldiers*, 104–5;
and Peterson, *Lincoln in American Memory*, 52–53.

50. Savage, *Standing Soldiers*, 106. Savage has dismissed Mills's design as "paternalistic," which "reinscribed subservience in the black body and reaffirmed the black man's
segregation from the civic realm of the hero." Such analysis not only is shaped by twen-
tieth- and twenty-first-century standards of racial equality, but it misses the fact that
Union and emancipation were merged together for many Unionists in the immediate
postwar years.

51. At least seven Lincoln monuments were erected between 1868 and 1874 according to Bullard, *Lincoln in Marble and Bronze*. Two statues by Henry Kirke Brown,
one in Brooklyn (1869) and the other in Union Square in New York (1870), featured
ostensibly simple figures of a cloaked Lincoln holding a scroll. Vinnie Ream's Lincoln,
commissioned by the government for the U.S. Capitol and unveiled in 1871, closely
resembled Brown's Union Square monument, again featuring the president with the
Emancipation Proclamation in hand (Bullard, *Lincoln in Marble and Bronze*, 25–45;
Savage, *Standing Soldiers*, 67, 81, 83).

52. Historians since have criticized the memorial for emasculating the slave and
reasserting "the old racial structure and power relations of slavery" (Savage, *Standing
Soldiers*, 119).

53. The monument's origins began in the immediate aftermath of Lincoln's assassination when Charlotte Scott, an ex-slave living in Ohio, entrusted five dollars to her
former master for a monument to the president. As word spread, other African Americans began collecting contributions, and eventually the Western Sanitary Commission
of St. Louis decided to sponsor the project as "Freedom's Memorial." Desiring a great
work of art, the Western Sanitary Commission asked every freedman in the country
to donate "one week's free work, or its equivalent" to the fundraising effort. Unlike the
previously mentioned Colored People's Educational Monument Association, which was
led by black activists and sought to build a school in Lincoln's name, the Freedmen's
Memorial project revealed a structural division between the black donors and white
organizers of the project (Blight, *Race and Reunion*, 196; Savage, *Standing Soldiers*,

90–94, 113–19; Bullard, *Lincoln in Marble and Bronze*, 64–72; Peterson, *Lincoln in American Memory*, 57–60). There were several competing designs for the Freedmen's Memorial, including one by Harriet Hosmer.

54. Frederick Douglass, "The Freedman's Monument to Abraham Lincoln: An Address Delivered in Washington, DC on 14 April 1876," in Blassingame et al., *Douglass Papers*, 427–40; Savage, *Standing Soldiers*, 113–19; Peterson, *Lincoln in American Memory*, 59–60. Savage argues that "Douglass at once swept aside the paternalistic argument that his race owed Lincoln a special debt of patronage." While Douglass might have rejected the notion of patronage, a closer reading of his speech indicates that he did hold Lincoln in esteem even if he found some of his motivations flawed.

55. White, *Lincoln's Greatest Speech*, 39–40.

56. Baruch and Beckman, *Civil War Union Monuments*, 59; image of monument accessed through http://upload.wikimedia.org/wikipedia/en/b/b4/Union_Monument_in_Vanceburg_propaganda.jpg, accessed July 18, 2010.

57. Marshall, *Creating a Confederate Kentucky*, 6.

58. De Forest, *Random Sketches*, 8–9.

59. *Liberator*, September 8, 1865.

60. *New York Tribune*, September 8, 1865.

61. Cowden, *Fifty-ninth Regiment*, 28.

62. Califf, *Record of the Services*, 1. When circumstances allowed, African Americans, like white U.S. veterans, recorded their wartime memories in regimentals as early as 1865 and 1866.

63. Williams quoted in Gannon, *Won Cause*, chap. 11.

64. Shaffer, *After the Glory*, 170.

65. Fleetwood quoted in Glatthaar, *Forged in Battle*, 231.

66. Shaffer argues that emancipation was "by far the most important legacy of the war. Hence, rather than seeing themselves as saviors of the Union, they remembered themselves as warriors in an army of liberation." I contend that the two cannot be so easily separated (Shaffer, *After the Glory*, 170).

67. Quotations from Gannon, *Won Cause*, chap. 11.

68. *New York Sun*, December 4, 1866; *Daily Phoenix* (Columbia, S.C.), November 23, 1866; *National Republican* (Washington, D.C.), August 10, 1867; Shaffer, *After the Glory*, 69–70, 159. Shaffer notes that the Colored Soldiers' and Sailors' League disappeared from the historical record in the early 1870s. The organization was active in 1887, responding to the efforts of the Lower South to exclude African Americans from the GAR (*Fort Worth Daily Gazette*, July 15, 1887).

69. *New York Times*, July 27, 1875, July 27, 1879, August 3, 1887. In 1886, Senator George F. Hoar of Massachusetts introduced a bill calling for a monument to African American soldiers and seamen (*Washington Bee*, December 18, 1886). A monument to the Colored Soldiers and Sailors would not be dedicated in Washington, D.C., until 1998.

70. GAR, *Proceedings of the National Encampment* (1870).

71. Gannon, *Won Cause*, 6. Barbara A. Gannon's recent book *Won Cause* offers the most comprehensive treatment of the interracial cooperation and nature of the GAR. She argues that not only did the GAR honor the black men who had fought for the Union, but it also welcomed them into the association during the height of segregation.

Conversely, scholars such as William C. Davies (*Patriotism on Parade*), Stuart McConnell (*Glorious Contentment*), and Donald Shaffer (*After the Glory*) have argued that the GAR treated black members poorly and imposed a segregationist paradigm on them.

72. Gannon, *Won Cause*, 25, 37–39, 45, 65, 7–79, 112.

73. Gannon, *Won Cause*, 38, 85–98, 100, 105, 107–8, 114; Schwalm, *Emancipation's Diaspora*, 237; Shaffer, *After the Glory*, 155. Gannon notes that all-black units are equally difficult to identify because the GAR records prove to be color-blind; they rarely identified the racial makeup of a post.

74. Gannon, *Won Cause*, 85, 99–114.

75. Gannon, *Won Cause*, 58–59, 68, 112–13, 119–21; Shaffer, *After the Glory*, 177. Addeman, *Reminiscences of Two Years*; Cowden, *Fifty-ninth Regiment*; Morgan, *Reminiscences of Service*, 5–6, 20. For more on the public memory of Fort Pillow, see Cimprich, *Fort Pillow*.

76. For a discussion of African Americans' participation in (Union) Memorial Days, see Gannon, *Won Cause*, 72–81; Blair, *Cities of the Dead*, 22, 134–36, 176; Shaffer, *After the Glory*, 171–72; and Blight, *Race and Reunion*, 76, 88, 270, 304–7, 315.

77. *Atchison (Kans.) Daily Globe*, September 22, 1884.

78. *New York Age*, January 7, 1888.

79. Quoted in Blair, *Cities of the Dead*, 137.

80. Lambert, *Address before Post No. 2*, 9–10.

81. In 1896, the GAR Department of the Potomac came together for the first celebration of Appomattox (*Washington Post*, April 10, 1896).

82. *New York Times*, May 15, 1871; GAR, Dept. of New York, Canby Post, *Memorial Day with the Canby Post*, 52.

83. *Franklin Repository* (Chambersburg, Pa.), June 10, 1868.

84. Emerson, *Letters*, 732 (Ellen Tucker Emerson to Edward Waldo Emerson, September 4, 1871).

85. Gillespie, *Secret to be Buried*, 395 (diary entry April 1880).

86. Unlike ex-Confederate women, northern women found opportunities to join associations with no direct ties to the war or the Union cause. For example, on May 10, 1866, while ex-Confederate women were initiating their memorial tributes, Elizabeth Cady Stanton, Susan B. Anthony, and other northern women were congregating to form the American Equal Rights Association in New York (Dubois, *Feminism and Suffrage*, 63; *Richmond Times*, May 11, 1866).

87. Briggs, *Reminiscences and Letters*, 240 (Caroline Clapp Briggs to Miss F.B., March 1, 1882).

88. *New York Times*, October 13, December 29, 1865, February 2, 1866, April 14, 1869, December 12, 1874.

89. *New York Times*, March 31, 1867. Former Confederate women did take on some of these tasks immediately after the war. By 1866, however, most Confederate women's associations tended to concentrate on the dead rather than the living (Janney, *Burying the Dead*, 43).

90. Two of the first women's clubs appeared in 1868, Sorosis in New York (dedicated to furthering the educational and social activities of women) and the New England Women's Club of Boston (Davies, *Patriotism on Parade*, 37).

91. GAR, *Proceedings of the National Encampment* (1870); WRC, *Proceedings of the Second National Convention* (1884).

92. Beath, *History of the Grand Army of the Republic*, 12, 14.

93. O'Leary, *To Die For*, 75.

94. WRC, *Proceedings of the Third National Convention* (1885); Carnahan, *Manual*, 41–43.

95. WRC, *Proceedings of the National Convention* (1883); WRC, *Proceedings of the Second National Convention* (1884).

96. WRC, *Proceedings of the Second National Convention* (1884); O'Leary, *To Die For*, 76–77.

97. In 1881, Commander Charles Houten, Department of New Jersey GAR, requested the various ladies' aid societies in the state to send representatives to Trenton to form a state organization. That December, the Loyal Ladies' League (LLL) became an auxiliary to the New Jersey GAR. During the next few years, Pennsylvania, California, and Kansas all formed LLLs. In 1884, when the WRC decided to admit "any loyal woman," the New Jersey LLL refused to affiliate. Two years later, the various LLLs met in Chicago where they formed the Ladies of the GAR (Carnahan, *Manual*, 44; Davies, *Patriotism on Parade*, 38). By 1926, the LGAR had included "ex-army nurses" within its folds.

98. Carnahan, *Manual*, 54. The LGAR noted consistently that the organization "shall not be auxiliary to any other order or organization" (LGAR, *Rules and Regulations*, 3).

99. Gannon, *Won Cause*, 47–56; O'Leary, *To Die For*, 82–90. WRC leaders succeeded in implementing state-level segregation in Tennessee (1890), Kentucky (1900), and Maryland (1900)—though Maryland later appears to have had some interracial activity (Morgan, *Women and Patriotism*; Gannon, *Won Cause*, 229–30n6).

100. WRC, *Journal of the Fifth National Convention* (1887).

101. WRC, *Journal of the Twelfth National Convention* (1894), 38.

102. Resolution Lafayette Post No. 140 of New York, January 2, 1894, Box 1, Abraham Gilbert Mills Papers, NYPL.

103. Lambert, *Address before Post No. 2*, 11. Lambert quoted from both Maj. Gen. George H. Thomas's report to the secretary of war in 1868 and Sherman on May 30, 1878.

104. GAR, Dept. of Minnesota, *Journal of Proceedings of the Eleventh Annual Encampment* (1891), 232.

105. Charles Devens, "Address of Charles Devens," in Loyal Legion, *Military Essay*, 1:84.

106. Davies, *Patriotism on Parade*, 249.

107. For historians who have argued that sectionalism influenced political discourse during Reconstruction, see Bensel, *Sectionalism and American Political Development*, xix; Silbey, *American Political Nation*, 139–40; Bradley, "House, Beast, and Bloody Shirt."

108. *Congressional Globe*, 39th Cong., 1st sess., May 8, 10, 1866, 2460, 2544; Blight, *Race and Reunion*, 51; Cloyd, *Haunted by Atrocity*, 37–38; Foner, *Reconstruction*.

109. For an excellent account of Grant's 1868 campaign, see Waugh, *Grant*, 119–22.

110. Foner, *Reconstruction*, 337–45; Curtis quoted in Blight, *Race and Reunion*, 103; Cloyd, *Haunted by Atrocity*, 37–38. Three former Confederate states (Virginia, Mississippi, and Texas) were still under martial rule during the election of 1868 and therefore ineligible to vote. For an account of the violence intrinsic in the 1868 election, see Foner, *Reconstruction*, 342–45.

111. Edwards, *Angels in the Machinery*, 60.

112. Gallman, "Anna Dickinson and the Election of 1872," in Fahs and Waugh, *Memory of the Civil War*, 162–63.

113. Waugh, *Grant*, 143–45; Gallman, "Anna Dickinson and the Election of 1872," in Fahs and Waugh, *Memory of the Civil War*, 162–63.

114. The doorkeeper's duties included enforcing the chamber's rules and announcing the visits of prominent statesmen such as the president.

115. Bradley, "House, Beast, and Bloody Shirt," quotations pp. 21, 22.

116. Logue, *To Appomattox and Beyond*, 98–99; Logue, "Union Veterans and Their Government," 426–30; Marten, *Sing Not War*, 303n7.

117. *Harper's Weekly*, November 9, 1867; *Harper's Weekly*, October 3, 1868; Cloyd, *Haunted by Atrocity*, 42–43.

118. Ohio Association of Union Ex-Prisoners of War, *Proceedings of the Ohio Association* (1884); Kimball, *Brinley Hall Album*, 147; Blight, *Race and Reunion*, 152; Cloyd, *Haunted by Atrocity*, 37–38. Cloyd observes that the personal narratives tended to be more strident than those that appeared before Wirz's trial. He notes that "the competition and popularity of the memoirs encouraged the polemical nature of the accounts" (Cloyd, *Haunted by Atrocity*, 39).

119. Cloyd, *Haunted by Atrocity*, 38.

120. Waugh, *Grant*, 169–70; Trudeau, "Start with the Basics," 54–55; Mahan, "Arsenal of History," 5–27, Garfield quoted p. 8; Irvine, "Genesis of the *Official Records*," 221–29. For a discussion of the white southerners' response to the publication, see chap. 6.

121. Sherman, *Memoirs*; Sheridan, *Personal Memoirs*, xii.

122. Joan Waugh's *U. S. Grant* offers a riveting account of Grant's determination to write his memoirs even as he was dying.

123. Waugh, *Grant*, 197–209.

124. Grant, *Personal Memoirs*, 2:630.

125. Waugh, *Grant*, 179–80, 190–91.

126. Grant, *Personal Memoirs*, 2:665.

127. Grant, *Personal Memoirs*, 1:103.

CHAPTER 5

1. Letter from G. N. Dexter, formerly quartermaster of the regiment to Capt. A. A. Winn, November 8, 1874, in *Veteran Reunion of the 3rd GA Regiment*.

2. *Veteran Reunion of the 3rd GA Regiment*. Katherine Du Pre Lumpkin wrote that her father attended the Union Point reunion, noting that it was the first ever of its kind in the South (Lumpkin, *Making of a Southerner*, 111).

3. *New York Times*, May 21, June 18, 1866.

4. On the Lost Cause, see for example Brundage, *Southern Past*; Fahs and Waugh,

Memory of the Civil War; Blair, *Cities of the Dead*; Blight, *Race and Reunion*; Gallagher and Nolan, *Myth of the Lost Cause*; Hale, *Making Whiteness*; and Foster, *Ghosts*.

5. Mitchell, *Hollywood Cemetery*, 71; *Richmond Times*, April 26, June 1, 1866; HMA minutes, June 10, 1867, MOC; Foster, *Ghosts*, 40–41, 59; *Richmond Daily Dispatch*, May 11, 1868. While men formed the basis of the Stuart Memorial Association, they relied on the Hollywood Memorial Association for assistance. For an example of men taking the lead in memorialization in the 1890s, see Crow, "In Memory of the Confederate Dead."

6. For discussion of monument inscriptions, see Brown, *Public Art of Civil War Commemoration*, 35–40.

7. The number of Confederate regimentals published in the 1860s was much lower than the number published by Union regiments. But a handful did appear. See, for example, Tunnard, *Southern Record* (1866); and Jones, *Historical Sketch of the Chatham Artillery* (1867).

8. Du Bose quoted in Blight, *Race and Reunion*, 158. For Alexander's memoir, see Alexander, *Fighting for the Confederacy*.

9. Blight, *Race and Reunion*, 78; Foster, *Ghosts*, 49. Daniel H. Hill preferred to publish reminiscences from men who fought in the war, but amateur poets sent scores of unsolicited works to his office. Historian Sarah Gardner notes that he rejected many of these, but a good many found their way into his publication. She estimates that circulation of his magazine never exceeded 12,000 (Gardner, *Blood and Irony*, 279n55).

10. The *Southern Opinion* was published between June 16, 1867, and May 1, 1869. Owned and operated by Pollard until his assassination in December 1868, precipitated by an article he printed on November 21, 1868, the paper changed hands twice in its last five months of publication. Messrs. W. D. Chesterman and Company bought the paper in December 1868 but sold it to D. S. Hardwick and Company in March 1869. J. Marshall Hanna, editor under Hardwick's ownership, chose to terminate the paper in May 1869, citing that its mission had been fulfilled.

11. *Southern Opinion* (Richmond), June 15, 26, 1867.

12. Foster, *Ghosts*, 49; Nolan, "Anatomy of the Myth," in Gallagher and Nolan, *Myth of the Lost Cause*, 13; Simpson, "Continuous Hammering and Mere Attrition," in Gallagher and Nolan, *Myth of the Lost Cause*, 148–53. The *Lost Cause* first appeared in 1866 but was rereleased in a revised edition the following year.

13. Both contemporaries and later historians hailed Robert E. Lee as the epitome of reconciliationist sentiment between 1865 and his death in 1870. Lee's most famous biographer, Douglas Southall Freeman, wrote that "Lee the warrior became Lee the conciliator. Within less than five months [after Appomattox], he was telling Southern men to abandon all opposition, to regard the United States as their country, and to labor for harmony and better understanding. Seldom had a famous man so completely reversed himself in so brief a time, and never more sincerely" (Freeman, *R. E. Lee*, 4:219). According to Gaines Foster, "Lee played an important role in leading southerners to accept defeat and to seek reunion" (Foster, *Ghosts*, 51). See also Smith, *Lee and Grant*, 302. For historians who offer a more complicated interpretation of Lee as outwardly exhibiting reconciliation but inwardly harboring violent emotions, see Gal-

lagher, *Lee and His Army*, 256–57; Nolan, *Lee Considered*, 134–35, 150–52; Connelly, *Marble Man*; Pryor, *Reading the Man*, 434–50.

14. Robert E. Lee to James Longstreet, October 29, 1867, Letterbook, Lee Family Papers, VHS; U.S. Congress, *Report of the Joint Committee on Reconstruction*, 129; Pryor, *Reading the Man*, 449; Fellman, *Making of Robert E. Lee*, 277. Michael Fellman contends that Lee's posture during the Joint Committee testimony was disingenuous as "he had been in constant communication with such men" (Fellman, *Making of Robert E. Lee*, 264).

15. Lee to Mrs. William Coulling of Richmond, May 5, Lee to Miss Ida Dodge of Lynchburg, May 11, Lee to Mr. William Beyers of Richmond, June 2, 1866, Letterbook, Lee Family Papers, VHS.

16. *Evening Telegraph* (Philadelphia), August 24, 1869. Gen. James Longstreet, too, elected not to attend. According to a Philadelphia newspaper, prominent officers of both sides had declined the invitation and only two Confederates attended (*Evening Telegraph*, August 25, 1869).

17. Robert E. Lee to Jubal A. Early, October 15, 1866, November 22, 1865, Letterbook, Lee Family Papers, VHS. For more discussion on the public and private expressions of Confederates such as Lee, see Fellman, *Making of Robert E. Lee*, 275–89; Harris, "Across the Bloody Chasm."

18. Fellman, *Making of Robert E. Lee*, 276.

19. Pryor, *Reading the Man*, 450.

20. Lee quoted in Pryor, *Reading the Man*, 450. For more on Lee harboring animosity toward the North, see Gallagher, *Lee and His Army*, 256–57.

21. *Staunton (Va.) Spectator*, September 8, 1868; Fellman, *Making of Robert E. Lee*, 286–87.

22. Lee quoted in Nolan, *Lee Considered*, 150–51. For more anti-Reconstruction quotations by Lee, see Fellman, *Making of Robert E. Lee*, 289–91. Johnston was the son of famed Confederate general Albert Sidney Johnston.

23. Marten, *Sing Not War*, 19–20, 246–48. Edward L. Ayers argues that respect for Confederate veterans decreased over time among white southerners (Ayers, *Promise*, 26–28, 335–58).

24. Foner, *Reconstruction*, 342; Foster, *Ghosts*, 48. Marten notes that "observers frequently commented on the high percentage of [Klan] members who were former Confederate soldiers" (Marten, *Sing Not War*, 65).

25. The Confederate Soldier's Association of Pickens County formed in the fall of 1866. For more on this group, see Poole, *Never Surrender*, 64, 123. The officers of the 3rd North Carolina commenced their organization after an 1866 funeral (Marten, *Sing Not War*, 12).

26. Women's leadership, however, did not preclude men from involvement in the movement. For further discussion of men's roles, see Janney, *Burying the Dead*, chaps. 2 and 3.

27. Foner, *Reconstruction*; Richardson, *West from Appomattox*.

28. Dabney H. Maury, "The Southern Historical Society: Its Origins and History," *SHSP* 18:349–65; Foster, *Ghosts*, 50–51; Trudeau, "Start with the Basics," 52–53. All

three organizations formed in 1869. The members of the SHS appointed Benjamin Morgan Palmer president and Dr. Joseph Jones secretary-treasurer, and selected other prominent Confederates as vice presidents of each southern state (not Confederate), including Robert E. Lee, Wade Hampton, D. H. Hill, and John C. Breckinridge. Despite mailing 6,000 circulars across the South and seeking the aid of newspapers, during 1869 the society gained little support outside of New Orleans. After several months, fewer than a hundred members had joined, and by early 1870 only forty-four members had contributed dues.

29. For a discussion of the gendered nature of Lee's memory battles that occurred between Confederate men and the LMAs, see Janney, *Burying the Dead*, chap. 4.

30. Gallagher, *Confederate War*, 85–89; Buck, *Road to Reunion*, 251; Wilson, *Baptized in Blood*, 48; Foster, *Ghosts*, 47; Connelly, *Marble Man*, 4, 25–26. For a classic example of the Lost Cause's veneration of Lee, see Early, *Campaigns of Gen. Robert E. Lee*.

31. *Richmond Daily Dispatch*, October 20, 21, 25, 1870; "The Monument to General Robert E. Lee: History of the Movement for Its Erection," *SHSP* 17:185–205; October 19, 1870, Lee Monument Association Records, LOV; Foster, *Ghosts*, 51.

32. Osborne, *Jubal*, xiii, 6–9, 18–21, 34–52, 390, 402–13; Gallagher, *Lee and His Generals*, 200–202.

33. Osborne, *Jubal*, xiii, 6–9, 18–21, 34–52, 390, 402–13; Early, *Memoir of the Last Year*. Early refused to take the amnesty oath to the U.S. government; however, he returned to the country after President Andrew Johnson issued an unconditional amnesty that ultimately pardoned all combatants against the United States during the war.

34. Apparently, Bradley T. Johnson and several of his fellow officers in the Army of Northern Virginia had been contemplating a veterans' organization just prior to Lee's death. In a letter dated October 25, 1870, Johnson asked Early to serve as the president of the Association of the Army of Northern Virginia. Johnson and his comrades had been planning the association for "some months" and had considered Lee for the presidency. But with Lee's passing, Johnson asked Early to take on the role. The group would serve to "preserve our old friendship, to collect materials for the history of the Army, and to cherish the names and fame of our dead comrades." Johnson suggested that Early might fuse his desire for a Lee monument association with this veterans' group (Bradley T. Johnson to Jubal A. Early, October 25, 1870, Jubal A. Early Papers, Library of Congress).

35. For more discussion of manhood/masculinity among both Union and Confederate soldiers during and after the Civil War, see Marten, *Sing Not War*, 65; McPherson, *For Cause and Comrades*, 6, 13, 25–31, 76–78; Berry, *All That Makes a Man*, 9–10, 171–73; Mitchell, *Civil War Soldiers*, 17–18, 42; Foster, *Ghosts*; Whites, *Civil War as a Crisis in Gender*, 160–224; Bardaglio, *Reconstructing the Household*, 129–36, and Edwards, *Gendered Strife and Confusion*, 111–19.

36. "To the Survivors of the Army and Navy of the Confederate States and to all the admirers of the Character of the late General Robert E. Lee, wherever they may reside," November 1870, Lee Monument Association Records, LOV; Jubal A. Early, Lynchburg, Virginia, October 24, 1870, reprinted in the *New York Times*, October 28, 1870.

37. Janney, *Burying the Dead*, 110; Osborne, *Jubal*, 440–41; Foster, *Ghosts*, 52–53. Early was elected president of the temporary Lee Monument Association, but later in

the meeting the group elected Jefferson Davis as the permanent president. Historian Gaines Foster argues that many white southerners rejected Early's resistance to the postwar world and instead embraced veterans such as John Brown Gordon who espoused a vision of the New South. Gary W. Gallagher, however, convincingly demonstrates that Early was pivotal in shaping a heroic image of Lee and of the Confederate military effort (Foster, *Ghosts*, 60–61; Gallagher, "Jubal A. Early, the Lost Cause, and Civil War History," in Gallagher and Nolan, *Myth of the Lost Cause*, 35–59).

38. Trudeau, "Start with the Basics," 52–53; Early, *Proceedings of the Southern Historical Convention*; Foster, *Ghosts*, 54–55. Despite his appointment of an all-Virginian executive committee, Early included representatives from twelve states. Many Virginians did lead the movement, but Gaines Foster overemphasizes the degree to which it was a Virginian movement. Neither was the Lost Cause message controlled by this coalition in the 1870s. Rather, a survey of Confederate reunion speeches and regimentals suggests that those from throughout the former Confederacy espoused similar messages.

39. Early, *Proceedings of the Southern Historical Convention*, 27, 32, 35–38, 43; Gallagher, "Jubal A. Early, the Lost Cause, and Civil War History," in Gallagher and Nolan, *Myth of the Lost Cause*, 43. Early offered a similar message in an address before the SHS at Richmond on October 29, 1873 (*New York Times*, October 30, 1873).

40. The word "vindicated" appears frequently in the pages of the *SHSP*. Karen Cox argues that the United Daughters of the Confederacy "raised the stakes of the Lost Cause by making it a movement about vindication, as well as memorialization" (Cox, *Dixie's Daughters*, 1).

41. GAR, Dept. of Indiana, *Journal of the Seventh Annual Session* (1886), 148.

42. "The Lost Cause," *SHSP* 16:234, 236.

43. Evans quoted in Gallagher and Nolan, *Myth of the Lost Cause*, 13.

44. Gallagher, *Lee and His Army*, 261; Trudeau, "Start with the Basics," 52–53. Trudeau notes that before 1876, the SHS released its material through publications such as *The Land We Love*, *The New Eclectic Magazine*, and *Southern Magazine*.

45. Gallagher, *Lee and His Generals*, 206–7; Jones, *Life and Letters of Robert Edward Lee*, 121 (letter quoted from Lee in early 1861); Buck, *Road to Reunion*, 251–52; Connelly and Bellows, *God and General Longstreet*, 25–27.

46. Gallagher, "Jubal A. Early, the Lost Cause, and Civil War History," in Gallagher and Nolan, *Myth of the Lost Cause*, 35–59, quotations pp. 41–42; Gallagher, *Lee and His Generals*, 199; Early, *Proceedings of the Southern Historical Convention*, 37–38, 27–28.

47. *Our Living Our Dead* (July 1873) quoted in Foster, *Ghosts*, 57–58.

48. Foster, *Ghosts*, 57. *Our Living Our Dead* ran from July 1873 through early 1876, folding because of low circulation.

49. Connelly, *Marble Man*, 61.

50. "Within a Stone's Throw of Independence at Gettysburg," *SHSP* 12:111–12; Gallagher, *Lee and His Generals*, 206–7; Foster, *Ghosts*, 58. While Longstreet was demonized by the Lost Cause orators, in the pantheon of Confederate heroes only Lee's trusted lieutenant Thomas "Stonewall" Jackson came close to generating a similar deified status (Gallagher, *Lee and His Generals*, 210).

51. Stephens, "Cornerstone Speech"; Stephens, *Constitutional View*, 1:12.

52. Most literature on the Lost Cause argues that former Confederates asserted the insignificance of slavery. Kenneth M. Stampp, for example, argued that Lost Cause spokesmen "denied that slavery had anything to do with the Confederate cause" (Stampp, *Imperiled Union*, 260). Alan Nolan observed that "Southerners' contention that slavery had nothing to do with the war was widely accepted" (Nolan, "Anatomy of the Myth," in Gallagher and Nolan, *Myth of the Lost Cause*, 20).

53. Croom, *War-history of Company "C."*

54. Tunnard, *Southern Record*, 21.

55. Davis, *Rise and Fall*, 1:66.

56. "Address of Colonel Edward McCrady, Jr.," *SHSP* 16:246.

57. Easley quoted in Poole, *Never Surrender*, 83.

58. "Slavery," Jubal Early Papers, Scrapbook, Library of Congress, quotation p. 12. This essay was written after the war, as indicated by Early's reference to the "late Confederate States." In 1915 his niece, Ruth Early, published a lengthier version of the essay. Early opens this piece by stating: "The struggle for independence made by the Southern States of the American Union, grew out of the questions of self-government arising mainly in regard to the institution of African slavery as it existed in those states" (Early, *Heritage of the South*, 11).

59. Johnston, *Address before the Literary Societies.*

60. "The Lost Cause," *SHSP* 16:235.

61. Hodge, *Sketch of the First Kentucky Brigade*, 3.

62. Early, *Proceedings of the Southern Historical Convention*, 27.

63. "Monument to the Confederate Dead at Fredericksburg," *SHSP* 18:401.

64. This is not to say that Confederates were not nationalists (see chapter 1). On the contrary, their understanding of the nation was filtered through a domestic lens.

65. Connelly and Bellow, *God and General Longstreet*, 22–28.

66. *Memphis Daily Appeal*, September 18, 1870.

67. On Reconstruction, see Foner, *Reconstruction*; Hahn, *Nation under Our Feet*; and Painter, *Standing at Armageddon*. For more on the Lost Cause as an act of defiance by white conservatives, see Poole, *Never Surrender*.

68. Ross, "Commemoration of Robert E. Lee's Death," 135–50 (quotation p. 146); *DeBow's Review*, October 1870.

69. Fellman, *Making of Robert E. Lee*, 192.

70. *Boston Daily Advertiser*, August 20, 1873; *New York Times*, October 30, 1873; *Bangor (Maine) Daily Whig & Courier*, August 22, 1873; Easley quoted in Poole, *Never Surrender*, 83; F. A. Porcher, "The Last Chapter in the History of Reconstruction in South Carolina," *SHSP* 12:173; Early, *Proceedings of the Southern Historical Convention*, 26.

71. Poole, *Never Surrender*, 59, 82–84, Easley quoted p. 83.

72. Gallagher, "Jubal A. Early, the Lost Cause, and Civil War History," in Gallagher and Nolan, *Myth of the Lost Cause*, 35–59 (quotation p. 42).

73. Dabney H. Maury, "Grant as a Soldier and Civilian," *SHSP* 5:238. Unlike Early, Maury did note that Grant had been a gracious victor at Vicksburg and Appomattox.

74. Joan Waugh points out that the attacks on Grant not only blemished his national

and international military stature, but, as intended, they also bolstered Lee's (Waugh, *Grant*, 186).

75. Eckert, *John Brown Gordon*, 149. Gordon was called to testify about the activities of the Klan.

76. Letter from G. N. Dexter, formerly quartermaster of the regiment to Capt. A. A. Winn, November 8, 1874, in *Veteran Reunion of the 3rd GA Regiment*.

77. *Veteran Reunion of the 3rd GA Regiment*.

78. Gaines Foster argues that Early and the Virginians' anti-northern tenor dissuaded other Confederates from joining their efforts: "Most southerners did not wish to keep alive the passions of the war by refighting battles and issues" (Foster, *Ghosts*, 47–75, quotation p. 62). Foster slights the degree to which anti-northern sentiment remained in the 1870s.

79. Quoted in Cloyd, *Haunted by Atrocity*, 41–42.

80. Blaine quoted in Cloyd, *Haunted by Atrocity*, 51. Congressman Benjamin Hill of Georgia had taken to the floor to sternly object, enlivening a spirited debate in the newspapers.

81. *SHSP* 1:113–16; Cloyd, *Haunted by Atrocity*, 52.

82. Democratic leaders were at odds over the proper use of the paramilitary groups. In contrast to Hampton's policy of "force without violence," Martin Witherspoon Gary and his Edgefield County supporters advocated a "shot gun policy" that explicitly endorsed fraud and violence to terrify African American and Republican voters (Poole, *Never Surrender*, 118–19). For more on the violence in South Carolina during 1876, including the Hamburg Massacre, see Foner, *Reconstruction*, 570–75.

83. Poole, *Never Surrender*, 116–35, quotation p. 122; Foner, *Reconstruction*, 570–75; Baker, *What Reconstruction Meant*, 18–19, 54–55. Baker estimates that as many as 30,000 white men were under arms as riflemen during the 1876 campaign.

84. Poole, *Never Surrender*, 119–21, 134; Baker, *What Reconstruction Meant*, 31; Wilson, *Baptized in Blood*, 37.

85. "Reunion of Virginia Division, A.N.V. Association," *SHSP* 14:184–85.

86. In focusing on the 1880s and 1890s, many scholars of the Lost Cause have argued that it served primarily as a nostalgic look at the past (see for example Foster, *Ghosts*; Ayers, *Promise*, 334–38). For the argument that the Lost Cause of the 1870s was more politically driven, see Poole, *Never Surrender*, 134–35; Janney, *Burying the Dead*, chaps. 2–3.

87. Numerous brigade and state level veterans' associations met during this time. For example, in 1871, more than 12,000 veterans met in Huntsville, Missouri, for a reunion. In 1874, veterans gathered in Galveston, Texas, for a grand reunion. The following year, the 3rd Georgia, Mahone's Old Brigade, Mosby's 43rd Battalion of Cavalry, and Hampton's Legion all met for reunions (*Lynchburg Daily Virginian*, April 13, May 12, and May 17, 1875; *Daily Phoenix* [Columbia, S.C.], August 25, 1871, July 15, 1875).

88. While Foster's argument that the aristocratic bias of Early's groups and their contentious personalities hampered their efforts seems likely, his assertion that the majority of white southerners rejected their use of the Confederate past appears less probable, as the remainder of this chapter demonstrates (Foster, *Ghosts*, 61–62).

89. Foster, *Ghosts*, 91.

90. *Daily Arkansas Gazette*, October 28, 1879.

91. Speech of Thomas T. Munford to Confederate Veterans at Lynchburg, c. 1884, Munford-Ellis Family Papers, DU, emphasis in original.

92. Foster notes that the end of Reconstruction removed the political importance of issues of the war for veterans, but reunions would seem to suggest otherwise (Foster, *Ghosts*, 67, 83, 89–90).

93. "Tribute to the Confederate Dead," *SHSP* 10:174–78.

94. *St. Louis Globe-Democrat*, September 10, 1881.

95. Garfield had been shot by Charles Guiteau on July 2, 1881. Surviving the attack, he suffered throughout the summer before succumbing to his injuries on September 19, 1881. See Millard, *Destiny of the Republic*.

96. *New York Times*, August 24, 1881; *County Paper* (Oregon, Mo.), September 23, 1881; *Sacramento Daily Record-Union*, August 23, 1881. Newspapers spell the name both "Grigsby" and "Grisby."

97. *County Paper* (Oregon, Mo.), September 23, 1881; *St. Louis Globe-Democrat*, August 21, 1881.

98. *Jacksonport Herald* reprinted in *Daily Arkansas Gazette*, October 28, 1879.

99. Foster, *Ghosts*, 128–29. Foster notes that between 1886 and 1899, more than sixty percent of Confederate monuments featured the lone soldier rather than a funerary symbol such as a pyramid.

100. Foster, *Ghosts*, 131.

101. Foster, *Ghosts*, 104–12; Davies, *Patriotism on Parade*, 40–41; Blight, *Race and Reunion*, 272; Marten, *Sing Not War*, 149–52.

102. Blight, *Race and Reunion*, 272. While testifying before Congress in 1871, Gordon denied involvement with the Klan; he did, however, concede to be associated with a secret "peace police" organization whose goal was the "preservation of peace" (Eckert, *John Brown Gordon*, 145–49).

103. Foster, *Ghosts*, 111; Blight, *Race and Reunion*, 127.

104. Foster observes that the decision to elect Gordon commander, as opposed to a Virginian such as Jubal Early or Fitzhugh Lee, underscores the discontinuity between the two phases of the veterans' movement (Foster, *Ghosts*, 110). But a closer examination of the rhetoric of the 1870s and late 1880s/early 1890s suggests that Confederate veterans promoted a similar message in both phases.

105. Gordon, *Reminiscences of the Civil War*, 444.

106. Foster, *Ghosts*, 111.

107. GAR, Dept. of Minn., *Journal of Proceedings of the Eleventh Annual Encampment*, 232.

108. Wm. C. P. Breckenridge, "The Ex-Confederate and What He Has Done in Peace," Address delivered before the Association of the Army of Northern Virginia, October 36, 1892, *SHSP* 20:227.

CHAPTER 6

1. Ammen, *Caverns of Luray*, Strother quoted pp. 44–47; *Harper's Weekly*, January 11, 1879; *Frank Leslie's Illustrated Newspaper*, July 2, 1881.

2. *Reunion of Ex-Soldiers of the North and South*, 5; *North American* (Philadelphia), July 14, 1881.

3. *Page Courier* (Luray, Va.), July 14, 1881.

4. *Reunion of Ex-soldiers of the North and South*, 5; *Page Courier* (Luray, Va.), July 28, 1881.

5. "In the 1880s and 1890s," writes David Blight, "the practice of reconciliation and fraternalism emerged as dominant in veterans' culture." For historians who have emphasized reunion and reconciliation, see Buck, *Road to Reunion, 1865–1900*; Blight, *Race and Reunion*, 2–5, 65, 265, quotation p. 198; Silber, *Romance of Reunion*; Smith, *Golden Age of Battlefield Preservation*; Fellman, *Making of Robert E. Lee*, 304; Campbell, *When Sherman Marched North*, 105. For those who have highlighted the complexities of reconciliation and the persistence of sectional animosities, see Neff, *Honoring the Civil War Dead*; Reardon, *Pickett's Charge*; Coski, *Confederate Battle Flag*, 67; Waugh, *Grant*; Gallagher, *Causes Won*; Gallagher, *Union War*; Gannon, *Won Cause*; O'Leary, *To Die For*, 121–28; Marten, *Sing Not War*, 273; Harris, "Across the Bloody Chasm."

6. For historians who contend reconciliation was based largely on shared northern and southern ideas about white supremacy, a forgetting of emancipation, and an acquiescence to the Lost Cause, see Blight, *Race and Reunion*, 2–5, 65, 198, 265; Silber, *Romance of Reunion*; Smith, *Golden Age*; Fellman, *Making of Robert E. Lee*, 304; O'Leary, *To Die For*, 108, 134, 195.

7. Harris, "Slavery, Emancipation," 267; Harris, "Across the Bloody Chasm."

8. John S. Mosby to Eppa Hunton, November 18, 1909, Papers of John Singleton Mosby, UVA; McConnell, *Glorious Contentment*, 85. For discussion of the Gilded Age, see Edwards, *New Spirits*.

9. McConnell, *Glorious Contentment*, 151; Weeks, *Gettysburg*, 14–17, 35, 59–60.

10. *Annals of the War*, i–iv.

11. Johnston, "Dalton-Atlanta Operations," in *Annals of the War*, 330–41; Imboden, "Fire, Sword, and Halter," in *Annals of the War*, 169–83; Brookee-Rawle, "Right Flank at Gettysburg," in *Annals of the War*, 467–84; Northcott, "Union View of the Exchange of Prisoners," in *Annals of the War*, 184–90; Judge Robert Ould, "Exchange of Prisoners," in *Annals of the War*, 32–59; Blight, *Race and Reunion*, 164–68; Gallagher, "Introduction," in *Annals of the War*, v–x.

12. "Literary Notices," *SHSP* 11 (December 1883): 576; Charles M. Blackford, "The Trials and Trial of Jefferson Davis," *SHSP* 29 (1901): 57; Mahan, "Arsenal of History: *Official Records of the War of the Rebellion*," 5–27. Mahan notes that some former Confederates questioned the accuracy of the series, but these misgivings were quite rare.

13. Gallagher, "Introduction to the *Southern Bivouac*," in *Southern Bivouac*, 1:i–xii, quotations p. v; Marshall, *Creating a Confederate Kentucky*, 89–90. In 1885, Basil Duke and Richard W. Knott became the new editors of the magazine. Along with transforming it into a literary journal, the editors began to publish more pieces espousing the

"proper" role of African Americans in society. In 1886, the *Century* magazine purchased the *Southern Bivouac*.

14. Blight, *Race and Reunion*, 173–75; *Battles and Leaders*, 1:iii–iv; Pettegrew, "'Soldier's Faith,'" 56. The four-volume set sold more than 75,000 copies in 1888 (Blight, *Race and Reunion*, 431n10).

15. *Battles and Leaders*, 1:ix.

16. Blight, *Race and Reunion*, 173–75; Johnson quoted in Waugh, *Grant*, 169.

17. For examples of thanks for Blue-Gray excursions, see R. E. Lee Camp, Sons of Confederate Veterans Collection (hereafter Lee Camp Records), Box 2, VHS.

18. "What the Centennial Ought to Accomplish," *Scribner's Monthly* 10 (August 1876): 509–10.

19. *New York Tribune*, June 18, 1875. Paul Buck notes that on this occasion, veterans from Charleston, South Carolina, returned the battle flag of the 54th Massachusetts to the town of Lexington. I have been unable to find primary sources confirming this (Buck, *Road to Reunion*, 134–35).

20. Govan and Livingood, *Chattanooga Country*, 306–7. The following year Union and Confederate veterans in Chattanooga joined each other's respective Memorial Day services.

21. A. B. Lawrence, Warsaw, N.Y., to Col. M. E. Bradley, October 21, 1892, Lee Camp Records, Box 2, VHS; Marten, *Sing Not War*, 252, 258. For a discussion of how northern tourism fostered the culture of reconciliation, see Cox, *Dreaming of Dixie*, 130–31.

22. Gosson, *Post-bellum Campaigns of the Blue and Gray*.

23. *House Reports*, 52th Cong., 2nd sess., H. Rept. 2188, 1–4.

24. *Christian Union*, August 26, 1874.

25. Harris, "Across the Bloody Chasm," 16.

26. Rogers, *Record of the Rhode Island Excursion*, 27, emphasis added. For another example of soldiers as the "first to lay aside the angry partisan feelings," see *Anderson (S.C.) Intelligencer*, September 25, 1879.

27. Rogers, *Record of the Rhode Island Excursion to Gettysburg*, 21.

28. New York State Monuments Commission, *Final Report on the Battlefield of Gettysburg*, 1:250–57. Flower was not a veteran but had spent the war years running a jewelry store. He later served as the president of the New York Railroad before becoming governor in 1891.

29. For example, on May 10, 1877, the anniversary of Gen. Thomas J. "Stonewall" Jackson's death, the "boys in blue" of Chattanooga, Tennessee, accompanied a procession of those clad in gray to the Confederate cemetery. Wishing to reciprocate, on May 30, the "boys in gray" agreed to appear without their rebel uniforms or battle flags in the Federal Memorial Day services (Govan and Livingood, *Chattanooga Country*, 306–8).

30. Nearly every example of cemeteries that contained both Union and Confederate soldiers tended to be those which included Confederate POWs.

31. Lee Camp Papers, Box 2, VHS; *Washington Post*, May 27, 1894; *Trenton Evening News*, May 31, 1885.

32. All of these men, along with Grant, had graduated from the U.S. Military Academy at West Point. Johnston likewise attended the funeral of Sherman in 1891.

33. Waugh, *Grant*, 216–37, 241, quotation p. 236. For an excellent account of Grant's funeral and its message of reconciliation, see Waugh, *Grant*, chap. 5.

34. Waugh, *Grant*, quotations pp. 237, 247.

35. Waugh, *Grant*, 236–38, quotation p. 237.

36. Gordon, *Reminiscences of the Civil War*, 444.

37. Chamberlain, *"Bayonet! Forward,"* 159.

38. Marvel, *Lee's Last Retreat*, 198; Marvel, *Place Called Appomattox*, ix, 259–62. Marvel provides a wonderful account of how both Gordon and Chamberlain reimagined the roles they played during the surrender.

39. See for example the speech of Governor McKinley in Boynton, *Dedication*, 341.

40. Colonel Mullikin's Oration, October 25, 1888, in Maryland Gettysburg Monument Commission, *Report of the State of Maryland*, 72–76.

41. *New York Times*, May 31, 1895. Contrary to historians' descriptions of the monument as evidence of reconciliation, the placement and dedication of a monument to Confederate veterans on northern soil was especially divisive among Union veterans. See, for example, *Washington Times*, May 22, 1895; *National Tribune* (Washington, D.C.), May 23, 1895.

42. Kimball, *International Cotton Exposition*, 2.

43. Kimball, *International Cotton Exposition*, 135–39.

44. *CV* 3 (June 1895): 177. For more on northern tourists to the South, see Silber, *Romance of Reunion*, 66–92; and McIntyre, *Souvenirs of the Old South.*

45. Lears, *Rebirth of a Nation*, 201–8.

46. *Watchman*, October 3, 1895.

47. *Cincinnati Enquirer* reprinted in *Louisiana Democrat*, May 12, 1875.

48. O'Leary, *To Die For*, 121–28. O'Leary notes that "Grand Army veterans often expressed strong hostility towards the South and wanted to affirm the victory of the Union," though she overestimates the degree to which Union veterans became more willing "to accept that it was not treason but the South's belief in the righteousness of its cause that had led the South into rebellion" (127).

49. GAR, *National Encampment* (1892), 213–14.

50. *St. Louis Republic*, May 27, 1903.

51. For historians who contend reconciliation was based largely on an acquiescence to the Lost Cause, see Blight, *Race and Reunion*, 2–5, 65, 198, 265; Silber, *Romance of Reunion*; Fellman, *Making of Robert E. Lee*, 304.

52. Clement A. Evans, "Contributions of the South to the Greatness of the American Union," delivered before the Association of the Army of Northern Virginia, October 10, 1895, Richmond, Virginia, *SHSP* 23, 15.

53. Christian, *Confederate Cause*, 26.

54. Blight, *American Oracle*, 159.

55. Fellman, *Making of Robert E. Lee*, 304; Drum quoted in Coski, *Confederate Battle Flag*, 67.

56. *Kansas City Times*, June 16, 1887.

57. *Atchison (Kans.) Daily Champion*, June 16, 1887.

58. *Milwaukee Sentinel*, June 17, 1887. Although many GAR departments supported Fairchild, numerous Democratic newspapers denounced his remarks as instigating sec-

tional bitterness (see for example *New York Times*, June 20, 1887, which had switched from the Republican Party to support Cleveland and the Democrats in 1884).

59. *Arkansas Gazette*, June 17, 1887; Coski, *Confederate Battle Flag*, 67–69.

60. Bachelder served as the Superintendent of Tablets and Legends beginning in 1883. It was he who suggested the criteria for inscribing and positioning monuments. That is, monuments were to mark points from which units launched their attack—the so-called battle line regulations (Weeks, *Gettysburg*, 24–25).

61. Reardon, *Pickett's Charge*, 91–96, Butler quoted p. 96; *Maine Farmer*, April 21, 1887. The marker would ostensibly mark the spot where Confederate general Lewis A. Armistead fell, thus not overriding the battle line regulations.

62. Reardon, *Pickett's Charge*, 97–99; *Galveston Daily News* (Houston, Tex.), July 6, 1887; *Fayetteville (N.C.) Observer*, July 14, 1887; quotation in *Daily Picayune* (New Orleans), July 9, 1887.

63. Quoted in Reardon, *Pickett's Charge*, 110. It is likely that some of the Union veterans responded this way after visiting the field and finding a Confederate monument erected on Culp's Hill. In November 1886, the 1st (2nd) Maryland had requested permission from the Gettysburg Battlefield Memorial Association to place the monument on private property. But the Abe Patterson Post GAR of Philadelphia was enlivened by the placement, noting that it was a "sacrilege" to allow an "intrusion by traitors upon sacred soil" (*Winchester (Va.) Times*, November 6, 1889). I would like to thank my student David Graham for sharing this story with me.

64. Reardon, *Pickett's Charge*, 108–13; Gobin quoted in Linenthal, *Sacred Ground*, 95; *Daily Evening Bulletin* (San Francisco), July 2, 1888. Reardon notes that approximately 300 Confederates attended.

65. Reardon, *Pickett's Charge*, 103–6, quotation p. 105. In 1898, the Lee Camp debated whether to attend a reunion in Philadelphia, citing the Pennsylvanians' refusal to march under the Confederate flag in 1888 (*Richmond Dispatch*, July 26, 30, 1898).

66. Boynton, *Chattanooga and Chickamauga*, article originally appeared on August 17, 1888.

67. The first Confederate monument at Gettysburg was erected by the 1st (2nd) Maryland in 1886.

68. *SHSP* 16:339–48.

69. *Galveston Daily News*, August 27, 1889; Smith, *Chickamauga Memorial*, 19–21; CMA, *Proceedings at Chattanooga*, 7, 15–20. For the most comprehensive account of the creation of Chickamauga and Chattanooga National Military Park, see Smith, *Chickamauga Memorial*. For an equally compelling and thorough account of the first five national military parks, see Smith, *Golden Age*.

70. CMA, *Proceedings at Chattanooga*, 136–41; Smith, *Chickamauga Memorial*, 22.

71. CMA, *Proceedings at Chattanooga*, 136–41.

72. *St. Paul Daily News*, September 21, 1889; *Los Angeles Times*, September 21, 1889; *Daily Inter Ocean* (Chicago), September 21, 1889; CMA, *Proceedings at Chattanooga*, 29–31; Smith, *Chickamauga Memorial*, 20.

73. CMA, *Proceedings at Chattanooga*, 136–41; Smith, *Chickamauga Memorial*, 22. The enabling legislation, like the battlefield itself, was to be a joint effort among Union

and Confederate veterans. Three commissioners would be appointed by the secretary of war, one a Union veteran of the battle (Brevet Brig. Gen. Joseph S. Fullerton) who would also serve as chairman of the commission, one a Confederate veteran of the battle (Alexander P. Stewart), and finally a Union veteran still on active duty (Capt. Sanford C. Kellogg). Boynton, who had precipitated the whole idea, would serve as the commission's historian and secretary.

74. Foster, *Ghosts*, 104–12; Davies, *Patriotism on Parade*, 40–41; Blight, *Race and Reunion*, 272; Pencak, *Encyclopedia of the Veteran in America*, 1:136.

75. *CV* 1 (December 1893): 353. Initially, there were several competing publications, including the *Confederate War Journal Illustrated*, edited by Marcus J. Wright and Ben LaBree, and endorsed by John B. Gordon as the most important publication of its kind. As historian John A. Simpson points out, the *War Journal* differed from the *CV* by publishing only contemporary accounts of the Civil War rather than post-bellum narratives. When the *War Journal* went out of business in less than two years, LaBree started another monthly of a similar format called the *Lost Cause*. Becoming the official organ of the UCV was no easy task for Cunningham, in large part because of personal disputes with Gordon (Simpson, *S. A. Cunningham*, 90–95).

76. Simpson, *S. A. Cunningham*, 95–100, 159; Foster, *Ghosts*, 106, 108; Davies, *Patriotism on Parade*, 112. Simpson points out that circulation for the *CV* peaked in 1902, but it "sustained itself about the twenty-thousand mark for many years." Foster notes that the Sons were horrified that the abbreviation USCV might be confused with "United States Colored Volunteers" and changed their name.

77. *Daily Inter Ocean* (Chicago), May 27 and 29, 1890; *Bismarck Daily Tribune*, May 28, 1890; Wilson, "Monument Avenue, Richmond," 105. William Blair notes that "it is likely that a majority of white Americans believed . . . that there was nothing to be concerned about." Instead, "white criticism came primarily from Republican newspapers" (Blair, *Cities of the Dead*, 155–57).

78. *National Tribune* (Washington. D.C.), June 5, 1890.

79. *New York Times*, May 30, 1890; Foster, *Ghosts*, 100–101; Blight, *Race and Reunion*, 267–69; Savage, *Standing Soldiers*, 150–51; Wilson, "Monument Avenue, Richmond," 105.

80. Ex-Confederates from Maryland and Virginia participated in the procession at the dedication of Grant's Monument on April 27, 1897. For an excellent account of the creation of Grant's Monument, popularly known as Grant's Tomb, see Waugh, *Grant*, 262–301.

81. *Richmond Planet*, May 3, 1890.

82. *New York Times*, April 10, 12, 13, 1890; Blair, *Cities of the Dead*, 158–59.

83. See, for example, "Address of Asa B. Isham," MOLLUS, Ohio Commandery, *Sketches of War History 1861–1865*, 2:215, 232.

84. *Grand Army Record* 5 (December 1889): 4, in Davies, *Patriotism on Parade*, 254.

85. *National Tribune* (Washington, D.C.), December 19, 1889; *New York Times*, August 9, 1890. The court-martial revolved around Gray's attempts to "make the recalcitrant members of his command make amends." When they refused to do so, he "chartered nine colored posts . . . and said that if they (his opponents) would not parade in

the Davis procession they would be made to walk side by side with the negroes." General Alger, commander-in-chief of the GAR, disapproved the sentence of the court-martial in August 1890.

86. *National Tribune* (Washington, D.C.), December 12, 1889; January 9, 16, February 27, 1890. Davis was initially interred in New Orleans, but in 1893 his remains were disinterred and reburied in Richmond's Hollywood Cemetery. Historian Donald E. Collins notes that most of the non-southern press printed news of Davis's death objectively and without evident bias (Collins, *Death and Resurrection of Jefferson Davis*, 55–56).

87. George M. Finch, "In the Beginning," read on October 1, 1884, in MOLLUS, Ohio Commandery, *Sketches of War History 1861–1865*, 1:29.

88. New York Monuments Commission, *Final Report on the Battlefield of Gettysburg*, 2:521.

89. GAR, Dept. of Minnesota, *Journal of Proceedings of the Twelfth Annual Encampment* (1892), 236.

90. McConnell, *Glorious Contentment*, 224–26; *Morning Oregonian* (Portland), October 11, 1894.

91. GAR, *Journal of the Twenty-ninth Encampment of the GAR, Louisville, KY*, 1895, 422.

92. Under the rubric of education, GAR posts embarked on an effort to instill their values in the next generation through textbook campaigns, calls for displaying the American flag over every public school house, and patriotic instruction through military drills in schools (McConnell, *Glorious Contentment*, chap. 7). For a discussion of the southern textbook debate, see McPherson, "Long-Legged Yankee Lies."

93. *Irish World and American Industrial Liberator* (New York), February 17, 1894; McConnell, *Glorious Contentment*, 225–26; GAR, *Journal of the Twenty-ninth Encampment of the GAR, Louisville, KY*, 1895, 422.

94. Christian, *Confederate Cause*, 4.

95. Dawson, *Our Women in the War*, 5.

96. Davies, *Patriotism on Parade*, 234–35.

97. Lumpkin, *Making of a Southerner*, 111–13.

98. Christian, *Confederate Cause*, 13, 25. Christian was quoting British historian Percy Greg.

99. *Unveiling and Dedication of Monument to Hood's Texas Brigade*, 33.

100. Lafayette McLaws to Andrew Jackson McBride, July 3, 1895, A. J. McBride Papers Atlanta History Center. Transcript courtesy of Keith Bohannon.

101. Beard, *Address of Hon. John S. Beard of Pensacola*.

102. *Ladies Home Journal* reprinted in "The Heart of America," *CV* 3 (December 1895): 354–55.

103. Silber, *Romance of Reunion*, 93–95, 109–20. Silber explains that the marriage metaphor was not nearly as apolitical as novels and plays suggested. Rather, it implied that the masculine North had tamed and subdued the feminine South.

104. The 1880 presidential election pitted two former Union generals against each other—James A. Garfield as the Republican candidate and Winfield Scott Hancock as the Democratic candidate. A hero in the South because of his short tenure as com-

mander of the Fifth Military District during Reconstruction (from which he was ousted), every state of the former Confederacy voted for the one-time Army of the Potomac general. For more on Hancock and the election, see Taylor, "General Hancock: Soldier of the Gilded Age," 187–96; Millard, *Destiny of the Republic*, 57–62.

105. Silber, *Romance of Reunion*, 99.

106. Goodwyn, *Democratic Promise*, 259.

107. For more on the Populist Party see Goodwyn, *Democratic Promise*, and Kazin, *Populist Persuasion*. Blight argues that Populism was "hostile to the Lost Cause tradition" in part because it "brought blacks into political life more vigorously than at any time since radical Reconstruction" (Blight, *Race and Reunion*, 294).

108. *New York Times*, October 12, 1896. For the argument that McKinley's 1896 campaign marshaled a reconciliationist memory of the war, see Kelly, "Election of 1896." Rather than forgetting the war, Kelly argues that McKinley's campaign reminded voters of the perils of sectional (this time the South and West united against the Northeast) and class divisions that would erupt if the Democratic/Populist candidate William Jennings Bryan were elected. I do not agree, however, with Kelly's contention that this marked the end of the bloody shirt. Quite the contrary, I would argue that the memory of the war continued to be invoked to garner Union veterans' vote. The message might have evolved to focus on the threats of labor unrest and Bryan's silver coinage (whereby pensions would be devalued), but the strategy of inducing soldiers to "vote as they shot" had not.

109. Marten, *Sing Not War*, 271; Chalker, "Fitzgerald," 397–405; *New York Times*, April 20, 1895; *News and Observer* (Raleigh, N.C.), April 20, 1895; *Macon Telegraph*, November 9, 1895; *Washington Post*, January 29 and March 29, 1896; *Salt Lake Semi-Weekly Tribune*, March 24, 1896; *Atchison (Kans.) Daily Globe*, May 5 and June 11, 1896.

110. Marten, *Sing Not War*, 271; Chalker, "Fitzgerald," 404.

111. *Blue and Gray*, March 1894; Marten, *Sing Not War*, 273.

112. *Washington Post*, June 4, 1894.

113. *SHSP* 22:336–80; *Washington Post*, May 31, 1894.

114. *Milwaukee Sentinel*, May 31, 1894; *North American*, May 31, 1894; *Washington Post*, June 1 and 5, 1894.

115. *Galveston Daily News*, May 31, 1894; *News-Observer-Chronicle* (Raleigh, N.C.), June 1, 1894; *Atlanta Journal* reprinted in the *Washington Post*, June 5, 1894.

116. Letter from Commander Columbia Post, No. 706, Dept. of Illinois, GAR, Chicago to Lee Camp, October 11, 1892, Lee Camp Papers, VHS.

117. J. G. Everest, Chairman of Com., Columbia Post, No. 706, Dept. of Illinois, GAR, Chicago, June 14, 1894, to Commander of R. E. Lee Camp, Lee Camp Papers, VHS.

118. *Chicago Daily Tribune*, June 14 and 29, 1894; *Washington Post*, June 27, 1894.

119. *SHSP* 22:383–86. The debate would not end with the Lee Camp's response. Rather, the Columbia Post responded in kind, again defending the Union cause and going so far as to ask the Confederate veterans to repudiate their cause if they were indeed loyal to the Union.

120. *Los Angeles Times*, September 15, 1895; *Atlanta Constitution*, September 17, 1895.

121. *Los Angeles Times*, September 20, 1895; Smith, *Golden Age*, 66–67; Smith, *Chickamauga Memorial*, 53–57.

122. Osborne, "Letters of Senator Edward Cary Walthall to Robert W. Banks," 191 (Walthall [ex-Confederate General, Army of Tennessee] to Robert W. Banks [ex-Confederate regimental adjutant and staff officer to Walthall], Grenada, Miss., September 4, 1895). Thanks to Keith Bohannon for bringing this letter to my attention.

123. Boynton, *Dedication*, 27–28.

124. *Los Angeles Times*, September 19 and 20, 1895.

125. Boynton, *Dedication*, 304.

126. Boynton, *Dedication*, 89.

127. *New York Times*, September 20, 1895.

128. Stewart quoted in Paige and Greene, *Administrative History*, 38 (Stewart to Fullerton, July 17, 1894, Ezra A. Carman Papers, Manuscript Division, New York Public Library); Smith, *Chickamauga Memorial*, 72.

129. *New York Times*, September 21, 1895; *San Francisco Call*, September 21, 1895; Boynton, *Dedication*, 181–83; LaFantasie, *Gettysburg Requiem*, 246–47.

130. *CV* 3, no. 10 (October 1895): 292–93.

131. *New York Tribune*, July 21, 1900; *Omaha Daily Bee*, July 20, 1900. Several Confederate associations subsequently protested Gordon's appearance at the national GAR encampment later that summer.

132. Smith, *Golden Age*, 36–37, 48, 211. The momentum to preserve the heroic fields continued, with bills for seventeen proposed parks reaching Congress by 1904. But as Timothy Smith points out, no new Civil War parks were established until the mid-1920s.

133. *Unveiling and Dedication of Monument to Hood's Texas Brigade*, 176–77.

134. For a newspaper article discussing this, see "Joint Reunion of Confederate and Federal Veterans Planned," *St. Louis Republic*, May 27, 1903.

135. Gallagher, "Introduction," *Annals of War*, xii.

136. Historian Nina Silber argues that northern middle-class men (nonveterans) "increasingly set the dominant tone on the reunion question" and "their voices gradually drowned out the protests and alternative visions" offered by groups like the GAR who were "outside the mainstream of reconciliationist politics" (Silber, *Romance of Reunion*, 11, 59–61, 98).

137. In 1885 there were 1,449,000 Union veterans in civilian life. By 1900, that number had decreased to 1,000,000 (Skocpol, *Protecting Soldiers and Mothers*, 109). The number of Confederate veterans in civilian life is more difficult to determine, although James Marten notes that in 1893 more than 27,000 Confederate veterans were living in state soldiers' homes or receiving state pensions (Marten, *Sing Not War*, 17).

CHAPTER 7

1. *New York Times*, September 21, 1895.

2. *New York Times*, September 21, 1895; Boynton, *Dedication*, 181–83; LaFantasie, *Gettysburg Requiem*, 246–47.

3. Boynton, *Dedication*, 239–40. Patrick Kelly observes that Altgeld was one of the

chief targets of the Republican campaign in 1896. Republicans linked him closely to anarchy and class warfare, especially because he had pardoned the Haymarket anarchists and challenged the legality of President Cleveland's actions during the 1894 Pullman Strike (Kelly, "Election of 1896," 267).

4. *New York Times*, September 20, 1895; Boynton, *Dedication*, 36.

5. Boynton, *Dedication*, 239.

6. Boynton, *Dedication*, 123.

7. Varon, *Disunion!*.

8. On the era of segregation, see Ayers, *Promise*, 132–59; Woodward, *Strange Career of Jim Crow*; Hale, *Making Whiteness*; Gilmore, *Gender and Jim Crow*; Kantrowitz, *Ben Tillman*. Lynching was not restricted to the states of the former Confederacy during this period. For example, in 1897, a mob in Urbana, Ohio, lynched a black man named Charles Mitchell for allegedly assaulting a white woman (Blight, "Shaw Memorial," in Blatt et al., *Hope and Glory*, 89).

9. Blight, *Race and Reunion*, 2; Fellman, *Making of Robert E. Lee*, quotation p. 304; Linenthal, *Sacred Ground*, 91–93; Foster, *Ghosts*, 194; McConnell, *Glorious Contentment*, 181; Shaffer, *After the Glory*, 169; Fahs, "Feminized Civil War," 1487; Clark, *Defining Moments*, 193; O'Leary, *To Die For*, 29–68; Madison, "Civil War Memories," 198–230; Schwalm, *Emancipation's Diaspora*, 219, 255. For example, Blight notes, "By 1897 the sectional reunion was virtually complete, founded on a racial apartheid that was becoming the law and practice of the land" (Blight, "Shaw Memorial," in Blatt et al., *Hope and Glory*, 87).

10. Bederman, *Manliness and Civilization*; Russet, *Sexual Science*.

11. Foner, *Reconstruction*; Richardson, *West from Appomattox*; Richardson, *Death of Reconstruction*.

12. *Michigan at Gettysburg*, 29–39.

13. *Reunion and Dedication of the Monument at Arlington*.

14. "A War Incident Recalled—the Lees," *Grand Army Sentinel* 2 (May 20, 1886): 324, in Davies, *Patriotism on Parade*, 254–55.

15. Pennsylvania Antietam Battlefield Memorial Commission, *Pennsylvania at Antietam*, 157. This was from a speech by Dr. S. M. Whistler of the 130th Pennsylvania at monument dedication in 1906.

16. Blight, *Race and Reunion*, 65. David Blight argues, conversely, that "reconciliationist practices overtook the emancipationist legacy of the Civil War." A substantial number of scholars have agreed with Blight on this point. For those who have disagreed, arguing that Union soldiers did not forget emancipation, see Gallagher, *Union War*; Gannon, *Won Cause*; Waugh, *Grant*; Hunt, *Good Men*; Harris, "Across the Bloody Chasm"; Madison, "Civil War Memories," 221–23.

17. *Chicago Daily*, May 31, 1895. Hanes did observe that U.S. soldiers had fought to save the Union, but he believed that the moral question of slavery had been just as much of a factor.

18. New York State Monuments Commission, *Final Report on the Battlefield of Gettysburg*, 1:240.

19. *Report of the Unveiling*, 19.

20. Laney Souvenir Company, *Laney's Gettysburg Battlefield*.

21. Smith et al., *Addresses Delivered*, 20.

22. Smith et al., *Addresses Delivered*, 27. Thanks to Mark Johnson for the research he did in finding these Antietam speeches.

23. Indiana Commission, *Indiana at Antietam*, 26.

24. Pennsylvania Antietam Battlefield Memorial Commission, *Pennsylvania at Antietam*, 157.

25. These attitudes embodied what Robert Penn Warren described as the "Treasury of Virtue" (Warren, *Legacy of the Civil War*, 59–66).

26. Mowris, *History of the One Hundred and Seventeenth Regiment*, 205–6.

27. H. G. Hunter to Officers and members of the Lee Camp, June 25, 1891, Lee Camp Collection, VHS.

28. *Western Christian Advocate*, March 9, 1881; Millard, *Destiny of the Republic*, 78–79.

29. Jeffrey, *Abolitionists Remember*, 155–56, 163; Gardner, *Blood and Irony*, editor's quotation p. 81; Henry Goddard Thomas, "Colored Troops at Petersburg," *Century* 34 (1887): 777–82.

30. "Union Sentiment among Confederate Veterans," *Century* 34 (1887): 309; James Lane Allen, "Mrs. Stowe's 'Uncle Tom' at Home in Kentucky," *Century* 34 (1887): 855–67.

31. Gilder quoted in Gardner, *Blood and Irony*, 81.

32. Larry Gara notes that northerners' distinction between slavery and the slave power "helps explain how Americans could repress a rebellion led by a slave oligarchy and at the same time perpetuate a racist bias" (Gara, "Slavery and the Slave Power," 6).

33. Powell, *Colored Soldier*, 10–11. Powell noted that he earnestly protested presenting a paper on this topic.

34. Henry Goddard Thomas, "Colored Troops at Petersburg," *Century* 34 (1887): 778, 781; Gannon, *Won Cause*, 8. Historian Robert Hunt notes that some white U.S. veterans believed that the USCT aroused too much vitriol among Confederate soldiers, making combat more difficult than it might have been (Hunt, *Good Men*, 167n33).

35. *Roanoke Times*, June 30, 1893; *North American* (Philadelphia), July 3, 1893.

36. *Southern Argus* (Baxter Springs, Kans.), September 17, 1891.

37. *Guthrie Daily Leader*, October 11, 1895.

38. Gannon, *Won Cause*, 28–34, quotations pp. 29, 30.

39. For historians who focus the exclusion of black comrades and posts from the southern GAR, see Davies, *Patriotism*, 267–69; McConnell, *Glorious Contentment*, 213–17; and Shaffer, *After the Glory*, 143–55. Shaffer notes that the Lower South proved more resistant to black and integrated posts than did the Upper South.

40. Quoted in Gannon, *Won Cause*, 32,

41. David Blight states emphatically that "there is no evidence that a black veteran attended the festivities" (Blight, *Race and Reunion*, 206). The absence of USCT veterans simply cannot be confirmed. African American newspapers covering the event included the *Savannah Tribune* (August 31, 1895) and the Indianapolis *Freeman* (September 28, 1895).

42. *News-Herald* (Hillsboro, Ohio), September 26, 1895; *Zion's Herald*, October 2, 1895. According to the Indianapolis *Freeman*, September 28, 1895, "no colored troops" were represented in the grand procession. But neither did many other veterans in atten-

dance, both white Union veterans and Confederate veterans, march in the procession. Instead, the procession was composed of regular U.S. troops (represented by the 17th U.S. Infantry) and the state guards of Ohio, Tennessee, and Georgia.

43. As historian Barbara Gannon has argued, not only did the GAR welcome black veterans into the association during the height of segregation, but also its records rarely identified the racial makeup of a post (Gannon, *Won Cause*, 38, 85–98, 100, 105, 107–8, 114, 207). Chattanooga's "Chickamauga" Post No. 22 (founded September 1884) was an all-black post. I have been unable to find any response by this or any other black GAR post to the proceedings.

44. *National Tribune* (Washington, D.C.), September 19, 1895. This quotation was reprinted in newspapers from Kansas to Washington State.

45. Terrill, *Campaign of the Fourteenth Regiment New Jersey Volunteers*, 131–32.

46. MOLLUS, Minnesota Commandery, "Glimpses of the Nation's Struggle," in *Papers Read Before the Minnesota Commandery*, 3:377.

47. "School Histories in the South," *CV* 7 (November 1899): 500–509. By blaming historians rather than the GAR (who was itself encouraging the publication of such texts), Confederate veterans might still join hands with their former foes over the bloody chasm.

48. "Justice to the South—True History," *CV* 1 (November 1893): 323.

49. Foster, *Ghosts*, 118–19; Gallagher and Nolan, *Myth of the Lost Cause*, 15, 96; Harris, "Across the Bloody Chasm," 207–10; "Speech of Hon. John H. Reagan," *CV* 5 (July 1897): 343–44.

50. Thomas Rosser, 1901 speech, Papers of Thomas Lafayette Rosser Jr. and the Rosser and Gordon Families, UVA.

51. John S. Mosby to Judge Reuben Page, June 11, 1902, Papers of John Singleton Mosby, UVA.

52. First Kentucky Brigade, C.S.A.: Scrapbook, 1882–1925, KHS. Caldwell did note that while slavery was a direct cause of the war, "a corollary of the main proposition involved in the mighty struggle . . . [was] the fight of local self-government."

53. Christian, *Confederate Cause*.

54. Davis, *Rise and Fall*.

55. As discussed in chapter 1, many nonslaveholders reaped the benefits of living in a slave society.

56. Beard, *Address of Hon. John S. Beard of Pensacola*; *SHSP* 22:336–80; *Washington Post*, May 31, 1894.

57. "School Histories in the South," *CV* 7 (November 1899): 500–509.

58. *Richmond Dispatch*, February 23, 1896; *In Memoriam Sempiternam*, 45.

59. Gallagher and Nolan, *Myth of the Lost Cause*, 15–16, 96; Stonebraker, *Rebel of '61*, 7, quotation by Bradley T. Johnson.

60. Johnson, *Address Delivered*, 12–13; *Richmond Times-Dispatch*, February 23, 1896.

61. Foster, *Ghosts*, 23; Baker, *What Reconstruction Meant*, 82; *The Century* 2 (June 1887), 309.

62. First Kentucky Brigade, C.S.A.: Scrapbook, 1882–1925, KHS.

63. Jeffrey, *Abolitionists Remember*, 221.

64. *Annual Reunion of Pegram Battalion Association* (1886), 32.

65. Gallagher and Nolan, *Myth of the Lost Cause*, 14; Wilson, *Baptized in Blood*, 4, 68, 102; Hillyer, "Relics of Reconciliation," 50.

66. *CV* 1 (May 1893): 136.

67. Hale, *Making Whiteness*, 43–84; Blight, *Race and Reunion*, 216–30; Savage, *Standing Soldiers*, 155–57; "Monuments at Fort Mill, S.C.," *CV* 7 (May 1899): 209–11.

68. Periodical from 1880 quoted in Wilson, *Baptized in Blood*, 103; Savage, *Standing Soldiers*, 155–57.

69. Shaffer, *After the Glory*, 175–76; Jordan, *Black Confederates*, 185–200. It is impossible to determine precisely how many of these men accompanied the rebel armies, but it was no doubt a small minority compared to the 180,000 black men who served in the USCT. For examples of Confederates inviting black men to veterans' reunions, see *Weekly Pelican* (New Orleans), June 11, 1887; *Wichita Eagle*, September 5, 1889. For an account of slaves and freedmen being coerced into labor for the Confederacy during the war, see Brasher, *Peninsula Campaign*.

70. In recent decades, there has been a rise in the popular notion that thousands of African American soldiers voluntarily fought in the Confederate armies. On this topic, see Blight, "Shaw Memorial in the Landscape of Civil War Memory," in Blatt et al., *Hope and Glory*, 80; Levine, *Confederate Emancipation*, 13.

71. For more on this, see chapter 9.

72. Silber, *Romance of Reunion*, 124, 139–40; Blight, *Race and Reunion*, 211–54; Janney, "'One of the Best Loved'"; McElya, *Clinging to Mammy*. "Much of the emotional impact of this literature was due to the fact that black voices narrated to white audiences stories of courtships, of Blue-Gray fraternalism, of reconciliation itself." Through such literature, "a civil war among whites," Blight notes, "is mended by the wit, wisdom, and sacred memories of faithful blacks" (Blight, *Race and Reunion*, 224).

73. For more on the complicated and contradictory nature of humans, see Dew, *Apostles of Disunion*, 81.

74. Harris, "Across the Bloody Chasm," 185.

75. Blair, *Cities of the Dead*, 134–36. For an excellent discussion of race and Union Memorial Days, see Gannon, *Won Cause*, 72–81.

76. *Daily Inter Ocean* (Chicago), September 23, 1880; *St. Louis Globe-Democrat*, June 20, 1884. The Republican Party clubs were known as Garfield and Arthur Clubs.

77. *St. Louis Globe-Democrat*, June 20, 1884.

78. Quoted in Baker, *What Reconstruction Meant*, 77.

79. *New York Times*, September 23, 1885.

80. Clark, *Defining Moments*, 5, 11, 167–69, 196; Shaffer, *After the Glory*, 173. For an excellent account of the divisions within black memory and the changes over time, see Clark, *Defining Moments*, chaps. 4 and 5.

81. *Richmond Planet*, October 18, 1890. Williams observed that he had been born in 1856.

82. *Richmond Planet*, October 11, 1890. For a thorough account of the planning and convention, see Blair, *Cities of the Dead*, 161–67.

83. *Richmond Planet*, October 11 and 18, 1890; Blair, *Cities of the Dead*, 164–65.

84. *Richmond Dispatch*, October 17, 1890; *Richmond Planet*, October 18, 1890; Blair, *Cities of the Dead*, 166.

85. *New York Times*, October 14, 1890; *Richmond Dispatch*, October 18, 1890; *Richmond Planet*, October 11 and 18, 1890; Blair, *Cities of the Dead*, 163, 166.

86. Blair, *Cities of the Dead*, 166–67; *Appeal* (St. Paul, Minn.), January 3, 1891; *Richmond Dispatch*, January 2 and 3, 1891; *Washington Bee*, December 27, 1890; *Fort Worth Daily Gazette*, December 6, 1890.

87. Quoted in Blair, *Cities of the Dead*, 166–67.

88. Blair, *Cities of the Dead*, 167–68.

89. *Richmond Planet*, December 20, 1890.

90. Blair, *Cities of the Dead*, 168.

91. Gannon, *Won Cause*, 28–34; *Fort Worth Gazette*, October 20, 1895.

92. *Wichita Eagle*, January 11, 1890.

93. *New York Sun*, August 26, 1898.

94. *National Tribune* (Washington, D.C.), August 11, 1887; *Washington Bee*, August 6, 1887.

95. *Kansas City Journal*, June 1, 1897. For more on the thirty-two-year effort to create the monument, see Richardson, "Taken from Life"; Greenthal, "Augustus Saint-Gaudens and the Shaw Memorial"; and Brown, "Reconstructing Boston," in Blatt et al., *Hope and Glory*, 94–95, 116–29, 146–51.

96. Blight, *Race and Reunion*, 338–44; Whitfield, "Sacred in History and Art," 3–27; *New York Times*, June 1, 1897; *Richmond Planet*, June 5, 1897; Savage, *Standing Soldiers*, 193–97; James Barnes, "Shaw Memorial," *Harper's Weekly*, May 29, 1897.

97. *New York Times*, June 1, 1897; Washington, *Up from Slavery*, 250.

98. Brown, "Reconstructing Boston," in Blatt et al., *Hope and Glory*, 151–52. The monument committee initially invited a veteran, Col. Thomas Livermore, to deliver the day's speech. At the request of the Shaw family, James was selected after Livermore declined. Historian Thomas J. Brown notes that James's absence from the war not only weighed on him, but it remained a matter of concern for the regiment's surviving officers. The veterans ultimately chose Henry Lee Higginson to deliver an address the evening before the dedication.

99. James, *Memories and Studies*, 41, 43, 45, 57. For more on James's oration, see Savage, *Standing Soldiers*, 204–7.

100. Blight, *Race and Reunion*, 342–43; Whitfield, "Sacred in History," 13–15; *New York Times*, June 1, 1897; *Richmond Planet*, June 5, 1897; Washington, "A Speech at the Unveiling of the Robert Gould Shaw Memorial," May 31, 1897, in Harlan, *Papers of Booker T. Washington*, 4:286 (accessed via http://www.historycooperative.org/btw/volumes.html); Washington, *Up From Slavery*, 253. I have been unable to determine the composition of the audience.

101. Blatt et al., *Hope and Glory*, 28–30, 89, 111–14, 177–78, Carney quoted pp. 112–14; *Richmond Planet*, May 31, 1890; *Alexandria Gazette*, May 15, 1895. In the 1920s, members of the WRC, GAR, and Spanish-American War veterans erected a memorial to Carney in Norfolk, Virginia (Gannon, *Won Cause*, 76).

102. Washington, "A Speech at the Unveiling of the Robert Gould Shaw Memorial,"

May 31, 1897, in Harlan, *Papers of Booker T. Washington*, 4:287–88. For another reference to the war having not been in vain, see Washington, "An Article in *Leslie's Weekly Illustrated*," June 17, 1897, in Harlan, *Papers of Booker T. Washington*, 4:302.

103. Harlan, *Papers of Booker T. Washington*, 4:287; Blight, *Race and Reunion*, 343.

104. Clark, *Defining Moments*, quotation p. 149; *Washington Bee*, August 6, 1887. For an example of calls for colored widows' pensions, see the *Washington Bee*, April 20, 1889.

105. Clark, *Defining Moments*, 149.

106. Quoted in Savage, *Standing Soldiers*, 152.

107. *Richmond Planet*, May 31, 1890.

108. *New York Age, State Capital* (Springfield, Ill.), and *National Home Protector* (Baltimore) all quoted in *Richmond Planet*, June 7 and 14, 1890.

109. *Daily Inter Ocean* (Chicago), May 5, 1893.

110. *Washington Bee*, May 31, 1890.

111. *Richmond Planet*, June 14, 1890. For a discussion of black laborers who erected the monument, see Savage, *Standing Soldiers*, 153.

112. *New York Times*, May 30, 1890.

113. For more on the "faithful slave," see Hale, *Making Whiteness*, 97–119; McElya, *Clinging to Mammy*.

114. Quotations from Clark, *Defining Moments*, 179–81.

115. Schwalm, *Emancipation's Diaspora*, 222–24. Kathleen Ann Clark points out that despite the difference in approach to slavery, "the majority of African American spokespersons were united in their characterization of slavery as a time of unparalleled human cruelty and oppression — in marked contrast to the romanticized portrayals increasingly set forth by whites" (Clark, *Defining Moments*, 181).

116. Jefferson Manly Falkner to Booker T. Washington, October 29, 1902, in Harlan, *Papers of Booker T. Washington*, 6:563–64. Falkner noted that he would follow Washington's request and "avoid publicity" of the $100 donation, though he believed that Washington's "generosity and good will" should be shared.

117. Clark, *Defining Moments*, 150–54, 182; *New York Evangelist*, June 16, 1887. Vance served two terms as governor of North Carolina, first during the war (1862–65) and then after Reconstruction (1877–79). For an account by an African American leader that Emancipation Days served as "a dangerous source of race antagonism," see Clark, *Defining Moments*, 183. For one such incident, see the dispute between the National Emancipation Association and the mayor of Warrenton, Virginia, over the Washington Zouaves attending Emancipation Day in September 1899: *New York Times*, September 21, 1899; *Richmond Times*, September 17 and 20, 1899; *New York Sun*, September 19, 1899; *Evening Times* (Washington, D.C.), September 16, 1899; *Clark Courier* (Berryville, Va.), September 27, 1899.

118. Washington, "An Address at the National Peace Jubilee," October 16, 1898, in Harlan, *Papers of Booker T. Washington*, 4:491.

119. Clark, *Defining Moments*, 184.

120. Clark, *Defining Moments*, 183.

121. Gannon, *Won Cause*, 36.

122. *Alexandria Gazette*, May 15 and 17, 1895; *Daily Public Ledger* (Maysville, Ky.),

May 9, 1895. Numerous white GAR posts, including the entire Department of Nebraska, likewise protested the monument.

123. Blight, *Frederick Douglass' Civil War*, 217–18.

124. This was a phrase coined by John Hay.

125. Lears, *Rebirth of a Nation*, 207; Traxel, *1898*, 121; Blight, *Race and Reunion*, 346.

126. Records of the Adjutant General's Office (hereafter RG 94), entry 13, NARA contains 11 boxes of letters from individuals, many of them Union or Confederate veterans, offering their service during the Spanish-American War. One typical letter from R. B. Foster of New Castle, Virginia, reads: "I know what war means, and as I once fought against the grand old U.S. flag I now desire to offer my services to you with the hope that you may give me a chance to have the honor of protecting . . . the flag against which I fought" (R. B. Foster to Secretary of War, April 4, 1898, RG 94 e. 13, Box 181, NARA).

127. Jonathan W. Gee to General Alger, Secretary of War, April 4, 1898, RG 94 e. 13, Box 181, NARA.

128. Benjamin K. Keyser to President McKinley, April 2, 1898, RG 94, e. 13 Box 181, NARA. Emphasis in original.

129. Quoted in Foster, *Ghosts*, 146.

130. *CV* 7 (July 1898): 304.

131. Traxel, *1898*, 164.

132. For historians who argue that the Spanish-American War was the most important factor in cementing reconciliation, see Trask, *War with Spain*; Silber, *Romance of Reunion*; Pressly, *Americans Interpret Their Civil War*, 137; Lears, *Rebirth of a Nation*; Marvel, *Lee's Last Retreat*, 198; Krowl, "'In the Spirit of Fraternity,'" 175.

133. William A. Blair notes that support for the war among white southerners was at best mixed. The chance to prove their loyalty and the potential for increased cotton markets helped convinced them otherwise (Blair, *Cities of the Dead*, 180).

134. Other well-known Confederates who joined the U.S. Army during the Spanish-American War included William C. Oates and John S. Mosby.

135. For the best treatment of the South as feminized by defeat, see Silber, *Romance of Reunion*.

136. Traxel, *1898*, 122, 144; Silber, *Romance of Reunion*, 178–79; *Butte Weekly Miner* (Mont.), July 7, 1898.

137. "Patriotism in the South," *CV* 6 (July 1898): 325.

138. "Southern History," *CV* 7 (June 1899): 246.

139. For discussion of the dual nature of nationalism and identity, see Potter, "Historian's Use of Nationalism," 924–50.

140. Gaines Foster argues that the Spanish-American War helped vindicate the South and assure northern respect (Foster, *Ghosts*, 145–49). For a discussion of how the war made northerners accept white southern manliness, see Silber, *Romance of Reunion*, 178; Pettegrew, "Soldier's Faith," 61–62.

141. *Iowa State Bystander*, quoted in Blight, *Race and Reunion*, 348.

142. *Richmond Planet*, May 7, 1898; Ayers, *Promise*, 328.

143. Not all white southerners felt this way. The *Harrisonburg Spirit* (Virginia) supported not only African American regiments, but also black officers. Mitchell pointed out that "we have thousands of liberal minded white people in Virginian who are

friendly to our people and will uphold them in any legitimate effort for their material advancement" (*Richmond Planet*, June 25, 1898).

144. *Richmond Planet*, July 16, 1898.

145. *Outlook*, July 2, 1898. For an assessment of Higginson's gradual disillusionment with other abolitionists, military leaders, and the federal government, see Poole, "Memory and the Abolitionist Heritage."

146. Ayers, *Promise*, 329–30.

147. *New York Sun*, July 4, 1898; Traxel, *1898*, 209–10. Traxel points out that many newspapers rang with white supremacist language. The *New York Tribune*, for example, noted that the conduct of black soldiers showed that "their African nature has not been entirely eliminated by generations of civilization."

148. Washington, "An Address at the National Peace Jubilee," October 16, 1898, in Harlan, *Papers of Booker T. Washington*, 4:490–92; Washington, *Up from Slavery*, 254–55; *New York Times*, October 20, 1898; *New York Evangelist*, October 20, 1898. Harlan notes that a slightly different version of the speech appeared in Washington's 1901 *Story of My Life and Work* (Harlan, *Papers of Booker T. Washington*, 4:492).

149. Blight, *Race and Reunion*, 324–27, 331. Blight argues that Washington's "brand of reconciliation" as delivered in the Atlanta Compromise Speech was "on Southern terms." It was "a complex mixture of purposeful forgetting, a theory of 'race-development' . . . and interracial cooperation" (quotation p. 331).

150. See for example "New Colored Soldier," *The Independent*, June 16, 1898; Henry Ossian Flipper to Booker T. Washington, December 12, 1898, in Harlan, *Papers of Booker T. Washington*, 4:529.

151. Douglass quoted in Blight, *Race and Reunion*, 349.

152. Silber, *Race and Reunion*, 136–37. For a discussion of white supremacy and the Chinese Exclusion Act of 1882, see Lears, *Rebirth of a Nation*, 98–99, 110–16. According to Anglo-Saxonism, white peoples had already proven themselves capable of self-government and democracy. Any nonwhite group, whether black, Filipino, Chinese, or Native American, was understood to be unqualified and ill suited to vote, hold elected office, or, in the instance of the Chinese, even to become citizens.

153. Bederman, *Manliness and Civilization*; Painter, *Standing at Armageddon*, 149–56; Lears, *Rebirth*, 92–96.

154. For examples of white southerners worried about the instituting reconstruction governments abroad, see Ayers, *Promise*, 333.

155. *New York Times*, May 13, 1899; "Southern History," *CV* 7 (June 1899): 248.

156. Blair observes that some white southerners held an opposing view: they did not want the United States to "assume the role of overseas carpetbaggers" (Blair, *Cities of the Dead*, 180).

157. Quoted in Blight, *Race and Reunion*, 352.

158. "Union Soldier's Tribute," *CV* 7 (June 1899): 272.

159. "Southern History," *CV* 7 (June 1899): 246.

160. Historian William A. Blair argues that McKinley's desire for three things led to this proclamation: "reconciliation of the sectional heart, consolidation of southern support for overseas expansion, and reclamation of his reputation in racial affairs." Prior to his arrival in Atlanta, the president had visited Tuskegee, where he endorsed the work

of Booker T. Washington (Blair, *Cities of the Dead*, 179–81). For more on white southerners' reluctant support of the war, see Ayers, *Promise*, 328–29, 332–33.

161. *New York Times*, December 15, 1898.

162. *National Tribune* (Washington, D.C.), December 22, 1898. For more outpourings of white southern enthusiasm, see Blair, *Cities of the Dead*, 182–83.

163. *Richmond Times*, December 17, 1898. Representative David de Armond, Democrat of Missouri, stated on December 16, 1898, that the president should extend benefits to maimed and poor Confederates. John Franklin Rixey, Democrat of Virginia, introduced a bill that would open the National Soldiers' Homes to Confederate veterans. Within weeks, Senator Marion Butler, Populist of North Carolina, proposed an amendment to the appropriations bill providing for the payment of pensions to Confederate veterans as well as Union veterans (*New York Times*, January 27, 1899).

164. *National Tribune* (Washington, D.C.), December 29, 1898. For an exception, see letter from George W. Healey of Iowa.

165. *National Tribune* (Washington, D.C.), December 22, 1898. See the *National Tribune*, January 12 and February 2, 1899, for other letters protesting the proposals.

166. *Richmond Dispatch*, January 18, 1899; "Concerning Pensions for Confederates," *CV* 7 (January 1899): 25. Some Confederate Camps did favor pensions and assistance with Confederate graves. The Joseph E. Johnston Confederate Veterans of Dalton, Georgia, for example, observed that accepting federal pensions and care for their graves would be vindication of the southern cause and would eliminate sectional discord (*National Tribune* (Washington, D.C.), April 20, 1899).

167. *New York Times*, May 13, 1899; *Evening Bulletin* (Maysville, Ky.), May 13, 1899; *National Tribune* (Washington, D.C.), May 25, 1899.

168. For the "trial by battle argument," see Nicoletti, "American Civil War as a Trial by Battle," 71–110.

169. *National Tribune* (Washington, D.C.), March 12, 1896. In the North, white and black Unionists continued to attend Memorial Days together in many instances. But the color line became more visible in the South.

170. Baker, *What Reconstruction Meant*, 82. Baker notes that Memorial Day in Mobile, Alabama, had been reserved for whites only in 1892. For subsequent celebrations of Memorial Day in Florence by the Blue and Gray Memorial Association, see *Watchman and Southron* (Sumter, S.C.), June 4, 1902.

171. *Evening Bulletin* (Maysville, Ky.), May 16, 1902; *National Tribune* (Washington, D.C.), May 22, 1902; *Albuquerque Daily Citizen*, May 15, 1902; State Soldiers' and Sailors' Monument—Indianapolis, http://maxkade.iupui.edu/soldiers.html (accessed May 23, 2011). The proposal for the monument had been recommended by wartime governor Oliver P. Morton in 1887. Much of the work had been completed by 1898, but the formal dedication did not occur until 1902. Intended to commemorate Union soldiers, by the monument's dedication state planners had decided it should honor all Hoosier soldiers from the Revolution through the Spanish-American War. There are also four bronze statues of George Rogers Clark, Governor William Henry Harrison, Governor James Whitcomb, and Governor Oliver P. Morton to commemorate the various periods of Indiana history.

172. Madison, "Civil War Memories," 222.

CHAPTER 8

1. *San Francisco Call*, July 22, 1911; *Richmond Times-Dispatch*, July 22, 1911; *Washington Herald*, July 22, 1911.

2. *El Paso Herald*, July 22, 1911; *Crittenden Record-Press* (Marion, Ky.), July 27, 1911. For example, just before the president's address, forty-eight young women—far too young to remember the war—representing the states of the Union clasped hands, formed a circle, and sang an anthem composed especially for the event.

3. Some historians have suggested that women played a special role in reconciliation. See, for example, Morgan, *Women and Patriotism*, 10–12, 20–22, 37; Censer, *Reconstruction*, 244–49; Johnson, "Sallie Chapin," 87–104.

4. *Washington Post*, July 23, 1911.

5. WRC, *Journal of the Twenty-ninth National Convention* (1911), 395–96.

6. Minnesota Vicksburg Monument Commission, *Minnesota in the Campaigns of Vicksburg*.

7. Dawson, *Our Women in the War*.

8. This is not to say that Confederates were not nationalists (see chapter 1). On the contrary, their understanding of the nation was filtered through a domestic lens.

9. Silber, *Gender and the Sectional Conflict*, 74–76, quotation p. 77.

10. Silber, *Gender and the Sectional Conflict*, 83–84; Schwalm, *Emancipation's Diaspora*, 233.

11. Moore, *Women of the War*; Brockett and Vaughn, *Woman's Work in the Civil War*; Schultz, *Women at the Front*, 12; Fahs, "Feminized Civil War," 1461–94.

12. Moore, *Memorial Ceremonies*; Silber, *Gender and the Sectional Conflict*, 83–84, 88; Schwalm, *Emancipation's Diaspora*, 233.

13. Savage, *Standing Soldiers*, 111–12; *Frank Leslie's Illustrated Newspaper*, January 30, 1886; *Washington Post*, September 14, 1895, December 22, 1896, October 5, 1911; Martin, *Confederate Monuments at Gettysburg*. In 1895, the UCV launched a campaign to place a monument to Confederate women on the grounds of every southern state capitol. The goal was only partially realized. Only seven states built such monuments between 1912 and 1926—in part because of women's objections in favor of a commemoration they deemed more appropriate, such as retirement homes, colleges, or scholarship funds (Mills, "Gratitude and Gender Wars: Monuments to Women of the Sixties," 183; Brown, *Public Art of Civil War Commemoration*, 69). A monument to Gettysburg's Civil War women was erected in 2002 in Gettysburg's Evergreen Cemetery. The statue honors Elizabeth Thorn, who helped bury the first ninety-one soldiers from the battle (Virtual Gettysburg, http://www.virtualgettysburg.com/exhibit /monuments/feature.html, accessed May 1, 2008).

14. Johnson, *Campfire and Battle-field*, 533–40.

15. GAR, Dept. of Kansas, *Mother Bickerdyke Day*. In the twentieth century, the monuments built to Union women were almost exclusively memorials to nurses, including the Massachusetts State House memorial to nurses; Mother Bickerdyke in Galesburg, Illinois, 1904; Clara Barton at Antietam National Military Park, 1962; and Mary Sturges, Kansas City, Kansas.

16. Silber, *Gender and the Sectional Conflict*, 13, 20–22, 88.

17. WRC, *Journal of the Second National Convention* (1884), 13.

18. Schultz, *Women at the Front*, 189; "Mrs. M. A. Bickerdyke," Report No. 9 to accompany bill H.R. 700, January 12, 1886, U.S. Serials Set; Silber, *Daughters*, 272–74. Silber observes, "Perhaps the most unfortunate, albeit unintended, consequence of the WRC's priorities was that they contributed to the diminishing place of Union women in American memory" (273).

19. Livermore quoted in Silber, *Gender and the Sectional Conflict*, 84–85.

20. WRC, *Journal of the Second National Convention* (1884).

21. Silber, *Gender and the Sectional Conflict*, 85–86. Silber suggests that because northern veterans focused much of their energy on securing pensions, "northern women may have also had a heightened awareness of suffering among those who either did not receive adequate pensions or did not qualify for them" (87).

22. Marten, *Sing Not War*, 20. Maris Vinovskis estimates that sixty-one percent of southern white men of military age (13–43) in 1860 fought in the Confederate armies. Gary Gallagher suggests this number is conservative at best, arguing that seventy-five to eighty-five percent served (Vinovskis, "Have Social Historians Lost the Civil War?," 40; Gallagher, *Confederate War*, 29).

23. Marten, *Sing Not War*, 19–21, 53, 77, 245–51. For the argument that Union soldiers placed God and country above their obligation to their women, see Silber, *Gender and the Sectional Conflict*, 1–36.

24. *Southern Opinion* (Richmond), July 27, 1867.

25. *Boston Daily Advertiser*, August 20, 1873; *Georgia Weekly Telegraph*, September 2, 1873; *Boston Daily Whig & Courier*, August 22, 1873; *New York Times*, August 25, 1873. For a stern rebuke of Davis's speech, see W. T. Sherman to Col. Thos. T. Munford, August 22, 1873, John W. Daniels Papers, Box 22, UVA.

26. Silber, *Romance of Reunion*. Silber argues that northern men in particular understood southern white women's sectional animosities as based on "nothing but emotion, and therefore lacking in reason and logic" (Silber, *Romance of Reunion*, 50).

27. Here I borrow from Cecilia O'Leary, who argues that the GAR was forced to grapple with "the contradictory impulses of sectional animosity and their ardent passion for national unity" (O'Leary, *To Die For*, 121).

28. Johnson, "Sallie Chapin," 2:87–104, quotation p. 92.

29. For historians who argue that the WCTU played a pivotal role in national reconciliation, see Blum, *Reforging the White Republic*, 14–15, 177–208; Silber, *Romance of Reunion*, 103–5; Gaughan, *Last Battle of the Civil War*, 183; Dunlap, "In the Name of the Home." For a discussion of the Daughters of the American Revolution's efforts to facilitate reconciliation, see Morgan, *Women and Patriotism*, 45–46, 85–86, 142–45, 190 (n. 47); O'Leary, *To Die For*, 81; and Davies, *Patriotism on Parade*, 277–80.

30. Johnson, "Sallie Chapin," 92–93; Gardner, *Blood and Irony*, 55–56, 60, *Fitz-Hugh St. Clair* quoted p. 56. The editors of the *SHSP* thanked Chapin for her novel, noting that it served as a model for young men of the South (*SHSP* 5 [June 1878]: 304).

31. Quoted in Johnson, "Sallie Chapin," 93.

32. Gordon quoted in Johnson, "No North, No South," 4.

33. The Daughters of the American Revolution similarly sought to avoid sectionalism in the name of their organization. As historian Cecilia O'Leary points out, they

attempted to erase discussions of slavery, emancipation, and race relations from their national dialogue (O'Leary, *To Die For*, 80–81).

34. Dunlap and Johnson both note that the WCTU was able to convince many southern white women to join by conceding state rights. As Johnson writes, "Southerners were free to practice segregation and to ignore the national's endorsement of the home protection ballot, or woman suffrage. Both in questions of African American participation and woman suffrage this was imperative to encouraging white Southerners to remain in the national" (Dunlap, "In the Name of the Home"; Johnson, "Sallie Chapin," 93).

35. Among women dedicated to remembering the war, LaSalle Corbell Pickett stood alone as a devout reconciliationist. See Janney, "'One of the Best Loved,'" 370–406.

36. *New York Times*, June 25, 26, 1893; *Roanoke Times*, April 28, 1897; Cashin, *First Lady*, 7–8, 279–82, 299, 306, 311. Former Confederates tended to criticize Varina Davis for her decision to live in New York City and her frequent refusals to attend Lost Cause functions.

37. *Chicago Daily Tribune*, February 12, 13, 1891, May 16, 1897; and *New York Times*, February 8, 1891; Cashin, *First Lady*, 282.

38. Fitzhugh Brundage observes that southern white women frequently employed their position as Confederate memorialists to move into other social causes such as prohibition, social welfare for needy mothers and children, and even suffrage (Brundage, *Southern Past*, 12–54).

39. Cox, *Dixie's Daughters*, 16–29; Poppenheim, *History of the United*, 8; O'Leary, *To Die For*, 82; Morgan, *Women and Patriotism*, 28–30; Davies, *Patriotism on Parade*, 40–41; *CV* 5 (January 1897): 34; *CV* 5 (October 1897): 499; Foster, *Ghosts*, 172. The UDC employed the same organizational structure as the WRC with its three-tiered organization of national offices, state departments, and local corps. Membership figures are often difficult to determine. In the earliest years, the UDC recorded the number of chapters, not members. Moreover, conflicting reports were published in the *CV* and published minutes of the annual conventions.

40. Cox, *Dixie's Daughters*, 34–39. Cox notes that "of the fifteen women elected president-general of the UDC between 1894 and 1919, more than half were born after 1850" (37). For comparison with the membership in the LMAs, see Janney, *Burying the Dead*, chap. 6.

41. Raines quoted in Cox, *Dixie's Daughters*, 141.

42. Worried that they were being eclipsed by the immensely popular Daughters, women of the LMAs joined together under the banner of the Confederated Southern Memorial Association in 1900 (Janney, *Burying the Dead*, 178–83).

43. Cox, *Dixie's Daughters*, 3, 32, 96, 106, 143, 158.

44. UDC, *Minutes of the Sixth Annual Convention* (1900), 68–69.

45. UDC, North Carolina Division, *Sixth Annual Meeting* (1903), 12. Overman is listed as Mrs. William H. Overman in the minutes.

46. UDC, North Carolina Division, *Seventh Annual Meeting* (1904), 58. In the late 1890s, local chapters and state divisions of the UDC began chartering children's groups for the descendants of Confederate veterans between the ages of six and sixteen. Known as the Children of the Confederacy (CofC), the groups helped with commemorative

activities, but were conceived principally to generate enthusiasm for the Confederate past among the next generation of white southerners. Like the UDC, members were required to show proof of their lineage. The success of the state-level chapters convinced the general organization to establish the CofC as an official auxiliary in 1917 (Cox, *Dixie's Daughters*, 121–22, 134–39).

47. For more on the CMLS and the Confederate Museum, see Janney, *Burying the Dead*, 160–99.

48. For historians who have argued that historical memory was tied to power relations, see Brundage, *Southern Past*; Neff, *Honoring the Civil War Dead*; Hale, *Making Whiteness*; and Blight, *Race and Reunion*. For a discussion of the way in which the younger generation of white southerners felt it was being denied access to the life of their parents, see Carmichael, *Last Generation*.

49. North Carolina Division UDC, *Eighth Annual Convention* (1905), 61–62. Fowle is listed as "Mrs. Samuel Fowle" in the UDC minutes. A search of the on-line catalog at the East Carolina University archives reveals that she was Mary Payne Fowle, originally of Norfolk, Virginia (East Carolina University special collections, http://digital.lib.ecu.edu/special/ead/findingaids/0460/).

50. *Chicago Daily Tribune*, August 5, 1900; Davies, *Patriotism on Parade*, 38, 76; Morgan, *Women and Patriotism*, 12; UDC, *Minutes of the Seventh Annual Meeting* (1900), 9–37. The Women's Christian Temperance Union counted nearly 250,000 members. There were other, lesser-known Union women's organizations as well, including the Ladies of the Naval Veterans' Union Association, Dames of the Loyal Legion, and National Association of Nurses of the Civil War (Davies, *Patriotism on Parade*, 39).

51. O'Leary, *To Die For*, 92–94; Morgan, *Women and Patriotism*, 10, 38.

52. The conclusions about the WRC women are based on a survey of national presidents and other officers as well as some division level officers. Birth year, marital status, relatives' activity during the war, and relatives' membership in the GAR were all recorded. Of the twenty-three women who served as national president between 1883 and 1906, one was born in the 1820s, three in the 1830s, fourteen in the 1840s, and five in the 1850s. The same general pattern holds true for other national officers of the WRC. Thanks to Katie Martin for her invaluable help on this project.

53. Obituary of Kate B. Sherwood, printed in the *Democrat* (Ravena, Ohio), February 16, 1914, http://www.rootsweb.ancestry.com/~ohfulton/KateBSherwood.html, accessed February 10, 2012; Susan Augusta Pike Sanders, http://www.mchistory.org/popups/CemWalk%20Bios/Sanders_Sue_Pike.html, accessed February 10, 2012.

54. Child, *Letters of Lydia Maria Child*, 280 (Lydia Maria Child to Francis George Shaw, September, 1880).

55. LGAR founder quoted in Davies, *Patriotism*, 259.

56. WRC, *Proceedings of the Fifth National Convention* (1887). Such stark sentiments did not always reign. In 1901, the WRC's national chaplain celebrated the fact that the graves of both the blue and gray had been honored on Memorial Day (WRC, *Journal of the Nineteenth National Convention* [1901], 111–20).

57. *National Tribune* (Washington, D.C.), March 12, 1896.

58. Some historians have understood the WRC's efforts more in the vein of reconciliation. See, for example, O'Leary, *To Die For*, 97.

59. *National Tribune* (Washington, D.C.), March 12, 1896.

60. WRC, *Journal of the Eighth Annual Convention* (1890), 24.

61. Silber, *Gender and the Sectional Conflict*, 94; Morgan, *Women and Patriotism*, 2, 38–41. The division of labor between the GAR and WRC was not nearly as complete as Morgan suggests.

62. For an inference that patriotic instruction was indicative of the reconciliationist sentiment espoused by the WRC, see Morgan, *Women and Patriotism*, 38–41.

63. WRC, *Journal of the Twelfth Annual Convention* (1894), 296–97. In 1893, the WRC aligned itself with the National Council of Women, a coalition of women's groups that included groups like the WCTU, to further its patriotism campaign (Silber, *Daughters of the Union*, 272–73; O'Leary, *To Die For*, 98–99).

64. WRC, *Journal of the Twelfth Annual Convention* (1894), 190.

65. WRC, *Journal of the Twenty-ninth National Convention* (1911), 178–79. The five states were Alabama, Florida, Georgia, North Carolina, and South Carolina.

66. For discussion of how nationalism and sectionalism might coexist, see Potter, "Historian's Use of Nationalism," 931–32.

67. On the overlap between UDC and DAR membership, see O'Leary, *To Die For*, 80; Morgan, *Women and Patriotism*, 46, 174–75n49; Cox, *Dixie's Daughters*, 35, 39, 171n14. Davies notes that southern women were more likely to be members of both the UDC and DAR than northern women were to be members of both the WRC and DAR (Davies, *Patriotism on Parade*, 104).

68. Morgan, *Women and Patriotism*, 28–35, 71; "The Term 'Nation,'" *CV* (March 1901): 111. As Morgan points out, Dunovant's words met a stern resistance in the *Confederate Veteran*.

69. For discussion of distance between civilians and soldiers, see Marten, *Sing Not War*, 245–49.

70. I have been able to find only one reference—tellingly, by a Union woman—claiming that the bonds of widowhood and bereaved mothers might help foster national healing (*New York Times*, August 29, 1874).

71. Neff, *Honoring the Civil War Dead*, 12.

72. "The Term 'Nation,'" *CV* (March 1901): 111.

73. *St. Louis Republic*, May 27, 1903.

74. David Blight's thesis (that reconciliation was premised on a shared understanding of white supremacy and an agreement among Unionists and Confederates to forget the role of slavery in the war) has been extended to studies on women. Francesca Morgan argues, "In subscribing to race-based definitions of North-South reconciliation, the women of the WRC promoted an American nationalism based on race." Yet just as white Union veterans did not embrace reconciliation in the name of race and a forgetting of emancipation, neither did women (Morgan, *Women and Patriotism*, 10, 12–13, 20–21, 142, quotation p. 37; Dunlap, "In the Name of the Home").

75. WRC, *Journal of the Sixth Annual Convention* (1888), 274.

76. WRC, *Journal of the Twelfth Annual Convention* (1894), 38.

77. WRC, *Journal of the Thirteenth National Convention* (1895), 247.

78. WRC, *Journal of the Twenty-ninth National Convention* (1911), 231.

79. Morgan, *Women and Patriotism*, 39; Silber, *Gender and the Sectional Conflict*,

90–91; Gannon, *Won Cause*, 48–49. Some states, like Kentucky, detached their black corps, meaning that these corps reported directly to the national WRC headquarters. In other states, like Virginia and Mississippi, the WRC was all black and the white corps detached.

80. WRC, *Journal of the Ninth Annual Convention* (1891), 35; Schwalm, *Emancipation's Diaspora*, 239. As Barbara Gannon notes, black women's Civil War groups did not wither and die after segregation because their association with white women's groups was less important than their affiliation with their male counterparts in the all-black posts (Gannon, *Won Cause*, 49).

81. Silber, *Gender and the Sectional Conflict*, 91.

82. WRC, *Journal of the Twenty-ninth National Convention* (1911), 425–26.

83. WRC, *Journal of the Tenth National Convention* (1892), 126. Efforts to build the monument initiated with a USCT veteran, not the women. It was not completed until 1920.

84. Taylor, *Reminiscences of My Life*, 119–20, 133–36, 142.

85. *Chicago Daily Tribune*, May 16, 1897.

86. Hillyer, "Relics of Reconciliation," 51. For more on the CMLS and the Confederate Museum, see Janney, *Burying the Dead*, 160–99.

87. On "Mammy," see Hale, *Making Whiteness*, 98–104; McElya, *Clinging to Mammy*.

88. "Extract from 'Wrongs of History Righted,'" *CV* 23 (October 1915): 443–44.

89. "Faithful Family Servant," *CV* 19 (November 1911): 522–23; Hale, *Making Whiteness*, 51–74, 98–115; Cox, *Dreaming of Dixie*, 34–57; McEyla, *Clinging to Mammy*; Blight, *Race and Reunion*, 286.

90. "Requests by U.D.C. Historian," *CV* 20 (February 1912): 54–55.

91. Quoted in Cox, *Dixie's Daughters*, 104.

92. "Monument to Faithful Slaves," *CV* 13 (March 1905): 123.

93. Hale, *Making Whiteness*, 60–70; Foster, *Ghosts*, 140.

94. "Slave Monument Question," *CV* 12 (1904): 525; "Monument to Faithful Slaves," *CV* 13 (1905): 123. For discussion of southern white fears of black men, see Ayers, *Promise of the New South*, 154–59. Apparently, a majority of Daughters attending the 1907 annual convention agreed with Adams, and consideration of the proposal for a national monument was postponed.

95. Unidentified clippings, UDC Records, Scrapbooks, KHS; *Minneapolis Journal*, April 23, 1902; Marshall, *Creating a Confederate Kentucky*, 166–71. Henrietta Duke was also the sister of Confederate cavalry general John Hunt Morgan.

96. Undated clipping (probably February 1902), *Nashville Tennessee*, UDC Collection, Scrapbooks, KHS.

97. UDC Collection, Scrapbooks, KHS; *Adair County News* (Columbia, Ky.), February 19, 1902; *Princeton Union* (Princeton, Minn.), January 16, 1902; Marshall, *Creating a Confederate Kentucky*, 166–71.

98. Hagood quoted in Marshall, *Creating a Confederate Kentucky*, 169; *Washington Post*, undated clipping, UDC Collection, Scrapbooks, KHS; Taylor, *Reminiscences of My Life*, 139–40. I have been unable to find any other statements from WRC members regarding the protest.

99. Marshall, *Creating a Confederate Kentucky*, 170–71. For an extended discussion of the Lexington UDC's efforts, see Marshall, "1906 *Uncle Tom's Cabin* Law," 368–93.

100. UDC, *Minutes of the Twelfth Annual Meeting*, 139.

101. Cloyd, *Haunted by Atrocity*, 101–8.

102. In 1890, the GAR purchased the Andersonville grounds from a private owner. Unable to maintain the grounds, the GAR approached the WRC in 1895 about purchasing the property. The WRC did so, for one dollar, in 1896. In 1910, the WRC donated the Andersonville Prison Park over to the U.S. government (WRC, *Journal of the Thirteenth National Convention*, 34; WRC, *Journal of the Fourteenth National Convention*, 250).

103. GAR, *Journal of the Fortieth National Encampment* (1906), 111–16. For a fierce debate among members of the GAR as to how to stop the monument and whether or not to seek the UCV's assistance, see pp. 180–90.

104. GAR, *Journal of the Fortieth National Encampment* (1906), 111–16.

105. *Atlanta Constitution*, January 26, 1908. I would like to thank Jim Marten for the information about Tanner.

106. *Washington Post*, January 25, February 23, 1908; *New York Times*, February 2, 1908.

107. WRC, *Journal of the Twenty-sixth National Convention* (1908), 163–67.

108. Ball was born in Illinois in 1855. In 1873, she moved with her family to Kansas, where she taught public school and eventually served as a notary public. From 1876 to 1886, she held positions in committee clerkships for the Kansas legislature and served as a press reporter from 1877 to 1890. In 1881, she began her career as a journalist, writing for the Albuquerque *Daily Journal*, the Kansas City *Daily Times*, and other publications. In 1891, she moved to Washington, D.C., where she continued to contribute to periodicals. In 1887, she married H. M. Ball ("Ball, Mrs. Isabel Worrell," in Willard and Livermore, *American Women*, 1:50).

109. *The Sun*, January 26, 1908. Ball's statement is not only anti-UDC but also anti-immigrant. "I am distinctly disappointed in their idea of types of men. It is a well-known fact that Wirz was an ignorant, uncouth, foreigner, not even a naturalized citizen of the United States, that was selected for this horrible work just because he was ignorant and brutal and able to do his work without much urging."

110. GAR, *Journal of the Fortieth National Encampment* (1906), 180–90.

111. *Atlanta Constitution*, January 30, 1908.

112. Cloyd, *Haunted by Atrocity*, 106–7; *SHSP* 36:226–36.

113. Numerous former Confederate men did speak out against the proposed Wirz monument or at least ask that the UDC temper its inscription so as not to offend the North (*The Bookman*, March 1908; Cloyd, *Haunted by Atrocity*, 106; *Atlanta Constitution*, February 8, 1908).

114. Cloyd, *Haunted by Atrocity*, 107. For a complete text of the monument inscription, see http://www.nps.gov/ande/historyculture/wirz-mon.htm, accessed September 19, 2011.

115. Cox, *Dixie's Daughters*, 146–47; *Washington Post*, November 15, 1912; UDC, *Minutes of the Nineteenth Annual Convention*, 80.

116. UDC, *Minutes of the Nineteenth Annual Convention*, 8–9; *Washington Post*, November 13, 1912.

117. *Washington Post*, November 24, 1912; "Confederate Flag in Washington," *CV* (December 1912): 548–49; Cox, *Dixie's Daughters*, 148.

118. "Vicious Partisan Comment on the U.D.C.," *CV* 21 (1913): 217 (New York newspaper quotation).

119. *National Tribune* (Washington, D.C.), November 21, 1912.

120. Blair, *Cities of the Dead*, 174–79, 187–93; and Krowl, "In the Spirit of Fraternity." For an account of the Arlington property, see Gaughan, *Last Battle of the Civil War*.

121. Krowl, "In the Spirit of Fraternity," 168–69; "Confederate Dead at the North," *CV* 9 (May 1901): 196–98; UDC, *Minutes of the Eighth Annual Convention* (1901), 88–89; CSMA, *History of the CSMA*, 38–39.

122. CSMA, *History of the CSMA*, 38–39. The legislation was sponsored by two Civil War veterans, Brig. Gen. Marcus J. Wright, a Tennessean who fought for the Confederacy, and Senator Joseph R. Hawley, a brevetted Union major general from Connecticut. The bill provided $250,000 for disinterring the Confederates, furnishing each with a pine coffin, and reinterring the bodies at Arlington. One hundred and thirty-six Confederates had been buried at Arlington during the war. Another 128 had been buried at the Soldiers' Home Cemetery. These 264 soldiers constituted the initial interments in the new Confederate section. Not all white southerners approved of the Confederate section (Blair, *Cities of the Dead*, 174–79, 187–93; and Krowl, "In the Spirit of Fraternity").

123. Cox, *Dixie's Daughters*, 53–56, 68–71, 146–47; O'Leary, *To Die For*, 146; Poole, *On Hallowed Ground*, 116–17.

124. For a detailed account of the monument's planning and building, see Cox, *Dixie's Daughters*, 53–60, 68–71.

125. The UDC was not thrilled with the speech of Bryan, noting that it lacked in expressing tribute to the people of the South "who for decades had shown their merit in his unstinted indorsement [*sic*]" ("Laying the Corner Stone at Arlington," *CV* [December 1912]: 550).

126. *Washington Post*, November 13, 1912; *Richmond Times-Dispatch*, November 13, 1912. Interestingly, Herbert's speech sounded more like the Union Cause than the Lost Cause, observing that "questions that once divided the North and South are settled forever, and the Union is more complete than ever before."

127. Cox, *Dixie's Daughters*, 70–71; "Monument at Arlington," *CV* (July 1914): 292–97; *Washington Post*, June 5, 1914; *New York Times*, June 5, 1914.

128. *Commoner* (Lincoln, Neb.), June 1, 1914 (this date appears correct, as this was a monthly magazine).

129. McEyla, *Clinging to Mammy*, 128–31; Blair, *Cities of the Dead*, 201. For a more thorough description of the monument, see http://www.arlingtoncemetery.mil/visitor _information/Confederate_Memorial.html.

130. This is a reference to the tragedy *Cato* (written by Joseph Addison in 1712) in which the hero resists the tyranny of Julius Caesar and is thereafter acclaimed as an icon of republicanism, virtue, and liberty.

131. *Washington Post*, June 4, 1914.

132. Cox, *Dixie's Daughters*, 70–71; "Monument at Arlington," *CV* (July 1914): 292–97; *Washington Post*, June 5, 1914. Cox notes that "at the time of the unveiling, most

members of the UDC did not honestly believe that reconciliation had occurred between the North and South" (Cox, *Dixie's Daughters*, 71).

133. Cox, *Dixie's Daughters*, 146. Cox argues that the Arlington monument served as a "token of reconciliation" and represented "an important step toward vindicating" the Confederate cause (Cox, *Dixie's Daughters*, 68–69). I concur with her assessment of the monument as a symbol of vindication, but I do not believe that the UDC intended it as a token of reconciliation.

134. Ed Rogers to Charles W. Cowtan, September 13, 1916, Charles W. Cowtan Papers, NYPL Manuscripts and Archives Division, Folder—Correspondence, 1861–1916.

135. Cox, *Dixie's Daughters*, 143–44.

CHAPTER 9

1. Reardon, *Pickett's Charge*, 176–93.

2. *Washington Post*, July 1, 1913.

3. Quoted in Reardon, *Pickett's Charge*, 189–90.

4. Blight, *Race and Reunion*, 9.

5. *Richmond Times-Dispatch*, May 10, 1913.

6. "Gettysburg, Gettysburg," *CV* 21 (August 1913): 377.

7. *Chicago Daily Tribune*, July 3, 1913.

8. Gannon, *Won Cause*, 189; *Washington Bee*, June 24, 1913.

9. Reardon, *Pickett's Charge*, 188. For a discussion of the attendance and newspaper coverage of African American veterans at the reunion, see Gannon, *Won Cause*, 183–85.

10. Logue, *To Appomattox and Beyond*, 132, 137; Skocpol, *Protecting Soldiers*, 109, 132, 573n2.

11. Blight, *Race and Reunion*, 356.

12. *Washington Post*, March 30, 1906; *Daily Ardmoreite* (Ardmore, Okla.), July 10, 1907. The group appears to have been short-lived. It met in Jamestown in 1907 and held its second national encampment in St. Petersburg, Florida, in 1908, but after that I was unable to find any record of it (*Bisbee [Ariz.] Daily Review*, March 29, 1908).

13. Adams quoted in Blight, *Race and Reunion*, 360.

14. Congressman Poe of North Carolina asked for an appropriation of $250,000 for a Lee monument directly opposite the Grant Memorial then under construction at the base of the Capitol. An arch that would become known as the Lincoln Memorial Arch would be added across Pennsylvania Avenue, connecting the base of the Grant statue with the Lee statue (*The Citizen* [Honesdale, Pa.], August 16, 1912).

15. *Congressional Record*, 62nd Cong., 3rd sess., January 29, 1913, 2455. In 1887, proponents of such a bridge had suggested it be called the General Ulysses S. Grant Memorial Bridge. Construction of the bridge was finally authorized in 1925, and it opened in 1932 as the Arlington Memorial Bridge.

16. For an example of such sentiment among former Confederates, see *Unveiling and Dedication of Monument to Hood's Texas Brigade*, 176–77.

17. Sturgis, *Shall Congress Erect Statues*. I would like to thank Mike Parrish for supplying this pamphlet.

18. Novick, *That Noble Dream*, 74.

19. Historian Cecilia O'Leary argues that by Wilson's administration, both northern and southern whites had forgotten African Americans' participation in the war and the Union goal of emancipation (O'Leary, *To Die For*, chap. 8). She likewise discusses a "racialization of patriotism" (129).

20. GAR, *Journal of the Forty-eighth National Encampment* (1915), 264.

21. GAR, *Journal of the Fifty-fourth National Encampment* (1920), 203.

22. Sturgis, *Shall Congress Erect Statues*, 8–9. Emphasis added.

23. For a discussion of how the Union Cause has been forgotten, see Gallagher, *Union War*, 3–6.

24. Clark, *Defining Moments*, 202–4; for a discussion of Evacuation Day, see 217. William Blair observes that by the late nineteenth and early twentieth centuries, Emancipation Days no longer carried the same partisan emphasis they had in an earlier period (Blair, *Cities of the Dead*, 193).

25. Blight, *Race and Reunion*, 371.

26. *New York Times*, December 19, 1909. The article did note that at least one white southerner had suggested that "a good way to celebrate the abolition of slavery would be to pay for the slaves." According to an editorial that appeared in a Richmond newspaper, "The South has already paid more in pensions for Union soldiers that the total bill for slaves that were freed, and the South would bear a considerable part of the expense if the old slaveholders were reimbursed."

27. *The Outlook*, November 8, 1913; Blight, *Race and Reunion*, 374–75; Kachun, *Festivals of Freedom*, 247–48. Du Bois staged his production twice more, once in Washington in 1915 and again in Philadelphia in 1916.

28. In recent years, it seemed that the bitter rancor of the surrender had been forgotten. In the writings and public speeches of civilians such as LaSalle Corbell Pickett and veterans Joshua Chamberlain and John B. Gordon, Union armies had provided rations for starving Confederate troops, Lee's sword had been magnanimously returned by Grant, and Union soldiers had saluted their fallen foes at the surrender parade.

29. *Richmond Times-Dispatch*, April 25, 1913.

30. CMLS Minutes, MOC; *Virginia Gazette* (Williamsburg), May 8, 1913.

31. *Richmond Times-Dispatch*, May 10, 1913. At first the Lee Camp of Confederate Veterans agreed to cooperate in making the Richmond jubilee the grandest yet. But after intense pressure from the CMLS, in May the Lee Camp rescinded its earlier endorsement. The Pickett Camp UCV likewise joined the protest.

32. "Gov. Mann Doesn't Favor Gathering at Richmond in 1915," *CV* 21 (August 1913): 386; Reardon, *Pickett's Charge*, 196.

33. *Richmond News Leader*, April 3, 5, 1915.

34. *Richmond News Leader*, April 9, 1915.

35. Instead of a grand peace celebration embracing both Confederate and Union veterans, in 1915 the GAR and UCV opted only to hold separate reunions in their respective nation's former capitals.

36. There is an extensive literature on white supremacy. For some insightful examples, see Gilmore, *Gender and Jim Crow*; Kantrowitz, *Ben Tillman*; Ayers, *Promise*; Hale, *Making Whiteness*; Cox, *Dixie's Daughters*, 4–5, 13–15, 121–28.

37. Peterson, *Lincoln in American Memory*, 166.

38. Peterson, *Lincoln in American Memory*, 168; Sandage, "Marble House Divided," 138–39.

39. Brundage, "White Women and the Politics of Historical Memory in the New South," in Gilmore, Simon, and Daily, *Jumpin' Jim Crow*, 115–39; Hale, *Making Whiteness*, 61–62, 86; Cox, *Dixie's Daughters*, 2, 13–15, 39, 84–87, 121–28, 138–40. As historian Karen Cox notes, "There was nothing innocuous about imparting the Lost Cause narrative to a younger generation" (Cox, *Dixie's Daughters*, 122).

40. "Worse Than War," *CV* 21 (August 1913): 371, 376–77; [Gen. Henry T. Douglas], "The Confederate Soldier, 1861–1865," *CV* 29 (July 1916): 297. A survey of the *Confederate Veteran* reveals that there were eight articles published on Reconstruction up until 1904 with no year having more than three articles. In 1905, twelve articles appeared in a single year. This rate dropped again until 1915 when eleven articles appeared. The following year witnessed the highpoint with twenty-five articles produced.

41. Clark, *Defining Moments*, 193. For emphasis on Reconstruction see Novick, *That Noble Dream*, 74.

42. "Requests by U.D.C. Historian," *CV* 20 (February 1912): 54–55.

43. Clark, *Defining Moments*, 193, 210.

44. Blight, *Race and Reunion*, 357–58.

45. Foner, *Reconstruction*, xix, xx.

46. Thomas Nelson Page, "Dixie Book of Days," *CV* 29, no. 1 (January 1916): 28.

47. Peterson, *Lincoln in American Memory*, 168–69.

48. Cullen, *Civil War in Popular Culture*, 24–25; Chadwick, *Reel Civil War*, 97–101, 110–29; Blight, *Race and Reunion*, 373, 394–97; MacLean, *Behind the Mask of Chivalry*, xi, 23–25; Goodman, *Stories of Scottsboro*, 17.

49. *Congressional Record*, 63rd Cong., 2nd sess., July 8, 1914, pp. 11797–98; Blight, *Race and Reunion*, 372.

50. *Congressional Record*, 63rd Cong., 2nd sess., July 8, 1914, p. 11798.

51. *Tulsa Star*, July 30, 1915; *Broad Ax* (Salt Lake City), July 17, 1915; Blight, *Race and Reunion*, 373.

52. Kachun, *Festivals of Freedom*, 247; Blight, *Race and Reunion*, 373.

53. Blair, *Cities of the Dead*, 173; *Appeal* (Saint Paul, Minn.), August 28, 1915; *Broad Ax* (Salt Lake City), August 7, 1915. Both papers quoted the Norfolk *Star*. Kachun notes that similar affairs were held in Philadelphia, Chicago, Louisville, and Atlantic City between 1913 and 1916—all to "less than a resounding success" (Kachun, *Festivals of Freedom*, 249).

54. See for example *Richmond Planet*, April 10, 1915; *Chicago Defender*, July 13, 1918.

55. *Chicago Defender*, June 8, July 13, 1918; *National Tribune* (Washington, D.C.) quoted in the *Chicago Defender*, January 21, 1896.

56. Some GAR posts did endorse the film. For example, the Provo, Utah, post offered a showing to those over age seventy (*Ogden [Utah] Standard*, April 5, 1916).

57. Rev. A. J. Emerson, D.D., "The Birth of a Nation," *CV* 29 (March 1916): 141.

58. Mrs. S. E. F. Rose, "The Ku-Klux Klan and 'Birth of a Nation,'" *CV* 29 (April 1916): 157.

59. Chadwick, *Reel Civil War*, 121–27, 135, 136, 139; Cullen, *Civil War in Popular Culture*, 25.

60. Morgan, *Women and Patriotism*, 104, 119.

61. Morgan, *Women and Patriotism*, 112–14. For more on the UDC and the peace movement, see Cox, *Dixie's Daughters*, 150–57. Cox argues that World War I marked the achievement of national reconciliation "on the Daughters' terms."

62. In 1913, Congress appropriated $400,000 for a memorial commemorating the services of northern and southern women of the Civil War (note that this project was initiated by men, not women). The memorial societies were responsible for raising the remaining $300,000 necessary for three memorial windows ("Memorial Window to Women of the Sixties," *CV* 31 [July 1923]: 243; http://www.redcross.org/museum /history/square.asp, accessed November 16, 2011).

63. Quoted in Morgan, *Women and Patriotism*, 113. For more on the UDC during the First World War, see Gardner, *Blood and Irony*, 214–19.

64. Gardner, *Blood and Irony*, 214–19, quotation p. 217. The Cross of Honor had been awarded by the UDC since 1900 to all Confederate veterans who had faithfully served the cause (Foster, *Ghosts*, 157).

65. The relationship between the GAR and SUV had at times been tenuous. For example, the GAR objected to the use of military titles among men who had never served. By the 1890s, historian William Davies observes, relations had become more cordial. The groups held joint meetings and by 1895 more than 750 GAR members were also Sons members (Davies, *Patriotism on Parade*, 101).

66. Davies, *Patriotism on Parade*, 76. Davies notes that "between 1889 and 1901 the order had recruited 163,000 members, but at the end of the period they retained only 26,000."

67. GAR, *Journal of the Fifty-second Encampment* (1918), 60.

68. Morgan, *Women and Patriotism*, 118.

69. Foster, *Ghosts*, 7, 116, 172, Owen quoted p. 172.

70. Bulletin (number 2), "History, Definition, Principles, and Program," issued by Adjutant-in-Chief Walter L. Hopkins (ca. 1920s), MOC.

71. WRC, *Journal of the Twelfth National Convention* (1894), 60; WRC, *Journal of the Twenty-ninth National Convention* (1911), 61, 75. Among other organizations, the Ladies of the GAR numbered around 55,000 (WRC, *Journal of the Twenty-ninth National Convention* [1911], 61).

72. WRC, *Journal of the Thirty-eighth Annual Convention* (1920), 125–29; GAR, *Fifty-fourth National Encampment* (1920), 81, 213. In 1918, the number was 164,644 (GAR, *Journal of the Fifty-second Encampment* [1918], 63). The membership numbers in the WRC journal do not always match those in the GAR journal. Morgan argues that the WRC continued to admit only women who had been loyal to the Union Cause of 1861–65 (Morgan, *Women and Patriotism*, 160). The LGAR had more than 63,000 members in 1918 (GAR, *Journal of the Fifty-second Encampment* [1918], 187).

73. Gannon, *Won Cause*, 49. Leslie Schwalm notes that the Biddle Circle No. 38 WRC remained active in St. Paul–Minneapolis through at least 1956 (Schwalm, *Emancipation's Diaspora*, 239).

74. Quoted in Davies, *Patriotism on Parade*, 307–8.

75. Morgan, *Women and Patriotism*, 87, 111. Morgan notes that the WRC was the only women's patriotic organization to endorse woman's suffrage until shortly before the Nineteenth Amendment was ratified.

76. "Twenty-sixth Annual Convention, UDC," *CV* 28 (January 1920): 33.

77. Janney, *Burying the Dead*, chap. 6.

78. Brundage, "White Women and Historical Memory," in Gilmore, Simon, and Daily, *Jumpin' Jim Crow*, 115–39 (quotation p. 127); Hale, *Making Whiteness*, 61–62, 86; Cox, *Dixie's Daughters*, 2, 13–15, 39, 84–87, 121–28, 138–40; Morgan, *Women and Patriotism*, 116. Tellingly, the "apolitical" Daughters withheld support for nationwide woman's suffrage until the end.

79. Foster, *Ghosts*, 179.

80. *Washington Post*, April 24, 1922; Jacob, *Testament to Union*, 36–45.

81. *Washington Post*, April 27, 28, 1922; *New York Tribune*, April 28, 1922; *Tulsa Daily World*, April 28, 1922; *New York Times*, April 28, 1922; Jacob, *Testament to Union*, 49–50.

82. Many of these veterans initially called for a memorial road to Gettysburg rather than a stone monument. For debate, see *Congressional Record*, 62nd Cong., 3rd sess., January 29, 1913, 2234–40.

83. See for example the speech of William P. Borland of Missouri in *Congressional Record*, 62nd Cong., 3rd sess., January 29, 1913, 2234–35.

84. *Congressional Record*, 62nd Cong., 3rd sess., January 29, 1913, 2244.

85. *New York Tribune*, January 1, 1912; Peterson, *Lincoln in American Memory*, 206–14; Jacob, *Testament to Union*, 119–25; Houck, "Written in Stone," 161–65. A new Lincoln Memorial Committee was established in January 1911. In July, the Fine Arts Commission selected the Potomac Park Site. In December 1912, the Fine Arts Commission adopted Bacon's plan and recommended it to Congress. On January 29, 1913, Congress finally adopted the resolution.

86. Houck, "Written in Stone," 169–72.

87. Peterson, *Lincoln in American Memory*, 170–75; Grimké, "Abraham Lincoln and the Fruitage of His Proclamation," 51–52; Barr, "Anti-Lincoln Tradition," 152, 209–16.

88. Cortissoz quoted in Savage, "Politics of Memory," in Gillis, *Commemorations*, 149n33.

89. Sandage, "Marble House Divided," 139; Savage, "Politics of Memory," in Gillis, *Commemorations*, 140; Concklin, *Lincoln Memorial*, 45. Guerin elected not to portray the figures as black.

90. Sandage argues that Lincoln could not remain both the Great Emancipator and the Savior of the Union (Sandage, "Marble House Divided," 139).

91. "Throng at Dedication," *Washington Post*, May 31, 1922.

92. *New York Times*, May 31, 1922; *Washington Post*, May 31, 1922; Houck, "Written in Stone," 231; Concklin, *Lincoln Memorial*, 76–77.

93. *Washington Post*, May 31, 1922.

94. "Throng at Dedication," *Washington Post*, May 31, 1922.

95. Schwartz, "Collective Memory and History," 469.

96. "Taft Presents Memorial," *Washington Post*, May 31, 1922.

97. "Voices Wish Martyr Could See Blue and Gray Present," *Washington Post*, May 31, 1922.

98. Quoted in Fairclough, "Civil Rights and the Lincoln Memorial," 410–11.

99. Concklin, *Lincoln Memorial*, 79.

100. *Chicago Defender*, June 10, 1922.

101. Harding, *President Harding's Address*, 3.

102. For one example of the memory of slavery remaining among white GAR men, see Dept. of Minnesota, GAR, *Journal of Proceedings of the Fifty-fifth Annual Encampment* (1922), 207–11.

103. In other words, Blight's thesis of reconciliation based on white supremacy and the erasure of slavery from the conflict happened not among the war generation, but those living in the early twentieth century. For a similar argument, see Madison, "Civil War Memories," 199, 229.

104. *New York Tribune*, July 3, 1922. The pamphlet, "Truths of the War Conspiracy of 1861," was written by H. W. Johnstone of Georgia and published by Mildred Rutherford in 1921.

105. *Evening World* (New York), June 23, 1922; *Edgefield Advertiser*, June 28, 1922.

106. *New York Times*, June 22, 1922.

107. *New York Times*, June 29, 1922; Dept. of Minnesota, GAR, *Journal of Proceedings of the Fifty-fifth Annual Encampment* (1922), 207–11; *New York Tribune*, September 30, 1922. The resolutions at the national encampment were tabled.

108. *New York Times*, June 24, 1922.

109. *Chicago Defender*, July 15, 1922.

110. Peterson, *Lincoln in American Memory*, 250.

111. Barr, "Anti-Lincoln Tradition," 175; Tyler quoted in Peterson, *Lincoln in American Memory*, 253.

112. "President Abraham Lincoln," *CV* 17 (April 1909): 153–54.

113. Everett, *Davis, Lincoln, and the Kaiser*; Blacknall, *Lincoln as the South Should Know Him*, 2; Barr, "Anti-Lincoln Tradition," 152, 201–7, 229–31; Peterson, *Lincoln in American Memory*, 253. As Barr notes, not all anti-Lincolnites were white southerners. Everett wrote his pamphlet in response to an article that appeared in the *Saturday Evening Post* that compared Lincoln's government of 1861 with that of the allies in the Great War and the kaiser with the Confederate cause.

114. *Evening Public Ledger* (Philadelphia), June 28, 1922; Peterson, *Lincoln in American Memory*, 251.

115. *Columbia Evening Missourian*, November 8, 1922.

116. *New York Times*, July 3, 1922.

117. *Edgefield Advertiser*, June 28, 1922; "The Rutherford History Report," *CV* 30 (August 1922): 285. Not all Confederate organizations agreed. In a letter published in the *Confederate Veteran*, SCV Historian-in-Chief Arthur R. Jennings stood by the report ("That Lincoln Resolution—and Some Other Things," *CV* 30 [August 1922]: 285).

118. *New York Times*, February 14, 1928; Peterson, *Lincoln in American Memory*, 252, quoting *Times-Dispatch*. Robinson was born in 1872 and therefore had no personal memory of even Reconstruction.

119. The UDC had first considered a national monument to faithful slaves in 1904.

Renewed calls for a memorial surfaced in 1920. A memorial was finally dedicated in October 1931 at Harpers Ferry, West Virginia (Janney, "Written in Stone").

120. For a discussion of the mammy figure as asexual, see McEyla, *Clinging to Mammy*, 131, and Thurber, "Development of the Mammy Image and Mythology," 87–108. Ironically, Moton supported the Mammy Memorial; see McEyla, *Clinging to Mammy*, 157.

121. Morgan, *Women and Patriotism*, 145–46; McEyla, *Clinging to Mammy*, 152–55; *Washington Post*, February 17, 1923; For an excellent account of the Mammy Memorial debate, see McEyla, *Clinging to Mammy*, 140–234.

122. Chandler Owen, "Black Mammies," in *Messenger* 5, no. 4 (April 1923): 670.

123. McEyla, *Clinging to Mammy*, 203.

124. "From the President General," *CV* 32 (February 1924): 70; Morgan, *Women and Patriotism*, 227n74.

125. *New York Times*, August 25, 1930.

126. According to historian Theda Skocpol, by 1910 most Civil War veterans were age sixty-five or older (Skocpol, *Protecting Soldiers*, 132). In December 1930, only 48,991 Union veterans remained on the U.S. pension roles (*CV* 39 [January 1931]: 42). Only 500 Union veterans planned to attend the 1930 Memorial Day services (*Washington Post*, May 25, 1930).

127. *CV* 39 (September 1931): 323, 354 (October 1931): 391–94. In the spring of 1900, Julia A. Garside of the Southern Memorial Association of Fayetteville, Arkansas, issued a call for all LMAs to unite in one body to be called the Confederated Southern Memorial Association (CSMA). For more on the CSMA, see Janney, *Burying the Dead*, chap. 6.

128. *Times-Virginian* (Appomattox), August 14, 1930.

129. *Houston Post*, September 15, 1933.

130. Despite numerous proposals and congressional bills beginning in the 1890s calling for a national park to mark this special place, none materialized (*House Reports*, 58th Cong., 2nd sess., H. Rept. 2325, 3–5; Smith, *Golden Age*, 48; *Senate Report* 57th Cong., 1st sess., S. Rept. 1344). For an extended discussion of efforts to build the Peace Monument at Appomattox, see Janney, "War over the Shrine of Peace."

131. *Washington Post*, November 15, 1931.

132. Copy of Report of the Jury appointed to select design, to the Quartermaster General, March 9, 1932, Records of the Commission of Fine Arts (hereafter RG 66), NARA; *Washington Post*, March 12, 1932; *New York Times*, March 12, 1932.

133. C. A. DeSaussure, Commander-in-Chief of the UCV, to Quarter Master General Bash, April 20, 1932, Records of the National Park Service (hereafter RG 79), NARA.

134. Brig. Gen. L. H. Bash, Asst. to Quartermaster General, to Gen. C. A. DeSaussure, April 25, 1932, RG 79, NARA. Bash reiterates this argument in a second letter to C. A. DeSaussure on May 20, 1932, RG 79, NARA. Bash reminded the Confederate veteran that he was merely a servant of the federal government. But more important, the plan for the monument had originated not with the War Department but with congressional representatives from Virginia—and the chairman of the jury of architects was a Virginian and son of a Confederate soldier.

135. C. A. DeSaussure to Gen. L. H. Bash, May 26, 1932, RG 79, NARA.

136. C. A. DeSaussure to Gen. L. H. Bash, May 26, 1932, RG 79, NARA.

137. *Washington Post*, March 3, 1902.

138. Letter to *Richmond Times-Dispatch*, unknown publication date, in UDC Scrapbook C-9, MOC.

139. C. A. DeSaussure to Gen. L. H. Bash, May 26, 1932, RG 79, NARA.

140. C. A. DeSaussure to Gen. L. H. Bash, May 18, 1932, RG 79, NARA. Several southern communities did erect monuments to the "over-throw" of Reconstruction. In the early twentieth century, white residents of Colfax, Louisiana, began commemorating the site of the 1873 Colfax massacre, which they claimed had effectively ended Reconstruction. In 1921, they dedicated a monument at the site in memory of the three white men who died in the fight (Keith, *Colfax Massacre*, 167–69).

141. For discussion of the battle between the UDC, African American leaders, and the NAACP over the Heyward Shepherd monument in the 1920s and 1930s, see Janney, "Written in Stone."

142. For discussion of clashes between Ladies' Memorial Associations and Confederate veterans, see Janney, *Burying the Dead*, chap. 4.

143. "An Open letter to the Daughters of the Confederacy by Mary D. Carter," included in Mary D. Carter to Anna Jones, Appomattox UDC, September 21, 1932, RG 79, NARA. The *Confederate Veteran* regularly printed articles by Bowers in this period.

144. For discussion of southern white fears of black men, see Ayers, *Promise*, 154–59.

145. Mary D. Carter to Anna Jones, Appomattox UDC, September 21, 1932, RG 79, NARA. Not all UDC members in Virginia or elsewhere supported Carter. Anna Jones of the Appomattox UDC, for example, supported the Appomattox monument (S. L. Ferguson to Brigadier Gen. L. H. Bash, September 28, 1932, RG 79, NARA).

146. MacLean, *Behind the Mask*, 142–43; Ayers, *Promise*, 158–59; Carter, *Scottsboro*.

147. Baker, *What Reconstruction Meant*, 89.

148. Jackson County (Ala.) *Sentinel*, April 23, 1931, quoted in the *New York Times*, March 8, 1933.

149. F. Raymond Daniell, "Background Study of Scottsboro Case," *New York Times*, April 16, 1933.

150. "Lynchings Feared in Scottsboro Case," *New York Times*, November 10, 1933.

151. UDC Scrapbook C-9, MOC.

152. "An Open letter to the Daughters of the Confederacy by Mary D. Carter," included in Mary D. Carter to Anna Jones, Appomattox UDC, September 21, 1932, RG 79, NARA.

153. Mary Lois Sibley Eve to Gen. L. H. Bash, June 14, 1932, RG 79, NARA.

154. Virginius Dabney, "Action at Richmond Regretted in U.C.V.," *New York Times*, July 3, 1932.

155. Mary D. Carter to Anna Jones, Appomattox UDC, September 21, 1932, RG 79, NARA. Emphasis in original.

156. Possibly for fiscal reasons, the Appomattox community was not as vehemently anti-Grant and anti-Lincoln as the more vocal Confederate groups. The local UDC chapter, for example, did not support the more radical claims of Daughters such as Carter.

157. SCV Commander-in-Chief Walter L. Hopkins to Bash, September 14, 1933, RG 79.

158. "S. C. V. Scores Plan to Build Union Statues," *Richmond Times-Dispatch*, September 6, 1933.

159. William R. Dancy, "Article on Grant-Lee Statue is Called Misleading by Dancy," *Richmond Times-Dispatch*, October 1, 1933.

160. Even some of the Sons' own ranks broke with them following Dancy's divisive words. Henry W. Battle, former Chaplain-in-Chief of the SCV, noted that he had bitterly resented the monument when first proposed, but now he recognized the spirit of unity in which it was intended (Henry W. Battle, "Dr. Battle Sees No Objection to Monument," *Richmond Times-Dispatch*, October 1, 1933).

161. *New York Herald Tribune*, October 23, 1932; UDC Scrapbook C-9, MOC.

162. *Washington Post*, February 3, 1934; *New York Times*, March 4, 1934, emphasis added; *Richmond Times-Dispatch*, February 3, 1934.

163. *Washington Post*, February 3, 1934. A Virginia delegation, including former Representative Joel W. Flood, who had been one of the original proponents of the monument, introduced a bill in Congress for a battlefield park.

164. "Battlefield Project Approved," *Washington Post*, September 14, 1935.

165. *Chicago Defender*, September 21, November 2, 1929; *Pittsburgh Courier*, September 21, 1929; *CV* 36 (June 1928): 205; *New York Times*, September 14, 1929, August 28, 1930, September 14, 1937; *New York Times*, September 4, 1935; *Washington Herald*, November 19, 1935. Proposals for a joint encampment surfaced as early as 1917 and continued through at least 1937.

166. Newspaper quoted in Linenthal, *Sacred Ground*, 97.

167. Logue, *To Appomattox and Beyond*, 142. By 1930, fewer than 100,000 Union veterans survived.

168. Pencak, *Encyclopedia of the Veteran* 1:201. The GAR's papers were given to the Library of Congress and its artifacts to the Smithsonian and other museums.

169. *CV* 40 (November 1932): 406; Logue, *To Appomattox and Beyond*, 142.

170. Pencak, *Encyclopedia of the Veteran* 1:136, 201.

171. "From the President General," *CV* 32 (February 1924): 70; UDC, *Minutes of the Forty-sixth Annual Convention* (1939), 275; *Senate Report*, 79th Cong. 2nd sess., S. Rept. 1826, July 5, 1946, 1; *House Report* 87th Cong. 2nd sess., H. Rept. 2263, August 23, 1962, 1–2. The WRC had sought incorporation as early as 1946. As late as 1968, the UDC could still claim 819 chapters and 27,956 members (UDC, *Minutes of the Seventy-fifth Annual Convention* [1968], 224).

172. Gallagher, *Lee and His Army*, 255, 263–64; Dickson, *Sustaining Southern Identity*. The full title of the second collection is *Lee's Dispatches: Unpublished Letters of General Robert E. Lee, C.S.A. to Jefferson Davis and the War Department, Confederate States of America, 1862–1865*.

173. Freeman, *R. E. Lee*, 4:493; Gallagher, *Lee and His Army*, 265–69, 274–76; *New York Times*, February 10, 1935; *North American Review* 240 (June 1935), 184; Dickson, *Sustaining Southern Identity*, 113, 151. There have been numerous critiques of Freeman by historians. For two examples, see Connelly, *Marble Man*, and Nolan, *Lee Considered*, both of which are direct responses to Freeman, suggesting the extent of his influence. For more on the influence of Freeman, see Gallagher, "Introduction to the 1998 Edition," in Freeman, *South to Posterity*.

174. Chadwick, *Reel Civil War*, 187–88.

175. Gallagher, *Causes Won*, 46–51, 107; Chadwick, *Reel Civil War*, 189. Chadwick notes that Selznick did tone down the novel's harsh portrayal of Reconstruction (Chadwick, *Reel Civil War*, 197).

176. Gallagher, *Causes Won*, 50.

177. Du Bois, *Black Reconstruction*; Hale, *Making Whiteness*, 81–82. *Black Reconstruction* was ignored by the *American Historical Review* and initial sales were modest (1,984 copies had sold by 1938). But historian David Levering Lewis reminds us that critical reaction from the *New York Times, Herald Tribune*, and *World-Telegram* was exceptional (Lewis, "Introduction," in Du Bois, *Black Reconstruction*, xi).

178. Baker, *What Reconstruction Meant*, 84–85; Campbell, *When Sherman Marched North*, 48. For more on postbellum slave narratives, see Schwalm, *Emancipation's Diaspora*, 244–47.

179. Fairclough, "Civil Rights and the Lincoln Memorial," 414; Sandage, "Marble House Divided," 135–36. Initially Anderson had requested to perform at Constitution Hall. But the Daughters of the American Revolution (DAR), who owned the hall, refused to accommodate her because she was black. The denial became well known when Eleanor Roosevelt, a member of the DAR but also a supporter of civil rights, withdrew from the organization and promptly helped Anderson find another venue.

EPILOGUE

1. Grant quoted in Cook, *Troubled Commemorations*, 1. Cook offers an excellent overview of the Civil War Centennial Commission's efforts to commemorate the centennial.

2. Cook, *Troubled Commemorations*, 58, 78–83, quotation p. 83.

3. Cook provides a detailed account of early resistance to a national commission and the eventual establishment of state commissions in every southern state (Cook, *Troubled Commemorations*, 56–70).

4. Cook, *Troubled Commemorations*, 75, 88–119.

5. Blight, *American Oracle*, 12–19, quotation p. 18; *Jet Magazine*, April 6, 1961. The negative publicity led to the resignations of Grant and Karl S. Betts, executive director of the commission. President Kennedy appointed two academics in their place, Allan Nevins and James I. "Bud" Robertson. Although Nevins and his staff initially planned the services at the Lincoln Memorial without any African American speakers, protest from the black press caused him to relent. Mahalia Jackson was invited to sing, and Thurgood Marshall delivered brief remarks.

6. *Jet Magazine*, January 23, 1964.

7. Blight, *American Oracle*, 1–2, Sterling quotation p. 21.

8. Senator Jim Webb homepage, http://webb.senate.gov/newsroom/pressreleases /03-16-2011-01.cfm, accessed March 16, 2012; "Historians' Forum." Between the fall of 2009 and the spring of 2011, Senator Mary Landrieu (D-La.), Senator Jim Webb (D-Va.), and Congressman Jesse Jackson Jr. (D-Ill.) each introduced bills to establish a national commission to commemorate the 150th anniversary of the Civil War. But each of these efforts failed, dying in committee.

9. "Historians' Forum"; Virginia Sesquicentennial Commission, http://www.virginiacivilwar.org, accessed March 19, 2012.

10. A 2011 poll by CNN found that 42 percent of 824 adults surveyed did not believe slavery was a main cause of the war (CNN Opinion Research Poll, conducted April 9–10, 2011, http://politicalticker.blogs.cnn.com/2011/04/12/cnnopinion-research-poll-april-9-10-civil-war, accessed March 20, 2012).

11. "Historians' Forum," 384–85.

12. *Washington Post*, December 22, 2010; Clarence Page, "How We Still Fight the Civil War," *Chicago Tribune*, April 20, 2011. For a discussion of symbols of the Lost Cause increasingly coming under fire, see Gallagher, *Lee and His Generals*, 265–66.

13. Lafayette (Ind.) *Journal and Courier*, February 18, 2011; "Sons of Confederate Veterans Commemorate Jeff Davis Inauguration," Associated Press, February 19, 2011, http://blog.al.com/montgomery/2011/02/sons_of_confederate_veterans_c.html, accessed March 15, 2012.

14. The NAACP protested the Secession Ball but decided not to protest the Montgomery celebration for fear that it would only attract attention to the event.

15. *Washington Post*, December 22, 2010; Richard Fausset, "Birthplace of Confederacy Backs Away from the Anniversary Event," *Los Angeles Times*, February 18, 2011.

16. http://www.time.com/time/nation/article/0,8599,2055981,00.html, accessed March 19, 2012.

17. Gallagher, *Causes Won*, 4–10; "Historians' Forum," 382–83. Gallagher notes that even as Hollywood has opted to move away from Confederate-leaning films, the trend toward Confederate art has increased. For an excellent discussion of the controversies over the Confederate battle flag, see Coski, *Confederate Battle Flag*.

18. Presidential Proclamation—Civil War Sesquicentennial, http://www.whitehouse.gov, accessed April 14, 2011. Emphasis added. In 2009, a petition requested that Obama cease the White House tradition dating back to Wilson of sending a wreath to the Confederate Memorial in Arlington. In a more reconciliationist message than his 2011 speech, however, Obama chose to continue the practice but also sent a second wreath to the African American Civil War Memorial. (*Washington Post*, June 5, 2011).

19. Clarence Page, "How We Still Fight the Civil War," *Chicago Tribune*, April 20, 2011. His article also appeared in the *Poco Record* on April 23, 2011.

BIBLIOGRAPHY

PRIMARY SOURCES

Manuscripts

Alderman Library, University of Virginia, Charlottesville
    Cabell and Ellet Family Papers
    John W. Daniels Papers
    Sarah Ann Graves Strickler Fife Diary
    McCue and Martin Family Papers
    Papers of John Singleton Mosby
    William Henry Redman Diary
    Papers of Thomas Lafayette Rosser Jr. and the Rosser and Gordon Families
Eleanor S. Brockenbrough Library, Museum of the Confederacy, Richmond, Va.
    Confederate Memorial Literary Society Records
    Federal Records, U.S. Circuit Court, Virginia District
    Hollywood Memorial Association Records
    Oakwood Memorial Association Minutes
    Pamphlet Collection
    United Daughters of the Confederacy Scrapbooks
Gettysburg National Military Park, Gettysburg, Pa.
    General Historic Photographic Collection
    William H. Tipton Photographic Prints
Huntington Library, San Marino, Calif.
    Brock Collection
    Diary of Annie G. Dudley Davis
    Papers of George H. Mellish
    Nicholson Collection
    Manley Ebenezer Rice Papers
Kentucky Historical Society, Frankfort
    First Kentucky Brigade, C.S.A.: Scrapbook, 1882–1925
    United Daughters of the Confederacy Records, 1855–1999
Library of Congress, Washington, D.C.
    Jubal A. Early Papers
Library of Virginia, Richmond
    Lee Monument Association Records
    Petersburg Ladies' Memorial Association Minutes

Massachusetts Historical Society, Boston
    Henry J. Millard Letters
    William B. Stark Diary
National Archives, Washington, D.C.
    Records of the Adjutant General's Office (RG 94)
    Records of the Commission of Fine Arts (RG 66)
    Records of the National Park Service (RG 79)
    Records of the Office of the Judge Advocate General (RG 153)
    Records of the War Department (RG 393)
    Union Provost Marshal's File
New York Public Library, Rare Book and Manuscripts Division, New York City
    Charles W. Cowtan Papers
    Abraham Gilbert Mills Papers
Perkins Library, Special Collections Library, Duke University, Durham, N.C.
    Lucy Muse Walton Fletcher Diary
    Munford-Ellis Family Papers
Southern Historical Collection, University of North Carolina, Chapel Hill
    Henry A. Birdsall Diary
Virginia Historical Society, Richmond
    Aylett Family Papers
    Henry Clay Brock Diary
    James Henry Gardner Papers
    R. E. Lee Camp, Sons of Confederate Veterans Collection
    Lee Family Papers
    Wynne Family Papers

On-Line Databases

The American Presidency Project (accessed through http://www.presidency.ucsb
    .edu/ws/index.php?pid=72356&st=davis&st1)
    Andrew Johnson Proclamation, May 2, 1865
Booker T. Washington Papers, University of Illinois History Cooperative (accessed
    through http://www.historycooperative.org/btw/volumes.html)
North American Women's Letters and Diaries (accessed through http://
    alexanderstreet.com/products/nwld.htm)
    Diary of Mollie Dorsey Sanford
    Gaughan, *Letters of a Confederate Surgeon, 1861–1865*
Southern Historical Collection, University of North Carolina (accessed through
    http://www.lib.unc.edu/mss/shc/index.html)
    Henry A. Birdsall Diary
WPA Slave Narrative Project (accessed through "Born in Slavery: Slaves Narratives
    from the Federal Writers' Project, 1936–1938," http://memory.loc.gov/ammem
    /snhtml)
    Fanny Berry interview

Addeman, Joshua Melancthon. *Reminiscences of Two Years with the Colored Troops.* Providence, R.I.: N. Bangs Williams & Co., 1880.

Alexander, Edward Porter. *Fighting for the Confederacy: The Personal Recollections of General Edward Porter Alexander.* Edited by Gary W. Gallagher. Chapel Hill: University of North Carolina Press, 1989.

Ammen, S. Z. *The Caverns of Luray: An Illustrated Guide-book to the Caverns, Explaining the Manner of their Formation, their Peculiar Growths, their Geology, Chemistry, &c.* Philadelphia: Allen, Lane & Scott's Printing House, 1886.

Andrews, Eliza Francis. *The War-Time Journal of a Georgia Girl 1864–1865.* Edited by Spencer B. King Jr. New York: Appleton & Co., 1908.

Annals of the War, Written by Leading Participants North and South, Originally Published in the Philadelphia Weekly Times. Edited by Alexander K. McClure. 1879. Reprint, with an introduction by Gary W. Gallagher, New York: De Capo, 1994.

Annual Reunion of Pegram Battalion Association in the Hall of the House of Delegates, Richmond, Va., May 21st, 1886 When the Battle-flag of the Battalion Was Presented by Capt. W. Gordon McCabe, Adjutant. Richmond: Wm. Ellis Jones, 1886.

Appleton's Annual Cyclopedia and Register of Historic Events of the Year 1876. New York: D. Appleton, 1876.

Bartlett, John Russell. *The Soldiers' National Cemetery at Gettysburg: With the Proceedings at Its Consecration; at the Laying of the Corner-stone of the Monument, and at Its Dedication.* Providence, R.I.: Providence Press Company for the Board of Commissioners of the Soldiers' National Cemetery, 1874.

Basler, Roy P., Marion Dolores Pratt, and Lloyd A. Dunlap, eds. *The Collected Works of Abraham Lincoln.* 8 vols. New Brunswick, N.J.: Rutgers University Press, 1953.

Battles and Leaders of the Civil War: Being for the Most Part Contributions by Union and Confederate Officers. 4 vols. Introduction by Roy F. Nichols. 1884–1888. Reprint, New York: T. Yoseloff, 1956.

Beard, John S. *Address of Hon. John S. Beard of Pensacola at Defuniak Springs, Florida, March 16, 1901 at Reunion of First Florida Brigade, United Confederate Veterans.* N.p.: 1901.

Beath, Robert B. *History of the Grand Army of the Republic.* 2nd ed. Philadelphia: Burk and McFetridge, 1885.

Beecher, Harris H. *Record of the 114th Regiment, N.Y.S.V. Where It Went, What It Saw, and What It Did.* Norwich, N.Y.: J. F. Hubbard Jr., 1866.

Blacknall, O. W. *Lincoln as the South Should Know Him.* Raleigh, N.C.: Manly's Battery Chapter, Children of the Confederacy, 1915.

Blassingame, John W., Peter P. Hinks, L. Diane Barnes, Sean P. Adams, and Gerald Fulkerson, eds. *Frederick Douglass Papers.* Series 1, 5 vols. New Haven, Conn.: Yale University Press, 1979–1992.

Boudrye, Louis N. *Historic Records of the Fifth New York Cavalry, First Ira Harris Guard: Its Organization, Marches, Raids, Scouts, Engagements and General*

Services, during the Rebellion of 1861–1865. 3rd ed., enlarged. Albany, N.Y.:
J. Munsell, 1868.

Boynton, Henry Van Ness. *Chattanooga and Chickamauga: General H. V. Boynton's Letters to the Cincinnati Commercial Gazette.* Washington, D.C.: Geo. R. Gray Printer, 1891.

———. *Dedication of the Chickamauga and Chattanooga National Military Park, September 18–20, 1895: Report of the Joint Committee to Represent the Congress at the Dedication of the Chickamauga and Chattanooga National Military Park.* Washington, D.C.: Government Printing Office, 1896.

Briggs, Caroline. *Reminiscences and Letters of Caroline C. Briggs.* Edited by George S. Merriam. Boston: Houghton, Mifflin & Co., 1897.

Brockett, Linus Pierpont, and Mary C. Vaughn. *Woman's Work in the Civil War.* Philadelphia: Zeigler, McCurdy, and Co., 1867.

Brownell, William Howard. *War Lyrics and Other Poems.* Boston, 1866.

Butler, J. G. *The Martyr President: Our Grief and Our Duty.* Washington, D.C.: McGill & Witherow, 1865.

Califf, Joseph M. *Record of the Services of the Seventh Regiment, U.S. Colored Troops, from September, 1863, to November, 1866: by an Officer of the Regiment.* Providence, R.I.: E. L. Freeman & Co., 1878.

Carnahan, J. Worth. *Manual of the Civil War and Key to the Grand Army of the Republic and Kindred Societies.* Washington, D.C.: US Army & Navy Historical Association, 1899.

Chamberlain, Joshua Lawrence. *"Bayonet! Forward": My Civil War Reminiscences.* Introduction by Stan Clark. Gettysburg: Stan Clark Military Books, 1994.

Chambers, Henry A. *Diary of Captain Henry A. Chambers.* Edited by T. H. Pearce. Wendell, N.C., 1983.

Chester, John. *The Lesson of the Hour: Justice as Well as Mercy, a Discourse Preached on the Sabbath following the Assassination of the President, in the Capitol Hill Presbyterian Church, Washington, D.C.* Washington, D.C., 1865.

Chickamauga Memorial Association. *Proceedings at Chattanooga, Tenn. and Crawfish Springs, Ga., September 19 and 20, 1889.* Chattanooga Army of Cumberland Reunion Entertainment Committee, 1889.

Child, Lydia Maria. *Letters of Lydia Maria Child.* Edited by John G. Phillips Whittier. Boston: Houghton, Mifflin & Co., 1883.

Christian, George L. *The Confederate Cause and Its Defenders: An Address Delivered before the Grand Army of Confederate Veterans of Virginia, at the Annual Meeting Held at Culpepper C.H., Va., October 4, 1898.* Richmond: Wm. Ellis Jones, Book and Job Printer, 1898.

Clark, James Freeman. *Order of Services at Indiana-Place Chapel, On Easter Sunday, April 16, 1865, Being the Sunday after the Assassination of Abraham Lincoln.* Boston: Walker, Fuller, and Co., 1865.

Clark, James H. *The Iron-Hearted Regiment: Being an Account of the Battles, Marches and Gallant Deeds Performed by the 115th Regiment N.Y. Vols.* Albany, N.Y.: J. Munsell, 1865.

Concklin, Edward F. *The Lincoln Memorial: Prepared under the Direction of*

the Director of Public Buildings and Public Parks of the National Capital, by
Edward F. Concklin, Special Assistant. Washington, D.C.: U.S. Government
Printing Office, 1927.

Confederated Southern Memorial Association. *History of the Confederated Memorial
Associations*. New Orleans: Graham Press, 1904.

Cowden, Colonel Robert. *A Brief Sketch of the Organization and Services of the Fifty-
ninth Regiment of United States Colored Infantry, and Biographical Sketches.*
Dayton, Ohio: United Brethren Publishing House, 1883.

Croom, Wendell D. *The War-history of Company "C," (Beauregard Volunteers) Sixth
Georgia Regiment (infantry) with a Graphic Account of Each Member.* Fort Valley,
Ga.: Printed at the "Advertiser" office, 1879.

Daly, Mary Lydig. *Diary of a Union Lady, 1861–1865.* Edited by Harold Earl
Hammond. New York: Funk & Wagnalls, 1962.

Davidson, Nora Fontaine Maury. *Cullings from the Confederacy: A Collection of
Southern Poems, Original and Others, Popular during the War between the States,
and Incidents and Facts Worth Recalling.* Washington, D.C.: The Rufus H. Darby
Printing Co., 1903.

Dawson, Francis W. *Our Women in the War: An Address by Capt. Francis W. Dawson,
Delivered February 22, 1887, at the Fifth Annual Re-union of the Association of the
Maryland Line, at the Academy of Music, Baltimore, Md.* Charleston, S.C.: Walker,
Evans & Cogswell, 1887.

Dawson, Sarah Morgan. *The Civil War Diary of Sarah Morgan.* Edited by Charles
East. Athens: University of Georgia Press, 1991.

Davis, Jefferson. *The Rise and Fall of the Confederate Government.* 2 vols. New York:
D. Appleton and Co., 1881.

De Forest, Bartholomew B. S. *Random Sketches and Wandering Thoughts; or, What I
Saw in Camp, on the March, the Bivouac, the Battle Field and Hospital, While with
the Army in Virginia, North and South Carolina, during the Late Rebellion. With
a Historical Sketch of the Second Oswego Regiment, Eighty-first New York V. I.*
Albany, N.Y.: Avery Herrick, 1866.

Dennett, John Richard. *The South as It Is.* 1866. Reprint, edited by Caroline E.
Janney, Tuscaloosa: University of Alabama Press, 2010.

Dexter, Henry Martyn. *What Ought to Be Done with the Freedmen and with the
Rebels?: A Sermon Preached in the Berkeley Street Church, Boston, on Sunday
April 23, 1865.* Boston: Nichols & Noyes, 1865.

Dooley, John. *John Dooley, Confederate Soldier: His War Journal.* Edited by Joseph T.
Durkin. Washington, D.C.: Georgetown University Press, 1945.

Dowdey, Clifford, ed., and Louis H. Manarin, assoc. ed. *The Wartime Papers of R. E.
Lee.* 1961. Reprint, New York: Da Capo Press, 1987.

Du Bois, W. E. B. *Black Reconstruction: An Essay toward a History of the Part which
Black Folk Played in the Attempt to Reconstruct Democracy in America, 1860–
1880.* 1935. Reprint, with an introduction by David Levering, New York: Oxford
University Press, 2007.

Duffield, George, *The Nation's Wail: A Discourse Delivered in the First Presbyterian
Church on the Sabbath.* Detroit: Advertiser and Tribune Print, 1865.

Early, Jubal A. *The Campaigns of Gen. Robert E. Lee. An Address by Lieut. General Jubal A. Early before Washington and Lee University, January 19, 1872*. Baltimore: John Murphy, 1872.

———. *The Heritage of the South: A History of the Introduction of Slavery; Its Establishment from Colonial Times and Final Effect upon the Politics of the United States*. Edited by Ruth H. Early. Lynchburg, Va.: Press of Brown-Morrison, 1915.

———. *A Memoir of the Last Year of the War for Independence in the Confederate States of America*. Edited by Gary W. Gallagher. Columbia: University of South Carolina Press, 2001.

———. *Proceedings of the Southern Historical Convention, Which Assembled at the Montgomery White Sulphur Springs, Va. on the 14th of August, 1873, and of the Southern Historical Society as Reorganized*. Baltimore: Turnbull Brothers, 1873.

Edmonds, Sarah Emma. *Nurse and Spy in the Union Army: Comprising the Adventures and Experiences of a Woman in Hospitals, Camps, and Battle-fields*. Hartford, Conn.: W. S. Williams & Co., 1865.

Edmondston, Catherine. *Journal of a Secesh Lady: The Diary of Catherine Ann Devereux Edmondston, 1860–1866*. Edited by Beth G. Crabtree and James W. Patton. Raleigh: Division of Archives and History, Dept. of Cultural Resources, 1979.

Emerson, Ellen Tucker. *The Letters of Ellen Tucker Emerson, vol. 1*. Edited by Edith W. Gregg. Kent, Ohio: Kent State University Press, 1982.

Everett, Edward. *Address of Hon. Edward Everett*. Boston, 1864.

Everett, Lloyd Tilghman. *Davis, Lincoln, and the Kaiser Some Comparisons Compared (National and International Ethics, 1861 and 1914)*. Ballston, Va.: Yexid Publishing, 1917.

"A Few Words in Behalf of the Loyal Women of the United States / by One of Themselves." *Loyal Publication Society Papers*, No. 10. New York: W. C. Bryant & Co., 1863.

Gage, M. D. *From Vicksburg to Raleigh; or, A Complete History of the Twelfth Regiment Indiana Volunteer Infantry, and the Campaigns of Grant and Sherman, with an Outline of the Great Rebellion*. Chicago: Clarke & Co., 1865.

Garidel, Henri. *Exile in Richmond: The Confederate Journal of Henri Garidel*. Edited by Michael Bedout Chesson and Leslie Jean Roberts. Charlottesville: University of Virginia Press, 2001.

Gettysburg Battle-field Memorial Association: Announcement. Gettysburg, 1863.

Gillespie, Emily Hawley. *A Secret to Be Buried: The Diary and Life of Emily Hawley Gillespie, 1858–1888*. Edited by Judy Nolte Lensink. Iowa City: University of Iowa Press, 1989.

Gordon, John Brown. *Reminiscences of the Civil War*. Introduction by Ralph Lowell Eckert. 1903. Reprint, Baton Rouge: Louisiana State University Press, 1993.

Gosson, Louis C. *Post-bellum Campaigns of the Blue and Gray, 1881–1882*. Trenton, N.J.: Naar, Day & Naar, 1882.

Graf, LeRoy P., and Ralph W. Haskins. *The Papers of Andrew Johnson*. 16 vols. Knoxville: University of Tennessee Press, 1967–1969.

Grand Army of the Republic. *Journal of the National Encampment.* Publishers, dates, and places of publication vary.

———. *Proceedings of the National Encampment of the Grand Army of the Republic.* Publishers, dates, and places of publication vary.

Grand Army of the Republic, Department of Indiana. *Journal of the Seventh Annual Session of the Grand Army of the Republic, Department of Indiana, February 17 and 18, 1886.* Indianapolis: Hasselman-Journal Co., 1886.

Grand Army of the Republic, Department of Kansas. *Mother Bickerdyke Day, General Order No. 4, May 12, 1897, by Department of Kansas, GAR.* Topeka, Kansas, 1897.

Grand Army of the Republic, Department of Minnesota. *Journal of Proceedings of the Annual Encampment of the Department of Minnesota.* Minneapolis: Co-operative Printing Company, dates vary.

Grand Army of the Republic, Department of New York, Canby Post. *Memorial Day with the Canby Post, no. 17, Grand Army of the Republic, Gloversville, N.Y., Saturday, May 30th, '74.* Gloversville, N.Y.: Intelligencer Steam Printing House, 1874.

Grant, Ulysses S. *The Personal Memoirs of Ulysses S. Grant.* 2 vols. 1885. Reprint, Old Saybrook, Conn.: Konecky & Konecky, 1994.

Grimké, Archibald H. "Abraham Lincoln and the Fruitage of His Proclamation." *The American Missionary* 63 (January 1909): 51–53.

Hall, James E. *The Diary of a Confederate Soldier: James E. Hall.* Edited by Ruth Woods Dayton. Privately printed, 1961.

Hancock, Cornelia. *Letters of a Civil War Nurse: Cornelia Hancock, 1863–1865.* Edited by Henrietta Stratton Jaquette. Lincoln: University of Nebraska Press, 1998.

Harding, Warren G. *President Harding's Address at the Dedication of the Lincoln Memorial, Washington, D.C., 30 May 1922.* Washington, D.C.: Government Printing Office, 1922.

Hawks, Esther Hill. *A Woman Doctor's Civil War: Esther Hill Hawks' Diary.* Edited by Gerald Schwartz. Columbia: University of South Carolina Press, 1984.

Hodge, George B. *Sketch of the First Kentucky Brigade / by Its Adjutant General.* Frankfort: Printed at the Kentucky Yeoman Office, Major & Johnston, 1874.

Hollywood Memorial Association. *To the Women of the South . . . Our Designation Is "Hollywood Memorial Association of Richmond"—Pledged to Apply the Means Which May Be Provided to the Permanent Protection and Adornment of the Graves of the Confederate Dead Interred in Hollywood Cemetery.* Richmond, 1866.

Holt, John Lee. *I Wrote You the Word: The Poignant Letters of Private Holt.* Lynchburg, Va.: H. E. Howard, 1993.

Hubbs, G. Ward, ed. *Voices from Company D: Diaries by the Greensboro Guards, Fifth Alabama Infantry Regiment, Army of Northern Virginia.* Athens: University of Georgia Press, 2003.

In Memoriam Sempiternam. Richmond: Confederate Museum, 1896.

Indiana Commission. *Indiana at Antietam: Report of the Indiana Antietam Monument Commission and Ceremonies at the Dedication of the Monument.* Indianapolis: Aetna Press, 1911.

Jackson, Henry W. R. *The Southern Women of the Second American Revolution: Their Trials, &c. Yankee Barbarity Illustrated. Our Naval Victories and Exploits of Confederate War Steamers. Capture of Yankee Gunboats, &c.* Atlanta: Intelligencer Steam-Power Press, 1863.

James, William. *Memories and Studies.* New York: Longmans, Green, and Co., 1911.

Johnson, Bradley T. *An Address Delivered at the Dedication of the Confederate Memorial Hall Richmond, Va., February 22, 1896.* Richmond: Wm. Ellis Jones, 1896.

Johnson, Rossiter. *Campfire and Battle-field: History of the Conflicts and Campaigns of the Great Civil War in the United States.* New York: Knight & Brown, 1896.

Johnston, William Preston. *Address before the Literary Societies of Washington and Lee University, Lexington, VA, On Commencement Day, June 25, 1879, by William Preston Johnston.* Lexington, Va., 1879.

Jones, Charles C., Jr. *Historical Sketch of the Chatham Artillery during the Confederate Struggle for Independence.* Albany: J. Munsell, 1867.

Jones, J. B. *A Rebel War Clerk's Diary at the Confederate States Capital.* 2 vols. New York: Old Hickory Bookshop, 1935.

Jones, Rev. J. William. *Life and Letters of Robert Edward Lee: Soldier and Man.* New York: Neale Publishing Company, 1906.

Kean, Robert Garlick Hill. *Inside the Confederate Government: The Diary of Robert Garlick Hill Kean, Head of the Bureau of War.* Edited by Edward Younger. New York: Oxford University Press, 1957.

Kimball, Edward P., ed. *Brinley Hall Album and Post 10 Sketch Book.* Worcester, Mass.: F. S. Blanchard & Co., 1896.

Kimball, H. I. *International Cotton Exposition (Atlanta, Georgia, 1881): Report of the Director General.* New York: D. Appleton, 1882.

Ladies of the Grand Army of the Republic. *Rules and Regulations of the Ladies of the Grand Army of the Republic.* Chillicothe, Ohio: Scholl Print Company, 1926.

Lambert, William H. *Address before Post No. 2, Dep't of Penn'a, Grand Army of the Republic / by William H. Lambert; at Monument Cemetery, Philadelphia, Decoration Day, May 30, 1879.* Philadelphia: Press of Culbertson & Bache, 1879.

————. *Memorial Day Oration of William H. Lambert at the National Cemetery, Arlington, Va., May 30, 1883.* Philadelphia: Grant, Faires, & Rodgers, 1883.

Lane, David. *A Soldier's Diary: The Story of a Volunteer, 1862–1865.* Jackson, Mich., 1905.

Laney Souvenir Company. *Laney's Gettysburg Battlefield and Its Monuments.* Cumberland, Md.: Laney Souvenir Co., 1895.

LeConte, Emma. *When the World Ended: The Diary of Emma LeConte.* Edited by Earl Schenck Miers. New York: Oxford University Press, 1957.

LeGrand, Julia. *The Journal of Julia LeGrand, New Orleans 1862–1863.* Edited by Kate Mason Rowland and Agnes E. Croxall. Richmond: Everett Waddey Co., 1911.

Loyal Legion of the United States. *Military Essay and Recollections of the Pennsylvania Commandery of the Loyal Legion of the United States.* 2 vols. 1890. Reprint, Wilmington, N.C.: Broadfoot, 1995.

Lucas, Daniel R. *History of the 99th Indiana Infantry, Containing a Diary of*

Marches, Incidents, Biography of Officers and Complete Rolls. Lafayette, Ind.: Rosser & Spring, Book and Job Printers, 1865.

Lumpkin, Katherine Du Pre. *The Making of a Southerner*. 1946. Reprint, Athens: University of Georgia Press, 1991.

Lynch, John W., ed. *The Dorman-Marshbourne Letters, with Brief Accounts of the Tenth and Fifty-third Georgia Regiments, C.S.A.* Senoia, Ga.: Down South Publishing, 1995.

Mac El'Rey, Rev. J. H. *The Substance of Two Discourses on the Assassination of the President, St. James Episcopal Church, Wooster, Ohio, Easter Day, 1865*. Wooster, Ohio: Republican Steam Power Press, 1865.

Marcus, Jacob Rader, ed. *Memoirs of American Jews, 1775–1865*. Philadelphia: Jewish Publication Society of America, 1955.

Marks, Bayly Ellen, and Mark Norton Schatz, eds. *Between the North and South: A Maryland Journalist Views the Civil War: The Narrative of William Wilkins Glenn, 1861–1869*. Cranbury, N.J.: Associated University Presses, 1976.

Maryland Gettysburg Monument Commission. *Report of the State of Maryland Gettysburg Monument Commission: To His Excellency E. E. Jackson, Governor of Maryland, June 17th, 1891*. Baltimore: W. K. Boyle & Son, 1891.

McAllister, Robert. *The Civil War Letters of General Robert McAllister*. Edited by James I. Robertson Jr. New Brunswick, N.J.: Rutgers University Press, 1965.

McCook, Anson G. *Address before the Society of the Army of the Cumberland at Their Eleventh Reunion: Washington, November 19, 1879*. Cincinnati: R. Clarke & Co., 1879.

McNeill, Sallie. *The Uncompromising Diary of Sallie McNeill, 1858–1867*. Edited by Ginny McNeill Raska and Mary Lynne Gasaway Hill. College Station: Texas A&M University Press, 2009.

Memorial Day with the Canby Post, No. 17, Grand Army of the Republic, Gloversville, N.Y., Saturday, May 30th, '74. Gloversville, N.Y.: Intelligencer Steam Printing House, 1874.

Merrill, Samuel H. *The Campaigns of the First Maine and First District of Columbia Cavalry*. Portland, Me.: Bailey & Noyes, 1866.

Michigan at Gettysburg, July 1st, 2nd, 3rd, 1863. June 12th 1889. Proceedings Incident to the Dedication of the Michigan Monuments upon the Battlefield of Gettysburg, June 12th, 1889. Detroit: Winn & Hammond, 1889.

Military Order of the Loyal Legion, Minnesota Commandery. *Papers Read before the Minnesota Commandery of the Military Order of the Loyal Legion of the United States 1889–1892*. 6 vols. St. Paul: D. D. Merrill.

Military Order of the Loyal Legion, Commandery of Ohio. *Sketches of War History 1861–1865: Papers Read before the Ohio Commandery of the Military Order of the Loyal Legion of the United States 1883–1886*. 9 vols. Cincinnati: Robert Clarke & Co., 1888.

Military Order of the Loyal Legion, Commandery of the State of Wisconsin. *War Papers Read before the Commandery of the State of Wisconsin, Military Order of the Loyal Legion of the United States*. 3 vols. Milwaukee: Burdick, Armitage, & Allen, 1891–1903.

Minnesota Vicksburg Monument Commission. *Minnesota in the campaigns of Vicksburg, November, 1862–July, 1863 / an Address Delivered before the Minnesota Historical Society by General Lucius F. Hubbard, September 9th, 1907. Report of the Minnesota Vicksburg Monument Commission.* St. Paul: n.p., 1907.

Minnigh, Luther W. *The Battlefield of Gettysburg and National Military Park: The Mecca for Veterans, Patriots and Students of History.* Harrisburg, Pa.: Keystone Print, 1895.

Moore, Frank. *Memorial Ceremonies at the Graves of Our Soldiers: Saturday, May 30, 1868.* Washington, D.C. 1869.

———. *Women of the War: Their Heroism and Self-Sacrifice.* Hartford, Conn.: S. S. Scranton & Co., 1866.

Morgan, Thomas Jefferson. *Reminiscences of Service with Colored Troops in the Army of the Cumberland, 1863–65.* Providence, R.I.: Soldiers and Sailors Historical Society, 1885.

Mowris, James A. *A History of the One Hundred and Seventeenth Regiment, N.Y. Volunteers, (Fourth Oneida,) from the Date of Its Organization, August, 1862, Till That of Its Muster Out, June, 1865.* Hartford, Conn.: Case, Lockwood and Co., 1866.

National Lincoln Monument Association. *National Lincoln Monument Association: Incorporated by Act of Congress, March 30, 1867.* Washington, D.C.: Printed at the Great Republic Office, 1867.

———. *Organization and Design: Proceedings of the Board of Managers. Plan and Prospects. Appeal to the Public. Appendix.* Washington, D.C.: New National Era, 1870.

New York State Monuments Commission for the Battlefields of Gettysburg and Chattanooga. *Final Report on the Battlefield of Gettysburg.* 3 vols. Albany: J. B. Lyon Company, 1900.

Ohio Association of Union Ex-Prisoners of War. *Proceedings of the Ohio Association of Union Ex-Prisoners of War, at the Reunion Held at Dayton, O., July 29, 30 and 31, 1884, with Register of Members: Organized at Columbus, August 11, 1880, Reorganized at Cincinnati, September 15, 1881.* Columbus: Ohio State Journal Print, 1884.

Peirce, Taylor, and Catherine Peirce. *Dear Catherine, Dear Taylor: The Civil War Letters of a Union Soldier and His Wife.* Edited by Richard L. Kiper. Lawrence: University Press of Kansas, 2002.

Pember, Phoebe Yates. *A Southern Woman's Story.* 1879. Reprint, with an introduction by George C. Rable. Columbia: University of South Carolina Press, 2002.

Pennsylvania Antietam Battlefield Memorial Commission. *Pennsylvania at Antietam: Report of the Antietam Battlefield Memorial Commission of Pennsylvania.* Harrisburg: Harrisburg Publishing Co. and State Printer, 1906.

Peter, Frances. *A Union Woman in Civil War Kentucky: The Diary of Frances Peter.* Edited by John David Smith and William Cooper Jr. Lexington: University Press of Kentucky, 2000.

Petty, A. W. M. *A History of the Third Missouri Cavalry: From Its Organization at*

Palmyra, Missouri, 1861, up to November Sixth, 1864: with an Appendix and Recapitulation. Little Rock: J. Wm. Demby, 1865.

Poppenheim, Mary, et al. *The History of the United Daughters of the Confederacy*. 1938. Reprint, Raleigh, N.C.: Edwards & Broughton, 1955.

Potter, William J. *The National Tragedy: Four Sermons Delivered before the First Congregational Society, New Bedford, on the Life and Death of Abraham Lincoln*. New Bedford, Mass.: A. Taber & Brother, 1865.

Powell, E. Henry, Lt. Col. 10th USCT. *The Colored Soldier in the War of the Rebellion: Read before the Vermont Commandery of the Loyal Legion*. Imprint, 1893.

Reid, Whitelaw. *After the War: A Southern Tour: May 1, 1865–May 1, 1866*. Cincinnati: Moore, Wilstach & Baldwin, 1866.

Report of the Unveiling and Dedication of the Indiana Monument at Andersonville, Georgia (National Cemetery), Thursday, November 28, 1908. Indianapolis: Wm. B. Burford, 1909.

Reunion and Dedication of the Monument at Arlington National Cemetery Va., Wednesday, October 21, 1896, Second Connecticut Heavy Artillery. Hartford, Conn.: Hartford, Case, Lockwood & Brainard Co., 1897.

Reunion of Ex-Soldiers of the North and South: Held at Luray, Virginia, July 21, 1881: and at Carlisle, Pennsylvania: September 28, 1881: with the Addresses Delivered on Both Occasions: Published under the Auspices of Capt. Colwell Post No. 201, Grand Army of the Republic, of Carlisle, Pa. Carlisle, Pa.: Herald and Mirror Print, 1881.

Reunion of Post Phil Kearny, no. 8, G.A.R., at Irving Hall, March 25, 1868: Opening Address / Comrade H. E. Tremaine: Banner Presentation and Address; by Major-General J. Watts De Peyster: Response; by Post Commander, B. T. Morgan. New York: W. O. Bourne, 1868.

Rogers, Horatio, ed. *Record of the Rhode Island Excursion to Gettysburg, October 11–16, 1886: with the Dedicatory Services of the Battlefield Memorials of the Second Rhode Island Volunteers, and Batteries A and B, First R.I. light artillery*. Providence, R.I.: E. L. Freeman & Son, 1887.

Rogers, William M. *History of the One Hundred and Eighty-ninth Regiment of New-York Volunteers*. New York: John A. Gray & Green, 1865.

Ruffin, Edmund. *The Diary of Edmund Ruffin*. 3 vols. Edited by William Kauffman Scarborough. Baton Rouge: Louisiana State University Press, 1972.

Sheridan, Philip Henry. *Personal Memoirs of P. H. Sheridan, General, U.S. Army*. London: Chatto & Windus, 1888.

Sherman, William T. *Memoirs of General William T. Sherman*. 2 vols. New York: D. Appleton and Co., 1875.

Simmons, L. A., *The History of the 84th Reg't Ill. Vols*. Macomb, Ill.: Hampton Brothers, 1866.

Simon, John Y., ed. *The Papers of Ulysses S. Grant*, 31 vols. Carbondale: Southern Illinois University Press, 1967–.

Simpson, Brooks, LeRoy P. Graf, and John Muldowny, eds. *Advice after Appomattox: Reports to Andrew Johnson, 1865–1866*. Knoxville: University of Tennessee Press, 1987.

Smith, Benjamin T. *Private Smith's Journal: Recollections of the Late War.* Edited by Clyde C. Walton. Chicago: R. R. Donnelley & Sons, 1963.

Smith, James O., Franklin Murphy, and Theodore Roosevelt. *Addresses Delivered on the Occasion of the Dedication of the New Jersey Monument on the Battlefield of Antietam, September 17, 1903.* N.p.: M. Plum, 1903.

Soldiers' National Memorial Cemetery. *Oration of Major-General O. O. Howard and Speech of His Excellency A. G. Curtin: at the Laying of the Corner Stone of the Monument in the Soldiers' National Cemetery, at Gettysburg, July 4, 1865, with the Other Exercises of the Occasion.* Gettysburg: Aughinbaugh & Wible, 1865.

Speairs, Arabella, and William Beverly Pettit. *Civil War Letters of Arabella Speairs and William Beverley Pettit of Fluvanna County, Virginia, March 1862–May 1865.* 2 vols. Edited by Charles W. Turner. Roanoke: Virginia Lithography and Graphics, 1988.

Stephens, Alexander H. *A Constitutional View of the Late War Between the States: Its Causes, Character, Conduct and Results.* 2 vols. Chicago: Zeigler, McCurdy & Co., 1868–70.

————. *Recollections of Alexander H. Stephens: His Diary Kept When a Prisoner at Fort Warren, Boston Harbour, 1865.* Edited by Myrta Lockett Avary. 1910. Reprint, New York: Da Capo Press, 1971.

Stone, Kate. *Brokenburn: The Journal of Kate Stone 1861–1868.* Edited by John Q. Anderson. Baton Rouge: Louisiana State University Press, 1955.

Stonebraker, Joseph R. *A Rebel of '61.* New York: Wynkoop Hallenbeck Crawford Co., 1899.

Strong, George Templeton, *Diary of George Templeton Strong, Selections.* 3 vols. Edited by Allan Nevins and Milton Halsey Thomas. New York: Macmillan, 1952.

Sturgis, Thomas. *Shall Congress Erect Statues at National Expense to Confederate Officers in Washington?: Resolutions Adopted by the New York Commandery of the Military Order of the Loyal Legion, October 6th, 1909. Confederate Officers and the Right of Secession.* New York, 1910.

Taylor, Susie King. *Reminiscences of My Life: A Black Woman's Civil War Memoirs.* 1902. Reprint, edited by Patricia E. Romero and Willie Lee Rose, New York: Markus Wiener Publishing, 1988.

The Terrible Tragedy at Washington: Assassination of President Lincoln. Philadelphia: Barclay & Co., 1865.

Terrill, John Newton. *Campaign of the Fourteenth Regiment New Jersey Volunteers* 2nd ed. New Brunswick, N.J.: Daily Home News Press, 1884.

Towne, Laura M. *Letters and Diary of Laura M. Towne: Written from the Sea Islands of South Carolina, 1862–1884.* Edited by Rupert Sargent Holland. 1912. Reprint, New York: Negro Universities Press, 1969.

Trowbridge, J. T. *The Desolate South, 1865–1866: A Picture of the Battlefields and of the Devastated Confederacy.* Edited by Gordon Carroll. New York: Duell, Sloan and Pearce, 1956.

Tunnard, William H. *A Southern Record: The History of the Third Regiment Louisiana Infantry.* Baton Rouge: Printed for the Author, 1866.

United Daughters of the Confederacy. *Minutes of the Annual Convention*. Opelika,
Ala.: Post Publishing Co., dates vary.
United Daughters of the Confederacy, North Carolina Division. *Minutes of the
Annual Convention*. Raleigh, N.C.: Capital Printing Co., dates vary.
U.S. Congress. *Congressional Globe*. Washington, D.C.: Blair & Rives, 1834–1873.
U.S. Congress. *Congressional Record*. Washington, D.C.: Government Printing Office,
1873–.
U.S. Congress. *House Reports*.
U.S. Congress. Joint Committee on Reconstruction. *Report of the Joint Committee
on Reconstruction*, 39th Cong., 1st sess. Washington, D.C.: Government Printing
Office, 1966.
U.S. Congress. *Senate Reports*.
U.S. Sanitary Commission. *Narrative of Privations and Sufferings of the United States
Officers and Soldiers While Prisoners of War in the Hands of Rebel Authorities*.
Philadelphia, 1864.
U.S. War Department, *The War of the Rebellion: A Compilation of the Official Records
of the Union and Confederate Armies*, 128 vols. Washington, D.C.: Government
Printing Office, 1880–1901.
*Unveiling and Dedication of Monument to Hood's Texas Brigade on the Capitol
Grounds at Austin, Texas, Thursday, October Twenty-seven, Nineteen Hundred
and Ten and Minutes of the Thirty-ninth Annual Reunion of Hood's Texas Brigade
Association Held in Senate Chamber at Austin, Texas, October Twenty-six and
Twenty-seven, Nineteen Hundred and Ten, Together with a Short Monument and
Brigade Association History and Confederate Scrapbook*. Houston: F. B. Chilton,
1911.
Vanderslice, John M. *Gettysburg: A History of the Gettysburg Battle-field Memorial
Association, with an Account of the Battle, Giving Movements, Positions and Losses
of the Commands Engaged*. Philadelphia: Memorial Association, 1897.
*Veteran Reunion of the 3rd GA Regiment at Union Point, Georgia, July 30th and 31st,
1874*. Savannah, Ga.: S. J. M. Baker, 1875.
Walker, Georgiana Freeman. *Private Journal of Georgia Freeman Walker, 1862–
1865: with Selections from the Post-War Years, 1865–1876*. Edited by Dwight F.
Henderson. Tuscaloosa, Ala.: Confederate Publishing, 1963.
Washington, Booker T. *Up from Slavery*. New York: Doubleday, Page & Co., 1902.
Watson, William. *Letters of a Civil War Surgeon*. Edited by Paul Fatout. West
Lafayette, Ind.: Purdue Research Foundation, 1961.
Welles, Gideon. *Diary of Gideon Welles, Secretary of the Navy under Lincoln and
Johnson*. Edited by Howard K. Beale. 3 vols. New York: Norton, 1960.
Wert, J. Howard. *A Complete Hand-book of the Monuments and Indications and
Guide to the Positions on the Gettysburg Battlefield*. Harrisburg, Pa.: B. M.
Sturgeon & Co., 1886.
Wiatt, *Confederate Chaplain: William Edward Wiatt, An Annotated Diary*. Edited by
Alex L. Wiatt. Lynchburg, Va.: H. E. Howard, 1994.
Willard, Frances Elizabeth, and Mary A. Livermore, eds. *American Women: Fifteen
Hundred Biographies*, 2 vols. 1897. Reprint, Detroit: Gale Research Co., 1973.

Woman's Relief Corps. *Journal of the Annual Convention.* Publishers, dates, and places of publication vary.

———. *Journal of the National Convention.* Publishers, dates, and places of publication vary.

———. *Proceedings of the National Convention.* Publishers, dates, and places of publication vary.

Wood, George L. *The Seventh Regiment: A Record.* New York: James M. Miller, 1867.

Wood, Wales W. *A History of the Ninety-fifth Regiment Illinois Infantry Volunteers, from Its Organization in the Fall of 1862, until Its Final Discharge from the United States Service in 1865.* Chicago: Tribune Company, 1865.

Periodicals

Adair County News (Columbia, Ky.)
Albuquerque Daily Citizen
Alexandria Gazette
Anderson (S.C.) Intelligencer
Appeal (St. Paul, Minn.)
Arkansas Gazette
Atchison (Kans.) Daily Champion
Atchison (Kans.) Daily Globe
Atlanta Constitution
Baltimore American and Commercial Advertiser
Baltimore Sun
Bangor (Me.) Daily Whig & Courier
Bisbee (Ariz.) Daily Review
Bismarck Daily Tribune
Blue and Gray: The Patriotic Magazine
The Bookman
Boston Daily Advertiser
Boston Daily Whig & Courier
Boston Herald
Broad Ax (Salt Lake City)
Brownlow's Knoxville Whig
Butte Weekly Miner
Century
Charleston Courier
Charleston Mercury
Chicago Daily
Chicago Daily Tribune
Chicago Defender
Chicago Tribune
Christian Recorder
Christian Union

Circular
Citizen (Honesdale, Pa.)
Clark Courier (Berryville, Va.)
Cleveland Morning Leader
Columbia Evening Missourian
Commoner (Lincoln, Neb.)
Confederate Veteran
Constitutional Union
County Paper (Oregon, Mo.)
Crittenden Record-Press (Marion, Ky.)
Daily Ardmoreite (Ardmore, Okla.)
Daily Arkansas Gazette
Daily Evening Bulletin (San Francisco)
Daily Inter Ocean (Chicago)
Daily National Republican (Washington, D.C.)
Daily News and Herald (Savannah, Ga.)
Daily Ohio Statesmen
Daily Phoenix (Columbia, S.C.)
Daily Picayune
Daily Public Ledger (Maysville, Ky.)
Daily Richmond Examiner
DeBow's Review
Edgefield Advertiser
El Paso Herald
Evening Bulletin (Maysville, Ky.)
Evening Public Ledger (Philadelphia)
Evening Telegraph (Philadelphia)
Fayetteville (N.C.) Observer
Flag of Our Union
Fort Worth Daily Gazette
Frank Leslie's Illustrated Newspaper

Franklin Repository (Chambersburg, Pa.)
Freeman (Indianapolis)
Galveston Daily News
Georgia Weekly Telegraph
Guthrie Daily Leader
Harper's Weekly
Hopkinsville Kentuckian
Houston Post
Illinois Daily State Journal
Independent
Irish World and American Industrial Liberator
Jet Magazine
Journal and Courier (Lafayette, Ind.)
Kansas City Journal
Kansas City Times
Keowee (S.C.) Courier
Liberator
Los Angeles Times
Louisiana Democrat
Louisville Daily Journal
Lowell (Mass.) Daily Citizen and News
Lynchburg Daily Virginian
Lynchburg News
Macon Telegraph
Maine Farmer
Memphis Daily Appeal
The Messenger
Milwaukee Sentinel
Montgomery Mail
Morning Oregonian (Portland)
National Republican (Washington, D.C.)
National Tribune (Washington, D.C.)
New Orleans Times
New York Age
New York Daily News
New York Evangelist
New York Herald
New York Observer and Chronicle
New York Sun
New York Times
New York Daily Tribune
New York Tribune
News-Herald (Hillsboro, Ohio)

News and Observer (Raleigh, N.C.)
News-Observer-Chronicle (Raleigh, N.C.)
Norfolk Virginian
North American Review
Ogden (Utah) Standard
Ohio State Journal
Old Guard
Omaha Daily Bee
Outlook (N.Y.)
Page Courier (Luray, Va.)
Petersburg (Va.) Daily Index
Petersburg (Va.) Daily-Index Appeal
Pittsburgh Courier
Pittsfield (Mass.) Sun
Philadelphia Inquirer
Philadelphia Press
Princeton Union
Richmond Daily Dispatch
Richmond Dispatch
Richmond Enquirer
Richmond Examiner
Richmond News Leader
Richmond Planet
Richmond Times
Richmond Times-Dispatch
Richmond Whig
Roanoke Times
Sacramento Daily Record-Union
Salt Lake Semi-Weekly Tribune
San Francisco Call
Savannah Tribune
Scribner's Monthly
Southern Argus
Southern Bivouac
Southern Historical Society Papers
Southern Opinion (Richmond)
Southern Recorder (Milledgeville, Ga.)
St. Louis Globe-Democrat
St. Louis Republic
St. Paul Daily News
Staunton (Va.) Spectator
Texas Republican (Marshall, Tex.)
Times-Virginian (Appomattox)
Trenton Evening News
Trenton State Gazette

Tulsa Daily World
Tulsa Star
Valley Spirit (Chambersburg, Pa.)
Valley Virginian
Virginia Gazette
Washington Bee
Washington Herald
Washington Post

Watchman
The Watchman and Southron (Sumter,
S.C.)
Weekly Pelican (New Orleans)
Western Christian Advocate
Wichita Eagle
Winchester (Va.) Times
Zion's Herald (Ill.)

SECONDARY SOURCES

Books

Anderson, Benedict. *Imagined Communities: Reflections on the Origins and Spread of Nationalism*. New York: Verso, 1991.

Attie, Jeanie. *Patriotic Toil: Northern Women and the American Civil War*. Ithaca, N.Y.: Cornell University Press, 1998.

Ayers, Edward L. *In the Presence of Mine Enemies: War in the Heart of America, 1859–1863*. New York: W. W. Norton, 2003.

———. *The Promise of the New South: Life after Reconstruction*. New York: Oxford University Press, 1992.

Bailey, Fred Arthur. *Class and Tennessee's Confederate Generation*. Chapel Hill: University of North Carolina Press, 1987.

Baker, Bruce E. *What Reconstruction Meant: Historical Memory in the American South*. Charlottesville: University of Virginia Press, 2007.

Bardaglio, Peter W. *Reconstructing the Household: Families, Sex, and the Law in the Nineteenth Century South*. Chapel Hill: University of North Carolina Press, 1995.

Barton, Michael. *Goodmen: The Character of Civil War Soldiers*. University Park: Pennsylvania State University Press, 1981.

Baruch, Mildred C., and Ellen J. Beckman. *Civil War Union Monuments*. Washington, D.C.: Daughters of Union Veterans of the Civil War, 1978.

Bay, Mia. *The White Image in the Black Mind: African-American Ideas about White People, 1830–1925*. New York: Oxford University Press, 2000.

Bederman, Gail. *Manliness and Civilization: A Cultural History of Gender and Race in the United States, 1880–1917*. Chicago: University of Chicago Press, 1995.

Bensel, Richard Franklin. *Sectionalism and American Political Development, 1880–1980*. Madison: University of Wisconsin Press, 1984.

Beringer, Richard, Herman Hattaway, Archer Jones, and William N. Still Jr. *Why the South Lost the Civil War*. Athens: University of Georgia Press, 1986.

Berlin, Ira, Barbara J. Fields, Steven F. Miller, Joseph P. Reidy, and Leslie S. Rowland. *Slaves No More: Three Essays on Emancipation and the Civil War*. New York: Cambridge University Press, 1992.

Berry, Stephen William. *All That Makes a Man: Love and Ambition in the Civil War South*. New York: Oxford University Press, 2003.

Blair, William A. *Cities of the Dead: Contesting the Memory of the Civil War in the South, 1865–1914.* Chapel Hill: University of North Carolina Press, 2004.

Blair, William A., and William Pencak, eds. *Making and Remaking Pennsylvania's Civil War.* University Park: Pennsylvania State University Press, 2001.

Blanton, DeAnne, and Lauren M. Cook. *They Fought Like Demons: Women Soldiers in the American Civil War.* Baton Rouge: Louisiana State University Press, 2002.

Blatt, Martin H., Thomas J. Brown, and Donald Yacovone. *Hope and Glory: Essays on the Legacy of the 54th Massachusetts Regiment.* Amherst: University of Massachusetts Press, 2001.

Blight, David W. *American Oracle: The Civil War in the Civil Rights Era.* Cambridge, Mass.: Belknap Press of Harvard University Press, 2011.

———. *Beyond the Battlefield: Race, Memory, and the American Civil War.* Amherst: University of Massachusetts Press, 2002.

———. *Frederick Douglass' Civil War: Keeping Faith in Jubilee.* Baton Rouge: Louisiana State University Press, 1989.

———. *Race and Reunion: The Civil War in American Memory.* Cambridge, Mass.: Harvard University Press, 2001.

Blum, Edward J. *Reforging the White Republic: Race, Religion, and American Nationalism.* Baton Rouge: Louisiana State University Press, 2005.

Bonan, Gordon B. *The Edge of Mosby's Sword: The Life of Confederate Colonel William Henry Chapman.* Carbondale: Southern Illinois University Press, 2009.

Bonner, Robert E. *Colors and Blood: Flag Passions of the Confederate South.* Princeton, N.J.: Princeton University Press, 2002.

Brasher, Glenn David. *The Peninsula Campaign and the Necessity of Emancipation: African Americans and the Fight for Freedom.* Chapel Hill: University of North Carolina Press, 2012.

Brown, Thomas J. *The Public Art of Civil War Commemoration: A Brief History with Documents.* Boston: Bedford/St. Martin's, 2004.

Brundage, W. Fitzhugh. *The Southern Past: A Clash of Race and Memory.* Cambridge, Mass.: Harvard University Press, 2005.

———, ed. *Where These Memories Grow: History, Memory, and Southern Identity.* Chapel Hill: University of North Carolina Press, 2000.

Buck, Paul. *The Road to Reunion.* Boston: Little, Brown, 1937.

Bullard, F. Lauriston. *Lincoln in Marble and Bronze.* New Brunswick, N.J.: Rutgers University Press, 1952.

Calkins, Chris M. *The Appomattox Campaign: March 29–April 9, 1865.* Conshohocken, Pa.: Combined Books, 1997.

———. *The Battles of Appomattox Station and Appomattox Court House, April 8–9, 1865.* Lynchburg, Va.: H. E. Howard, 1987.

———. *The Final Bivouac: The Surrender Parade at Appomattox and the Disbanding of the Armies, April 10–May 20, 1865.* Lynchburg, Va.: H. E. Howard, 1988.

Campbell, Jacqueline Glass. *When Sherman Marched North from the Sea: Resistance on the Confederate Home Front.* Chapel Hill: University of North Carolina Press, 2003.

Carmichael, Peter S. *The Last Generation: Young Virginians in Peace, War, and Reunion*. Chapel Hill: University of North Carolina Press, 2005.

Carter, Dan T. *Scottsboro: A Tragedy of the American South*. Baton Rouge: Louisiana State University Press, 1969.

Cashin, Joan E. *The First Lady of the Confederacy: Varina Davis's Civil War*. Cambridge, Mass.: Belknap Press of Harvard University Press, 2006.

Catton, Bruce. *A Stillness at Appomattox*. Garden City, N.Y.: Doubleday, 1954.

———. *Never Call Retreat*. Garden City, N.Y.: Doubleday, 1965.

———. *This Hallowed Ground: The Story of the Union Side of the Civil War*. Garden City, N.Y.: Doubleday, 1956.

Censer, Jane Turner. *The Reconstruction of White Southern Womanhood, 1865–1900*. Baton Rouge: Louisiana State University Press, 2003.

Chadwick, Bruce. *The Reel Civil War: Mythmaking in American Film*. New York: Knopf, 2001.

Chesebrough, David B. *No Sorrow Like Our Sorrow: Northern Protestant Ministers and the Assassination of Lincoln*. Kent, Ohio: Kent State University Press, 1994.

Cimprich, John. *Fort Pillow, A Civil War Massacre, and Public Memory*. Baton Rouge: Louisiana State University Press, 2005.

Clampitt, Bradley R. *The Confederate Heartland: Military and Civilian Morale in the Western Confederacy*. Baton Rouge: Louisiana State University Press, 2011.

Clark, Kathleen. *Defining Moments: African American Commemoration and Political Culture in the South, 1863–1913*. Chapel Hill: University of North Carolina Press, 2005.

Clinton, Catherine, and Nina Silber, eds. *Divided Houses: Gender and the Civil War*. New York: Oxford University Press, 1992.

Cloyd, Benjamin G. *Haunted by Atrocity: Civil War Prisons in American Memory*. Baton Rouge: Louisiana State University Press, 2010.

Collins, Donald E. *The Death and Resurrection of Jefferson Davis*. Lanham, Md.: Rowman & Littlefield, 2005.

Connelly, Thomas L. *The Marble Man: Robert E. Lee and His Image in American Society*. Baton Rouge: Louisiana State University Press, 1977.

Connelly, Thomas L., and Barbara L. Bellows. *God and General Longstreet: The Lost Cause and the Southern Mind*. Baton Rouge: Louisiana State University Press, 1982.

Connerton, Paul. *How Societies Remember*. New York: Cambridge University Press, 1989.

Cook, Robert J. *Troubled Commemorations: The American Civil War Centennial, 1961–1965*. Baton Rouge: Louisiana State University Press, 2007.

Cooper, William J., Jr. *Jefferson Davis, American*. New York: Vintage, 2000.

Coski, John M. *The Confederate Battle Flag: America's Most Embattled Emblem*. Cambridge, Mass.: Harvard University Press, 2005.

Cox, Karen L. *Dixie's Daughters: The United Daughters of the Confederacy and the Preservation of Confederate Culture*. Gainesville: University Press of Florida, 2003.

———. *Dreaming of Dixie: How the South Was Created in American Popular Culture*. Chapel Hill: University of North Carolina Press, 2011.

Cullen, Jim. *The Civil War in Popular Culture: A Reuseable Past*. Washington, D.C.: Smithsonian Institution Press, 1995.

Davies, Wallace Evan. *Patriotism on Parade: The Story of Veterans' and Hereditary Organizations in America, 1783–1900*. Cambridge, Mass.: Harvard University Press, 1955.

Dawsey, Cyrus B., and James M. Dawsey. *The Confederados: Old South Immigrants in Brazil*. Tuscaloosa: University of Alabama Press, 1995.

Dearing, Mary R. *Veterans in Politics: The Story of the GAR*. Baton Rouge: Louisiana State University Press, 1952.

Dew, Charles. *Apostles of Disunion: Southern Secession Commissioners and the Causes of the Civil War*. Charlottesville: University Press of Virginia, 2001.

Dickson, Keith D. *Sustaining Southern Identity: Douglas Southall Freeman and Memory in the Modern South*. Baton Rouge: Louisiana State University Press, 2011.

Douglas, Ann. *The Feminization of American Culture*. London: Papermac, 1996.

Dubois, Ellen Carol. *Feminism and Suffrage: The Emergence of an Independent Women's Movement in America, 1848–1869*. Ithaca, N.Y.: Cornell University Press, 1978.

Eckert, Ralph Lowell. *John Brown Gordon: Soldier, Southerners, American*. Baton Rouge: Louisiana State University Press, 1989.

Edwards, Laura. *Gendered Strife and Confusion: The Political Culture of Reconstruction*. Urbana: University of Illinois Press, 1997.

Edwards, Rebecca. *Angels in the Machinery: Gender in American Party Politics from the Civil War to the Progressive Era*. New York: Oxford University Press, 1997.

Fahs, Alice. *The Imagined Civil War: Popular Literature of the North and South, 1861–1865*. Chapel Hill: University of North Carolina Press, 2001.

Fahs, Alice, and Joan Waugh, eds. *The Memory of the Civil War in American Culture*. Chapel Hill: University of North Carolina Press, 2004.

Faust, Drew Gilpin. *The Creation of Confederate Nationalism: Ideology and Identity in the Civil War South*. Baton Rouge: Louisiana State Press, 1988.

———. *Mothers of Invention: Women of the Slaveholding South in the American Civil War*. New York: Vintage Books, 1996.

———. *This Republic of Suffering: Death and the American Civil War*. New York: Alfred A. Knopf, 2008.

Fellman, Michael. *The Making of Robert E. Lee*. New York: Random House, 2000.

Fellman, Michael, Lesley J. Gordon, and Daniel Sutherland. *This Terrible War: The Civil War and Its Aftermath*. New York: Longman, 2003.

Fleche, Andre. *The Revolution of 1861: The American Civil War in the Age of Nationalist Conflict*. Chapel Hill: University of North Carolina Press, 2012.

Foner, Eric. *Free Soil, Free Labor: The Ideology of the Republican Party before the Civil War*. New York: Oxford University Press, 1995.

———. *Reconstruction: America's Unfinished Revolution*. New York: Harper and Row, 1988.

Foster, Gaines M. *Ghosts of the Confederacy: Defeat, the Lost Cause, and the Emergence of the New South*. New York: Oxford University Press, 1987.

Frederickson, George M. *The Inner Civil War: Northern Intellectuals and the Crisis of the Union*. New York: Harper & Row, 1968.

Freehling, William W. *The Road to Disunion*. New York: Oxford University Press, 1990.

———. *The South vs. The South: How Anti-Confederate Southerners Shaped the Course of the Civil War*. New York: Oxford University Press, 2001.

Freeman, Douglas Southall. *R. E. Lee: A Biography*. New York: Charles Scribner's Sons, 1947.

———. *The South to Posterity: An Introduction to the Writing of Confederate History*. 1939. Reprint, Baton Rouge: Louisiana State University Press, 1998.

Gallagher, Gary W. *Causes Won, Lost, and Forgotten: How Hollywood and Popular Art Shape What We Know about the Civil War*. Chapel Hill: University of North Carolina Press, 2008.

———. *The Confederate War: How Popular Will, Nationalism, and Military Strategy Could Not Stave Off Defeat*. Cambridge, Mass.: Harvard University Press, 1997.

———. *Lee and His Army in Confederate History*. Chapel Hill: University of North Carolina Press, 2001.

———. *Lee and His Generals in War and Memory*. Baton Rouge: Louisiana State University Press, 1998.

———. *Lee the Soldier*. Lincoln: University of Nebraska Press, 1996.

———. *The Union War*. Cambridge, Mass.: Harvard University Press, 2011.

Gallagher, Gary W., and Alan T. Nolan, eds. *The Myth of the Lost Cause and Civil War History*. Bloomington: Indiana University Press, 2000.

Gallman, J. Matthew. *America's Joan of Arc: The Life of Anna Elizabeth Dickinson*. New York: Oxford University Press, 2006.

———. *The North Fights the Civil War: The Home Front*. Chicago: Ivan R. Dee, 1994.

Gannon, Barbara A. *The Won Cause: Black and White Comradeship in the Grand Army of the Republic*. Chapel Hill: University of North Carolina Press, 2011.

Gardner, Sarah E. *Blood and Irony: Southern White Women's Narratives of the Civil War, 1861–1937*. Chapel Hill: University of North Carolina Press, 2004.

Gaughan, Anthony J. *The Last Battle of the Civil War: United States vs. Lee, 1861–1883*. Baton Rouge: Louisiana State University Press, 2011.

Genovese, Eugene. *The Political Economy of Slavery: Studies in the Economy and Society of the Slave South*. New York: Pantheon Books, 1965.

Giesberg, Judith Ann. *Army at Home: Women and the Civil War on the Northern Home Front*. Chapel Hill: University of North Carolina Press, 2009.

———. *Civil War Sisterhood: The U.S. Sanitary Commission and Women's Politics in Transition*. Boston: Northeastern University Press, 2000.

Gillis, John R., ed. *Commemorations: The Politics of National Identity*. Princeton, N.J.: Princeton University Press, 1994.

Gillispie, James M. *Andersonvilles of the North: The Myths of Realities of Northern Treatment of Civil War Confederate Prisoners*. Denton: University of North Texas Press, 2008.

Gilmore, Glenda Elizabeth. *Gender and Jim Crow: Women and the Politics of White*

Supremacy in North Carolina, 1896–1920. Chapel Hill: University of North
  Carolina Press, 1996.
Gilmore, Glenda, Bryant Simon, and Jane Daily, eds. *Jumpin' Jim Crow: Southern
  Politics from Civil War to Civil Rights*. Princeton, N.J.: Princeton University Press,
  2000.
Ginzberg, Lori D. *Women and the Work of Benevolence: Morality, Politics, and Class
  in the Nineteenth-Century United States*. New Haven, Conn.: Yale University Press,
  1990.
Glatthaar, Joseph T. *Forged in Battle: The Civil War Alliance of Black Soldiers and
  White Officers*. New York: Free Press, 1990.
———. *General Lee's Army: From Victory to Collapse*. New York: Free Press, 2008.
Goldfield, David. *Still Fighting the Civil War: The American South and Southern
  History*. Baton Rouge: Louisiana State University Press, 2002.
Goodman, James. *Stories of Scottsboro*. New York: Pantheon Books, 1994.
Goodwyn, Lawrence. *Democratic Promise: The Populist Moment in America*. New
  York: Oxford University Press, 1976.
Govan, Gilbert E., and James W. Livingood. *Chattanooga Country, 1540–1951: From
  Tomahawks to TVA*. New York: Dutton, 1952.
Grant, Susan-Mary. *North over South: Northern Nationalism and American Identity
  in the Antebellum Era*. Lawrence: University Press of Kansas, 2000.
Grimsley, Mark. *The Hard Hand of War: Union Military Policy toward Southern
  Civilians, 1861–1865*. New York: Cambridge University Press, 1995.
Hahn, Stephen. *A Nation under Our Feet: Black Political Struggles in the Rural South
  from Slavery to the Great Migration*. Cambridge, Mass.: Belknap Press of Harvard
  University Press, 2003.
———. *Roots of Southern Populism: Yeoman Farmers and the Transformation of the
  Georgia Upcountry, 1850–1880*. New York: Oxford University Press, 2006.
Halbwachs, Maurice. *The Collective Memory*. New York: Harper & Row, 1980.
Hale, Grace Elizabeth. *Making Whiteness: The Culture of Segregation in the South,
  1890–1940*. New York: Pantheon Books, 1998.
Harter, Eugene C. *The Lost Colony of the Confederacy*. Jackson: University Press of
  Mississippi, 1985.
Hess, Earl J. *Liberty, Virtue, and Progress: Northerners and Their War for the Union*.
  New York: New York University Press, 1988.
———. *The Union Soldier in Battle: Enduring the Ordeal of Combat*. Lawrence:
  University Press of Kansas, 1997.
Hettle, Wallace. *Inventing Stonewall Jackson: A Civil War Hero in History and
  Memory*. Baton Rouge: Louisiana State University Press, 2011.
Hobsbawm, Eric, and Terence Ranger, eds. *The Invention of Tradition*. Cambridge:
  Cambridge University Press, 1992.
Holberton, William B. *Homeward Bound: The Demobilization of the Union and
  Confederate Armies, 1865–1866*. Mechanicsburg, Pa.: Stackpole Books, 2001.
Holt, Michael F. *The Political Crisis of the 1850s*. New York: Wiley, 1978.
Hunt, Robert. *The Good Men Who Won the War: Army of the Cumberland Veterans
  and Emancipation Memory*. Tuscaloosa: University of Alabama Press, 2010.

Jacob, Kathryn Allamong. *Testament to Union: Civil War Monuments in Washington, D.C.* Baltimore: Johns Hopkins University Press, 1998.

Janney, Caroline E. *Burying the Dead but Not the Past: Ladies' Memorial Associations and the Lost Cause.* Chapel Hill: University of North Carolina Press, 2008.

Jeffrey, Julie Roy. *Abolitionists Remember: Antislavery Autobiographies and the Unfinished Work of Emancipation.* Chapel Hill: University of North Carolina Press, 2008.

Jordan, Ervin L., Jr. *Black Confederates and Afro-Yankees in Civil War Virginia.* Charlottesville: University Press of Virginia, 1995.

Kachun, Mitchell A. *Festivals of Freedom: Memory and Meaning in African-American Emancipation Celebrations, 1808–1915.* Amherst: University of Massachusetts Press, 2003.

Kammen, Michael. *Mystic Chords of Memory: The Transformation of Tradition in American Culture.* New York: Vintage Books, 1993.

Kantrowitz, Stephen. *Ben Tillman and the Reconstruction of White Supremacy.* Chapel Hill: University of North Carolina Press, 2000.

Kazin, Michael. *The Populist Persuasion: An American History.* Ithaca, N.Y.: Cornell University Press, 1998.

Keith, LeeAnna. *The Colfax Massacre: The Untold Story of Black Power, White Terror, and the Death of Reconstruction.* New York: Oxford University Press, 2008.

Laderman, Gary. *The Sacred Remains: American Attitudes toward Death, 1799–1883.* New Haven, Conn.: Yale University Press, 1996.

LaFantasie, Glenn W. *Gettysburg Requiem: The Life and Lost Causes of Confederate Colonel William C. Oates.* New York: Oxford University Press, 2006.

Lawson, Melinda. *Patriot Fires: Forging a New American Nationalism in the Civil War North.* Lawrence: University Press of Kansas, 2002.

Lears, T. J. Jackson. *Rebirth of a Nation: The Making of Modern America, 1877–1920.* New York: HarperCollins, 2009.

Leonard, Elizabeth D. *All the Daring of a Soldier: Women of the Civil War Armies.* New York: W. W. Norton, 1999.

———. *Lincoln's Avengers: Justice, Revenge, and Reunion after the Civil War.* New York: W. W. Norton, 2004.

———. *Lincoln's Forgotten Ally: Judge Advocate General Joseph Holt of Kentucky.* Chapel Hill: University of North Carolina Press, 2011.

Levine, Bruce. *Confederate Emancipation: Southern Plans to Free and Arm Slaves during the Civil War.* New York: Oxford University Press, 2006.

Linderman, Gerald F. *Embattled Courage: The Experience of Combat in the American Civil War.* New York: Free Press, 1987.

Linenthal, Edward Tabor. *Sacred Ground: Americans and Their Battlefields.* Urbana: University of Illinois Press, 1991.

Litwack, Leon F. *Been in the Storm Too Long: The Aftermath of Slavery.* New York: Vintage Books, 1979.

Logue, Larry M. *To Appomattox and Beyond: The Civil War Soldier in War and Peace.* Chicago: Ivan R. Dee, 1996.

Loughridge, Patricia R., and Edward D. C. Campbell Jr. *Women in Mourning.* Richmond: Museum of the Confederacy, 1985.

MacLean, Nancy. *Behind the Mask of Chivalry: The Making of the Second Ku Klux Klan.* New York: Oxford University Press, 1994.

Manning, Chandra. *What This Cruel War Was Over: Soldiers, Slavery, and the Civil War.* New York: Vintage Civil War Library, 2008.

Marshall, Anne E. *Creating a Confederate Kentucky: The Lost Cause and Civil War Memory in a Border State.* Chapel Hill: University of North Carolina Press, 2010.

Marten, James Alan. *Sing Not War: The Lives of Union and Confederate Veterans in Gilded Age America.* Chapel Hill: University of North Carolina Press, 2011.

Martin, David G. *Confederate Monuments at Gettysburg: The Gettysburg Battle Monuments, Volume I.* Hightstown, N.J.: Longstreet House, 1986.

Marvel, William. *Lee's Last Retreat: The Flight to Appomattox.* Chapel Hill: University of North Carolina Press, 2002.

————. *A Place Called Appomattox.* Chapel Hill: University of North Carolina Press, 2000.

Massey, Mary Elizabeth. *Bonnet Brigades.* New York: Knopf, 1966.

Mays, Thomas D. *Cumberland Blood: Champ Ferguson's Civil War.* Carbondale: Southern Illinois University Press, 2008.

McConnell, Stuart. *Glorious Contentment: The Grand Army of the Republic, 1865–1900.* Chapel Hill: University of North Carolina Press, 1992.

McCurry, Stephanie. *Confederate Reckoning: Power and Politics in the Civil War South.* Cambridge, Mass.: Harvard University Press, 2010.

McElya, Micki. *Clinging to Mammy: The Faithful Slave in Twentieth-Century America.* Cambridge, Mass.: Harvard University Press, 2007.

McIntyre, Rebecca Cawood. *Souvenirs of the Old South: Northern Tourism and Southern Mythology.* Gainesville: University Press of Florida, 2011.

McPherson, James M. *Battle Cry of Freedom: The Civil War Era.* New York: Oxford University Press, 1988.

————. *For Cause and Comrades: Why Men Fought in the Civil War.* New York: Oxford University Press, 1997.

————. *Ordeal by Fire: The Civil War and Reconstruction.* New York: Knopf, 1982.

————. *What They Fought For, 1861–1865.* New York: Doubleday, 1995.

Millard, Candice. *Destiny of the Republic: A Tale of Madness, Medicine, and the Murder of a President.* New York: Doubleday, 2011.

Mills, Cynthia, and Pamela H. Simpson, eds. *Monuments to the Lost Cause: Women, Art, and the Landscapes of Southern Memory.* Knoxville: University of Tennessee Press, 2003.

Mitchell, Mary H. *Hollywood Cemetery: The History of a Southern Shrine.* Richmond: Virginia State Library, 1985.

Mitchell, Reid. *Civil War Soldiers.* 1988. Reprint, New York: Penguin Books, 1997.

Morgan, Francesca. *Women and Patriotism in Jim Crow America.* Chapel Hill: University of North Carolina Press, 2005.

National Park Service. *Appomattox Court House,* Handbook 160. Washington, D.C.: Department of the Interior, 2003.

Neff, John R. *Honoring the Civil War Dead: Commemoration and the Problem of Reconciliation*. Lawrence: University Press of Kansas, 2005.

Nevins, Allan. *The Ordeal of the Union*. New York: Scribner, 1947.

Nolan, Alan T. *Lee Considered: General Robert E. Lee and Civil War History*. Chapel Hill: University of North Carolina Press, 1991.

Novick, Peter. *That Noble Dream: The "Objectivity Question" and the American Historical Profession*. Cambridge: Cambridge University Press, 1988.

O'Leary, Cecelia Elizabeth. *To Die For: The Paradox of American Patriotism*. Princeton, N.J.: Princeton University Press, 1999.

Osborne, Charles C. *Jubal: The Life and Times of General Jubal A. Early, CSA, Defender of the Lost Cause*. Chapel Hill, N.C.: Algonquin Books, 1992.

Osterweis, Rollin G. *The Myth of the Lost Cause, 1865–1900*. Hamden, Conn.: Archon Books, 1973.

Ott, Victoria E. *Confederate Daughters: Coming of Age in the Civil War*. Carbondale: Southern Illinois University Press, 2008.

Paige, John C., and Jerome A. Greene. *Administrative History of Chickamauga and Chattanooga National Military Park*. Denver: National Park Service, 1993.

Painter, Nell Irvin. *Standing at Armageddon: United States, 1877–1919*. New York: W. W. Norton, 1987.

Pencak, William, ed. *Encyclopedia of the Veteran in America*. ABC-CLIO, 2009.

Perman, Michael. *Reunion without Compromise: The South and Reconstruction, 1865–1868*. Cambridge: Cambridge University Press, 1973.

Peterson, Merrill D. *Lincoln in American Memory*. New York: Oxford University Press, 1994.

Phillips, Jason. *Diehard Rebels: The Confederate Culture of Invincibility*. Athens: University of Georgia Press, 2007.

Piehler, G. Kurt. *Remembering the American Way, 1783–1993*. Washington, D.C.: Smithsonian Institute Press, 1996.

Poole, Scott. *Never Surrender: Confederate Memory and Conservatism in the South Carolina Upcountry*. Athens: University of Georgia Press, 2004.

Potter, David Morris. *The Impending Crisis, 1848–1861*. New York: Harper & Row, 1976.

Pressly, Thomas. *Americans Interpret Their Civil War*. New York: Free Press, 1954.

Pryor, Elizabeth Brown. *Reading the Man: A Portrait of Robert E. Lee through His Private Letters*. New York: Viking, 2007.

Quigley, Paul. *Shifting Grounds: Nationalism and the American South, 1848–1865*. New York: Oxford University Press, 2012.

Rable, George C. *Civil Wars: Women and the Crisis of Southern Nationalism*. Urbana: University of Illinois Press, 1989.

———. *Fredericksburg! Fredericksburg!* Chapel Hill: University of North Carolina Press, 2002.

Ramage, James A. *Gray Ghost: The Life of Colonel John Singleton Mosby*. Lexington: University Press of Kentucky, 1999.

Reardon, Carol. *Pickett's Charge in History and Memory*. Chapel Hill: University of North Carolina Press, 1997.

Richardson, Heather Cox. *The Death of Reconstruction: Race, Labor, and Politics in the Post-Civil War North, 1865–1901*. Cambridge, Mass.: Harvard University Press, 2001.

———. *West from Appomattox: The Reconstruction of America after the Civil War*. New Haven, Conn.: Yale University Press, 2007.

Robertson, James I. *Soldiers Blue and Gray*. Columbia: University of South Carolina Press, 1988.

Royster, Charles. *Destructive War: William Tecumseh Sherman, Stonewall Jackson, and the Americans*. New York: Knopf, 1991.

Rubin, Anne Sarah. *A Shattered Nation: The Rise and Fall of the Confederacy, 1861–1868*. Chapel Hill: University of North Carolina Press, 2005.

Russet, Cynthia. *Sexual Science: The Victorian Construction of Womanhood*. Cambridge, Mass.: Harvard University Press, 2001.

Sanders, Charles W. *While in the Hands of the Enemy: Military Prisons of the Civil War*. Baton Rouge: Louisiana State University Press, 2005.

Savage, Kirk. *Standing Soldiers, Kneeling Slaves: Race, War, and Monument in Nineteenth-Century America*. Princeton, N.J.: Princeton University Press, 1997.

Schantz, Mark S. *Awaiting the Heavenly Country: The Civil War and America's Culture of Death*. Ithaca, N.Y.: Cornell University Press, 2008.

Schroeder, Patrick A. *The Confederate Cemetery at Appomattox*. Lynchburg, Va.: Schroeder Publications, 2005.

Schultz, Jane E. *Women at the Front: Hospital Workers in Civil War America*. Chapel Hill: University of North Carolina Press, 2004.

Schwalm, Leslie A. *Emancipation's Diaspora: Race and Reconstruction in the Upper Midwest*. Chapel Hill: University of North Carolina Press, 2009.

Schwartz, Barry. *Abraham Lincoln and the Forge of National Memory*. Chicago: University of Chicago Press, 2000.

Searcher, Victor. *The Farewell to Lincoln*. New York: Abington Press, 1965.

Shaffer, Donald Robert. *After the Glory: The Struggles of Black Civil War Veterans*. Lawrence: University Press of Kansas, 2004.

Sheehan-Dean, Aaron. *Why Confederates Fought: Family and Nation in Civil War Virginia*. Chapel Hill: University of North Carolina Press, 2007.

Silber, Nina. *Daughters of the Union: Northern Women Fight the Civil War*. Cambridge, Mass.: Harvard University Press, 2005.

———. *Gender and the Sectional Conflict*. Chapel Hill: University of North Carolina Press, 2008.

———. *Romance of Reunion: Northerners and the South, 1865–1900*. Chapel Hill: University of North Carolina Press, 1993.

Silbey, Joel H. *The American Political Nation, 1838–1893*. Stanford, Calif.: Stanford University Press, 1991.

Simpson, John A. *S. A. Cunningham and the Confederate Heritage*. Athens: University of Georgia Press, 1994.

Skocpol, Theda. *Protecting Soldiers and Mothers: The Political Origins of Social Policy in the United States*. Cambridge, Mass.: Harvard University Press, 1992.

Smith, Gene. *Lee and Grant: A Dual Biography*. New York: McGraw-Hill, 1984.

Smith, Timothy B. *A Chickamauga Memorial: The Establishment of America's First Civil War National Military Park*. Knoxville: University of Tennessee Press, 2009.
———. *The Golden Age of Battlefield Preservation: The Decade of the 1890s and the Establishment of America's First Five Military Parks*. Knoxville: University of Tennessee Press, 2008.
Stampp, Kenneth M. *The Imperiled Union: Essays on the Background of the Civil War*. New York: Oxford University Press, 1980.
Stiles, T. J. *Jesse James: Last Rebel of the Civil War*. New York: Knopf, 2002.
Summers, Mark W. *A Dangerous Stir: Fear, Paranoia, and the Making of Reconstruction*. Chapel Hill: University of North Carolina Press, 2009.
Sutherland, Daniel E. *A Savage Conflict: The Decisive Role of Guerrillas in the American Civil War*. Chapel Hill: University of North Carolina Press, 2009.
Taylor, Amy Murrell. *The Divided Family in Civil War America*. Chapel Hill: University of North Carolina Press, 2005.
Thelen, David, ed. *Memory and American History*. Bloomington: Indiana University Press, 1990.
Thomas, Emory M. *The Confederacy as a Revolutionary Experience*. 1971. Reprint, Columbia: University of South Carolina Press, 1991.
———. *Robert E. Lee: A Biography*. New York: W. W. Norton, 1995.
Thomas, W. I., and D. S. Thomas. *The Child in America: Behavior Problems and Programs*. New York: Knopf, 1928.
Toplin, Robert, ed. *Ken Burns's The Civil War: Historians Respond*. New York: Oxford University Press, 1996.
Townes, W. Stuart. *Enduring Legacy: Rhetoric and Ritual of the Lost Cause*. Tuscaloosa: University of Alabama Press, 2012.
Trask, David F. *The War with Spain in 1898*. New York: Macmillan, 1981.
Traxel, David. *1898: The Birth of the American Century*. New York: Knopf, 1998.
Trefousse, Hans L. *Andrew Johnson: A Biography*. New York: Norton, 1989.
Trudeau, Noah Andre. *Like Men of War: Black Troops in the Civil War, 1862–1865*. Boston: Little, Brown, 1998.
———. *Out of the Storm: The End of the Civil War, April-June 1865*. Boston: Little, Brown, 1994.
Turner, Thomas Reed. *Beware the People Weeping: Public Opinion and the Assassination of Abraham Lincoln*. Baton Rouge: Louisiana State University Press, 1982.
Varon, Elizabeth R. *Disunion! The Coming of the American Civil War, 1789–1859*. Chapel Hill: University of North Carolina Press, 2008.
———. *We Mean to Be Counted: White Women and Politics in Antebellum Virginia*. Chapel Hill: University of North Carolina Press, 1998.
Warren, Robert Penn. *The Legacy of the Civil War*. 1961. Reprint, with an introduction by Howard Jones, Lincoln: University of Nebraska Press, 1998.
Waugh, Joan. *U. S. Grant: American Hero, American Myth*. Chapel Hill: University of North Carolina Press, 2009.
Weeks, Jim. *Gettysburg: Memory, Market, and an American Shrine*. Princeton, N.J.: Princeton University Press, 2003.

White, Ronald C. *Lincoln's Greatest Speech: The Second Inaugural*. New York: Simon & Schuster, 2002.

Whites, LeeAnn. *The Civil War as a Crisis in Gender: Augusta, Georgia, 1860–1890*. Athens: University of Georgia Press, 1995.

Wilson, Charles Reagan. *Baptized in Blood: The Religion of the Lost Cause*. Athens: University of Georgia Press, 1980.

Winter, Jay. *Sites of Memory, Sites of Mourning: The Great War in European Cultural History*. Cambridge: Cambridge University Press, 1998.

Woodward, C. Vann. *Origins of the New South 1877–1913*. Baton Rouge: Louisiana State University Press, 1951.

———. *The Strange Career of Jim Crow*. New York: Oxford University Press, 1974.

Woodworth, Stephen E. *Nothing but Victory: The Army of Tennessee, 1861–1865*. New York: Knopf, 2005.

Articles and Papers

Anderson, David. "Down Memory Lane: Nostalgia for the Old South in Post-Civil War Plantation Reminiscences." *Journal of Southern History* 71 (February 2005): 105–36.

Andrew, Rod, Jr. "Soldiers, Christians, and Patriots: The Lost Cause and Southern Military Schools, 1865–1915." *Journal of Southern History* 64 (November 1998): 677–710.

Barr, Alwyn. "The Semi-Centennial of Texas Independence in 1886." *Southwestern Historical Quarterly* 91 (January 1988): 349–59.

Blair, William A. "Barbarians at Fredericksburg's Gate: The Impact of the Union Army on Civilians." In *The Fredericksburg Campaign: Decision on the Rappahannock*, edited by Gary W. Gallagher, 142–70. Chapel Hill: University of North Carolina Press, 1995.

———. "Friend or Foe: Treason and the Second Confiscation Act." In *Wars within a War: Controversy and Conflict over the American Civil War*, edited by Joan Waugh and Gary W. Gallagher, 27–51. Chapel Hill: University of North Carolina Press, 2009.

Bradley, Ed. "The House, the Beast, and the Bloody Shirt: The Doorkeeper Controversy of 1878." *Journal of the Gilded Age and Progressive Era* 3, no. 1 (January 2004): 14–34.

Brundage, W. Fitzhugh. "White Women and the Politics of Historical Memory." In *Jumpin' Jim Crow: Southern Politics from Civil War to Civil Rights*, edited by Glenda Gilmore, Bryant Simon, and Jane Daily, 115–39. Princeton, N.J.: Princeton University Press, 2000.

Burton, Crompton B. "'The Dear Old Regiment': Maine's Regimental Associations and the Memory of the American Civil War." *New England Quarterly* 84 (March 2011): 104–22.

Case, Sarah H. "The Historical Ideology of Mildred Lewis Rutherford: A Confederate Historian's New South Creed." *Journal of Southern History* 68 (August 2002): 599–628.

Chadick, Mary Cook. "Civil War Days in Huntsville." *Alabama Historical Quarterly* 2 (Summer 1974) 319–33.

Chalker, Fussell M. "Fitzgerald: A Place of Reconciliation." *Georgia Historical Quarterly* 55 (Fall 1971): 397–405.

Crow, Amy. "'In Memory of the Confederate Dead': Masculinity and the Politics of Memorial Work in Greensboro, North Carolina, 1894–1895." *North Carolina Historical Review* 83 (January 2006): 31–60.

Fahs, Alice. "The Feminized Civil War." *Journal of American History* 85 (March 1999): 1461–94.

Fairclough, Adam. "Civil Rights and the Lincoln Memorial: The Censored Speeches of Robert R. Moton (1922) and John Lewis (1963)." *Journal of Negro History* 82, no. 4 (Autumn 1997): 408–16.

Faust, Drew Gilpin. "'A Riddle of Death': Mortality and Meaning in the American Civil War." 34th Annual Robert Fortenbaugh Memorial Lecture. Gettysburg, Pa.: Gettysburg College, 1995.

Gallagher, Gary W. "An End and New Beginning." In *Appomattox Court House National Historic Park Handbook 160*. Washington, D.C.: U.S. Government Printing Office, 2002.

Gara, Larry. "Slavery and the Slave Power: A Crucial Distinction." *Civil War History* 15 (March 1969): 5–18.

Gorman, Michael D. "Lee the 'Devil' Discovered at Image of War Seminar: Derisive Graffiti Appears in 1865 Brady Photo of Lee." *Battlefield Photographer* 3, no. 1 (February 2006): 1, 3–4.

Govan, Thomas P. "Americans below the Potomac." In *The Southerner as American*, edited by Charles Grier Sellers Jr., 19–39. Chapel Hill: University of North Carolina Press, 1960.

Hacker, J. David. "A Census-Based Count of the Civil War Dead." *Civil War History* 57 (December 2011): 307–48.

Harris, M. Keith. "Slavery, Emancipation, and Veterans of the Union Cause: Commemorating Freedom in the Era of Reconciliation, 1885–1915." *Civil War History* 53 (September 2007): 264–90.

Hillyer, Reiko. "Relics of Reconciliation: The Confederate Museum and Civil War Memory in the New South." *Public Historian* 33 (November 2011): 35–62.

"Historians' Forum." *Civil War History* 57 (December 2011): 380–402.

Holzer, Harold. "With Malice toward Both: Abraham Lincoln and Jefferson Davis in Caricature." In *Wars within a War: Controversy and Conflict over the American Civil War*, edited by Joan Waugh and Gary W. Gallagher, 109–56. Chapel Hill: University of North Carolina Press, 2009.

Irvine, Dallas D. "The Genesis of the *Official Records*." *Mississippi Valley Historical Review* 24, no. 2 (September 1937): 221–29.

Janda, Lance. "Shutting the Gates of Mercy: The American Origins of Total War, 1860–1880." *Journal of Military History* 59, no. 1 (January 1995): 7–26.

Janney, Caroline E. "'One of the Best Loved, North and South': The Appropriation of National Reconciliation by LaSalle Corbell Pickett." *Virginia Magazine of History and Biography* 116, no. 4 (2008): 370–406.

———. "War over the Shrine of Peace: The Appomattox Peace Monument and Retreat from Reconciliation." *Journal of Southern History* 77, no. 1 (2011): 91–120.

———. "Written in Stone: Gender, Race, and the Heyward Shepherd Memorial." *Civil War History* 52, no. 2 (June 2006): 117–41.

Johnson, Joan Marie. "'No North, No South': Touring the South for the WCTU." Unpublished paper presented at the Southern Historical Association Meeting, Richmond, November 2007.

———. "Sallie Chapin: The Woman's Christian Temperance Union and Reconciliation after the Civil War." In *South Carolina Women, Their Lives and Times*, edited by Marjorie Julian Spruill, Valinda W. Littlefield, and Joan Marie Johnson, 2:87–104. Athens: University of Georgia Press, 2010.

Kelly, Patrick J. "The Election of 1896 and the Restructuring of Civil War Memory." *Civil War Memory* 49 (September 2003): 254–80.

Krowl, Michelle A. "'In the Spirit of Fraternity: The United States Government and the Burial of the Confederate Dead at Arlington National Cemetery, 1864–1914." *Virginia Magazine of History and Biography* 111, no. 2 (2003): 151–86.

Logue, Larry M. "Union Veterans and Their Government: The Effects of Public Policies on Private Lives." *Journal of Interdisciplinary History* 22 (Winter 1992): 411–34.

Madison, James. "Civil War Memories and 'Pardnership Forgittin',' 1865–1913." *Indiana Magazine of History* 99 (September 1999): 198–230.

Mahan, Harold E. "The Arsenal of History: *The Official Records of the War of the Rebellion.*" *Civil War History* 29, no. 1 (March 1983): 5–27.

Marshall, Anne E. "The 1906 *Uncle Tom's Cabin* Law and the Politics of Race and Memory in Early-Twentieth Century Kentucky." *Journal of the Civil War Era* 1, no. 3 (2011): 368–93.

McPherson, James M. "Antebellum Southern Exceptionalism: A New Look at an Old Question." *Civil War History* 50, no. 4 (2004): 418–33.

———. "The Long-Legged Yankee Lies: The Southern Textbook Crusade." In *The Memory of the Civil War in American Culture*, edited by Alice Fahs and Joan Waugh, 64–93. Chapel Hill: University of North Carolina Press, 2004.

Mills, Cynthia. "Gratitude and Gender Wars: Monuments to Women of the Sixties." In *Monuments to the Lost Cause: Women, Art, and the Landscapes of Southern Memory*, edited by Cynthia Mills and Pamela H. Simpson, 183–202. Knoxville: University of Tennessee Press, 2003.

Morgan, Edmund S. "The Puritan Ethic and the American Revolution." *William and Mary Quarterly* 24 (January 1967): 3–43.

Neely, Mark E., Jr. "Was the Civil War a Total War?" *Civil War History* 27 (March 1991): 5–28.

Nicoletti, Cynthia. "The American Civil War as a Trial by Battle." *Law and History Review* 28 (Spring 2010): 71–110.

Nora, Pierre. "Between History and Memory: Les Lieux de Mémoire." *Representations* 26 (Spring 1989): 7–25.

Osborn, George C., ed. "Letters of Senator Edward Cary Walthall to Robert W. Banks." *Journal of Mississippi History* 9 (July 1949): 185–203.

Parsons, Elaine Frantz. "Klan Skepticism and Denial in Reconstruction-Era Public Discourse." *Journal of Southern History* 77 (February 2011): 53–90.

Pettegrew, John. "'The Soldier's Faith': Turn-of-the-Century Memory of the Civil War." *Journal of Contemporary History* 96 (January 1996): 49–73.

Poole, W. Scott. "Memory and the Abolitionist Heritage: Thomas Wentworth Higginson and the Uncertain Meaning of the Civil War." *Civil War History* 52 (June 2005): 202–17.

Potter, David. "The Historian's Use of Nationalism and Vice Versa." *American Historical Review* 67, no. 4 (July 1962): 924–50.

Ross, Michael A. "The Commemoration of Robert E. Lee's Death and the Obstruction of Reconstruction New Orleans." *Civil War History* 51, no. 2 (June 2005): 135–50.

Sandage, Scott A. "A Marble House Divided: The Lincoln Memorial, the Civil Rights Movement, and the Politics of Memory, 1939–1963." *Journal of American History* 80 (June 1993): 135–67.

Schwartz, Barry. "Collective Memory and History: How Abraham Lincoln Became a Symbol of Racial Equality." *Sociological Quarterly* 38, no. 3 (Summer 1997): 469–96.

Taylor, John M. "General Hancock: Soldier of the Gilded Age." *Pennsylvania History* 32 (April 1965): 187–96.

Thurber, Cheryl. "The Development of the Mammy Image and Mythology." In *Southern Women: Histories and Identities*, edited by Virginia Bernhard, 87–108. Columbia: University of Missouri Press, 1992.

Trudeau, Noah Andre. "Start with the Basics: A Select Group of Essential Primary Sources Helps Tell the War's Stories." *Civil War Times Illustrated* 51, no. 4 (August 2012): 52–57.

Van Zelm, Antoinette G. "Virginia Women as Public Citizens: Emancipation Day Celebrations and Lost Cause Commemorations, 1863–1890." In *Negotiating Boundaries of Southern Womanhood: Dealing with Powers That Be*, edited by Janet L. Coryell et al. Columbia: University of Missouri Press, 2000.

Varon, Elizabeth R. "'The Last Hour of the Slaveholders' Rebellion': African American Discourse on Lee's Surrender at Appomattox." Paper presented at the Georgetown Nineteenth Century Workshop, March 22, 2010.

Vinovskis, Maris A. "Have Social Historians Lost the Civil War?: Some Preliminary Demographic Speculations." *Journal of American History* 76, no. 1 (June 1989): 34–58.

Whitfield, Stephen J. "Sacred in History and in Art: *The Shaw Memorial*." *New England Quarterly* 60, no. 1 (March 1987): 3–27.

Williams, Kenneth H., and Russell Harris. "Kentucky in 1860: A Statistical Overview." *The Register* 103 (Autumn 2005): 743–64.

Wilson, Richard Guy. "Monument Avenue, Richmond." In *Monuments to the Lost Cause: Women, Art, and the Landscapes of Southern Memory*, edited by Cynthia Mills and Pamela H. Simpson, 100–115. Knoxville: University of Tennessee Press, 2003.

Theses and Dissertations

Barr, John. "The Anti-Lincoln Tradition in American Life." Ph.D. dissertation, University of Houston, 2011.

Dunlap, Leslie Kathrin. "In the Name of the Home: Temperance Women and Southern Grass-Roots Politics, 1873–1933." Ph.D. dissertation, Northwestern University, 2001.

Harris, M. Keith. "Across the Bloody Chasm: Reconciliation in the Wake of the Civil War." Ph.D. dissertation, University of Virginia, 2009.

Houck, Jeanne B. "Written in Stone: Historical Memory and the Mall in Washington, D.C., 1861–1945." Ph.D. dissertation, New York University, 1993.

Kinsel, Amy. "'From These Honored Dead': Gettysburg in American Culture, 1863–1938." Ph.D. dissertation, Cornell University, 1992.

Luebke, Peter C. "Union Regimental Histories, 1865–1866." M.A. thesis, University of Virginia, 2007.

Websites

Alabama Local News (http://blog.al.com/montgomery/2011/02/sons_of_confederate_veterans_c.html)

Ancestery.Com (http://www.rootsweb.ancestry.com)

Andersonville National Historic Site (http://www.nps.gov/ande/historyculture/wirz-mon.htm)

CNN Opinion Poll (http://politicalticker.blogs.cnn.com/2011/04/12/cnnopinion-research-poll-april-9–10-civil-war/)

Civil War Sesquicentennial (http://www.whitehouse.gov)

Official Website of Arlington National Cemetery (http://www.arlingtoncemetery.mil/visitor_information/Confederate_Memorial.html)

Senator Jim Webb (Va.) Homepage (http://webb.senate.gov/newsroom/pressreleases/03–16–2011–01.cfm)

Susan Augusta Pike Sanders (http://www.mchistory.org/popups/CemWalk%20Bios/Sanders_Sue_Pike.html)

Time magazine (http://www.time.com/time/nation/article/0,8599,2055981,00.html)

Virginia Sesquicentennial Commission (http://www.virginiacivilwar.org/)

Virtual Gettysburg (http://www.virtualgettysburg.com/exhibit/monuments/feature.html)

INDEX

AANVA. *See* Association of the Army of Northern Virginia

Abolitionism, 14–16, 48, 52, 59, 81, 88, 98, 112, 208, 209, 277, 316 (n. 12). *See also* Emancipation

"Abraham Lincoln" (Brownell), 72, 331 (n. 167)

Adams, Charles Francis, II, 269

Adams, Mrs. W. Carleton, 255, 375 (n. 94)

Addams, Jane, 162

African American Civil War Memorial, 388 (n. 18)

African Americans: and American Legion, 282; and black codes in the South, 85–86; celebration by, following Confederate surrender, 48; civil rights for, 61, 113, 116, 119, 126, 203, 222, 228, 290; and civil rights movement of twentieth century, 305, 307–10; and Civil War Centennial Commission, 307–8; and Confederate Memorial Days, 210; at Confederate veterans' reunions, 210; contributions of, during Civil War, 84; disenfranchisement of, 8–9, 199, 210, 215, 275, 293; at Grand Review of Union soldiers, 70–71; Lee on freedmen, 65; and Lincoln Memorial, 285–86, 288–89, 305; lynchings and mob violence against, 162, 199, 210, 215, 220, 227, 275, 286, 291, 293, 361 (n. 8); mourning by, at Lincoln's death, 56; mourning by, for their soldiers, 75; and myth of black rapist, 255, 291, 297–98; newspapers and periodicals for, 219–20; and Niagara Movement, 275; and prohibition of interracial marriage, 86; racism against, 17, 36, 318 (n. 28); scholarship on, 315 (n. 16); and semi-centennial celebrations of emancipation, 272–73, 277–79; and Spanish-American War, 225–28; as state and federal officeholders, 105, 213,

366 (n. 117); stereotypes of, 204–5, 208, 210, 291, 368 (n. 147); and testimony in white courts, 86; and Union Memorial Days, 4, 8, 75, 100–101, 211–12, 273, 369 (n. 169); voting rights for, 61, 88, 97–98, 105, 113, 117, 139, 148, 203, 208, 228, 291, 333 (n. 27); in Woman's Relief Corps, 125. *See also* African American veterans; African American women; Emancipation; Emancipation Days; Segregation; Slavery; United States Colored Troops; White supremacy

African American veterans: on African American women during Civil War, 236; and Blue-Gray reunions, 205–6; and Chickamauga and Chattanooga dedication, 205–6, 362 (n. 41), 362–63 (n. 42); in Colored Soldiers' and Sailors' League, 117, 341 (n. 48), 342 (n. 53); and Gettysburg reunion (1913), 267; in Grand Army of the Republic, 8, 101, 117–20, 205–6, 215, 222, 342 (n. 68), 342–43 (n. 71), 363 (n. 43); and preservation of the Union, 115–20; relationship between white Union veterans and, 338 (n. 6); reunions of, 215; and Union and emancipation as dual legacy of Civil War, 105; and Union Memorial Days, 101; and United Confederate Veterans, 222

African American women: during Civil War, 236; Civil War groups of, 375 (n. 80); and mammy image, 8, 211, 254, 264, 292–93; in Woman's Relief Corps, 252–53, 283, 375 (n. 79)

Alabama: Emancipation Days in, 215; Grand Army of the Republic posts in, 205; Memorial Day celebrations in, 369 (n. 170); Scottsboro boys case in, 297–98; sesquicentennial celebration of Civil War in, 309, 310, 388 (n. 14)

Alabama (Thomas), 186

Battle, Henry W., 386 (n. 160)

Battlefield monuments. *See* Confederate monuments; Union monuments; *and specific monuments*

Battles and Leaders of the Civil War, 165–66, 198, 203–4, 354 (n. 14)

Baxter, Alice, 258

Beard, John S., 186

Beauregard, P. G. T., 149, 165

Beckman, Ellen J., 339 (n. 9)

Beecher, Harris H., 105, 339 (n. 8)

Beecher, Henry Ward, 52, 81, 341 (n. 49)

Behan, Katie, 261–62

Bell, John, 16

Belle Isle (Richmond prison), 28, 77, 152

Bellows, Dr., 341 (n. 49)

Beringer, Richard, 318 (n. 36)

Berlin, Ira, 340 (n. 31)

Berry, Fannie, 48

Betts, Karl S., 387 (n. 5)

Bickerdyke, Mother, 236, 370 (n. 15)

Birdsall, Henry, 58

Birth of a Nation, The, 256, 277, 279–80, 303

Bismarck, Otto von, 112

Black codes, 85–86

Black Reconstruction in America, 1860–1880 (Du Bois), 304, 387 (n. 177)

Blacks. *See* African Americans

Blaine, James, 152

Blair, William A., 317 (n. 17), 357 (n. 77), 367 (n. 133), 368 (nn. 156, 160), 379 (n. 24)

Bledsoe, Albert Taylor, 136

Blight, David W., 315 (nn. 14, 20), 337 (n. 113), 338 (nn. 124, 5), 353 (n. 5), 359 (n. 107), 361 (n. 16), 362 (n. 41), 364 (n. 72), 374 (n. 74), 383 (n. 103)

"Bloody shirt" rhetoric, 126–32, 151

Blue and the Gray, The, 186

Blue and Gray: The Patriotic American Magazine, 188

Blue-Gray magazines, 164–66

Blue-Gray organizations of veterans, 158

Blue-Gray reunions: and African Americans, 205–6; and "Americanness," 170–71, 263; at anniversary of battle of Bunker Hill, 166; Appomattox semi-centennial celebration, 274–75; Confederate veterans' view of, 173–74; criticisms of, 267; frequency of, 3, 167–68;

at Gettysburg, 175–76, 266–68, 274; last Reunion of the Blue and Gray, 300, 301; Manassas Peace Jubilee and Reunion, 232–34; motivations of veterans for, 166–67; parameters of, 167; and reconciliation, 6, 161, 162; tensions at, 3–4, 194–95; in twentieth century, 266–69; in Virginia, 160–61; women at, 232–34, 247, 370 (n. 2)

Blum, Edward, 314 (n. 12)

Bohannon, Keith, 360 (n. 122)

Bonner, M. J., 301

Booth, John Wilkes, 42, 56, 59, 64, 67, 328 (n. 109)

Boston Advertiser, 90

Bowers, Claude, 297

Boynton, Henry Van Ness, 177–78, 180, 357 (n. 73)

Brady, Mathew, 59, 60

Bragg, Braxton, 149

Bragg, Junius, 64

Brazil, 69

Breckinridge, John C., 159, 330–31 (n. 158), 348 (n. 28)

Briggs, Carolina, 122

Brisbin, James S., 101

Broaddus, Andrew, 161

Brooke-Rawle, William, 164

Brown, Henry Kirke, 341 (n. 51)

Brown, John, 14, 59, 61, 81, 119, 219, 273

Brown, Jonathan Mason, 100, 338 (n. 120)

Brown, Thomas J., 365 (n. 98)

Brown-Daggett, Eliza, 282

Brownell, Henry Howard, 72, 331 (n. 167)

Brownlow, William "Parson," 79

Brown v. Board of Education, 306–7

Brundage, W. Fitzhugh, 314 (n. 5), 372 (n. 38)

Bryan, St. George T. C., 267

Bryan, William Jennings, 225, 262, 359 (n. 108), 377 (n. 125)

Buck, Paul, 354 (n. 19)

Buel, Clarence C., 165–66

Buffalo Soldiers, 226

Bullard, F. Lauriston, 341 (n. 51)

Bull Run, battles of, 13, 73, 112. *See also* Manassas

Bull Run monuments, 73–74, 77, 106, 332 (n. 11)

Bunker Hill, battle of, 166

Burial Corps, U.S., 77–78, 91, 93

Confederate flag: at Blue-Gray reunions, 234; at Jefferson Davis's funeral, 183; at dedication of Lee monument in Richmond, 181–82; northern reactions to, 181–83, 194, 356 (n. 65); return of Confederate battle flags, 174–75, 246, 269; as symbol of treason, 183, 220, 234; and United Daughters of the Confederacy, 248–49, 260–61, 275

Confederate Memorial Days: activities during, 93–95; and African Americans, 210; compared with Union Memorial Days, 99–100; dates for, 93, 335 (n. 74), 336 (n. 90); Lee's refusal to attend, 137; and Lost Cause, 94–95, 134; northerners' negative reactions to, 95–96, 336 (n. 96); restrictions on, under Reconstruction, 98; and separate southern identity, 75; and southern white women, 93–100, 237, 258–59, 283. *See also* Union Memorial Days

Confederate Memorial Literary Society (CMLS), 244, 253, 274, 379 (n. 31)

Confederate monuments: Arlington Confederate Monument, 261–65, 377 (nn. 125–26), 377–78 (n. 132), 378 n. 133), 388 (n. 18); in Chicago, 171, 222, 355 (n. 41); design of, 156, 352 (n. 99); in 1880s, 156; to faithful slaves, 210, 254–55, 292–93, 297, 383–84 (n. 119); geography of, 135; at Gettysburg, 356 (nn. 63, 67); in Kentucky, 115; and Ladies' Memorial Associations, 135, 156; to Lee, 141–42, 181–82, 270, 271, 349 (n. 37); Lee's refusal to support, 137–38; and Lost Cause, 134–35; to southern white women, 236, 370 (n. 13); in Virginia, 134–35, 141, 176–77, 188–91; Wirz monument, 235, 256–59, 261, 262, 263, 376 (n. 113)

Confederate Museum (Richmond), 244, 253. *See also* White House of the Confederacy

Confederate Relief and Historical Association (Memphis), 140

Confederate soldiers: animosity of, following surrender, 42–45; at Appomattox Court House, 45–46; bravery and loyalty of, 43, 51, 86, 91, 94, 134, 144, 167, 170, 192, 193, 202–3, 216, 275, 326 (n. 56); brutality by, 12–13, 20, 28; exclusion of,

from Grand Review, 71; and hard-war policy of Union generals, 25–28; hatred and animosity of, toward enemy, 12–14, 19–24, 66; independent nation as Civil War goal of, 13; Lee's farewell order to, 43–44, 66, 86, 144, 324–25 (n. 11), 325 (n. 15); after Lincoln's assassination, 66; motivations of, 17–19, 316 (n. 6), 320 (n. 66); as prisoners of war, 28, 35, 41, 322 (n. 92), 323 (n. 109); resistance of, to Lee's surrender, 53, 64; return home by, after surrender, 41, 49, 139, 329 (nn. 122, 124); as slaveholders, 207, 318 (n. 34); statistics on, 238, 371 (n. 22). *See also* Confederate veterans

Confederate Soldier's Association (Pickens County, S.C.), 140, 347 (n. 25)

Confederate Survivor's Association of Augusta, Ga., 154

Confederate Survivors' Association of South Carolina, 140

Confederate Veteran: circulation of, 180–81, 357 (n. 76); compared with *Southern Historical Society Papers*, 180; competitors of, 357 (n. 75); Cunningham as editor of, 180, 209, 223, 357 (n. 75); founding of, 180

Confederate veterans: Cleveland's appointment of, to federal posts, 174, 175; as ex-prisoners of war, 151–52; hostility of, toward Union veterans, 186; northern view of, 202; organizations of, 139–40, 142, 153–54, 156–58, 348 (n. 34); pensions for, 229–30, 369 (nn. 163, 166); and praise for wartime sacrifices of southern white women, 235, 238–39; regimental histories by, 135–36, 163, 346 (n. 7); respect for, by southerners, 139, 347 (n. 23); reunions of, 133–34, 153–56, 157, 207, 209, 210, 277, 345 (n. 2), 351 (n. 87); on slavery, 207; soldiers' homes for, 221, 229, 248, 360 (n. 137), 369 (n. 163); and Spanish-American War, 223–25; statistics on, 268, 301, 302, 360 (n. 137); stories and conversations by, about wartime experiences, 185. *See also* Blue-Gray reunions; Lost Cause; Reconciliation; United Confederate Veterans

Confederate War Journal Illustrated, 357 (n. 75)

Hollywood Cemetery, 302; *Rise and Fall of the Confederate Government* by, 207; on southern white women, 238, 239; state holiday honoring, 248; and surrender terms, 5; and Union prisoners of war, 50; at White Sulphur Springs meeting, 142, 238

Davis, Varina, 67, 241–42, 253, 372 (n. 36)

Davis, William H., 285–86

Davis, Winnie, 241

Dawson, Francis W., 184, 235

Day, Hollen E., 248

De Armond, David, 369 (n. 163)

DeBaptist, Rev. R., 88

Decoration Day. *See* Confederate Memorial Days; Union Memorial Days

De Forest, Bartholomew B. S., 17

Dehart, R. P., 212

Democratic Party: and congressional election of 1867, 129; and Conscription Act (1863), 36; and emancipation, 317 (n. 24); on Emancipation Proclamation, 36; and "free labor" ideology, 15; and Lee, 50–51, 138–39; and Lincoln's plan for reconstruction, 35, 41; Peace Democrats/Copperheads, 16, 36, 245–46, 317 (n. 24), 320 (n. 67), 323–24 (n. 117); racism of, 36; and reconciliation, 81; and Redeemers, 20, 133, 142, 200; War Democrats, 36, 323–24 (n. 117); and white supremacy, 81

Dennett, John Richard, 87, 334 (n. 41)

Department of Interior, U.S., 300

De Peyster, J. Watts, 340 (n. 27)

Derrick, Rev. W. B., 205

DeSaussure, C. A., 294–96, 384 (n. 134)

Devens, Charles, 126

Dexter, George N., 133

Dickerson, Rev. Charles, 117

Dickerson, Samuel, 48

Dimon, Theodore, 29

"Dixie," 46, 166, 182

Dixon, Thomas, 255–56, 276

Dom Pedro II (emperor of Brazil), 69

Dooley, John, 53

Dorman, Alfred S., 53

Douglass, Frederick: black newspapers on, 219; and Freedmen's Memorial, 114; Grand Army of the Republic posts named after, 119; on Lincoln, 114, 286, 342 (n. 54); and National Lin-

coln Monument Association, 113, 341 (n. 48); pageant on, 273; on reconciliation, 58; on remembering Civil War and emancipation, 4, 7, 111, 201, 218, 222, 311

Douglass, Lewis H., 227, 256

Downing, George T., 213

Drum, R. C., 174

Du Bois, W. E. B., 272, 273, 304–5, 379 (n. 27), 387 (n. 177)

Du Bose, Dudley McIver, 135–36

Duffield, Rev. George, 59

Duffield, Henry M., 192

Duke, Basil, 255, 353–54 (n. 13)

Duke, Henrietta Morgan, 255, 375 (n. 95)

Dunlap, Leslie Kathrin, 372 (n. 34)

Dunn, Oscar J., 149

Dunning, William A., 276, 304

Dunovant, Adelia A., 249, 251, 374 (n. 68)

Early, Jubal A.: on African Americans, 220; on Army of Northern Virginia, 144; and Association of the Army of Northern Virginia, 142, 348 (n. 34); defense of slavery by, 146, 275; expatriation of, to Canada, 141, 330 (n. 158); federal indictment against, 68; on Grant, 150; and Grant's funeral, 169; and Lee Monument Association, 141–42, 349 (n. 37); and Lee Monument in Richmond, 182; and Lost Cause, 131, 141–44, 158, 159, 348 (n. 33), 350 (n. 58), 351 (n. 78), 351–52 (n. 88); military career of, 141; and reconciliation, 138; on Reconstruction, 149–50; refusal of, to contribute to *Battles and Leaders of the Civil War*, 165; refusal of parole or amnesty by, 68, 348 (n. 33); on remembering Civil War, 4–5, 311; return of, to United States (1869), 141, 348 (n. 33); on slavery, 8, 207, 253, 350 (n. 58); and Southern Historical Society, 142, 158, 349 (nn. 38–39); at White Sulphur Springs meeting, 142–43

Early, Ruth, 350 (n. 58)

Earnshaw, Chaplain William, 76

Easley, William King, 146, 149, 150

Edmonds, Sarah Emma, 320–21 (n. 69)

Eisenhower, Dwight D., 306–7

Ellet, Mary, 82

Ellyson, J. Taylor, 177, 274

Elmira Prison, 28, 151–52
Emancipation: Douglass on, 7, 111; and
    Emancipation Cause, 315 (n. 20), 332
    (n. 10); as goal/end result of Civil War,
    15–17, 51–52, 72, 77, 88, 111–16, 198,
    201–6, 208, 271, 289–90, 316 (n. 12),
    317 (nn. 19, 24–25), 332 (n. 10), 340
    (n. 31), 342 (n. 66), 361 (n. 17); impact
    of, on the South, 84–87, 207; John-
    son's concerns about, 83; Lincoln as
    Great Emancipator, 8, 62, 90–91, 115,
    286, 292, 305, 382 (n. 90); and Lin-
    coln Memorial, 285–89; and meaning
    of liberty, 113; preservation of the Union
    linked with, 111–17, 125–26, 289–90;
    and reconciliation, 199–206; and Re-
    publicans, 26, 317 (n. 24); responsi-
    bility of, 201–2; and reunion, 85; semi-
    centennial celebrations of, 272–73,
    277–79; southern view of impact of, on
    African Americans, 208–9, 253; and
    Thirteenth Amendment, 16–17, 105;
    Union Memorial Day rhetoric on, 100,
    338 (n. 119); United Daughters of the
    Confederacy on, 253–56; white Union
    veterans' attitude on, 7, 9, 340 (n. 40);
    and Woman's Relief Corps, 53. See also
    Abolitionism; Emancipation Days;
    Emancipation Proclamation
Emancipation Days: African Americans'
    celebration of generally, 8, 75, 219; be-
    ginning of, in 1857, 323 (n. 103); during
    Civil War, 33–34; dates for, 88–89, 212–
    14; festive nature of, 33, 87–91, 119–20,
    212; frequency of, 340 (n. 43); Grand
    National Celebration of Freedom in
    Richmond, 213–14; on New Year's Day,
    33, 87–88, 212, 214; political activism
    of, 213, 214–15, 379 (n. 24); as threat to
    safety of African Americans, 89–90, 334
    (n. 64), 335 (n. 75); in twentieth cen-
    tury, 272; whites' participation in, 221
Emancipation Proclamation: African
    Americans on, during Civil War, 33;
    anniversary celebrations of, 120, 212;
    beginning date of, 16, 33, 214; Confeder-
    ate leaders on, 26; Democratic Party on,
    36; and enlistment of African Ameri-
    cans, 16; Martin Luther King on, 307,
    308; and Lincoln monuments, 114; pre-
    liminary version of, 201, 307; reading of,

during Emancipation Day celebrations,
    90–91; as war measure, 16, 111, 286
Evacuation Day ceremonies, 8, 75, 89–90,
    272, 335 (n. 75). See also Emancipation
    Days
Evans, Clement A., 143, 173–74
Evans, William McKee, 300
Everett, Edward, 31
Ewell, Richard, 20, 68
Ewing, Hugh B., 16
Ezekiel, Moses, 263–64

Fairchild, Lucius, 174–76, 183, 355–56
    (n. 58)
Fair Oaks, battle of, 24
Faithful slaves, image of. See Lost Cause;
    Slavery
Falkner, Jefferson Manly, 366 (n. 116)
Fallows, Samuel, 113, 288
Faust, Drew Gilpin, 318 (n. 36), 320 (n. 59)
Federal Memorial Days. See Union Memo-
    rial Days
Federal Writers' Project, 305
Federated Patriotic Societies, 294
Ferguson, Champ, 80
Field, Charles William, 128
Field, James G., 187
Fields, Barbara J., 340 (n. 31)
Fifteenth Amendment, 105, 117, 148, 214
Finch, George M., 183
First World War. See Great War
Fitzgerald, Ga., 187–88
Fitzgerald, Philander H., 187–88
Fitz-Hugh St. Clair: The South Carolina
    Rebel Boy (Chapin), 240, 241
Flags. See American flag; Confederate flag
Fleche, Andre, 318 (n. 33)
Fleetwood, Christian, 117
Fletcher, Lucy, 84
Flood, Joel W., 386 (n. 163)
Florida: Emancipation Days in, 214, 221;
    Grand Army of the Republic in, 188;
    Woman's Relief Corps in, 283
Flower, Roswell P., 168, 354 (n. 28)
Foracker, Joseph B., 175
Fordyce, S. W., 224
Forrest, Nathan B., 55, 310
Fort Delaware, 139
Fort Donelson, 35
Fort Monroe, 67, 87, 242
Fort Pillow, 20, 26, 119, 226, 319 (n. 45)

Fort Sumter, 55–56, 59
Fort Wagner, 84, 119, 216, 217, 226
Fort Warren, 68, 86–87
Foster, Gaines, 346 (n. 13), 348 (n. 33), 349
    (nn. 37–38), 351 (n. 78), 351–52 (n. 88),
    352 (nn. 92, 99), 357 (n. 76)
Foster, Kate, 39
Foster, R. B., 367 (n. 126)
Fourteenth Amendment, 105, 140, 148, 214
Fourth of July. *See* July Fourth ceremonies
Fowle, Mary P., 245
Fowler, Abbie C., 246–47
Frank Leslie's Illustrated Newspaper, 29, 50
Fraternal organizations. *See specific orga-
    nizations*
Fredericksburg, battle of, 25, 33, 40, 107
Fredericksburg battlefield, 296
Freedmen and -women. *See* African Ameri-
    cans
Freedmen's Bureau, 77, 276
Freedmen's Memorial, 114–15, 341–42
    (n. 53)
Freedom. *See* Emancipation
Freedom Project, 340 (n. 31)
Free labor ideology, 15, 19, 202
Freeman, Douglas Southall, 302–3, 346
    (n. 13), 386–87 (n. 173)
Free Soil Party, 171
French, Daniel Chester, 285
Frietchie, Barbara, 320 (n. 68)
Fugitive Slave Act, 59
Fuller, Sarah E., 245
Fullerton, Joseph S., 357 (n. 73)

Gage, M. D., 111
Gallagher, Gary W., 315 (n. 20), 338–39
    (n. 7), 348 (n. 33), 371 (n. 22), 388
    (n. 17)
Gannon, Barbara A., 342 (n. 71), 343
    (n. 73), 363 (n. 43), 375 (n. 80)
GAR. *See* Grand Army of the Republic
Gara, Larry, 362 (n. 32)
Gardner, James Henry, 98
Gardner, Sarah, 346 (n. 9)
Gardner, Washington, 173, 263
Garfield, James A., 130, 155, 203, 246, 352
    (n. 95), 358 (n. 104)
Garrett, John W., 82
Garrison, William Lloyd, 48, 88
Garside, Julia A., 384 (n. 127)
Gary, Martin Witherspoon, 351 (n. 82)

GBMA. *See* Gettysburg Battlefield Memo-
    rial Association
Gender. *See* Northern white women; South-
    ern white women
Georgia: Atlanta Cotton Expositions in,
    171, 217; Blue-Gray reunion in, 194–95;
    Confederated Southern Memorial Asso-
    ciation in, 294; Confederate Memorial
    Day in, 93; Confederate Survivor's Asso-
    ciation of Augusta in, 154; Confederate
    veterans' groups in, 156, 369 (n. 166);
    Emancipation Day in, 221; Fitzgerald
    soldiers' colony in, 187–88; Grand Army
    of the Republic posts in, 205; readmis-
    sion of, to the Union, 133; Redeemers
    in, 133, 157; reunion of Confederate
    veterans in, 133–34, 345 (n. 2); United
    Daughters of the Confederacy in, 257,
    258
Georgia-Pacific Railroad, 158
Georgia regiments: 3rd, 133, 150, 351
    (n. 87); 6th, 19, 145
Gettysburg: Blue-Gray reunion (1913) at,
    266–69, 274; as commemorative site,
    31–33, 32, 88, 100, 107, 163, 201; GAR
    reunion at (1885), 122; *Laney's Gettys-
    burg* battlefield guide, 201; monuments
    at, 77, 100, 103, 106–7, 168, 176, 178, 179,
    200, 205, 332 (n. 11), 356 (nn. 60–63,
    67), 370 (n. 13); reinterment of south-
    ern soldiers buried at, 261; speeches at,
    201
Gettysburg, battle of: casualties from, 30,
    106, 107, 322 (n. 98), 356 (n. 61); Con-
    federate dead from, 30, 322 (n. 98); fifti-
    eth anniversary of, 10–11; Lee's defeat
    at, 32–33, 107, 144–45, 164; Pickett's
    Charge at, 175–76, 178, 266; significance
    of, 32–33, 40, 107, 164; silver anniver-
    sary of (1888), 176; site of, 338 (n. 1)
Gettysburg Address, 31, 228, 285, 286, 292
Gettysburg Battlefield Memorial Associa-
    tion (GBMA), 31–32, 103, 106–7, 138,
    175, 195, 237, 356 (n. 63)
Gettysburg national cemetery: black sol-
    dier buried in, 78; Cemetery Asso-
    ciation, 322 (n. 97); compared with
    Andersonville cemetery, 76; funding for,
    322 (n. 97); Lincoln's dedication of, 77;
    management of, 322 (n. 97); number of
    Union soldiers buried in, 322 (n. 97);

remembering Union dead at, 98; for Union dead, 30–33, 75

Gettysburg National Military Park, 195

Gibbons, J. R., 258

Gilder, Richard Watson, 204

Gill, Charles A., 100

Gillespie, Emily, 121

Glatthaar, Joseph T., 318 (n. 34), 327 (n. 85)

Glenn, William, 55

Glory, 309

Gobin, J. P. S., 176

Gone with the Wind, 303–4, 308, 387 (n. 175)

Gooden, Henry, 78

Goodlett, Caroline Meriwether, 242, 243

Gordon, Anna, 241

Gordon, John B.: at Appomattox Court House, 45–46, 170, 355 (n. 38), 379 (n. 28); at Blue-Gray reunion in Atlanta, 194–95; and Chickamauga national park, 178; on *Confederate War Journal Illustrated*, 357 (n. 75); on Grant's surrender terms, 150; and Ku Klux Klan, 351 (n. 75), 352 (n. 102); on Lee, 144; and Lee Monument in Richmond, 182; and Lost Cause, 157–58, 194; on reconciliation, 158, 194–95, 349 (n. 37), 360 (n. 131); on Reconstruction, 150; and United Confederate Veterans, 157–58, 352 (n. 104); on white supremacy, 158

Govan's Brigade, 154

Graham, David, 356 (n. 63)

Graham, Ezekiel D., 19

Graham, Robert, 100

Grand Army of Confederate Veterans of Virginia, 185

Grand Army of the Republic (GAR): African American veterans in, 8, 101, 117–20, 205–6, 215, 222, 342 (n. 68), 342–43 (n. 71), 363 (n. 43); and Andersonville monuments, 257; and Andersonville Prison Park, 376 (n. 102); and Appomattox celebrations, 274, 343 (n. 81); and Arlington Confederate Monument, 263, 264; and *The Birth of a Nation*, 279, 380 (n. 56); and Blue-Gray reunions, 160–61, 166, 247; and Carney monument in Norfolk, Va., 365 (n. 101); and commemoration of Lincoln's life, 294; and Confederate flag, 183, 234; and

Confederate graves, 102, 229; and Confederate monument at Gettysburg, 356 (n. 63); and Jefferson Davis's funeral, 183; and Emancipation Days, 119–20; ending of, 302; and Fitzgerald soldiers' colony, 188; founding of, 108; goals and motto of, 109–10, 120, 123, 184; Grant as member of, 131; and Grant equestrian statue, 284; and Grant's funeral, 169; hostility between white southerners and, 4, 9, 355 (n. 48); and joint encampment with United Confederate Veterans, 195, 301; and Lee Monument, 181; and Lincoln Memorial, 287; local club rooms of, 110; membership statistics for, 108–9, 153, 163; and Memorial Days, 99, 100, 119, 121, 202–3, 287, 337 (n. 114); and monument to unknown Confederate dead in national cemetery, 262; national encampments of, 110, 173, 183, 191, 205, 206, 230, 251–52, 257, 264, 302; newspaper of, 110; origins of, 108; papers and artifacts of, to Library of Congress and Smithsonian, 386 (n. 170); parade of, in Detroit, 270; and pensions and soldiers' homes for Confederate veterans, 229; and pensions for veterans, 109, 110; and publication of official records of Civil War, 130; records of, 343 (n. 73); rejection of Lost Cause by, 126; and return of Confederate battle flags, 174–75; reunions of, 121, 122, 379 (n. 35); and rightness of Union cause, 110, 173; and school textbooks, 183–84, 242, 358 (n. 92); and sectional animosity versus national unity, 371 (n. 27); and Sons of Union Veterans, 381 (n. 65); in South, 186, 205, 362 (n. 39); in twentieth century, 268, 302; and United Confederate Veterans and United Daughters of the Confederacy resolution on Lincoln, 291; women's auxiliaries of, 123–25, 238, 344 (n. 97)

Grand Army Record, 183

Grand Review, 69–72, 331 (n. 162)

Grant, Fred, 169

Grant, Julia Dent, 241–42, 253

Grant, Ulysses S.: black newspapers on, 219; and celebrations following Confederate surrender, 47; criticisms of military record of, 131, 137, 150, 351 (n. 74);

death and funeral of, 130, 169–70, 174;
and Freedmen's Memorial, 114; and
Grand Review of Union soldiers, 69–70;
on Lee, 131; memoirs by, 111, 130–31,
236, 345 (n. 122); military education of,
354 (n. 32); monuments to, 182, 242,
284, 295–300, 357 (n. 80); order stopping soldiers' revelry at end of Civil
War, 42–43, 45; and pardon for Lee, 66;
and peace conference with Confederate commissioners, 37; and Petersburg
siege, 37; and presidential election of
1868, 127, 129, 131, 138; and prisoner
exchange system, 150, 164; and punishment of Confederate leaders, 67–68;
on reconciliation, 131; and Reconstruction, 150–51, 170, 297; reelection of, in
1872, 128, 157–58; on righteousness of
Union Cause, 192; rumors of attempted
assassination of, 57, 67; scandals and
corruption of presidency of, 127; on
slavery as cause of Civil War, 111, 112;
and surrender of Confederates at Appomattox Court House, 35, 40–41, 131,
170; surrender terms of, 5, 34, 35–36,
41, 48–51, 57, 63, 81, 150, 151, 158, 170,
173, 284, 294, 329 (n. 124), 330 (n. 154),
351 (n. 73)
Grant, Ulysses S., III, 306, 387 (n. 5)
Grant's Monument, 182, 242, 357 (n. 80)
Graves. *See* Burial of Confederate dead;
    Burial of Union dead; Confederate
    cemeteries; National cemeteries; *and*
    specific cemeteries
Gray, Jacob, 183, 357–58 (n. 85)
"Gray shirt" rhetoric, 152
Great Depression, 294, 298, 299, 303, 305
Great War, 10, 269, 271, 280–82, 291, 381
    (n. 61)
Greeley, Horace, 116, 127–28, 157–58
Green, Bessie, 121
Greg, Percy, 358 (n. 98)
Griffith, D. W., 256, 277, 303
Grigsby, W. H., 155, 159
Grimké, Archibald, 286
Grimsley, Mark, 317 (n. 19)
Guerin, Jules, 286–87, 382 (n. 89)
Guiteau, Charles, 352 (n. 95)

Hagood, L. M., 255–56
Hall, James, 34, 323 (n. 109)

Halleck, Henry, 68
Hallowell, Edward N., 116
Hampton, Wade, 142, 149, 152–53, 171, 348
    (n. 28), 351 (nn. 82, 87)
Hancock, Cornelia, 34
Hancock, Winfield Scott, 169, 187, 358–59
    (n. 104)
Hanes, Rev. Myron, 201, 361 (n. 17)
Hanly, J. Frank, 201
Hanna, J. Marshall, 346 (n. 10)
Harding, R. J., 195
Harding, Warren G., 287–90
Harlan, James, 49
Harnden, Henry, 113
Harper's Weekly, 28, 129, 161
Harris, Belle C., 252
Harris, Joel Chandler, 209–10, 254
Harrison, Benjamin, 129, 180, 181
Harrison, Hubert, 286
Hattaway, Herman, 318 (n. 36)
Hawley, Marcus J., 377 (n. 122)
Hayes, Rutherford B., 153
Hearst, William Randolph, 222
Henderson, R. H., 161
Henry, Patrick, 18
Henry, Robert Randolph, 267
Herbert, Hilary, 262, 377 (n. 126)
Herbert, Sidney, 151
Herold, David, 67
Higginson, Henry Lee, 365 (n. 98), 368
    (n. 145)
Higginson, Thomas Wentworth, 226
Hill, Benjamin, 351 (n. 80)
Hill, Daniel Harvey, 68, 136, 346 (n. 9), 348
    (n. 28)
HMA. *See* Hollywood Memorial Associa-
    tion
Hoar, George F., 342 (n. 69)
Holberton, William B., 331 (n. 5)
Hollyhock (Union gunboat), 64
Hollywood Cemetery, 93, 94, 95, 98, 302,
    358 (n. 86)
Hollywood Memorial Association (HMA),
    92, 135, 141–42, 346 (n. 5)
Holstein, Charles L., 110
Holt, Joseph, 67, 81
Holt, Thomas Michael, 221
Hood, John B., 149, 165
Hood's Texas Brigade, 185, 223
Hood's Texas Brigade Association, 195
Hopkins, Walter L., 282

Hosmer, Harriet, 342 (n. 53)
Hours at Home, 29
Houston, Charles, 344 (n. 97)
Howard, Bronson, 186
Howard, O. O., 77, 198
Hull, Sara, 257
Humphreys, John M., 66
Hunt, Robert, 362 (n. 34)
Hunter, Charles, 221
Hunter, David, 163–64
Hunter, H. G., 202–3

Illinois: Emancipation Day celebration in, 212; race riot in Springfield, 275; United Confederate Veterans posts in, 180. *See also* Chicago
Illinois regiments: 84th, 48; 95th, 111
Imboden, John D., 163–64
Immigration, 108–9, 140, 202, 211, 238, 247, 271, 283, 376 (n. 109)
Indiana: Civil War monument in Indianapolis, 8, 230–31, 369 (n. 171); Emancipation Days in, 212; Grand Army of the Republic posts in, 118, 183, 271; Lincoln's funeral train in, 63; presidential election of 1888 in, 129; Union Memorial Day in, 100
Indiana regiment, 12th, 111
Industrialization, 154, 162, 172, 202, 211, 245
Iowa: Emancipation Day in, 33, 88; Grand Army of the Republic in, 118–19; veterans' reunion in, 121
Iowa regiments: 12th, 121; 22nd, 51, 61

Jackson, Andrew, 114, 193
Jackson, Giles B., 278, 279
Jackson, Henry W. R., 12, 23
Jackson, Jesse, Jr., 388 (n. 8)
Jackson, Mahalia, 387 (n. 5)
Jackson, Thomas J. "Stonewall": bravery of and praise for, 94, 303, 350 (n. 50); commemorations of death of, 94, 336 (n. 90), 354 (n. 29); death of, 94, 142, 241; and defiance of Barbara Frietchie, 320 (n. 68); monument to, 135, 137–38; on patriotism of southern women, 23; textbook depictions of, 184; on Union dead, 20
James, William, 216–17, 365 (n. 98)
Jet, 308

Johnson, Andrew: amnesty and pardons by, to former Confederates, 61, 81, 83–84, 85, 348 (n. 33); and Emancipation Day celebration, 89; and execution of assassination conspirators, 97; at Gettysburg monument dedication, 77, 332 (n. 11); at Grand Review of Union soldiers, 69–71; and impact of emancipation, 83; impeachment of, 127; on Lincoln's assassination, 67; and Lincoln's funeral, 62; on punishment for treason, 61–62, 95, 181; reconciliation and Reconstruction policy of, 61–62, 77, 78, 81, 82, 83, 97, 329 (n. 122); reelection hopes of, 83; and restoration of Union, 81; on Sherman's surrender terms, 63; veto of Civil Rights Act by, 89; as vice presidential candidate, 36
Johnson, Bradley T., 147, 208–9, 348 (n. 34)
Johnson, Joan Marie, 372 (n. 34)
Johnson, Robert Underwood, 165–66
Johnson, Rossiter, 236
Johnston, Albert Sidney, 347 (n. 22)
Johnston, Joseph E.: at Grant's funeral, 169; and Lee Monument in Richmond, 182; after Lee's surrender, 53, 55; and Sherman's funeral, 354 (n. 32); surrender of, to Sherman at Durham Station, 63, 71, 93, 330 (n. 154); writings by, 163, 165
Johnston, William Preston, 139, 147, 347 (n. 22)
Johnstone, H. W., 383 (n. 104)
Jones, Anna, 385 (n. 145)
Jones, Archer, 318 (n. 36)
Jones, Charles Colcock, Jr., 19
Jones, John B., 26
Jones, Joseph, 348 (n. 28)
Jones, J. William, 143, 164, 185
Julian, Ira, 209
July Fourth ceremonies, 75, 120, 219, 221, 224, 332 (n. 11)
Juneteenth, 75, 88, 212

Kachun, Mitchell A., 380 (n. 53)
Kansas: African American veterans' reunion in, 215; Emancipation Days in, 119–20, 212; Loyal Ladies' League in, 344 (n. 97); protest against *The Birth of a Nation* in, 279
Kean, Robert Garlick Hill, 85

Kellogg, Sanford C., 357 (n. 73)

Kelly, Patrick J., 359 (n. 108), 360–61 (n. 3)

Kennedy, John F., 307, 387 (n. 5)

Kennedy, Mrs. John A., 123

Kentucky: African American protests against *The Clansman* and *The Birth of a Nation* in, 255–56; Confederate monuments in, 115; guerrilla fighting in, during Civil War, 27, 80; pro-slavery Unionists in, 16, 115; rejection of Thirteenth Amendment by, 16–17; semicentennial celebration of emancipation in Louisville, 273; Union Memorial Days in, 100–101; Union monuments in, 115; United Daughters of the Confederacy in, 255–56; U.S. Army recruits from, 317 (n. 26); Woman's Relief Corps in, 283, 344 (n. 99), 375 (n. 79)

Kentucky's Orphan Brigade, 207, 209

Kimball, Hannibal, 171

King, Martin Luther, Jr., 307, 308, 310

Kingsolving, Wythe Leigh, 292

Kinne, Elizabeth D'Arcy, 125, 246

Kirby Smith, Edmund, 64, 330 (n. 158)

Kirkland, Caroline, 321 (n. 70)

Kirk's Ferry Rangers, 21

Kirk's Raiders, 58

Knott, Richard W., 353–54 (n. 13)

Ku Klux Klan, 127, 139–40, 157, 256, 276, 280, 291, 297, 310, 347 (n. 24), 351 (n. 75), 352 (n. 102)

Labor disputes, 109, 140, 162, 211, 247

LaBree, Ben, 357 (n. 75)

Ladd, Luther, 332 (n. 9)

Ladies' Aid Society, 124, 245

Ladies' Memorial Associations (LMAs): and Confederate cemeteries, 92; and Confederated Southern Memorial Association, 261–62, 372 (n. 42), 384 (n. 127); and Confederate monuments, 135, 156; on emancipation, 253; founding of, 335 (n. 78); and Lost Cause, 9, 125, 135, 283; membership statistics of, 153, 245; members of, 240, 243; and Memorial Days, 93–100, 238, 283; naming of, 244; northern counterparts of, 233; organization of, 335 (nn. 79–80); purpose of, 335 (n. 80); and reinterment of Confederate dead, 261, 335 (n. 81),

338 (n. 127); resistance to reconciliation by, 7, 134, 243

Ladies of the GAR (LGAR): membership of, 124, 243, 344 (n. 97), 381 (n. 71); membership statistics on, 381 (nn. 71–72); organization of, 344 (n. 98); and praise for war contributions of women, 236; and resistance to reconciliation, 7, 233, 246, 251

Ladies of the Naval Veterans' Union Association, 373 (n. 50)

Ladies' Union Relief Association (LURA), 122–23

LaGrand, Julia, 26

Lamar, Lucius Q. C., 174

Lamar, Mrs., 298–99

Lambert, William H., 111, 120, 344 (n. 103)

Land We Love, The, 136, 346 (n. 9), 349 (n. 44)

Lane, David, 58

Langston, John Mercer, 213

Layton, Julia Mason, 252

LeConte, Emma, 22–23

Lee, Fitzhugh, 53, 68, 138, 142, 169–70, 182, 224, 225

Lee, "Light Horse Harry," 143

Lee, Robert E.: and amnesty oath, 68; Arlington property of, in Union hands, 20, 50–51, 137, 262, 270; attitude of, toward Yankees, 20; black newspapers on, 219–20; on black soldiers, 226; burning effigy of, 89; as commander of Army of Northern Virginia, 18–19, 32–33; and Confederate nationalism, 18–19; death of, 140–41, 169, 346 (n. 13); defense of Jefferson Davis by, 65; and Democratic Party, 138–39; "devil" epithet against, 59; on Emancipation Proclamation, 26; family background of, 143; farewell order of, after Confederate surrender, 43–44, 66, 86, 144, 324–25 (n. 11), 325 (n. 15); federal indictment against, for treason, 68, 84; first interview by, after Lincoln's assassination, 65; on freedmen, 65; Freeman's biography of, 302–3; Gettysburg defeat of, 32–33, 107, 144–45; Grant's criticisms of, 131; Grant's surrender terms for, 5, 35, 41, 48–51, 57, 63, 81, 150, 151, 158, 173, 294, 330 (n. 154), 351 (n. 73); on hard-war policy of Union, 84; on Lincoln's assassination, 65; and Lost Cause, 42, 43–44, 65, 137–38, 140–41, 143–44, 169, 181–82; monuments to, 141–42, 181–82, 219–20, 270, 271, 295–300, 349 (n. 37), 378 (n. 14); northern attitudes toward, after surrender, 50–51, 222; opposition of, to Confederate expatriation after Civil War, 68; Overland Campaign of, 131; parole for, 65, 66, 68; photograph of, 59, 60; portraits of, in schools, 275; praise for, 131, 134, 137, 141, 269, 294, 302–3; as president of Washington College, 137; and reconciliation, 65, 137–39, 329 (n. 135), 346–47 (n. 13), 347 (n. 14); on Reconstruction, 138; refusal of, to repudiate Confederate cause, 65; on reunion, 65, 96; as slaveholder, 146, 200, 264; and Southern Historical Society, 348 (n. 28); state holiday honoring, 248; on state rights, 65, 96; surrender of, at Appomattox Court House, 40–46, 120, 134, 170, 330 (n. 154); textbook depictions of, 184; at White Sulphur Springs meeting, 138–39

Lee, Robert E. (grandson), 263

Lee, Stephen D., 171–72, 184, 228

Lee, Susan P., 185

Lee Camp of Confederate Veterans: and Appomattox semi-centennial celebration, 274, 379 (n. 31); and dedication of monument to Pickett in Richmond, 177; and dedication of Richmond Soldiers' and Sailors' Monument, 189–91, 359 (n. 119); and Gettysburg semi-centennial celebration, 267; northern contacts with, 167, 189–91, 202–3, 359 (n. 119); and Philadelphia reunion, 356 (n. 65); photograph of, 157; statewide confederation of, 156

Lee Monument Association, 141–42, 349 (n. 37)

Lee's Dispatches (Freeman), 302

Lee's Lieutenants (Freeman), 303

Leon Hunters, 134–35

Leopard's Spots, The (Dixon), 276

Lewis, David Levering, 387 (n. 177)

Lewis, Rev. Gen. L. M., 155

LGAR. *See* Ladies of the GAR

Libby Prison (Richmond), 28, 152

Liberal Republican Party, 127–28, 187

Liberty, meaning of, 113. *See also* Emancipation

Lincoln, Abraham: attitude of, toward slavery, 91, 114, 146, 286, 317 (n. 19); black newspapers on, 219; and black soldiers, 26, 56, 226; and celebration following Confederate surrender, 46–47; as danger to slaveholding South, 18; Douglass on, 114, 286, 342 (n. 54); and emancipation linked with preservation of the Union, 113, 289; funeral of, 62–63; Gettysburg Address by, 31, 228, 285, 286, 292; at Gettysburg cemetery dedication, 77; as Great Emancipator, 8, 62, 90–91, 115, 286, 292, 305, 382 (n. 90); hard-war policy of, 25; monuments to, 113–15, 269, 285–94, 341 (nn. 48–54); national reactions to death of, 56–63; and peace conference with Confederate commissioners, 37; poem on, 331 (n. 167); positive attitudes toward, after Lee's surrender, 56; on preservation of the Union, 91; reconciliation policies of, 5, 34–35, 37–38, 41, 47–48, 49, 52, 78, 292, 323 (n. 112); reelection of, in 1864, 36–37, 115, 324 (n. 119); as Savior of the Union, 324 (n. 5), 382 (n. 90); on secession, 15, 47, 323 (n. 112); second inaugural address of, 37–38, 52, 115, 146, 286; southern animus toward, 20–21, 64, 197, 267, 290–92, 294; southerners' praise for, 292; symbols and titles representing memory of, 71, 72, 324 (n. 5); textbook depictions of, 183, 290–92; and Union soldiers, 114–15; writings and pageant on, 203–4, 273

Lincoln, Abraham, assassination of: African Americans' reactions to, 56, 58, 327 (n. 85); by Booth, 42, 56, 59, 64, 67, 328 (n. 109); calls for punishment and retribution against Confederates following, 41–42, 58–59, 61–62, 66–69; capture and trial of alleged conspirators involved in, 66–67, 83; Confederates' reactions to, 329 (n. 126); execution of conspirators to, 78–79, 97; Lee on, 65; mourning following, 56, 62–64; and

sectional animosities, 169; Union sol-
diers' reactions to, 58, 61, 71–72; vio-
lence in different cities following, 57–58
Lincoln, Mary, 62
Lincoln, Robert Todd, 287
Lincoln, Tad, 62
Lincoln, Willie, 62
Lincoln Memorial, 269, 285–90, 305, 382
  (n. 85)
Lincoln Memorial Commission, 285–86
Lippincott's, 210
Livermore, Mary, 237
Livermore, Thomas, 365 (n. 98)
LMA. *See* Ladies' Memorial Associations
Logan, John A., 98–99, 108, 117–18, 119, 291
Logan, Mary, 291
Longstreet, Helen Dortch, 292
Longstreet, James: black militia in New
  Orleans under command of, 149; federal
  indictment against, 68; and Gettysburg
  battle, 144–45, 164; and Gettysburg
  Battle Memorial Association meet-
  ing, 347 (n. 16); and Lee Monument in
  Richmond, 182; Lost Cause orators on,
  144–45, 349–50 (n. 50); and Republican Party, 139; as surveyor of customs
  of port of New Orleans, 131; writings
  by, 165
Lost Cause: Americanism of, 248–49; black
  newspapers on, 219–20; and bravery of
  Confederate soldiers, 86, 91, 134, 216,
  225, 275; as category of memory, 10, 315
  (n. 20); and Civil War as defensive war,
  147, 158, 185, 190–91, 208, 235; coinage
  of term, 136–37; and Confederate cemeteries generally, 75; Confederate flag as
  emblem of, 181–83, 194, 220, 234, 356
  (n. 65); and Confederate monuments,
  134–35, 156; and Confederate veterans'
  reunions, 153–56; and conflicts and tensions over reconciliation, 6–7, 174–86,
  188–96; and defense of slavery, 134, 139,
  145, 146, 150, 197, 209–11, 275; and denial of Civil War as act of treason, 65,
  87, 126, 185–86; and denial of slavery
  as cause of Civil War, 8, 86–87, 134, 137,
  145–47, 148, 202, 206–9, 350 (n. 52);
  and denunciation of Reconstruction,
  134, 148–53, 158; and denunciation of
  Union Cause, 185, 189–90, 193–94, 197–
98; and distinctive southern identity, 10,
134, 136, 153, 159; and Early, 131, 141–
44, 158, 159, 348 (n. 33), 350 (n. 58), 351
(n. 78), 351–52 (n. 88); in 1880s, 154–59,
351 (n. 86); in 1890s, 180–86; gendered
nature of, 54, 142; and *Gone with the
Wind*, 303–4, 308; and John B. Gordon,
157–58; and "gray shirt" rhetoric, 152;
happy- and loyal-slave tenet of, 8, 197,
209–11, 220, 222, 254, 275, 278, 292–
93, 297; and just nature of Civil War, 65,
87, 94–95, 126, 133–34, 143, 147, 154–55,
158, 159, 173–74, 185–86, 189, 194, 355
(n. 48); and Lee, 42, 43–44, 65, 137–38,
140–41, 143–44, 148, 149, 169, 181–82;
and Memorial Days, 94–95, 134; northern reactions to, 103, 234; periodicals
on, 136, 180–81, 357 (n. 75–76); Pollards' defense of, 136–37; and praise for
wartime sacrifices of southern white
women, 94, 99, 235, 238–39, 275; and
regimental histories, 135–36; and reunions of Confederate veterans, 133–34;
scholarship on, 315 (n. 17); and school
textbooks, 183–85, 188, 206, 207–8,
242, 243, 244, 247, 248, 275, 290–92;
and secession as constitutional right,
87, 134, 139, 143, 147; and sesquicentennial of Civil War, 309–10; and southern white women, 9–10, 54, 123, 125,
135, 140, 234–35, 238–45, 259, 283–84,
295–301, 304, 349 (n. 40); and Spanish-
American War, 224–25, 229–30;
superior-numbers argument of, 86, 91,
94, 132, 134, 137, 144, 151, 158, 167, 189,
190, 296, 302; tenets of, 86–87, 126, 134,
137, 144–48, 158–59, 174; in twentieth
century, 272, 274–78, 283–84, 302–5; in
twenty-first century, 309–10; on Union
prisons during Civil War, 322 (n. 92).
See also Confederate veterans; Southerners; United Confederate Veterans;
White supremacy
Lost Cause (journal), 357 (n. 75)
*Lost Cause, The: A New Southern History
  of the War of the Confederates* (Pollard),
  136–37, 346 (n. 12)
Louisiana: black occupying troops in, 85;
  Colfax massacre in, 385 (n. 140); disenfranchisement of African Americans in,

199; Grand Army of the Republic posts in, 205; Lincoln's Reconstruction policy toward, 323 (n. 112); Reconstruction in, 142, 148–49, 385 (n. 140); and United Confederate Veterans, 156–57. *See also* New Orleans

Louisiana regiment, 3rd, 145

Love, Rev. Emanuel K., 221

Loyal Guard (Union Veteran Legion), 339 (n. 24)

Loyal Ladies' Leagues, 344 (n. 97)

Loyal Legion, 130

Luebke, Peter, 339 (n. 7)

Lumpkin, Katherine Du Pre, 185, 345 (n. 2)

LURA (Ladies' Union Relief Association), 122–23

Luray Caverns, 161

Lynching, 162, 199, 210, 220, 227, 275, 286, 291, 293, 305, 361 (n. 8)

MacEl'Rey, Rev. J. H., 58

Maddox, James E., 233

Magruder, Henry, 80

Magruder, John B., 330 (n. 158)

Mahan, Harold E., 353 (n. 12)

Mahone's Old Brigade, 351 (n. 87)

Maine, 123

Manassas, battles of, 128, 161. *See also* Bull Run

Manassas commemorative observances, 76–77, 88, 100, 269

Manassas Peace Jubilee and Reunion, 232–34

Manderson, Charles F., 192

Mann, William H., 10–11, 266, 274

Manning, Chandra, 316 (nn. 11–12), 318 (n. 28), 340 (n. 31)

Markham, Thomas R., 154–55

Marriage: and coverture, 124; as metaphor for reconciliation, 187, 239, 358 (n. 103); prohibition of interracial, 86

Marshall, Charles, 325 (n. 15)

Marshall, Thomas, 201

Marshall, Thurgood, 387 (n. 5)

Marten, James, 338 (n. 4), 347 (n. 24), 360 (n. 137)

Martin, Thomas S., 278

Marvel, William, 355 (n. 38)

Maryland: Confederate patriotism in, following Lee's surrender, 54–55; pro-slavery Unionists in, 16; reactions to Lincoln's assassination in, 57, 61; reunions of Rosser's Cavalry Brigade and Artillery in, 154; Sanitary Fair in, 32; violence in Westminster following Lincoln's assassination, 57; Woman's Relief Corps in, 344 (n. 99)

Maryland regiment, 2nd, 339 (n. 18), 356 (n. 67)

Mason, Landon R., 267

Massachusetts: and Blue-Gray reunion, 166; monuments to Union soldiers in, 332 (n. 9); New England Women's Club in Boston, 343 (n. 90); review of 54th Massachusetts regiment of USCT in Boston, 115–16; Shaw Memorial in Boston, 8, 215–19, 226, 365 (n. 98); veterans' reunions in, 121, 215; Woman's Relief Corps in, 123, 253

Massachusetts regiments: 1st, 179; 2nd, 107; 5th Cavalry, 215, 216; 24th, 87–88; 32nd, 46; 34th, 49; 54th, 115–16, 215–19, 226, 354 (n. 19); 55th, 215, 216

Maury, Dabney H., 150, 351 (n. 73)

Maury, Matthew Fontaine, 330 (n. 158)

Maximilian (emperor of Mexico), 330 (n. 158)

McAllister, Robert, 42, 51

McBride, Robert W., 271

McClellan, George B., 36, 144, 165, 323 (n. 117), 324 (n. 119)

McClure, Alexander K., 163–64

McConaughy, David, 31–32

McConnell, Stuart, 342–43 (n. 71)

McCrady, Edward, Jr., 146, 153

McCurry, Stephanie, 320 (n. 59)

McDonald, William N., 165

McGuire, Hunter, 206, 208

McKinlay, Whitefield, 289

McKinley, William: on care of Confederate graves, 228–29, 261; on reconciliation, 187, 358 (n. 108), 368 (n. 160); and Spanish-American War, 223, 224, 226; and Tuskegee Institute, 368–69 (n. 160)

McLaws, Lafayette, 186

McNeill, Sallie, 86

McPherson, Edward, 103, 338 (n. 1)

McPherson, James, 323–24 (n. 117)

Meade, George, 69, 322 (n. 98)

Meek, C. A., 279

National Tribune, 110, 119, 183, 229, 246, 261, 279

National Veterans' Association of the Blue and the Gray and their Sons, 269, 378 (n. 12)

Neff, John R., 328 (n. 121), 331 (n. 168), 332 (n. 20), 337 (n. 109), 338 (n. 114)

Negro Historical and Industrial Association, 278

Nevins, Allan, 387 (n. 5)

New Deal, 298, 299, 305

New Eclectic Magazine, The, 349 (n. 44)

New Hampshire, 112–13, 123

New Jersey, 47, 273, 344 (n. 97)

New Jersey regiment, 14th, 206

New Orleans: celebration in, at end of Civil War, 47; mourning for Lee in, 148, 149; reactions in, to Lincoln's assassination, 58, 63–64; rebel and Union gunboats in, after Civil War, 64; Reconstruction in, 148–49; Southern Historical Society in, 142, 348 (n. 28); Unionists' animosity toward Jefferson Davis in, 50; Union occupation of, during Civil War, 26, 34–35; and United Confederate Veterans, 156–57

New York (state), 102, 121

New York City: African American veterans' reunion in, 215; celebration in after Confederate surrender, 47; Grant's funeral in, 169; Grant's Monument in, 182, 242, 357 (n. 80); Lincoln monuments in, 341 (n. 51); Lincoln's funeral train in, 62; mourning in, following Lincoln's assassination, 56, 62; National Emancipation Exposition in, 273; violence in, following Lincoln's assassination, 57

New York regiments: 5th Cavalry, 34; 7th, 182; 64th, 183; 71st, 224; 81st, 17; 104th, 107; 114th, 105; 117th, 202; 189th Volunteers, 51–52

Niagara Movement, 275

Nineteenth Amendment, 382 (n. 75)

NLMA (National Lincoln Monument Association), 113–14, 341 (n. 48)

Noble, John W., 173

Nolan, Alan, 350 (n. 52)

Noland, William C., 295

Norfolk, Va.: Carney monument in, 365 (n. 101); Emancipation Days in, 33, 89, 120, 334 (n. 64), 335 (n. 75); monument to black soldiers in cemetery in, 253, 375 (n. 83)

North Carolina: Confederate Memorial Days in, 98; Emancipation Days in, 214, 221; pro-slavery Unionists in, 16; racial reconciliation in, 221; railroads not segregated in, 199; Southern Historical Society of, 144; Union Memorial Days in, 99; United Daughters of the Confederacy in, 261; violence against African Americans in Wilmington in, 227; Woman's Relief Corps in, 283

North Carolina regiments: 3rd, 140, 347 (n. 25); 49th, 43

Northcott, Robert S., 164

Northerners: commerce between South and, 82, 96, 171–72, 271; Confederate definition and depiction of Yankees, 12, 19, 20–21, 25–26; Confederate women's hatred of Yankees, 21–23; criticisms by, of reunions for Confederate veterans, 155; and family reconciliations with former Confederates, 82; on Lost Cause, 103; negative reactions of, to Confederate Memorial Days, 95–96, 336 (n. 96); and reconciliation, 52–53, 81–83, 96, 101, 102, 172–73, 260, 333 (n. 29); relationship between Union veterans and civilians, 104, 107–8, 238; and sectional differences in antebellum period, 19; and white supremacy, 200. *See also* Abolitionism; Northern white women; Reconciliation; Union soldiers; Union veterans

Northern white women: battlefield relics of, during Civil War, 24; at Blue-Gray reunions, 247; Civil War experiences of, 235, 236; disabled veterans in families of, 121–22; on emancipation, 251–52; friendships between southern white women and, 239–42; and Grand Army of the Republic, 121, 123–25, 344 (n. 97); and Great War, 280–81; inconspicuous role of, in Union memory, 235–38; and Memorial Days, 121, 237; memorialization activities by, 9, 238; monument honoring, 381 (n. 62); as nurses during Civil War, 236, 237, 370 (n. 15); patriotism of, during Civil War, 24, 236–37, 320 (n. 68), 321 (n. 70); and

Pollard, Edward A., 136–37, 346 (n. 12)
Pollard, H. Rives, 136, 346 (n. 10)
Pool, Stephen D., 144
Populist Party, 187, 359 (nn. 107–8)
Porter, David D., 37
Port Hudson, battle of, 119
Potter, Rev. William, 59
Powell, E. Henry, 204, 362 (n. 33)
Powell, Lewis, 67
Presidential election of 1864, 36–37, 324 (n. 119)
Presidential election of 1868, 127, 129, 131, 138–39
Presidential election of 1876, 153, 351 (nn. 82–83)
Presidential election of 1880, 358–59 (n. 104)
Presidential election of 1888, 128–29
Presidential election of 1896, 187, 359 (n. 108), 360–61 (n. 3)
Price, Sterling, 330 (n. 158)
Prisoners of war: African Americans as, 28, 321 (n. 78); at Andersonville Prison, 28, 76, 79–80, 104, 129, 152; Confederate soldiers as, 28, 35, 41, 136, 151–52, 322 (n. 92), 323 (n. 109); exchange system for, 28, 41, 150, 164; graves of, 76, 189–90, 331 (n. 8), 332 (n. 20), 333 (n. 22); monument to Confederate prisoners of war, 171; newspaper images of, 28–29, 50; punishment for mistreatment of, 79–80, 83; Union soldiers as, 28, 29, 41, 49–50, 79–80, 129–30, 321 (n. 78), 322 (n. 92); Union veterans' experiences as, 129–30
Puritanism, 189, 193

Quantrill, William, 27, 155
Quigley, Paul, 318 (nn. 33, 36)

Race. See African Americans; African American women; Emancipation; Segregation; Slavery; White supremacy
Race riots, 275, 286
Railroads, 82, 158, 199
Raines, Anna Davenport, 242, 243
Randolph, Janet Weaver, 261
Rankin, Henry B., 291
Rankin, Jeannette, 280
Reagan, John H., 68, 207, 330 (n. 153)
Ream, Vinnie, 341 (n. 51)

Reardon, Carol, 356 (n. 64)
Reconciliation: and American centennial celebrations, 166, 182; and "Americanness," 170–71, 180, 187, 195, 248–49, 263, 266; and business interests, 171–72; conflicts and tensions over, in 1880s and 1890s, 6–7, 52–53, 174–86, 188–98, 360 (n. 136); and emancipation, 199–206; of family members, 82; and Fitzgerald soldiers' colony, 188; Garfield on, 203; gendered nature of, 168, 187, 232–34, 358 (n. 103); John B. Gordon on, 158, 349 (n. 37); Grant on, 131; and Grant's funeral, 169–70, 174; and Grant's surrender terms, 151, 158, 170, 284; and Great War, 280–81; Johnson's amnesty and pardons to former Confederates, 81, 83–84, 85; Johnson's approach to, 61–62, 77, 78, 81, 82, 83, 97, 329 (n. 122); and Lee, 65, 137–39, 329 (n. 135), 346–47 (n. 13), 347 (n. 14); Lincoln's approach to, 5, 34–35, 37–38, 41, 47–48, 49, 52, 78, 323 (n. 112); marriage and family metaphors for, 52, 187, 239, 358 (n. 103); and McKinley's call for care of Confederate graves, 228–29, 261; meanings of, 6; and myth of Appomattox, 170; northern reactions to and interpretations of, 52–53, 81–83, 96, 101, 102, 172–73, 260, 333 (n. 29); and northern views of Confederate veterans, 202; and northern white women, 7, 234, 246–47, 249–51; periodicals supporting, 164–66, 198, 203–4, 354 (n. 14); in popular culture of 1880s and 1890s, 186–87, 210–11; and Populist Party, 187; and return of Confederate battle flags, 174–75, 246, 269; reunion distinguished from, 5–7, 74, 82–83, 102, 311; and romance of reunion, 187, 358 (n. 103), 364 (n. 72); scholarship on, 314–15 (n. 13), 353 (nn. 5–6); southern reactions to and interpretations of, 96, 173–74, 259–60, 336 (n. 99); southern white women's resistance to, 7, 9–10, 69, 233–35, 238–39, 242–45, 249–51, 256–65, 371 (n. 26); and Spanish-American War, 222–31; Taft on, 260; Union Memorial Days rhetoric on, 101, 338 (n. 124); versus retribution against Confederates, following Lincoln's assassination,

northern press on, 20; power of, 15, 18, 208, 210; relationship between poor class of white southerners and, 202; relationship between southern non-slaveholders and, 18; and secession, 61. *See also* Slavery; Southerners; White supremacy

Slavery: African Americans on legacy of, 220–22, 366 (n. 115); as cause of Civil War, 4, 8, 13, 15–17, 18, 31, 52, 73, 86–87, 100, 105, 111–15, 145, 159, 198, 200–201, 206, 207, 271, 276, 290, 309, 318 (n. 35), 340 (nn. 31, 33), 361 (n. 17), 363 (n. 52), 388 (n. 10); and Confiscation Acts of 1861 and 1862, 26, 317 (n. 19), 321 (n. 76); contributions of slaves to Confederate war efforts, 16, 210, 278, 317 (n. 18), 364 (nn. 69–70); corruption of South by, 59, 73; cruelty and oppression of, 112, 209, 211, 305, 366 (n. 115); defense of, 84–85, 134, 139, 145, 146, 150, 197, 209–11, 275; Douglass on, 4; flight of slaves to Union lines during Civil War, 317 (n. 19); in *Gone with the Wind*, 304; Lincoln's attitude toward, 91, 114, 146, 286, 317 (n. 19); Lost Cause rhetoric on, 8, 86–87, 134, 137, 145–47, 148, 197, 206–11, 350 (n. 52); monuments to faithful slaves, 210, 254–55, 292–93, 383–84 (n. 119); as morally reprehensible, 201, 202; North as complicit in system of, 81, 146; pro-slavery Unionists in border regions during Civil War, 16–17, 115; and southern nonslaveholders' support of Confederacy, 18; statistics on, 16, 84, 206, 251; in territories, 14, 15; U.S. Constitution's slave clauses, 286; white southerners' attitudes toward, 8–9; and white southerners' images of happy and faithful slaves, 8, 197, 209–11, 220, 221–22, 254–55, 264, 275, 278, 292–93, 297, 383–84 (n. 119); white Union veterans' attitude on, 7–8. *See also* Abolitionism; Emancipation

Slocum, Henry W., 70
Smith, Benjamin T., 57
Smith, Gerritt, 81, 333 (n. 29)
Smith, Timothy, 360 (n. 132)
Snead, Claiborne, 151
Society of Cincinnati, 108

Society of the Army of Tennessee, 108, 154, 169
Society of the Army of the Cumberland, 108, 154, 169, 177–78
Society of the Army of the Potomac, 108, 154, 169
Solari, Mary M., 254
Soldiers' Aid Societies, 123
Soldiers' homes for veterans, 104, 110, 125, 139, 221, 229, 247, 248, 360 (n. 137), 369 (n. 163)
Soldiers' monuments. *See* Confederate monuments; Union monuments; *and specific monuments*
Soldier's Tribune, 104
Sons of Confederate Veterans (SCV), 180, 275, 282, 299, 310, 357 (n. 76), 386 (n. 160)
Sons of Union Veterans (SUV), 109, 124, 281–82, 381 (nn. 65–66)
Sons of Veterans of the United States, 109
South Carolina: and Blue-Gray reunion, 166; Confederate veterans' groups in, 140, 347 (n. 25); disenfranchisement of African Americans in, 199; Emancipation Days in, 212; Fort Mill monument to faithful slaves in, 210; Grand Army of the Republic posts in, 205, 230, 264; Hampton's "Red Shirts" in, 152–53, 351 (n. 82); Memorial Days in, 93, 230; organization for black Union soldiers in Charleston, 117; raising American flag over Fort Sumter after Lee's surrender, 55–56; remembering Union dead in Charleston, 98; secession of, 240; segregation in, 230; sesquicentennial celebration of Civil War in, 309–10; Woman's Relief Corps in, 283
South Carolina regiments: 1st Volunteers, 226; 5th Cavalry, 240
South Carolina Survivors' Association, 150
Southern Alliance, 187
Southern Bivouac, 164–65, 353–54 (n. 13)
Southerners (white): amnesty and pardons for, by Johnson, 61, 81, 83–84, 85, 97; attitudes of northerners toward, from 1865–1869, 59, 61, 77; and black codes, 85–86; and black occupying troops, 85; commerce between North and, 82, 96, 171–72, 271; corruption of, by slavery,

Tyler, John, 291
Tyler, Julia, 57
Tyler, Lyon Gardiner, 291

UDC. *See* United Daughters of the Confederacy
Uncle Tom's Cabin (Stowe), 209, 211, 255, 256, 276
Union, preservation of: and African American veterans, 115–20; and Constitutional Union Party, 16; as goal during and after Civil War, 5–6, 9, 13, 14–15, 31, 38, 39, 51, 52, 68, 72, 77, 100, 104–5, 116, 117, 173, 289–90, 316 (n. 11), 317 (n. 24); and Johnson, 81; Lee on, 143; Lincoln on, 91. *See also* Reconciliation; Reunion; Union Cause
Union Cause: American flag as symbol of, 272; "bloody shirt" rhetoric of, 126–32, 151; Confederate denunciations of, during 1890s, 189–90, 193–94, 197–98; demise of, in popular imagination, 10, 269, 272, 281; Emancipationist Cause distinguished from, 332 (n. 10); emancipation linked with, 111–17, 125–26, 289–90; and Lincoln Memorial, 285, 287–88; and northern white women, 125–26, 245; and regimental histories, 105; reunion as goal of, 9, 41, 68, 153, 162, 247, 311; righteousness of, proclaimed by veterans, 110, 115, 131, 173, 186, 192; Theodore Roosevelt on, 201; scholarship on, as category of memory, 315 (nn. 19–20); and sesquicentennial of Civil War, 310–11; in twentieth century, 301–2; in twenty-first century, 310–11; Booker T. Washington on, 218. *See also* Reconciliation; Reunion; Union, preservation of
Union cemeteries. *See* Burial of Union dead; National cemeteries; *and specific cemeteries*
Union Ex-Prisoners of War, 109
Union Memorial Days: and African Americans, 4, 8, 75, 100–101, 119, 211–12, 273, 369 (n. 169); in Arlington National Cemetery, 4, 102, 111; in border states, 100–101; compared with Confederate Memorial Days, 99–100, 121; compared with Emancipation Days, 120; criticisms of, 99; declining attendance at,

104; decoration of graves on, 117; description of, 99–100; and Douglass's speech at Arlington National Cemetery in 1871, 4; and Grand Army of the Republic, 99, 100, 119, 121, 287, 337 (n. 114); male leadership for, 121, 237; number of states sponsoring, 102; origins of, 98, 336 (n. 88); purpose of, 120; and reconciliation, 338 (n. 124); white southerners' negative reactions to, 99, 101; women's participation in, 121, 237. *See also* Confederate Memorial Days
Union monuments: to African American soldiers and sailors, 117, 119, 293, 342 (n. 69); in Connecticut, 119; geography of, 135; in Indianapolis, 8, 230–31, 369 (n. 171); in Kentucky, 115; in Massachusetts, 332 (n. 9); in New Hampshire, 112–13; to nurses, 370 (n. 15); in Ohio, 100, 119; in Pennsylvania, 332 (n. 9), 339 (n. 11); survey of, 339 (n. 9); symbols and inscriptions on, 106, 193; and Union Cause, 107. *See also specific monuments*
Union Party, 36, 323 (n. 116)
Union Signal, 241
Union soldiers: attitudes of, toward Grant's surrender terms, 48–49; Confederate ballad on, 21; Confederate women's hatred of, 21–23; feelings of, after surrender, 42–45, 66; Grand Review of, 69–72; and hard-war policy, 25–28; hatred and animosity of, toward the enemy, 12–14, 19–24, 66; and Lincoln, 114–15; and Lincoln's assassination, 58, 61, 71–72; motivations of, 14–17, 316 (n. 6), 317 (nn. 10–11), 320 (n. 66); as prisoners of war, 28, 29, 41, 49–50, 79–80, 321 (n. 78), 322 (n. 92); return home by, after Confederate surrender, 75, 331 (n. 5); revelry by, following surrender, 42–45; statistics on, 238; and surrender of Confederates at Appomattox Court House, 40–46. *See also* Emancipation; Northerners; Union veterans; United States Colored Troops
Union Veteran Legion, 109, 257, 339 (n. 24)
Union veterans: on African American suffrage and equal rights, 113; attitude of, on emancipation, 7, 9, 111–15, 340 (n. 40); as ex-prisoners of war, 129–30;

families of, 121–23; hostility of Confederate veterans toward, 186; and Lincoln Memorial, 289–90; memories of, 105; on northern white women's role during Civil War, 235–36; pensions for, 109, 110, 188, 229, 369 (n. 163), 371 (n. 21), 379 (n. 26), 384 (n. 126); physical and mental disabilities of, 121–22, 338 (n. 4); and presidential election of 1888, 128–29; reactions by, to Lost Cause, 126; regimental histories by, 104, 105, 163, 236, 338–39 (n. 7), 342 (n. 62); relationship between African American veterans and, 338 (n. 6); relationship between northern civilians and, 104, 107–8, 238; and return of Confederate battle flags, 174–75; reunions of, 108, 109, 121, 122, 150; on righteousness of Union Cause, 110, 115, 131, 173, 186, 192; statistics on, 268, 301, 302, 360 (n. 137); and Union and emancipation as dual legacies of Civil War, 104–5. *See also* African American veterans; Blue-Gray reunions; Grand Army of the Republic; Reconciliation

Union Veterans' Union, 109

Union War Prisoners' Association, 129

Union women. *See* Northern white women

United Confederate Veterans (UCV): and African American veterans, 222; and Appomattox Peace Monument, 295–96, 300; and *The Birth of a Nation*, 280; and care of Confederate graves, 229; and commemoration of Lincoln's life, 294; ending of, 302; and Fitzgerald soldiers' colony, 188; founding of, 134, 156–57, 159, 180; Gordon as first commander of, 157–58, 352 (n. 104); and Grant equestrian statue, 284; hostility between white northerners and, 4, 9, 190; and joint encampment with Grand Army of the Republic, 195, 301; and Lincoln as personally responsible for Civil War, 290–92; membership statistics for, 180; organization of, 157; and pensions for Confederate veterans, 229; periodical published by, 180–81, 357 (nn. 75–76); reunions of, 277, 280, 290, 379 (n. 35); and school textbooks, 184–85, 290–92; and Sons of Confederate Veterans, 282;

in twentieth century, 268, 302; and white supremacy, 227–28

United Daughters of the Confederacy (UDC): activities of, 242–43, 248; and Appomattox Peace Monument, 297–99, 301, 385 (n. 145); and Appomattox semi-centennial celebration, 274; and Arlington Confederate Monument, 261–65, 377 (nn. 125–26), 377–78 (n. 132), 378 (n. 33); and Blue-Gray reunions, 234; characteristics of members of, 243, 250–51, 372 (n. 40); children's auxiliaries of, 244, 275, 372–73 (n. 46); and commemoration of Lincoln's life, 294; convention of, in 1912 in Washington, D.C., 259–61; on emancipation, 253–56; and faithful slave monuments, 254–55, 292–93, 297, 383–84 (n. 119); founding of, 180, 242–43; and Great War, 280–81; and Lincoln as personally responsible for Civil War, 290–92; and Lost Cause, 9, 10, 275, 295–301, 304, 349 (n. 40); membership requirements for, 243; membership statistics of, 243, 283, 293, 302; and memory of Reconstruction, 256, 269, 276, 297–98; northern counterparts of, 233; organization of, 282, 372 (n. 39); patriotism of, 248–49, 260, 280–81; and proposed monument to Jefferson Davis in Washington, D.C., 264; purpose of, 243–44, 251, 265; resistance to reconciliation by, 7, 234, 235, 243–44, 249–51, 256–65, 349 (n. 40); and restoration of McLean House at Appomattox, 300; textbook campaign of, 248, 275, 290–92; in twentieth century, 269, 283, 293–94, 297–99, 302, 381 (n. 64), 382 (n. 78); and *Uncle Tom's Cabin* theater production, 255, 256; and Wirz monument, 235, 256–59, 261, 262, 263, 376 (n. 113)

United Sons of Confederate Veterans, 180, 357 (n. 76)

United States Colored Troops (USCT): at battle of the Crater (Petersburg), 17, 26; bravery of, 91, 116, 119, 203, 204, 215–17; burial of, in national cemeteries, 78, 118, 332 (n. 17); Confederate guerrilla attacks against, 27, 80; Confederates' response to, 39, 45; and defeat of Con-

federacy, 45, 91, 335 (n. 72); and emancipation, 8, 31, 117; and Emancipation
Days, 33; and Emancipation Proclamation, 16; enlistment of, due to military necessity, 116–17; exclusion of, from
Grand Review, 70–71, 331 (n. 162); at
Fort Pillow, 20, 119, 226, 319 (n. 45); at
Fort Wagner, 84, 119, 216, 217, 226; and
graves of Union dead, 76; from Kentucky, 317 (n. 26); at Lincoln's funeral,
62; at Lincoln's second inauguration,
38; manual labor by, for constructing
field works, 317 (n. 20); and Medal of
Honor for Carney, 217; monuments to,
117, 119, 293, 342 (n. 69); pay scale for,
286; at Petersburg, 203, 204; prejudice
against and stereotypes of, 119, 204–5,
362 (n. 34); as prisoners of war, 28, 321
(n. 78); reactions of, to Lincoln's death,
56, 58, 327 (n. 85); regimental histories
of, 342 (n. 62); return home by, 115–16;
Shaw Memorial honoring, 215–19, 226,
365 (n. 98); statistics on, 317 (n. 26),
364 (n. 69); after surrender, 45; in Texas
and Union-occupied cities, 45, 71, 85.
See also African American veterans
University of Florida, 291
USCT. *See* United States Colored Troops

Vale, Joseph G., 112
Vance, Zebulon, 221, 366 (n. 117)
Vanderslice, John, 184
Van DerVeer, Ferdinand, 177–78
Van Der Voort, Paul, 123, 124
Vardaman, James, 235
Varon, Elizabeth, 45
Veterans. *See* African American veterans;
Confederate veterans; Grand Army of
the Republic; Union veterans; United
Confederate Veterans; *and other veter-
ans' groups*
Vicksburg, battle of, 25, 32, 35, 131
Vicksburg National Military Park, 195
Vincent, Strong, 107, 339 (n. 11)
Vinovskis, Maris, 371 (n. 22)
Virginia: attitudes toward reunion and
reconciliation among white residents
of, 96; and Blue-Gray reunion, 160–61,
166; Confederate Memorial Days in, 93,
94–95, 98; Confederate monuments in,

134–35, 141, 176–77, 188–91, 219–20;
Confederate veterans' groups in, 142,
156; Emancipation Days and Evacuation Days in, 33, 87–90, 120, 213–14,
334 (n. 64), 335 (nn. 69, 75); Fort Monroe in, 67; Grand Army of Confederate Veterans in, 185; Ladies' Memorial
Associations in, 335 (n. 78), 336 (n. 90);
Lincoln's Reconstruction policy toward,
323 (n. 112); Luray Caverns in, 161; martial rule in, 345 (n. 110); race relations
in, 367–68 (n. 143); railroads in, 82,
199; reactions to Lincoln's assassination
in, 64; reunions of Confederate veterans in, 351 (n. 87); school textbooks in,
185, 206; secession by, 137; sesquicentennial celebrations of Civil War in, 309,
388 (n. 14); slaveholders as Confederate
soldiers in, 318 (n. 34); Union Memorial
Days in, 99; Union monument to black
soldiers in, 253, 375 (n. 83); Woman's
Relief Corps in, 283, 375 (n. 79). *See also*
Norfolk, Va.; Richmond, Va.
Virginia regiments: 1st, 169; 31st, 45
Voting rights: for African Americans, 61,
88, 97–98, 105, 113, 117, 139, 148, 203,
208, 228, 291, 333 (n. 27); disenfranchisement of African Americans, 8–9,
199, 210, 215, 275, 293; and Union
veterans' lack of support for African
American suffrage, 113; for women,
162, 245, 249–50, 283, 343 (n. 86), 372
(nn. 34, 38), 382 (n. 75)

Wade-Davis Bill (1864), 35
Wallace, George, 310
Wallis, S. Teakle, 21
Walthall, Edward Cary, 191–92
War Department, U.S., 45, 47, 129–30, 174,
295–96, 299–301
Warner, William, 110
*War of the Rebellion: A Compilation of the
Official Records of the Union and Con-
federate Armies (OR)*, 129–30, 164, 165,
353 (n. 12)
Washington, Booker T.: "Atlanta Com-
promise" speech by, 218–19, 289,
368 (n. 149); on civil rights for Afri-
can Americans, 222; donation by, to
Confederate soldiers' home, 221, 366

(n. 116); on reconciliation, 218–19, 227, 368 (n. 149); on semi-centennial celebration of emancipation, 272; at Shaw Memorial dedication, 217–19, 221; on slavery, 221–22; on Spanish-American War, 226–27; and Tuskegee Institute, 217, 218, 288, 368–69 (n. 160); on Union Cause, 218

Washington, D.C.: Marian Anderson's performance in, 305, 387 (n. 179); celebrations in, after Confederate surrender, 46–47; Emancipation Day in, 88–89; Grand Review of Union soldiers in, 69–72; Grant equestrian statue in, 284–85; Andrew Jackson monument in, 114; Lincoln Memorial in, 269, 285–90, 305, 382 (n. 85); Lincoln monuments for, 113–15, 341 (n. 51); Lincoln's funeral in, 62–63; monument to colored soldiers and sailors in, 342 (n. 69); proposed Jefferson Davis monument in, 264; proposed Lee monument in, 270, 271, 378 (n. 14); proposed Lincoln-Lee-Grant memorials in, 270, 378 (n. 15); proposed mammy monument in, 292–93; trial of co-conspirators for Lincoln's assassination in, 67; United Daughters of the Confederacy convention in, 259–61; violence in, following Lincoln's assassination, 57

Washington, George, 143, 146, 181

Watson, William, 49

Waugh, Joan, 345 (n. 122), 351 (n. 74)

WCTU. See Woman's Christian Temperance Union

Weaver, James B., 187

Weaver, Samuel, 29

Webb, Alexander S., 175

Webb, Jim, 387–88 (n. 8)

Weeks, Jim, 339 (n. 10)

Weeks, John W., 284

Welles, Gideon, 57, 71

Western Sanitary Commission, 341 (n. 53)

Wheeler, Joseph, 224, 226, 271

Whipple, Captain, 134–35

Whistler, S. M., 201–2

Whitcomb, Governor James, 369 (n. 171)

White, A. R., 286

White, Frank, 278

White, Samuel, 210

White House of the Confederacy, 208, 253. See also Confederate Museum

White northerners. See Northerners; Northern white women

White southerners. See Southerners; Southern white women

White supremacy: and Anglo-Saxonism, 227; and The Birth of a Nation, 256, 277, 279–80, 303; and Democratic Party, 81; and disenfranchisement of African Americans, 199; John B. Gordon on, 158; and Lost Cause, 8–9; in newspapers, 368 (n. 147); and nonslaveholders' support of Confederacy, 18; against nonwhite groups generally, 368 (n. 152); and northerners, 200; and reconciliation, 199–200, 315 (n. 14), 374 (n. 74), 383 (n. 103); scholarship on, 379 (n. 36). See also Lost Cause; Lynching; Segregation; Slave oligarchy

White women. See Northern white women; Southern white women

Whitney, Addison, 332 (n. 9)

Whittier, John Greenleaf, 320 (n. 68)

Wiatt, William, 324 (n. 1)

Wilderness, battle of, 131

Wilderness battlefield, 76

Wiley, Belle, 120

Willard, Frances E., 240–41

Willett, J. W., 294

Williams, George F., 44

Williams, George W., 213–14, 364 (n. 81)

Williams, George Washington, 116–17

Williams, Madeline A., 307

Williams, Thomas, 95

Williamsburg, battle of, 20

Wills, David, 29

Wills, Helen DeBerniere, 244

Wilson, Henry, 48

Wilson, Woodrow, 260, 263, 278, 280, 379 (n. 19), 388 (n. 18)

Wilson's Creek, battle of, 155

Winn, C. A., 151

Wirz, Henry, 28, 76, 79–80, 256–59, 261, 376 (n. 109)

Wirz monument, 235, 256–59, 261, 262, 263, 376 (n. 113)

Wisconsin, 175, 273

Wittenmyer, Annie, 247, 251

Wolcott, Roger, 216

Woman's Christian Temperance Union (WCTU), 240–41, 243, 245, 372 (n. 34), 373 (n. 50), 374 (n. 63); Woman's Relief Corps members in, 245

Woman's Relief Corps (WRC): African American women in, 252–53, 283, 375 (n. 79); and Andersonville Prison Park, 257–58, 376 (n. 102); and Arlington Confederate Monument, 262, 263; and attitude toward United Daughters of the Confederacy, 234; and Blue-Gray reunions, 247; and Carney monument, 365 (n. 101); characteristics of members of, 245, 250–51, 373 (n. 52); and emancipation, 53; founding of, 123–25; and Great War, 280–81; incorporation of, by Congress, 302, 386 (n. 171); membership of, 124–25, 250–51, 282–83, 344 (n. 97); membership statistics of, 245, 282–83, 302, 381 (n. 72), 386 (n. 171); and Memorial Day, 247, 373 (n. 56); as official auxiliary of Grand Army of the Republic, 123–24, 238; patriotic instruction campaign of, 247–48, 265, 272, 283, 374 (n. 63); on patriotism of northern white women, 237; photograph of, 250; and praise for war contributions of women, 236; priorities of, 371 (n. 18); and race-based reconciliation, 374 (n. 74); and resistance to reconciliation, 7, 233, 246, 250–51; segregation of, in the South, 125, 245, 252, 283, 344 (n. 99); in twentieth century, 282–83, 302, 381 (n. 73), 382 (n. 75); on Wirz monument, 257–58

Woman's rights movement, 162, 241

Woman's suffrage, 243, 245, 249–50, 283, 343 (n. 86), 372 (nn. 34, 38), 382 (n. 75)

Women. *See* African American women; Northern white women; Southern white women; *and specific organizations*

Wood, Wales, 111

Woodbury, Urban A., 194

Woolson, Albert, 302

Works Progress Administration, 305

World War I. *See* Great War

WRC. *See* Woman's Relief Corps

Wright, Marcus J., 130, 357 (n. 75), 377 (n. 122)

Wright, Uriel, 96–97

Yateman, J. E., 341 (n. 49)

Young, Bennett, 263

Young Women's Christian Association (YWCA), 243, 245